THE RESTORATION NEW TESTAMENT COMMENTARY IN QUESTION AND ANSWER FORM

A Catechetical Commentary

BY

WILLIAM HURTE

OLD PATHS PUBLISHING COMPANY
Rosemead, California
1964

To

THE ENTIRE BROTHERHOOD OF

BELIEVERS IN JESUS THROUGHOUT THE WORLD,

This Book,

WHICH HAS BEEN WRITTEN FOR THEIR EDIFICATION

AND HELP IN THE KNOWLEDGE OF HIS WILL,

IS MOST AFFECTIONATELY INSCRIBED

BY

THE AUTHOR.

PREFACE.

A FEW words will suffice to inform the reader of the circumstances which led me to commence the present volume of Biblical exposition. During my previous Christian life, I had been diligently seeking to understand the Scriptures, but without a thought of writing, in the present form, for the instruction of others, what I was then trying to learn myself, until very unexpectedly prompted to do so by a casual remark of a brother in the Lord. The remark of this brother was scarcely addressed to me, but was the utterance of a deep, anxious feeling, and, from the earnestness and solemnity of his manner, very deeply impressed my spirit. Indeed, it made him, although unconsciously, an instrument in the Lord's hand of stirring me up to begin what I have now completed, and to this circumstance I will briefly refer.

At the close of 1879, I was in the north of Scotland, preaching in the fishing villages along the Banffshire coast, and teaching as I had opportunity those who were meeting together as Churches of Christ. I found among these brethren generally a yearning desire to understand the Scriptures, and during the time I was among them, every available opportunity of giving and receiving instruction was eagerly embraced. We seldom met on the road, or by appointment in their cottages, but I found that they had ready for proposal some Scriptural difficulty, or some text which I was asked to explain, very often to quite a goodly number of persons who had gathered to receive instruction. To myself it was a deeply-interesting exercise, and I felt thankful that I had previously been led to examine these very difficulties which they then felt, and could explain them to their apparent general satisfaction. While these conversations were going on, I did sometimes feel a desire that they could have been written down, that others in like need of instruction might also share it with them, but had no thought just then of attempting it myself.

During my stay in the north I spent a week in one of the inland villages, and by request passed an evening with one of the few brethren there. After tea he opened his Testament, and said,

" Here is a chapter which we purpose on Lord's Day to read in the church, but there are some things in it which I do not understand, and I would like you to explain them to me if you can." We at once began to examine them in the light of context and other portions, and ascertained what appeared to be their meaning, and for which he expressed thanks. During our conversation, he was led to say, "Oh that there were some one in the church who could open to my understanding the meaning of God's Word!" This utterance, which was expressed with a deep sigh, went to my heart, and before I spoke, I inwardly prayed that God would raise up some one who would give in a book the instruction which he and many others desired to possess. My prayer was almost instantly followed by what was to me a rather startling thought. Why not try and meet this need yourself? Why wait for others to supply what may be your own duty to provide? Do the best you can, and God will help you. I did not mention my thoughts to this good brother, whose deep sigh had so suddenly started them within me, but could not help pondering them even while I remained with him ; and as I walked along to my lodging, and through the hours of the night, these new thoughts very deeply exercised my mind. I felt as if I had this work to do, and yet I shrank from it as I thought of all that was involved in writing and printing what I saw was really needed. However, I felt that I could do something towards this necessary instruction of my brethren, and my responsibility to do the best I could was so laid upon my heart, that before the following night I had actually commenced the work which the reader has now before him.

The catechetical method adopted in this volume has arisen from the circumstances which led me to begin the work. I had been hearing and answering the enquiries of brethren upon the meaning of texts of Scripture during the preceding two months, and this formed a model for me when I began to write. Indeed, I seemed to be only carrying forward with my pen what we had been doing in our social gatherings ; and I may here state that these brethren, and others in need of similar instruction, have been continually kept before me.

When I commenced I had no intention of writing so lengthily as I have done, but only to take up a few of the principal difficulties which occur in the Gospels and Epistles, and about which almost every young Christian is sure to desire information. I found, however, upon careful examination, that almost every chapter had its difficulties, or at least what seemed to me to be such, and that every Gospel and Epistle had its special place in the New Economy, which was not always perceived by those who read them, and which to overlook must be a loss to all who do so. I resolved, therefore, to meet as many of these as I could, and so, to give connection and completeness to the whole, I have gone through the entire New Testament.

I have asked and answered in this volume about 4000 questions, all of which are intended to unfold the meaning of the Scriptures, and to make as intelligible as I could the great scheme of redemption which the Holy Spirit has unfolded in it. Thousands more might have been added, but in doing so I should have increased the size of the book beyond what it was thought advisable to do.

I very much regret the brevity of many of the answers given, but had no choice, than, either to reduce the number of questions or to be thus brief. I have, however, omitted nothing that I thought would help to the understanding of any paragraph, or verse, or word, and by condensing the answers, I have been able to answer more questions than I could have done if I had expanded and proved everything I have said. Some of the answers given will possibly be new and startling to some who have been reading the New Testament as a mere text-book, and in the light of what we may term "present day religion"; but I would beg all such to examine what is said in the light of the context or of the plan of redemption, which should always be kept before us in our study of divine revelation; and the correctness of the answers or remarks will then become more apparent.

The work is by no means an exhaustive one. It is simply a help to any who may be seeking to understand what Jesus taught, and what apostles have preached and written of the grace and love and purpose of God. I trust that I have removed from those revelations of God some doctrinal and textual difficulties, which previous training and our Authorised Version may have fixed in the mind of almost every reader of the Scriptures. I fully expect that all such, by a careful and impartial reading of this book, will be better able to understand the New Covenant in Christ Jesus, than they were before doing so.

That such a volume, arranged in this catechetical method, is needed, I have no doubt whatever, especially by young converts, and also by many others who have failed to obtain the teaching which belongs to their Christian standing. The many questions that have been put to myself about the meaning of texts of Scripture during the past thirty years, and the many queries which from month to month appear in periodicals about spiritual things, have made it manifest that some such help is really needed, and has had considerable weight in stirring me up to try and meet it in my own feeble manner, and to persevere until I have completed what I began.

For some years my early morning hours have been devoted to the writing of this volume, and during this consecutive study of the New Testament my own heart has often been refreshed and cheered by its hallowed truths. In this exercise I have had my own spiritual recompense, and now invite the reader to share with me this feast of heavenly manna. This spiritual food that has come down from heaven to us is God's gift of love; but to enjoy it each must gather for his own eating, or receive for his own need, what other hands may have gathered and prepared. My own part in the work I have done is very much like that of a father, who after years of gathering of the manna for himself, and others to whom he has ministered, now seeks to guide his children and friends in their own necessary search for a daily supply of spiritual food, and to help them to discern between what is from heaven and that which is of the earth. In many instances it has been necessary to remove the rubbish which careless hands or misdirected spirits have thrown over it, to the trouble and loss of many earnest seekers. God's Word is perfect, and nothing that is of any value can ever be added to it by man; but it is a loss not to be estimated when anything that God has revealed is hidden from us, either by mistranslation or misinterpretation, and to remove these wherever we can is both our duty and our privilege.

If the reader does not find here every question answered that he might have proposed, or every difficulty removed that he may feel, I trust he will not under-estimate on that account the help that is afforded in many things, but will see that there is still much work to be done, and will strive to share it with those who have laboured before him in this great field.

To Him who is worthy, even our Lord Jesus, be all the glory. Amen.

W. H.

EDINBURGH, *October* 1884.

MATTHEW.

CHAPTER I.

1. *Matthew begins his book at the birth of Jesus Christ, by asserting that He is the "son of David," the "son of Abraham." Why does He mention this special relationship to David and Abraham?*

David received the promise of a son, whom in spirit or prophecy he called Lord, who while He was to be his successor, as the anointed ruler over God's people, was also to sit at the right hand of God; and Abraham received the promise of a seed, in whom all nations should be blessed. Prior to the birth of Jesus, no seed of Abraham had ever been a source of blessing to *all* nations; and no son of David had ever been exalted to the right hand of God. The promise, therefore, remained to be fulfilled in some one yet to appear, as God's promises could not be broken. In heading this birth-roll with "Jesus Christ, son of David, son of Abraham," Matthew assumes that in Jesus the promise made to both David and Abraham was fulfilled. Through Jesus blessing *had* reached all nations; and He was also seated at the right hand of God. This register, therefore, is given from Abraham to Joseph, and as Jesus was the son of the latter by Mary, He became heir to the throne of David.

Would the genealogical roll which Matthew copied be carefully preserved from illegal names?

The whole nation would be interested in having a correct register of the heirs to the throne of David, while the Sanhedrin, who had charge of such matters, would carefully preserve the documents from all illegal names. This national register of all heirs to the throne would, doubtless, be accessible to all interested in it, so that even Pilate, ere he mocked the Jews by writing over the cross, "This is Jesus the King of the Jews," may have consulted it. By this public roll the right of Jesus to the throne of David was established, and if "son of David," then He was also "son of Abraham."

3–6. *Is it not strange that four women who were foreigners should be included in this genealogy, and be reckoned in the line of the Messiah?*

It may appear strange that these women should be incorporated into this separated family of Abraham, but at the same time it is deeply suggestive of the "ways of God," when in the dispensation of the gospel He gathered "strangers and foreigners" into the "holy nation," "thus making of twain one new man."

Are the different methods by which these women obtained a place for their seed among the Messiah's ancestors typical of the manner in which the Gentiles were introduced among the people of God?

The incidents connected with their admission into the family of Abraham are most striking. Tamar had to compel Judah, the father of her seed, to confess that it had a right to a place in the family by producing,

A

when required, the pledges he had given her (Gen. xxxviii. 25). Rahab, by her faith in the testimony given by the messengers, escaped judgment, and by marriage became one of the nation. Ruth, the Moabitish damsel, was first a gleaner, and then the wife of Boaz her kinsman redeemer; while she that was of "Uriah the Hittite," though the seed which she obtained through unfaithfulness was not permitted to live, yet bore a son who ruled from the river to the ends of the earth.

What points in the acceptance of Christ by the Gentiles were typified in the cases of these women?

We find that while Peter was willing to preach the Gospel in the house of Cornelius a Gentile, and thus sow the seed by which they were begotten into life, he was not ready to admit them into the family, until he saw the pledges in the gift of tongues, when he exclaimed, "Can any man forbid water, that these should not be immersed, who have received the Holy Spirit as well as we? and he commanded them to be immersed in the name of the Lord Jesus." Thus were these Gentiles placed on the heavenly roll, and their right to be there was never again disproved. And even Jesus, who was born of a faithless nation, and died for their sin, yet being raised from the dead, had all authority given into His hand.

17. *"Fourteen generations," but the second list contains only thirteen names. How is this?*

If these names are arranged in three columns, just as Matthew formed them into divisions, the numbers will be found to be correct. From Abraham to David is one column, and there are exactly fourteen names; from David, who now heads the second column, to Josias, there are fourteen names; and from Jechonias to Christ, who is also included in the list, there are the names of fourteen persons.

18. *Was the conception of Jesus while His mother was still a virgin an absolute necessity?*

As He who should bruise the head of the serpent was to be the seed of the woman, not of the man, the conception had to take place while Mary was still a virgin, thus fulfilling two prophecies, "Behold a virgin shall conceive and bear a son, and shall call his name Immanuel" (Isaiah vii. 14), and, "the Lord hath created a new thing in the earth, a woman shall compass a man" (Jer. xxxi. 22). The conception in virginity, and also the birth in marriage, were absolutely necessary, as by them was solved a problem which God alone could solve, viz., how Jesus could be the Son of God and yet become flesh; how He could be the seed of the virgin, and also heir to the throne of David. Thus both were fulfilled, and Jesus became "son of man," and also "king of the Jews."

21. *"Thou shalt call his name Jesus." What does this name indicate?*

In the name Jesus, meaning Jehovah Saviour, there is a distinct reference to both the past and the present. As Jehovah He was the one God of Israel under the old covenant; as Saviour He is the deliverer of all who trust and obey Him under the new. The name, therefore, ought to have prompted the inquiry of every Jew, and should furnish instruction to every Gentile. It is a most precious name, for though suggestive of our ruin, it is also of our deliverance.

CHAPTER II.

1. *"Behold there came wise men from the East to Jerusalem." Did this visit take place immediately after the birth of Jesus?*

Most likely the interesting events recorded by Luke—viz., the change from the stable to a house, the journey to Jerusalem at the end of three and thirty days of the purification of Mary, the joyous reception of the child and His parents by Simeon and Anna in the temple—all preceded this visit, which was followed by the flight into Egypt.

3. *Why was Herod so much troubled about this " born king of the Jews " ?*

Herod was an Idumean by birth, and therefore an usurper of the throne of David. To hear of one born with a legal claim to that throne might well trouble him.

4–6. *Why did Herod ask the scribes and chief priests where this king should be born?*

Because the place of His birth had been predicted, and having formed an evil design against Him, he sought the information in order to carry out his purpose.

Why did he send the wise men to seek the babe when he might have sent an armed force?

That would have defeated his purpose. The child had first to be discovered, and this search they were best fitted, as he thought, to accomplish, and then, under pretext of worship, he might suddenly destroy this claimant and rival to the throne. But being disappointed in their return with the necessary information, he at once decided to kill all the babes in Bethlehem, that thus he might effect the death of the new born king of the Jews.

16. *Must not Herod have been an exceedingly bad man to have ordered such a wholesale murder?*

One cannot but shudder at such an act of cold-blooded murder ; but if Herod had previously refused to accept a position to which he had no rightful claim, this terrible crime would never have stained his life. To maintain himself on a throne of which he was not a rightful occupant, he had to seek the life of the son of David. The facts are very suggestive, and pregnant with lessons to all. The most appalling acts of many a life are only the end of a series. It is not so much great crimes that we need to watch against as the beginnings of wrong. The first glass may seem but a small matter, but how often it has led to a drunkard's grave. The first small theft may appear but trivial, but it has often led to prison, and dishonour that was never removed. The first departures from the appointments of Jesus have led to apostacy and ruin. Let us all beware of *first* indulgences of evil, of *first* neglects of duty, or, if sinful deeds have already been committed, let us confess them and forsake them, lest they lead to greater sins.

17, 18. *How was the prophecy " Rachel weeping for her children," fulfilled in the slaughter of the infants in Bethlehem?*

The event referred to by Jeremiah, in the passage quoted by Matthew, was the departure of the captives of Judah and Benjamin from Ramah, where they had been assembled by Nebuzar-adan prior to their departure to Babylon. Under the figure of Rachel weeping and mourning for her children as if they were never to return again, the prophet described the crowd who accompanied the captives to Rachel's tomb on the border of Benjamin, lamenting over their exile as a permanent one. Bidding her dry her tears, Jeremiah comforts her by saying that " they shall come again from the land of the enemy." Keeping this before us, we see that this prophecy was fulfilled, not in the cruel death of the children, but in the departure of Jesus their deliverer to Egypt. Those who knew of the flight of Joseph (and doubtless his friends would be aware of it) would thereby have all their hopes extinguished. But as the promise was given to Rachel that *her* children should return, so also would God bring back *His* Son, as had been declared by another prophet, "Out of Egypt have I called my son."

Why are the interesting events recorded by Luke, which occurred between the birth of Jesus and the flight into Egypt, omitted by Matthew?

As Matthew is giving us the history of a royal successor to David, his whole narrative is in harmony with his object, and instead of the purification in the Temple, the rapture of Simeon, etc., he recounts the visits of illustrious persons, with homage and gifts of gold, frankincense and myrrh, all worthy of a prince. Matthew is writing about a king, and therefore he speaks so frequently about the kingdom over which, in due time, this king would reign.

CHAPTER III.

1. *"In those days came John the Baptist." Is Baptist a proper designation?*

Baptistes should be rendered immerser, as the word expresses his work, not his title. He is distinguished not so much by his preaching as by his immersing in water those who believed in the coming Messiah.

2. *Was this "kingdom of heaven" a new theme to the nation of Israel?*

As a prophecy it was old and familiar to all, but the proclamation of it being "at hand" must have been new and startling. As every Jew had his own ideal of this promised kingdom, and depicted it in glowing colours, the news of its approach must have aroused the deepest interest.

What did he mean by it being "at hand"?

He meant that it was near, not merely as to time, but as it was to be entered by accepting the truth concerning Jesus, it was as near as the proclamation could make it; for by accepting the truth the obedient at once became subjects of this new and heavenly administration. When Jesus afterwards said, "Blessed are the poor in spirit, for theirs is the kingdom of heaven," He evidently shows that to all such it had a veritable existence.

5, 6. *Matthew here says that "Jerusalem, and all Judea, and all the region round about Jordan," went out and were baptised by John, and that Pharisees and Sadducees also went, whom he would not baptise. Who were the former persons?*

Jesus afterwards speaks of them as publicans and harlots, who repented at the preaching of John, and Matthew here calls them sinners, as they confessed their sins, which the Pharisees never did. This very large class of persons who thronged to hear John were those who felt that they needed mercy, and not the law, which they had broken. Their teachers expounded the law of Moses, with a good deal of tradition mixed up with it, which only condemned those who failed to keep it; while John proclaimed remission of sins to all who accepted the coming Messiah, and so drew to Him a multitude of hearts, and effected a great reformation of life. This is the class of persons who are spoken of when it said, Jerusalem and all Judea, etc., went out to John and were immersed by him.

7-9. *Why did John rebuke the Pharisees and Sadducees when they came to his immersion?*

Because they came to him as the seed of Abraham, and not as sinners needing a Saviour. They wished to be immersed on the ground of having the old covenant, and not accepting the provision to be enjoyed through the new. How could they flee from coming wrath, when they did not believe that they were in danger of it? John had therefore to show to them that their fleshly relation to Abraham was of no value, and that out of stones, *i.e.*, the down-trodden ones of the nation, God, through Jesus, was able to raise up children to Abraham.

What was the result of this plain speaking?

The rejection of John as their teacher, and thus the rejection of the counsel of God.

10–12. *John immersed in water, but the Coming One was to immerse in the Holy Spirit and fire. Are these latter two aspects of one blessing?*

They are two distinct manifestations of what the Psalmist calls "mercy and judgment,"—the former shown at Pentecost (Acts ii.), when the apostles received the promised immersion in the Spirit, in order to insure a faithful proclamation of the new covenant to the house of Israel and of Judah, and by which they began to cleanse the threshing floor, and to gather His wheat into the garner, *i.e.*, the church; the latter at the destruction of Jerusalem, when the chaff, *i.e.*, the rejectors of Christ, was burned with unquenchable fire.

Does the term "fire" mean a literal flame?

Certainly not. It is a symbol of the judgment of God, and was frequently so used by the prophets. The fire of which John here speaks was the invasion of Jerusalem, A.D. 71, by the Romans, who utterly destroyed the nationality and ecclesiastical polity of the Jews, as foretold by Malachi (iv. 1), "The day that cometh shall burn them up, saith the Lord of Hosts, that it shall leave them neither root nor branch."

The fire is said to be unquenchable. Does this refer to time or eternity?

It is the judgment of the Jewish dispensation or age, and its effects still continue upon all who cling to the old economy. John refers to its operation in time, not in eternity. Paul expresses the same truth in another figure, when he says, "Let their eyes be darkened, that they may not see, and bow down their back alway." (Rom. xi. 10.)

Is the fleshly standing of the Jew of no value in this dispensation?

It is of no value whatever, because the covenant that pertained to the flesh is out of date, and "the circumcision" now are they "who worship God in spirit, and rejoice in Christ Jesus, and have no confidence in the flesh" (Phil. iii. 3); "He is a Jew who is one inwardly, and circumcision is that of the heart, in the spirit, not in the letter, whose praise is not of men, but of God" (Rom. ii. 29). The only hope for a Jew in this dispensation is in the Gospel of Jesus, and he is as welcome to trust in Him as any Gentile can be, "For there is no difference between Jew and Greek, for the same Lord over all is rich unto all that call upon Him" (Rom. x. 12).

13. *Of the life of Jesus between the return of Joseph from Egypt and His own immersion by John, Matthew says nothing at all. Is not this silence a great loss to us?*

It is only in keeping with the history of many of God's distinguished servants. What do we know of the life of Moses during those forty years' sojourn in the land of Midian, save that he kept the flock of Jethro, thus learning lessons of patience and humility, all of which were needed by him when shepherding the flock of God? Or what do we know about David before his anointing by Samuel, except that he kept his father's sheep, played on the harp, and that he was a skilful and exact marksman with the sling? We only know that they were being secretly trained for their future life and action, and the results are manifest to us, when a nation is the charge, and Goliath of

Gath the mark for the sling and the stone. We may wonder as to the manner in which Jesus spent those twenty years or more; but that incident recorded by Luke, when He was in that circle of learned Rabbis, both hearing and asking them questions, will show how He had been employed. That hidden life of Jesus, if we may so term it, was one of untiring study of the will of God. Every type and symbol, every prophecy and precept, is so thoroughly made His own, that when He enters the field of service for God He commits no mistakes. The great secret of His perfect life as a servant, and as a Son, is His perfect knowledge of the revealed will of God, and His complete subjection to it. One great reason why our service is so imperfect, even when the heart is sincere, is our imperfect knowledge of His Word. If the Scriptures are not our daily study, how can we become acquainted with their teaching? If poetry and history, languages and science, news and romance, are eagerly devoured, while the Word of God is seldom read, how can the life be other than a spiritually barren one? In His life of Scripture study and active service, He has left us a bright example.

13–17. *What distance did Jesus travel in order to be immersed?*

Matthew says that He came from Galilee to Jordan, where John was immersing, which some say was about a hundred miles, and the lesson which that long journey supplies should not be overlooked. Jesus did not wait for favourable circumstances, but overcame the difficulties which distance put in His way. John was far off, but Jesus could travel; and by His obedience He obtained the recognition of God, and the anointing of the Spirit.

The immersion of the people by John had reference to their past sins;

but as Jesus had no sin, why was He immersed?

In the immersion appointed by God, there is not only a burial, but also a rising again, and these acts have relation both to the past and to the future. The past life of a sinner is one of obedience to sin, but in the truly repentant heart there is in this ordinance a burial of the past, and a rising again to a life of obedience to God. Jesus, prior to His immersion, though He had no sin, was yet by the law of Moses placed under parental and other restraints, and fully complied with them; but when He rose from that grave of water, He rose to give His life to God in a new service. From that voluntary surrender of Himself He was a whole burnt offering, a sacrifice and an offering to God for a sweet-smelling savour.

What are the most prominent matters connected with the immersion of Jesus?

(1.) His prompt obedience to God: "Suffer it to be so now, for thus it becometh us to fulfil all righteousness." (2.) His anointing by the Spirit, by which He became the Christ, *i.e.*, the anointed of God. (3.) God's recognition of Him as His Son; for years He had been known only as the son of Joseph and Mary, but from that time He was to be known and confessed as the Son of God.

CHAPTER IV.

1–11. *" Tempted of the devil." Was such a trial necessary for Jesus?*

The temptation was doubtless necessary to the "second man," the head of a new creation, and under the circumstances it was unavoidable. He was sure to be opposed by Satan, the great foe of humanity, who was indeed the god of the age, over which he had power, and could exercise it against all who came within the range of his operations. Then Jesus had not only to conquer for Himself, but He had also to show to all who should accept Him as their leader, that all spiritual conquests must be gained by means of truth. He did not overcome Satan by physical omnipotence, but by the omnipotence of truth.

Had this spiritual conflict and conquest of Christ over Satan any typical illustration in the conduct of the saints of old?

There is a very striking illustration in the case of David, who, when sent after his anointing to carry provision to his brethren, heard the defiant challenge of the giant of Gath, accepted it, and with a sling and a stone brought the proud boaster to the earth.

Did Satan follow any definite plan in these temptations?

The temptations were evidently arranged so as to bear upon the circumstances in which He was placed. He was hungry, in poverty and obscurity, so the temptations were adapted to these conditions. Satan's liberty to do this must have been the result of God's permission, for since man yielded to the first temptation, God has given to Satan power in circumstances which he can now use for purposes of evil, so that none, not even Jesus Himself, could be free, when He came within the sphere in which Satan is allowed to work. Here we see Jesus in poverty, and Satan uses His condition to provoke an unlawful use of power, and thus to break His trust in God His Father.

Does a change of circumstances, then, only alter the form of temptation, never remove it?

This is a truth that should never be forgotten, and the example of Jesus should be deeply studied in this respect. He never sought to change circumstances, but to improve them, and if evil, to overcome them by the truth. We are ever seeking to change our trying circumstances, and looking for change as our only hope. Too often, alas! we think of being better only in a better position, and so mistake the purpose of trial. It is not change that we should seek, but conquest through patient endurance. Poverty may be a snare, but riches may be a far greater one ; to be unnoticed may be humiliating, but to be admired and caressed may be positively dangerous. Every position will have its own peculiar dangers, against which we must "watch and pray, lest we enter into temptation."

Jesus met the three temptations with the Word of God. Is His method an example to us?

There is no other way of meeting temptation successfully, and if we only use the truth as Jesus used it, we too shall triumph. His pathway of humble dependence was clearly marked out for Him by the Spirit. Satan endeavoured to turn Him from it, but He nobly resisted and waited upon God. God has revealed to us in His Word every thing He wishes us to do ; Satan ever seeks to work in us disobedience to His will. The test is often a severe one—some fleshy gratification, some pecuniary gain, some worldly elevation, is urgently pressed upon our acceptance ; whether we shall yield on some vain pretext, or resist and please God, is often a solemn crisis fraught with consequences which eternity alone can reveal.

Why would it have been wrong for Jesus to have turned the stones into bread when He had power to do it?

Because by doing so He would have failed as an example of trust in God. How could He have asked His disciples to prove God's faithfulness by their patient endurance had He relieved His own need by omnipotence ? There is not a trial, even pinching poverty and hunger, which He has not felt ; and there is not a difficulty in which He has not proved the faithfulness of God.

Is the departure of Satan, and the visit of the angels, a proof of triumph and deliverance ?

A very manifest one ; Satan leaves the field, and angels attend to relieve the needs of Jesus. This is always the case when God is trusted. He watches the very day and hour when deliverance should come, and those who trust Him shall never be confounded.

12. *Did not the imprisonment of John prove a sad loss to the work of proclamation ?*

It would appear as such at the time, the labourers being so few and the work so important, but as the Lord of the harvest called in other labourers, first twelve, and afterwards seventy, the loss was amply supplied. Every city and village in the land heard the Gospel of the Kingdom, and saw the evidences of its truth, so the work begun by John was most efficiently sustained.

13–16. *Why is it said that light did spring up in those morally dark regions adjoining Capernaum, when Jesus went to dwell there ?*

Because wherever Jesus went He made known the truth that enlightens dark minds, and as Isaiah had mentioned these border lands as sharing the blessings attending His dwelling in Capernaum, Matthew carefully notes that " the people which sat in darkness saw a great light." This simple incident should be a lesson to us that wherever we go we should carry the light of truth with us. The truth of God shines through the medium of teaching and living, and He who has enlightened our dark minds expects us to both live and teach His truth.

18–22. *The calling of these fisher-men by the Sea of Galilee was seemingly very sudden. Had they ever met with Jesus before ?*

John in his Gospel, chap. i., describes a previous interview, when so firm a conviction of Jesus being the Messiah had taken hold of their minds, that they went along with Him, and saw further convincing proofs of this truth. They appear to have then returned to their usual employment, but when again met by Jesus, were desired to follow Him : so their life-work began.

They had to leave their boats and nets. What compensation did Jesus offer them ?

We do not read of any inducement being offered by Him to secure their services. The work itself was an honour to be coveted, and the loss was ultimately a gain, as they afterwards learned. They left nets, and boats, and friends, to follow Jesus, and He gave them a throne and glory. Though He promised nothing at first, He was not unrighteous to forget their work and labour of love.

23–25. *" And they brought unto Him all sick people that were taken with divers diseases," etc. Why does Matthew give us this terrible picture ?*

Not to reveal the sad condition of humanity, but to show that Jesus could meet it in its most dreadful form. His ministry was one of loving pity for those who were in trouble, and a wondrous revelation of the heart of God.

CHAPTER V.

1. *To whom does this discourse delivered on the Mount specially refer ?*

A proper understanding of its application as well as its meaning is very important. It was delivered to the disciples of Jesus, or those who had put themselves under His teaching when separated from the multitude, and was intended for their instruction in the principles of the new institution—the kingdom which God was about to set up, and over which in due time Jesus was to reign. Moses was the ruler under God in the Jewish institution, by the laws and statutes given through him, and which were in harmony with it as a fleshly typical institution. The great Teacher, who was also to be a ruler; thus early in His ministry, made known to His disciples the principles of the new reign, assuring them that unless their righteousness exceeded that of the Scribes and Pharisees, they should in no wise enter into the kingdom of heaven.

If in this discourse the principles of the new reign were presented, when did they come into operation, or, in other words, when did the kingdom of heaven begin?

It began with their acceptance of the principles and truths on which it was based. When the laws were received the reign began, when the required poverty of spirit was a reality the kingdom became the portion of those who realised it.

Why were the multitude not present with the disciples when Jesus delivered this memorable discourse?

The multitudes had been deeply interested in seeing the miracles, and to hear that the kingdom was at hand was most exciting, and aroused their ideal expectation, but few cared to learn how they might become subjects of it, and it has always been so. Preaching is generally about something that can be talked about and discussed with others, while teaching is more searching, and deals with the heart and the life, and but few care to be thus dealt with. The teaching of Jesus (and He was a pattern to all teachers) was like a mirror, in which men could see their own hearts reflected, not at all a pleasant sight; and this was the principal reason why the disciples, not the multitude, the learners, not the hearers, came to Him in the Mount, " and when He was set, He opened His mouth and taught them."

3. *What did He teach them?*

A secret which all desire to know, but to the knowledge of which few attain—the secret of a blessed or happy life, because it is learned only by those who do the things which lead into the kingdom.

Was the kingdom spoken of a visible one?

Jesus said nothing about it being visible. He told them who would possess it or be its subjects, and from this teaching something of its nature and existence may be learned. It may appear strange that God should set up a kingdom that could not be seen, but its visibility or otherwise must depend upon the medium through which it is to be viewed. If it was to be seen only through the truth, then the believing alone could see it, but if through a fleshly medium, then all might see it. Jesus Himself was the Son of God, but only those who believed the testimony could see this divine relation, the unbelieving saw Him only as the son of Joseph. The Pharisees, not understanding His teaching respecting the kingdom, were looking for it in a tangible form, and had to be told " the kingdom of God cometh not with observation," *i.e.*, with outward show, neither shall ye say, lo here! or lo there! for, behold, the kingdom of God is within you, *lit.*, in the midst of you (Luke xvii. 21). These persons, looking for it coming in material tangibility and pomp, could not see it, although existing among them —not, of course, in Christ-rejecting Pharisees, but in truth-loving disciples. It is " within," said Jesus, not without, to be felt in the heart, not seen with the eye. Paul expressed the same truth when he wrote, " The kingdom of God is not meat and drink," *lit.*, eating and drinking, " but righteousness, peace, and joy in a holy spirit " (Rom. xiv. 17). There were harlots and publicans who in poverty of spirit received the kingdom of God as a little child, and entered into it; and there were Scribes and Pharisees who could not, and never did see it. Jesus came to to make known the truth which begets a new life in him who receives it, and whenever this truth is so received, the reign of God is begun. It may be called the " new reign," or as Jesus termed it, " the kingdom of heaven," *lit.*, the heavens, but this was what He was speaking about when He said, " Blessed are the poor in spirit, for theirs is the kingdom of heaven." It may appear strange to some that complete emptiness of that in which the Pharisees rested should be a qualification for entering the kingdom, yet it was so, and so it remains.

What did Jesus mean when He said " the meek shall inherit the earth " ? Were they to possess land ?

The people to whom Jesus made His proclamations had received the land of Palestine as national property, but this possession failed to meet the deep need felt by many hearts, hence their waiting for the kingdom of God. The flesh might be satisfied with the earth, but the heart yearned for something which earth could not bestow. When the kingdom of heaven, therefore, was proclaimed, and its associated blessings were offered to men, for the sake of Christ they forsook houses, lands, and all that flesh held dear; thus proving that they understood Jesus to refer not to secular but to spiritual privileges. It is true that Jesus uses the term earth in the promise made to the meek, but the truth must not

be overlooked that in stating the privileges of the new covenant, both Christ and His apostles employ those terms which denoted the privileges of the old covenant. As the old was a type of the new, the Law a shadow of the Faith, we must not expect to find the shadow and the substance the same thing. Jerusalem the antitype is not the old city of the types ; the earth of the better promises is not the earth of the old inheritance ; the holy nation of the faith is not the old nation of the tribes of Israel ; and, to prevent such mistakes, many of the old terms have some qualifying word affixed to them explaining the nature of the thing referred to. Hence " *Heavenly* Jerusalem," " *Holy* nation," " *New* Covenant," " *Better* hope," was sufficient to inform even a Jew that a new order of things was presented, and though many of the terms belonging to the new dispensation are not so plain and definite they must not be put in the wrong list. When reading of the old institution we should remember that we are among fleshly and material things ; and when reading or speaking of the new institution, whether from prophets or apostles, from Isaiah or from Paul, we must not apply their description of spiritual things, although clothed in earthly and material language, to some carnal scheme. Our first great care, when reading the Spirit's teaching, should be to ascertain to which dispensation it belongs, and at the same time to keep before us the great landmarks laid down for our guidance, viz., that "the Faith" follows "the Law;" the spiritual the natural ; the temple of " living stones " the temple of " hewn stones," and that this order is not to be reversed. To make a carnal economy succeed a spiritual one is to adopt a course which has no countenance in divine revelation. To be undiscerning in the dispensational application of terms used by the Holy Spirit is to draw a veil over the truth, and make ourselves the victims of delusion and disappointment.

13–16. *"Ye are the salt of the earth," "Ye are the light of the world." Had this teaching a special application to the disciples that heard Jesus, or does it apply to all believers?*

We should not overlook the special relation in which these disciples stood to Him from whom they received the truth, of which salt is a symbol; and to the earth, *i.e.*, the Jewish people, who as far as they received the truth were preserved from corruption; and to the light as a symbol of the gospel shining through them into the world, *i.e.*, the nations. These disciples were the first to receive the truth of the kingdom and the light of the gospel, thus becoming the medium through which it spread among the two sections of the human family. Believers now are merely the receivers of light through the apostles' testimony, and require themselves to walk in the light, and so commend it to others, who may be induced to accept it also. Jesus is here speaking of the responsibility of those first disciples to the Jews, their own brethren, and to the nations. The importance of these twelve men being true to the trust committed to them was greater than that of any others who have lived since their time. Who can measure the consequences to the world had the salt in them become savourless, and their light been placed under a bushel?

Were the succeeding directions and instructions in this discourse given specially to those who heard Him, and if so, what have we to do with them?

The instructions were doubtless specific, but it is our privilege also to learn from them what is pleasing to Him, and in faith and love to practise what He has enjoined.

17. *Why had Jesus to tell them that He had not come to destroy the law and the prophets?*

The Jews, from want of the spirit of loving obedience, regarded the law as an intolerable burden, and they thought that the new teacher, the Messiah, would set it aside, and introduce an easier code of obligations. This He assured them He would not do, for He came not to destroy or loose down, but to fulfil.

18. *"Till heaven and earth pass." What is meant by these words?*

The removal of the Jewish institution, heaven and earth as symbols, were frequently applied to them by the prophets (see Isaiah i. 2), and thus we are prepared for such an application. When we remember that the law had its threatenings or judgments as well as its claims, it was a most solemn utterance indeed when He said, all should be fulfilled, He met all its claims, but its judgments fell on them because of their disobedience.

19. *"The least in the kingdom of heaven." How can any be esteemed least in heaven?*

It is not heaven that Jesus is speaking of, but the kingdom of heaven upon the earth. It is where men can term God-appointed commands non-essential, and neglect them, and teach others to do the same. Such persons, although they have entered the kingdom by accepting Christ, are, by slighting His claims in some matters, disapproved by Him, and called the least in the kingdom. What the ultimate issue may be will depend upon subsequent behaviour. If such repent they will be forgiven, if they continue to oppose, their rejection must follow. Many of the Jews were thrust out of the kingdom, while others repented and found in it an abiding place.

21, 22. *To the ancients it was said, "Thou shalt not kill," but why did Jesus forbid anger?*

Because while a murderer would be amenable to a Roman tribunal, anger would be judged by God. A libel on character could be dealt with by the Council or Sanhedrin; but the spiteful word would expose the utterer to hell fire, *lit.*, the Gehenna of fire. As there were two courts of justice, at one of which small offences were tried, and at the other greater crimes, so Jesus reminds them of a still higher court, even God's, where the spirit that prompts all words and actions will be judged by Him.

25, 26. *Why does Jesus urge speedy agreement with an adversary ?*

The advice is based on sound wisdom. It is always best, if at all possible, to cease contentions before they are carried into a court of justice. If the adversary can be appeased, the matter is ended; but if it is put into the hands of judges, then the consequences must be endured even to the uttermost farthing. Possibly there was also in this advice a lesson for the nation to consider. They had made God their adversary, and it would be well for them to make an agreement before the matter went to judgment, because, if it proceeded thus far, the utmost penalty would be inflicted.

27, 28. *What effect was the Saviour's reference to adultery intended to produce ?*

Purity of heart as well as life. Not only was the act to be avoided, but even the evil desire was to be regarded as sinning against God.

29, 30. *Is the right eye and the right hand to be literally separated from the body ?*

Both the eye and the hand are harmless unless prompted to sin by an evil mind, but the actions of which they are the symbols are to be separated from the life. The teaching of Jesus plainly intimates that the dearest thing on earth must be sac-rificed or cut off, if it cause us to stumble.

What is meant by the whole body being " cast into hell " ?

Literally it is the Gehenna, the place of burning or judgment, and is terribly suggestive of the doom of those who rejected the reign of God. It was a prophetic warning of the doom of the nation, when the whole body would suffer in that burning fire of siege and famine, slaughter and death. Better, far better, would it have been for them to have suffered every conceivable loss for the kingdom of God, than this entire loss in the Gehenna of fire.

31, 32. *Why did Jesus refer to the law of divorce ?*

Because, as then applied, it was a violation of the law of God. True, Moses had given them the law of divorce in the matter of uncleanness, but they had made it apply to every form of dislike which a man might take to his wife, and when written on a legal form, he could place it in her hand, send her away, and thus free himself from the marriage bond. Fornication was the only cause for which a man was allowed by God to put away his wife ; every other reason was evil in His sight. To such a height had this iniquity of divorce risen in the days of Malachi, that God thus spoke through him, "And this have ye done again, covering the altar of the Lord with tears, with weeping, and with crying out (of divorced wives), insomuch that He regardeth not the offering any more, or receiveth it with goodwill at your hands (ii. 13–16). Nor had the evil at all abated in the days of Christ, so that it was needful to warn His disciples against it, lest they should be ensnared by popular example, and forget the law of God.

33–37. *Is the Saviour's injunction against swearing to be obeyed under all circumstances ?*

Most certainly; nothing can be plainer than "But I say unto you, swear not at all," and, to prevent His words being misunderstood, He adds, "But let your speech be yea, yea; nay, nay; for whatsoever is more than these cometh of evil."

38, 39. *It was Moses who said, "Eye for eye, tooth for tooth," but Jesus taught His disciples not to resist evil. How are these contrary teachings reconciled?*

Both are consistent. The law given by Moses required justice, but Jesus came to show mercy, and asks His disciples to manifest His spirit in their dealings with others. They might follow Moses, and revenge in full measure, with tongue or fist, every word or blow dealt by others, but doing so they could not be the disciples of Jesus. It is certainly not in human nature to turn the left cheek to him who has smitten the right, but it is Christ-like, and to follow His example and teaching will glorify Him.

40. *The Saviour directs His disciples not to resist those who would sue them at the law. Would not the rights of those who do so be sorely trampled upon?*

All such would have God for their advocate and defender, and happy is he who has the God of Jacob for his helper. There are thousands who have followed their own course in the matter of resistance, who afterwards would have been glad had they adopted the advice of Jesus. Getting and retaining our rights in this world is not everything; there are hearts to be won for Christ, and the manifestation of His spirit in peace, meekness, and unselfishness, will go much further in effecting this desirable object than strife, war, and law suits, which too often make this world a hell upon earth.

44. *"Love your enemies." How is it possible to do this?*

By having the spirit of Him who loved us, even when we were His enemies. Still it is well to understand that it is not mere affection that is called for, but loving action. His own spirit of love being our guide, He makes His sun to shine on the evil and the good. "Be ye therefore perfect, as your Father who is in heaven is perfect."

CHAPTER VI.

1–8. *"Take heed that ye do not your alms before men." Why does Jesus warn His disciples against public display?*

It may be well to state that the word alms, in ver. 1, is, *lit.*, righteousness, and includes both the alms-giving, prayer, and fasting afterwards named. It was needful that Jesus should warn His disciples against public display in doing these things, not only because human nature is so prone to it, but the practice of the Pharisees was very ensnaring in this respect. In almsgiving, a trumpet was sounded to intimate the act, and the corners of the broad ways where many were passing were selected at which to offer prayers, all to be seen of men. "Verily I say unto you, they have their reward." Men see and praise them, but God approves not of their work.

Is it wrong to tell others what we do for God in our religious service?

Yes; if it is simply to let them see how good, or holy, or benevolent we are. It is sounding the trumpet, and we may lose the divine reward through it. We must seek to live before God, not before men.

"Enter into thy closet." Is is absolutely necessary to have a closet or secret place for prayer?

Yes; but let us fully understand what a closet really means. The public street in which we are walking, or the shop in which we are serving may be our closet, because from thence, unheard by others, our prayers may ascend to our Father, who seeth in secret, and He who seeth in secret will reward thee. The word "openly" is possibly an interpolation, and should be omitted.

9–13. *"After this manner therefore pray ye," etc. Why did Jesus teach His disciples this prayer?*

Because in their transition from Judaism they required to understand their relation to God, to His kingdom, and to one another; and this their divine teacher kindly supplied.

Was this prayer, generally called the Lord's prayer, intended for use through all time?

It seems to have been intended only for that introductory period, as those who were converted by the apostles were taught by inspiration to pray, and also to sing. Some of its petitions will always be applicable, but not as a general form of prayer.

16–18. *Is fasting appointed by God, and is it in force as a law under the present dispensation?*

Fasting was appointed under the law in connection with the day of atonement or expiation, when the Jews were commanded to afflict their souls, or fast from even to even. But in addition to this God-appointed fast—a type of the deep exercise of heart and separation from evil which would take place under the Gospel, in reconciliation to God —there were many other men-appointed fasts, even as the Pharisees fasted twice a week with disfigured faces, and thus compelled men to own their piety and zeal. It was not before God they fasted, but before men, and from them they had their reward. "When thou fastest," said Jesus, "do not be like them; let God alone know what you do, and by Him you will be rewarded." Fasting was not commanded by Jesus, but has His approval when done in

a proper spirit. Then we have the example of the church at Antioch, which fasted and prayed, ere they sent Paul and Barnabas on their mission to the Gentiles. With many Christians, however, daily abstinence, or fasting from mere indulgences which would prove injurious to the inner man, is needed. The end of fasting is restraint of the body, and this has to be daily maintained, if its members are to be servants to righteousness unto holiness.

19–21. *"Lay not up for yourselves treasures upon earth." How is one to know whether their treasure is on earth or in heaven?*

By noting what is most esteemed, carnal or spiritual things. That which is the heart's treasures will have the most of its interest and attention; and a little careful observation will make this manifest to all. We may all know whether worldly or spiritual conversation is most interesting to us; whether the house of prayer or scenes of vanity are most attractive; whether Christ or self hold the first place. Whatever rules the heart and the life decides where our treasure is.

24. *"Ye cannot serve God and mammon." What is mammon?*

Mammon was the name of the Syrian god of riches, the obtaining of which, by whatever means, was held to be pleasing to it. To serve mammon was understood by the Jews to be devotedness to the obtaining of wealth.

25. *"Take no thought for your life." Did the Saviour wish them to be careless of life?*

No. It was over-anxiousness, *i.e.*, a divided mind, against which He bids them beware. He wished them to know that God cared for them, and this should free them from anxiety, but not from any duty which might lawfully devolve upon them.

Was this injunction meant only for

those who then followed Him, or for disciples in every age?

It was addressed to those who had left all and followed Him, but every disciple in every age should fully confide in God. This precept of Jesus really meant, do not trust in circumstances, trust in God.

May we, then, still appropriate the same helpful facts which they were called to consider?

The very same. God is still clothing the grass, and painting the flowers, and feeding the birds, and thus is still furnishing proofs of His continued care over His creatures. The neglect of these things would be a positive loss of needed instruction.

What did Jesus mean by asking, Is not the life more than meat?

The question supplies its own answer. God gave the life, and will He not give food to sustain it? He made the body, will He not give clothing for it? Who will dare deny that He will.

CHAPTER VII.

1, 2. *Why did Jesus forbid His disciples to sit in judgment on each other?*

There are several reasons for His doing so. (1.) There is a natural proneness in man to do this, while the habit is a spiritually unhealthy one, and injurious in many ways to one's own mind. (2.) All have failed before God, and, to say the least, it is very unbecoming in those who themselves have failed to sit in judgment on the shortcomings of others. It is displeasing to our Heavenly Father to hear His children recounting, on every occasion, the failings of each other, instead of hiding them in brotherly love. (3.) God Himself claims this prerogative of judging them, as an apostle teaches, "Why dost thou judge thy brother, or why dost thou set at nought thy brother? for we shall all stand before

the judgment-seat of Christ" (Rom. xiv. 10). (4.) According to the judgment and measure we bestow upon others will be our own, and this cannot fail because God has declared it. The season may be a long one, but the harvest will come, and when it does arrive, it will resemble in kind the seed sown. David once shed innocent blood, and though the Lord forgave his sin, the sword never departed from his house. Ebedmelech, the Ethiopian, did but a neighbourly action when he procured the release of Jeremiah from the dungeon, where otherwise he must have died; but he received a blessed return when the word came to him from the Lord, "Thy life shall be a prey unto thee, because thou hast put thy trust in Me." "Judge not, that ye be not judged," is a precept we should consider; and instead of measuring out evil in word and deed, it will be better to " scatter seeds of kindness for our reaping by and by."

3–5. *Is the mote and the beam connected with judging each other?*

It is a most pointed appeal to those who judge, and the charge of hypocrisy was justly deserved. It was a professed regard to righteousness to point out the mote, *i.e.*, the small splinter in a brother's eye, while the beam in their own was not even thought of. Let self-improvement be your first work, and then you will be better fitted to improve others.

6. *What does Jesus mean by "dogs" and "swine," to which the "holy" must not be given?*

These dogs and swine were symbols of men of like dispositions and habits, who turned back to the errors they had once renounced. The Jews, as is mentioned by Peter in his Second Epistle, furnished many sad illustrations of this return to old habits. These words of Jesus were prophetic warnings respecting them.

Should this command of Jesus pre-

vent us from seeking the salvation of the unsaved ?

Certainly not ; the cases are widely different. The salvation of the unsaved should be sought by every possible means ; but those " who had tasted of the good word of God, and the powers of the world to come," *i.e.*, the Spirit's gifts in the new dispensation, and had renounced such for Judaism, were in a hopeless condition.

7–11. Is the privilege of asking and receiving favours from God conferred unconditionally ?

It is bestowed only through Christ, and those who desire needful mercies must seek them through Him. Jesus does not name the medium of access, but it is always implied. Even under the law blessings could be enjoyed only through obedience to its requirements, and in these the Coming One was always set forth in some appointed type, so that faith in a coming Messiah was required, ere spiritual blessing could be obtained. The illustration of a father's conduct towards his son is doubtless given to show that, as a parent would not disappoint a child in its proper request for food, neither would their heavenly Father disappoint the earnest request of His children.

12. " Whatsoever ye would that men should do to you, do ye even so to them," etc. What is the special relation of this appeal ?

It stands related to the entire paragraph. He had told them not to judge others, when their own life would not bear a close inspection. He also showed them how God their Father treated His needy suppliants, "giving good things to those who ask Him." " Therefore, all things whatsoever ye would that men should do to you, do ye even so to them."

13, 14. " Enter ye in at the strait gate." What does this mean ?

Gate and door are symbols which are frequently used in the Bible, and must not be confounded with each other. Both are means of entrance, but each has a special application. " Gate " here is a symbol of law, justice, righteousness, and authoritative claim ; whilst " door " is a symbol of grace, by which Jesus designates Himself. " I am the door," said He, but He is never called the gate. He entered by the gate Himself, as stated in Ps. cxviii. 19, " Open to me the gates of righteousness, I will go into them, and will praise the Lord." His own teaching, as given in this discourse to disciples, was a strait gate to many ; but the claims were divine, and to realise the end desired obedience had to be rendered. Hence, " it hath been said by them of old time," and " but I say unto you," must be carefully distinguished.

If divine claims are represented by the strait gate, what is meant by wide is the gate ?

The wide gate also represents authority or claims, but not of God, but " traditions of the elders," which Scribes and Pharisees kept open, to the ruin of all who entered thereat, because it was the way of disobedience to God.

" Few there be that find it." Is this applicable to all time ?

Jesus was speaking only of that time. His words strictly are, " few are those finding it," while many were entering through the wide gate leading to destruction.

Does the word " destruction" mean annihilation ?

No. It means a change from a former state, whether applied to persons or things, but never total extinction of being. The prodigal son was lost, *lit.*, destroyed, when in the far country, yet he returned to his father's house. The sheep of the house of Israel were lost, *i.e.*, gone to destruction, yet Jesus came to seek and save them. Dr Ellicot says, " I question whether a single passage can be adduced in which it (the word destruction) means in relation to material things more than the breaking up of their outward form and beauty, or in spiritual things more than what may be described as the wretchedness of a wasted life. We must not therefore attach the idea of annihilation to the word destruction."

15–20. *"Beware of false prophets." In what did the danger of heeding them consist?*

In being led to believe that the judgment of God would not overtake the nation in its degeneracy, as had been foretold by the prophets, and also by John. The evil fruit proved the tree to be evil, and would be hewn down and cast into the fire. Beware of them, said Jesus, whatever their profession may be, or you may be ensnared by them.

22, 23. *"I never knew you." Who were these rejected ones, and when was the day of their rejection?*

They were disciples who became faithless to Christ, although they had received some gifts of power, and, as they plead, had cast out devils or demons. The day of their rejection was that which overtook the guilty nation in which the faithless suffered through their rejection of Christ.

24–27. *What did Jesus intend to teach by the houses built on the rock and on the sand?*

The consequences of obedience and disobedience to all who heard Him. Those who heard and obeyed, would not be swept away by the coming storm ; while those who heard and were disobedient, would not be able to stand against it.

CHAPTER VIII.

We have here an account of a leper healed by Christ. Was pure sympathy His only object in doing this?

There was sympathy doubtless, but Jesus had a far higher object in view than the relief of bodily suffering. He came to cleanse the impure in heart and life, to cure the spiritually diseased, and to give life to those spiritually dead ; and to show His fitness to work in this latter field, He began to work in the former. He asked men to receive His mind-enlightening truth, but first of all He gave sight to the blind. He came to quicken into spiritual life, and, to encourage men to believe on Him, He quickened into life those physically dead. Thus this ministry among the sick was intended to help in the higher ministry of salvation, by drawing out their obedient trust in Himself as the God-provided Saviour.

Why did the leper say, "Lord, if thou wilt, thou canst make me clean"?

Because he had not received any promise that Jesus would heal him. There was modesty as well as confidence in his faith. He believed that Jesus had the power, but felt that he had no right to claim it.

Why did Jesus send him to the priest when He had healed him?

Because though He had healed him by the power of God, there was a law for his cleansing by the priest, and Jesus would not set aside any arrangement of God. The leper would have to be sprinkled with blood, washed with water, and anointed with oil (Levit. xiv.), and thus he would obtain a place in the congregation and family, which by his leprosy had been forfeited. Now the priest being appointed by God to do this, must be acknowledged, so the healed leper was sent to the priest to receive from him priestly cleansing.

Was the cleansing of the leper a type of any Christian privilege?

It was probably a type of the acceptance of believing Gentiles, who were once afar off, like defiled lepers,

B

but now are brought nigh by the blood of Christ.

5-10. *Why did Jesus marvel at the faith of this centurion ?*

The centurion was a Roman official stationed at Capernaum, in charge of soldiers, for the protection of Roman interests. No special effort had been made by Jesus for his benefit, but being a thoughtful observant man, and having confidence in the sympathy and power of Jesus, he ventured to ask Him to heal his servant. No sooner did Jesus reply, " I will come and heal him," than the strong faith of the man began to show itself. In felt unworthiness of such a visit, he at once proposed that Jesus should command, and his servant should be healed. His reference to his own authority over the soldiers stationed under him was most expressive : I have but to command, and I am obeyed, so you have but to speak the word only, and my servant shall be healed. Jesus was honoured by it, and granted his request.

11, 12. *What did Jesus mean by " Many shall come from the east and west, and shall sit down with Abraham, etc., in the kingdom of God " ?*

It was a prophetic declaration of the gathering of the nations to Himself whenever the opportunity should be given, because this gathering together of the outlying nations in the reign of God was to be when Jesus was exalted, and acknowledged by them, as He had been by Abraham, etc., previously. Jacob, when speaking of the Shiloh, said, " Unto Him shall the gathering of the people, *lit.*, peoples, be " (Gen. xlix. 10), and in this man's faith Jesus saw a proof that the Gentiles were ready to accept the grace of God and confirm the prophecies which had been given.

14-17. *" That it might be fulfilled."* *Why does Matthew connect so closely those cures of diseases with this prophecy by Isaiah ?*

The prophet had foretold that the Messiah would do these things, and had Jesus failed, even in the cure of sicknesses, this claim to be the Messiah would have been forfeited. So even this prophecy was fulfilled, " Himself took (away) our infirmities, and bore (removed) our sicknesses."

19, 20. *"Master, I will follow thee."* *Did this scribe understand what following Jesus implied ?*

It is evident that he did not, and Jesus at once undeceived him, by stating his own true position. It was fleshly position the man sought, and Jesus had nothing of that kind to offer, being, as He said, worse off than the foxes and birds of the air.

21. *" Suffer me first to go and bury my father."* *How could Jesus refuse this request ?*

It was not present burial that he wanted to perform, but to stay at home till his father's death, and then resume discipleship. We cannot think that Jesus would repress the desire of a son to perform the last token of respect to a parent ; but the man wished to make an agreement for future service, which Jesus would not accept. To-day was the claim of Christ, a more convenient day was the plan of this would-be disciple.

23. *This crossing the lake seems like separating Himself from the multitude. Why did He act thus?*

Because He saw that they were more anxious to have their diseases cured than to learn the truths He taught ; it therefore was necessary for them to be left to ponder over what He had already said and done.

24-26. *Why were the disciples afraid of the storm when Jesus was in the boat with them ?*

Because of their lack of faith and patience, and both were needed in that storm. Their work just then was to carry Jesus over the lake, and though He was sleeping, the tempest could not have frustrated His command to them to do so. In their fear and impatience they were overcome, and had to be rebuked. We have need to watch ourselves, lest we also become affected by circumstances, and faint and fear when we should be strong in the might of our Redeemer. In the voyage of this life storms will arise, and test our faith and patience. We need patient continuance, for the promise can only be received after we have done the will of God.

28–30. Matthew says that two men possessed with devils met Jesus in this country of the Gergesenes, while Mark and Luke, who seem to narrate the same event, speak only of one. Is it one event which is described by the three evangelists?

I am inclined to think that one event is referred to by all. That there were two men out of whom devils were cast is certain, because Matthew names two, while Mark and Luke name only one, who was so strikingly distinguished by his request to be with Jesus, and the peculiar mission given to him instead.

"Possessed with devils." What were these?

It is, *lit.*, demons, and so we should read, instead of devils, in every other place. There is but one devil, there are many demons. If we accept the testimony of Josephus, who expresses the conviction, not only of his own nation but also of all antiquity, they were the spirits of wicked men, who, entering into living beings on earth, controlled them as we find in the New Testament. This view is certainly sustained by the records of the evangelists, who speak of them as evil and unclean spirits, as entering into men, as being cast out and returning to the abyss from whence they came. How they could possess men, and why such manifestations

have ceased (if indeed they have ceased), we cannot say. That there were such, and that they acknowledged Jesus of Nazareth as the Son of God, is beyond all question, and full of interest to us who believe in Him as our Almighty Saviour.

32–34. The destruction of so many swine by these ejected demons was a most serious loss. How can this act of Jesus, who gave them permission to enter the swine, be justified?

The violation of God's law by those who kept those unclean animals was a more serious matter than their destruction, which must be regarded as a practical rebuke for their disregard of His claims. We are sorry that they thought more of their swine than of Jesus, as they "besought Him to depart out of their coasts."

CHAPTER IX.

1. *"And he entered into a ship and passed over, and came into his own city." What city was this?*

Capernaum, His adopted city, here called "His own city," while Nazareth of Galilee was "His own country" (Mark vi. 1). It is well to note these distinctions when reading His life.

2–8. This palsied man was brought to Jesus to be cured of his palsy. Why did Jesus declare first of all the forgiveness of his sins?

This act of remission of sins, so promptly tendered by Jesus, proves that a physical cure was not the greatest need felt by the man. There was a consciousness of unforgiven sin which lay far heavier on his heart than his bodily helplessness. He, no doubt, wished to be cured, but he more earnestly desired forgiveness, and this earnest desire was met by Jesus. This forgiving of sin also served another purpose. It aroused a slumbering jealousy against Him in certain scribes, who inwardly charged

Him with blasphemy, thus giving Him an opportunity of proving His authority. His proposed test was in the form of a question, "Which is easier to say, Thy sins be forgiven thee, or to say, Arise, and walk?" The helpless cripple lay before them, and every one must have felt that nothing less than the power of God could effect a cure. While all eyes were fixed on the paralytic, Jesus said, "But that ye may know that the Son of man hath power on earth to forgive sins (then said He to the sick of the palsy,) Arise, take up thy bed, and go to thine house ; and he arose, and departed to his house."

9. *Was not the call of Matthew to follow Jesus a very abrupt one?*

To all appearance the call was abrupt, and the response to it without deliberation, but in all probability the preparation for it had been sufficient. Matthew, doubtless, was a thoughtful man, and the visits of Jesus to Capernaum had not been unheeded by him. Then he had the writings of the prophets, with which he could compare the facts he observed and the signs he saw done by Jesus, and thus slowly, but surely, the conviction became rooted in his mind that this stranger was, indeed, the promised Messiah. He then needed only an opportunity to confess his faith; and as Jesus passed by the custom house on that ever-memorable day, the opportunity was given. "Follow me," said Jesus, "and he arose and followed Him." His instant decision was a most important step, as by so doing he became enrolled among the apostles of Jesus, which a few days' delay would have prevented, even had he afterwards become a disciple.

10. *Why did Matthew invite Jesus to a public entertainment in his house?*

There were two reasons at least : first, he showed that he was not ashamed of Jesus, but received Him into his house ; and second, he gave to many other publicans an opportunity of hearing his newly accepted teacher.

On what ground did the Pharisees object to Jesus eating with publicans and sinners?

On a traditional precept which made it defiling to do so; and they marvelled that Jesus should violate the traditions of the elders. His reply is full of heavenly compassion. He had come among men as a physician among the sick, and as a Saviour for sinners, and not for the righteous, who need no change of heart or life.

16–18. *Why did Jesus speak of an "old garment and new cloth" and "of new wine and old bottles?"*

To teach John's disciples, who came to inquire about fasting, that the "old garment" of Pharisaism could not be patched with the new cloth from heaven's loom, which would only spoil the character of both ; and that the old bottles of Judaic form could not hold the wine which flowed from the true vine. Fasting was only appropriate to seasons of trial, and never at marriage festivals.

18–31. *In these fourteen verses there are three striking cases of cure—the ruler's daughter who was dead, the woman with an issue of blood, and two blind men. Why are these recorded?*

To show that Jesus always responded to faith, no matter who manifested it. Each of these persons expressed their confidence that Jesus had power to relieve their need. The ruler said, "My daughter is even now dead : but come and lay thy hand upon her, and she shall live." The woman said (though within herself), "If I may but touch His garment, I shall be whole." The blind men, in response to the question of Jesus, "Believe ye that I am able to do this?" said, "Yea, Lord," and at once He granted their desire.

Why did Jesus charge these blind men not to make the cure known?

Lest it should cause trouble both to the blind men and Himself. The Pharisees were continually watching to turn all His doings against Him, and caution was required to enable Him to continue His good work.

32–34. *Jesus was here charged with casting out a demon by the prince of the demons. Is this an instance of their evil course?*

It is just one of the many instances in which they sought to hinder His influence among the people, and accounts for the reserve He had occasionally to practise.

35. *Jesus visited all the cities and villages. Was this all over Palestine?*

It was in Galilee, I presume, where He could pursue His work more unhindered than in Judea, the stronghold of Pharisees. But His personal visits only revealed the need there was for more labourers in the great harvest field.

38. *Who was the "Lord of the harvest"?*

God Himself, who was earnestly looking for fruit from this great Jewish field, into which He had then sent His own Son to labour. With Him, and under Him, others were also being led forth to gather some fruit for God.

Why does Jesus urge them to pray for more labourers?

There is much wisdom in the direction. Those who pray are the most likely to feel and work, and it was such persons Jesus wished to have associated with Himself while thus labouring for God.

CHAPTER X.

1. *In recording the sending forth of the twelve disciples, afterwards called apostles, Matthew has said nothing of their previous election to* apostleship. *Were they not chosen from among other disciples?*

Their being named as "His twelve" implies that they had been separated from other disciples, though Matthew records only his own separation for this work.

Why did Jesus give them power against unclean spirits, etc.?

To prove the divine authority of Him who sent them, and thus prepare the people to receive the truth proclaimed.

2–4. *"Now the names of the twelve apostles are these; Simon,"* etc. *Have these names any peculiar signification?*

Some of them are indicative of the faith and piety of parents or friends who gave them: as John, which means Jah or Jehovah, is gracious; Matthew, gift of Jah; Alpheus, taught of Jah; Lebbeus, lion of Jah; Thaddeus, breast of Jah; one of spiritual relation: as Peter, which means a rock stone, a name given by Jesus upon his confession of Him as the rock-foundation; and two of birthplace or location: as Simon the Cananæan, *i.e.,* of Cana of Galilee, not Canaanite as in C.V.; and Judas Iscariot, *i.e.,* the man of Carioth, or of the city.

5. *Why did He forbid them to visit the Gentiles, and the cities of the Samaritans?*

Not because He did not care for them, for they were included in His final commission, and would be visited in due time, but until that time arrived, the "lost sheep of the house of Israel" were to have all their attention.

7. *"The kingdom of heaven is at hand." What were the people to understand by this proclamation?*

That the promised reign of God was so near that they might place themselves under it. It was not proclaimed to satisfy mere curiosity, but for honest reception; and being a reign by means of the truth, their acceptance of the truth procured their admission into it. The truth as proclaimed by Jesus and His apostles formed the basis of a new rule of God over man, and even those who under the old rule of God by the law given through Moses had forfeited by disobedience their position, might through a change of mind become the subjects of a new administration.

9, 10. *"Provide neither gold, nor silver," etc. Why forbidden—these necessary things?*

That they might prove in all their need the providence of God, and be thus assured that their mission was according to His will.

11–13. *If any house rejected their salutation of peace, it was to return to them again. What did Jesus mean by this?*

The salutation, "Peace be to this house," was the first token of a friendly mission, and if accepted, other blessings followed, but if rejected, he who bestowed it received a blessing. It is a remarkable fact, that good thoughts and deeds are never lost; if not accepted by those for whom they are intended, the heart of the giver is always blessed.

14. *The dust was to be shaken off their feet against any house or city that rejected their message. Can this still be done by preachers of the gospel?*

Not without authority from God. Even preachers require to be careful not to usurp authority which they have not received. It is the ambassador from the throne that must be regarded, and not the person who merely repeats his message. These apostles were to leave the dust of their feet as a witness against those who rejected their message, but when a bishop or a pope attempts to imitate them, it is perfectly ridiculous. Of course, when the curses of preachers and popes were enforced by law, it was a serious matter to lie under their ban, but this power being withdrawn, their curse need not be heeded.

15. *How shall it be more tolerable for Sodom, etc., in judgment, than for these gospel-rejecting cities?*

The contrast is not between the burning up of Sodom with fire, etc., and the desolating of Jewish cities by Roman armies, though both judgments were inflicted for transgression; but between Christ-rejecting Jews, and Lot-rejecting Sodomites in that yet future day when God shall judge the world in righteousness, by that man whom He hath ordained.

16. *"Be ye therefore wise as serpents." How do serpents show wisdom?*

By fleeing from danger when escape is possible. A serpent, though armed with a deadly sting, seldom uses it unless provoked to do so. It was as if He had said, You have power to punish these wolfish men among whom I am sending you, but do not heedlessly arouse hostility. In your mission be both wise and harmless.

17–22. *Was the persecution here spoken of by Jesus confined to their first tour, or did it extend over the entire period of their mission as apostles?*

This warning of Jesus was doubtless prophetic of what was to happen to them during their entire mission to the nation till the destruction of Jerusalem. The Jews never ceased to persecute till that overthrow, and their power to continue persecution then ceased.

23. *"Verily I say to you, ye shall not have gone over the cities of Israel till the Son of man be come." What coming is referred to here?*

His coming in judgment upon that nation, a coming which followed this specially merciful but rejected mission. The mission of the apostles was to con-

fluence with Pharisees, nor that of Jesus, who freely mixed with all classes, could win them from their corrupt ways.

Malachi the prophet announced the reappearing of Elijah. How could the mission of John fulfil this prediction?

To represent one person or his work by the name of another may appear strange to us, but this had been frequently done. The name of Esau, Jacob, Israel, David, etc., is often applied to their descendants and successors, and when so used must be accepted. Besides, persons who have filled a typical place in the arrangement of God, never return to be its antitype, although they may supply the name to another whom God may raise up to be so. The angel Gabriel announced to Zechariah that his son should go before Jesus, in the spirit and power of Elijah, and here He assured His disciples that John fulfilled the prophecy.

20–24. What may we learn from the woes pronounced against Chorazin, etc.?

We learn that greater privileges bring greater responsibilities, and, if not improved, heavier judgments.

What is the meaning of "thou, Capernaum, which art exalted unto heaven"?

The revised version reads, "And thou, Capernaum, shalt thou be exalted to heaven? thou shalt go down unto Hades," which shows that while her hopes were exaltation, her doom was dishonour and the grave. Her thought was preferment, her end was judgment.

25. Who were these "wise and prudent," from whom some things were hid, and who the "babes," to whom they were revealed?

The wise and prudent were the scribes and rulers of that day, who, having refused the simple testimony that the kingdom of heaven had ap-

proached, were denied the privilege of knowing that Jesus was the Christ. It was not the way of salvation that had been hid from them, nor the message of judgment upon persistent transgressors, for these were fully revealed; but having turned a deaf ear to these things, it pleased God to hide from them the dignity of His own Son. To the "babes," His disciples, this was revealed, and confessed by them. And, when returning from their mission on one occasion, they came to Him with joy and said, "Lord, even the demons are subject unto us, through Thy name." As these wise ones, the sages of that day, refused to be instructed by Jesus and His disciples, so the power of His name was hid from them, and in this He rejoiced and thanked His Father, as their ignorance of this truth helped on His mission among those who were anxious to receive it. Their annoyance of Him in His work was great; but had they known what even His disciples knew, it might have been much greater.

CHAPTER XII.

1–8. When the Pharisees charged the disciples of Jesus with violating the law of the sabbath, was the Saviour's vindication of their conduct thoroughly satisfactory?

The Pharisees had a traditional law, that to pluck ears of corn on the sabbath was to work, and it was to this they objected. The cases of David and the priests brought forward by Jesus were to the point, as they proved that even law was not so strict as to set aside absolute necessity. The disciples were hungry, and to pluck ears of corn on the sabbath was no violation of the law of God.

What did Jesus mean by saying, "In this place is one greater than the temple"?

Scholars have now decided that the correct reading is, "A greater thing than the temple (service) is here." Jesus had just spoken about David and the temple service, and now gently hints at the contrast. David ate of the holy bread, priests work in the temple, but here are labourers in a higher service, and why may not they eat a few ears of corn on the sabbath day? "If ye had known what this meaneth, I desire mercy and not sacrifice, ye would not have condemned the guiltless. For the Son of man (their Master) is Lord even of the sabbath day."

9. *Why did Jesus go to their synagogue when His doing so was likely to renew the attack?*

God's law was to be read there, and worship offered to Him, and probable consequences were not allowed to interfere with known obligations.

"*And behold there was a man which had his hand withered.*" Did he go for the same purpose?

Very likely, and a most blessed thing it was for him that he was in the way of obedience on that occasion. No sooner, however, do the Pharisees observe this man, than they put to Jesus the question, "Is it lawful to heal on the sabbath days? that they might accuse Him." His reply brought the matter very close to themselves, and when asked what they would do if one of their own sheep had fallen into a pit, no answer was required, and He at once healed the man and let him go.

17–21. *In narrating the quiet way in which Jesus performed these miracles, Matthew applies to Him a very striking prophecy from Isaiah. How does it apply to His earthly mission?*

Its fulfilment embraces a longer period than His sojourn on earth, because it refers to ministry among the Gentiles, which did not commence while He sojourned on the earth. This prophecy includes events which succeed each other, from the august scene which took place at His immersion, to the judgment which descended upon the nation of Israel when He was seated upon His throne in glory. Then there are events which come in between these two extremes, and the spirit and character of His work are briefly but graphically detailed : "He shall not strive nor cry, neither shall any man hear His voice (as a conqueror) in the street. The bruised reed will He not break (but will seek to bind it up), and the smoking flax or wick (of the lamp) will He not quench, till He send forth judgment unto victory." The quotation of this prophecy in connection with the murderous spirit of the Pharisees was evidently intended to prove, not only the patience of Jesus for a season, but the wrath that in due time would fall upon them.

22–30. *When Jesus healed the man possessed with a demon, why did the Pharisees accuse Him of working under Beelzebub?*

That they might' destroy His influence over the people, who were ready to confess Him to be the Son of God. Their charge, however, was made to appear most foolish, and by His power over demons the kingdom of God was demonstrated to be a reality.

31, 32. *In what did blasphemy or speaking against the Holy Spirit consist?*

In asserting that the power by which Jesus cast out demons was derived from an unclean spirit. To ignore the power of the Holy Spirit in Him was a crime of the greatest magnitude.

Why could it not be forgiven, "*neither in this world, neither in the world to come?*"

We should read, *neither in this*

age (the Jewish), *nor in the coming one* (the Christian). It will, however, be well to understand what Jesus here means by forgiveness. It is a great mistake to suppose that Jesus declares that there is a sin or blasphemy against the Holy Spirit which will not be forgiven although the transgressor submit to the God-appointed conditions of pardon. This thought we should not for a moment entertain. Forgiveness is used here in relation to judgment, which God will not set aside. Paul's address to the Athenians will help us to understand this matter. " The times of this ignorance God winked at," *i.e.*, overlooked, or did not bring judgment upon them for their vice and idolatry, thus forgiving them ; also in Psalm lxxviii. 37, 38, where it is written of Israel, " For their heart was not right with Him, neither were they stedfast in His covenant. But He, being full of compassion, forgave their iniquity, and destroyed them not ; yea, many a time turned He His anger away," *i.e.*, He did not bring judgment upon them. Here, however, Jesus plainly teaches that His own testimony might be rejected, and not bring wrath upon them, but when the presence or power of the Holy Spirit in His miracles was denied, then judgment was inevitable. This sin would not be passed over by God.

33–37. "*For by thy words thou shalt be justified, and by thy words thou shalt be condemned.*" *Is not this a new basis of judgment ?*

No ; but in this statement Jesus strikes at the root of a common delusion, viz., that the heart is better than the tongue. It is not a new principle of judgment, but a warning against deception. God will judge men according to their real character, but the tongue reveals the condition of the heart. The tree is known by its fruit, and the

heart by the utterance of the tongue. If we watch our tongues we may learn our true condition, and from the teaching of Jesus we may learn true wisdom. " Make the tree good, and the fruit (will be) good."

38, 39. "*Master, we would see a sign from heaven.*" *Why refuse this request ?*

Because their purpose was an evil one. They wanted a sign that would minister to their exaltation, and he could not encourage their pride of heart ; so He urges them to use the sign they already had in Jonah, who, after being three days and three nights in the belly of the fish, was received by the Ninevites as a prophet of God. They might reject His ministry during His life, but if His resurrection did not convince them that He was the Son of God, then their case was hopeless.

40. "*The Son of man shall be three days and three nights in the heart of the earth.*" *Is this statement not contrary to fact ?*

Not contrary to fact, but only contrary to tradition, which says that He was crucified on Friday, and if this was true, then He was not three nights in the earth or sepulchre. The evangelists do not name the day of His death, but only the day of His rising again, and as He was to be three days and three nights in the heart of the earth, He must have died on Thursday. Tradition may be received in some matters as a help, but should never be allowed to set aside the Scriptures. If Christ died on Friday, neither man nor angel could prove that He was three nights in the tomb.

42. *Why should a queen of the south, coming to hear the wisdom of Solomon, condemn that generation ?*

Solomon was reputed to have the wisdom of God, and she came to prove him " concerning the name of the Lord" (1 Kings x. 1.) She was doubtless a worshipper of idols, and came to test a man who was a witness for God, and acknowledged that the wisdom of the living God dwelt in him. In this she would condemn that generation, who refused to accept that greater than Solomon, who had come to them.

43–45. *" When the unclean spirit is gone out of a man," etc. To what does Jesus refer?*

The statement about a man with an unclean spirit is very suggestive, and the application of it to that nation, when we appeal to facts, is not far to seek. We might ask, how should an unclean spirit have possession of a man, except that by his evil desires he has first prepared a dwelling for it in his own heart, for unclean spirits do not dwell in those who are pure in heart. And when, by certain causes, the practice of evil is hindered, or the unclean spirit, for want of room to work, may be said to have gone out of a man, the man becomes restless to return to evil, and if it is not possible to follow out the same course, other spirits are selected to dwell there, and the last state of that man is worse than the first. "Even so," said Jesus, "shall it be also unto this wicked generation." The nation had been guilty of idolatry, but by the chastisement of God in the Babylonish captivity, this unclean spirit had gone out from them; yet being bent on evil, they had taken other spirits more unclean than the first, so that Jesus had to call them a "generation of vipers," worse indeed than at the first.

45–50. *What lesson may be learned from the teaching of Jesus about relationship?*

A very important one, viz., that if obedient to His Father, we shall be as brother or sister or mother to Him, and that such relationship to Him,

through the truth, is far higher than through the flesh.

CHAPTER XIII.

1. *It is here stated that Jesus "spake many things unto them in parables." Was this a new method of instruction?*

Not a new method, as parables are mentioned in the Old Testament, but one which was now adopted by Jesus for the first time. It also evidently marks an epoch in His ministry, and this should be carefully noted, as it may help us to perceive the difference between His earlier and and His later teaching, as well as find in it a reason for the change.

What is the object of the first of these seven parables?

To show the result of His own preaching of the kingdom of heaven being at hand, among those who previously heard His proclamation. It is not any similitude of the kingdom itself, nor any illustration of what might afterward occur in the labours of any of His servants; but the results of His own efforts are set forth in this parable of the sower, some of whose scattered seed fell on the beaten path, some on ground with rock beneath, some among thorns which afterwards sprung up and choked it, and some on ground which brought forth fruit.

Why did He say, "He who hath ears to hear, let him hear"?

Because the parable was designed for instruction, but its lesson could be understood only by the attentive mind. A truth was hid in the parable, but it was not so concealed that the earnest seeker could not find it. Jesus, therefore, in this fine enigmatical sentence, seeks to awaken the necessary interest.

10–13. *Why did Jesus speak to them in parables?*

The disciples, observing the change

from plain testimony to parables, asked the same question, and the answer of Jesus, which is of more than ordinary interest, and which will help us to understand some principles connected with the divine administration, is here recorded. " Jesus answered and said unto them, Unto you (who have received me as the Messiah) it is given to know the mysteries, *lit.*, secrets, of the kingdom of heaven ; but unto them (who have not received me) it is not given. For whosoever hath (received me), to him shall be given, and he shall have abundance ; but whosoever hath not (received me), from him shall be taken away even (that privilege of hearing) which he hath. Therefore speak I to them in parables ; because they seeing see not (me), and hearing they hear not (me), neither do they understand."

14, 15. *"And in them is fulfilled the prophecy of Isaiah, which saith, by hearing ye shall hear, and shall not understand," etc. Was this quoted to show what God had done in them judicially ?*

It was rather to show what they themselves had done. " Their eyes have they closed." This voluntary act will account for all that follows. This wilful closing of their eyes affected both heart and ears, and was the cause of their rejection of God's Son, who had come to save them. Very early in His ministry the scribes, Pharisees, and rulers of the synagogues decided not to accept Christ, and this decision explains their subsequent conduct towards Him, even to the taking of His life. It should never be thought, even for one moment, that God did anything to hinder their salvation. The gift of His Son, the loving ministry of Jesus, the proclamation of salvation to them after they had put Jesus to death, as well as His long suffering, forbid such a thought. God did intimate by His

prophet what would be the result of wilful rejection of the truth, and now Jesus calls the attention of His disciples to the striking manner in which it was being fulfilled.

18–23. *In the parable, the fowls of the air are said to pick up the seed sown, while in this exposition He speaks only of the evil one catching away that which was sown in the heart. Why this difference ?*

The difference is not a contradiction, but only a fuller view of the agencies of evil that are at work to prevent the attainment of good. The birds of the air are symbols of the scribes, priests, and Pharisees, who by vain reasonings and terrible threats hindered very many from receiving the truth which Jesus taught; then, behind all this, there was the wicked one, who by this means prevented the truth from taking root, so that it became like as seed that fell upon the beaten path. The people over whom the traditions of Pharisees, etc., prevailed, left no spot in their minds open for the truth, and though heard by them, and often with astonishment, there was no harvest for the sower ; but this is only one of the four different classes of hearers that listened to His proclamations.

The second class received the seed into " stony places." What do these represent ?

The circumstances surrounding those who heard the word, which, though unperceived by them at the time, eventually proved a fatal obstruction. They heard that the kingdom was at hand with joy ; but when trial and persecution arose on account of it, they stumbled, and bore no fruit.

What were the thorns which choked the up-growing seed of this third class ?

Anxiety about the world, the influence of riches, and the desire for things which the kingdom did not supply; these choked the word, and it became unfruitful.

To what do you attribute the fruitfulness of the fourth class?

To the causes assigned by Jesus, and to no other. He names but three causes, which, when combined, never fail to produce the desired effect, viz., hearing, understanding, and obeying the word spoken; or, in other words, there was attention, knowledge, and practice, from which fruit in varied proportion will always follow.

Is it right to pray, as some do, that a preached Gospel may produce fruit, in some thirty, some sixty, and some a hundred fold?

No. Jesus is here stating a fact, not giving directions for prayer. He would rather it had been this high return in all; but it was only as thirty-fold in some, and he just states it. It is very questionable about asking for results in preaching. Paul asked for an open door—a "free course," *i.e.*, an opportunity for preaching the word, that all who desired might receive it. Men are turned to God by His Gospel, and not by His absolute omnipotence, and this should always be remembered, even in prayer to Him.

24–32. *"Another parable put he forth,"* etc. *To what period does this parable of the good seed and the tares sown in the same field apply?*

To the time of the Saviour's personal ministry. He was the sower of the good seed, the Jewish field being His appointed sphere of service, and into the minds of all who were ready for its reception He cast the life-giving truth of God—truth which prophets had before revealed concerning Himself, and which was applied by Him with such force and aptness as astonished all who heard Him, and instructed those who waited for the kingdom of God. But as the disciples afterward asked Him the meaning of the "tares of the field," His reply to their question must be considered.

31, 32. *The kingdom of heaven is here said to be "like a grain of mustard seed." When was the kingdom so small? and over what period was its growth to extend? and what are the birds of the air that should lodge in its branches?*

The kingdom of heaven was the rule or reign of God by the truth concerning Jesus, and when first proclaimed and accepted was exceedingly small—so small, indeed, that it might have seemed an easy thing to crush the rising blade. But He who planted the seed in that Jewish field, watched over and protected it under most adverse circumstances, until it grew and made room for itself in the earth. "A little one shall become a thousand, and a small one a strong nation," said the Lord by Isaiah, and we may surely mark its fulfilment going on. There were but few confessors of Jesus as the Son of God in the days of His flesh, but there are thousands upon thousands now, and their influence is certainly being felt in the world. Everywhere national authority protects those who accept the Christian religion, and wish to serve Christ according to the New Testament. It has indeed become a great tree, when compared with its first appearance in the field, and it is still growing, and spreading forth its branches in the earth. We do indeed sit under the vine and the fig-tree, none daring to make us afraid, and for these privileges we acknowledge Him who is at God's right hand. Then, in the midst of these granted favours, under the spreading branches of this heaven-planted tree, the birds of the air, *i.e.*, sectarian teachers, who draw away disciples after them, and giving to them some self-elected name, do shelter themselves. We note that at first the birds of the air, *i.e.*, Jewish teachers, sought to pick up the seed sown, but when it grew, then teachers of like spirit seek to avail themselves of its protected rights. In the present day we have quite a number of ecclesiastical organisations which assume to be Christian, or, as they mostly prefer to be called, evangelical, which were unknown in the days of the apostles, except as prophetically revealed to Timothy, as those who shall " turn away their ears from the truth," or, as in another letter, " some shall depart from the faith."

33. *This parable of the leaven hid in three measures of meal was also spoken to the multitude. What does it represent ?*

Two things are to be specially noted here—(1.) The kingdom, the divine administration through the truth, to which the woman had access. (2.) The woman herself, who hid the leaven in the meal till all was leavened. In the latter the apostacy, which is caused by the woman (a symbol of the church), is before us. She hid or secretly mixed the leaven of false doctrine with the truth, until corruption appeared in every part. For example, take the church of the middle ages on which to test this saying of Christ, " till the whole was leavened." There was not a truth, ordinance, or precept which she had not changed and perverted. It is indeed a sad thought that the meal, a symbol of the truth which the apostles of Jesus put into the hands of the woman, *i.e.*, the church, should have been so leavened with false teaching. It is, however, a blessed truth that the New Testament, the source of the truth, is pure, because given to us by the Holy Spirit, and from this heavenly source the pure bread of life may be procured. In the days when the woman sat upon the scarlet coloured beast, and could shut up the oracles of God, men could not compare truth and error together ; but now, that barrier being removed, all who will may have the truth of God instead of the traditions of men.

There were three measures of meal in which the leaven was hid. What do the three measures represent ?

The truth of God prepared and given in history, law, and prophecy, each of which was corrupted by the church for her own selfish purposes.

36–43. *" Declare unto us the parable of the tares of the field." Are there not still some difficulties, even after the explanation given by Jesus ?*

Not if we read, *so shall it be at the end of this age*, instead of " the end of the world," because we shall then see that Jesus refers to the end of the Jewish dispensation, and all must be understood in harmony with it. It was indeed a harvest, for God sent forth His reapers, the angels, *lit.*, messengers, and the tares, the children of the wicked one, were cast into the furnace of fire, a symbol of God's wrath upon Christ-rejecting Jews, who received error rather than truth, and so become tares in the field of the world, and were then cast out into the furnace.

Does the word " angels " or messengers define who were to be employed in this work of gathering out the wheat and burning up the tares ?

Who these were must be learned from the context, or from history, or from both. The apostles of Jesus doubtless were the messengers who, from Pentecost onward, gathered in the wheat into the barn or church, while the Roman army gathered up the tares and burned them in the fire. This was the end of the age predicted by Jesus.

44–46. *Were the three parables that follow delivered to His disciples or to the multitude ?*

To the disciples ; but as Jesus explained only the last of the three, the knowledge gained from His exposition of it must have been deemed sufficient to guide them in understanding the others.

What is the difference between the "pearl of great price" and the "treasure hid in the field," as there is finding, buying, and selling in both parables?

The treasure hid in the field, and the pearls gathered in the ocean, reveal at once the different circumstances of those to whom the one treasure is available. It is in the field that the Jew could seek and find Christ, for whom Paul, when he found it, counted all else as dregs ; and it is in the ocean (a symbol of the nations among whom so many of them were scattered) that the pearl-seeking merchant, the Grecian Jew so-called, must find the pearl of great price. The Gospel was to be preached among all nations, that all of the scattered seed of Abraham after the flesh might hear it, and "then," said Jesus, "shall the end (of the dispensation) come." (Matt. xxiv. 14.)

47. *What was the object of the parable of the net cast into the sea?*

To show the result of this wider effort among the Jews of the provinces, whose synagogues Paul and others never failed to enter to prove that Jesus was the Christ. Here the net was cast into the sea and drawn to shore, where they gathered the good into vessels—*i.e.*, the churches of the saints—and cast the bad away. Such was the close of the gracious administration of the kingdom of heaven among those to whom the Word of God first came.

52. *What were the "things new and old" which the instructed scribe would bring out of his treasure?*

The old were the prophecies concerning the kingdom, and the new the Saviour's teaching by which it was entered.

CHAPTER XIV.

1–12. *Who was Herod the tetrarch, and what is a tetrarch?*

He was Herod Antipas, son of Herod the Great, who divided his kingdom among his sons, bequeathing to Herod Antipas the district of Galilee and Perea. Thus he was known as a tetrarch—*lit.*, a ruler over a fourth part of a kingdom.

Herod first imprisoned and then beheaded John. Why did he commit this great crime?

There was a complication of causes which it may be well to consider. When Herod first became acquainted with John he had no thought of doing either of these wicked deeds, yet both were done by him, and for which he now stands charged before God. John was a good and faithful man, whom Herod gladly heard, and for a time profited by his exhortations. But the hour of temptation came and formed a solemn crisis in the life of the king. He first coveted, and then took his brother Philip's wife, thus becoming a fornicator. When John reproved the king for his sin, his proud heart rose up against it, and he cast John into prison. He would, indeed, have put him to death, but he feared the people, and so John remained in prison. Then came Herod's birthday, and the feast and the dancing of the damsel, and Herod's rash vow to her, and her strange, very strange, request for the head of John the Baptist in a charger or tray. The request, however, was not her own, but that of her mother, who used her for this wicked deed, and thus the good man's life was taken.

Is there any lesson for us in this sad narrative?

Yes ; a very important one—viz., to beware of the first step in the path of evil. The first glass of strong drink has been the first step to many a drunkard's grave ; the first act of dishonesty has led many to prison, shame, and ruin. The Christian's first neglect of prayer, reading the Scriptures, neglect of the Lord's table and worship, upon some vain pretext, may have seemed but a small matter, but eternal consequences have followed that first act of disobedience. Let us watch against the first neglect of duty, the first act of sin, whatever the inducement may be. If we once step aside the path may never be regained. We might confess the sin and be forgiven, but we may find that we have not the humble mind that will do so, and then our ruin is certain.

13–33. The Saviour is here shown in close relation with want, sickness, and danger. Are such narratives of any personal advantage?

They may be so, if they are rightly used. Trials, necessities, and dangers are sure to be a part of the lot of every human being, and it must be encouraging to have such a record of such a Saviour. It is with this very Saviour, who fed the multitude, who healed all these sick people, and who caught the hand of Peter when sinking, that we have to do. To be able to count upon His sympathy and gracious help in time of need is no ordinary privilege. We see in Him boundless sympathy and never-failing power. The disciples may ask Him to send the multitude away because the place is desert, but His reply is, "they need not depart, give ye them to eat." There are but "five loaves and two small fishes," but with them He supplies their wants, and meets the need of all. How blessed, how safe, to look to Him who sticketh closer than a brother.

CHAPTER XV.

1–6. What was this " tradition of
c

the elders," the non-observance of which by the disciples of Jesus was challenged by the scribes and Pharisees?

The Jews held that God gave to Moses two sets of laws, one of which was written, the other, delivered orally, was then handed down from generation to generation. Then it is said that these traditions, which, in the time of Jesus, were extolled by the scribes and Pharisees above the written law of Moses, were afterwards committed to writing by Rabbi Jehuda, and termed the Mishna. The tradition which the disciples had neglected at that time was that the hands should always be washed immediately before eating.

How were the disciples free from these traditions?

As Galileans they lived outside the territory over which the influence of the Pharisees extended, that being chiefly in Judea, and their own Master did not put them under human tradition. On this occasion a company of scribes and Pharisees, attracted by the fame of Jesus, had gone down from Jerusalem to Gennesaret, and at once raise a question that they think will damage His character as a teacher, but only to learn that their traditions were more serious infringements of the commands of God than eating with unwashed hands.

Does honour to parents involve their support?

Most certainly it did, and for a son to refuse such help, even by giving it to God's temple, was a violation of His command. The scribes, etc., were disbursers of such gifts to the temple service, and by their tradition encouraged men in this act of dishonour, and received from Jesus a justly merited rebuke. It was selfishness which led them so to act, and their glaring hypocrisy is justly exposed.

7–9. Jesus declared that Isaiah had prophesied concerning their evil deeds. Does not this look like fore-ordination ?

The prophet is simply foretelling the conduct of men who would set aside the authority of God, but, *à priori*, position is always either stated or supposed. These people had accepted man's teaching instead of God's, and this hypocrisy was the result. God does not say by the prophet that men will commit this or that evil, irrespective of anything preceding it. He states what will be done by men who reject Him, and His statements are verified by facts. The prophet spoke of their sham worship, but the people had first of all forsaken God in their hearts. The thing is repeated every day by men who become first faithless, and then hypocrites.

10–20. " Not that which goeth into the mouth defileth a man." Why introduce this matter of eating ?

It was a word for the multitude, who were greatly influenced by the teaching of the Pharisees. Jesus wished them to know that man is not defiled by what goes into his mouth, but by that which comes out of it. Even the disciples had to be instructed in this important matter of what really constituted defilement.

21–28. Why did Jesus at first refuse the request of this woman of Canaan, and afterwards grant it ?

He did not refuse, but only did not reply at first to her desire. He had a special mission given Him to the lost sheep of the house of Israel, and this was outside the house, and called for thought. Her faith, however, in His power to help her was tested, and when she took her true place as a dog under the table, requesting that even the crumbs might fall for her eating, her request was fully met.

CHAPTER XVI.

1–3. " A sign from heaven" was desired by these Pharisees and Sadducees. Why did Jesus deny their request ?

Because their design in asking it was evil. They had evidently no faith in His mission, as they were continually perverting both His words and His works. Had they only carefully noted the signs already given, they would not have asked for more.

They could foretell the weather from the appearance of the sky. Why did Jesus refer to this ?

To show their hypocrisy in asking a sign in support of His mission, when the signs already afforded them had received no attention, and awakened no interest. They could foretell weather from observation, but had bestowed no thought upon the signs of the times, *lit.*, seasons. It was sheer hypocrisy to ask any sign from Jesus.

4. How was Jonah a type to that generation ?

His burial in the belly of the fish, and his issuing therefrom, was a type of the death and resurrection of Jesus; and was recorded for their instruction, but being neglected by them, no other should be given.

13–19. Why did Jesus enquire concerning the opinions held by the people concerning Himself ?

Possibly to obtain that result which afterwards followed in the noble, intelligent confession of Peter, but it led to a sad disclosure respecting the thoughts of the people. It is evident that the latter had utterly failed to profit by all that had been done to prove the divine Sonship of Jesus. God had proclaimed from the heavens, " This is My beloved Son." Signs and wonders had been wrought to confirm it, and this is the result— " Some say Thou art John the Baptist, some Elias," etc. This was all the length the nation had reached. He was in the world, and the world knew Him not.

How is this misapprehension of Christ by the people to be explained ?

It is evident that they reasoned, rather than received the testimony given with its accompanying proofs. It was easy to think that John had risen from the dead, or that Elijah had returned to the world, but Jesus was neither the one nor the other. As long as men reason instead of believing the truth, they are sure to be the victims of mistake and deception.

Why did the confession of His Sonship by Peter cause Jesus to exclaim so rapturously, " Blessed art thou, Simon, son of Jonas" ?

Because this great truth of the new covenant, which must be believed and confessed by all who become His disciples, had really been accepted by one heart, and confessed by one mouth to the glory of God. Up to this time it was an unanswered question whether Jesus of Nazareth, the anointed Son of God, would be confessed by any one. In Peter's clear and open confession this question was settled, and time alone could manifest how far his example would be followed.

What did Jesus mean when He said, " flesh and blood hath not revealed it to thee, but My Father who is in heaven" ?

This truth which Peter confessed, and which was designed to be the creed of the new dispensation, was not from man but from God the Father, whose declaration from the heavens Peter here repeats, having doubtless heard it at the Jordan, and accepted it as true.

What did Jesus mean by " this rock" ?

Most certainly Himself. He is the *Petra*, the rock on which the Church is built, and not *Petros*, a

stone, or piece of a rock, as Peter is called.

" On this rock will I build My Church." Can we learn from this statement when His Church came into existence ?

No. We simply learn that the building of the Church was future. He did not say, I have built, or, I am building, but " I will build My Church," and history must inform us when this wondrous structure commenced. The "Acts of the Apostles" has furnished the information, and from this record by Luke we can learn its rise and progress.

When He said " the gates of hell shall not prevail against it," did He mean the Church ?

It is, *lit.*, the gates of *hades, i.e.,* the unseen state, and possibly refers to the truth which He had just uttered respecting Himself. He had just affirmed, " Upon this rock I will build My Church ; " but when called to enter death's dominion, this truth seemed imperilled. But the gates of hades, a periphrasis for death, could not hold Him, and He returned to do all He had spoken.

What were the " keys of the kingdom of heaven" which were given to Peter ?

The authority to declare in the name of Jesus, to Jews and Gentiles, the terms on which they would be admitted into it, both as set up on earth in grace, and as established in glory. This he did in his two sermons, one preached to Jews at Pentecost (Acts ii.), the other preached to Gentiles (Acts x.), by submission to which they became subjects of the kingdom established on earth ; and in his two letters written to those two classes in relation to the heavenly kingdom.

What does to " bind" and to " loose" indicate ?

To enact or appoint, and to abrogate or cut away the things not required, which Peter in proclaiming the way of access had to do, and to do it with the assurance that he was declaring the will of God. " Whatsoever thou shalt bind on earth shall be, *lit.*, shall have been, bound in heaven ; and what thou shalt loose on earth shall be, *lit.*, shall have been, loosed in heaven. It was a heaven-arranged plan which Peter proclaimed.

20. *Why did Jesus charge His disciples to tell no man that He was the Christ ?*

In chap. xviii. 9 Jesus adds, " till the Son of man be risen again from the dead." For a season their testimony was limited, but when Jesus was enthroned, all restraint was removed. To everything there is a season, and the disciples had to observe this.

21, 22. *Why did Peter rebuke Christ, when told of His shame and death ?*

Because he reasoned upon the testimony of Christ instead of believing it, and thus proved that he had failed to see its necessity. He had just been honoured for his confession of Jesus as the anointed Son of God, and now has to be rebuked for refusing this preparatory revelation of the death of Jesus.

23. *" Get thee behind me, Satan." Was this not a very harsh rebuke to call Peter Satan ?*

It would be better to read *adversary*, for this is what is meant. Peter was opposing Christ, and was therefore an adversary to Him. And as his example would be a cause of stumbling to others, the rebuke was justly deserved.

24. *Why did Jesus speak of self-denial as the common lot of all who would follow Him ?*

Peter had just said, " Be it far from Thee," or more strictly, pity Thyself, Lord, this shall not be unto Thee, and Jesus took occasion to show that others, if they would follow Him, might also have to forfeit life in being His disciples. It was not that He alone must bear the cross, but His disciples must bear it also.

28. *What did Jesus mean by saying that some of them should not die till they saw Him coming in His kingdom ?*

Expositors have selected three events as a fulfilment of this utterance, viz., the transfiguration, Pentecost, and the destruction of Jerusalem ; each selecting that manifestation which was judged the most appropriate. One writer suggests that possibly the three are intended. We may say that there is no force whatever in applying the words of Jesus " shall not taste of death " to the transfiguration, which was only six days after ; or even to the scene at Pentecost, which followed in about two years. We are therefore shut up to the conclusion that the judgment upon Jerusalem, at which a few, and only a few, had not tasted death when it took place, was really intended. Then He did come, not for the first time in His kingdom, but was then manifest in the power of His kingdom, against those who had rejected Him.

CHAPTER XVII.

1–9. *When Jesus was transfigured in presence of three of His disciples, what was done to Him ?*

He was changed, or *lit.*, had another form. These disciples saw Him then as we would see Him now could we see Him in glory.

What was the object of this change ?

That testimony of His glorification might be given in due time. It is no small matter, even to those who now believe in Him, that three reliable witnesses have seen Him glorified. From Peter's Second Epistle we see how much he makes of this event. " We have not followed cunningly-devised fables when we made known to you the power and coming of our Lord Jesus Christ, but were eye-witnesses of His majesty."

Why did Moses and Elijah appear in this scene?

We must be guided in our reply by what occurred on that occasion. Moses, the law-giver of that dispensation, and Elijah, the representative of the prophets, appear together with Jesus, the anointed of God, and, in presence of these selected witnesses, lay down their commissions at His feet, while God from heaven exclaims, *This is My beloved Son, in whom I delighted: hear ye Him.* This transfer of authority from these servants under the old economy to a Son who was to rule in the new, would be remembered by them when their testimony for Jesus would begin.

10–13. *Malachi affirmed that Elijah would precede the Messiah. Was it wrong for the scribes to expect him first?*

The prophet gave the name of the worker for the work to be done, and this was only in harmony with other prophecies, as Israel for his seed, David for Christ, etc. But when John came in the spirit and power of Elijah, as affirmed by Gabriel, it should have sufficed. The reason, however, why the scribes appealed to this prophecy, was in order to disprove the claims of Christ to be the Messiah. The veritable Elijah had not come, and from this they held that Jesus was an impostor. The affirmation of Jesus that John was the Elijah that was to come, has for ever settled this question.

14–21. *How could the disciples fail to cast out this demon when they had received power to cast them out?*

The answer of Jesus was most instructive to them. He had bestowed upon them this gift, but they had now to learn by failure, which must have been very humbling to them,

that it could be exercised only in reference to Him. They had evidently acted independently of Him, hence their failure on this occasion (ver. 21) presents a difficulty, because it intimates that some demons require also prayer and fasting for their expulsion, and thus implies that others do not. Some MSS. omit the verse, and it may not have been spoken by Jesus.

When Jesus spoke of the grain of mustard seed, did He teach that a small measure of faith would suffice to remove a mountain?

It is not the small measure of faith that Jesus commends, but the faith that would rise with the occasion The tiny grain grew into a tree in due time. If you had faith like that, said Jesus, you would be equal to every difficulty.

Can any Christian apply to himself the promise, "And nothing shall be impossible to you"?

No. It can only apply to those who had the gift of power. Christians can appropriate any promise made to them as God's children, but the working of miracles was a special gift bestowed only upon a few. It was true to the apostles in relation to their work, but not to others.

24–27. *Was this half shekel tax a Jewish or a Roman tax?*

Doubtless a Roman head tax, as it was demanded at Capernaum, at the receipt of custom. The half shekel of the temple was paid at Jerusalem to the priests, and not to Roman officials, as here. The Saviour did not wish to offend even these rulers of the land, and the fish was caught to meet the demand.

CHAPTER XVIII.

1–6. *"Who is the greatest in the kingdom of heaven"? Why did the disciples ask this question?*

From the answer of Jesus it would seem that the question had been asked from fleshly motives. They evidently did not understand the nature of the kingdom about which they were asking, but had conceived the idea of pomp and place and power. Possibly they were jealous because Peter had already received a promise of distinction, and three of them had witnessed His transfiguration ; they therefore somewhat anxiously press the question, who should be the greatest?

Why did He select a little child to instruct and answer them?

Because the absence of ambition is so marked in a child, and this was largely manifest in their question. They were seeking fleshly position, and required to learn that in the kingdom of heaven the most humble were the greatest, and that in order to ascend they must descend. It must indeed have been a severe reproof when He said " Except ye be converted," or turn from your fleshly ambition, "you shall not enter into the kingdom of heaven " at all. He who has opened it could not admit you in the spirit you now possess.

7. *" It must needs be that offences come." Why " must needs be"?*

These offences were snares, or causes of stumbling, which would arise from the condition of the nation. Their pride, lust of power, and blind submission to tradition, would imperil the progress of all who sought to follow Jesus. Under the circumstances it could not be otherwise than that snares would abound, but as God had given all necessary directions for life and godliness, neither the ensnarers nor the ensnared would escape condemnation. And, as it was then, so it is still. There abound snares of every type, religious and worldly, which must be dangerous to all, but exceedingly perplexing to some. Only think of the many religious sects that exist in the world, each claiming to be right, and presenting its claims for acceptance by others. How difficult for an anxious person to know which is right, and in the uncertainty he may choose a false one, or possibly reject all.

Then again, think of the worldliness of many professing Christians, whose habits of life are a strange mixture of piety and vanity, devotion and gossip, a psalm and a song, the Bible and the novel, each having its place and performance in the drama of life. How perplexing and ensnaring must all this be to one who looks to such for example—and examples all such certainly are either for good or evil. These and many such like evils abound in the world and in the church, and it must needs be that causes of stumbling will come.

8, 9. *How can these evils be overcome?*

By sacrifice and self-denial on the one hand, and by unfaltering obedience to the requirements of the kingdom of heaven.

15–17. *" If thy brother trespass against thee," etc. Must these directions of Jesus be always followed?*

Yes, when the matters involved are as stated by Jesus. If there is trespass, *lit.*, sin, against a brother, then " go and tell him his fault, *lit.*, correct him, between thee and him alone, and if he hear thee, thou hast gained thy brother." Now in taking action under this law of trespass, when we feel we ought to do so, let us first of all be sure that we have done nothing to provoke the alleged trespass, and that trespass was really intended, and was not merely the result of unforeseen circumstances. A little patience and self-inspection may compel us to view the alleged trespass in another light, and lead us to see that our own previous action has done so much to cause it, that we have our own share in the fault. It is possible for one so to act or speak as to force out words or actions from brethren that ought not to be, but we, having caused it, should rather confess the whole wrong than seek any redress. Then let it be "alone," not telling others first, or even speaking of it to others, but to him alone, and if he hear thee, thou hast gained rather than estranged thy brother. Then should this fail, action may be taken as further directed by Jesus.

20. *"Where two or three are gathered together in My name, there am I." Is this because they are few?*
No. Neither the few nor many can claim His promised presence or approval, but only as met in, *lit.*, into, His name. It is the name, *i.e.*, the authority by which they are gathered, that secures the promise, and not numbers nor place.

21, 22. *The brother who trespassed was if possible to be gained by the course suggested, and if won, forgiven. Why is Peter so anxious to know how often this might be renewed?*
There is, one fears, something suspicious about this question, and yet one is glad that Peter asked it. He thought seven times a great length of forbearance, but seventy times seven far exceeds it, and, while it is a great claim upon our hearts, it shows also the heart of Him who makes it. Will God do less to us than He requires from us? I think not, and our failings may require as much from Him.

23–35. *What is this similitude of the kingdom intended to teach?*
Not only the graciousness of God in forgiving so many offences, but also His claim upon all who receive forgiveness, to manifest the same spirit towards others. Peter may have been annoyed at the very large claim made by Jesus upon him, but it should have prompted him to reflect upon the large measure of forgiveness shown to him.

CHAPTER XIX.

3–9. *"Is it lawful for a man to put away his wife for every cause?" Is there anything suspicious in this question?*
It is always indicative of an unsubjected spirit when men seek to alter the arrangements of God. His will demands obedience, and man's heart, thus put to the test, too often seeks vain excuses to set that will aside. It is instructive, however, to note how their question is met by Jesus. They asked about putting away, and He at once refers to God's law concerning marriage. He made the two one flesh, and adds, "What therefore God hath joined together, let not man put asunder." This reply should have been sufficient, but it was not what they wanted, and at once they appeal to Moses, but only to receive a rebuke. "They say unto Him, why did Moses then command to give a writing of divorcement?" This appeal to Moses seemed a triumph for the moment. Will the Teacher set aside the great lawgiver? But Jesus had no fault to find with Moses. Moses wrote you this precept, but it is a witness against you, because it shows the hardness of your heart. The law of God is not changed; it is you who have changed, and now you are seeking to be approved by God's law.

13–15. *What may be learnt from Jesus putting His hands on these little children?*
A very important truth, viz., that infants can be the subjects of His holy benediction. The little child, though in unfavourable circumstances through the first man's transgression, is undefiled by personal guilt, and upon such He could lay His hands and pray. It is a striking fact that

infants undefiled by personal sin, and disciples made clean through His word, were both the subjects of His blessing.

21. *This young man was told to sell all that he had and follow Jesus, and he should have treasure in heaven. Is this a standing test?*

This charge of Jesus to part with all was a special test, and no one else can personally apply it. The claims of Christ on this age are made known by His apostles, and these are to guide us in our discipleship. Neither the selling of property nor retaining it is to us a condition of discipleship, but the receiving of Christ; and when accepted as our Lord, He must guide us in all things.

27-30. *What was the nature of this reward promised by Jesus to His disciples?*

There are several things stated here which may help to explain both the nature of the reward, and the time of its bestowal. (1.) It was to be in the " regeneration," *i.e.*, the new state or the Christian economy. (2.) It was to be when the Son of man sat upon the " throne of His glory," which was when seated at the right hand of God, or as Paul speaks of Him " crowned with glory and honour." (3.) They were to sit upon " twelve thrones," —symbols of administrative authority—" judging," *i.e.*, delivering to the nation of the Jews the new laws of the exalted Messiah, who was to be known among them as " Lord and Christ," *i.e.*, the anointed Lord. This honour was specially bestowed upon those who continued with Him in His temptation, and while others who had "forsaken houses, brethren," etc., should have their hundredfold reward, this administrative honour was specially conferred upon the twelve. Thus the " first " disciples being denied this special honour became last, and the " last," the

twelve chosen to it, became first in the kingdom of heaven.

CHAPTER XX.

1-16. *In what period was this similitude of the kingdom going on?*

This hiring of labourers was doubtless taking place during the ministry of Jesus, but to understand it fully it is necessary to notice carefully the well-defined symbols employed. The " vineyard " is said by the prophets to be the " house of Israel " (Isaiah v. 7), while " day," a part of a cycle of time, or a dispensation, is occasionally applied to His own lifetime, and " hour," a section of the day, is a still more limited period, and marks off the varied elections to labour that took place. We must also remember that this similitude of the kingdom is an explanation of the saying, " Many that are first shall be last; and the last first." Jesus had been speaking about the honour of administration which was to be conferred only upon twelve of the labourers, while many had been employed to make it known. There were disciples of John employed in relation to the kingdom, and " other seventy also" sent out by Christ, each expecting a promised reward, and looking for it more in the way of merit, than a manifestation of grace, as shown to some. Now it is from these disappointed ones that the murmuring arises when the steward gives to each his hire. The twelve might be deemed not so worthy of the recompense received as some others, but there was grace as well as right in the bestowal of the penny. The " goodman of the house " justified himself in thus dispensing his gifts. " Is it not lawful," he said, " for me to do what I will with my own? Is thine eye evil because I am good? So the last shall be first, and the first last; for many be called, but few chosen " (to the high honour of administration in My kingdom).

20–23. *Had the mother of Zebedee's children any right to claim for her two sons the highest seats in the kingdom ?*

None whatever, except the pride of parental ambition, possibly prompted by her sons, who, knowing that they were chosen with the twelve for administration, began to aspire to the highest seats, not knowing for what they were asking.

Was the answer of Jesus calculated to undeceive them ?

It should have done so, as He clearly intimated that His own exaltation must succeed His immersion in suffering, and if they would share His honour, they must drink of His cup, etc. Not that suffering would ensure the highest seat; that would only be given to those for whom it had been prepared of the Father.

24–28. *The ten disciples were indignant at the ambition of their two brethren. Was their indignation a just one ?*

It was the indignation of selfishness at seeing their two brethren seeking to forestall them in their own ambitious designs. Jesus, however, has a lesson for them all—that of His own life. " The Son of man came not to be ministered unto, but to minister, and to give His life a ransom for many"; and assured them that if they would be great and chief, they must become servants to their brethren.

29–34. *What lesson may we gather from the cure of these two blind men ?*

A deeply instructive one, viz., that God will never fail to respond to trusting supplication. He loves to honour intelligent faith. These blind men owned Jesus as the son of David, and were healed by Him in response to their faith.

CHAPTER XXI.

1–11. *The obtaining of this colt, on which Jesus rode into Jerusalem, was by His own direction. Why did He do so ?*

It had been marked out for Him by the Prophet Zechariah, and at the last stage of His journey, He arranges to fulfil the prediction. His familiarity with the Scriptures, and His readiness to embody them in His own life, are most suggestive examples for us. The great programme of His ministry had been drawn out by the Spirit, and to its fulfilment He resolutely sets Himself without a single reservation.

Is this entry of Jesus into Jerusalem to be regarded as an act of self-exaltation ?

No, rather as an act of humiliation. The prophet had written, " Tell ye the daughter of Zion, Behold thy king cometh unto thee, meek, and sitting upon an ass, and a colt the foal of an ass." He who had made clouds His chariot, and walked upon the wings of the wind, who might have had angels for His attendants, and archangels following in His train, sat upon an ass, followed by Galileans, peasants, and other pious hearts, on their way to keep the feast at Jerusalem. It is true there was a little enthusiasm manifested by these simple-minded people, who would gladly have ushered in the triumph of their Messiah ; for they cut down branches from the trees, and spread their garments in the way, and shouted Hosanna to the son of David, but this was no part of His arrangement. He was simply fulfilling the Scriptures, while the multitude sought to make it a season of triumph, and usher in His reign, which action only rendered Him more contemptible in the eyes of envious priests and scribes.

12-14. *Why was the temple the first place visited by Jesus after He entered the city?*

Because the temple was His Father's house, and He went there to honour His Father's claims. Though a son He became a servant—a Jew made under the law, and God was honoured by obedience to all its institutions. But before He can worship He must drive out the mercenary intruders, who have made the "house of prayer" a den of robbers. He must worship, but He must first of all testify against the evil of those who have so dishonoured God.

Why were the money changers and sellers of doves carrying on their business in the temple?

The condition of the nation had made the trade necessary—the people who came from the country and from the provinces to keep the feasts, and pay the half shekel at the appointed time, could not pay it in Roman or other foreign coin; hence those persons were present with half shekels of Jewish coin, which they exchanged at a profit. Doves also were offered in sacrifice, and were thus for sale to those requiring them. These things had become necessities under the circumstances, but fraud and robbery were largely practised on foreign Jews. The priests, who profited by allowing the trade to be carried on in some part of the temple, also conniving therein. Robbery and worship were thus carried on under the same roof, a sad illustration of the degeneracy of which man is capable.

15, 16. *Why did the singing of the children disturb the priests so much?*

It was not the singing, but the song that annoyed them. The children having caught up the strain from the multitude, followed Him into the temple, chanting Hosanna, Hosanna to the son of David! This making Jesus of Nazareth the subject of such a song, was most provoking to those who were ready to put Him to death, and yet, said Jesus to the priests when they complained about it, it is one of your own psalms they are singing. "Have ye never read, out of the mouths of babes and sucklings thou hast perfected praise?" This psalm also, the chorus of which the children were chanting, was one of the processional psalms, and had its fulfilment that day in Him who had come in the name of the Lord.

18-21. *" Let no fruit grow on thee for ever." Why did Jesus pronounce such a withering sentence on this barren tree?*

It was in order to teach a lesson more valuable than the tree, and far more solemn than its death. He had been disappointed in a nation that should have borne fruit for God, but had failed to do so, and the withered tree stood as a warning to whoever would receive the lesson it was intended to teach.

20, 21. *Could the astonished disciples understand about the mountain being removed and cast into the sea?*

Not unless they first understood the prophetic action of Jesus in withering the fig-tree. The time came when they had to do with that symbolical mountain, and in the gift of prophecy pronounce its doom and removal for ever, both of which sad events came to pass. The Jew remains, but the nation is gone. As a mountain cast into the sea, a symbol of the nations, so have they sunk among the people, holding no position among them except their own personality.

28-32. *Why did Jesus refer to these two sons?*

To show them a picture of their own conduct. They had professed their willingness to obey God, but manifested their disobedience, while harlots and publicans, who at first refused to obey, afterward repented and obeyed God.

CHAPTER XXII.

1–14. *Where was this parable of the kingdom of heaven delivered?*

In Jerusalem or its vicinity, and to those priests and their confederates in religion, who had rejected Jesus as the Christ of God. The parable gives a twofold view—first, of the gracious provision made by God for their reception, and then of the insulting rejection of that provision.

Who are represented by the king and his son?

God and His Son Jesus, between whom and believers a marriage union was to take place, followed by a feast, or, as the prophet Isaiah foretells, "A feast of fat things, of wine on the lees"—*i.e.*, Gospel privileges so richly provided for those who accept Him as their bridegroom and friend.

Who are represented by the "servants" and those "that were bidden to the wedding"?

The invited ones, to whom the feast had been made known by John, were the priests and Pharisees, to whom Jesus delivered this parable, and were those "bidden to the wedding," Jesus having said, "John came unto you in the way of righteousness, and ye believed him not." Thus John and his disciples were the first "servants" inviting them to the wedding, "but they would not come." Then "other servants," the disciples of Jesus, with a more definite message, are sent out, and the prepared dinner, oxen and fatlings killed, and all things ready, opens to us the Gospel proclamation, when it is rejected by the nation, who actually murder some of those who are sent to them, and this is followed by their own sad doom of destruction. This section, from verses 3–7, covers the entire period, from the preaching of John to the destruction of Jerusalem, which is revealed in the king sending forth his armies, destroying those murderers, and burning up their city.

In verse 9 we have the servants sent out into the highways to invite another class of persons to the wedding. Who were these?

It is important for our understanding of this new section of the parable to observe that it is the same servants who are sent out to another class of persons, who are said to have been in the *highways*. Now this term scarcely conveys the meaning intended by *diexodus toon odoon*, which, *meton.*, refers to those who had gone out, or departed from the way, and who are to be followed by these servants and invited to the marriage. Note that we have two classes continually kept before us in the Saviour's ministry—viz., scribes and Pharisees, who form one class, and are referred to in the first section of this parable; and publicans and sinners, who form the second class, and are dealt with in the second part of it. We have no difficulty in deciding that it is to this latter class, who had really gone out of the right path, or highway, but were to hear that the Good Shepherd had come to seek and to save those that were lost, that are here referred to. There was, as we read in several places, quite a rush of this latter class to the feast, and the wedding was furnished with guests. Still, though the invitation was general, and the response to it apparently large, yet as there were conditions of enjoyment, all had to be tested by the king, as to whether or not they had on the required wedding garment.

What was this wedding garment?

Christ Jesus, as made known in the glad tidings, and who was put on by obedience to the truth ; but the profession of all such had to be tested in due time.

When did the examination take place ?

When the church was formed upon the basis of the apostles' proclamation, that Jesus, though He had been crucified, had been raised from the dead, and made Lord of all. Those who accepted Him as their Lord then, and many who had previously been baptised as His disciples did so at Pentecost, and those who did not were rejected, and not admitted to the feast. The man without a wedding garment was a representative of a large class, who claimed to be guests on other grounds than faith in a risen and exalted Jesus, but the claim was not allowed.

What was the outer darkness into which this man was cast ?

That state into which the Gospel arrangement cast or placed every Jew who rejected it, and into which not a single ray of light ever enters. Prophecy, previous to the coming of Jesus, was as a light shining in a dark place until day should dawn, and the morning star should arise in their hearts. But when the day opened by the Gospel of a risen Jesus, the night lights of the old economy were all extinguished, never more to be relighted. Judaism has continued from the first preaching of Christ till now, but it is like a dark cavern surrounding with gloom all who abide in it, because the true hope of glory, or divine assurance of salvation, can never enter the mind of one of them so long as they abide there. The phrase "outer darkness" is most expressive. It is the darkness outside His kingdom and church, where the light of His presence alone is found. Called they were, this can never be questioned; chosen they were not, except those

who received Him. The " gnashing of teeth " very fitly represents the rage manifested by some when the apostles refused to own them as the people of God. Indeed, this very term is used by Luke when referring to the result of the charge of Stephen, " They gnashed upon him with their teeth."

15–22. *The Pharisees and Herodians were not one in politics, why then did they unite to entangle Jesus?*

Both were opposed to Jesus, and only united to crush His influence by means of a crafty political question, and judged that His answer would bring Him into disgrace with either the Patrician or the Roman party. The Pharisees paid tribute, but only under protest, while the others keenly looked after the interests of the Herodian family. So jointly, after acknowledging His fearlessness of men, they ask Him, " Is it lawful to give tribute unto Cæsar or not ? " Had this enquiry been an honest one, His questioners might have obtained some valuable information, but by this question they were seeking to destroy both His character and His liberty. Discerning their motive, He asks to see the tribute money, and they brought to Him a penny, or denarius, " and He said to them, Whose is this image and superscription ? They say unto Him, Cæsar's." And, as if he said, Well, you are trading with Cæsar's coin, pay him what belongs to him, and give God His due also. Thus confounded, they left Him and went their way.

23–33. *The Sadducees are the next to try their hand at disputation. On what do they base their argument ?*

On the denial of a truth, and then they propound a query based upon their own negation. They bring forward a case of a woman, who was said to have had seven husbands, to prove the absurdity of a resurrection in which they did not believe. The patient reply of Jesus (and the difference between His answer to the Sadducees and that given to the Pharisees should be noted) not only meets their difficulties, but points out its cause. "Ye do err," said he, "not knowing the Scriptures, nor the power of God ; for in the resurrection they neither marry nor are given in marriage, but are as the angels of God in heaven." He then quotes the saying of God to Moses, "I am the God of Abraham," etc. They are, therefore, alive to Him ; for He is now their God, and in the resurrection they will be reclothed and fitted for their heavenly state.

34–40. *"Master, which is the great commandment in the law ?" Was this a renewal of the controversy?*

Yes ; and it is sad to think that the last few days of Jesus were so embittered with controversy. First, the Pharisees, with the Herodians, assail Him with a political question, then the Sadducees charge Him with teaching an absurdity, and now the Pharisees alone, with a lawyer for a spokesman, propound a knotty question about the law. His answer is very direct : "Thou shalt love the Lord thy God with all thy heart," etc. This is the first and great commandment ; and then added, the "second is like unto it, Thou shalt love thy neighbour as thyself," this latter being a truth for their conscience greatly needed by this class.

CHAPTER XXIII.

Was Jesus still in Jerusalem when He delivered this denunciatory address?

He was either in the city or its suburbs, as He had come up to the Passover, and as God's Lamb He was kept there that He might be ready for sacrifice. Still He must work for the truth, and after answering all the subtle questions with which the divided sects of that ancient city sought to entangle Him, He delivered this final public address, one of the most scathing that ever fell from His lips. The language employed may be thought too strong, but as His exposure of their life and spirit is studied, the conclusion will be that it was right in Him to thoroughly unmask the evil of their hearts. The only part to which objections might be made is the "woe" pronounced not less than eight times in this chapter, but this had been declared long before by the prophets, against those sins practised by them so openly. He is therefore only making application of that which had been written against evil-doers.

1. *The opponents of Jesus seem to have retired. Why did He deliver this address to the multitude and to His disciples?*

To warn them of the danger of being led by these "blind guides." Many of those who listened to Him were from Galilee and the other side of the Jordan, so for their sakes He made this exposure, and pointed out the fearful end of those whose advantages should have led to better results.

2–6. *What did He mean by "the scribes and Pharisees sit in Moses' seat"?*

The scribes were writers of the law, while the Pharisees read or directed the reading of the law : thus they sat in the seat of the great lawgiver. There was nothing wrong in this part of their work, for Jesus exhorts the people to observe the things they wrote and read. What they read, or bid you observe from Moses, that observe and do, but their works you must reject, because they are fashioned by tradition, and selfish love of authority. Love of praise, love of exaltation is prominent in all they do, therefore be not ye like them.

7–12. *"Be ye not called Rabbi." Who are specially warned here ?*

His disciples, who in the new institution, would have temptations to receive the honour of men. The Pharisees had sought exaltation, and they are warned against it. Had the warning of Jesus been heeded by all, we should never have heard of the "man of sin," sitting in the temple of God. Not only should these honours not be sought, but we must beware of giving them to any simply because they profess to serve Jesus.

13. *"Woe unto you." What is the signification of this woe ?*

Coming judgment that was sure to overtake them on account of their hypocrisy and apostacy from the truth.

" Ye shut up the kingdom of heaven against men." How could they do this ?

By shutting out the testimony by which men entered into it. By their refusal to endorse its proclamation, they excited suspicion in those who did not think for themselves, and by threatened expulsion from the synagogue of all who became His disciples, many were deterred from accepting Him as their teacher.

14. *How did they devour widows' houses ?*

By applying to their own use officially the profits or dues which were appointed by the law for the widows of priests. Thus they devoured their houses or means of support, making their own pretended pious service a plea for their claims.

15. *How was their proselytism so condemnable ?*

Their false or traditional teaching mixed up with the law produced false practice, so that the proselyte became worse by adopting it than if he had remained in heathenism.

16–22. *How did these scribes and Pharisees show their blindness in the distinctions they made about swearing ?*

By making distinctions where none existed, thus encouraging falsehood, without a sense of wrong. For instance, they taught, "Whoever swears by the temple, it is nothing"— that is, there is no sin, though you do not fulfil your vow ; but "whoever swears by the gold of the temple, he is a debtor," *i.e.,* under obligation to perform it ; and so with the altar, and the throne of God. Jesus showed them that the temple and the gold, the altar and the gift upon it, the throne and its occupant, were one, and they were blind and foolish in teaching that men could vow and yet not be under obligation.

23. *" Ye tithe mint and anise," etc. Why was it wrong to do this ?*

There was nothing wrong in it if any chose to do so, but it was their motive that Jesus condemned. They sought by these petty acts to convey the impression that they were exceedingly strict in keeping the law, in which God commanded the tithing of corn, while their omission of judgment, mercy, and faith, proved their deep-dyed hypocrisy. They proverbially strained out a gnat and swallowed a camel.

25. *"Woe unto you, for ye make clean the outside of the cup and platter." What was there wrong in this ?*

Nothing whatever, if only what was in them had been cleanly got and used. But when the livings of widows were intemperately devoured, the words "extortion and excess" were most appropriate, and defiled even their traditionally cleansed vessels. It was their sin to which He points in this proverbial admonition, "Blind Pharisee, cleanse first that which is within the cup and dish, that the outside of them may be clean also."

27–32. *Why did Jesus condemn*

the garnishing of the sepulchres of the righteous ?

Because these were the tombs of murdered prophets and just men, and if they had only been rightly affected towards them, they would have mourned over them instead of garnishing them.

34–36. *Why should all the righteous blood shed upon the earth be visited upon that generation ?*

Every recorded murder had the disapprobation of God connected with it, and every repetition of such a crime was, in addition to its criminality, a rejection of the divine testimony against the evil. Thus every crime was in the face of a divine protest, and in the death of Jesus their guilt reached a climax, and judgment long deferred was to be visited on that generation.

CHAPTER XXIV.

1. *Why were the disciples so anxious to call the attention of Jesus to the buildings of the temple ?*

Probably on account of the solemn words He had just spoken concerning Jerusalem, the people, and their house left desolate. To them it was a sad utterance, for their heart still clung to the temple which for the time being was the place of communion with God. He had just briefly stated its doom, and His attention is called to it in order to excite His sympathy on its behalf. His reply, however, extinguished all hope for its preservation, and they next sought to know the time of the end of their beautiful temple, and of its associated calamities.

3. *How many questions did the disciples ask Jesus, and what does privately mean ?*

According to Mark, there were four of His disciples who came to Him on the Mount of Olives, when both the multitude and the other disciples were absent. This is what

he means by privately. Then they asked Him two questions, which presumably included all they desired to know, a full grasp of which will greatly assist us to understand the very full and careful answers of Jesus. If the questions proposed are not understood, a misunderstanding and a misapplication of the events detailed, is almost certain. They ask (1.) " When shall these things be ? " *i.e.*, the destruction of the temple, of which He had previously spoken ; and (2.) " What shall be the sign of Thy coming," *lit.*, presence or manifestation in connection with this overthrow, " and of the end of the world," *lit.*, the completion or ending of the age. This second is like a double question, and yet it is really one. They understood that His manifestation was to terminate the age, and they ask what will be the sign when this shall come to pass. It will make a great difference in our reading of the Saviour's answers, whether we read this second question as referring to the end of the material universe, or to the end of the Jewish age. We must therefore be certain that it is *aeon* and not *kosmos* which they use, and a glance at the Greek text will suffice.

4. " *Take heed that no man deceive you.*" *Deceive them in what respect ?*

In relation to His personal manifestation, which was not intended, but only a manifestation in power. Some would come in His name and deceive many, but they were not to hearken to such. He assured them that He should not be visibly present at all, so that there need be no mistake. Every person assuming to be the Christ was a deceiver and not to be followed. This matter is again referred to in ver. 23.

6–8. *Why did He exhort them not to be troubled by wars and rumours of wars, when the overthrow was to be by a war ?*

The strife of nations and the rumours of wars would be continually heard of, but as these were only the beginning of sorrows, they were not to be moved by them, *i.e.*, they were to take no action on account of them. It was for the war that would desolate the city, destroy the temple, scatter the people, and close the age, for which they were to watch, and the signs of its approach, being also the sign of His power in judging them, was very carefully given.

9–13. *" Then shall they deliver you up,"* etc. *When were these afflictions endured by them ?*

In the interval that occurred between their proclamation of the ascended Jesus, and the occurrence of the Roman siege. The " Acts of the Apostles," the letters of Paul and of Peter, furnish abundant evidence that they did suffer all these things. It need cause no surprise that many thus severely tested should fail, and that only those who continued faithful to the end enjoyed the deliverance.

14. *Why was the end or judgment delayed until the Gospel of the kingdom was everywhere proclaimed, and for whose benefit was this done ?*

For the Jews, the people who were to be judged, and who were at that time scattered over the Roman empire or world ; the *oikoumene*, or that which is ruled over. That it was the Jews to whom the Gospel was to be preached, is plain from the statement that it was to be preached in the world, not for the conversion of the nations, as the commission directs, but for a witness to them that God did not bring this judgment upon His ancient people without first seeking to win them to His Son. That such a witness was borne, the labours of Paul fully attest. Not a synagogue or colony was overlooked by him in any city he visited. Even when sent to Rome as a prisoner, his first effort was to call together the chief of the Jews and preach to them the kingdom of God. The disciples asked about the end of the age, and He here replies, that the Gospel shall be preached all over the world, *i.e.*, wherever the scattered people are, and *then* shall the end come. This is certainly not very definite as to the time, but before He closes, the limit of its extension is clearly given by bounding it within that generation.

15–20. *They were to flee from Jerusalem and Judea when they saw the " abomination of desolation."* *What was this ?*

The Roman army with their eagle-mounted banners, which, when planted upon their holy places, were indeed an abomination. As soon as this army entered Judea they were to flee to the mountains, and those in the city were to leave it at once. The one upon the housetop must not delay his flight by entering his house, or the gates would be closed, and flight impossible. The one in the field must not enter the city even for his garment, or he might never get out again. They must either escape to the mountains or be exposed to the siege.

What may we learn from His direction to them to pray that certain favourable circumstances might occur ?

That these were in God's hands, and that He would grant them in answer to prayer. The judgment would come, but He could send it in summer instead of winter, which to them would be a great favour. God can lighten burdens He will not altogether remove, and can stay His rough wind in the day of His east wind.

21. *Some persons affirm that what is called the " great tribulation," is yet future. Is this true ?*

Not if this teaching of Jesus is to be accepted. He says that there had not been any like it from the beginning, to that time, and never should be. This is decisive, and should be accepted. The great tribulation spoken of in Revelation vii. is the same as mentioned here, and out of which many are brought.

23–27. *Why does Jesus refer to the lightning when instructing His disciples to beware of false Christs and false prophets?*

He told them that such should arise and affirm His personal presence, here or there, in the " desert," or in " the secret chambers," but, said He, " believe it not. For as the lightning cometh out of the east, and shineth even unto the west ; so shall also the coming, or manifestation, of the Son of man be." That is, my coming, *lit.*, presence, will be as the lightning, whose source may be in the east, but the flash or stroke is in the west. The source of this tribulation will be the throne of the glory upon which I shall be sitting, but the stroke will fall upon Jerusalem and the nation of Israel. " For where the carcase is, there will the eagles be gathered together."

29. *In speaking of the darkening of the sun, moon, and stars, which was to follow this visitation, does He not refer to the end of the world?*

In order to see that these terms are used as symbols of the nation of Israel, and do not refer to the planets of the heavens, we must note the word *immediately*. Jesus had just spoken of the eagles gathering to the carcase, which all understand to denote the Roman army besieging Jerusalem, and like vultures devouring the already dead body of the nation. Then He adds, " Immediately after the tribulation of those days, *i.e.*, at once, directly, shall the sun be darkened," etc. Now we know that these things did not befall the luminaries of the sky, and must therefore be applied to the

nation to whom these symbols had been long familiar. When Joseph had his dream of the subjection of his brethren to him, he saw the sun, moon, and eleven stars bow down to him, which Jacob at once applied to himself and his family. From that overthrow the Jews ceased to be light-bearers to the world, and Christ, the apostles, and the church, fill this high and responsible position.

30. " *And then shall appear the sign of the Son of man in heaven.*" *Is this an answer to their question, " and what shall be the sign of thy coming?*"

They asked for a sign of His coming, and here He states very definitely, when you see all these lights put out, and the powers of this once exalted system shaken into confusion, then you will see the sign of the Son of man in heaven. They will mourn, but your redemption from their power will then be effected.

Is it not strange that Jesus, when giving them a sign of His power, should pass over all the demonstrations of the Spirit from Pentecost onward, and fix upon this last evidence as a sign for them?

It does appear strange at first, but a similar answer was given to Moses when God sent him to deliver Israel. Moses asked for a token or sign that he was sent by God, and the reply was, " When thou hast brought forth the people out of Egypt, ye shall serve God upon this mountain " (Exod. iii. 12). All the previous signs that were to be done in Egypt and the Red Sea are thus passed over, and this latter sign, when Israel should stand as worshippers at Horeb, was given instead of them. So with Jesus. In giving them a sign of His exaltation, He passed over all the signs which were to go on for thirty years or more previous to that, and gives this last evidence in the overthrow of the nation. The

D

destruction of Jerusalem, its temple and worship, was the final demonstration of the Father, that Jesus whom they crucified was His exalted Son. The sign was a fearful one to all concerned. From that terrible shaking the old institution became a wreck. Alas, that they should still cling to it, when they might enter the new covenant, and be for ever blest.

What does He mean by "and they shall see the Son of man coming in the clouds of heaven with power and great glory"?

It is, *lit.*, *upon* the cloud, and is a further revelation in symbol of the manner of His coming. The clouds here are a symbol of the Roman army by which He overthrew the nation. The prophets frequently so used this symbol, " Behold the Lord rideth upon a swift cloud, *i.e.*, the Chaldean army, and shall come into Egypt " (Isaiah xix. 1). The Roman army were the clouds upon which He should ride for judgment upon that people.

31. *" And He shall send His angels." Were these celestial beings?*

They are simply His *messengers*, gathering out by His testimony His elect from the four winds, before the judgment descended upon the rejectors of His grace.

34. *What did He mean by " This generation shall not pass till all these things be fulfilled "?*

That the Jews then living were to see all the predictions then delivered exhaustively fulfilled. *Genea*, the word used by Jesus, cannot be stretched beyond the generation then existing. Some of course would die, even some of the apostles passed away by death, but others lived to see the prophecy an accomplished fact. Numbers who had seen Jesus crucified, saw that destructive siege which happened only about thirty-seven years after. " This generation " therefore forms an important link of the chain which binds all these events together.

35. *" Heaven and earth shall pass away, but My words shall not pass away." What does this mean?*

" Heaven " and " earth " are used by the prophets of Israel, as symbols of the nations. Thus Isaiah speaks (i. 2), " Hear, O heavens, and give ear, O earth." These, said Jesus, shall pass away, but my words, *i.e.*, my truth, shall not pass away. It shall abide when all this is removed. Or as Paul writes to the Hebrews, " The things which are shaken will be removed, but the things which cannot be shaken will remain."

37–39. *Why does He refer to the days of Noah?*

To show that as the people then did not believe the testimony of Noah concerning the coming deluge that was to take them away ; so the Jews would not believe His word concerning His coming in judgment.

40. *How, in that siege, would one be taken out of the field, and the other left?*

His word, when believed, would take one out of the field and another from the mill, and send them to the mountain, and so they would escape, while the unbelieving would remain and perish.

42. *Does " watch therefore " apply to these events concerning Jerusalem?*

Most certainly. The approach of the desolater, foretold by Daniel as well as Jesus, was to be seen before every way of escape was closed, and for this they were to watch and flee away at once.

Can this exhortation be applied either to death or the personal return of the Lord?

No. We cannot watch even for death, for its approach is invisible. We may be ready for it by being in Christ, and that is what all should be. Then as to the Lord's return we cannot watch for it, because it must be invisible to mortal sight. The living can flee nowhere then, because they will be changed in a moment, in the twinkling of an eye. The Thessalonians were not watching but waiting for God's Son from heaven, having turned from idols to serve the living and true God. This is the attitude believers are now called upon to occupy.

45–51. *Who is this "ruler over His household"?*

The teacher in the church, upon whom rested the obligation to instruct the saints of that period, respecting these coming calamities, that all might be prepared to meet them. If he was faithful, he would give all timely instruction, but if careless he would be surprised and cut off in his sins.

CHAPTER XXV.

THE BRIDEGROOM AND THE VIRGINS.

1–13. *When did this similitude of the kingdom of heaven take place?*

At the destruction of Jerusalem, as is clearly indicated by the first word, "Then," *i.e.*, at that time, will all these things occur. In the preceding paragraph Jesus spoke of the wise servant who faithfully waited for his lord and was honoured, and of the foolish servant who, through his evil reasonings and practice, was unprepared and punished. Here also reference is made to wise and foolish persons, who are compared to virgins waiting for the bridegroom—the wise having lamps with oil in them, the foolish with lamps, but no oil in them.

Who is the Bridegroom spoken of in this similitude?

The Lord Jesus, who was taking out of the way of judgment all who in loving confidence acted under His instruction, and who also marked out the hopeless doom of those who had not His word abiding in them, in

the day that should burn as an oven, and when the proud, etc., should be as stubble.

Who are represented by the virgins?

Those who had been instructed about the judgment coming on the nation, whether personally by Jesus, or by the faithful servants under Him. The wise virgins are those who, having heard and believed the careful teaching of Jesus respecting the judgment, held it fast, and knew what to do when the crisis came upon them; while the foolish virgins represent those who, though professedly believing the warnings of the judgment, had not treasured up His directions, and had to seek instructions from their own teachers when the crisis came.

What is meant by "oil in their vessels"?

Having their understanding enlightened by the teaching of Jesus respecting the coming crisis. In the Old Testament the olive and its oil are used as symbols of the Spirit and His revelations, which, when received and used as oil in a lamp, was a light upon their path. The wise virgins possessed the teaching of Jesus, and used it for their escape, while the foolish who neglected it were in darkness and confusion when the Bridegroom came.

What is meant by "the Bridegroom tarried"?

The delay in the execution of judgment, which being put back nearly forty years from the ascension of Jesus, there could be no action in relation to His directions about escape. "They all slumbered and slept" very properly expresses the necessary quiescent state of that period.

What is meant by the "midnight"?

The dispensation is figuratively termed a day, which virtually closed when God's Lamb was offered in sacrifice. The typical lamb of their passover was to be killed at the going down of the sun (Deut. xvi. 6), and the day closed with its death, and a new day commenced in gloom and darkness. The death of Jesus, the antitypical Lamb, therefore closed that dispensational day, and a new day began in the shade and gloom of the past. Yet, though the dispensational day then virtually closed, it went on in ever-deepening gloom of night until "the days of vengeance," called by Jesus "midnight," and then the day passed away for ever.

The foolish asked the wise for oil, i.e., *instruction. Why was it refused?*

The banners of the imperial hosts were waving in the land, and it had become a time for action, not instruction. " I must away " was about all that any believer then could say to his neighbour. It was flee or perish.

While the foolish virgins went to seek oil, or obtain instruction how to act, the " door was shut." What door was this?

The gates of Jerusalem, which were shut by official order, and the avenues of escape from the land, which the Romans soon closed.

Why is the " watch therefore " repeated here?

The time of the occurrence of these things was not revealed, but only preceding events, and for the appearance of these they must watch.

As this simile of the kingdom does not directly apply to us, what instruction may we derive from it?

There are indirect lessons which apply to all time, and these should be carefully noted. We may learn from it—(1.) that the words of Jesus are true, and will all be fulfilled; (2.) that it is important to carefully note His directions, and implicitly obey them; and (3.), never to expect blessings except through the appointed means.

THE TALENTS.

14–30. *Why did Jesus deliver this parable or simile of the talents given by the master to his servants?*

To show the importance of using, and increasing by use, the deposit of knowledge already bestowed by Himself. The revelations of dispensational judgment and deliverance had been given in varied measure even to His disciples, or, as in the simile, one received five talents, another two, and another one, but each had received sufficient for trading, i.e., each had received sufficient knowledge of coming events to provoke research and further enquiry, which would be sure to lead to further knowledge of these things.

Did Jesus speak of coming judgment to any but His disciples?

He frequently spoke of it to the multitude and to the scribes in parables, such as that of the vineyard let out to husbandmen, and the marriage made by the king for his son, in which judgment was plainly declared. This testimony delivered to them about the king sending his armies and destroying the murderers, and burning up their city, may be counted as only "one talent;" but, had it been used aright, much more could have been learnt, not only of the judgment, but of deliverance. Instead, however, of using it for enquiry, they buried it in unbelief, and abused the giver when condemned for their neglect.

"After a long time the lord of those servants came, and reckoned with them." To what period does Jesus here refer?

To the judgment already spoken of, the destruction of Jerusalem. It is the persons to whom the talents were given that are here called to account, and are rewarded or punished according to their use or neglect. This simile is inseparably connected with the preceding one by the first word "for," which introduces the reason why watchfulness was required. If no revelation of preceding signs had been given, there could have been no responsibility in relation to this calamity; but these were ample, and all were involved thereby. "For, as a man travelling into a far country," who gave talents to his servants, who having received them were held accountable, so had Jesus, preparatory to His departure, deposited with His servants valuable deposits of truth, for which He held them accountable.

What is the outer darkness into which the unprofitable servant was cast, with weeping and gnashing of teeth?

Outer darkness is here a symbol of the state into which the unprofitable servant was cast by this final rejection of God. Up to this period of judgment, the old institution, by its temple sacrifices and priesthood, was an uncancelled bond of fleshly union; but when God destroyed the whole institution, and scattered it so thoroughly that the subjects of it have never been able to put it together again, He dissolved the last tie which held them to Himself as a people. Every avenue of approach to Him which that institution opened was closed for ever, and as they refused to enter by Christ the door, they were left in outer darkness, weeping, a symbol of their grief at being thus treated, and gnashing their teeth, illustrative of the revengeful spirit which raged within them.

THE JUDGMENT.

31–46. *Is Jesus in this section speaking of the final judgment of the world?*

Considering its close relation to the preceding similes and prophecy, it seems rather to be of that dispensational judgment which closed the age of which He is speaking, the punishment of which to the Jew still continues, being everlasting, *lit.*, age-enduring.

But is this not to take place when He shall "come in His glory," and "sit upon the throne of His glory"?

Yes, and He is now seated upon the throne of His glory. *We see Jesus,* said Paul, *who was made lower than the* (former) *messengers by the suffering of death, crowned with glory and honour.* And when He came in power, and overturned the people who put Him to death, He did, indeed, as the "Son of man, come in His glory," a glory in which even His faithful disciples were called to share.

The approval, or condemnation of those brought before Him, is made to rest upon their treatment of His disciples. How was this?

Because by their treatment of His disciples they showed their faith or unbelief in Himself. While Jesus maintained a personal ministry on earth, much respect and honour was shown to Him by those who derived personal benefit from His healing helping power, but when the work passed into the hands of others, they were treated much upon their own merits. Few of them recognised the claims of Jesus in His disciples, but treated them most indignantly, as the "Acts of the Apostles" fully show. Jesus, however, reckoned the treatment shown to His disciples by the Jews during that period as done to Himself, and rewarded or punished accordingly.

CHAPTER XXVI.

3–6. *Why did the chief priests, scribes, and elders assemble for consultation just before the passover?*

They wished to seize and kill Jesus, and, in order to effect their object, it was necessary to adopt some plan before His many friends from the country assembled, hence this consultation at the palace of the high priest. There were difficulties in connection with His apprehension, and these had to be met.

How did they overcome these difficulties ?

By means of a faithless disciple, who, knowing their desire, volunteered for a sum of money to deliver Him into their hands when His friends were absent.

6–13. *This woman, who anointed Jesus in the house of Simon, is said to have done a work so good that it should have a place in testimony with His gospel. In what did its greatness consist ?*

In her manifest faith in His testimony concerning His death. Not one of His disciples believed that He would be crucified, but she, having believed, ventured to anoint beforehand His body for burial. This act of faith was as fragrant to His spirit as the perfume that filled the room. The anointing showed her faith, and pleased her Lord.

14–16. *"They covenanted with him for thirty pieces of silver." Did Judas or the council fix the price ?*

There were two parties in the transaction, each having their own interest. Judas, we presume, would desire a high price for betrayal, and they, wishing to degrade Jesus, offered for His arrest the price of a slave. It was a base and humiliating contract, but Jesus patiently endured it all.

17–19. *"My time is at hand." This message was sent by Jesus, when seeking a room in which to keep the passover. What did He mean ?*

It is strictly, *my season is near, i.e.,* my opportunity of attending to the feast is the present: "I will keep the passover at thy house with My disciples." The next day, the preparation day proper, when many lambs were slain for the feast, Jesus

was God's paschal lamb, so He partook of it the night previous.

20. *In Egypt the Israelites stood to eat the passover, but here we read "He sat down with the twelve." Why this difference of posture ?*

The entire dispensation was typical, so that even position at the passover feast is not without instruction. In Egypt they partook of it by God's command, with sandalled feet and girded loins, and staff in hand, standing ready to leave at the given signal, a most impressive type of the sinner, who upon his believing in Christ should stand ready to pass through the waters of baptism, under his newly accepted leader. In Canaan they sat or reclined, a fit expression of deliverance or rest from their former bondage, and also a type of the rest of the believer in Jesus.

21–25. *"One of you shall betray Me." How could Judas say, "Master, is it I ?"*

He had already agreed to betray Him, and had received into his hand the price of blood, and was, therefore, capable of this insolent address.

Was he present at the institution of the memorial feast ?

John records that Jesus gave the passover sop to Judas, who immediately went out. As a Jew he had a right to the passover feast, but as a betrayer he could have no interest in the new arrangement, and possibly knew nothing of it; besides, he had to meet with the council and arrange for betrayal, and so left early.

26–28. *Our version reads, "Jesus took bread, and blessed it." Is this proper ?*

Our translators added the word "it," which should be omitted. Jesus took bread, and blessed—*i.e.,* gave thanks to God.

Does the giving of thanks before the breaking of bread, etc., differ from ordinary prayer and supplication ?

The prayers and supplications of saints on other occasions may include everything needful, but on this occasion there should be simply thanksgiving for that which is enjoyed through Christ. Asking forgiveness of sins, or any other privilege, is altogether out of place. There should be at His table intelligent recognition of our deliverance from judgment by Him. To sit at His table and not see Him as our Saviour is confusion. If we have accepted Him in loving trust, and are walking in obedience to Him, we should take our place at His table as accepted guests, fully assured that all the privileges of the new covenant are ours, and for this surely we may give thanks.

On the table of the Lord there is a loaf and a cup. Why should there be two elements in commemorating one event ?

As there are two elements used at the feast, so there are two aspects of Christ's work to be distinctly recognised by us :—(1.) That He gave His life in service for us, and taking the bread should be regarded as a renewal of our obligation to give our lives in service to Him ; to eat of the loaf should be felt as a solemn pledge by us to reproduce His life in our own—to live Christ over again in the true spirit of service ; and (2.) that He gave His blood to seal the covenant by which we have remission of our sins, and all other provided favours. When we drink of the cup, we are accepting the pledge that all new covenant blessings are ours. To have a doubt respecting this would not only dishonour Him, but hinder our own joy and thanksgiving.

29. *" I will not henceforth drink of this fruit of the vine." Had Jesus partaken of it ?*

Yes, but this was at the passover ; for, though mentioned after instituting the memorial feast, it was spoken in relation to the passover cup, of which He partook with the rest, but would do it no more until He drank it new with them in His Father's kingdom. That is, before another passover occurred, they should unite in the joy of another deliverance. This is what He means by drinking it new with them in His Father's kingdom.

31. *" All ye shall be offended because of Me this night." Why should the smiting of Jesus offend His disciples ?*

It will be better to read, *stumbled* because of Me. The disciples had refused His testimony concerning His sufferings and death, and when they saw Him smitten and afflicted, they were confused and troubled. Had they believed the prophecy, " I will smite the shepherd," they would have been prepared for the event.

33–35. *" I will never be offended." Was Peter sincere in this confident assertion ?*

I would not for a moment question his sincerity ; but he did not know the power of the circumstances by which he would be surrounded on that eventful night. Peter did not believe that Jesus would die and rise again, and when he saw Him in the hands of His enemies, he was ready to count Him an impostor, and by earnest protest sought to clear himself of all association with Him.

36. *Why did Jesus go to Gethsemane ?*

To seek strength for His approaching trial and death. He had often taught His disciples to trust God and fear not, and now He is called upon to practise His own teaching, and submit Himself entirely to God. It is deeply instructive to see Him yielding up His own will, to do the will of His Father, although to do so was to give up His life.

39. *" Father, if it be possible, let this cup pass from Me." What cup was this ?*

It was not the hour and power of darkness, of which the malicious Jews and thoughtless Gentiles had full possession, because, according to John, He would not ask to be saved from it; neither could it be the forsaking of God, for that had been foretold and accepted; nor was it His death, for prophets had written that He should be cut off, and He had come from the Father to fulfil them. But there was one trial becoming apparent, the removal or mitigation of which He desired. The twelve, who up to this time had continued with Him in His temptations, were about to give way; one had already agreed to betray Him, another He knew would deny Him, while those He had taken with Him into the garden to watch were asleep. He plainly saw the extent of the desertion He would have to endure, and prayed that if possible this cup, this trial added to all the rest, might pass from Him. "Nevertheless, not as I will, but as Thou wilt,"—if it please Thee, I will drink this cup also. The death He is called to die will rend every tie of friendship, and beget suspicion in the hearts of all, and yet He is willing to endure everything that man may be saved. The tramp of feet descending Mount Olivet, is now heard; He knows their errand, and is now ready to meet them. He at once arouses the sleeping disciples with, "Sleep ye now, and take rest." Behold! the betrayer is at hand!

47–54. Was Judas responsible to the priests for His arrest?

No; only for His betrayal into the hands of the soldiers, who were present to arrest Him. Judas gave the sign, and they took hold of Him. Two courses were open to Him, one of which He must choose—either to yield unresistingly and let things take their course, or to resist and hinder their purpose. Why He did not choose the latter, but submitted to the former, reveals the true spirit of obedience. "Thinkest thou," He said to him who cut off the man's ear, "that I cannot now pray to My Father, and He shall presently give Me more than twelve legions of angels? But how then shall the Scriptures be fulfilled, that thus it must be?" How dear to His heart was the fulfilling of the Scriptures, although it was to cost Him His life.

56. "Then all the disciples forsook Him and fled." Was He then drinking the dreaded cup?

Yes; it was the first He had to drink. Not a disciple remained to cheer Him as He passed over Olivet, and He who had succoured so many, had to commence His trial alone. The scribes and elders, with Caiaphas, the high priest, were anxiously waiting for Him in Jerusalem, and the servants and soldiers hurried Him on to suffer judgment at their hands.

THE TRIAL OF JESUS BEFORE THE COUNCIL.

59. Why were false witnesses allowed to appear in this preparatory trial, and why did Jesus not reply to them?

Their unjust proceedings arose from their bitter hatred to Jesus, and led them to seek His death, even by falsehood. In refusing to answer their false accusations He was fulfilling the Scriptures, which said, "Like a lamb dumb before his shearer, so opened He not His mouth."

63. "Tell us whether Thou be the Christ the Son of God." Why did Jesus reply to this challenge of the high priest?

Because the truth of God was at stake. Jesus could be silent before false witnesses, but He must speak when called upon to witness for the truth. It was then He witnessed the good confession, and was charged with blasphemy, and deemed worthy of death.

" Ye shall see the Son of man sitting at the right hand of power," etc. Did they understand Him?

They neither understood nor believed His word until they were as chaff in the midst of the burning. They knew the meaning of His words only when the descending axe of judgment was hewing them down as fuel for the unquenchable fire, and instead of being humbled into penitence, they were maddened into obdurate rage.

65. *Why did the high priest rend his clothes on hearing the witness of Jesus?*

He accounted it blasphemy, and the rending of the clothes was commanded by a Rabbinical law, and formally preceded the passing of the sentence of death, of which Jesus was then accounted worthy.

67. *" Then did they spit in His face, and buffeted Him." Who were those who did so?*

Roman officials and servants of the high priest; but the act was brutal, and also illegal, because Jesus was then not officially condemned.

CHAPTER XXVII.

THE TRIAL OF JESUS BEFORE THE SANHEDRIN.

1. *" When the morning was come," etc. Was this a second trial?*

Apparently the entire Sanhedrin, or " whole council," were summoned early in the morning, and thus legally assembled, conducted what may be called a second trial, of which Matthew gives no report. According to Luke, whose account of it shows that there was a very brief examination of the points at issue, the decision of the first council was confirmed—viz., that the prisoner was worthy of death, and after this examination by the great council, He could be formally brought before Pilate for sentence of death, which he alone could pronounce.

3. *Why did Matthew record the death of Judas?*

There are at least two reasons which are worthy of notice :—(1.) His striking testimony to the innocency of Jesus before the chief priests and elders— " I have sinned, in that I have betrayed innocent blood "; and (2.) the solemn warning furnished in his sad end to all opposers of Christ.

4. *" What is that to us? see thou to that." What did they mean?*

What they really intended by this brief, hasty reply is : What is (your thought of His innocency) to us? thou wilt see (in a little while for thyself that He is not innocent).

Did Judas expect that Jesus would be condemned?

Judas knew that He had power to deliver Himself, and fully expected that He would do so, but he was disappointed. He had sold Him into their hands, and there He remained until condemned to die, and His condemnation, of which he had been the first agent, overwhelmed him with remorse.

It is said here that he " repented himself." Is not this a proof of penitence?

It is, strictly, *having regretted* (it)—*i.e.*, what he had done—but it was too late. Jesus was condemned to death. There was no penitence in the mind of Judas, it was the consequences he regretted, not the crime, and the remorse arising therefrom became insupportable. He did not even seek mercy had God been disposed to forgive him on Gospel terms, but rushed into death with suicidal hands, and now stands as a warning to others, not to seek wealth by unlawful means.

Would the crime of Judas have been as great, had Jesus prevented the arrest?

It could have made no difference before God. He measures crime by intentions, not by results.

THE TRIAL OF JESUS BEFORE PILATE.

11–14. *"And Jesus stood before the governor, and the governor asked Him, Art Thou the King of the Jews?" Why did this question of Pilate differ from that of the council?*

As the governor of the nation on behalf of Cæsar, Pilate could be anxious only about rivalry and sedition, while the chief priests and elders were jealous of His influence as a religious teacher. Pilate's question was a very proper one, and Jesus answered it without hesitancy, but when accused by the priests and elders, He answered nothing; and even when Pilate called His attention to their charges, He still made no reply.

15–18. *Why was Pilate the first to remind them of the favour granted them of having a political prisoner released to them at that feast?*

In the hope that they would allow him to release Jesus, but in this he was disappointed. A notable prisoner, called Barabbas, was chosen for this favour, and Jesus was left in his hands for judgment.

24. *Why did Pilate wash his hands before passing sentence on Jesus?*

To free himself from blame, while granting the Jews their request.

Was he free from blame?

Certainly not. He was conscious that Jesus had done no evil to make Him worthy of death, and even declared Him to be a "just person"—a striking testimony from His judge; and, yet, to please the Jews, he condemned Him to be crucified. It was the Jews who alone clamoured for His blood, but, as the representative of Roman authority, his act in condemning Jesus involved the Gentile nations in a confederacy that effected His death. The Gentiles would not have put Him to death but for the Jews, and the Jews could not without out the Gentiles, but together they crucified the Son of God.

Pilate affirmed the innocency of Jesus before the Jews. What official reason could he assign to Cæsar for His death?

Doubtless the alleged kingship of Jesus. He had declared to Pilate that He was a king, and on this charge His execution was effected. The scarlet robe and reed in His hand, the crown of thorns, and the "Hail! King of the Jews!" on bended knee, all indicate that this was the accusation given to the soldiers, and their barbarous mockery was based upon it. Over His head upon the cross this accusation was written :—"This is Jesus, the King of the Jews." Pilate did not believe it, but he had no other charge, and this would be assigned as the cause of His death in his despatch to Cæsar.

45. *Was the darkness, which lasted from the sixth to the ninth hour, caused by an eclipse?*

It was always full moon at the passover, when there could not be a natural eclipse of the sun. It was God who cast a sable covering over the great orb of day, and made the sun a mourner, when its Creator was giving up His life.

46. *That loud cry, Eli, Eli, etc., seems not to have been understood. How could they mistake His words?*

They were not Jews, but Romans who mistook His words. He was not calling for Elias, but repeating the first sentence of the xxii. Psalm in Hebrew, thus proving it to be fulfilled in Himself.

51. *"The veil of the temple was rent in twain." What did this rending express?*

This veil covered the entrance to the holy of holies, and was typical of the flesh of Christ. When Jesus died, this veil was rent open, and the way of access was set forth in this last shadow of the institution. Through His death and resurrection a way is now opened into glory.

57—60. *How was it that Joseph of Arimathœa was so prepared for the burial of Jesus?*

Just as the woman was prepared to anoint Him beforehand for His burial. We account for this entire preparation, and being ready for the crisis, to Joseph's previous reception of his Master's teaching. The tomb, the clean linen cloth, were prepared in faith. The prophet said that He would make His grave with the rich, and Joseph, a rich man, prepared it, and so honoured his gracious Lord.

CHAPTER XXVIII.

1. *"The first day of the week came Mary Magdalene, etc., to the sepulchre." Why was this visit delayed so long?*

Their object in visiting the sepulchre was to anoint the body of Jesus, and this was their first opportunity to do so. Assuming as true that Jesus was crucified on Thursday the preparation day, then Friday being a passover sabbath, on which no servile work could be done, and Saturday a seventh-day sabbath, they could not have gone earlier than they did. "In the end of the sabbath, *lit.*, sabbaths, as it began to dawn towards the first of the week," they came to see the sepulchre.

Why were the women so ready to visit the sepulchre when the apostles went only when summoned by them?

They had a work of love to perform on the dead body of Jesus, and this brought them where they expected to find it, a work which the men never purposed to do. Besides, a guard of soldiers had been placed there, and of these they were afraid, a fear which never entered into the hearts of these women. They stood by Him to the last of His agony, saw Him taken down from the cross, and borne to the sepulchre, and when the sabbaths are past they again seek His supposed lifeless body.

2—4. *"And, behold, there was a great earthquake." Was this the cause of the soldiers' flight?*

Had our translators rendered *seismos* by heart-quake instead of earthquake they would have been nearer the truth. An angel of the Lord descended from heaven, whose countenance was like lightning, and rolled away the stone, "and for fear of him the keepers (not the earth) did shake, and became as dead men." Fear caused their flight, and the sepulchre was left under angelic guard.

Why were the women not afraid when they saw the angel?

He said unto them, "Fear not ye; for I know that ye seek Jesus who was crucified. He is not here; for He is risen, as He said."

11—15. *How did the watch manage their part of the story?*

They gave a faithful report to the chief priests, who, seeing that they were defeated, agreed together with the elders to affirm and maintain a lie. A large sum of money was offered to the soldiers to say that the disciples had stolen the body while they slept. This bribe was accepted by them, and this lie was circulated; Pilate was persuaded not to investigate the matter, while the Jews generally gladly accepted this deception, and fastened upon themselves and their children the last link of the chain of unbelief. Those self-imposed fetters have never been broken, but bind their spirits still. No intelligent Jew denies the crucifixion of Jesus, but His resurrection is denied by nearly all of them. The apostles afterward affirmed His resurrection in their presence, and as His dead body was never produced to refute their testimony, it stands an indisputable fact.

18. *"All power or authority is given to me in heaven and on earth." Why in heaven as well as on earth?*

Because while it is on earth He must be obeyed, as alone having authority here, it is into heaven the obedient are to be admitted, and authority is granted to Him in order to personally admit them there. It is a blessed truth to all who have received Him as their Saviour and Lord on earth, to know that He can admit them into the Father's glorious home, and that all the resources of heaven are in His hands.

19, 20. *The disciples were commanded to teach the nations, to baptise and teach all things commanded them. Why have we the word "teach" twice in this commission?*

It would be more correct to read, *Going therefore, disciple ye all the nations, immersing them into the name of the Father, and of the Son, and of the Holy Spirit: teaching them to observe all things whatsoever I have commanded you: and, lo, I am with you alway, unto the end of the age.* The version of the commission as given by Mark (xvi. 15, 16), " Go ye into all the world, and preach the Gospel to every creature ; he that believeth and is baptised shall be saved," should always be laid alongside of that given Matthew. From this twofold version we can clearly understand what the apostles had to do in carrying out the will of Jesus, viz., to preach the Gospel of Christ, and immerse those who were willing to receive Him, into the ever sacred names of Father, Son, and Holy Spirit, and then to instruct them in all the commands of Christ Jesus ; while those to whom the Gospel came had to hear, obey, and be blest.

Is the commission of Christ to regulate both preaching and obedience all through the dispensation?

Christ has issued no other. There must therefore be conformity to His authority as made known and proclaimed by the apostles, or His promise of salvation cannot be claimed. The apostolic proclamation, which was endorsed by the Spirit, still remains in the world, and must be accepted by implicit obedience, or rejected in disobedience by all who hear it. Blessed are all they who learn His will, and in loving trust obey Him.

MARK.

CHAPTER I.

What is there peculiar to this " Gospel according to Mark"?

The difference between this record and those by Matthew, Luke, and John, could scarcely be overlooked ; and arises chiefly from the fact that in this Gospel Jesus is presented under an entirely new aspect. Mark is evidently setting forth Jesus as the *Servant* both of God and man, hence service has a large place in this record of His life. Then, in keeping with this specific object, many things are omitted here which we find in the other Gospels. Mark gives no account of the birth of Jesus, or of

His genealogy, or discourse on the mount. The parables of the kingdom, so fully given by Matthew, and the discussions between Christ and the Pharisees, so fully reported by John, are scarcely noticed in this Gospel. It is not as the king waiting for His kingdom that we see Jesus here, but as the girded Levite, the willing worker, the sympathising friend of all in distress. It will be both instructive and refreshing to note these peculiar features of this Gospel of Mark.

1. *Why does he call the mission of John, " The beginning of the Gospel of Jesus Christ " ?*

John was the forerunner of Christ, as the prophet had written, so that when he appeared as a herald in the wilderness, the Master was at hand. John was to Jesus as the twilight to the day that follows it. When he announced the kingdom at hand, it was the beginning of the good tidings.

4. *John preached " the baptism of repentance for the remission of sins." Were those who accepted the proclamation forgiven by God ?*

Most certainly. God's promise could not fail to all who accepted it on the terms proposed.

5. *" Confessing their sins." Is confession of sins a pre-requisite of baptism ?*

It was then, because as Jews they had failed under the law ; but now, under the apostolic proclamation, it is Jesus, the anointed Son of God, who must be confessed with the mouth, and believed in with the heart, a previous conviction of sin being always implied.

8. *" He shall baptise you with the Holy Spirit." Was this promised to all believers ?*

Facts will best explain this and many other statements. The promise was fulfilled only in the apostles, but in them for manifestation and help to all.

9. *Jesus was baptised of John in Jordan. Why was He baptised ?*

To do the will of His Father, to whom, by His baptism, He became subject in all things. In His immersion in the Jordan He buried all His own claims, and rose from that grave of waters only to yield to the righteous claims of God.

12. *Was the temptation a part of the will of God ?*

It was necessary that He who came to serve God perfectly must first conquer the adversary ; hence the Spirit leads Him at once into circumstances where the conflict should commence and the conquest be obtained.

The first Adam was tempted in the garden, but Jesus was tempted in the wilderness. Why did the circumstances differ so widely ?

It was sin that had made the difference. The transgression of the first Adam had turned the garden into a wilderness, and the Second Man came into this wilderness that He might change it into a garden. The thorns and briars grew everywhere, and Jesus accepted the scene with all its disadvantages, and gained the victory under most trying circumstances. Not only was Satan there, but the wild beasts, that, according to the prophecy in Ps. xci., He might tread under foot " the lion, and the adder, the young lion and the dragon," and thus leave the scene a conqueror. Mark alone records about the wild beasts, but the note is in harmony with prophecy. True, we get but a glimpse of this scene, but it is quite sufficient to show us how sin had changed everything.

Is there any lesson for us in this temptation of Jesus ?

There is one which it would be well for us to study, and learn from it the course we should pursue. Jesus sought to change nothing in

that sad scene, but, by the truth,
faith, and patience, He triumphed
over all. Satan, and wild beasts,
and a barren wilderness were before
Him, but armed with truth alone,
He enters, and leaves the scene a
conqueror. It is not a change of
scene that we should seek, but conquest in that into which we may be
led.

*Does the word " immediately " in-
dicate the action of the Spirit or of
Jesus ?*

It is connected with the Spirit,
who, as the accepted guide of Jesus,
urges Him at once into the field of
action. But the word is so often
used by Mark to express the action
of Christ that it deserves special
notice. The word *eutheos* is used by
Mark about forty times, variously
rendered "immediately," "straightway," etc. The word is in strict
keeping with the design of the Gospel,
and expresses so fully the spirit of
the true Servant. When work had
to be done, or trials endured, or
sufferings relieved, then this word
eutheos, "immediately," is used to
show the promptitude of response.
No time is wasted through delay ;
no opportunity is lost through indifference—He is on the spot at once,
attending to what is for the good of
man, and the glory of God. How
impressive this example for all the
servants of God, and how sharply
does His life and spirit reprove our
cold delays.

14. *Was the imprisonment of John
a signal for Jesus to begin His service ?*

He had already commenced His
labours ; but Mark does not note
His previous work. It is the field,
and the workers, as they appear in
succession, that are presented to our
view. John is the first, and then he
is put in prison, and at once Jesus
comes forward and takes up the
work. No interval is allowed, and no

time is lost. This is in perfect keeping with the testimony of Mark.

15. *" The time is fulfilled, and the
kingdom of God is at hand." What
does this denote ?*

It is, *lit., the season has been fulfilled, i.e.,* the old dispensation is
about to close ; and there is only one
message for Israel now, viz., "The
kingdom of God is at hand : Repent
ye, and believe the Gospel."

*Why does Jesus put repentance be-
fore faith, when no person can repent
without first believing ?*

Faith is belief of testimony, while
repentance, or a change of mind, is a
result of belief. Repentance, therefore, can never precede that which
produces it. Nor does it in the case
before us. Jesus called upon the
Jews to repent, and believe the Gospel ; but their previous relation to
prophetic testimony must not be
overlooked by us, nor the testimony
of John that so many of them had
rejected, and in their blindness were
clinging to tradition as their only
hope and plea. Having therefore
prophecy, which so plainly announced
the coming kingdom of God, *i.e.,* an
entire change of administration, and
the testimony of both John and Jesus
that it was near, it was quite appropriate for Him to say, " Repent ye,
and believe the glad tidings."

16. *Is the calling of the disciples
connected with the service of Jesus ?*

Yes. Not only is He ready to
labour Himself, but also to take up
other willing hearts and hands, to
help in the same service. So here
we have Him meeting with four
willing workers, and they are asked
to follow Him, which implies no less
than service with Him. We see
here the beginning of that joint participation in the great work of redemption, afterward so clearly expressed in His prayer, " I in them,
and Thou in Me." And, though
now on the throne, He is still direct-

ing the service He so earnestly commenced below.

29–31. *Mark records the cure of Simon's wife's mother. Does not this rather show power than service?*

Yes, if we overlook that part of it, which is so characteristic of this Gospel, He "took her by the hand, and lifted her up." Now contrast this with Matthew (iii. 15), "He touched her hand, and the fever left her," and with Luke (iv. 39), "He stood over her, and rebuked the fever," and the difference is striking. In Matthew and Luke's account of the cure we see the king healing with a word and a touch, but in Mark we see Him as the Servant, putting forth His hand, helping the sick one to rise from her bed; and thus showing to all fellow-workers that, in order to be efficient, they must use the hand as well as the tongue, and lift up as well as direct. Jesus needs such workers; may we all be ready to learn of Him.

40. *Is there anything in the cure of this leper, that will further show the character of His service?*

There is compassion mixed with service. "And Jesus, moved with compassion, put forth His hand." A compassionate heart is joined with a willing hand: a still further lesson to all His disciples. We must serve in this world, but let our service be full of sympathy.

CHAPTER II.

1. *What house was this in which Jesus apparently was hid?*

Most likely it was Peter's, as it was in his house that Jesus cured his wife's mother, and afterwards received her domestic ministrations. Peter had removed to Capernaum, where he and Andrew held joint-possession of a house (i. 29), and in it He would most likely abide, when in that city.

Is the aspect of Jesus as the Ser-

vant *of all fully sustained in this chapter?*

What strikes one so much here is, not merely that He is the willing Servant, but the amount of work done by Him. Not only is He ready to respond to every call, to teach on every occasion, to cure every applicant, but passes from one case to another with a rapidity which surprises all who know that the labourer needs rest. Of this He seldom avails Himself, for so long as there is work to be done, the heavenly toiler toils on, caring only for others who may need His help. First we have Him teaching the anxious, and opening up to them the truth of the kingdom (verse 2); then forgiving and healing a palsied man, and reasoning with the scribes who charge Him with blasphemy (verses 3–12); then we have Him teaching the multitude by the sea side (verse 13); and again, calling a disciple and becoming a guest at his house, where He has to defend His associations with publicans and sinners, before captious Pharisees (verses 14–16). In this way all are relieved, all are healed and instructed, and if any are left unblessed by Him, it is because of their pride or unbelief.

CHAPTER III.

1–4. *It was in the presence of Pharisees that watched Him, and of a poor cripple that needed His help, that Jesus put the question, "Is it lawful to do good on the Sabbath day?" Why did He add, "Or to do evil"?*

To show them that, according to their own tradition, to refuse to do good, when the opportunity occurred, was to do evil—to refuse to save life, when able to do so, was to kill. They had thus supplied Him with a traditional warrant to heal the withered hand, and frustrated their purpose to raise an accusation against Him. No wonder that He was grieved at the hardness of their heart; and while they were silenced by His question, He healed the man in the presence of them all. This question of Jesus, however, apart from its bearing on those who watched Him that they might accuse Him, presents a very solemn aspect of responsibility, which all would do well to ponder, viz., that to refuse or neglect to do good when we might do so, is really to do evil before Him who judges according to opportunity.

Why should the Pharisees object to Christ healing on the Sabbath, when the Rabbis allowed healing in cases of life and death ?

The "withered hand" was a standing infirmity that might be attended to on some other day, so that to heal it on the sabbath violated traditional law.

6. *Why did the Pharisees take counsel with Herodians?*

Possibly in order to consult whether they might not make the healing of the man a punishable offence, as the Jews had legal protection in all their services. In healing the man with a withered hand Jesus had sinned against traditional law; and it became a question whether or not they might take action against Him. The Herodians were not friendly to Pilate, whose authority protected the Jews in their worship and religious laws; but they were easily persuaded to make common cause with the Pharisees against Jesus, whom both hated.

7. *How did He escape their united plot?*

He quietly withdrew into another place, and those who were interested in His work and teaching followed Him, and were instructed and healed.

14. *"And Jesus ordained twelve"* (apostles). *Why only twelve?*

There is no reason given for this special number, and we judge it must be a fulfilment of some preceding type of the old economy. There were twelve tribes in the one nation, and here we have an apostle for each tribe, that no part of the nation might seem to be overlooked. Then there were twelve loaves on the table of shewbread, typical of a twelvefold administration which is fulfilled in these twelve proclaimers of one message. The new dispensation was certainly mapped out in the old, for the lines are too plain and numerous to be mistaken, and this suggests a reason for much that Jesus did. He was ever fulfilling the Scriptures, both its types and precepts, and thus did He honour God by whose directions all was given.

16-19. *Is there anything suggestive in the order of the names of the twelve ?*

Matthew, Mark, and Luke record the names of the apostles, but each in different order, except that all give Peter the first place on the list, and Judas Iscariot the last. Thus all acknowledge the high position assigned to Peter, and modestly hint the position in which Judas placed himself.

Were all the twelve Jews ?

We presume they were all Galilean Jews, except "*Judas Iscariot.*" Scholars now read *Ish kerioth, i.e.,* "a man of Kerioth," a city of Judah, instead of "Iscariot." If this be correct then Judas was of Judea, and was thus closely connected with the ruling powers of the nation, which may have had some influence over him in furthering their wishes when desirous to arrest Jesus.

20. *The multitude being so great, they could not so much as eat bread. Why does Mark record this seemingly trifling matter ?*

Mark alone records this fact, and this little event is in perfect keeping with his object. It is of Jesus as a

Servant that He is writing, and here we see the servant allowing the pressure of work to set aside His own rightful claims. It is the work, and not His food, that He is concerned about. Well might God thus speak of Him, " Behold my Servant whom I uphold, mine Elect in whom my soul delighteth."

CHAPTER IV.

1–20. *This chapter opens with the parable of the sower. What has this parable to do with Mark's special object in writing this Gospel ?*

You will notice in it a striking contrast between the multitude who press upon Him to hear the word, and the very little fruit that follows. The Servant is obliged to enter into a boat to give all an opportunity of hearing, and this parable shows us how little fruit rewarded the Sower's toil.

The parable reveals both the hindrances and the success. Is this the special object of it ?

It simply describes both, and is so far of great importance. The results of hearing the Gospel are often accounted for in a different way from that described by Jesus, and it is well to learn the causes of success or non-success from Him who understood it thoroughly.

Do you mean, as to there being fruit or no fruit ?

Yes. It is possible to blame God when there is no fruit, when the cause is really with man. There is divine provision in the seed sown, but there is responsibility in receiving or rejecting it, and this is a very important aspect of the matter. Man is too ready to blame God, when the blame lies at his own door. In this parable we may learn what God does in providing and sowing the seed, and we may also learn what is man's relation to it. In the first in-

stance, Satan comes and takes away the word sown ; but it is from careless and unprepared hearts. Then, in the second instance, the stony ground hinders the seed from taking deep root ; but this is neither more nor less than unsubdued nature opposed to truth. Then, in the third instance, we see that choking weeds are there, not from any foreordination of God, but from the love of riches, worldly anxiety, and the lust of other things. These certainly hinder the ripening of the fruit ; but man, not God, is the cause. And in the last instance, where there is fruit, we see how man co-operated with God. Having heard the word, he received it, and brought forth fruit unto life eternal.

21, 22. *Has this lighted candle any connection with the parable of the sower ?*

It is the same truth but another figure. The sower does not sow his seed to lose it, but to obtain a harvest ; and the candle is not lighted to be hid, but to shine. This parable was intended to meet a large class of persons who thought that the religion of Jesus was mere devotion ; hence the need of explaining matters. Truth was not for ornament, but practice—not merely to set the head right, but the heart and life. So He adds, " He that hath ears to hear, let him hear."

24. *Why did Jesus warn them to take heed in hearing ?*

Because both the matter and the manner of hearing was of vital importance. To hear truth, instead of tradition ; and to hear, *i.e.*, obey Christ, instead of misleading Pharisees, involved results that differed very widely. Well might Jesus say, " Take heed what ye hear."

26–29. *What did Jesus intend to teach by this parable of the kingdom ?*

It is intended to illustrate His previous statement, " For he that

E

hath, to him shall be given." In the case of the man who sowed seed in the ground, Jesus points to certain helpful influences which were silently at work, both in the blade and the ripening corn. "So," He adds, "is the kingdom of God." It is as if He had said, those who receive the truth in an obedient spirit, will receive help and confirmation, unobserved it may be by others, until the fruit is ripe for the sickle. There is a fine enigmatical lesson in this simile of the seed "cast into the ground" for all who will ponder it. Where the truth is received in love, the helping influences of Heaven will push it forward to a glorious issue.

CHAPTER V.

1. "*Into the country of the Gadarenes.*" *In Matthew viii.* 28, *we read Gergesenes. Why have we this difference?*

We may just state, from corrected readings of these places, that in Matthew we should read "Gadarenes," while in Mark and Luke we should read "Gergesenes."

But why have we two places named, when there is only one event?

There were two places, "Gadara" and "Gergesa," which evidently gave names to the district or country in which this event occurred. Matthew gives the one, and Mark and Luke the other.

6–8. *Mark tells us that this demoniac* "*worshipped Jesus,*" *and also cried out,* "*what have I to do with Thee? . . . torment me not,*" *etc. Were these things done and said by the man, or by the demons?*

By both. The man worshipped, the demons spoke through the man. He adored, they feared, while Jesus dealt with both according to His sympathy, wisdom, and power.

12. *Did not the man plead for the demons?*

It was rather the demons pleading for themselves through the man, and the request to enter the swine is clearly their own.

Was it through fear of torment?

This is clearly the reason on their part; but it also contains a solemn intimation, that in the abyss from which they had been loosed for a season, there is torment which they sorely dread.

18–20. "*He prayed Him that he might be with Him.*" *What was his chief reason for this desire?*

The poor man had been delivered by Jesus, and we cannot wonder at his desire to remain with his Saviour and friend. He might even fear, if left by himself, the demoniac possession might again take place.

Did the command of Jesus to go home and tell his friends what He had done for him, become an assurance of safety?

If he was to be a witness to them of the power and sympathy of Jesus, he must be able to show it in his person; and as he was sent for the purpose of witnessing to the power of Jesus, he at once accepted this guarantee of safety. The man evidently understood that as long as engaged in this mission there could be no repossession by demons, so Mark adds, "he departed, and began to publish in Decapolis how great things Jesus had done for him: and all did marvel."

What is meant by Decapolis?

It literally means ten cities, and was thus named by the Romans upon their conquest of Syria. Over this district of cities this grateful man travelled, a witness to all of the gracious power of Jesus.

CHAPTER VI.

1–6. *Why does Mark give such a brief account of the visit of Jesus to Nazareth?*

His brevity of detail is no doubt in keeping with his object; and while many things are omitted which Luke records, we are richly compensated by a record of other important matters which are not even named by the other evangelists. We just note one here. After Jesus marvelled at their unbelief, Mark adds, "And He went round about the villages, teaching." Foiled in His attempts to instruct and bless the people of Nazareth, He enters into other villages and places, that they might hear the gracious words that proceeded from His lips. What a lesson does this`furnish to all workers in the cause of Christ. Our work may fail in effecting good in some places, and with some people, but let us not cease our efforts on this account. There is another village, let us go there. There is another person, let us speak again of the truth that will bless all that receive it.

7–12. Is not this account of the sending forth of the twelve very brief?

Yes, when compared with the record of Matthew. But then Mark has an eye to service, and in keeping with this object, he alone notes the sending them forth by two and two; which shows how wisely and efficiently He arranged the labourers that were given to help Him. He did not send them out altogether, as time would have been lost, nor singly, though they might have been in twelve villages on the same day; but by two and two, so that there might be a full testimony to the people, and companionship and help to each other.

What was the " scrip" they were not to take ?

The scrip was a wallet or small bag which the traveller suspended from his shoulders, in which food, etc., could be deposited. The disciples thus sent out were to start without bread, and not to have a scrip in which any might afterward be put. Thus were they called to depend on God, not only from day to day, but from meal to meal, and thus they proved His guardian care.

13. Mark alone tells of the anointing with oil. Why did Jesus appoint it in connection with healing ?

In order to test the faith both of the healer and the sick. The disciples had to show their own faith in Jesus by anointing the sick, the sick by allowing it to be done, and in the cure which always followed, Jesus was thereby honoured.

14. Among the varied reports as to who Jesus was, why did Herod decide that He was John risen from the dead ?

Nothing but a desire that it might be so. It would have been a relief to Herod had John come to life again. He had been ensnared in putting him to death, and, as John's murderer, the act must have haunted his spirit. If Herod felt any relief by this thought, it was a vain relief, for he remained a murderer still.

29. Were those who buried his body the disciples of John ?

We assume that they were. During his imprisonment, they would be intensely anxious about their teacher, and the burial of his headless body would be their last expression of regard.

30. The apostles gathered themselves together and told Jesus all things. Was this on their return from their missionary tour ?

Yes. They had been sent out by Him, two and two, and by His direction they again meet, and give Him a report of their labours. There were two departments of their labours— teaching and healing; and they tell Jesus both what they had done, and what they had taught.

31. Why did Jesus ask them to rest awhile ?

Because, though but seldom resting Himself, He well knew how much these earnest workers required rest, and to obtain this necessary leisure they enter into a boat, and sail higher up the lake. No sooner, however, do they put to shore, than the crowds again assemble, and Jesus, being full of compassion, taught and fed the anxious but unstable multitude.

CHAPTER VII.

1. *Where did this meeting between Christ and the Pharisees take place ?*

We presume that it was in Capernaum, as in the previous chapter Mark says, that Jesus and His disciples came into the land of Gennesaret, in which district Capernaum is situated. These Pharisees and scribes had come from Jerusalem, and were possibly a select controversial party, who often followed Jesus on purpose to dispute with Him. Their object was to confound the new Teacher, but they were as often confounded themselves.

2–4. *Mark here explains the meaning of " defiled," and also about different washings. Why does he give these explanations ?*

His explanation of these matters at once assures us that he is writing to Gentiles who were unacquainted with these Jewish customs, and thus proves helpful to us all. *" For the Pharisees, and all the Jews, except they wash their hands oft, or with care, eat not." " And when they come from the market, except they wash, they eat not." Why does Mark repeat his explanation about washing, since the former washing must cover the latter ?*

It is our translators that have failed to render correctly what they did when they came from the market. Mark states that they never eat, except they wash their hands carefully ; but when they come from the market, they do not eat, except they immerse themselves, because of contact with those they held to be unclean. For this reason an immersion of the whole body was deemed necessary.

6–8. *Though the washing and immersion were traditional, yet both were useful to the body. Why did Jesus accuse them of hypocrisy ?*

Because they made the external washings a cover for internal wickedness. They washed their hands, and immersed their bodies with traditional care, but their spirit and practice were evil. The application to them of " hypocrites " was therefore just.

How could Isaiah prophesy of them ?

The prophet sketched characters, and to whomsoever they applied, of them it was written, whether good or evil. The Word is like a glass, into which, if a man look, he will see a face, and may know whether it belongs to him or not. Now Isaiah sketched the portrait of a hypocrite, and Jesus said, There is your face. They would not own it, but Jesus wrote their name under it.

May this not suggest a practical method of still using the Scriptures ?

Most certainly. This is what God wishes us to do. The Holy Spirit has sketched every variety of character in His book. The saint and the sinner, the pure and the impure, the hypocrite and the true, have all their portraits drawn to life ; and if we search carefully and honestly, we may find our own. In fact, the Bible is like a wardrobe full of garments, where each may find the dress that exactly fits him. To take the robe that does not belong to us is a daring assumption, and would subject us to a challenge. For an unbeliever to take what is the right of a believer, a proud person to assume the garb of humility, and an evil heart to profess purity, can only be a momentary gain, because the King will come in to see the guests, and all hearts are naked and opened before Him.

9. *It was a bold charge against these Pharisees to say that they had rejected the commandment of God by their tradition. Was this true?*

They had not professedly rejected God, but they had done so practically. To put a man's law in the place of God's, and to follow tradition instead of truth, is really to reject Him. It was so then,—it is so still. In many ways this is done now, while the doers of it are as undiscerning as were the Pharisees. The charge which Jesus made against them is fully sustained. The "corban," or gift of property to the temple, was allowed to make null all other claims upon it. Even the parents of the giver had no claim upon the honour or support of the donor, and thus, by a human law, God's law was set aside.

14, 15. *Is this instruction about defilement, connected with the "eating bread with unwashen hands"?*

It was an effort to instruct the people in what really defiles the man. The Pharisees held that to eat bread, without first washing the hands, defiled the eaters; but Jesus taught them that it was not what was eaten that defiled, but that which came from within.

17-23. *Was it not dulness of apprehension, when the disciples failed to understand this little parable?*

Possibly it might be; but one feels glad they had to ask Him again concerning it. The reply of Jesus is most valuable, and should be deeply pondered by all. Jesus plainly teaches that the heart and the act are inseparable, and that evil thoughts and acts defile the doer. According to Jesus, there cannot be an action, mental or physical, apart from the mind that conceives it, and for every action the conceiver is responsible.

24. *Why did Jesus refuse the request of this Syrophenician woman?*

He did not absolutely refuse her, but said that the children must first be attended to, and that it was not meet to take the children's bread and cast it to dogs. The term "dogs" may appear degrading, but the woman took the place assigned her by Jesus, and asked for the crumbs that fell from the children's table. Her reply was the answer of submissive faith, and received a gracious return from Jesus.

CHAPTER VIII.

1-9. *The multitude had been three days with Jesus; had they been without food all that time?*

Possibly not; but at the end of three days their supply was exhausted, and He must either help them or they must suffer.

Did Jesus feel responsible for their need?

In a great measure. His teaching and miracles had induced them to remain longer than their own resources could have warranted them to do, and now that He must withdraw, He must either leave them hungry and faint, or supply their need miraculously. He decided to supply them, and this miracle is the result—a fitting close to His heavenly teaching.

11-13. *Was the "sign from heaven," which the Pharisees demanded, something greater than the signs already shown to them?*

What they demanded was something like that which had been shown to their fathers. The manna from heaven by Moses, the thunder by Samuel, and the consuming fire by Elijah, were facts in their history; and they asked for a repetition of these from the new Rabbi. But as their demand was the fruit of unbelief, He could not answer their requests. If healing the sick, and feeding thousands with a few loaves and fishes, were not sufficient to convince them that He was the Son of God, He must refuse to answer their unjust claim. That deep sigh that rose from His spirit showed how deeply He felt this evidence of their misguided hearts.

14, 15. *What was this leaven of the Pharisees, and of Herod ?*

A spirit of hypocrisy—an insincere profession.

Why did He warn His disciples against it ?

Because they were in as much danger as others, and hypocrisy in one thing leads to hypocrisy in another.

16. *What did their mistake respecting this leaven indicate ?*

A lack of discernment, or what is worse, a want of faith. They failed to discern that He, who had fed thousands in their need, could surely supply them. "How is it that ye do not understand?" was a most fitting reproof.

22–26. *When the eyes of the blind man were touched by Jesus, he saw men as trees walking. What does this mean ?*

Defective vision. He could see a little, but could not discern men from trees, except by their motion. But when Jesus touched his eyes again he saw every man clearly.

27–30. *How could the confession of Jesus as the Son of God be so important, when He charged His disciples to tell no man of Him ?*

This restraint was only for a while; but when He was risen from the dead they had to testify and prove Him to be the Son of God.

31–33. *Why were the disciples so unwilling to receive the testimony of Jesus concerning His sufferings and death ?*

Because they reasoned from their own conclusions, instead of believing His word.

Was not this " Get thee behind Me, Satan," a rather severe reproof ?

It would be better to read, *Get thee behind Me, adversary,* which on this occasion Peter had become. The testimony of Jesus was opposed by him, and this reproof was justly deserved.

34. *Is this teaching about taking up the cross based upon the revelation of Jesus concerning His own sufferings and death ?*

He wished them to understand that not only must He suffer, but all that would follow Him, must also suffer ere they triumph with Him.

CHAPTER IX.

1. *What did Jesus mean by the kingdom of God coming with power ?*

It had come in testimony and blessing to those who received it as little children ; but it did also come in power and judgment to those Jews who rejected it. Such an event they did not think possible to them, but their sad experience proved the truth of this prophecy. Some of those who were then with Him lived to see its fulfilment—the sign of the Son of man in heaven.

1–8. *What was the purpose of the transfiguration of Christ ?*

To show His elected witnesses what their despised Master would be when His sufferings and death were past. They had seen, and would still further see, His shame ; but they also saw Him glorified ; and though they made no use of the fact while He was on earth, yet after His ascension it was of immense value. The glory to which He ascended was His promise to them, and so became their hope. They knew He could be glorified, for they had seen Him changed ; and they knew He was glorified, for they saw Him ascend.

9, 10. *Why did Jesus restrain their testimony till after His resurrection ?*

They neither believed nor understood about His resurrection, and therefore were not prepared to give testimony concerning the glory that should follow. Besides, there was order even in testimony, and they were therefore forbidden to tell what they had seen till He was risen from the dead.

11. *Malachi wrote that Elijah should come before the great and dreadful day of the Lord. Were the scribes wrong in expecting Him ?*

The prophet really gives the name of this noble defender of the claims of God, but the fulfilment was afterward shown to be its true exposition, and this was declared by Gabriel to Zacharias before the birth of his son. This is not the only instance in which the name of one person has been used for another who should fill a similar position. The name of David was given by Ezekiel as the prince and king of God's nation, who should rule over them for ever (xxxvii. 24, 25), and yet it was shown to be Jesus who should do this, as declared by Gabriel to Mary. We have therefore to be guided in our understanding of these things by revealed facts, and the fitness of things, and if we fail to do this we shall become the dupes of perverted imagination.

14–29. *Was it not humbling to Christ to see His disciples so signally fail to cast the demon from this child ?*

He must have felt it keenly, as there was no lack of power to do this, but only a want of preparation in them as stewards of that power, and this they afterwards learned. " This kind can come forth by nothing, but by prayer and fasting," said Jesus, and this is of immense importance to all who wish to labour effectually for

Christ. We see, from this instance, that He would not hide the personal failure, even of His own disciples, but allowed them to be put to shame before the people. We may also learn that success in His cause is not unconditional, and those who labour for Him must do so in conformity with His will.

33–37. *What did the dispute of the disciples by the way indicate ?*

Very marked ignorance of the Saviour's teaching, and of the kingdom of God. They disputed " who should be the greatest," presuming that Christ should fill a place similar to the kings of the earth. The child set in the midst of them was to rebuke their aspirations, and instruct their hearts. By it Jesus said, If you want to be high in God's kingdom, you must be humble. Under that reign everything is contrary to the desire of the flesh.

38. *Was it jealousy that led the disciples to forbid the man who was casting out demons ?*

It was jealousy, or ignorance, or both, and the Saviour's instruction respecting it is most valuable to all disciples. The sphere of service which a brother or sister may choose may easily be undervalued by us ; but when Christ is honoured, we should rather encourage than forbid.

42. *Is the child of verse 36 the same as " one of these little ones " named here ?*

No. The former is a child in age, the latter in disposition, i.e., a believer. To cause such a one to stumble would incur the displeasure of God. It is a fearful crime to cause a disciple to stumble.

43. *Is this undying worm and unquenched fire literal, or symbolic of judgment ? Is it fulfilled in time, or does it stand over for eternity ?*

We are inclined to think it is a symbol of the nation that rejected Christ, and is being fulfilled in their present dispersion and reproach. Their rejection by God is an ever gnawing worm, and His continued displeasure an unquenched flame ; and to have been saved from such a judgment no sacrifice could have been too great.

48. *Every one shall be salted with fire. What does this mean?*

The perpetuity of the punishment inflicted. Salt is a symbol of truth, which preserves, and as they are salted with fire—*i.e.*, judgment—so, as a people, the Jews are continued in the wrath inflicted upon them. This applies only to time, and from which any who accept of Christ escape ; but this judgment of God continues on all who continue to reject His unspeakable gift. This punishment was inflicted in time, and is distinct from that which must follow the judgment of the great day.

CHAPTER X.

2–9. *" Is it lawful for a man to put away his wife ?" Why did they put this strange question to Jesus ?*

It was a tempting question, and was intended to lead Him either to approve their practice or deny the authority of Moses. He did not, however, approve their practice, but asked what Moses commanded, and at once they adduce the law concerning divorce.

It must be presumed that Jesus had condemned the frequent practice of divorce, but how could it be wrong when Moses commanded it ?

The answer of Jesus discloses a sad fact, viz., that Moses had to frame a precept to meet their badness of heart. It was not the only instance in which he had to do this ; but it came from their instability, and led to evil. God made the two one flesh, said Jesus, and what He joined, let not man put asunder. It is as if Jesus had said, This precept of di-

vorce does not show that you are right in following it. It is a liberty which, if you were what you ought to be, you would not avail yourselves of. It is an open door through which, if you feared God, you would never pass.

10–12. *What made the disciples so anxious for further explanation ?*

Divorce among the Jews was so common in the days of Christ, and as apparently sanctioned by Moses, they had not perceived the evil, and were surprised that Jesus should go back to the first institution of marriage, and prove from it that divorce and remarriage was a sin against God's law.

13. *Jesus said, " Suffer the little children to come unto Me." Does this form a precedent for sprinkling or immersing them ?*

By no means. The two things have no connection with each other. Jesus could take them in His arms, and supplicate blessing upon them, and every benevolent heart might follow His example ; but to sprinkle water either upon them or upon any others, is what He neither did or commanded to be done.

17–22. *This young man, who came to Jesus, appeared very anxious to obtain eternal life. Was not this command of Jesus to sell all that he had, and give to the poor, a very stringent one ?*

Yes, very indeed ; but Jesus could set nothing less before him. The stringency of the command arose out of circumstances. To keep the law, was far easier than to be identified with Jesus, as the latter would involve the loss of all by force. Jesus knew what would follow if the young man became His disciple, and at once proposed the test, but found him not ready to bear such a cross.

23. *If riches are such a barrier in the way of sincere discipleship, would*

*it not be better neither to seek nor pos-
sess them ?*

Riches are by many inherited from others, and should not be cast away, but used so as to secure God's approval. To be even intrusted with them calls for great watchfulness, but to seek them specially is to imperil our spiritual life.

32 – 34. *What occasioned the amazement and fear of the disciples ?*

I presume it was the revelations which Jesus made concerning His end ; and though placed first in the narrative, their amazement and fear is an effect of the disclosure of what awaited Him in Jerusalem.

35. *What was it that led these sons of Zebedee to seek the first seats in the kingdom ?*

Selfish ambition—a lusting of the flesh. Had they received the previous teaching of Jesus, they would not have made such a foolish request.

38. *Was His own pathway to the throne presented to reprove their ambition ?*

It was rather to instruct them that suffering precedes glory. They had accepted the truth that He was to have a throne and royal dignity, but overlooked the way of ascent. Had they known this, they would not have aspired to the position. "Ye know not what ye ask," was a most cutting reproof. "Can ye drink of the cup that I drink of ? They said, we are able," but understood not what they said.

41. *Was the displeasure of the ten, against James and John, justifiable ?*

By no means. It was a temptation by which they were overcome, and so rendered evil for evil. The two were ambitious, the ten were envious, and all lacked the love that thinketh no evil. We all need to watch lest the sin of a brother lead us to sin also. If his angry word, or evil deed, provoke anger and evil in me, wherein do I excel ? "Be not overcome of evil, but overcome evil with good."

42–45. *Jesus here recommends serving, rather than ruling. Is this possible to all ?*

Yes, but not without the mind of Christ. The aspiration of the flesh is for power, rule, fame, and such things, and it is only by having the Spirit of Jesus that we can choose the lowly path of service. If we accept of Him as our guide, then we see Him giving His life a ransom for others. This is the spirit of true service, and to this He invites us,— "Take my yoke upon you, and learn of me."

46–52. *Why did blind Bartimeus call Jesus "Son of David," when the people called Him "Jesus of Nazareth" ?*

Because he believed Him to be the promised one, and by faith obtained a cure. Their faith went back only to Nazareth, while he believed that He was David's Son and Lord. He honoured Jesus by His faith, and was rewarded by receiving sight.

CHAPTER XI.

1. *Was this the Saviour's last journey to Jerusalem ?*

Yes, and a number of incidents that occurred on the way are carefully noted. A great number of people had joined Him at Jericho, on their way to the great feast, and following, saw His power and heard His teaching. At Bethany the colt of an ass was obtained, and from that place Jesus rode into Jerusalem.

Was this ovation by the multitude specially arranged by Jesus ?

I think not. He was simply fulfilling the Scriptures, and these simple Galileans seized the opportunity of expressing their faith in Him as the promised king. The garments and branches spread in the way, with hosannas ringing in the air, as He passed over the Mount of Olives, was quite a demonstration, but was unsought by Him. He knew that in a few days their hopes would perish, and their carnal expectations die out. So, after He got into the city, He dismounted, and went to the temple, and the crowd gradually dispersed. In the evening He retraced His steps to Bethany, possibly to the quiet home of Martha and Mary, who no doubt waited to gather fresh instruction from His lips.

12–14. *Jesus was disappointed in the fig-tree; but if its time of fig-bearing had not arrived, was it right in Him to curse it?*

I do not think that Jesus would expect natural impossibilities. It is likely that it was neither to the season of the year, nor to its age, that Mark refers when he says, " The time of figs was not," but rather to its barrenness. Both its age and season, and His own hunger, properly demanded fruit, but there was none for Him. So He forbad its further growth, and the blighted tree stood a type of the fruitless nation that yielded no fruit.

15. *Was it right in Jesus to put those money changers and merchants out of the temple in such an unceremonious way?*

They had no right to make a market-place of His Father's house. It was zeal for God that led Him so to act.

18. *Why were the scribes and priests so wrathful against Him?*

Because He not only rebuked their sin in thus allowing the temple to be defiled, but took from them a revenue obtained from the traders.

20. *The withered tree surprised the disciples. What did Jesus intend them to learn from it?*

A lesson on the power of faith—a

power which, Jesus assured them, they should wield as well as He. Indeed, whatever they should require for their work should be forthcoming in response to their faith.

Should the power to remove a mountain, cast out a demon, or shake off the dust of their feet against city or nation, be limited to the apostles?

By no means. Let him that has the power or authority to do so, use it ; but let none assume the authority when they do not possess it.

25, 26. *Why is God's forgiveness of tresspasses based upon our forgiveness of others?*

Forgiveness is an act of grace, and He who shows it has a right to claim it from others.

27–33. *Had these priests, scribes, and elders any right to question Jesus about His authority?*

As teachers under the law they had a measure of responsibility ; but as they had ignored the evidence of His authority, which had previously been given, it was an insolent demand. One does not wonder that they were put to shame.

CHAPTER XII.

1–12. *Was this parable about the vineyard given for instruction?*

Yes ; but instruction about judgment, not about privilege. Their treatment of the messengers already sent was strong presumptive evidence how they would treat the Son. So Jesus sketched the whole picture, and in its revealings they read a prophecy of their own doom.

Why did Jesus quote the cxviii. Psalm about the rejected stone becoming the head of the corner?

In order to show them that if they persisted in their rejection of Him, this prophecy would be fulfilled in their own experience. They might reject Christ, the God-appointed stone, but God would exalt Him, to their annoyance and shame.

How is it that nearly all the controversies with Jesus took place at Jerusalem ?

Jerusalem was the stronghold of most of the religious and political sects of the nation, and the visits of Jesus to it, at the appointed feasts, always brought out the opposition of one or other of these parties. We have here three separate attacks on Jesus, which followed each other in quick succession; and, as we read His reply to the Pharisees and Herodians, then to the Sadducees, and then to a scribe, we can only marvel at the patience and wisdom with which all are answered.

41–44. "*And there came a certain poor widow, and she threw in two mites, which make a farthing.*" *Why did not Mark just say, she gave a farthing ?*

Had she given a mite, the smallest coin in circulation, or even a farthing, the value of two mites, it might not have been noticed by Jesus. The woman, a poor widow, had only two mites, which together make but a farthing, and it would seem only her duty to keep one for herself. But she gave both, and thus gave her all. Let us not miss the object for which it was noticed and written. It was not the mite that arrested the attention of Jesus, but because it was her all. Others gave "of their abundance," she "all her living."

CHAPTER XIII.

1, 2. "*Master, see what manner of stones.*" *Why did this disciple call the attention of Jesus to the stones of the temple ?*

Possibly something that He had previously spoken respecting its doom —a doom which this disciple thought should never come upon it. The reply of Jesus, however, was so positive that all hope of its preservation was taken away.

3, 4. *Was it the statement, that not a stone should be left upon a stone, that led the four disciples to ask for particulars of this sad event ?*

Being assured by Jesus that this overthrow would take place, they naturally enquire : — (1.) "When shall these things be ? " and (2.) "What shall be the sign when all these things shall be fulfilled ? "

Why did Jesus reveal so minutely to His disciples the doom of the temple and city ?

Because they had to teach those who would be directly involved in the overthrow; and as the whole brotherhood had to be prepared for it by them, they were fully instructed in all things needful for the escape of the saints.

5. *Why did He warn against deception by false Christs ?*

Because it was rumoured that Christ would come in person and deliver His people from this calamity ; and this led some evil men to assume to be the Christ, and thus deceived many. Josephus names several persons who assumed to be deliverers of the people, and led away numbers, who perished with them in their vain attempts to remove the Roman yoke.

Why did He urge them not to be troubled at the report of wars and earthquakes and famines ?

Because, while these things would be associated with the predicted judgment, they would occur previous to it, and without caution, would possibly excite alarm and unnecessary flight.

9. *Why did He refer to their own persecutions prior to this judgment ?*

That they might be prepared for the treatment they would have to meet with, and to assure them that, in their trials before kings and rulers, they would not be forsaken by Him.

10. *Was this publishing of the Gospel " among all nations " to the nations, or did it specially concern the Jews ?*

Jesus was speaking directly about the judgment coming on the temple, and on the people of the Jews ; we must therefore connect this publishing of the Gospel among the nations specially with them. Not only were the apostles to preach to the whole creation, but inside this circle they were to speak to the " Jew first," that the Gospel, if not accepted, should be a witness against him.

14. *What is meant by this "abomination of desolation" ?*

It is from the Septuagint version that we get this peculiar designation of the scourge that God employed in punishing that nation. In Luke's version this is said to be " Jerusalem compassed with armies "—a Gentile power treading on holy ground, or the sanctified portion of the priests, and one which made the nation desolate. When you see the approach of this army, said Jesus, then, not before, you must flee to the mountains.

15. *Why must they be so hasty in their flight ?*

Because only on their prompt action could they escape. A man on the housetop that descended to flee, but first went in to fit himself with garments and encounter friends, might find, in that short delay, that the gates had been closed, and escape impossible. We presume that after the first alarm there was a brief space of time in which all who believed the words of Jesus might escape from the city and country, but that their escape depended upon their prompt obedience to the direction of Jesus.

19. *" For in those days shall be affliction." In what would it consist ?*

Of all that was endured in that terrible siege, which was the judgment of that dispensation. It may be well to note that the same Greek word in Matt. xxiv. 21 is rendered " tribulation," and in Luke xxi. 22 this is spoken of as " the days of vengeance."

In Rev. vii. 14 we also read of the " great tribulation." Is this the same tribulation, or is it one yet to come ?

Some expositors affirm that it is a tribulation which is yet to come, and which they term "the great tribulation," *i.e.*, the greatest of all that have transpired. But this idea will not agree with the words of Jesus in this Gospel:—" For in these days " (of the destruction of the temple, etc.) "shall be affliction " —*lit.*, tribulation—"such as was not from the beginning of the creation. . . . neither shall be." When Jesus therefore affirms that this Jewish crisis was to be the greatest of all that had occurred, or that ever should occur, those who are still looking for a greater must have made a mistake.

24. *Is the darkened sun, and moon, and falling stars, the literal orbs of heaven ?*

They are symbolical orbs—*i.e.*, the nation of Israel so designated. After that great overthrow they ceased to be light-bearers for God and the world, and this high honour was given to the disciples of Jesus. " Ye are the light of the world," not the people of Israel.

26. *Jesus here states that when these things occurred they would then see Him. Was this to be a visible view of His person, or a manifestation of His power ?*

Facts must help us to obtain a correct answer. He did not personally appear in that judgment, but said they should see Him " coming in clouds," which we understand from the context, and use of "clouds" in symbol, to refer to hosts or armies, and through these the power and glory of Jesus would be seen. These were the executioners of the wrath of the Lamb against that people.

30. *Did the judgment upon Jeru-salem by Titus exhaust the predic-tions of this chapter?*

If language can settle this matter, this verse should decide it :—" This generation shall not pass, till all these things be done."

Some persons render it, this race *shall* not pass, etc. *Can this render-ing be sustained?*

Not from *genea*, which is correctly rendered by " generation," a word which only applies to the people then living, and never to those who should live afterward.

32. *Jesus here says that the time of this judgment was unknown to men, to angels, and even to the Son. Why could not Jesus know it?*

While on earth Jesus filled the place of a servant; and, as He taught, " The servant knoweth not what his Lord doeth," so, the " time of the end " in the sealed book was not opened, even by Himself.

33. *How could they watch for His coming?*

By watching for the signs which revealed it. Whether the army came at midnight or in the morning, they were to note the approach, and flee to the mountains.

CHAPTER XIV.

1. *Why did the priests and scribes fear to arrest Jesus on the feast day?*

Because they knew that many of his personal friends would be present, and might prevent their purpose ; hence their meeting to arrange how best to do it.

3–9. *Was this feast held in Beth-any a parting feast?*

To one person it was so, and pos-sibly only one ; and though Jesus had said much to His disciples about leaving them, they neither under-stood nor believed His words.

How do you know there was one?

By the declaration of Jesus, that the woman who anointed His head had done it for His burying. This act of anointing, which properly be-longed to the dead, was here per-formed upon Jesus while living, and thus she showed her faith in His testimony that He should be cruci-fied.

Why was the act of this woman to travel through the world alongside His Gospel?

Because, while among the twelve not one was found to believe that He would die on the cross, or by wicked hands, this woman did be-lieve it, and thus honoured His testi-mony. Woman was indeed the first to believe the lie of the serpent, and thus helped on man's ruin, but was also the first among His disciples to believe that the woman's seed would give His life to redeem from that ruin. This simple appreciating trust could not be overlooked by Jesus, hence His declaration, that the re-port of her faith should be told along with His Gospel throughout the world, for a memorial of her. Whatever may be the weakness of woman, she is certainly distinguished by her trust. Too often, alas ! she has trusted and been deceived, but in trusting the word of Jesus she was not deceived. Solomon, when writ-ing about faithfulness, said, " One man among a thousand have I found ; but a woman among all those have I not found." But the greater than Solomon sought also, and while among men He found not one that believed the testimony of His death, He did find a woman that honoured His word by her trust.

10. *Who was the first to suggest the betrayal of Jesus?*

Judas was the first, because he went unto the chief priests, and made the proposal. They could never have thought that a disciple would do such a deed; but he let them know that, for a price, he might be induced to do it. To them it was an unexpected and opportune proposal, and they were glad, and offered him money.

What was it that made Judas do such a deed?

The love of money led him into the snare, and but for such a desire he could never have conceived the thought of getting money in such a base manner.

12. *The passover was to be kept by families or households. Would you call Jesus and His disciples a household?*

The people were to join together according to their eating of the lamb, and Jesus and His disciples formed a company, He as their head being responsible for the necessary provision; hence the disciples are sent to make ready the passover.

Might He not have escaped death by neglecting the passover?

Yes, but that would have been disobedience to the will of God, and this had no place in His life. Hence when the time came He was there to keep it, although He knew it would lead to His own death. The path of duty was to Him the path of death, but it also proved the path of life.

13. *Jesus spoke of His betrayal in the presence of all His disciples. Why did He do this?*

He has not told us the reason, but His revelation of the purpose of Judas shows how He could read his heart. Jesus knew what he was prepared to do, yet took no precaution to hinder his purpose. It was a friend that was sitting at His table that was going to betray Him, and yet He upbraids him not.

18. *" It were good for that man if he had never been born." Was this intended to deter Judas?*

Whether intended or not, it should have done so. He had an opportunity of balancing the thirty pieces of silver against this fearful doom, which Jesus plainly utters in his hearing. Had he done this before instead of after the deed, it would have saved him from that suicidal death which followed his terrible remorse. Judas is a type of millions who weigh consequences after, instead of before, the act by which they are developed.

22–24. *" This is My body " and " This is My blood." What did He mean?*

Just what Paul meant when he said, "That rock was Christ," *i.e.*, it set forth Christ. The bread and the cup set forth His life and His blood, so freely given for them.

25. *" I will drink no more of the fruit of the vine, until that day," etc. What did He mean?*

That he would drink no more of the passover cup until its antitype was a realised fact. For although both Matthew and Mark place this utterance as spoken after the institution of the memorial feast, yet, according to Luke, whose account of it must be read to form a correct understanding of its application, it was spoken after the passover, to which He directly alludes—I will not drink it again, until I drink it in a new institution.

" Until that day that I drink it new in the kingdom of God." Did He literally do this?

Peter says that they did eat and drink with Him after He was raised from the dead, but possibly he did not refer to the memorial institution. It is more likely that Jesus refers to their united joy in the fulfilment of these types in the kingdom of God. The joy was both new and mutual.

26. *Why did they sing at the close of the feast?*

The passover feast was a memorial of deliverance, and praise was fitting for the occasion. Jewish writers say that Ps. cxv.–cxviii. were always sung at that feast, the last closing the festive scene. We are much inclined to think that one or all of these psalms were chanted by Jesus and His disciples on that memorable night. How adapted they were to His confiding heart! How full of praise, of trust, of hope, of triumph, are their brief yet soul-inspiring sentences! Often had they been chanted by the households of Israel, but to none were they more appropriate than to Him who that night led the joyous and prophetic as well as retrospective song. It is the blessed privilege of disciples of Jesus to sing them still, and feel their heart-cheering influence, as chanting them with Him who, though in the heavens, is the leader of their praise.

27. *Why was the smiting of the Shepherd a cause of stumbling to the sheep?*

Because they expected glory without suffering, and were offended—*i.e.*, stumbled—when they saw Him suffer and die.

29. *Was not Peter's declaration, "although all shall be offended, yet not I," an empty boast?*

It was a sincere one, I have no doubt; but was made in ignorance of the circumstances that followed. The power of circumstances cannot be known before they occur, and thousands have sinned and fallen, who no more thought of doing so than Peter did before that eventful hour when he denied Jesus with oaths and curses. It is given us to know that no temptation will happen to us but such as is common to man, but, if such as those which have happened to the people of God should come upon us, we have yet to prove what we should do. Great is our weakness, but great is His strength on whom we may rely. Let us not boast, but trust God in our trial.

32. *Why did Jesus go to Gethsemane?*

It was His "*proseucha*" or place for prayer when at Jerusalem, and He went as He was wont, to seek help in His time of need. He sought retirement with His Father, and found it in that solitary shade. His course is very suggestive, and should be a lesson to us all. His time was very limited, but the greatest part of that night was spent in (1.) helping others ; and (2.) in seeking help for Himself.

41. *Why did He say, "sleep on now, and take rest, it is enough," etc.?*

One hardly likes to think that there was a tinge of reproach in His words, and yet it seems very like it. He had asked them to watch with Him, but they went to sleep, and now it is as if He said, your watchfulness is no longer needed, for the hour is come. Others read it as a question, "Do ye sleep now and take rest? Rise up, let us go," etc.

44. *Judas betrayed Jesus with a kiss. Why with a kiss?*

It was the token agreed upon by Judas and the band ; but is at the same time deeply suggestive that there must have existed between Jesus and His disciples a very loving familiarity. That kiss was the profession of continued love ; but it was with him the kiss of deceit. Jesus did as He was ever wont, and met His absent disciple with a kiss ; but that disciple went prepared to make it the sign of betrayal. He knew that Jesus would be ready to receive it, and bid the band closely watch that no mistake might be made. The kiss was given, and the arrest took place.

53. *Jesus was taken to the palace*

of the high priest. Why take Him there ?

A council was held there, of which he was president or judge. Their object was to obtain a conviction against Jesus, and in the morning secure His condemnation by Pilate the Roman judge. This previous conviction was necessary; hence these preliminary efforts to secure it.

54. *Why did Peter follow Him "afar off" ?*

Intense anxiety to know the issue led him to follow the crowd, while fear of being implicated in the trial kept him at a distance. Through another disciple he got into the palace, and mingled with the servants to see what the end would be.

55. *Why did the council allow false witnesses to testify against Jesus?*

They professed to be true witnesses, but in the trial their witness failed through want of agreement, and so failed to convict Him.

Why did *Jesus hold His peace when falsely charged by these witnesses?*

Because He would not reply to falsehood, but when challenged, " Art thou the Christ, the Son of the blessed?" He at once replied, " I am."

62–64. *Why did they call this blasphemy ?*

Because they did not believe His witness, and counting Him to be a man only, they heard His witness as a blasphemous assumption, and judged Him worthy of death.

CHAPTER XV.

Why did they call together this second and larger meeting ?

It was in order to obtain the verdict of the whole council, who in the meantime had been summoned to attend, and by an official decision Jesus was bound and sent to Pilate as one worthy of death.

2. *Why did Pilate question Jesus?*

In order to know whether He pleaded guilty or not guilty. He had patiently heard the charges of the council, and then asked if they were true, and marvelled when Jesus made no reply. The life of Jesus was in that hour placed in his hands, and he no doubt felt his heavy responsibility, and therefore turned from the accusers to the accused, that he might decide between them justly.

5. *Why did Jesus make no reply to His accusers ?*

It was written of Him in the prophets " so opened He not His mouth," and this writing was His guide, even amid the clamour of false accusation, so that afterward an apostle could write of Him, " when He was reviled, He reviled not again," and presents Him as an example to those whose behaviour in Christ was falsely accused.

14, 15. *If Pilate saw no evil in Jesus, how could he justify himself in condemning Him ?*

He did what too many have done both before and since—blamed others for the deed which has stained his own life.

16–20. *Why had these Roman soldiers to attend to the crucifixion of Jesus ?*

The sentence was passed by the governor, and they were its executioners ; and without mercy or sympathy they begin their barbarous work—scourging, torturing, and then they nailed Him to the cross.

These soldiers could have no personal spite against Jesus. Why were they so cruel ?

I very much fear that the promptings and bribes of the Jewish multitude had much to do with their cruelty. It was an opportunity for winning favour, and they were not slow to use it. The more they degraded Jesus, the greater the approval of Pharisees and priests. Their plaudits urged on these time-serving soldiers, and most shameful things were done by them.

21. *Why did they compel Simon to bear His cross?*

Not sympathy with Jesus, for that was never shown during His trial; but rather to degrade another, whose humiliation would give intense pleasure to the foes of Christ. It was an unplotted humiliation of a well-known sympathiser with Christ: "him they compel to bear His cross."

27. *Why did they crucify the thieves with Jesus?*

They were then under sentence of death; but to execute them that day could only have been prompted by a desire to further degrade Jesus. To crucify Him with these men was to make Him appear as vile as they. So, according to Isaiah, His death was with the wicked.

30. "*Descend now from the cross, that we may see and believe.*" *Why refuse their request?*

They proposed it as a test, but alas for them, they, like many other infidels, demanded a self-proposed proof, while overlooking all others that He had given. To have answered their request, even though they had been convinced by it, would have deranged the whole plan of God. His surrender of Himself left their request ungranted, and from this we may learn that it is possible to tempt God by unreasonable claims, and come to false conclusions because He denies them. They asked Jesus to descend from the cross, and because He did not, they would not believe Him to be the Christ.

33. *Was the darkness caused by an eclipse of the sun?*

Astronomers say that a natural eclipse of the sun was not possible then, as there was a full moon at the passover. A veil must therefore have been thrown over it by the

F

hand of God, and thus the sun became a mourner for Him who created it.

CHAPTER XVI.

1. *Was anointing the body a matter of custom or affection?*

It was a custom, dictated by affection; but in the case of Jesus, the manner of His death prevented these women from doing it at the time. Their early visit to the sepulchre, to anoint His body, only showed their want of faith in His word.

Why did the women think more about the stone than the guard of the sepulchre?

The guard was a private precaution, and possibly they knew nothing about it. They knew the stone was there, but knew not how to get it away.

5. *Why was this young man stationed at the sepulchre?*

To relieve the anxieties of these first visitors, and tell them that Jesus was risen, and also to send them with the message to His sorrowing disciples.

9–20. *On what grounds are objections raised against the authenticity of this section?*

The principal reason is that the section is not found, either in the Sinaitic or Vatican MSS., and this omission presents a difficulty. Then scholars tell us that Jerome, who lived in the fourth century, affirms that it was wanting in most of the Greek copies of his day; and this testimony also adds to the difficulty.

Is there anything to be said in its favour?

Yes, a good deal. Scholars say that the section is found in the Alexandrian and the Cambridge MSS., which are said to be as old as those that omit it. It is also found in twelve uncial MSS., said to be as old as the former MSS., and in all the cursive MSS. (so called from the form of the letters), though the last occasionally note that they were not found in some existing MSS. Then, in addition to this evidence, the section is quoted by Irenæus and Tatian, who lived in the second century, and quote from it, as written by Mark. It is also quoted by Hypolytus and Dionysius of Alexandria in the third century ; and as these writers lived earlier than Jerome, his testimony is quite set aside by theirs. Then we are told that all the ancient versions from the Greek, as the Peshito Syriac, the old Italic, the Sahidic, and Coptic, all of which were written before the time of Jerome, contain this section. There is therefore so much evidence in its favour that no scholar has ventured to expunge it from the book.

How then has the difficulty been created ?

Scholars are now pretty well agreed that Mark wrote this closing section from verses 9–20 ; but before he did so, his Gospel got into the hands of copyists, who wrote as they found it. This will account for the two facts— (1.) that there were copies of Mark's Gospel without these closing verses ; and (2.) these verses being afterward written by him, they were known and affirmed to have been written by Mark. We therefore accept the portion with all confidence, and use it as inspired truth.

Does not this account of the resurrection seem very much like an appendix to the brief notice already given by Mark?

There is no doubt about it being an addition to the Gospel. Some circumstances unknown to us hindered the full detail which might have been given. We have therefore a recapitulation of things connected with the resurrection. Then we have the commission, the ascension of Jesus, and the going forth of the disciples with the glad message.

Does the commission, as given by Mark, supply any additional information ?

We only get new aspects of it, which help us to better understand His requirements and promises. We learn here that it is the will of Jesus that the whole creation should know that He died for their sins, was buried, and rose again from the dead. And that he who believes, and is immersed, shall be saved ; but he who believes not shall be condemned.

Is the order of these requirements— preaching, believing, and immersion, an irrevocable one ?

It is the order given by Jesus, and no person, or body of persons, have power to reverse His will. Those who do so are not only disobedient themselves, but encourage it in others, and thereby incur a fearful responsibility. Preaching the Gospel is the first part of the arrangement of Christ, and is in order to lead men to believe in Him ; immersion, which He has appointed for all His disciples, is to follow faith, and thus assurance of His promise is attained.

Is there no other way of obtaining assurance of this promise of the Lord Jesus than by submitting to immersion ?

There is no other way revealed by the apostles of Jesus, and to assume the possession and enjoyment of it by any other method is only to deceive ourselves. We may lay down other premises, and assume other methods of acceptance, but who can be sure that Jesus will accept of them ? We may assume that sincere faith, without immersion in water, is quite sufficient; but we should have to wait until we see Jesus before we can know whether or not our plan will stand. We ought to discern the difference between reasoning out of our own hearts to any conclusion we may happen to come to, and believing and acting upon the divine testimony, or we may become the dupes of our own folly. The commission of the Lord Jesus not only exhibits the grace of God in perfect adaptedness to man's need, but is a plain, authoritative declaration of the way by which the provision of that grace is to be reached. It has come from Christ, by the Spirit, through the apostles, and now stands unrevoked, until the Lord returns. To assume to have found in the New Testament any direction, or law, or arrangement differing from this, is only allowing ourselves to be imposed upon by a false conception. When we obey Christ, we have the assurance of His own testimony, and know it from His own revelation, and unless Christ is false, it must be true. Neither angels that surround His throne, nor demons from the abyss, nor men on earth, could Scripturally deny the claim of those who believe, and are immersed according to the directions of Jesus, to the promise, "shall be saved." Nor do we see how any person who neglects or alters the arrangements of Christ can Scripturally claim His promise. We know that men have, and may still form, plans of their own, and may presume, and reason, and expect, etc., that they will obtain the promise of Christ after their fashion; but to believe that they will secure what is desired is impossible, because the testimony is wanting, and when there is no testimony there can be no faith. These matters claim the attention of all men, but especially

of those who have altered the arrangements of Christ. Let Christ be honoured by our obedience, and we can have no difficulty, but if we disobey, there is no certainty of blessing.

17–20. *"And these signs shall follow them that believe,"* etc. *Does this promise apply to the apostles only, or to those who believed their message?*

To the apostles, and not to those who believed their message. In verse 14, we read that Jesus "appeared to the eleven as they sat at meat, and upbraided them with their unbelief and hardness of heart." Then follows the commission for the work of proclamation, and this promise of confirmation in their work. They should be able to expel demons; to speak with tongues; to be unaffected by the bite of serpents; and to lay hands on the sick for their recovery. Now, every one of these promises was verified in the apostles of Jesus, but not in those who believed their testimony. To those who believed their word, gifts were imparted by the laying on of the hands of the apostles; but this promise in Mark was for themselves. So we read, in conclusion, "After the Lord had spoken unto them, He was received up into heaven, and sat on the right hand of God. And they went forth and preached everywhere, the Lord working with them, and confirming the word with signs following."

LUKE.

CHAPTER I.

1–4. *For what purpose did Luke write this "Treatise"?*

To give to a person called Theophilus a true and orderly account of

the birth, life, teaching, death, and resurrection of the Lord Jesus.

Is it not strange that this Gospel, which was at first only a private document, should afterwards become a public testimony for Christ?

The epistles of Paul to Timothy, Titus, and Philemon, were also written to individuals; but, from their value to the cause of Christ, and truth in general, and having been written by an apostle of Christ, they have become the property of the saints in every age.

What is the special object of this Gospel?

To show to Theophilus that Christ came to save and bless the nations of the earth. In this Gospel we see Jesus as the antitype of Jacob, who, though married to Leah the first-born, was also serving for Rachel the younger, who in due time became his bride.

Why should this special feature of this Gospel be presented to Theophilus?

He was no doubt a Gentile, and probably Luke also, and as they had been brought to rest in Jesus as their Saviour, it pleased the Holy Spirit to show by Luke, how much the life and ministry of Jesus, though special to the Jews, was nevertheless in harmony with God's purpose to bless the nations. To Theophilus, and also many other Gentiles, this would be deeply instructive.

Why does Luke narrate the birth of John the Baptist and other attendant circumstances?

The birth of John has a close relation to his theme, and is of historical value in confirming the truth of prophecy. A forerunner of Jesus was to appear, and Luke states the facts of his appearing.

Zacharias, the father of John, is said to be " of the course of Abia." What does this mean?

King David divided the priesthood into twenty-four courses or divisions, each course bearing the name of one of the families descended from Eleazar or Ithamar, sons of Aaron; that of Abia or Abijah (1 Chron. xxiv. 10), being the eighth. As upon them devolved the duty of directing and arranging the temple service, they had to leave their homes in the suburbs of the cities of refuge, and sojourn in Jerusalem the allotted time of service. Zacharias, who dwelt in the hill country of Judea, was burning incense in the temple at Jerusalem, when Gabriel appeared to him and foretold the birth of a son.

10. *Zacharias was burning incense in the temple, while the people were praying without. Is there any connection between incense and prayer?*

Under the law, the burning of incense was a type of intercession or worship, and the pious of that age evidently so understood it. While he burned incense within, the people were praying without. That golden altar, from which the priest took fire to burn fragrant incense, was a beautiful type of Jesus, the medium of all acceptable worship.

13. *Zacharias had long prayed for a son ; why did he doubt when told by Gabriel that his prayer was heard?*

His faith rested upon the power of the flesh, and when that was changed his faith was gone. His faith had been deceptive, and he had not perceived it; and when it became manifest, he had to be humbled. Zacharias knew from the prophecies that some one must go before the Messiah, and he had long prayed that the favour of such a son might be given to him. He had prayed no doubt as long as nature held out any hope, but when nature forbade his hope he had ceased. When Gabriel said, " Thy prayer is heard ; and thy wife Elisabeth shall bear thee a son," he questioned the declaration on the ground of natural inability, and was struck dumb for his unbelief.

26. *In the sixth month the angel Gabriel was sent to Nazareth, to a virgin espoused to Joseph, etc. The sixth month from what?*

From the conception of Elisabeth, the wife of Zacharias; so that Jesus was six months younger than John.

A son was promised to Eve, who should bruise the head of the serpent. Was this Son of Mary the promised one?

Yes; Jesus is the woman's seed, not man's; and in Him believers are a new creation, and are predestinated unto a new and heavenly inheritance.

32, 33. *"He shall be great, . . . and He shall reign over the house of Jacob for ever." Has this reign commenced?*

According to Peter (Acts ii. 30), this promise made to David was fulfilled when God seated Jesus at His own right hand in the heavens. David expected that the rule of His Son and Lord would be a spiritual rule, *i.e.*, a rule which would have truth alone for its sceptre; or, as here explained, "He shall reign over the house of Jacob for ever." When Jacob prevailed with God, and obtained blessing, he became a type or head of the house over which Jesus should reign. The house of Jacob, therefore, over which Jesus was to reign, was composed of those who, like Jacob, prevail with God through Jesus. So Paul reasons with the Hebrews. "But Christ as a Son over His own house; whose house are we, if we hold fast the confidence and the rejoicing of the hope firm unto the end" (chap. iii. 6). It was as believers that they formed the house of Jacob, and thus the house of the exalted Son of God. To expect a carnal reign for Christ, or a reign over mere nationality, is to pervert the great object for which He ascended on high, and sent His Gospel through the world. The truth is His sceptre, and the rod of His strength.

Mary, as well as Zacharias, questioned the word of the angel. Why was she commended, and he condemned?

There was a wide difference in their questions. His arose from unbelief, hers from a want of knowledge. He asks, "*Whereby* shall I know this, *seeing I am an old man?*" thus doubting the power of God; while she asks, "*How* shall this be, *seeing I know not a man?*" She did not doubt, but inquired, and when informed, she nobly yields herself: "Be it unto me according to thy word," although this would involve her in much shame.

36. *Why did the angel tell her of the conception of Elisabeth, the barren one?*

Possibly to encourage and instruct her that this thing was of God.

As Mary and Elisabeth were cousins, the latter being a daughter of Aaron, Mary must also have been of the tribe of Levi. Is there any Scripture that speaks otherwise?

I know of none, nor is there any difficulty even though she was really of that tribe.

How could Jesus be of the seed of David if His mother was of the tribe of Levi?

She was married to Joseph, and thus her tribal relation to the priestly house of Aaron terminated; while Joseph, being of the line of David, and heir to his throne, Jesus, being his son by marriage with Mary, became David's seed and heir.

39. *When Mary visited Elisabeth, she was accosted by her as "the mother of my Lord." How did she know this?*

By the Holy Spirit she had just received.

For what are these two women most distinguished?

For their simple trust, and, what is always associated with trust, joy in the Lord. Their faith led to adoring gratitude, and this grand triumphant song from the lips of Mary is the expression of her faith, love, and humility, that is truly refreshing to read. The things which God had promised long before are taken hold of by her in the full assurance of faith.

CHAPTER II.

1–7. Why does Luke refer to the taxing by the order of Cæsar Augustus ?

To show an important link in the chain of causes which led to the birth of Jesus in Bethlehem. Augustus passed a decree in Rome, that all the world—*lit.*, the habitable—or the kingdoms over which his imperial power extended, should be enrolled, and the time fixed for Bethlehem, the place where Joseph and Mary had to be registered, proved to be the time of the birth of Jesus. The inn, already crowded by previously arrived guests, could afford no accommodation to them ; and, as a last resource, they had to occupy a shed or place usually occupied by cattle, hastily fitted up for the occasion ; and while waiting their turn for enrolment, the birth of Jesus took place. It was no plan on their part to be in Bethlehem at that time ; they were simply yielding to the mandate of Augustus, and Jesus being born while they were there, the prophecy concerning the place of His birth was fulfilled.

Historians say that Cyrenius was not governor of Syria till some twelve years after this registration by order of Augustus. How can this be reconciled with Luke's account ?

Two words will make his record agree with facts, and we presume these should be appended to it. " This taxing was made *under* Cyrenius, *afterward* governor of Syria." Luke would not contradict facts, and this reading is in harmony with them.

8–12. Why did Luke tell Theophilus about the angelic visitors to the shepherds ?

Because their message to these men, while interesting to every Christ-expecting Jew, contained a fragment of news in which he, as a Gentile, would find special pleasure. The " good tidings of great joy " to them, was also " to all people." Jesus might live among the Jews, and care specially for the lost sheep of the house of Israel for a season, but the glad " Fear not ! " was intended for a far wider circle than that Jewish flock, and in due time would be proclaimed among the nations of the earth.

21. Jesus was circumcised when eight days old. How was this needful for Him ?

By His birth He was made of a woman, and by His being circumcised He was made under the law, that He might redeem those that were under the law, even by being cut off for their sins.

22. The " days of her purification." How many were these ?

According to the law of Moses, three and thirty days were required after circumcision, before the mother could visit the sanctuary of God, so that before her purification was effected she was confined altogether forty-one days.

Why were these turtle doves appointed by God ?

They were not only appointed for purification, but were also substitutionary offerings, for by these being offered to God, the child obtained a right to live. Every Israelite was redeemed to God, and his life was purchased by the life of a victim. It might be a lamb or turtle doves according to ability, but it was only when that life was offered, that the child could be presented to the Lord.

25–35. Would not Joseph and

Mary be surprised at the words of Simeon?

They were scarcely prepared for such a manifestation of joy. Not only was it revealed to Simeon that he should see the Lord's Anointed, but the prophecies of His great mission were clearly unfolded by him. The angel had told Mary what her child was to be, while Simeon tells her what He is to do. His mission involved the destiny of nations, and even a sword would pierce through her own soul.

What does he mean by the sword piercing her soul?

He no doubt refers to her bitter anguish when she would see Him hanging on the cross, but this she could not then understand. She might often ponder its meaning, but the sight alone could reveal it.

Why was Simeon so full of joy?

Because the promise so long delayed was then fulfilled. During four thousand years the faithful had been looking for this child, and now Simeon gazes upon the long-expected one. True, it is but a babe that he holds in his arms, but it is enough, he sees God's salvation, and can leave all the rest with a covenant-keeping God.

Presuming that Theophilus was a Gentile, how would Simeon's testimony interest him personally?

Simeon had the gift of prophecy, and spoke of God's salvation as " prepared before the face of all people," *lit.*, peoples. " A light to enlighten the Gentiles," *lit.*, for revelation to the nations. Surely this must have been interesting to Theophilus.

36. Anna, a prophetess, is also named, who " lived with a husband seven years from her virginity." What does this mean?

That her husband died seven years after their marriage, and at his decease she took up her abode at the temple, remaining a devout worshipper till she was eighty-four years of age.

How could she dwell in the temple?

By the temple we understand some one of the chambers in its precincts, and during that long stage of widowhood, which some think was eighty-four years, she had waited to see the salvation of God. How strong was her faith, and how persevering her devotion to Him she waited so long to see! She knew, along with Simeon and others, that the time of the promised " Messiah the Prince " was near, and eagerly waited its fulfilment. Nor did she wait in vain, but was permitted to gaze upon Him she waited to behold, and with a glad heart spake of Him to all them that were looking for " redemption in Jerusalem."

41–52. Why did Jesus go up to Jerusalem with His parents at twelve years of age?

At twelve a male took upon himself the responsibility of keeping the law, and no doubt the parents of Jesus had to present Him before the appointed officials in order to obtain their formal acceptance of Him as a " Son of the law," as such were called by them. It was, we presume, this official meeting of Jesus and the rulers, that led to that recorded debate with the doctors where his sorrowing parents afterwards found Him. In their first formal examination of Him, they must have found Him a youth of rare knowledge of the law, and may have felt ashamed before Him. We judge that they drew Him into this debate about the time of His parents' departure, and on their return from their first halting-place, they ultimately found Him in the midst of the doctors, with whom for three days, at appointed hours, the discussion had been prolonged.

" How is it that ye sought Me?

wist ye not that I must be about My
Father's business?" Why make such
a reply?

The Revised Version reads, "How
is it that ye *sought* Me? wist ye not
that I must be in My Father's house?"
and in this corrected reading we may
see the full force of His reply.

"*And He went down with them.*"
Why yield to their request?

"Honour thy father and thy
mother," was a law of God, and at
once He yielded obedience to His
Father's will.

CHAPTER III.

1. *Why does Luke give dates and
names of kings and governors who
ruled at the time of Christ's ministry?*

His object was to supply historical evidence that would be useful to Theophilus whenever it might
be called for; and so names distinctly the year when John commenced his proclamation of the
baptism of repentance, and thus
heralded forth the coming of the
Messiah.

2. *Luke names Annas and Caiaphas as being high priests together.
How could there be two high priests
at the same time?*

There could properly be but one
high priest. Annas was the priest
of the nation, but had been deposed
from office by Valerius Gratus, a
former Roman procurator, and another arbitrarily put in his place;
indeed, Caiaphas was the fourth
high priest from the deposition of
Annas. Annas was legally the high
priest, and was so regarded by the
people, while Caiaphas held office by
Roman prerogative, so Luke names
them both, as they seem to have
acted conjointly.

3. "*And he came into all the country
about Jordan, preaching the baptism
of repentance for the remission of*

sins." *Is not this a strange way of
recording his mission?*

It is a simple statement of this
God-provided blessing, the remission
of sins, and how they could enjoy it.
John preached the kingdom at hand,
and immersed all who honestly received his testimony into remission
of sins; but none were immersed except those who showed the required
change of heart, and to all who did
so the promise of remission was fully
declared.

5. "*Every valley shall be filled,*"
etc. *Is not this symbolic description of the work to be done likely to
cause some misunderstanding of its
nature?*

To say that valleys should be filled,
and mountains and hills brought low,
etc., might lead some to think of physical transformations to be effected,
but no person who had learned from
the Scriptures the nature of man's
need, and God's provision to meet
that need, could ever make such a
mistake. The Jews, through their
carnal mind, mistook these and other
prophecies of the Messiah's work, and
were looking for a change of circumstances rather than a change of heart
and life; but neither the ministry of
John, nor that of Christ and His
apostles, furnished any support for
such a vain expectation. No doubt
the people of Israel were painfully
conscious of many existing evils, and
would have hailed a Messiah that
would have removed them, but they
entirely failed to perceive the causes
which had produced these evils, and
were therefore looking for their removal in a way that God never intended. John's proclamation that a
way should be prepared for the royal
visitor, and that obstructions should
be removed out of the way of His
approach, had awakened great expectations; but the obstructions were
within, not without; in their mental,
and not in their physical condition;

and to the removal of these alone His ministry was directed.

The prophecy, " every valley shall be filled," etc., is from Isaiah ; but what is there in it to interest Theophilus ?

The first part of this prophecy has special reference to the condition of the Jewish people, a condition which the ministry of John was designed to remove, by leading them to lay aside their differences, and unitedly accept the approaching Lord; but to this he added, or rather expounded the prophecy, "And all flesh shall see the salvation of God," and this statement, which applied to Gentiles, must surely have interested Theophilus.

7. *" O generation of vipers, who hath warned you to flee from the wrath to come ?" Why is John so severe ?*

Because they trusted in their fleshly relation to Abraham, and ignored the necessity of a change of heart and life. They were altogether impure, but saw not their uncleanness. Who could warn them of coming wrath when they did not believe in it?

10–14. *"And the people asked him, saying, What shall we do then?" Had these people been baptised?*

I presume they had, as they seem to have honestly accepted John's proclamation, and now seek directions for their new life. There were three classes who thus sought instruction, and received warnings against their most easily besetting sins. The selfish were exhorted to acts of benevolence ; the publicans, to strict justice in their claims; and the soldiers, to become guardians of public interest, and abstain from tyranny and false accusation.

Is John not approving of a military profession, by giving direction to these soldiers ?

We should not conclude that these men were trained warriors, but were filling a position very similar to our police, and were required for public protection. They exercised their calling among the people, and were exhorted to avoid all injustice and false accusation.

15. *Why did the people think that John might possibly be the Messiah ?*

The very searching character of his ministry might possibly induce this thought; but his denial of being the Christ at once decided this matter.

In recording the immersion of Jesus, Luke states that He was praying when the Holy Spirit descended upon Him. What is the import of this notice?

The notice of this act of prayer is very interesting, though both Matthew and Mark omit it. It is peculiar to Luke, who, in addition to this instance, refers to Jesus praying on eight other occasions, and thus showing that on most great occasions Jesus availed Himself of this privilege. It is from Luke that we understand that Jesus had left the river, and had possibly fallen upon His knees in prayer before the heavens were opened, and the Spirit descended upon Him.

21–37. *Why does the genealogy of Jesus given by Luke differ from that given by Matthew ?*

The reason is found in the genealogy itself. Matthew traces it from Abraham and David, through Solomon the king, to Joseph, while Luke traces it up to David through the line of his son Nathan. Both lines were needed to sustain an unbroken relation with David, as twice they are made to assist each other. At the Babylonish captivity the two lines united in Zerubbabel ; and again move on separately until they unite in Joseph, the husband of Mary, the mother of Jesus, who, as the reputed son of Joseph, became heir to the throne of David, and in due time was anointed and exalted to rule over the people of God. And as Jesus ever lives, there can be no other legal claimant to that throne.

Matthew says that "Jacob begat Joseph the husband of Mary," while Luke says that he was "of Heli." How can this be?

Since Jacob of the line of Solomon begat Joseph, he must be his natural father, and as Joseph was also "of Heli," Jacob must have married Heli's widow, of whom Joseph was born, and became his legal heir; thus both lines terminate in him.

38. *Why does Luke trace the genealogy of Jesus up to Adam?*

It is in keeping with his whole treatise. Jesus as a Saviour was provided for man as man, and not as a Jew merely. Abraham had a claim for his seed, because Jesus was promised to him, but Adam had a prior claim for all humanity, having received the promise of the deliverer on their behalf. And though Christ Jesus was first preached to the Jews, He was also to be proclaimed to the nations descended from Adam.

CHAPTER IV.

1. *What is to be understood by Jesus being "full of the Holy Spirit"? and "led by the Spirit"?*

Two things are here distinctly intimated :—(1.) That Jesus possessed all needful power of the Spirit for signs, wonders, and confirmation of His testimony ; and (2.) that He was thoroughly subject to the guidance of the Spirit in all things. When it is said that Jesus was "led by—*lit., in*—the Spirit," we understand that He fully yielded up Himself to do all that had been before appointed for Him to pass through. The temptation was the first step in His new service, and in the spirit of loving obedience He is prepared to accept of it.

2. *Why was Jesus, the Holy One, allowed to be tempted of the devil?*

When Jesus came into the scene over which the tempter ruled, temptation was unavoidable, and the wilderness was selected as the arena for a fair contest. The circumstances necessary to develop all that Satan wished to use on the occasion were allowed, and Jesus was fully tested by him, and fully overcame all his temptations.

Of what use is a knowledge of these temptations to us?

To show us not only that Satan can be conquered, but how all disciples may conquer him. Jesus overcame Satan by the truth, and by this alone. The sling and the stone of truth were all the weapons He employed against this daring foe, and by these He overcame.

Can His disciples conquer as He conquered?

By obedience to God they may triumph in every instance, and by yielding to the temptations of Satan they fall before him. In these three notable instances, Jesus has illustrated the whole secret of successful warfare. He refused to do what Satan suggested, and supplied a reason from the written Word why He should not yield to His temptations.

14–24. *Why does Luke speak of His return into Galilee?*

Not of His return merely, but His return in the power of the Spirit. He had left Nazareth, and had been immersed by John, and anointed by the Spirit, and visited Capernaum, where some miracles were done, and then returned into Galilee, passing from one synagogue to another, healing and instructing the people, until He reached Nazareth, where He had been brought up. But when He rejoined them in their synagogue service, it was not as of old in piety alone, but in the power of the

Spirit, and with a fame of wondrous things which He had done in Capernaum; and, as He unrolled the scroll of the prophet Isaiah and read, "The Spirit of the Lord is upon me," and applied it to Himself, He had, alas! to witness their wonder, and ultimately to escape from their wrath.

Why did they not receive His testimony?

Because they could not reconcile His low earthly relationship with His exalted claims, and so rejected Him altogether. In fact, they sought to take His life.

25. *Why did Jesus refer to the case of the widow of Sarepta?*

Simply to show an instance in which there had been a prophet in their nation, with power to help, as was shown in the relief of this poor Sidonian, and yet in their unbelief the people failed to take advantage of it.

27. *Why did He allude to the cure of Naaman?*

To bring the matter of their unbelief still more clearly before them. There were, said Jesus, "many lepers in Israel, in the time of Elisha, but none of them was cleansed, except Naaman, the Syrian." Some had been healed by Jesus in Capernaum, and also in Galilee, but He had to leave Nazareth without doing any mighty works, because of their unbelief. The cases of Naaman and the widow proved that God could cure and help the needy, but through rejection of His appointed messengers His help was forfeited by others.

Did they understand this reference as a rebuke?

Yes; and in the spirit of revenge they sought His life. He had come to them as the prophet of God, but instead of receiving Him they tried to throw Him down the hill and thus destroy Him. Not only was a precious opportunity lost, but their own hearts were hardened thereby.

Is a want of faith in Jesus the reason why people are not blessed now?

Most certainly, although we might rather say it is a want of obedience. Most people profess to have faith, but have no assurance of blessing, for the simple reason that they are not obedient. By obedience we prove our faith, and thus receive the promise made to us.

Would it be right to say that God is more willing to bless than men are to be blest?

This is strikingly manifest in the case before us. Jesus went to Nazareth full of the power of the Spirit, and sought to do them good, but had to leave them through their unbelief, without bestowing a single blessing. When the Saviour reached Capernaum, He was gladly received, and the demonised and diseased came and proved His power to heal and bless.

CHAPTER V.

1–3. *Was it the crowding of the people that led Jesus to ask the use of Simon's boat?*

The intense pressure brought to bear upon Him rendered it difficult for the multitude to hear Him, and the boats on the lake just met this difficulty. So He went into one of them, and asked the owner, who happened to be Simon, to thrust out a little from the land, and so give the people on the beach an opportunity to hear. Simon good-naturedly granted the request of the stranger, and listened with the people.

4–12. *Did that address produce any effect on the mind of Simon?*

We do not read that it did, but something that followed not only affected him but deeply stirred his heart. Jesus had in a certain way borrowed his boat, and taken up his time, and at the close He wishes to repay him, and so directs him to launch out in the deep, and let down their nets for a draught. Peter at once referred to their useless toil through the night, but, urged by the stranger, he tried again, and they enclosed a great multitude of fishes, and their net began to break. To the servants on the boat this was a most exciting scene, their partners in the other boat were invited to help, and soon both were filled with the fish. If Simon Peter was unmoved by the discourse, he deeply felt the miracle.

What was it that led him to confess himself as a sinful man ?

The deep conviction that he stood in the presence of a divine being, with his heart laid bare to His gaze. It is a solemn thing for any man to find himself in the presence of one who can read his heart, and that was where Peter found he stood. The pleasure produced by the unexpected large catch of fish entirely disappeared from his mind under the deep sense of his sin. It is deeply suggestive of that condition of mind, which all will experience in the presence of a heart-searching God. This miraculous draught of fishes convinced all of the power of Jesus, and induced James, and John, and Peter to follow Him ; but in Peter's heart a deep wound was made that required the " Fear not " of Jesus to heal.

12–25. *Why does Luke give in this chapter so many instances of the power of Jesus ?*

To confirm the faith of Theophilus in that previous statement, that Jesus returned from His temptation in the power of the Spirit ; and though His mission and power was questioned and rejected by His own people at Nazareth, yet He went forth to make it known in rich blessing to others.

In this chapter there is quite a cluster of evidences, proving that Jesus of Nazareth was the anointed of God, and which should be read consecutively for this purpose, and would doubtless be as satisfactory to this end to others as they must have been to Theophilus. First, he notes the casting out of a demon, then the curing of Simon's wife's mother, then follows the account of the miraculous draught of fishes, also the cleansing of a leper, and the curing of a man sick of the palsy. These striking proofs of the power of Jesus, as the prophet that should come into the world, are so orderly grouped together as to leave nothing more to be desired. Indeed, the chief portion of his record after this is occupied with the teaching of Jesus, and the four miracles that are noted are given for another purpose.

27–32. *In what way would the record of this parting feast interest Theophilus ?*

It would enable him to see that Jesus, who met so freely with these varied classes, was no respecter of persons, and that He looked, not at their rank or class, but at their great need of the sympathy and salvation of God. A priest was no more to Jesus than a publican, nor a Pharisee than a sinner. It was not their social or ecclesiastical standing that He respected, but their relation to God. These publicans and sinners were the lost sheep of the house of Israel, and the love which led Him first to seek their salvation, led Him to seek the salvation of the " ends of the earth."

30. *Why was this eating and drinking with publicans and sinners condemned by the Pharisees ?*

Because they trusted in themselves that they were righteous, and despised others ; and when Jesus the Messiah sat down with publicans and sinners, He completely ignored their pretended sanctity, and silently proved it to be a sham. No wonder that their self-esteem was deeply wounded.

33. *Why did the Pharisees present the fasting and prayers of their disciples as a contrast to the non-observance of these things by the disciples of Jesus?*

Fasting and formal prayer were popular in that day, and those who practised these things were honoured by the people. Their allusion to it, therefore, was in order to damage the claims and character of Jesus in the eyes of those who were beginning to respect Him.

34. *Is the simile of the bridegroom an appropriate answer to their inquiry?*

It is very instructive, no doubt. He claimed to be the bridegroom, and had come to claim His bride, and it would be unseemly to fast in the bride-chamber, where there should be joy. When He was taken from them they would fast, but not until then.

36. *Is the parable of the old garment and the old bottles applied to their ascetic life?*

It is intended to show them that the new truths which He taught His disciples could never be fettered with their pharisaic system. And as new wine would burst the old wine-skins, so would the truth old systems. The truths He taught required a new spirit in order to their proper development.

39. *Why did Jesus say, "No man also having drunk old wine straightway desireth new," etc.?*

Straightway, i.e., at once, desireth new; as if the change was not easily effected. To pass from tradition to truth, from Moses to Christ, from self to God, was not an easy transition. Time as well as truth would be required, and in many cases neither would avail.

CHAPTER VI.

1. *What is meant by "the second sabbath after the first"?*

A more correct reading is, "And it came to pass on a sabbath that He went," etc. This removes the difficulty created by the present reading, —a reading which many scholars now reject.

2. *Assuming that the disciples were hungry, why did the Pharisees blame them for rubbing out ears of corn on the sabbath?*

Because it was a violation of their traditional law which forbad reaping and thrashing on the sabbath; and in one of their specifications of what reaping and thrashing included, they affirmed, that to pluck with the hand an ear of corn was reaping, and to rub it out was thrashing, and therefore not lawful to be done. Jesus, however, defended the disciples by appealing to the Scriptures, and thus proved that, while they understood tradition, they misunderstood God.

6. *On another sabbath, a man with a withered hand was in the synagogue. Why did they not accuse Him after healing the man, when they were watching to do so?*

Because He knew their purpose, and by a few plain, common-sense questions in the presence of the cripple, entirely frustrated their evil design; and when He had healed him they began to meditate something worse than accusation. They were determined to uphold tradition, although it should hinder the cripple from being healed, and when Jesus ignored their tradition they were filled with madness.

13. *"And continued all night in prayer to God." Why did Luke refer to this night of prayer?*

He alone has recorded it, but the reasons are not given. The choice of twelve men, who were to be His witnesses to the world, and the ambassadors of the administration which was to continue till He should return from heaven, involved most solemn issues. We do not wonder that He who taught His disciples to pray in all their need, should Himself on this occasion continue all night in prayer to God, or *lit.*, was continuing all night in the prayer of God.

The prayer of God. What does this mean?

Simply that He was using those God-given teachings of the Scripture which were appropriate for the occasion. Jesus did not pray as we too often do, just what we think or feel, but used for His need the revelations of God. The Bible is given to teach us not only how to live, but how to pray, and it will be well to be thus guided.

20–49. *Is Luke giving a new version of the discourse on the mount?*

No. It might rather be called an epitome of that discourse—a selection from the Saviour's teaching, but sufficient to instruct Theophilus and all other Gentiles in the requirements of the new institution. Luke says that Jesus delivered it to His disciples, and clearly unfolds what must be the spirit and character of those who follow Him. Matthew's report of this discourse was no doubt quite adapted to Jewish surroundings, while this briefer report by Luke is more adapted to Gentiles in whatever position they might be placed. Hence we notice that the scribes and Pharisees are not named here, nor are the courts of law and other Jewish matters even mentioned. The selection is made to meet circumstances, and precepts are given here which have a claim on all disciples. The claims which are made are purity of heart, sincerity of mind, separation from all evil, and conformity to the will of God in all things. This is what Luke shows

to be required in discipleship, and to all who thus obey Jesus He promises eternal security.

CHAPTER VII.

1–10. *Why does Luke record the cure of this centurion's servant?*

It is in harmony with his whole treatise. This centurion was a Gentile, and most likely his servant also, and this favour shown to Gentiles was a most refreshing fact to notice. Matthew records the cure as well as Luke, but the difference between the two is striking. First, Luke notes that he seeks for help through the elders of the Jews, and though a man of official standing, he seeks for blessing through this channel, because God had put the Jew first. Then we notice again that he presents nothing of his own work or merit to induce help from Jesus. He had done a great deal, but had nothing to say about it. The Jews might and did speak of his benevolence, for he had built for them a synagogue, but his only plea was the need of his servant, and when a messenger announced the coming of Jesus to his house, he sent to prevent Him as being unworthy of such honour, and simply requested Him to "say in a word, and my servant shall be healed." His faith was truly wonderful for a Gentile, and Jesus said that Israel with all her advantages had not furnished such an instance.

11–18. *Why does Luke record this case of the widow of Nain?*

It was a striking manifestation of sympathy with a bereaved widow, but it is not merely because of sympathy being shown that Luke records it. This widow was a Gentile, and though many of the citizens were sympathising with her, there were none to seek the help of Jesus on her behalf. Nor does He wait for that, but in tender compassion bids her dry her tears, and raises her son to life. This wondrous grace to a poor Gentile Luke cannot omit. It was a token for good in which some hearts would find special interest. These drops of rain upon their thirsty ground, gave hopes of a coming shower. Indeed, the rumour of what Jesus had done went throughout all Judea, and all the region round about, and even the disciples of John showed him of all these things.

19–28. Was it this peculiar display of sympathy and grace that stirred the heart of John to send such a message to Christ?

John doubtless expected great things for his own people, and this seemed a digression from the course he had marked out for his Lord. His disciples supplied him with information of what was going on, and he became perplexed when he found that his preconceived plans were not carried out. Indeed he was offended,—*i.e.*, stumbled,—and therefore sent this strange message to Jesus, " Art thou He that should come, or do we look for another?" The Master, however, bore with the weakness of His servant, and made His messengers the witnesses of His power and grace. " Go your way," said He, " and tell John what things ye have seen and heard."

29, 30. How did the publicans justify God in being immersed by John?

God had sent him to proclaim remission of sins to all immersed penitents, and all who obeyed the requirements of God's messenger honoured or justified the God who sent him; while the Pharisees, in refusing His counsel, rejected it against themselves. The immersion of the penitent might seem a small matter, but to those who believed John's preaching it was an accept-

ance of God's judgment against their past sins, and of a new life under the Messiah, while those who refused, ignored the truth both of their sin and of His grace.

31–35. Why did Jesus compare that generation to children in the market-place?

The comparison was intended as a solemn rebuke to these Pharisees and lawyers. It was as if he had said, no matter what is done, you are not affected by it for good. Whether it is the servant or the Son that calls upon you, there is no response for God.

36–50. Was it not rather strange for Jesus to go to the house of a Pharisee when He had so severely condemned the whole fraternity?

The Saviour accepted every opportunity of doing good, and whether invited by friend or foe, He readily accepted the invitation as a season for doing good. He did not make the circumstances, but simply used them, and the result was often deeply interesting. He did not ask Simon the Pharisee to entertain Him, nor the woman the sinner to follow Him there: both acted freely, and we learn the result.

Why did Luke record the case of the woman in Simon's house?

The case was one of special interest to all who knew they must either receive mercy or perish. The priests and Pharisees had no gospel for the guilty; they could judge and condemn all that were so, and for this they were too ready. But Jesus brought tidings of mercy for the guilty, and this poor woman, having heard, believed the message, and followed into Simon's house to anoint the beautiful feet that had brought it.

Did she go there to wash His feet?

No; she went there to anoint His feet. The washing—*lit.*, wetting—of His feet with tears, was no part of her plan, but as she stood behind Him love gently pressed them out, and having no towel at hand, her hair was used to wipe off the tears she could not restrain.

Did she go there to be forgiven?

No; she went there to express her love for forgiveness already received, and it was while she was doing this that Simon inwardly condemned his guest for allowing a well-known sinner to touch Him.

Why did Jesus refer to the case of these two debtors?

In order to show Simon the state of his own heart towards his guests. He could easily decide which of the debtors was under the greatest obligations to their creditor; and when told to look at the woman, her tears, her kiss, her ointment, and contrast these with his own cold reception, he would see at a glance, not only that he felt no obligation to Jesus, but that He read his heart by his utter neglect of even common social respect.

"Her sins, which are many, are all forgiven." Was this spoken for Simon's information?

It was to show him the cause of her strange action, and was also spoken to her that she might "Go in peace," although her action had been questioned.

CHAPTER VIII.

1. *As Luke is giving an orderly account of the life of Jesus, is there anything special to be noticed in this chapter?*

The word "afterward" marks a new movement in the life of Jesus—a fresh development of that mission of mercy which He had so graciously begun. Prior to this time, His labours had been confined chiefly to Galilee, and had been a demonstration of the power of the Spirit in Him there; but here we have Him starting on a mission tour through the whole land. Every city and village is visited, and though the twelve are with Him, yet He is the great worker in the field—sowing the seed on the varied soils over which He passed, and then in a parable marking the result. This detail of His own ministry in chap. viii. is followed by the ministry of the twelve in chap. ix., and the ministry of the seventy in chap. x., and thus the whole range of service is consecutively described.

5–15. *Was this parable of the sower intended to have a special or a general application?*

The parable was intended for those who heard the glad tidings of the kingdom of heaven, and marks in simile the nature and extent of their acceptance and rejection of the message; but any one may yet use it as a test of their own condition in relation to the Gospel of the Lord Jesus. Is there any fruit for God, is a question for all hearts now, and not merely for the time when He sowed the good seed.

Do the hindrances of which the sower speaks, when expounding the parable, arise out of circumstances, or a wrong condition of mind?

They arise out of both, because while the "way side," "the rock," and "the thorns," indicate the sphere of certain agencies, yet these similes can only be applied to persons in certain conditions of mind, and for these each one is responsible, or there could be no judgment. The "way side," according to Jesus, is the sphere where Satan ruled—the hard trodden uncultivated path—the mind over which tradition prevailed instead of truth. Into such a mind truth could not enter, so long as men's traditions held it in subjection. Then "the rock" is something hidden in self, and intercepts the striking down of the roots of the seed sown in the heart, and unless dug up, and thrown out, there will be no fruit. Then " the thorns " are things outside ; some worldly influences which surround, and if allowed, will choke the growth of the seed. The " good ground " is an honest heart, that having heard the word keeps it, and brings forth fruit with patience. Thus while the heavenly Sower, through one medium or other, may bring the truth to our minds, we individually become responsible for the result. If there is fallow ground, it must be broken up ; or thorns, they must be removed, or there will be no fruit unto life eternal.

16–18. *Is the " lighted candle," and " take heed," connected with the parable of the sower ?*

They are new lessons from the same Teacher, and intended for the same people, and for both heart and life. If the candle or lamp was not allowed to shine, the oil would be withdrawn, and if the truth brought nigh was not appreciated, it would be taken away.

19–21. *Do these proposed terms of relationship still remain in force ?*

Most certainly. Through the flesh Jesus had His mother and His brethren, but through reception of the truth a higher relation is formed by all who obey it. Indeed, that fleshly relationship has been dissolved by death, but by the truth an eternal relationship is formed through faith in Jesus.

22. *Why did Jesus cross the lake ?*

Because on other side of it there were lost sheep of the house of Israel.

Why were the disciples afraid in that storm ?

Because of their want of faith in Jesus. That storm proved a test of their hearts, the true state of which they could only learn in the trial. The difference between fear and trust is here strikingly manifest ; Jesus

could sleep in the storm while they were in great terror.

26–56. *We have three miracles recorded in this chapter. Why are they given ?*

These three miracles have a very important connection with the ministry of Jesus. In these three cases we have an illustration of man's threefold condition from which He came to release him, viz., the power of Satan, of disease, and of death. The restoration of the demonised man, the woman with her issue of blood, and the daughter of Jairus to their former state, are signs of what He is able to do spiritually for all who receive Him. It was not merely to cast out demons and heal issues of blood that He came into the world, but to cast out those evil passions that rule over men, and render them unfit for fellowship with God. In His gracious power He met the one, and by His truth He is seeking to meet the other. Blessed are all they who receive His healing and helping grace.

CHAPTER IX.

1, 2. *Is the subject of ministry continued in this chapter ?*

Yes, but here we get the ministry of the twelve. Jesus first went over the field Himself, and here we see Him sending others on the same errand. It is service multiplied by calling other workers to help in the proclamation. True, the message differed somewhat from its first proclamation by John ; then it was, " The kingdom of heaven is at hand," now the twelve are to preach it as a reality. " He sent them to preach the kingdom of God, and to heal the sick." These messengers carried the truth that reunited to God all who received it. The good seed of the kingdom was from heaven, so that by whomsoever received, the claims of heaven were acknowledged ; and

G

by means of the truth, divine rule was established.

3–6. *"Take nothing for your journey, neither staves, nor scrip, neither bread nor money." Why send them without personal resources?*

They were going out as His servants, and He undertook to care for them day by day. The extra garment which He forbad them to take was one generally worn for ornament or display, and this He did not allow.

Should the servants of Jesus go out to labour now in this dependent condition?

There are no special directions to others how they are to act in relation to these every-day necessities. There are examples in the Word which show that some may go forth as the fowls of the air, and get their daily wants supplied, while others take the place of the labouring ox and feed upon the corn while they are threshing. Whoever works for Christ sincerely, and trusts in Him, will not be forsaken. It is the work, and not the hire, that should fill the mind of the servants of Christ.

10. *Why did Jesus take His disciples into a desert place?*

Possibly it was selected that they might quietly tell Him how they succeeded, but this privacy was soon intruded upon by the people who followed them, and these soon increased to a multitude.

12–17. *"Send the multitude away," said the disciples to Jesus. Was this a want of faith or sympathy?*

Possibly both, but one feels a little ashamed of their suggestion to their gracious Master. They had proved a good deal of His grace and power in their late journey, and seem unwilling to let others share it with them. "Send them away," said the disciples. "Give ye them to eat," said Jesus. Blessed Master, help us to have more of Thy spirit.

The abundant supply for the multitude was produced miraculously by Jesus. Why did He give thanks for that which He had so provided?

"All things are of God," and the action of Jesus furnishes a striking illustration of how God is to be honoured in all His gifts. The man who makes abundance by his skill and industry, should after all thank God for the store. Jesus was God's servant, and, by the power bestowed on Him, He met the need of this multitude, but He did not forget to thank God for the supply.

18. *"Whom say the people that I am?" What does this question suggest?*

A very sad truth indeed. The Messiah had come into the world according to the prophets, and they did not know Him. Their opinions varied, but all failed to see in Him the Son of God.

28. *Only three of His disciples were allowed to see Him transfigured on the Mount. Why restrict the sight to so few?*

The glorification of Jesus was not intended for public testimony, like His resurrection, and was therefore witnessed by only three of the disciples, and even these had to keep it secret until after He was raised from the dead. To themselves, and to all who believed their testimony, it must have greatly strengthened their faith in the hope of glory. It was a tangible illustration of what Jesus now is, and what the saints will be when they are with Him.

30. *How could Moses and Elijah appear on the Mount with Jesus?*

We might say by the power of God, but this answer sheds no light upon the process by which God brought them together. Moses was buried in the land of Moab, and Elijah was taken up without dying, but both were in the keeping of God, and when He required them He could produce them. The case is powerfully suggestive, not only of glorification, but of the present existence of those who have departed this life.

37–57. *In these twenty verses there are several manifest failures, both in the spirit and action of the disciples. Why has Luke recorded these failures?*

I cannot think that it would be merely to expose their weakness, but rather to show the teaching of Jesus in relation to each of the things in which they so signally failed. First of all, they failed to cast out the unclean spirit, and have to learn that it was because they were seeking to exalt themselves rather than Christ, and must have been humbled to learn that they had power, but because of their spirit they could not use it. Then again, we have them contending together which of them should be the greatest, and by the little child set in the midst, they have to be reproved for their ambition. A case of petty exclusivism is next disclosed by John, in which they had forbidden a man who was casting out a demon, simply because he followed not with them. They had counted upon their Master's approval, but were justly disappointed, and instructed to pursue a wiser course. The last of these failures was perhaps the most condemnable of all, in seeking to bring down fire upon a Samaritan village, because they were unwilling to receive Jesus. To witness these sad manifestations of spirit must have been most painful to Himself, but as a patient teacher of all that is good, He quietly seeks to lead them to manifest a more loving spirit, and to do good rather than evil.

CHAPTER X.

1. *"After these things the Lord appointed other seventy also." Why does Luke alone record this mission?*

Why the other evangelists did not refer to it we cannot say, but the mission itself is a fact, and it is in keeping with the object of his treatise to record it. The field was wide, and the labourers were multiplied according to the great need of the people of Israel. These three missions, beginning with Jesus Himself, then the twelve, then the seventy, which, from a given place, widen out into the whole land of Israel, are a beautiful illustration of that world-wide mission of which he has afterwards to become the historian.

4. *Among the peculiar directions given by Jesus to these seventy we find, " And salute no man by the way." Why so uncourteous?*

The direction was suggestive of the character of their message. It was not courtesy, but life and death, about which they were employed. The ordinary salutation of " peace, peace," which indicates that all is well, would contradict their message. They were sent to people that were all wrong, and sought to lead them to feel it.

5, 6. *Why were they to say " Peace " to every house they entered?*

Because they carried a message of peace, not to the building, but to the people, who either rejected or responded to it. If the message of peace was accepted, peace was enjoyed, but if rejected, they had the reflex blessing of their salutation. The disciple that seeks to bless others cannot fail, either to bless them or be blest himself, for " peace be unto you " cannot fall to the ground.

7. *" Go not from house to house " —i.e., for the purpose of getting food. Why give such directions?*

The purport of His instruction was, be more concerned about your message than your meat. You will be supplied, but take what is given to you.

They were to wipe off the dust of their feet against Christ-rejecting cities. What may we learn from this?

A very solemn lesson—viz., that privilege enjoyed brings responsibility, while privilege neglected brings judgment. It was a greater crime to reject Christ than to reject Moses.

17–20. *According to Jesus, the recording their names in heaven was of greater value than the power to expel demons. Had they overlooked this?*

They were evidently flushed with joy at their signal triumph, and had overlooked their higher privilege in association with Christ. He therefore shows them that relationship with God was of more value than gift. It is a question which each one may profitably apply to his own heart. Which gives me most joy, position or union with Christ? If it is power or gift, let me beware ; if it be Christ, let me rejoice, because in Him I have all things.

21. *Who were these "wise and prudent," from whom some things were hid; and "babes," to whom things were revealed?*

The "wise and prudent" were the rulers and teachers of that age, who did not discern the full power of Jesus ; while the "babes" were the seventy, and such as they, who saw in His power to expel demons the greatest proof of His deity. It was to them the crowning proof of His Messiahship, which they held fast until they saw Him as the risen One.

25. *"What shall I do to inherit eternal life?" Why did this lawyer ask such a question?*

Not to obtain any instruction from Jesus, but rather that he might ensnare Him in His reply. He was no doubt agreeably surprised at being called upon to exhibit his own attainment in a knowledge of the law, and felt somewhat flattered by the approval of the new Teacher. Jesus declared that he had " answered right ; this do, and thou shalt live." It was no doubt a very easy thing for him to repeat, " Thou shalt love the Lord thy God with all thy heart," etc., " and thy neighbour as thyself," and very pleasant to be commended for his reply. The thing, however, was not complete, another step and justification of himself would be attained, and the mission of the Teacher would be seen to be useless. So he ventures to ask Jesus one more question :— " And who is my neighbour?" The reply is a deeply interesting sketch of an unfortunate man, who in his travel from Jerusalem to Jericho fell among thieves, and, after being robbed and wounded, was left half dead. The priest and Levite, who happened to pass, heeded him not, but he was at last happily rescued by a kind-hearted Samaritan, who did for him all that he required. The question, " Which now of these three was neighbour to him that fell among the thieves?" was quite natural, and the reply could scarcely have been otherwise than, " He that showed mercy on him." But when Jesus said to him, "Go, and do thou likewise," he must have felt that his professed keeping of the law was only a sham.

Does this man who fell among thieves represent any particular class of persons?

Yes ; and as the illustrations used by Jesus were generally sketches of actually existing things, the persons represented were never far to seek. There were among them a large class of persons, who, on their wayward journey from the city of peace to

46284

the city of the curse, had been both robbed and wounded. Who these were, we have only to notice where the ministry of Jesus was so often exercised, and the oil and wine of teaching and consolation so often applied, and we may then see who were the persons the priest and the Levite always passed by. When did they ever pity and help a publican or a sinner? Never.

Did this good Samaritan represent Jesus?

This character is in beautiful keeping with His life. His eye ever beamed with compassion for the sufferer, and His hand was ever ready to help the needy. He certainly did visit wretched, ruined, wounded sinners on this earth, and actually changed places with them. Heaven and glory is His rightful place, while dishonour and the dust is the fallen condition of the sinner, and the contrast of position is most striking. But see how Jesus reverses this state of things, and actually leaves His high seat in order that the sinner may be exalted. This is no dream, it is a reality, and we marvel at the grace of our God.

38–42. Martha received Jesus into her house as a guest, but Mary sat at His feet, and heard His word. What made the difference between these two sisters?

Their different estimate of the truth which Jesus taught. To entertain her guest was Martha's highest thought, while to learn the truth was the one thought of Mary, and for this all else was laid aside. She chose the good part—*i.e.,* the truth ; and this she proved by afterward anointing Him for His burial.

"One thing is needful." Was this teaching or reproof?

It was reproof to Martha doubtless, because it showed that He was not pleased with her domestic anxiety. She was evidently more concerned about the body than the mind, about serving than learning, and this was painful to the Teacher who had become her guest, and was most anxious to instruct her in divine things.

When Jesus said, " But one thing is needful," did He refer to something spiritual?

I think not, but rather to the preparation she was making for the coming meal. She was preparing many things for His enjoyment, when one thing would have been sufficient. Jesus would rather she had come and heard the teaching which her sister so eagerly embraced than have cumbered herself with much serving or preparation of food.

CHAPTER XI.

1. *" Lord, teach us to pray." Why had they to ask for instruction in prayer?*

Because in the new relationship to God, into which they had been called, they felt the need of their Master's teaching; and as John had instructed His disciples, it formed a precedent for their request.

Did Moses teach men to pray?

As the law-giver of the people he could not do so, since the law and prayer can have no fit relation to each other. In the law of Moses God set forth His claims on those who chose to occupy this ground before Him, and judgment followed violation of it. Prayer was allowed, and directed by the Spirit under that dispensation, but it was rather through the priesthood of Aaron, which shadowed forth the promised Messiah, than through the law.

What does the privilege of prayer imply?

Acceptance of Christ, and dependence on God for all things through Him. Prayer is a privilege which God has opened to those who accept of a gracious mediator.

2–5. In this prayer which Jesus taught His disciples there is but one petition relating to the body? Is it not strange that it should be so briefly noticed?

This one petition covered all their need for the day, and beyond this nothing more was required. The six remaining petitions relate to spiritual things, and show by their number that God's claims stand higher than the claims of self.

Can the petition for daily supply be used by believers now?

I suppose it could be used by them; but where is the disciple that would be satisfied with it? A supply for the day only would be too limited for most suppliants. Provision for a month, a year, or even a life-time is more frequently sought for.

5–9. What did Jesus intend to teach by the case of the man who by importunity obtained three loaves from his friend at midnight?

A striking illustration of the difference between God and man. By imploring and continued urging this man got what he needed, but, said Jesus, God is waiting for you to ask Him, that He may bestow on you His blessing. He will not say, I cannot rise and give thee, but, Ask and ye shall receive.

11. "If a son shall ask bread of any of you that is a father," etc. What is this intended to teach?

The deep parental feeling of God. That He should take the action of a parent to illustrate His own care is truly wonderful. God wishes to give the good, not the injurious, blessing, not judgment.

13. The giving of the Holy Spirit is here said to follow asking, while Peter (Acts v. 32) speaks of the bestowal through obedience. How can these differences be reconciled?

Luke and Peter do not refer to the same thing. A correct rendering of Luke would be *a holy spirit*, or as David prays, "a right spirit." This is sustained by the version of Matthew (vii. 11), who terms the promise "good things." Luke therefore refers to the suppliant's own spirit, while Peter refers to the Holy Spirit.

14, 15. "He casteth out devils by Beelzebub the chief," etc. Why did they raise this false report?

It was a striking manifestation of power, and by this false charge they sought to damage His reputation.

16. "And others, tempting Him, sought of Him a sign from heaven." How could it be wrong in them to do so?

They asked this sign in order to test His power; but as this could only have gratified their worldly ambition, He refused their request. However, before He left them He pointed out what acceptance of Himself implied, as illustrated in Jonah the prophet. It was as a risen one that the Ninevites accepted Jonah, and as such they would have to accept of Him. It was a sign from earth, even His own resurrection, that would be given them, and if they failed to profit by this, the men of Nineveh would condemn them.

24–26. The man out of whom the unclean spirit was cast took to himself seven other spirits, and became worse than at the first. To what does He apply this illustration?

The context furnishes no light upon this strange case, but an answer may be gathered from the history of the nation. God had purged from them the spirit of idolatry by a scourging captivity in Babylon, and when they returned to their house, they found it, as it were, swept and garnished. Instead, however, of remaining separate from uncleanness, they took other wicked spirits, and in the days of Christ they were worse than at their captivity.

27. The woman that said, "Blessed is the womb that bare thee," seems to have made a mistake. In what did this consist?

In judging that a fleshly relationship would secure all needed good; and Jesus gave her to know that obedience to the truth was of far higher import. To be the mother of that Son was indeed an earthly honour, but to be obedient to that Son, would secure heavenly honour.

37–44. This is the second visit of Jesus to the houses of Pharisees by special invitation. Is it not strange that they should invite Him when He generally reproved them?

It is difficult to say why they should invite Him as a guest, but it is instructive to notice how willingly He attends to their requests, and how faithful He is to all who are present. The Pharisee who invited Him to dine was the first to open the attack on this occasion, but his ears must have been made to tingle ere Jesus closed His reply. His exposure of their hypocrisy not only showed how He knew their hearts, but how abominable their service was in the sight of God. Their liberality and piety was universally applauded; but the way in which their wealth was obtained, and the self-seeking of their devotions, led Him to declare that a fearful doom awaited them. "Woe unto you, Pharisees!"

45. Why did this lawyer feel reproached by these fearful charges of Christ?

Because he felt that the lawyers, on whose behalf he entered a protest, were implicated in this condemnation of the Pharisees. Traditional law was the basis of the whole system, and as Jesus had condemned the tithing and external sanctity of this popular sect, He had condemned those who had the legal oversight of these things. No wonder, then, that this lawyer felt aggrieved by these denunciatory charges of Jesus.

50. How could the shed blood of all the righteous men, from Abel to Zacharias, be charged on that generation?

Because they had the Scriptures, which condemned those who put the faithful to death, and in putting Christ to death, the object of the faith of Abel, and all who suffered as he for their faith, they incurred the guilt of rejecting all this weight of testimony, as well as their own personal crime.

CHAPTER XII.

1–3. "They trod one upon another." What does this indicate?

Intense earnestness. The people were so eager to hear Jesus, that neighbourly respect was set aside. Each one struggled with his fellow to get near enough to hear His wonderful words.

What was this "leaven of the Pharisees"?

It was the doctrine of externalism —fair outside, though foul within. A profession of sincerity without reality. Jesus labelled it hypocrisy, and said to His disciples, "Beware of it."

4. "Be not afraid of them that kill the body." Why refer to this possible doom?

Because He knew that if they were faithful, they would be persecuted even unto death. But as man could only kill the body, they were not to fear him, but rather to fear God, who could cast the unfaithful into hell.

"Cast into hell." What did Jesus mean by this?

The word here rendered hell, is strictly *gehenna*, a place of judicial punishment outside of Jerusalem. But as Jesus uses the term to denote the place of punishment to which God consigns the faithless in another state, we must conclude that *gehenna* is used as a symbol of that state.

This revelation of such a future doom should stir all hearts to obey Him who alone has power to inflict it.

6, 7. *How would God's care for sparrows be an indication that He would care for His faithful ones?*

Jesus reasoned from the lesser to the greater, and gives this as His conclusion. God cares for sparrows, but you are of more value than many sparrows, therefore God cares for you. This is, however, more than reason to us, it is revelation, and opens up to disciples a most gracious view of God's overseeing care.

13-15. *"Master, speak to my brother," etc. Why did this man seek the help of Jesus to obtain a portion of his brother's inheritance?*

Because he was covetous, and would have used Jesus to obtain that to which he had no legal right.

16-21. *The ground of this rich man brought forth plentifully. Was there anything wrong in this abundance?*

No. It should have been a matter of thankfulness, as it might have been used for good; but instead of this the opportunity became a snare, and the man planned for his own ease. We need to watch even our mercies, lest they should lead us to forget the Giver. To lay up earthly treasures instead of heavenly, must be an eternal loss to all who do so.

22. *The course recommended by the Saviour to His disciples prohibited all earthly aspiration. Was this just to them as men having claims and rights in the world?*

They had accepted Him as their Teacher, and these were the lessons and maxims that He gave for the ordering of their lives. He prohibited them from seeking or possessing this world's goods, but promised them that God would provide, and give to them a kingdom and portion that would not perish, and

this would more than balance all their sacrifice.

33. *Were the directions to sell all, and have nothing but their God-provided daily portion, special to them, or intended for all time?*

These directions were specially connected with the disruption of things belonging to that dispensation. The possession of property would have been a snare to the disciple of Jesus at that trying period, and life alone was promised to those who patiently endured to the end. Had they possessed much worldly goods at the destruction of Jerusalem, it would most likely have hindered their escape at the only time it could have been effected.

36. *How could they wait and watch for their Lord, if He has not yet come?*

The coming to which Jesus alludes, and for which they were to watch, was not a coming in person, but in power to judge the nation, and to scatter it as the chaff of the summer threshing-floor. To deny His presence on that occasion, or to affirm that He did not come in that national overthrow, is to refuse Him one of the signs which He claimed as a proof of His exaltation. " Then shall appear the sign of the Son of man in heaven" (Matt. xxiv. 30).

41. *Peter asked if the parable of the faithful servant was spoken to them specially, or to all. How do you understand His reply?*

I understand Him to say, It is not to you alone that I am speaking thus; there are others involved in this event as well as you, and all who are faithful when the Lord comes, He will recompense, while the unfaithful will suffer His displeasure.

Is this punishment of few stripes, or many stripes, to take place in eternity?

It is doubtless connected with the judgment of which the Saviour was speaking, and would be realised in the measure spoken of, when He fulfilled His word. It was in time, and connected with that final dissolving of the Jewish commonwealth, that these few or many stripes would be inflicted on those who knew or did not know the Master's will.

45. *"My lord delayeth his coming." Was this named as a possible thought of some ?*

No doubt there was delay in the execution of the judgment that was to fall upon the nation, and when the delay was used for fleshly purposes it became a snare. Had their faith and patience been matured by it, they would have been ready whenever the Master did appear; but when used for the purposes of lust and tyranny, as is evident from the epistle of James, then surprise and ruin was certain.

49. *"I am come to send fire on the earth." What kind of fire is this ?*

Judgment, of which fire is a symbol. Yet, this fire which He kindled, was not the direct object of His visit, but is rather a result of rejected grace.

50. *"But I have a baptism to be baptised with." What does this mean?*

His immersion in suffering, the overwhelming nature of which had been fully made known by the prophets. It had been written of Him, " All thy waves and thy billows are gone over me " (Ps. xlii. 7); and for its fulfilment He was painfully anxious.

CHAPTER XIII.

1–3. *Why did these persons tell Jesus of the slaughter of the Galileans ?*

Galilee was a district in which Jesus could labour with greater liberty than in Judea, being out of the jurisdiction of Pilate, who keenly watched over Roman interests. As Jesus was a Galilean, it was expected that He would complain of the injustice of Pilate, and thus involve Himself. In this, however, they were disappointed, as from this painful fact He drew a most solemn and instructive warning. These men had suffered death while unrighteously resisting a power that had dominion over them, and, said He, " unless you repent, you will likewise perish," *i.e.*, perish by the same power.

4, 5. *Who brought forward the sad disaster at Siloam ?*

It was referred to by Jesus in order to correct public sentiment regarding these sufferers, but of the event we know nothing beyond what is here stated. We may judge that it was looked upon as a divine visitation for some supposed infringment of public right, and Jesus repeats His own solemn warning, that unless there was a change in them they would perish in a similar manner— referring doubtless to the judgment which came upon their city.

6–9. *Is the parable of the barren fig tree connected with these warnings?*

It is an exposition of the goodness of God to them as a nation, and of their neglect of a great opportunity afforded them for improvement. If they did improve it, well, but if not, an inevitable doom awaited them.

What was the vineyard in which the fig tree was planted ?

The whole economy, which included both the law and the prophets, and which was in force when Christ was speaking to them.

What did the fig tree represent ?

The nation as it then stood before God; no longer called a vine—its former designation when brought out of Egypt—but a fig tree, a tree which ordinarily grew by the wayside, but here planted in a vineyard for the richer culture and protection it afforded. The " certain man who had a fig tree planted in his vineyard," fully shows what God had so graciously done in prolonging the dispensation, with all its privileges, to a people who had justly forfeited them, and who therefore had no claim to their continuance. As a fig tree in a vineyard, to which place it had no right, but was still allowed to remain, so the people of Israel were allowed to continue year after year, until their remaining in the vineyard could no longer be allowed.

What do the three years represent ?

The three years of Christ's ministry, when under His culture there should have been fruit for God ; but as there was none, its doom was declared, " cut it down," etc.

Why was this threatened doom not executed at once ?

The doom of the tree was delayed through the pleading of the dresser of the vineyard. His desire was to give it a further opportunity, and facts in the history of the nation, of whom this tree was a symbol, prove that this reprieve was shown. The crisis was delayed, but the opportunity not being improved, judgment became inevitable.

10–17. The ruler of the synagogue was indignant at Christ healing a poor woman on the sabbath, but was not the reply of Jesus, " thou hypocrite" rather severe ?

It does appear harsh, but then it was true, as Jesus proved by appealing to his own action in relieving his ox or ass, and then condemning Him for helping an afflicted daughter of Abraham. To be a ruler of the synagogue, and then set a higher estimate upon his ass than upon one of Abraham's children, was only varnished hypocrisy.

18–22. Luke gives but two of the seven parables recorded by Matthew (chap. xiii.) Why make this selection ?

The selection is in keeping with the design of his treatise. The truth, of which the grain of mustard seed is a symbol, was cast into the garden, and would become a great tree ; and the leaven, a symbol of corrupting error, would be hid by the woman in the meal, and work through all the measures of it ; and if understood by Theophilus, these matters would be of special interest.

23. " Lord, are there few that be saved?" Was this a mere speculative enquiry ?

The sentence should read, *Lord, are there few being saved ?* or in other words, is your work at all successful ? It appears like a friendly enquiry, and Jesus turns it to a practical account, by urging the man himself to enter into the strait gate.

24. What was this strait gate, through which some were not able to enter ?

Two distinct things are here referred to—the "strait gate," or as some MSS. read, the *narrow door,* and the " house," of which it was the entrance. This narrow door was possibly the claims of Jesus put forth in His teaching, which, if accepted, opened their way into all the privileges of the house, but if refused, the Master might rise and close the door, after which entrance became impossible. It is not that many shall not be able to enter in at the door, but having neglected—*i.e.,* refused—to enter by the door, they should not be able to enter into the house.

29. " And they shall come from the east," etc. Who are these ?

Those Jews who, during that first pentecostal season of spiritual blessing, went up to Jerusalem, and through the preaching of the Gospel by Peter, did come and " sit down in the kingdom of God."

31. " Get thee out, for Herod will kill Thee." Had these Pharisees any authority to say this ?

No ; it was said to intimidate

Him. They had told Him of Pilate, and that did not trouble Him, and now they seek to frighten Him by warning Him of Herod ; but He fears neither the one nor the other.

32. " *Go ye and tell that fox.*" *Does He refer to Herod ?***

I think not. Herod, the tetrarch, had never interfered with Jesus, nor in any way hindered His ministry. It is more likely to be the person who sent these time-serving Pharisees, to whom Jesus sent this justly deserved rebuke, and plainly informs him that He would not turn aside till all His work was accomplished.

CHAPTER XIV.

1–4. *We have here an account of Jesus being once more at the table of a Pharisee. Why did they watch Him?*

Because a sick man was present, and it being the sabbath, they watched to see if He would heal him. This is the third time that Luke records about Jesus being a guest at the houses of Pharisees, and on each occasion something occurred which was to them most provoking. The first visit is recorded in chap. vii., and on that occasion a " woman which was a sinner " followed Him and anointed His feet, much to the annoyance of the host. Then, in chap. xi., we have Him sitting down at the table of a Pharisee with unwashen hands, to him a very great insult. And here " there was a certain man before Him which had the dropsy," and, though they were watching Him, He healed the man, and let him go.

Why did Jesus become the assailant on this occasion ?

He only did what it was very sad He should have to do, viz., defend an act of gracious power, and did so by a very homely appeal :—
" Which of you shall have an ass or an ox fallen into a pit, and will

not straightway pull him out on the sabbath day ? " To this question there was no reply.

7–11. *Was this parable about the chief rooms at feasts put forth for direction or condemnation ?*

For both I presume. He had marked their ambitious spirit in choosing the chief seats, and desired to instruct them in a wiser policy. Whether or not His advice was taken, the truths He uttered remain. " Whosoever exalteth himself shall be abased ; and he that humbleth himself shall be exalted."

12–14. "*When thou makest a dinner, or a supper, call not thy friends, etc., but call the poor, the maimed,*" *etc. Was not this strange advice ?*

Very strange indeed. It is quite a reversal of human plans, and advice which few will care to follow. Still it is God-like, and what Jesus did Himself. He made a feast, not for beings of heavenly rank, but for the poor and maimed of this world, looking only for a recompense in glory. Besides, the Saviour advances a principle of immense importance for all to know. If in the good done mere human applause is sought, the higher approval of God will not be given ; but if what is done is done for Christ's sake, then, as a work of faith and a labour of love, it will be rewarded at the resurrection of the just.

15–24. "*Blessed is he that shall eat bread in the kingdom of God.*" *Did this man understand what he was saying ?*

I should judge from the Saviour's reply that it was more the outburst of carnal fancy than of enlightened judgment. Under the figure of a great supper, which a certain man made, he was shown that this kingdom had been opened, but that possessions, wealth, and pleasure, had been preferred to its spiritual privileges by those to whom its favours had first been offered. If the poor and blind, etc., were afterwards called in, and the former denied the repast, it was because they had slighted the proffered boon.

25-27. "*And there went great multitudes with Him.*" *Why did these crowds follow Jesus?*

Selfishness was doubtless their secret motive, because all failed to apprehend the nature of His mission. It was this which led Him to deliver this searching address, in which He plainly states that if they wished to be His disciples, father, and mother, and wife, and children, and brethren, and sisters, yea, and even life also, might have to be sacrificed for Him ; and this matter He urged them to carefully consider. They had been induced to think that it would be a grand thing to be a disciple of one who could heal them when sick, feed them when hungry, and meet all their need, but this was a very low view of the character of His mission. True, He had done many signs among them, but these were in order to lead them to accept Him as a Saviour from sin, and every evil way, and unless these things were desired, their discipleship would prove a failure.

Was His allusion to the building a tower, and going to war, intended to induce reflection ere they became His disciples?

It was usually a simple reference to what is usually done both in building and war. Men generally count the cost, and act accordingly. The cross will have to be borne if you follow Me, therefore consider beforehand whether or not you can forsake all for Me.

CHAPTER XV.

1. *What occasioned the delivery of these three parables recorded in this chapter?*

The murmuring of the scribes and Pharisees against Jesus, on account of His great attention to publicans and sinners.

Who were these publicans and sinners?

The publicans were collectors of the Roman tribute, and those of them that were Jews were thoroughly despised by their brethren, and by traditional law were excluded from temple privileges. The sinners, so called, were a large class of persons, who through immorality of life, insubordination to tradition, and other sins, had forfeited their religious standing ; and being excommunicated by the Pharisees, they were held to be without hope.

Why did these persons gather round Jesus?

Because He spoke to them of a compassionate God, and had even forgiven those who penitently sought His blessing. The kingdom He preached was indeed entered by some of them, and by His teaching they had been led into a purer form of life. We do not wonder that so many of this class should gather round Him to hear His words of peace and love.

2. *Who were these scribes and Pharisees?*

The scribes were the professional writers of the Scriptures, and "traditions of the elders," while the Pharisees were the most popular religious sect of that day ; and who carried out these traditions to the very letter. Between these two there was a close affinity, each party being necessary for the existence of the other ; hence they generally combined their opposition to Christ ; and unitedly sought to weaken His influence. Here it is said they murmured, and thus indignantly frowned upon His work of love.

3-7. *What is the object of this parable of the lost sheep?*

Several important objects are fulfilled by it, which it would be well to notice—(1.) That it is a defence of His own conduct, by a personal appeal to those who murmured at Him, "What man of you, having an hundred sheep, and should lose one of them," what would you do? Would you not seek it, and when found, would you not rejoice over your sheep? And, "I say to you, that likewise joy shall be in heaven over one sinner that repenteth." (2.) It was a concession that the sinners whom He sought had gone astray from the flock, but as you will seek your sheep when lost, so am I seeking those who have been lost from the flock of My Father.

8–10. Why have we a second parable to describe the lost?

There were two classes of persons who were the objects of complaint. There were sinners, who are fitly represented by a lost sheep, because of their wandering from the fold, and publicans, who are more fitly described by the piece of silver lost in the house. And as silver is valuable, and worth seeking after, so the woman seeks and finds her lost piece, and, with friends and neighbours who have sympathised, there is mutual joy in her dwelling. And Jesus repeats, "And likewise I say unto you, there is joy in the presence of the angels of God over one sinner that repenteth."

"There is joy in the presence of the angels." Is it the joy of angels to which Jesus alludes?

No; it is the joy of God, the owner of the sheep that had gone astray, and of the piece of silver that had been lost; a joy in which angels, like the neighbours and friends, may participate, but the source of the joy can only be looked for in the bosom of Him who now sees these lost ones restored.

11–32. What is the object of this parable of the prodigal son?

We see in it a striking difference between the heart of the Father, and the heart of the brother in the reception of this returned wanderer. The father's joy and the brother's frown present a most striking contrast.

Who are represented by these two sons?

The two classes named in the beginning of the chapter. The publicans and sinners are represented by the younger, while the scribes and Pharisees are seen in the elder brother. The younger had left his home and led a very dissipated life; while the elder had remained at home and kept himself free from vice.

Who is the father of these two sons?

God; who under the dispensation had been Father to both—to publicans and sinners, who had set themselves free from His claims, and to scribes and Pharisees, who still remained about the temple, the Father's house.

It is said by some that Jews and Gentiles are pictured in this family scene. Is it so?

The real actors in the scene are plainly stated, and I feel sure these murmuring scribes would see their own portrait in this murmuring elder brother.

CHAPTER XVI.

1–8. What lesson did Jesus seek to convey to His disciples by this account of the unjust steward?

The importance of strict faithfulness in all things committed to their trust; and, while spoken to His disciples, was also intended for covetous Pharisees who had used their position for selfish purposes. And, as they were listening to Him, it was needful to give them this severe rebuke.

What was the object of this unjust steward in reducing the rightful claims of his lord?

In order that he might ingratiate himself into the favour of those whose debts were unjustly reduced by him. So the hundred measures of oil, which one really owed to his lord, were set down fifty, and the hundred measures of wheat were set down fourscore. Formerly he had appropriated this overplus to himself, and thus defrauded his lord, and now that he has been accused of injustice, and is about to be called to account for it, he foresees the evil coming upon him, and still further unjustly plans to meet it. To make friends of his lord's debtors was his only hope, probably hinting that as he had shown favour to them, they would have to return it by receiving him into their houses.

How could his lord commend him when really a loser by his unjust dealings?

It was his crafty cleverness that his lord humorously noticed or praised, but declared him an unjust steward. Julian the apostate, a most bitter enemy to Christ, is said to have applied this to Him, and declared that by commending the unjust steward Jesus encouraged cheating.

What did Jesus mean by " the children of this world are in their generation wiser than the children of light"?

Not that they were wiser than believers who had counted all loss for Christ, but that they were wiser than scribes, Pharisees, and others who had God's law, and made such a poor use of it. The "children of this world"—*lit., sons of this age*—had opportunities which some of them improved, but these blind leaders did not avail themselves of the advantages of their position. "Children of light" He might call them, for they had God's Word, and God's

Son; but they were not wise in their generation, for they turned away from the truth, and followed the traditions of men.

9–12. *"And I say unto you, make yourselves friends of the mammon of unrighteousness," etc. Is not this strange advice for Jesus to give?*

Not when understood. I am inclined to think it was ironically spoken to them, and by His tone and look was known to be so. It is as if He had said to these Pharisees who afterward derided Him, well, make yourselves friends of the mammon of unrighteousness, *i.e.*, riches unrighteously obtained by devouring widows' houses, etc., and like this man, get a habitation that will serve you all your life, and what will you have then? Your riches will fail, and this age will come to a close, and you will then have nothing left. The case of the unjust steward must ever be kept before us, in order to understand this address, which was certainly intended for the Pharisees. This steward first defrauded his lord, and then when about to be put out of office, he turns to the people to serve his need. This was a true portrait of these unfaithful stewards of God's patrimony, and the advice which Jesus ultimately gives them is worthy of being pondered by all.

13. *"No servant can serve two masters." Can riches or mammon be a master?*

Riches can and do rule the hearts of all who yield to their influence, and if they rule, God cannot. Our actions must decide whether God or earthly things rule our spirit, as these will manifest who is our master.

14. *Why did the Pharisees deride Him when they heard these things?*

Because they consciously felt His powerful appeals, and contemptuously ignored His instruction.

16. *"The law and the prophets were until John." Did their autho-*

rity cease when John began to preach?

No; but the shadows of the one, and the prophecies of the other began then to be fulfilled. The preaching of the kingdom of God, so long foretold by prophets, commenced a new era, and as it was opened by divine authority, it could be lawfully entered. Those who accepted the new Teacher were released from the yoke of the law, and many that were condemned by it, were fully and freely forgiven by Him. No wonder that men pressed into the kingdom of God.

Is there any distinction to be made between the "kingdom of God is at hand," and the "kingdom of God is preached"?

Most certainly. The former showed that it was still future, though near, the latter that it was opened, or how could men press into it if it had no existence.

19–31. Is this account of the rich man and Lazarus a parable, or did it really occur?

Luke does not say that it was a parable, but reports Jesus as saying that there *was* a certain rich man; and that there *was* a beggar who *was* laid at his gate full of sores, etc., and he would be a bold man who dare affirm that there never were such men, and that these things which are said to have occurred never did take place.

But are there not difficulties in connection with this account that render it liable to rejection as a literal occurrence?

There are some things which are strange to us, but we must not reject them on that account. Angels carrying Lazarus to Abraham's bosom, and Abraham talking with the rich man, are both outside of our experience, but must be received as unquestioned testimony, whether it be according to our ideas or not. It will be right to say, that the word translated hell is *hades*, the unseen, in which place both Lazarus and the rich man were located after death, and in which we get a glimpse of their separate condition through this uncovering of the unseen by Jesus. But suppose we admit that it is a parable, and not a real occurrence, we are led to ask, Is the parable itself based on fiction? Can it be possible that Jesus would sketch these experiences as felt after death, if there was no such thing? Consciousness in the intermediate state is certainly taught by Jesus in this sketch, and even if admitted to be a simile to illustrate the condition of the nation after its dispensational death, yet that condition is set forth by what is affirmed to have taken place after natural death, so that either there is consciousness in that state, or Jesus has deceived us.

The rich man prayed for relief in his suffering. Why was his prayer not granted?

He was told by Abraham that no change in his condition could take place, and that Lazarus could not cross the fixed chasm that was between them, to minister to his relief. The expectation of deliverance from purgatorial suffering entertained by some has no support from this case.

Why was his prayer for his five brethren denied?

On the ground that God had spoken already by Moses and the prophets; and if these were not regarded, other messengers would fail to bring them to a change of mind.

Why does Abraham say that one from the dead would not be regarded?

It was prophetic of the unbelief of the class for whom this message was intended, for one did arise out from among the dead, and yet they repented not.

CHAPTER XVII.

1, 2. *Why " impossible but that offences will come" ? Could not God prevent them ?*

Yes ; if He prevented man's freedom of action, but this He does not see fit to do. He wishes man to yield to love, and not physical necessity. The condition of society as it then existed was before the mind of Jesus when He uttered these words, and He well knew that while the rulers of the nation rejected Him, and persecuted His disciples, there would be causes of offence— *i.e.*, stumbling—to all who wished to follow Him.

The offenders were under a great condemnation, but would the offended be excused ?

There can be no excuse in fearing and believing man rather than God, and it is well when those that stumble are delivered and forgiven.

3, 4. *Is this " take heed to yourselves" connected with offences ?*

It is a selected case for personal application. A brother may offend a brother, which, alas ! too often occurs. Now, there are two ways, either of which an offended brother may take :—(1.) He may act vindictively towards his brother, and avenge himself—this is the way of the flesh ; or (2.) He may show him his wrong in the spirit of meekness, and upon his repentance forgive him—this is Christ's way, and of this effort to restore they were never to weary.

5. *What has the increase of faith to do with this God-like spirit of forgiveness ?*

Very much indeed. In fact, all the difference between taking God's way and our own is involved in believing or not believing the teaching of Jesus.

6. " *If ye had faith as a grain of mustard seed.*" *Does Jesus teach here that a little faith would suffice for this occasion ?*

Not a little faith, but a growing faith,—a faith that will rise with difficulties, and overcome them.

Could any believer have faith enough to remove a sycamine tree ?

Yes ; if he had a promise, or a command to do so, not otherwise. Jesus was speaking to those who had received the power to work miracles, but the exercise of it required faith in Him who gave it, and when this was wanting there was signal failure, as the case of the demoniac fully shows (chap. ix. 40). The disciples had received power, but were not in a condition to use it. The fact is suggestive to all who labour for Christ. There should not only be the gift, but preparedness of mind to use it.

12–19. *There were ten lepers healed, but only one returned to thank the Healer. How was this ?*

This blessing came to them rather indirectly, as many other blessings do to those who enjoy them, and this became a test of their condition of heart. These lepers appealed to Jesus for sympathy, and He sent them to the priest, and " as they went they were healed." The cure came rather unexpectedly, but there was no mistaking it, and now, who should be thanked for the cure ? It was a question for their hearts, on which they did not decide alike. They had left the presence of Jesus uncured, and the change seemed to reach them like a general providence, and thus became a question as to who had a right to be acknowledged. So nine decided to go on to the priest, and but one, and he a Samaritan, returned to thank the Healer. If he must go to the priest, it shall be afterward, but Jesus must first be acknowledged. The nine must first go to the priest, and after they had been there they were hardly likely to return and thank Jesus, at least we do not hear of them doing so. There is a lesson in this simple narrative for us. We often seek for needed favours from God, which after all may reach us in an ordinary manner, and we may be ensnared into attributing our favours to circumstances rather than to Him who is the source of all blessing. God is our helper, and desires to be remembered by all to whom His help has been shown.

20. *"And when He was demanded of the Pharisees when the kingdom of God should come,"* etc. *Does His reply help us to understand anything of its nature ?*

I think so, but our understanding of His teaching will greatly depend upon the ideas we may have previously formed respecting it. According to Jesus, the kingdom had come, for publicans and harlots had entered into it, and yet the Pharisees had not even seen it. It was among them, and yet they had not recognised it, because they were looking for a kingdom in which national display would everywhere demonstrate its existence, instead of one in which truth should rule the hearts of obedient, loving subjects. The reign of heaven was not local, here or there, but within the obedient heart. This teaching of Jesus to the Pharisees forbids the thought of locality or external display of the kingdom of God under the present gracious administration. Even before Pilate, when Jesus admitted that He was a king, He patiently explained to him that His kingdom was not of this world, else would His servants fight. It is well to ponder these statements, that we may be preserved from expecting what God has never intended to give. Thousands have been disappointed by unwarranted expectations, and thousands more

are seeking and looking for unpromised things.

22. *What are these " days of the Son of man " which some would desire to see ?*

The period of His ministry, which was a season of blessing to many. It would be in the time of judgment upon the Jews when these days would be remembered, but looked for then in vain.

24. *What has the lightning to do with this threatened judgment ?*

It is an illustration of the peculiar relation which Jesus sustained to that judgment which was afterwards to fall upon the nation. For as the lightning may have its source in one part of the heavens, and shine and strike in some other part under heaven, even so should it be when the power of Jesus should be revealed. He should be on the throne at God's right hand, when the full consuming power of judgment should descend from Him upon the nation at Jerusalem.

26–30. *Why does He refer to the days of Noah and Lot ?*

Simply to show that the unbelief which prevailed previous to the judgment in their day would prevail when His judgment was manifest among them—men would not believe it until overtaken by it.

Jesus speaks of marriage in the days of Noah, but not in the days of Lot. Why this omission?

The omission is a sad revelation of the condition of Sodom. Among them the marriage relation was almost set aside, so that Jesus could not say of them, " they married." They were ripe for judgment, but heeded it not. So will this generation be, said Jesus, when the Son of man is revealed.

Can these days of Noah and Lot apply to any other period than that Jewish judgment of which He is here speaking ?

H

The disciples asked Him, " Where, Lord ? " that is, where will these things happen, and His reply has settled the matter for all who will receive it. " Wheresoever the body is, there will the eagles be gathered together." These Roman eagles did descend and devour the corrupted carcase of the nation. The Jew still lives, but his civil polity as a nation is no more. We cannot apply it to that which has no existence.

CHAPTER XVIII.

1–8. *What did Jesus mean by "men ought always to pray, and not to faint" ?*

That they ought to persevere until the much-needed and promised deliverance was obtained. It was a special lesson for the direction of His disciples under their approaching trials, and an assurance that God would appear on their behalf.

Was the parable intended to show the value of perseverance ?

Jesus shows, by the success of the importunate widow, who obtained her request from an unfeeling judge, how much more likely they would be to obtain redress from God, who was really interested in their welfare.

Who were these " elect " that required vengeance to be shown on their behalf ?

They were the saints that suffered during the period that preceded the judgment which came upon the Jewish nation. After the ascension of Jesus His disciples were sorely persecuted, as we may gather from the " Acts of the Apostles," which must have caused much crying out for deliverance. God heard their sighs for relief, and though He did bear long with their enemies and oppressors, He at last avenged or rather vindicated His chosen ones, and set them free from their cruelty.

" *When the Son of man cometh,*

shall He find faith on the earth ? " *To what period does this apply ?*

To the period of judgment that was coming on the nation, and of which He had just been speaking. That God would respond to the cry of His suffering children was certain, and that judgment would overturn their oppressors ,had been most solemnly declared ; but would they believe His testimony ? His question, " When the Son of man cometh (in judgment on this generation), shall He find faith on the earth ? " plainly intimates that He would not.

Is it right to connect this sentence, " the Son of man cometh" with that Jewish judgment, when it is generally applied to His return in person ?

Jesus Himself has so connected it, as the context in several places clearly proves. He declared to His disciples that some of them should not taste of death till they saw Him coming in His kingdom. This event, therefore, which some of their eyes should behold before death, is called by Him His " coming," and as such we must receive it. This coming, or presence in power by judgment, closed that dispensation, and is quite distinct from His return in person to judge the world.

9–14. " *Two men went up into the temple to pray.*" *Does Jesus refer to what actually took place ?*

It is very likely that some who heard it would see in it a sketch of their own worship. The Pharisees frequently went to the temple to count up their own works, especially those which included fasting, prayer, and alms, while publicans, so discouraged by public censure, scarcely dared to hope for mercy. It is a deeply interesting matter to read the Saviour's review of these two worshippers, and it must have startled some of those self-righteous ones, to hear Jesus declare that this pleading publican went down to his house justified rather than the Pharisee.

Why should the publican who could say nothing for himself, be justified rather than the man who could say so much?

Because the latter took the ground of his own self-imposed righteousness, which God could not accept; while the former sought God's propitiousness, and He could be gracious through the promised sacrifice. He had said by the prophet, "Though your sins be as scarlet, they shall be as white as snow," and the publican took this provided ground before God and obtained His mercy.

Why did the publican stand afar off?

I understand that the Jews had framed a traditional law, that no publican should be allowed to approach the temple within a specified number of spaces, and this law kept him far off from the place to which as a son of Abraham he had a legal right. But, though compelled to stand at a distance, his prayer could reach God.

15–17. Was it superstition that led these parents to seek for their children the touch of the Saviour's hand?

This is quite possible, and while Jesus granted their request, He made it the occasion of valuable instruction from which all might profit. It was as if He had said, if you want the kingdom, you must become childlike.

18–24. Was it mere compliment in this ruler to say to Jesus " Good Master"?

It was complimentary no doubt, but his address involved more than he thought of or intended. He gave to Jesus a divine title, and Jesus reminded him of what he had done.

Why does Jesus direct him to the law when he asks for eternal life?

As a Jew he was bound to keep these God-given precepts, but when he affirmed that for years he had kept them, he revealed the true state of his mind. If keeping the law would secure the privilege he desired, he was prepared to support his claim; but when Jesus applied the test of sacrificing all and becoming His disciple, he shrank from the offer and went away sorrowful. The man desired eternal life, but the test was too great for him.

25–30. Why should riches have been such a hindrance in entering the kingdom of God?

The difficulty arose out of the circumstances which surrounded the ministry of Jesus. The civil powers were so much opposed to Him, that to become His disciple not only endangered property, but even life itself. Peter said, we have left all and followed Thee; but how few that had this world's goods would leave them for the sake of the despised Nazarene. " How hardly shall they that have riches enter into the kingdom of God." A blessed recompense awaited all who accepted Jesus at any cost, but how few were found to do this.

31–34. Why could the twelve not understand about His death?

Because they reasoned against its possibility instead of believing His word. The testimony of His death and resurrection was for their faith, not their reason, and failing to believe, they could not understand.

CHAPTER XIX.

1–10. Zaccheus the publican seems to have been very anxious about Jesus. Why was there no open door for his access to Christ?

It was tradition that had closed the door, not God, and he, like many others, accepted this traditional verdict as of God, when it was only of man. The decision of the religious rulers of that day was, even if Jesus of Nazareth be a prophet, you, being a publican, have no right to speak to Him, so all that he attempted was a look, and on account of the crowd, he being little of stature, had to climb a tree in the way as his only apparent chance of seeing Him. *Zaccheus must have been startled at this proposed visit to his house, while others were annoyed. How could Jesus justify Himself in so doing ?*

Jesus assigned two reasons for His going to the house of Zaccheus, and to the first of these a Pharisee could hardly object, viz., that he was a son of Abraham, and therefore salvation should come to him. But a still higher reason was, that Jesus had come to seek and save the lost, and, although they murmured at Him going to be the guest of a sinner, it did not hinder Him responding to the craving of an earnest heart.

" Behold, Lord, the half of my goods I give to the poor," etc. Was this declaration made under the tree, or in after conversation ?

The Lord spent the day with Zaccheus, and I judge this to be the fruit of that interview. When he saw the grace of God, he was prepared both for restitution and benevolence.

11–27. *What was this parable about the nobleman intended to teach ?*

It was to correct their thought about Himself and the kingdom of God. They expected that Christ, the claimant to the throne of David, would at once declare His power and set them free from their enemies, and this carnal idea had to be corrected. The kingdom of God, which was indeed set up—for some had entered it by accepting the truth which Jesus proclaimed—and which kingdom was soon to be transferred to Him, was not a reign in which mere physical force would triumph over the force of Cæsar ; but a reign of righteous-

ness, peace, and joy in renewed hearts and lives. Instead of looking for this, they were looking to regain national power and glory, and a Messiah who could not do this was not the Messiah they expected. This parable was delivered to correct their false notion.

How could it do this ?

It presented a picture of God's arrangements, of which they should have taken advantage. The parable is doubtless based on facts with which they were familiar. According to Josephus, their own rulers, Herod, Archelaus, and Antipas, had to visit Rome in order to be invested with the imperial authority which their rule in the provinces necessarily called for ; but, when so invested, it was unlawful to refuse submission. His own departure to heaven, and His return in judgment upon that nation, is the true exposition of the parable ; and having deposited talents ere He departed— *i.e.*, revelations of this judgment—on His return He would know what every man had gained by trading. If this deposit of knowledge had been rightly used He would reward, but if not, they would be judged as wicked servants.

28–40. *Why did Jesus send for the colt ?*

To fulfil a prophecy which had been given of Him by Zechariah (ix. 9), and thus He obeyed the direction of the Spirit.

Was His riding into Jerusalem an act of triumph ?

It was rather an act of humility than of triumph, of meekness than of pomp and show. No doubt the simple-minded Galileans that accompanied Him were quite ready to usher Him into Jerusalem as "The king that cometh in the name of the Lord," but they knew not that He was riding on to shame and death, before that triumph could begin.

This thought is impressively rendered by Milman—

" Ride on ! ride on in majesty !
In lowly pomp ride on to die :
Bow Thy meek head to mortal pain,
Then take, O Lord, Thy power and
    reign."

Was there anything done by Jesus, on that short journey from Bethany to Jerusalem, that was likely to foster the hope of a national triumph ?

I think not, but rather the contrary. He had indeed, by fulfilling the prophecy of Zechariah, claimed to be the promised king, but the traits of His character were meekness, lowliness, and salvation ; and ere He left that lowly seat, instead of encouraging the vain hope of the nation, He, amid falling tears, foretold its fearful doom. In fact, through their unbelieving rejection of the great purpose for which He came, a crisis had arrived that nothing could change.

42. *"The things which belong unto thy peace." What things were these ?*
It is strictly *the things for thy peace,* and these were what He had made known during His ministry among them. Had His teaching been accepted, repentance and a new life would have followed, and thus they would have been saved from judgment.

"But now they are hid from thine eyes." How were these things hidden from them ?
By their unbelieving rejection of the truth as taught by Jesus a crisis in the history of the nation had arrived, and their doom was inevitable. "Their eyes have they closed," said Matthew (xiii. 15), and thus both life and judgment were hidden from them.

CHAPTER XX.

1. *Why did the priests and scribes challenge the authority of Jesus ?*
It was a combined effort to terminate His increasing influence as a teacher of the people. The hierarchy of that day claimed absolute authority as teachers, and forbad all others to meddle with these matters. John's right to baptise the people was questioned by them, and his reply was that God had sent him ; but when they demanded the authority of Jesus, He first of all asked them to decide a very simple matter, and made His own reply to depend on theirs.

4. *"The baptism of John, was it from heaven, or of men ?" Why ask such a question ?*
They had had to do with John's testimony, and rejected it, so He asks them for a reason. If John was self-sent, you did perfectly right, but if God sent him, what do you say for yourselves ? but they refused to answer His question through fear of being condemned, and so forfeited His reply.

9–16. *Was it their behaviour on this occasion that led Him to deliver this parable ?*
Not on this occasion merely, but during the whole of His mission they had shown this truth-rejecting spirit, and in the parable Jesus gives this graphic view of the character of their opposition. John, and the twelve, and the seventy, had all been employed about this vineyard, and their treatment of the servants was a matter of history; but when the Son was given up to their power, they killed Him and cast Him out, and that sin made their judgment a righteous one. It was an easy thing to say "God forbid," as He pictured the miserable end of the occupiers of this vineyard, but they had to learn by sad experience what they would not learn by testimony, viz., that sin and suffering follow each other:

17. *Why did Jesus quote from the 118th Psalm about the exalted stone ?*
It was to meet their "God forbid," or *lit.,* let it not be. That

quotation distinctly implied, You exalt yourselves by rejecting the God-provided stone, but God will make that stone the head of the corner, and then it will put you down.

18. *The stone was to break those who fell on it, while those on whom it fell were to be ground to powder. Does Jesus here speak of mercy and judgment, or a twofold judgment?*

Of a twofold judgment I presume. The Pharisees, scribes, and priests, who fell upon that stone were broken or crushed by its rising again; but when that stone fell on the nation, it did "grind to powder,"—or *lit., winnow,*—*i.e.*, as chaff is winnowed, or lifted up for the wind to drive away. *How could you prove this to be the application intended by Jesus?*

History proves the latter, for the nation was indeed winnowed and scattered; and (ver. 19) shows the former, for the "chief priests and scribes . . . . perceived that He had spoken this parable against them."

20-26. *"And they watched Him, and sent forth spies." Why did they do this?*

This wily question about paying tribute to Cæsar was their first attempt to cast Him out of the vineyard, but the effort only rebounded to their own shame.

"Is it lawful for us to give tribute unto Cæsar or not?" Why did the spies ask this question?

It was a political intrigue, and was intended to ensnare the Teacher. Their question was put so directly that they felt sure He would either say yes or no, but His answer only confounded them. "Show me a penny," said Jesus, and a penny was brought. "Whose image and superscription hath it? They answered and said, Cæsar's." The purport of His reply was, Well, then, why do you tempt me? In trading with Cæsar's coin, you own his sovereignty, and should give him his due.

"Render, therefore, to Cæsar the things which be Cæsar's, and to God the things which be God's . . . and they marvelled at His answer, and held their peace."

27-38. *Did the Sadducees, who next assailed Jesus, think of succeeding in argument better than their neighbours?*

No doubt they did, but soon found that their own defeat was as manifest as theirs. True, they assumed a resurrection, for the sake of argument, though absolutely denying future existence; but in bringing forward the strange case of the woman who had in her lifetime seven husbands, they gave Jesus the opportunity of a reply for which we should feel truly thankful.

Did Jesus intend His reply as a rebuke?

I think not. His reply is simply instructive; and it is interesting to note how different opposers are treated by Jesus. These Sadducees were not crafty opposers like the Pharisees, and were not denounced by Him. They were ignorant, but sincere though in error, and He tried to instruct them. The differences between this world and that are briefly but fully stated. In this world, said He, they marry, but in that, they neither marry nor are given in marriage; in this they die, but in that they never die, but are as the angels, being the children of God.

Does Jesus quote from Moses, in relation to Abraham, Isaac, and Jacob, to prove an intermediate state?

No, but to prove their resurrection,—a truth which these Sadducees denied. Jesus held that this truth was taught by Moses, when at the burning bush he called Jehovah the God of Abraham, etc. Hence it is shown that their death was not their annihilation.

41. *The Christ as David's Son, and*

yet his Lord, was a great puzzle to the scribes. Why did Jesus ask them to settle this perplexing question?

In order that, as they were unwilling to receive the solution of it in Himself, they might see their own ignorance.

Why did He charge them with devouring widows' houses? What was the nature of this crime?

These were widows of priests who had a portion allotted by the law, but whose patrimony was taken from them by traditional law, and transferred to these scribes and Pharisees. Jesus had to charge them with living on plunder, though for appearance they made long prayers.

CHAPTER XXI.

1. What treasury was this into which the people were casting their gifts?

It was the receiving chest of the temple into which the worshippers cast their free-will offerings.

2-4. On what principle could Jesus say that the two mites of this widow were more than the large gifts of the rich?

He measured the gifts by their individual resources, and not by the gifts themselves. The widow gave her all, they but a part of their substance. It was a new way of reckoning the value of gifts, but being God's way, it is worthy of being pondered. Many persons in giving a small sum term it the widow's mite, and as Jesus spoke so favourably of her mites, they conclude that the smallest gifts are thankfully received by Him. But her two mites were her all, and which of us have ever given that?

5, 6. Was it a measure of national pride that prompted this reference to the stones of the temple?

Possibly it was; but in order to prepare them for His teaching upon its approaching doom, He at once said that, beautiful as were these stones, the days were coming in which there should not be left one stone upon another.

7. Their question as to the time when this should take place was quite natural. Was the Saviour's answer sufficiently plain to determine when these things should come to pass?

The time as to date was not given, but the circumstances that were to reveal it were given with great minuteness, and for these they had to wait and watch. The time, therefore, was only to be known by the appearance of the events predicted.

8. Why did He say " Take heed that no man deceive you"?

Because deceivers would make capital out of His predictions, and announce themselves as " the Christ," and deceive the unwary. Do not go after them, said Jesus, but follow my directions.

9-19. How many things does He direct them to hear unmoved?

He said there would be false Christs, but these they were not to follow; and there would be wars and commotions among the nations, but these they were not to regard; earthquakes and famines were to occur, but none of these were the judgment predicted, but only signs of the disturbed state of society which would precede the crisis coming on the land. And though this beginning of sorrows would involve them in suffering, it would also furnish a testimony helpful to their own faith.

Could these directions be helpful only to those persons then living?

The predicted events were to occur in that generation, and could be directly helpful only to the persons who lived in the circle of their occurrence.

20, 21. What things were to move them to personal action?

The surrounding of Jerusalem

with armies was to be to them the signal of the approaching desolation, and at the approach of those armies they were to flee to the mountains, and allow nothing whatever to hinder their flight.

22. *What does He mean by, " For these be the days of vengeance," etc. ?*

The prophets foretold the day with many of its associations, as in Isaiah xxxiv. 8, and having that prophecy in their hands, they could study and learn its fearful character. Jesus therefore notes it, not as a new arrangement of God, but as a fulfilling of previously-declared judgment against their transgressions.

23, 24. *" Woe to them that are with child, and to them that give suck in those days." Does this apply to the disciples of Christ, or to those who suffered in the siege ?*

No woe rested upon His disciples, although they had to endure much trial ; it must therefore apply to unbelievers, and history records how terrible it was to be a mother in that siege, when hunger pressed them even to eat their own offspring.

Were the terrible things, which in these two verses Jesus affirms should take place, all fulfilled in that siege ?

Every one of them, without a single exception. There was distress without measure, and wrath unto the uttermost ; the sword devoured its thousands, and a multitude of captives were drafted off into Roman provinces ; while the ploughing up of the foundation of the temple, shows how completely Jerusalem was trodden under foot of the Gentiles.

" Till the times of the Gentiles be fulfilled." Is there any hope for Jerusalem in this declaration ?

Not a ray of hope in the verse itself, and to append one to it is to do so without authority. The times of the Jews extended from the giving of the law, to the judgment here predicted, and the times—*lit.*, seasons—of the Gentiles will extend to the period of Christ's return, and, guided by this prediction, we venture to affirm that their nationality will never be restored. Indeed, the prophet Jeremiah (chap. xix.) was commanded to take a potter's earthen bottle, and of the elders of the people, and of the elders of the priests, and to go forth into the valley of the son of Hinnom, and to declare in their hearing the events of this very siege. Let us carefully note his words as he breaks the bottle in their sight. "Thus saith the Lord of Hosts ; even so will I break this people and this city, as one breaketh a potter's vessel, that *cannot be made whole again."* We venture to say that the prophecy of this chapter was never fulfilled till the destruction by Titus, and this broken bottle, the symbol of a broken people, forbids all hope of restored nationality. Besides, God, having formed out of believers "a holy nation," is not likely to form again a secular one, or, indeed, one of any kind in addition to the Church, which is now His body.

25. *"And there shall be signs in the sun, and in the moon, and in the stars." Does He refer to the orbs of heaven ?*

No; it is the nation so designated. Jesus only repeats the language of the prophets, and these signs are the distress, perplexity, and revolution that was to occur among the people so visited. "I will shake the heavens and the earth, saith the Lord of Hosts" (Haggai ii. 6).

27. *What is meant by the Son of man coming in a cloud ?*

To those who heard Jesus this was sufficient to indicate the nature of His coming. That He did not come in person, but by the Roman army, the executioners of His wrath, is plain to all who will receive history for proof.

28. *What was this approaching redemption which His disciples were to expect ?*

Redemption from the persecuting spirit and power of the Jewish nation, the first great enemy of the disciples of Christ. From that time to the present they have had no power to persecute the saints.

32. *Was there anything said by Jesus to limit these things to that period ?*

He gave most definite instruction respecting the application of His words, " Verily I say to you, this generation shall not pass till all be fulfilled ;" and as " generation " applies strictly to the people then living, we must conclude that all was then fulfilled. Besides, he urges upon them the necessity of personal attention to sobriety, and freedom from secular ties, in order that they might be better prepared both in spirit and body for that sad event.

CHAPTER XXII.

1. *Why is the passover called the " feast of unleavened bread " ?*

Because during a period of seven days at the passover, the Jews eat unleavened bread, hence the two institutions were combined as one feast.

2. *Why does Luke refer to this feast in connection with their plot to kill Jesus ?*

Because they knew that He would be there to keep the feast, hence their plot in view of His visit to Jerusalem.

3. *How did Satan enter into Judas ?*

By his consent to betray Jesus he became a tool of Satan, a ready instrument for his work. By yielding to the temptation, Satan became his master.

7–14. *Was the man in whose house Jesus sought a place to eat the passover a friend, or a mere provider of rooms on that occasion ?*

From the message sent by Jesus, " The Teacher saith *unto thee*," I should judge that he was a disciple, and therefore gladly responded to the Teacher's request. The large upper room was furnished for the occasion, and there Peter and John prepared the passover, and at the appointed hour Jesus and His disciples sat down together.

15. *Why did Jesus so earnestly desire that passover ?*

Because that passover finished the typical age, and with His death all the prophecies concerning it came to an end. At that feast the sixty-nine weeks of Daniel's prophecy — the hebdomads or weeks of years—were completed, and He willingly yielded Himself to be and do all that was required of Him.

16–18. *" I will not any more eat thereof, until it be fulfilled in the kingdom of God." What did He mean by this ?*

The passover feast was typical, as well as memorial, and ere another passover returned, its antitype would be manifest in His death, which was the basis of a new administration. The passover, which was the first and the basis of the six feasts that followed, was not to be repeated until all had their fulfilment in Christian privileges.

" *And He took bread, and gave thanks, and brake, and gave to them, saying, This is My body which is given for you." How could the bread be His body ?*

The bread was not His body, nor did He intend His words to convey any such meaning, although many read the sentence as if He so taught. The Church of Rome holds that the bread is changed into His body by the act of the officiating priest (transubstantiation), while the Lutheran

Church holds that it is changed in the act of partaking of it (consubstantiation), both being in error respecting it; arising, we presume, through connecting statements which are really distinct. What Jesus did when He took bread, and brake it, and gave it to them to eat in remembrance of Him; and what He affirmed in saying, "This is My body which is given for you," must not be welded into one sentence. To do this is to make Him say what is not true, and what is not even common sense. Let us read His words, "This is my body which is given for you," or, *This body of Mine is given on behalf of you*, as a distinct truth, which it was very important to keep before their minds when partaking of the loaf, and we shall then have— what fact and testimony so abundantly confirm, viz.—a loving Saviour giving up His life for us. In giving them bread—*lit.*, a loaf—in the eating of which they might remember Him, it was not merely that they should recall in memory the giving up of Himself for them, but that in partaking of it they should have the opportunity of renewing their obligation to reproduce His life in their own. Breaking the loaf was not to symbolise His sufferings or death, as we have that in the blood, but for individual eating and participation in the life He lived and gave in service for them. True, in 1 Cor. xi. 24, we read, "This is my body which is *broken* for you;" but Biblical scholars in general have decided that "broken" should not be retained in this verse, and when omitted we should read, as in the version by Luke, "This is My body which is given for you." It may be well to note that we have four inspired versions of the institution of the memorial feast, just as we have four versions of the commission, and it is needful to read them all to form a correct understanding of what is intended. For instance, both Matthew and Mark record "This is My body," but omit "which is given for you," as supplied by Luke and Paul. It seems therefore necessary that when the briefer version is used, the fuller record should always be mentally supplied, and then we should be able to discern, not only what His disciples were to do in remembrance of Him, but also what He had done in giving Himself for them.

20. "*This cup is the new testament in My blood.*" How could the cup be the testament or covenant?

The cup was not the new testament, any more than the bread was His body; but we have here two distinct statements in relation to the cup and the covenant, just as we get in relation to the bread and His body. In order to understand this sentence, it will be well to read Matthew's version of this part of the institution. "And He took the cup and gave thanks, and gave it to them, saying, Drink ye all of it; for this is My blood of the new covenant, which is shed for many for the remission of sins" (chap. xxvi. 27, 28). From this we learn that neither the cup nor the blood is the new covenant, but were only complements of it. The facts of the case are simply these,—God made a new covenant, and Jesus sealed it with His blood, and gave to them the cup out of which they were to drink—the cup being a pledge to them that all the privileges of the new covenant were conferred upon them.

21. *Why does Jesus refer to the betrayer?*

He seems to have been startled with the thought that one was eating with Him as a professed friend, who yet was really an evil-plotting enemy. "But behold, the hand of him that betrayeth Me is with Me on the table."

22. *Why so openly refer to the sad doom of the betrayer, when the betrayal was predetermined?*

Not a predetermined act for Judas, but a predetermined degradation for Christ. The betrayal of man by his fellow had been common to every age, and to this deep insult Jesus was ready to submit. The betrayal of Christ by Judas, was not through any foreordination of God, but through covetousness, which had really become the governing purpose of his mind. To hear his doom pronounced, and yet betray Jesus, shows how powerfully this evil prevailed in his heart. To betray a guilty person merely for gain would be base enough, but Judas knew that Jesus was innocent, and yet betrayed Him for thirty pieces of silver.

24–27. *What was the occasion of the strife among His disciples?*

Their misunderstanding of the nature of the kingdom of God. Their carnal thought led to selfish ambition, and a desire for fleshly pre-eminence. To Peter the keys had already been promised, and this distinction granted to him may have started this rivalry, which must have been painful for Jesus to witness. His own example, " But I am among you as He that serveth," should have been a timely and instructive rebuke. Indeed, we do not think a repetition of it was ever again needed, as this rivalry was never again attempted.

28–30. *The continued faithfulness of the disciples was highly appreciated by Jesus. Did they then understand the nature of this promised reward?*

I think not. It was only when Jesus ascended to glory, and the Spirit descended at Pentecost, and the proclamation of salvation and condemnation began, that the nature of the reward promised by Jesus was really understood.

When did they sit on thrones?

We may answer this question by asking another, When did they sit at His table in His kingdom? and if facts are allowed to speak, the memorable scenes of the first Pentecost after His ascension will fully answer both. On that day, constrained and guided by the Holy Spirit, they began to deliver in princely authority the laws, statutes, ordinances, judgments, and promises of their exalted king ; at whose table, on that first day of the week, they sat as rulers under Him in the new administration. From that day those who accepted Jesus the Nazarene as the anointed Lord, did so through the preaching and teaching of these apostles. Then was fulfilled the word of the prophet (Isaiah xxxii. 1), " Behold a king shall reign in righteousness, and princes shall rule in judgment."

31–34. " *Simon, Simon, behold Satan desired you,*" etc. *Was this past or future?*

The desire or plot had been already formed, for Jesus knew about it, but the onslaught of the enemy had yet to be made. Peter evidently understood the trial to be before him, and expressed himself ready to meet any emergency. It was easy, no doubt, for him to say, " I am ready to go with Thee, both into prison and to death," but, while he knew his own willingness, he knew not the power of the circumstances that so soon would surround him. Jesus, however, knew and prayed for His disciple, that in that special trial his faith might not fail. Of this intercession Peter knew nothing until told of it, and this aspect of the pleading of Christ is very suggestive. We often think of His life, death, and ascension, let us not forget that He is making intercession for us. Out of our sight and hearing there are pleadings connected with our life always going on. It is a most cheering truth that we have a sympathising High Priest above.

35–38. *" When I sent you without purse,"* etc., *" lacked ye anything ? "* *" But now, he that hath a purse, let him take it."* Why this change ?

Jesus never failed to sustain His disciples while they were employed on that special mission, and His constant supply of their need furnished to them a special evidence that He was indeed the Son of God. But, when carrying on their work under the advocacy of the Spirit, this special providence and oversight of God would only be shared by them in common with other saints. And although He would never cease to care for them, yet they must use and husband their resources, since all they had would be needed in their future day of trial.

37. *What did Jesus mean by " the things concerning Me have an end " ?*

That all which had been written of Him would be fulfilled, even to His death with transgressors.

39. *Why did Jesus go to the Mount of Olives ?*

To pray — to seek help in His approaching trial. From Luke adding, " as He was wont," we judge that when at Jerusalem the Mount of Olives, and that part of it, the Garden of Gethsemane, was the closet into which Jesus retired to pray. From the regularity of His visits to this spot, Judas could count upon finding Him there, and though, like the beloved Daniel, He knew that persistence in His wonted course would end in His arrest, He delayed not to be in His chosen place. It is in the light of this record that we see a reason for His haste from the upper room, as recorded by John, " Arise, let us go hence." The time was drawing nigh, and He hasted away to be where He was wont.

42. *" Remove this cup."* What cup was this ?

I do not think it was death, because He came to die, and never shrank from it. It is more likely to be some trial associated with His death, and while asking its removal, He would not claim anything except in harmony with His Father's will.

43. *In what way did this angel from heaven strengthen Him ?*

Scholars say that the authenticity of this verse is doubtful, being omitted in many MSS. The following verse about the sweat of blood is likewise not well sustained. Both verses are therefore placed in brackets.

46. *" Why sleep ye ? rise and pray, lest ye enter into temptation."* What may we learn from this direction ?

We may learn that prayer is an unfailing resource in every trial. God can help when all other helpers fail, and to look to Him is all-important.

48. *Why did Jesus challenge this deceitful kiss of Judas ?*

It was as if He had said, Why not appear in your true character ? Why come with a kiss, when war is in your heart ?

50. *Why did Jesus heal the man whose ear had been cut off ?*

To fulfil His own teaching, " Bless them that curse you."

53. *" This is your hour and the power of darkness."* What does this mean ?

That for the season He was given up into their hands, to do with Him what they pleased. It is " your hour," *i.e.,* your opportunity for gratifying the base desire which has possessed you, " and the power of darkness," *i.e.,* of the authority of your rulers into whose hands I am now given. Jesus began to reason with them about the course they were pursuing, but reason was in vain. He might as well have reasoned with a wolf upon the propriety of relinquishing his hold o the lamb that had fallen into his power, as persuade these priests and elders to give up the victim of their hate. He was given up to their will, and they held Him till they had compassed His death.

54–62. *Was it fear that led Peter to deny his Master ?*

Not exactly through fear, but a change of circumstances occurred for which he was not prepared. Had he believed Christ he would have been ready for the event, but when he saw Jesus in the hands of sinful men, he lost confidence in Him as the Messiah, and thus his courage failed. There was fear doubtless, but his fear arose from his unbelief, and led to a threefold denial of his Master.

Where was Jesus when Peter denied Him ?

In the palace of the high priest, where, sitting with others, a maid discerned him,—*lit.*, by the light of the fire,— and charged him with being one of the disciples of Jesus.

66. *What was this council into which the elders, etc., led Jesus ?*

It was, *lit.*, the Sanhedrin or great council, and was formed of priests, scribes, and elders, whose decision was final among the Jews. Jesus had been tried before Annas, an ex-high priest, and Caiaphas, the actual high priest, which trials took place in the night, in connection with which we have many memorable events recorded. Then as soon as it was day, Jesus was led into the council or Sanhedrin and condemned as worthy of death. In each of these places much cruelty and insult was shown by His accusers ; for in addition to blindfolding Him and blasphemously speaking against Him, there are not less than five different words used by the evangelists in describing the cruel violent treatment He received at their hands.

CHAPTER XXIII.

1. *Why did they take Jesus to Pilate ?*

Pilate was the Roman governor of Judea, and as the Jews desired that Jesus should be crucified, he alone could order His execution. Hence after judging Him worthy of death, they led Him unto Pilate that he might pass the sentence.

2. *In seeking His condemnation by Pilate had they not to bring forward their charges against Him ?*

Yes, and with these they are prepared ; but in presenting their plea to Pilate, we at once discover their duplicity. Before the high priest they had condemned Him on the charge of witnessing to His divine sonship ; but before Pilate they are silent on this charge, and accuse Him as a political offender, even making Himself a king.

4–12. *Did Pilate accept their charge ?*

No. Contrary to their expectation, he decided to ask the prisoner as to the truth of the chief of these charges, and when asked, " Art thou the king of the Jews ?" Jesus assured him that He was, but according to John, He explained to Pilate's satisfaction that His kingdom was not of this world, and he had to return the charge into their hands as not proven against Him.

Why did his decision not end the trial ?

When, Pilate replied that he found no fault in Him, the chief priests were so exasperated by this favourable decision, that, fearing lest Jesus should escape out of their hand, they renewed their charge, and affirmed that from Galilee to Jerusalem He had stirred up the people.

Was it their naming of Galilee that led Pilate to send Jesus to Herod ?

No, but it led to enquiry, and

when he found that Jesus was strictly a Galilean, and as Herod was at the time also holding an official court in Jerusalem, He was passed on to him for trial. No doubt Pilate would feel relieved from a very serious responsibility, but the relief was only for a very short period.

Did the accusers of Jesus go along with Him to Herod ?

They seem to have mustered in full force before him, but the paragraph which contains the account of the trial only reveals the shameful character of the whole proceeding. Herod was exceeding glad to see Jesus, and hoped to have seen some miracle done by Him ; but when neither questions nor accusations, neither mockery nor derision, could move Jesus even to speak to him, he was provoked exceedingly, and returned Him to Pilate arrayed in a gorgeous robe.

Why did Jesus refuse to speak to Herod, when He answered the questions of Pilate ?

Between Herod and Pilate there was a striking difference. Pilate's questions were on the side of justice, while Herod's were for personal gratification. Up to this time Pilate had shown true nobility of character, while Herod was the truckling murderer of John. The silence of Jesus was a most fitting rebuke, and after He had been treated with great contempt, He was sent again to Pilate. On this occasion, however, instead of reopening the trial, Pilate declared that the conviction of Jesus had not been effected, and proposed to chastise and release Him. This announcement at once raised such a clamour, and the purpose of Pilate was so much shaken by it, that he ultimately yielded and gave orders for His crucifixion.

27–29. Were the women that bewailed Him, as He passed on to Calvary, His disciples ?

No ; for although their motherly sympathy moved them even to tears, their hearts were not drawn to Him as a Saviour. It is sad to think that He should have to tell them to weep for themselves and their children, in view of their approaching doom.

30. " Then shall they begin to say to the mountains, fall on us ; and to the hills, cover us." When did this take place ?

At the siege and overthrow of Jerusalem. John, who in Rev. chap. vii. 16, uses these very symbols in detailing that event, has not only fixed the true application of that part of the Revelation, but has enabled us to see that these approaching sorrows were before the mind of Jesus, when on His way to Calvary. These daughters wept over Him, but should rather have wept for themselves.

31. " If they do these things in a green tree." To what did Jesus refer ?

To Himself, to whom these soldiers had been so cruel in the day of His trial ; and by " the dry " to these " daughters of Jerusalem " to whom, in the day of their approaching trial, Roman soldiers would cause unmitigated sufferings.

39–43. What was it that led one of these malefactors to defend Jesus against the railing of the other ?

A deep conviction that He was unjustly nailed to that cross.

" Lord, remember me when Thou comest into Thy kingdom." Was it not a strange petition to ask under such circumstances ?

Very strange indeed. Possibly there was not another person in the world, that would have asked the same thing under such circumstances as this dying robber. During His ministry Jesus taught His disciples that He would die by wicked hands, and be raised from death to life and glory ; and, that this man believed His testimony, is proved by his request. There was not another being in the universe except Jesus, who was then dying on the cross, to whom such a request was really appropriate, as He alone could grant his petition, and to Him, helpless as He was, the dying man cried out, " Lord, remember me when Thou comest into Thy kingdom." A clearer manifestation of faith in Jesus could not have been given, and it must have been truly refreshing to Him when dying on the cross to hear the man at His side own Him as Lord, and ask to be remembered in His future triumph.

Do you not consider this malefactor as being previously a very bad man ?

The terms " thief "—*lit., robber*— and " malefactor "—*i.e., evil-doer*— give us a most unfavourable view of the man. I am, however, inclined to think that his crimes arose more from his opposition to the Roman yoke, under which his countrymen groaned as slaves, than to a bad, immoral principle that is attached to the name of thief. It was, I presume, his opposition to Roman tyranny that led to his arrest and death. He had refused the yoke, and suffered as an outlaw against the dominant power of Rome. That he had heard Jesus during His ministry, and understood the truth of His claims, can scarcely be doubted, and on the cross he had an opportunity of expressing his faith.

" *To-day shalt thou be with Me in paradise.*" *What did this mean ?*

That he would have a realisation of blessing sooner than he expected.

Was His promise to be fulfilled that very day ?

Most certainly. There could be no force in His words if the promise was deferred thousands of years.

That day both entered into Hades,— *i.e.*, the unseen state,—and an entrance into paradise, which was in the unseen, and into which Jesus entered, was also promised to this dying malefactor. Both entered into paradise that day, while, three days after, Jesus left it to reoccupy the body He had abandoned on the earth, and in due time to ascend to heaven.

It was a very sudden change from the cross, a penalty of broken law, to the paradise of God. How could he be so soon prepared for it ?

On the ground on which any person is prepared for it—viz., by a reception of Jesus, the Son of God. This preparation is absolutely necessary, both for the church, for paradise, or for glory. When Christ is received, and we are permitted to live a while on the earth, and are guided by Him, we shall enter His church ; and if called to leave the earth, we shall enter paradise, and when He shall come again, we shall enter glory. We must not look upon the reception of this dying man as a mere arbitrary act of the Lord Jesus, but the manifestation of His grace according to His own revealed will. His acceptance differed nothing from that of Abel or of Paul, it was only the circumstances that were peculiar.

Some read, To-day, I say to thee, thou shalt be with Me in paradise— i.e., *at some future time. Is this correct ?*

Jesus went to paradise after death, and it must be then or never, as at His ascension He went to heaven, not paradise.

50–53. Joseph of Arimathæa " begged the body of Jesus " for burial. Why did he do this ?

He had doubtless read and believed the prophecy by Isaiah (liii. 9), that His grave should be with the rich, and he was ready for the emergency, and prepared to do the will of God. That he believed the Scriptures concerning the death and burial of Jesus is evident, for the tomb, and the great stone, and the linen, were all ready for the hour.

54. *"And that day was the preparation, and the sabbath drew on."* What *"preparation"* and *"sabbath"* was this?

It was in the evening of the preparation day of the passover, when all the lambs were killed for the feast, that Jesus was crucified, and on that evening, when He was laid in the tomb, the people in Jerusalem were keeping the passover. The sabbath here referred to is not a seventh-day sabbath, but a passover sabbath, on which no servile work was allowed. We should read, *and a sabbath drew on.*

CHAPTER XXIV.

1-8. *Were the spices, brought by these women to the sepulchre, tokens of affection to Christ?*

They were tokens of affection toward His lifeless body, but were also proofs of their unbelief. Had they believed His word, they would have gone forth to meet Him, and not to embalm His body.

Did the empty sepulchre undeceive them?

No; it only perplexed them, because they did not even think of His resurrection, and it was only when the shining ones announced that He was risen, that His words were recalled to their minds.

9. *Why were the women the first to learn from the angels that Jesus had risen?*

They were the first to go to the sepuchre, and this was their recompense. They also were made the first bearers of the glad message. It is a fitting sequel to the sad fact, that those who were the first to

cause the need of a Saviour, should have the privilege of first making known that He was risen from the dead. The eleven first heard from the women that Jesus was alive again, but their words were as idle tales.

12. *Was Peter convinced by the empty sepulchre that Jesus was risen?*

Not fully. He was only filled with wonder when he saw the orderly way in which the linen clothes were laid, and further evidence was required ere he would believe that Jesus was alive.

13-24. *Why were these two disciples going to Emmaus?*

It was possibly the home of one or both of them, and having waited to the third day without obtaining any reliable evidence about Jesus, they decided to wait no longer, and started for their homes. Still their minds were anxious, and the events of the preceding days became the theme of their conversation. It was while they were thus conversing, with sad looks and sadder hearts, that Jesus drew nigh, and asked the purport of their trouble, and, thinking Him to be a stranger, they related the whole matter of His death, and rumours of His resurrection, but of which they were not yet satisfied.

25. *Why did He call them fools, etc.?*

It is strictly "thoughtless"—*i.e.,* without the intelligence which a hearty reception of prophecy would have given them, especially upon the one source of their difficulty, viz., that the suffering of the Messiah must precede His glory. This at once became His theme, and from Moses and the prophets, the Divine Expositor opened up these great truths, and made them so plain that I presume they wondered how they had overlooked them.

29. *Why did they press Him to abide with them?*

The reason assigned was that the day was far spent, but possibly there was a secret desire to learn more of the things of which they had already heard so much; and also that He might share with them their evening meal.

31. *How did they get to know Him at the table?*

Their eyes, which had been holden, were opened, and at once they knew Him, but in a moment He was gone from their sight. No doubt they were much startled by this unexpected appearance, and after gazing in wonder upon the vacant seat, they decided to return with the good news to Jerusalem. Having arrived there, the eleven are found gathered together, and each party has to report an appearance of their Lord.

33. *Why did the eleven gather on that first day of the week?*

By a previous direction of Jesus, and in order to commemorate His death.

Did He enter by the door, or supernaturally?

It was while they were talking together, the doors being shut, that He appeared in their midst, and must therefore have entered in a supernatural way. At first they were affrighted, and thought a spirit was before them, and were convinced of their mistake only by handling His body, and seeing Him partake of food.

44. *Did the death and resurrection of Jesus fulfil all that Moses and the prophets had written concerning Him?*

Not all. The preaching of repentance and remission of sins in His name among all nations had to follow, and of these things both Moses and the prophets had written.

"And behold I send the promise of My Father upon you." What promise was this?

The promise of the Spirit, and in the fulfilment of it they would be endued with power, and fitted to sustain a perfect ministry among men.

50. *"And He lifted up His hands and blessed them." What did those uplifted hands indicate?*

Priestly benediction; and a more fitting close to His loving ministry on earth could not be conceived. It was under those uplifted hands, and that benediction of peace, they were to carry on their labours during His absence. No wonder that they returned to Jerusalem with great joy, and while waiting for the promise, were continually praising and blessing God.

JOHN.

CHAPTER I.

1-3. *"In the beginning was the Word." To what period of time does John refer?*

To the creation of the world—to the time when all things that are began to be.

What does he mean by "The Word"?

It is a term by which he designates Him who was made flesh, and as he writes, "Dwelt among us, and we beheld His glory." We have therefore no difficulty whatever in deciding that Jesus, who became incarnate, was previously with God, and was God.

Why is Jesus called the "Word"?

It is used as a symbolic term, in

I

order to show that Jesus is the revealer of God. For just as words
reveal man's heart, thoughts, and
purposes, so by Jesus the character,
thoughts, and purposes of God are
revealed to man.

*John gives no account of the birth
of Jesus. Why does he omit so interesting a matter ?*

John is writing to prove that
Jesus was the Son of God, hence
His deity and pre-existence are the
great matters to be proved in this
record. During the life of Jesus the
scribes and Pharisees denied His
pre-existence, and when He said to
them on one occasion, " Before
Abraham was, I am, they took up
stones to cast at Him." After the return of Jesus to His Father, although
mighty works were done in His name,
they still refused to own Him as the
anointed Son of God. The testimony
of the apostles was set at nought, and
those who did believe it were persecuted and driven away. Now this
gospel of John is the last gracious
testimony of Heaven to this Christ-
rejecting nation of the Jews, and on
their behalf this record was made.
The mightiest proofs that His life
and teaching could furnish are here
presented, not to show that such a
person as Jesus of Nazareth was born
and lived among them, but that He
was sent from the Father to be their
Lord and Saviour.

*4, 5. " In Him was life." To what
life does John refer ?*

Not only to the life which is
evolved in creation, but to that also
which is through the Gospel—for
both natural and spiritual life are
from Him who was, and is, and is to
come.

How is He the light of men ?

By the truth, which enlightens all
who receive it.

*What was the darkness in which
the light was shining, yet was not
comprehended by it ?*

The ignorance of the Jews among
whom He taught, but who through
unbelief did not lay hold of the
truth.

*Why did he refer to John the
forerunner ?*

It is simply to show the contrast
between a witness of the light and
Him that was the true light.

9. *" Which lighteth every man that
cometh into the world." How can this
be true when so many are in darkness ?*

Jesus has revealed all truth necessary for the enlightening of all men ;
but as this light can only enter by
the understanding, through belief of
the truth, these conditions are always
involved. If men are not enlightened, it is either a want of knowledge
or a rejection of the truth.

10. *" The world knew Him not."
Is it of the Jews that John makes
this charge ?*

Yes ; they had ceased to be God's
people, and were fitly termed "the
world" by Christ Himself. They
knew Jesus only as the son of
Joseph, but never apprehended
either His divine character or His
mission.

11. *" He came unto His own, and
His own received Him not." Is it to
His coming to them in general, or to
something special that John refers ?*

John doubtless refers to a special
case, the particulars of which Luke
(chap. iv.) has carefully detailed.
We must, therefore, observe that
" own," which is repeated in this
verse, is (in Greek) first in the
neuter and then in the masculine
gender ; and this should be carefully
noted, in order to make a right application of this twofold reference.
We may, therefore, read, " He came
unto His own [home or city, *i.e.*,
Nazareth], and His own [people] received Him not." We are told by
Luke that, after His baptism and
temptation, He returned in the power

of the Spirit into Galilee, and the fame of His great works followed Him into Nazareth. Here, however, instead of being received as the Christ, they sought to take His life. It is to this rejection that John refers.

12. "*His own received Him not, but as many as received Him, to them gave He power,*" etc. *What are we to understand by this?*

That the people generally, both in Nazareth and in the nation, did not receive Him as the Messiah of God; but there were some who did so, and for these the high privilege of sonship was prepared.

"*To them gave He power to become the sons of God.*" *What power was this?*

It is *lit.* authority, or right to be so, and was conferred on all who did receive Him. The proclamation of the kingdom of God as a reign of truth and righteousness had opened up to the nation a gracious arrangement for union with God as their Father. In His own immersion in water, to which Jesus had been led by the will of God, and was thus begotten by the truth, and born out of the womb of water, He became the first-born of a new family, and was publicly owned by God the Father as His Son. Thus did He not only set an example to others, but was empowered to bestow this high privilege of sonship on all who in loving obedience received Him as the anointed of God, or in other words, all who confided in Him, and were baptised according to His will, became His disciples. Hence John adds (iv. 1, 2), that Jesus made and baptised disciples, who being born out of water and of the Spirit entered the kingdom and family of God. And all such were taught by Him to approach God as "Our Father which art in heaven."

What does John mean by "not of blood, nor of the will of the flesh," etc.?

That this spiritual relationship was effected by a new arrangement, and was altogether independent of fleshly relation to Abraham, or indeed of any plan of man. God proposed and adapted it to all His creatures, and those who accepted it were begotten of Him.

14. "*And the Word was made flesh.*" *What is implied in this statement?*

Both His pre-existence, and His incarnation. When John says, "The Word became flesh," he plainly intimates that He existed before He did so, and that the Word who became flesh was Jehovah, whose glory the prophet Isaiah had seen. Hence the word "became" clearly indicates that He who "was with God," before the world was, and "was God," took upon Himself this new form of existence in order to redeem men from ruin and death.

15. "*John bare witness of Him.*" *Why refer to this witness?*

Because John's testimony was in harmony with the purpose of this Gospel. John affirmed that Jesus was superior to himself, and was not only preferred before him, but was before him.

16. "*And of His fulness have all we received, and grace for grace.*" *What does this mean?*

We shall best understand his meaning by carefully noting what they did receive as the witnesses of His grace. They not only received the Holy Spirit, with demonstrations of power, but also many spiritual gifts and privileges which were all bestowed in the name of Jesus. In fact, the Church, the body of Christ, in its manifest possession of gifts and graces, was the fulness of Him who filleth all in all. These gifts and graces had never been possessed before, and John is careful to note that all were derived from Jesus. By "grace for grace" I understand him to mean, favour upon favour, abundance of favour—one favour pressing upon another until the grace became manifold. The grace bestowed on them, was all through the grace that dwelt in Him.

18. *"No man hath seen God at any time." How can this be reconciled with Exod. xxiv.* 10, *"And they saw the God of Israel"?*

The elders of Israel did indeed see Jehovah, the God of Israel, as also did Isaiah, who wrote (chap. vi. 1) "I saw also the Lord,"—*lit.*, Jehovah. We therefore judge that Jesus here refers to the Father, whom no man hath seen or can see, but who was manifest of old by Him who was known as Jehovah, and again by Him, when known as Jesus.

19–28. *John alone records this interview between the priests and John the immerser. Why does he narrate it?*

John is writing for conviction, and this open confession of the harbinger of Christ concerning his work as made known by the prophets, is most valuable. "I am not the Christ," said John; I am only a preparer of "the way of the Lord."

Why did they make his baptising of the people a point of dispute?

Because it initiated into a new service, and was understood to change the standing of those who submitted to it. They might therefore well say, Why do you baptise? if you are not the Christ, nor Elias, nor that prophet. John's answer was plain, I immerse in water unto repentance, but the Master is among you, and then greater things will be done by Him. The witness of this distinguished messenger is most valuable in this Gospel record.

Had Jesus been immersed when the priests and Levites made this enquiry of John?

That He had been immersed there can be no doubt, else he would not have said He is among you, though you know Him not. John had immersed Him, and had seen the Spirit descend and rest upon Him; but after His immersion He had withdrawn into the wilderness, and had not reappeared to him previous to this interview with these officials from Jerusalem.

29–34. *"The next day John seeth Jesus coming unto him." Was it the day following his testimony to the Pharisees?*

This appears almost certain. After His temptation in the wilderness which continued during forty days, He again appeared to John and received his public testimony that He was the Christ.

"And I knew Him not." How does this agree with Matt. iii. 13, *where it is said that John refused to immerse Him, and must therefore have known who He was?*

John may have known Him to have been a holy person, but only as the Messiah, when the appointed sign was given. When the Spirit rested upon Him then he knew Him as the one who should immerse in the Holy Spirit.

35–42. *The witness borne by John on the second day was a private one. Why was it given?*

For the sake of the two disciples who were standing with him when Jesus passed by, and upon his testimony one of them followed Jesus, and after being satisfied that he had found the Messiah, sought out his brother Simon, and brought him to Jesus. When Jesus beheld him, He gave to him the name of Cephas, which means Peter, *i.e.*, a stone, a term suggestive of a most important and vital relation to Himself as the rock-foundation. This last may be called John's third witness to Christ. His first witness was to the priests and Levites who had been sent from Jerusalem to ask him, "Who art

Thou?" This witness should have borne much fruit, but reasoning and unbelief prevented this result. His second witness was before the multitude when Jesus Himself was present, and was intended to prepare them to receive His ministry. The third witness was private, and led some of his own disciples to follow Christ. Thus officially, publicly, and privately, did John witness to the Lamb of God ; a witness which was afterward used by Jesus in His controversies with the Jews, with great effect.

43. *" The day following Jesus would go forth into Galilee." Was this a third day ?*

Yes ; and on this day there is a further gathering to Him of those who became His disciples. The personal influence of those who had found the Messiah was soon in operation, and brother brought brother, and friend brought friend to Jesus, until five loving hearts were firmly knit to Him.

46. *Why was Nathaniel so unwilling to receive Jesus of Nazareth as the promised Messiah ?*

The prophets had written that the coming One should be born in Bethlehem, but Philip spoke of Him as " Jesus of Nazareth, the son of Joseph," and as such he was unwilling to receive Him. However, a word about the fig-tree removed his difficulty, and at once he confessed Jesus as the Son of God.

51. *What did Jesus mean by " angels ascending and descending upon the Son of man " ?*

Just what they were afterward permitted to see. At the sepulchre, and upon Mount Olivet, angels descended and ascended and conversed about Him who now spoke with the wondering Nathaniel. Heaven was indeed opened to earth by the visits of these celestial beings.

CHAPTER II.

1–10. Is it not strange that Jesus should attend a marriage feast ?

Not at all. Marriage was an institution of God, and Jesus could honour it with His presence. It is evident that Jesus mixed freely with the people, and never stood aloof from them unless it was most prudent to do so. Hence we find Him in scenes of joy, as well as sorrow; in the cottage of the lowly, as well as the mansions of rich Pharisees. Indeed, He never seems to have refused an invitation from any that wished to have Him for a guest. It is, however, well to notice one feature in all His visits. He never went but as a teacher, and every invitation was taken up as an opportunity for usefulness. In this aspect He is a striking example to all His disciples.

Why did His mother say to Him, " They have no wine " ?

Because she evidently believed in His power to supply what was needed for the occasion.

Why did He say to her, " Woman, what have I to do with thee ? Mine hour is not yet come " ?

His words reveal a very important feature of His life, which, from His immersion to His death, was ever manifest—viz., that all must be done to the glory of God. It was as if He had said, I am not now under your control, nor indeed under my own : I am now God's servant, and whatever is done by Me must be done for His glory. So that when He said, " Woman, what have I to do with thee "—*lit., What to thee and to Me, woman ?* (is this matter of supply ?)—she perfectly understood Him to mean that it must be done for no other purpose than to glorify God, and to reveal His own subjection to the Father. John tells us that this end was secured, and that in this "beginning of miracles" the five disciples who followed Him saw His glory, and believed on Him as the Messiah.

There were six waterpots of stone, containing two or three firkins apiece. What is a firkin?

It is *lit.* a measure, and as rendered by Josephus is a bath, about nine gallons.

Why command to fill them to the brim?

That all might see that no deception was practised, but that a real miracle was wrought.

When did the change from water to wine take place?

In drawing it from the vessel. In the pot it was water, and remained water as all could see, but in drawing it out for the guests it was wine. This provision for the occasion was a proof of divine power in Jesus, and while it met the necessity of the season, must have solemnised all hearts that partook of it, and with the closing of the feast the miracle ceased.

Some persons charge Jesus with encouraging intemperance. Is this charge a just one?

If the drugged intoxicating drink of the present day is the standard by which such persons measure the provision made by Jesus, I do not wonder at the charge ; but we should be careful not to liken the wine supplied by Jesus to the wretched outcome of man's vile sensuality. What Jesus did was right, and ought never to be questioned.

Is there any dispensational teaching in this marriage feast?

I am inclined to think so, and this thought is sustained by the many remarkable things associated with the ministry of Jesus. The wine of the old Jewish marriage feast was all done when Jesus and His disciples were called to share in

its festivities. He alone could and did supply what was needful. As out of water, the symbol of death, wine was drawn by His direction to supply this feast : so from His own ministry in life and death, there did flow out the new wine of the new marriage feast. Still, as the wine on that occasion was obtained only in the drawing, so now joy comes only through believing. They drew to prove the luscious supply, so must we draw from the smitten rock, to taste and see how good the Lord is.

11. *Why does John note this as the "beginning of miracles," leading to conviction of those who became His disciples?*

Because it was the first of a series of signs given to prove that Jesus was the Son of God, and is recorded by John to convince others of this same great truth. Here he distinctly states that the first miracle secured the confidence of those who had left all and followed Him, and then goes on to record many others, in order that those who read may believe that Jesus is the Christ, the Son of God.

13–17. *Jesus found in the temple some that were making it a place of merchandise. Why did He drive them out?*

If we read, *And, making a scourge out of rushes, He drove them all out of the temple, both the sheep and the oxen;* we shall see that it was the cattle and not the people that He drove out. Every house in Jerusalem was being cleansed from leaven, but His Father's house was defiled by their unrighteous traffic. The cattle therefore were driven out, the tables of the money changers were thrown over, and them that sold doves were commanded to take them away. It was no doubt a very unexpected interference with their business, but none dared to resist.

18–22. The Jews asked Him for a sign. Why did they demand it ?

No doubt they were highly offended at what He had done, and demanded proof for His authority to interfere with their arrangements.

" Jesus answered and said unto them, Destroy this temple, and in three days I will raise it up." What force was there in the sign He proposed ?

The force of truth and omniscience; and, although the Jews mistook the saying, and applied it to their magnificent temple, yet it was afterwards remembered by His disciples, and strengthened their faith when He was raised from the dead.

23–25. Many were led by His miracles to believe in Him. Why was He so doubtful of their professed faith ?

Because He knew their fickleness of mind, which in their after conduct became so manifest. He knew what was in man, and therefore did not commit Himself to them.

CHAPTER III.

1–4. Did this interview with Nicodemus occur while Jesus was at this passover feast in Jerusalem ?

This is almost certain, and but for the division made by the chapter commencing here, and the omission by our translators, who failed to render a little but very important Greek particle, this would have been apparent. The word which has been passed unrecognised is the conjunctive particle *de*, usually rendered *but*, and serves to call attention to the fact that the word or clause with which it stands is to be distinguished from something preceding, and usually having an *opposing* or *adversative* force. See Lex. Now to supply this neglected *but* we shall see at a glance the connection, and may also gather from it a very instructive

lesson. John had just said of some Jews, " But Jesus did not commit Himself to them, . . . for He knew what was in man," and then adds, *" But there was a man named Nicodemus,"* etc., and to this man Jesus did commit Himself, and in some retired place, under the cover of night, He unfolded to his wondering mind the truth and love of God, just showing that wherever there is a heart for Christ, Christ is ready to meet that heart. Nicodemus really wanted instruction, and Jesus was ready to impart it.

What led Nicodemus to the conclusion that Jesus was sent by God ?

The miracles he saw done by Him, and over which he had thoughtfully pondered until he could say, " We know that Thou art a Teacher come from God ; for no man can do these miracles that Thou doest except God be with Him."

Were the teachings of Jesus on that night a reply to his questions ?

They were rather a reply to his need, which Jesus knew better than himself, and at once began to teach him the lessons he required to learn.

What lessons did Jesus teach him on this occasion ?

There were at least two, which to him were both new and difficult to receive. The first was, that in order to have a place in the kingdom of God, he must be born again, a statement which implied that he must have a new life. He, in common with all his brethren, vainly thought that his relation to Abraham gave him a claim to all divine favours; he therefore marvelled at the Teacher's first lesson, " Ye must be born again." The second lesson taught him by Jesus was possibly as perplexing as the first, viz., that God loved not the Jew only, but the whole world, and, in giving His Son, had made provision for " whosoever believeth in Him." Nicodemus required to know these divine lessons, and though he marvelled at them, they were at last fully received by his confiding spirit.

Is " born again" a proper rendering of the Greek word anothem ?

In the margin we read " born from above," and scholars tell us that these alternate renderings of this word have been used from the time of Chrysostom in the fourth century, who refers to both renderings as common in his day. No doubt the word used by Jesus, here rendered " again," and in the margin " from above," has a definite meaning which neither of these renderings fully express, and which possibly no single word in our language will fully render. This much, however, is plainly taught, that a natural birth will not secure spiritual privileges to any one. Nicodemus was a Jew, and by his natural birth a right to all the privileges of that dispensation were secured, but he has now to learn that unless " born again, he cannot [even] see the kingdom of God."

" Cannot see the kingdom of God." Why should it be invisible to those outside of it ?

Because it is a reign by means of the truth concerning Jesus; and only those who are obedient to Him can see the sceptre of His royal hand. Obedience to Christ is a voluntary acceptance of the reign of God, which unbelievers fail to recognise. If the kingdom of God had come with observation or outward show, even spiritually blind Pharisees might have seen it, but though among them in those who were obedient, they saw it not.

5–7. Why did Jesus say to Nicodemus, " Except a man be born of water and the Spirit, he cannot enter the kingdom of God " ?

To correct his mistake in supposing that Jesus spoke of a natural birth. The birth spoken of was to follow a

begetting by the truth, and this is the reason why the Spirit is associated with the birth. The birth was to be *lit. out of* water ; immersion in water of those who believe in Jesus having been appointed by Him. We may also conclude, that as none could enter or be subjects of this kingdom unless thus born, all who thus became obedient did really enter into it.

May not water be used here as a symbol of the truth ?

The Spirit Himself is the symbol of the truth, and His name is frequently used in the Bible for the testimony which is from Him, and we are not likely to have two symbols in one sentence for the same thing. Besides, we know that immersion in water is appointed for all disciples, and it is not strange that Jesus should tell Nicodemus of this Heaven-appointed way. He never omitted to make known the will of God, whatever His professed servants may do, and it is from Him we must learn the whole will of God. It is, therefore, from a womb of water that the newly-begotten of the truth come forth into the kingdom of God.

Is it not harsh to assert that a man cannot enter the kingdom of God without immersion ?

It may appear so ; but when we consider that immersion in water of penitent believing confessors of the Lord Jesus is His own appointed way of admission, and publicly announced in His name, we should not count it harsh to be so instructed. Immersion in water of those who believe, is a positive institution, and one which cannot be changed without challenging the divine prerogative to do as He wills. When Jesus affirms that we cannot enter into the kingdom of God without this birth of water and the Spirit, it would be bold of any one to say that we can. It is far better to obey, than to question the arrangements of Heaven. We may reason that if we are only sincere, one way is as good as another, but if we thus take upon us to act out some human plan, we assume a very serious responsibility.

What did Jesus mean by " That which is born of the flesh is flesh ; and that which is born of the Spirit is spirit " ?

The sentence is elliptical, and easily supplemented. " That which is born of the flesh is (a child of the) flesh, and that which is born of the Spirit is (a child of the) spirit. That which is born is a child in both cases, but the difference is as wide as the causes that produce them. A birth of the flesh gave a right to fleshly standing and privilege, but " flesh and blood cannot inherit the kingdom of God ; " therefore Jesus could say, " Marvel not that I said unto thee, ye must be born again."

8–10. Why does Jesus refer to the wind, to illustrate the birth of a child of God ?

Our translators have made Him do so, but scholars have decided that it should read *Spirit* and not " wind." Hence it would be better to read, *The Spirit breathes where He wills,* that is, He sends the life-begetting message by whomsoever He pleases, *and thou hearest the voice—i.e.,* the message—*but knowest not whence it comes,* NOR WHITHER IT GOES.

When Jesus said " Thou knowest not whence it cometh," etc., was it spoken of Nicodemus specially, or does it apply to every one ?

To him most certainly, and must have been a reproof to a " master of Israel," not to know that the Spirit of God selected His own messengers to convey His own truth. But to say that no one knows, or can know these things, is an unwarrantable application of the Saviour's words.

What does Jesus mean by " So is every one that is born of the Spirit " ?

In this way they are born, or more strictly begotten, that is, by the message of the truth, which is a life-begetting message in all who receive it.

11. " We speak that we do know, . . . and ye receive not our witness." Is this an illustration of the Spirit breathing by whom He will, and the testimony not heard ?

It is a practical illustration of this very complaint made. Jesus had spoken to them of judgment coming upon the nation, and they had not believed His testimony, how would they then believe in heavenly things ?

13. " The Son of man who is in heaven." How could this be true of Jesus when conversing with Nicodemus ?

If we read it as John's testimony, and not the testimony of Jesus, as if spoken by Him, there will be no difficulty. When John wrote, Jesus was in heaven, though not when He spoke to Nicodemus.

14. Why did Jesus refer to the brazen serpent ?

In order to teach Nicodemus what he yet required to learn of the love of God, and His gracious provision for a sin-ruined world. No doubt he thought the favour of God was limited to his own people, but now learns that it is otherwise. The serpents were in the camp and bit the people, and when the serpent of brass was lifted up, there was no limit to its healing power, when used as Moses directed. To believe, and to look upon the serpent of brass and be healed, were God's arrangements for all alike. So in the lifting up of the Son of man, " whosoever " opens up to all the healing blessings of His grace.

16. " For God so loved the world that He gave His only begotten Son." Why did Jesus make this very blessed declaration to Nicodemus ?

Simply to show him the reason why all men might believe and ob-

tain everlasting life. It might surprise him to hear that the love of
God was not limited to the Jewish
nation, but had been manifested
to the world by giving His Son to
die for it—a truth he required to
learn, in order that he might understand why God could save either
Jew or Gentile.

*Is the love of God to every human
being an unquestioned fact ?*

No; but it ought to be. I have
questioned it myself, but it was when
I reasoned instead of believing the
testimony of Jesus.

17. *" For God sent not His Son
into the world to condemn the world ;"
but in chap. ix. 39, Jesus says,
" For judgment I am come into this
world."   How can these sayings be
reconciled ?*

There is no disagreement between
them. The former sentence applies
to the world, the latter to Himself.
Hence we may read the latter statement, *To suffer judgment came I into
the world.*

22. *" And there He tarried with
them and baptised."   Did Jesus do
this personally ?*

In chap. iv. 2, we read that
"Jesus Himself baptised not, but His
disciples."

23. *" And John also was baptising
in Ænon near to Salim."   How could
these divine missions go on at the same
time ?*

We must not suppose that they
were continued in opposition to each
other.   When Jesus was baptised
He retired into the wilderness, and
John continued to preach the " baptism of repentance for the remission
of sins " until Jesus reappeared, and
received John's public witness, that
He was indeed the Lamb of God.
From that time the two missions
were united, and even two of John's
disciples   followed   Jesus.   John
selected Ænon because there was
much water, but those who were
baptised by him evidently became
the disciples of Christ.

CHAPTER IV.

1–3. *" When therefore the Lord
knew how that the Pharisees had
heard," etc.   Why did He leave
Judea for Galilee on this account?*

Because He knew how violently
they would oppose Him in His mission, while in many parts of Galilee
He could pursue His work unhindered.

*Why does he refer to Jesus not
immersing His disciples ?*

The contrast between John and
Jesus is still before us.   John immersed the disciples made by him
with his own hands, Jesus did not,
but His disciples ; and this incidental reference is instructive in at
least two aspects.   (1.) That discipleship to Jesus involved immersion.
(2.) That immersion by the hands of
others under the direction and sanction of Jesus was sufficient.

4. *Why " must needs go through
Samaria " ?*

Because Samaria lay between Judea
and Galilee, and as Jesus passed
through it, this memorable event at
the well of Jacob occurred.

5. *" The parcel of ground that
Jacob gave to his son Joseph."   Why
did the Jews hold this spot in such
memorable interest ?*

It was the scenes connected with
it that made it so full of interest.
It was here that Abraham pitched
his tent upon his first entrance into
the land of Canaan, and it was here
that God gave to him the promise
that his seed should possess that
land, although the Canaanite was
still in it, and he as yet had no seed.
It was here also that Jacob halted
on his return from Padan-aram, and
pitched his tent, and set up his
altar, having first purchased it of the
sons of Hamor for a hundred pieces

of silver. This parcel of ground was Jacob's dying gift to his beloved Joseph—a gift of hallowed memories and triumphing faith. I quote the bequeathment (Gen. xlviii. 22), as rendered by Kalisch, "Moreover I give to thee one portion above thy brethren, which *I take* out of the hand of the Amorite with my sword and my bow." It is not what he had done, but what he would do by the victorious hand of his children. This special gift was held sacred in dividing the land, as this portion was given to the sons of Joseph, whose bones were buried there. We do not wonder that John should note this object of special interest, near to which was Jacob's well, upon which Jesus now rested. The truth concerning Him that was to come had been entwined with all their history as a people; and now in Him who was sitting by that well, their long delayed expectations were fulfilled.

6. *Was this meeting of Jesus and this woman by the well providential or accidental?*

I would not call it either one or the other. The result was not in the meeting, but in the use that was made of it. Jesus was on His journey to Galilee, and was resting there while His disciples were gone to the village to buy meat, and the woman coming to draw water, Jesus embraced the opportunity of teaching her the truth, and the result was truly wonderful. We ought to learn a lesson from this circumstance, and be ever ready to speak and act for Christ. We are not responsible for results, but for action in harmony with truth. Nor should we be hindered by real difficulties. Jesus was weary and hungry, but these were set aside to instruct one dark mind in the truths of God.

7–9. *The woman's reply to Jesus, when He asked for a drink of water,* reveals a sad state of feeling between Jews and Samaritans. What was the cause of it?

The estrangement between them began when the ten tribes revolted from Judah, and having formed a new kingdom, with Samaria for their capital, their hostility toward each other was prolonged for centuries. It was, however, greatly intensified after the Assyrian captivity, chiefly on account of the influx of foreigners, who adopted the law of Moses as a religious code, built a temple upon Mount Gerizim, and set up a rival claim to be called the people of God. So fearful had their resentment of each other become, that when Jesus asked this woman for a drink of water, she was fairly startled.

10. *"If thou knewest the gift of God," said Jesus. What gift was this?*

Himself. He was God's gift, and was by her side ready to tell her the wondrous words of peace that alone could satisfy her thirsty spirit.

What was this living water He would have given to her?

The truth, that gave life to all who received it.

Why do you say that water in chap. iii. 5, is literal water, while here you say it means truth?

You must notice the term "living" appended to it, and this at once shows us that the term was used by Jesus symbolically. Water itself is used as a symbol of death, but when it is called the "water of life," or "living water," we learn that out of death life has come. Or in other words, Jesus has died that man might live, and His word of truth gives life to those who receive it.

16. *How did Jesus raise the thought of this woman above the water of the well?*

By revealing to her some facts of her life, which were known only to herself and God; and the exposure,

" he whom thou now hast is not thy husband," made her feel that she stood in the presence of a prophet of God.

Why did Jesus not answer her vexed question about the right place of worship ?

He did answer her, and His answer supplied to her most important instruction. He informed her that the contention was of no value, for the hour was coming when worship in both places would cease ; and that unless God was worshipped in spirit and truth it could not be accepted.

" *God is Spirit, and they that worship Him must worship in spirit and in truth." What does this mean ?*

It means most emphatically that the material worship of that age was about to close. Ritualistic service, whether in Jerusalem or Gerizim, was about to receive its final interdict, and God, who is Spirit, must be worshipped in spirit and in truth, *i.e.,* by Jesus.

25. *Why did the disciples marvel that He talked with the woman ?*

It is strictly *with a woman*, and to do so publicly was contrary to rabbinical precept. By this marvel of the disciples, John reveals to us how much they were still under the power of tradition. Jesus, however, was unfettered by it, and man or woman, in public or private, all were alike the objects of His care.

28–30. *Why did she go to tell the men of the city about Him ?*

He had told her that He was the Messiah, and His revelations of her own life had sent the truth deep into her mind. They, with herself, were looking for Him, and under the deep conviction that this might be the Christ, she called them out to judge for themselves.

What was the result of this interview ?

(1.) The woman herself was enlightened and convicted, and led to believe in Him as the Messiah. (2.) A whole city was brought out to hear, and also believed in Him. And (3.) it is not improbable, that this interview prepared the way for the visit of Philip the evangelist, which was attended with such gracious results. Jesus specially named Samaria in His commission to His disciples, remembering doubtless this interesting visit as He did so.

46–54. *Was this nobleman, who came to seek a cure for his son, a private or an official person ?*

The term " *basilikos,"* which John uses, denotes him to be an official person in relation to the king, but the nature of the office is not indicated beyond that he was a king's man, a courtier, who held some office under the Herodian government.

When Jesus said, " Except ye see signs and wonders ye will not believe," did He apply it to this man ?

No ; but to unbelieving Jews. This man had strong faith in Jesus, and had travelled twenty-five miles to meet Him, and when Jesus said to him, " Thy son liveth," he believed, and went home expecting to find it as Jesus had said. The meeting with his servants only confirmed his faith, and when he found that the healing began at the same time that Jesus spoke to him, he not only believed himself, but his whole house also.

CHAPTER V.

1–15. *On the return of Jesus to Jerusalem He is said to have healed a sick man at Bethesda. What was this Bethesda ?*

The meaning of the word is *house of mercy,* possibly a kind of infirmary, and in its porches, or chambers, the sick had shelter and provision.

Did healing really follow dipping in that pool ?

As this account of the angel, and the healing power of the pool is not found in many ancient MSS., scholars have decided that it is spurious, and from " waiting " of verse 3, to the close of verse 4, should be omitted, and the narrative is complete without it. The pool may have had its medicinal virtues, which would be sought by an eager and superstitious throng, but as Jesus passed by He healed this man, and though it was the sabbath He bid him take up his bed and go away.

Why did the Jews find fault with him for carrying his bed on the sabbath ?

They were simply upholding the law, which forbade the carrying of any burden on the sabbath ; but as He who had made him whole told him to take up his bed and walk, it became his defence when challenged by the Jews.

The Saviour afterward found the man in the temple, and gave him a most solemn charge. What did He mean by " sin no more, lest a worse thing come upon thee " ?

Two things are evidently implied in this solemn charge by Jesus. (1.) That his long affliction was a result of sinful violation of the laws of health and righteousness ; and (2.) that there was in the future something even worse than his present affliction, and this he was urged to avoid by a present reformation.

16-18. *The Jews sought to slay Jesus. On what grounds did they seek to do this ?*

On the ground of lawlessness and blasphemy. He had commanded the healed man to carry away his bed, He had also called God His Father, and for these things they sought His life, although he had a perfect right to do both.

" *My Father worketh hitherto, and I work." What work was this ?*

It was God's vindication of His righteousness and grace, which from the fall of man He had ever sought to manifest. In creation God worked and then rested—*i.e.*, found satisfaction in the work of His hands ; but when sin entered, that rest was broken up, and God had to work again in order to find a resting-place. At the altar, where faithful worshippers could offer their sacrificial symbols of the Coming One, God could meet and bless them ; and from the typical mercy-seat sprinkled with blood, He could speak words of grace and peace ; but it was only in Christ Jesus, the true mercy-seat, where God could find an abiding rest. To that rest, a result of His work for ages and generations, God is now inviting men to come. Christ healing on the sabbath was to the Jews a sin, but to Him a demonstration of the grace of God.

19. *What did He mean by " the Son can do nothing of Himself " ?*

That He did not work alone in His great mission. It was neither independence nor inferiority, but harmony, as he afterwards affirmed : " I and My Father are one "—*i.e.*, We are united in this great work of redemption. Jesus was not only a Son, united with the Father, but a Servant serving under the great Master ; but the Jews understood none of these things. The prophets had spoken of the Messiah under both aspects, but tradition had blinded the eyes of those before whom these things were manifested.

20, 21. *What were these " greater works " that would yet astonish them ?*

Quickening and raising the dead are specially named, and possibly judgment, which in the future would be inflicted by Him, is also intended.

22-27. *Jesus speaks of life and judgment as transferred to Himself.*

Does not this seem like inferiority of standing?

Yes, of standing or position, but not of nature. To overlook the fact that "the Word was made flesh," and that He who was Jehovah Elohim became a servant, is sure to lead to misapprehension and mistake. It was as the Lord Jesus Christ (titles obtained in redemption work), the once crucified, risen, and exalted One, that He became able to do for those who trust Him that which as Jehovah He could not have done. He died that He might live; He served that He might reign; He descended first into the lower parts of the earth, that He might ascend up far above all heavens; and then fill with all gracious things those who receive Him.

Has man no liberty of dealing with God except through His Son?

There is no alternative. We can hear God only through Jesus, and must honour the Father through the Son. The whole is summed up in one declaration: "For the Father judgeth no man, but hath committed all judgment unto the Son: that all men should honour the Son, even as they honour the Father. He that honoureth not the Son honoureth not the Father which hath sent Him."

"The dead shall hear the voice of the Son of God: and they that hear shall live." What death and life is this?

It is of spiritual death and life He is speaking here, because it was then going on, and would be more largely manifest in that coming hour of Gospel proclamation by His apostles. The reception of His word of truth gave life to all that received it then, and would do so to the end of the age.

28, 29. *"All that are in the graves shall hear His voice, and shall come forth." Is this a literal resurrection?*

Yes. It is those who are physically dead, that Jesus says will be raised to life again.

Will all that have lived on the earth live again? and will their resurrection take place together?

The Saviour's words furnish an answer to both questions. To the first the reply is, "*All* that are in the graves shall hear His voice, and shall come forth;" and outside of this "all" there are none. His reply to the second question is equally plain, "the *hour* is coming *in which all* that are in the graves shall hear His voice, and shall come forth." The hour in which the resurrection of all shall take place is a definite, though but a brief period. It is not a year, nor a month, nor a day, nor a moment, the smallest point of time, but the appointed hour when all shall be raised from death. There are things associated with the resurrection that will be done in a moment, as the change of the living at the sound of the last trump; but to the resurrection the hour will be given. Nor is there anything in the Word contrary to this. We read in 1 Thess. iv., that the "dead in Christ shall rise first," but this rising of the dead in Christ, is, before the living, who shall be changed and ascend, to meet the Lord in the air. We also read in Rev. xx. of the first resurrection, but this is not a physical but a symbolic resurrection. We do not, then, find any other scripture that might lead us to take any other view of these words of Christ than this, viz., that in the appointed hour, both the workers of good and of evil, will rise from their graves, *i.e.*, from death; and, according to Paul, in the appointed day Christ will judge the world in righteousness (Acts xvii. 31).

Can the destiny of those who are raised be clearly understood from these words of Christ?

To a certain extent there is positive plainness in these statements which all may understand. Jesus affirms that one class will be raised to life, and the other to condemnation, but the nature of these results can only be known by experience.

30–36. *"I can of mine own self do nothing." Why does Jesus here appeal to witnesses?*

Because His true nature and mission was denied, so He appeals to witness borne to Him—(1.) by John, (2.) by the signs and works done by Himself in confirmation of His mission, and (3.) by the Father who at His baptism owned Him as His beloved Son. His appeal therefore to this threefold witness was important.

"If I bear witness of Myself, My witness is not true." How could this be?

He meant that His witness would not be legal, as under the law the witness of one could not be accepted.

37. *"Ye have neither heard His voice, nor seen His form." Why does He refer to this?*

Some translate, *Have ye not heard His voice?* for God spake both at Sinai and the Jordan, *and have ye not had visions of His form?* referring to their prophets. It was therefore an appeal to them on behalf of Himself.

38. *"And ye have not His word abiding in you." How does He sustain this grave charge?*

By showing that they had refused to accept Him as the Son of God, when both John and the Father had borne witness to His Sonship.

39. *"Search the Scriptures." This is often quoted as a command by Jesus for Bible reading. Was it spoken for this purpose?*

No. If we read it, *Ye search the Scriptures, because ye think that in them ye have eternal life ; and they are they which bear witness of Me ; and ye are not willing to come to Me, that ye may have life*, we shall see more clearly the bearing of His words.

The Jews read the Scriptures, but were so influenced by tradition that they made no practical use of them. Life in the coming Messiah was plainly revealed in those holy writings, but when He came they received Him not. The Scriptures were therefore read in vain.

" Ye will not come to Me." Ought this verse to be quoted to prove man's freedom of will?

Jesus is not referring to power, but to action. It was not a question of freedom or necessity, but of choice. Every man does choose or wills ; this is assumed, but his choice is governed by his state of mind. If he loves evil, he will choose it, and reject Christ as his Lord ; but if he loves good, he will accept of Christ and be guided by Him. Jesus states what they had done, not what they could or could not do, and thus will He have to do with all men, to their approval or condemnation.

Why do these controversies recorded by John differ so much from the records of the other evangelists?

The addresses and debates recorded by John are nearly all Judean ; while the others give us more of His teaching in Galilee. The jealousy, the unbelief, and the unwillingness of these priests, scribes, and Pharisees, who literally swarmed in Judea, to receive His claims, were the cause of these controversies which John has specially recorded. This will also account for the subjects which on these occasions were debated, and for the greater signs which were done to convince them that He was the Christ.

CHAPTER VI.

1, 2. *Why did the multitude follow Jesus across the sea of Galilee?*

It was mere curiosity, and led to no practical result. It was only to see what was done, and not to learn obedience, that they followed Jesus.

It began and ended in wonder, while the great object of Christ was frustrated by their carnal motives.

4. *Why does John note that the passover was nigh at hand?*

Possibly to account for the multitude that had been gathered on this occasion. It appears that after He had crossed the lake He was not only followed by a great number out of mere curiosity, but having reached the main road on which Galileans were travelling to the feast, the company then increased to a multitude.

5–11. *John records here the feeding of five thousand men with five loaves and two small fishes. Why perform this miracle?*

To meet their necessity, not to show His power. Doubtless He felt the responsibility of having detained this great crowd, who by this delay had come to be in need of food, and by a miracle He met their need.

Why did He ask Philip where sufficient bread could be obtained?

It was to prove him, and his answer shows how entirely he had overlooked the power of Jesus. He thinks only of a natural way of meeting the difficulty, and that not being present he has nothing else to propose. Even Andrew, who had found the lad with his five barley loaves and two small fishes, said, " but what are they among so many?" These, however, furnished all He needed, and from these the five thousand were fed.

12–14. *Is it not strange that Jesus, who could feed thousands upon a few loaves and fishes, should be so careful about fragments?*

There is a fine moral lesson in this twofold direction of Jesus. There were but a few loaves and fishes, and yet He bade them feed the multitude; and the power of God made them equal to their need; and though there were many fragments when all were fed, He will not allow a fragment to be wasted. There is a lesson for us in this happy mien of faith and economy. How often we are called to minister to human need, both physically and spiritually, and refuse to do so because we think our supply of loaves and fishes too small for the demand, and when our supply is large we are in danger of wasting the fragments that remain. When the path of duty opens to us, and we shrink through unbelief, may we hear the Master saying, "Give ye them to eat," and we too may have fragments to gather up that will rebuke our unbelief. The disciples had more at the end than at the beginning, and this is very suggestive to all who are willing to serve Christ.

Why did John record the result of this miracle upon the people?

To show to those to whom he wrote its effects upon the minds of those who witnessed it. They said, " this is of a truth that prophet that should come into the world," and John wrote these things that others might believe that Jesus was the Son of God.

15. *Why did they wish to make Him a king?*

Because they knew from the prophets that the Messiah was to reign, but knew not the steps by which He was to rise to His throne. They did not even receive His own testimony that He must suffer and die before He could reign, and so He had to disappoint them to pursue His own spirit-marked path.

16–26. *Why were the people so puzzled to find Jesus at Capernaum?*

They had been fed by Jesus miraculously on the other side of the lake, and when the evening came the disciples embarked in a boat to recross the lake, but did not take Jesus with them. On the following day they sought but could not find Him, and then took ship and went to Capernaum. On finding Jesus they asked how He came there, but received no reply. John, however, tells us of His pathway over the deep waters, and after reaching His toiling disciples, and speaking to them words of cheer, they soon reached the shore of Capernaum.

Why did Jesus not tell them how He had reached the city? might it not have produced conviction?

They had already witnessed what should have been sufficient to prove that He was the Son of God; but the sign had failed to those who followed Him, and it would be in vain to tell them of another. Their motive was a fleshly one, and Jesus had to rebuke them. " Ye seek Me, not because ye saw the miracles, but because ye did eat of the loaves and were filled." It would have been well for them had they followed His advice, " Labour not (only) for the meat which perisheth, but for that meat which endureth unto everlasting life."

28. " *What shall we do, that we might work the works of God?" Does not this enquiry indicate that they were sincere?*

The sequel proved their insincerity, because when directed to believe in Himself as the work of God, they showed their unbelief by demanding a proof that they should do so.

30. " *What sign showest Thou?" Was it wrong to ask a sign?*

Not if it had been asked to obtain confirmation of the truth, but this was not their purpose. Their appeal to Moses proves that their motives were carnal. It was bread they wanted, not truth.

To believe in Christ seemed a small demand. Did this include all He required?

To believe in Jesus Christ as the Son of God covered the whole claim of God, because this involved full subjection to Christ. Faith and action are inseparable, for where there is no action there is no faith.

32–35. *Why did Jesus say, " Moses gave you not that bread from heaven"?*

Moses was only a servant ; God was the giver, even of that bread which their fathers did eat in the desert ; and He who gave the manna, had now given to them His well-beloved Son, the true bread from heaven—the bread which giveth life unto the world.

" Lord, evermore give us this bread.' Was this a sincere prayer?

Yes, but it was prompted by carnality and ignorance. They were like the woman of Samaria, who wanted the ever-springing water that she might neither thirst, nor have to draw. They wanted bread that would prevent both hunger and labour, and when Jesus said, " I am the bread of life," they were vexed and disappointed. They claimed that Jesus should either do for them as Moses had done for their fathers, or renounce all claim to be their leader. The difference between the two leaders was clearly understood by them, and the latter they distinctly rejected, because His mission was spiritual instead of carnal.

37–42. " *All that the Father giveth Me shall come to Me." Have we not here an election of persons who are given by God to Christ?*

Most certainly, but let us not mistake who they are, and why and when they are given. If we assume that this gift of persons to Christ was made in a past eternity, and without any revealed reason, we shall most seriously pervert the teaching of Christ. He is trying to show them that it was not as the nation of Israel, nor as the fleshly seed of Abraham, that they were to be given to Him, but as those, and only those, who believed in Him. Such, He assured them, would come to Him,

K

and these formed the Father's gift to Himself. Those believing in Him were to be the flock of God, and He had become their shepherd, and would give His life for them, and would also give life to them, and raise them up at the last day. The truth which Jesus wished to teach to these Jews, who had been blinded by tradition, was not only important to them, but to all other persons at all periods of time. Christ is God's way of acceptance and salvation, and He has revealed no other, and all are invited to come by Him. Those who understand God by believing His word, will trust in Christ, and thus be given to Him.

It will be important, however, to observe here, that when Christ came into the world, it was to introduce an entire change of administration. The Jews, who for fifteen centuries had been acknowledged as the people of God through the law of Moses, which was only a shadow of good things to come, had then, either to accept of the substance, or be left even without the shadow. They had either to accept of Christ, as their fathers, at the death of Moses, accepted of Joshua to lead them into their typical inheritance, or they must be left, as they would have been had they refused, with no alternative but condemnation. It was the persistent determination of these Jews to uphold the validity of their law-relation to God, and their persevering rejection of His teaching, that occasioned those bitter controversies which John has so largely recorded, and in which they were so often put to shame. To carefully note this state of mind, which was fully developed in these discussions, will, we think, furnish a key to these controversies, and also to many things that were said by Jesus to them. To apply these words to other men,

and to other things than as applied by Him, will often be no less than a perversion of the truth. Thousands of times, I assume, this 37th verse has been quoted to prove that some are not given to Christ, because they do not come to Him; and this affirmation that "All that the Father giveth Me shall come to Me," is held to prove their assertion. Now it is perfectly true that God has not given unbelievers, whether Jews or Gentiles, to be the flock of Christ, but to use this truth as the reason for their unbelief or not coming to Christ, is a most serious misapplication of truth. We would therefore suggest, and the statement will apply to every part of Scripture, that not only should the context of verses be read, but also the context of dispensation and circumstances, which should always be pondered together. It is not always what we may find in the chapter or book that is alone sufficient to determine the meaning and force of some statements in it, but we shall have very frequently to note the persons and the economy with which it stands related. Both in the gospels and the epistles this is largely overlooked, and often leads expositors to wholesale misapplication of the apostles' teaching.

"*And this is the Father's will which hath sent Me, that of all which He hath given Me I should lose nothing, but should raise it up again at the last day.*" Why object to these declarations?

Because they looked no further than His fleshly relationship, and for a son of Joseph, whose father and mother they knew, to affirm that He came down from heaven, and would raise the dead, was more than they could endure. They did not believe in His superhuman origin, and therefore rejected His declarations as false.

44. "*No man can come to Me,*

except the Father which hath sent Me draw him." Must not this arrangement set aside human responsibility?

If God drew men to Christ by irresistible force, as the tides of the ocean are drawn by the moon, there would be an end to all responsibility; but mind and matter are not controlled by the same law. Men are drawn to Christ by the teaching of the Spirit concerning Him, and when He is accepted the object is secured. Jesus appeared on the earth, there is no doubt, under most unfavourable circumstances, but the prophets had described Him just as He was, and those who accepted the teaching as fulfilled in Him were led to exclaim, "Thou art the Son of God," "Thou art the king of Israel." To wait for some emotional impulse to impel the heart to accept of Christ, instead of seeking instruction from the Bible how to act in relation to Him, is sure to lead to deception all who do so.

53–59. "Except ye eat the flesh of the Son of man," etc. What does this mean?

The controversies of centuries over these words have come down to our own day; nor are they likely to cease so long as it is possible to use these words of Christ both literally and symbolically. The eating of His flesh, and drinking of His blood in the memorial feast, is by many supposed to be what the Saviour here taught; but when we remember that spiritual life must always precede partaking of that commemorative feast, we must demur to the thought of life being received in partaking of it. We feel therefore shut up to say, that Jesus is here speaking by metonomy, of the Gospel arrangement for salvation. Christ Jesus died for sins, and was raised again for justification, and in order to salvation men must believe in Him as set forth in the Gospel. By His

"flesh" Jesus evidently refers to His incarnation, and by His "blood," to His death; and the reception of these facts in faith, is most appropriately set forth by eating and drinking.

60. "This is a hard saying." Did they mean that it was hard to understand?

No; but that it was hard to receive it. They did not wish to accept His teaching concerning His death, resurrection, and ascension, and this was the cause of their difficulty. Indeed, some would not receive it, and walked no more with Him.

70. "One of you is a devil." What did He mean by this strong language?

It is, *lit.*, an adversary, and refers to Judas, who betrayed Him into the hands of sinners.

CHAPTER VII.

1. "Jesus would not walk in Jewry." What place is intended?

In the older English versions, Jewry was generally used to denote Judea, but has been retained only three times in our common version. Judea is intended, and should be so rendered in each instance.

3–5. "For neither did His brethren believe in Him." Who are referred to here?

His fleshly kindred, who had not then believed in Him as the Messiah.

Why were they so urgent for Him to go up to Jerusalem at the "feast of tabernacles"?

In order that His claims should be tested, and, if false, disproved. They knew that the powers in Jerusalem were ready to contest His claims, and His friends also were anxious to urge on the trial.

7. "The world cannot hate you, but me it hateth." Why should the world hate Jesus?

Because of His testimony against their tradition and hypocrisy. Again and again He had convicted them of making void the law of God by their tradition, and faithfully warned them of the woes that would overtake them unless they repented. They, however, refused to change, and only hated Him for His faithful words.

10. *Jesus had left Judea because of the murderous spirit of the Jews (ver.* 1), *but here again returned to Jerusalem. Why does He do this?*

Because the feast of tabernacles had come, and whatever their opposition might be He would not be deterred from doing the will of His Father. He had, indeed, said to His brethren in Galilee, when urging Him to go up to the feast, " My time is not yet come," and they have to start without Him; but, in the midst of the feast, He is found teaching in the temple, as He always did when in Jerusalem, and thus working the works of the Father that sent Him.

14. *" Jesus went up into the temple and taught." Was it legally right for Him to do so?*

That part of the temple in which He was teaching was not the inner shrine or holy place, where only the priests could enter, but the porch, to which all worshippers had access. Here, as a " Teacher sent from God," He could converse with and teach those that gathered to hear His wondrous words.

15. *The Saviour's grasp of the truth seems to have astonished the Jews, and yet they said He had never learned. What did they mean?*

That He had not been taught in the schools of the Rabbis ; but His teaching fully proved that He had studied in the school of God, and was familiar with the Scriptures. Jesus had purposely shunned the Targums or interpretations of the elders, but the 119th Psalm, which

was certainly true of Him, was a prophetic witness how much He valued the statutes, laws, and judgments of God. That Psalm was embodied in His life, and in this voluntary acceptance of God's will He is a pattern to all believers.

21–23. *" I have done one work, and ye all marvel." To what does He refer?*

To the miracle performed at Bethesda (chap. v.) ; and, though it was done at a previous visit to Jerusalem, they had neither forgotten nor forgiven the offence against traditional law. On that occasion He had healed on the sabbath, and also directed the man to take up his bed and walk, and the discussion upon His right to do so was evidently renewed by them on His return. Jesus tried to show them their inconsistency in condemning Him for this work of mercy, when on the sabbath they would circumcise a man, lest the law should be broken, but His appeal was of no avail.

37. *Why did Jesus invite them to come to Him, when they did not believe in Him?*

Some of them did not believe in Him, but there were others who were deeply impressed with what they had witnessed, and it was to these He announced Himself as the only satisfying portion, " If any man thirst let him come unto Me, and drink," *i.e.*, believe in Me, and you shall be satisfied.

38. *" He that believeth on Me, as the Scriptures hath said, out of his belly shall flow rivers of living water." What does He mean by this.*

John explains that He referred to the time when the Spirit would be given, and when, from the hearts and lips of those who received Him, the truth should flow as water from a fountain. It is a prophetic utterance, fulfilled at Pentecost and onward. This living water was the truth which the apostles and others should preach and teach.

Where do the Scriptures say " out of his belly shall flow rivers of living water" ?

We do not know of any place where it is so recorded. We think it should be read as a promise made by Jesus Himself to those who should believe on Him, as the Scriptures of the prophets teach.

39. *" The Holy Spirit was not yet given." Are not facts against this statement ?*

Yes, and this should lead us to examine the sentence, which possibly may misstate the case. We know that the Spirit was given prior to that period. He was in the prophets, for they spake by Him. He was also in John the Baptist, and Simeon, and Christ. But on looking at this word *" given,"* we observe its italic letters, and thus know that our translators have added the word, and have thus made John contradict facts. To read "The Holy Spirit was not yet" seems incomplete, but then, what shall we add? Thomson, in his "Notes on the New Testament," says, that the Cambridge MS. has the words *" ep áutous"* upon them, and here we get, at least, a hint of what is required. The Spirit was promised, but was not yet upon them,—*i.e.* the disciples,—because Jesus was not yet glorified.

40–43. *Why should there be a division about the birthplace of Jesus?*

The prophets had written that He should be of the town of Bethlehem, while He had become known as the prophet of Nazareth of Galilee; so there was a division among the people. Had they sought reliable information on those matters they would have learned that both were true.

45–49. *Who were those who should have apprehended Jesus.*

They were Roman officials who had been sent by the Pharisees to apprehend Him. They seem, however, to have been so impressed with His address, that they returned without doing so, and declared, "Never man spake like this man."

Why did the Pharisees say, " Have any of the rulers or of the Pharisees believed on Him ?"

It was in order to shame these officers out of the respect which they had formed for this new Teacher. It was intended as a rebuke, whether felt to be so or not.

" But this people who knoweth not the law are cursed." To whom did the Pharisees apply this remark ?

To these Gentile officers, and it was a most degrading reflection upon them.

50,51. *Where was Nicodemus when he spoke a word for Jesus ?*

He was in the Sanhedrin, or great council, and though he only asked that justice might be done to Him, he was answered by a most reproachful taunt.

CHAPTER VIII.

1–11. *Is this section of eleven verses authentic ?*

Scholars have decided that it was not written by John, but judge that it was written in the apostolic age. The section commences with the last verse of the seventh chapter, and apparently intercepts John's record. The early copyists were fully aware that it was not written by him; but the case appears to have been so well authenticated, that, while placing it in different positions in the Gospel, very few of them rejected it. We receive it therefore as having occurred as narrated, but presume that it was not written, but only added, by John to his Gospel.

The woman was said to have been taken in an act for which the law condemned her to death by stoning. Why did they bring her to Jesus ?

It was in order to find an accusation against Him. No doubt they were prepared to accuse Him whichever side He took, and were even strong in the assurance of an easy triumph, but were doomed to a humbling disappointment. They might have retired when He wrote on the ground instead of answering them ; but instead of doing so, they continued to press for a reply. The reply was given at last, and seemed to cover the whole ground,—the sin of the woman, the justice of the law, and then, on certain terms, He proposed to make them the executioners ; " He that is without sin among you, let him first cast a stone at her ; and again He stooped down and wrote on the ground."

What did He write ?

This is not stated here ; but one ancient MS. adds, that He was writing down their sins. Now we cannot affirm that it was so ; but we are sure that either what He wrote or said produced a marked effect upon them. The fact of their own sin was evidently forced upon their attention, and fearing an exposure, more serious even than the crime of the woman, one by one they withdrew, till Jesus and the woman were left alone. Not a single accuser remained to press the claims of violated law.

Alone with Jesus. How did it terminate ?

With admonition to sin no more.

" Neither do I condemn thee." Did He overlook her sin ?

He speaks of it judicially. Moses condemned the sin ; but the witnesses who should have been the executioners were gone, and Jesus was not going to take their place, so He bids her sin no more. Jesus would rather lead from sin than execute the sentence against it.

She called Him Lord. Did she know who He was ?

Possibly not ; but there was in her that reverential courtesy which arises in the presence of a superior being, which she doubtless felt Him to be.

12. *How was Jesus the light of the world ?*

By the truth He taught and lived. That which was true and pure before God fell from His lips, and was embodied in His life, and all who received the truth and obeyed it, walked in the light.

What is meant by walking in darkness ?

Walking is a figure of life in action ; darkness of error, sin, evil, in fact anything contrary to the will of God. To live in opposition to God is to walk in darkness, while to obey Him is to walk in the light.

14–20. *In chap. v. 31, Jesus says, " If I bear record of Myself, My record is not true," while here He says, " My record is true." How do you harmonise these statements ?*

We must consider the Saviour's intention in each statement in order to understand them. The latter statement applies to Himself as a witness to the truth, while the former applies to their reception of it. " My record is not true " to you who will not receive it. This is the reason why other witnesses were called into court, as that of John and the Father to sustain His own. Here He appeals to the law that required two witnesses, and thus His own and the Father's were sufficient to establish His claim.

24. *" Ye shall die in your sins." Was not this a hasty conclusion ?*

They could only be saved by receiving Him, but this they refused to do ; and though the witness borne to His Messiahship was most ample, yet being rejected there was no alternative but ruin.

31–33. *" Then said Jesus to those Jews that believed on Him," etc. Why should they be called believers, when their reply proved the reverse ?*

They had been most favourably impressed with the evidences of His Messiahship, but failed to perceive its spiritual purpose, and this failure soon became manifest. When Jesus exhorted them to continue in the truth, in order to obtain deliverance from evil, their true condition became at once manifest. They were really trusting in their relation to Abraham, and when the truth was plainly spoken, they at once rejected Christ.

34. *Was there not some misunderstanding between them and Jesus?*

This is very evident; Jesus was speaking of their spiritual relation, while they thought only of their natural state. They objected to His statement about freedom, as being to them a false insinuation, and made a vapouring defence of never being in bondage to any man. This led Jesus to faithfully state their standing before God as sinners, and by a simile proved that they were slaves of sin. And as slaves were liable to removal, their remaining in the house of God was only a matter of time and circumstances. "The son abideth ever, but the servant"—*lit.* slave—"abideth not in the house for for ever."

How could they boast of freedom when facts were against it?

Pride blinded their eyes. They said they were never in bondage, but the Babylonian captivity, and their present subjection to Cæsar, bore witness against them; and even their plot to kill Jesus proved that they were the slaves of sin, and children of the evil one.

44. "*Ye are of your father the devil.*" *On what does the Saviour rest this grave charge?*

Upon their practice of evil. The fruit shows the kind of tree on which it grows. Sin connects men with Satan, as righteousness connects with God. The lusts of your father, the devil, ye will do, said Jesus,

therefore you are his children. It is by this teaching we should decide our relationship, and not by any reasoning of our own. Pride of heart will lead to a false estimate of our condition, but truth will be eye-salve to our eyes. We have need to beware of ourselves, lest we should be biassed in our decision by self-love, instead of the truth of God.

CHAPTER IX.

1. "*A man blind from his birth.*" *Why does John specially note this?*

It was a most striking case, and may have thus differed from others who had been healed by Jesus. With many, blindness is caused by accident and disease, but here was a man blind from his birth, and yet sight was given to him by Jesus. In his case there could be no deception.

2–4. "*Who did sin, this man or his parents, that he was born blind?*" *Why ask such a question?*

The words of God by Moses, "Visiting the iniquities of the fathers upon the children," may have suggested the latter part of it, while traditional thought may have suggested the former. Jesus at once assures them that previous sin was not the cause of his blindness; and while the sin of parents may often cause the sufferings of their children, it was not so in this case. "Neither hath this man sinned, nor his parents : but that the works of God should be made manifest in him."

"*I must work the works of Him that sent Me.*" *Was this miracle a work of God?*

Yes; it was a most striking manifestation, both of the power of God, and of the grace of Him who wrought it. We have to remember that He was just fleeing from the fury of the Pharisees, who had taken up stones to cast at Him, when He saw this man who was blind from his birth. It was an opportunity for giving another proof of His divine mission, and at once he embraced it, saying, " I must work the works of Him that sent Me while it is day."

5. *"As long as I am in the world, I am the light of the world." What did He mean ?*

It was spoken in relation to the miracle He was about to perform. He had just been driven from the temple on account of His teaching and miracles, and here He was about to repeat what had made them so angry, and it might appear strange for Him to do so ; but here He shows the reason : " I am (here as) the light of the world," and I must therefore reveal God, whatever may follow. "And when He had said this, He spat on the ground," etc.

6. *Why did Jesus put moistened clay upon this man's eyes, and send him to the pool, when He could have healed with a word ?*

If to give the man sight was the only object He sought to accomplish, it might have been so done, but He made the cure to depend upon the man's faith, and gave him an opportunity of showing it. The result secured his conviction, and also knowledge, that He who had given him sight was the Son of God.

8. *Were the neighbours the first to enquire about the means of the cure ?*

The man, we presume, would soon reach home, and both neighbours and parents would be greatly excited about him receiving his sight. Some could hardly believe that it was the man who sat and begged, but he assured them that he was the person. The rumour of this cure soon spread through Jerusalem, and at last the man was brought to the Pharisees, the leaders of the synagogue, and to whom, as a member, he was personally responsible. The trial was a most interesting one. First the man was questioned about the cure, and gave a simple account of the whole matter, but his testimony was doubted until his parents were called, who assured the court that he was their son, and that he was born blind, but how his eyes were opened they could not tell. " He is of age," said they, " ask him : he shall speak for himself."

Why were his parents so cautious about this matter ?

The Jews had agreed that if any man confessed that Jesus was the Anointed, he should be put out of the synagogue. This threat deterred many from even listening to Jesus, and his parents, thus afraid, threw the whole responsibility of answering upon himself.

24–38. *Was it their refusal to answer that led to the man's re-examination ?*

When they refused to answer through fear, the man was recalled, and in the simplicity of his honest heart became more than a match for these Christ-rejecting Pharisees. With a good share of common sense, and the simple fact that Jesus had opened his eyes, he dealt some heavy blows upon their carping criticism about Him. " This man is a sinner," they said. " Whether he be a sinner or no, I know not : one thing I know, that, whereas I was blind, now I see." " We know not whence He is," again they reply. This is marvellous, he rejoins, " and yet He has opened my eyes." These keen thrusts of the poor beggar so annoyed them that the discussion ended with expulsion from the synagogue. Fearlessly and nobly the man fought out his artless defence of Jesus, and suffered for so doing, but a blessed reward followed in seeing Jesus, and learning from Himself that He was the Son of God. *After the man was cast out, Jesus found him. Did He purposely seek him out?*

It is very like Jesus that He should do so. The man improved what he had received, and more was given. He had been honest to his convictions as far as he knew, and Jesus met him and declared Himself to be the Son of God, and he confessed his faith and worshipped.

Why did John record this miracle?

To support his great proposition, that Jesus was the Son of God. Here was a great miracle performed, the reality of which none could question, and though the doer of it was rejected through prejudice, it was left as a witness against them.

39. *"For judgment I am come into the world." How can we harmonise this statement with chap. iii. 17— For God sent not His Son into the world to judge the world?*

He came not to judge the world, but to save it, and He must therefore refer, not to judgment to be passed upon others, but judgment to be endured by Himself. The Pharisees had already denounced Him as a sinner, but in the face of this opprobrium cast upon Him He gave sight to this blind man. To endure judgment He came into this world, that they which see not might see, and that they which see might be made blind. The case of this blind man affords a striking comment upon these words of Jesus. He was spiritually as well as literally blind, but when his eyes were opened by Jesus he saw the truth, and believed on Him as the Son of God. The Pharisees saw the power of Christ, but rejected the evidence, and remained in their blindness and sin.

CHAPTER X.

1–6. *Is the parable of the shepherd and his flock connected with the preceding miracle?*

It was evidently delivered to those Pharisees who gathered about Jesus after it was known that He had given sight to the blind man. Instead of accepting the sign with joy, they were greatly annoyed by it, and sought to discredit His work in every possible way. The parable was delivered for a twofold purpose; first, to unmask the hypocrisy of these blind leaders of the blind; and second, to comfort and help those who received Him as the good Shepherd.

Is this parable a picture of shepherd work in Palestine?

A more simple description could hardly be given than this brief sketch drawn by Jesus—the fold, the flock, the porter or night-watch, and the shepherd calling his flock, are all true to life.

How was it they did not understand it?

It was not the parable, but the truth embodied in it they did not understand. The parable contained teaching which they failed to perceive, and this led to further exposition, by which the relation of the shepherd and his flock was more fully taught.

7. *Jesus afterward calls Himself the good shepherd. How is He also the door?*

Because by Him men enter into the fold, and, when united to His flock, He becomes their shepherd.

8. *"All that ever came before Me are thieves and robbers." To whom does He refer?*

Not to the prophets, nor even to John, for though before Him in point of time, they never sought to usurp His place. But there were those in His day who assumed the prerogative to bind and loose, to shut the kingdom, and to open it, a right granted only to Jesus. Their unlawful appropriation of this power justly exposed them to this charge—" thieves and robbers; but the sheep did not hear them."

9. *"I am the door." Why do some say that baptism is the door into the fold?*

Because they do not discern things that differ. It is not a *thing* but a person who is the door. Everything that Christ appointed is important, but He alone is the entrance. Faith and confession and immersion all tend to Jesus, but He is the door into salvation, and all are invited to enter by Him.

"Shall go in and out, and find pasture." To what does Jesus refer?

To privilege in two aspects, viz., safety and provision. Jesus gives both protection and truth to those who receive Him.

10. *Would this contrast between Christ the good shepherd and pretenders be understood by these Pharisees?*

Possibly not, although very plain. Their purpose was plunder, power, and control of the people for self-interest; His to give life to the flock, by giving His own.

"That they might have it more abundantly." What does this mean?

That they might have life with abundance, — *i.e.,* with privilege. There are facts which produce life in those who receive them; and there are truths which sustain that life when it is produced.

11. *What is a hireling?*

One who works for hire, and who would not be working in that department were it not for personal advantage. And, though the word applies to any hired worker, Jesus specially applies it to those religious workers,—scribes, Pharisees, etc.,—whose chief interest was the gain derived from their position, and not from any love for the flock over whom they had charge.

Ought not men to be supported in preaching?

Yes, supported, but not hired. Jesus was supported in His labours, and so were the apostles, but not hired. Kind hands and loving hearts ministered to them of their substance, and so had fellowship with them in their work. Think of Jesus stipulating for a salary before He would preach the Gospel of the kingdom; or the apostles striking a bargain before starting on a missionary tour! We should be startled at such a thought, and yet the greater part of the preaching and spiritual labour of the present day is done on this principle. Jesus and His apostles have set us an example in labouring freely in the Gospel field; and God in supplying their need.

15. *"I lay down My life for the sheep." Does not this imply limited atonement?*

No. Jesus is simply speaking of Himself as the "good shepherd," who gave His life, in contrast with hirelings who fled when danger was seen. Then we should understand that the term sheep or flock is here strictly applied to Jews, who were indeed God's ancient flock, "The people of His pasture, and the sheep of His hand." True, they had gone astray, and so were "lost sheep," but, as the "Shepherd of Israel," He had come to seek and save them. The term sheep is never applied to Gentiles in the Scriptures, and when His death is spoken of in relation to them, it is, "Who gave Himself a ransom for all, to be testified in due time."

16. *"And other sheep I have which are not of this fold." Who are these?*

They are those who through the Gospel, even from among the nations, believed in His name, and so were united with His flock. Or, as in another figure, they became members of His body.

17, 18. *"I lay down My life." "No man taketh it from Me." What did He mean?*

That His death was a voluntary one, and that without His will, His life could not have been taken, no not even on the cross. He had the power or right to surrender His life, and He had authority to receive it again, and of this right He fully availed Himself, both in dying and being raised.

22–27. The cure of the blind man, and the delivery of the parable of the good shepherd, seem to have occurred at the feast of tabernacles. Why does John here refer to the "feast of dedication"? Were these held together?

It is said that there were two months between these feasts, and Jesus had been away and returned to Jerusalem, but of this no notice is taken here. The subject of the parable is, however, again introduced, and applied to them with telling effect, " Ye are not of My sheep, as I said unto you."

Why did He so positively apply this charge to them?

Because of the proofs they had furnished of its truth. The sheep hear the shepherd's voice : they had not heard His voice, therefore were not of His flock.

28. " They shall never perish." Is not this absolute security?

Yes, but security to be enjoyed, only through obedience to Christ the good shepherd.

30. " I and My Father are one." In what respect?

In securing the safety of those who trust in Him.

CHAPTER XI.

The visits of Jesus to the home of Lazarus and his sisters appear to have been frequent. Why did He go there so often?

To instruct them in the truth which they manifestly desired to understand—especially Mary, who is said to have sat at His feet, and heard His words. Her anointing of the Teacher beforehand for His burial was a manifest proof that she had profited by His teaching ; and the truth of His sacrificial death, which even His apostles would not believe, was received and held fast by her.

1–3. When Lazarus was taken sick, why did the sisters send word to Jesus?

Because they believed that He could cure his sickness, and thus prevent his death, and therefore sent a messenger to acquaint Jesus with their trial.

" Behold he whom thou lovest is sick." Why appeal to the affection of Jesus?

It is not difficult to see the reason why they appeal to His love. They wished to obtain His help in their need, and this must have appeared to them their strongest plea. It did not, however, succeed, because, as if deaf to their entreaty, He allowed Lazarus to die.

4. " This sickness is not unto death." Why then did Jesus allow him to die?

To give to those Christ-rejecting Jews at Jerusalem another proof, the highest He could give them, that He was indeed the Son of God ; and whether received or rejected, it would be for the glory of God.

5. John says that Jesus loved them, and yet the trial deepens into death. Is such a trial consistent with love?

We might answer it by asking, Did God love His Son? and yet He gave Him up to death, thus involving Him in the greatest trial possible. God had a gracious purpose to accomplish, which could only be effected by His death, and to effect it He spared Him not. The Father even forsook His Son when on the cross, but His love must not be questioned. Hence, in harmony with this principle, many of God's dear children are called to suffer, but we should not for a moment doubt His love to them.

7. *Why did Jesus go into Judea again when His enemies there sought to take His life?*

To honour His Father by doing His work. If God could be honoured, self was not considered.

9. *"Are there not twelve hours in the day?" Why does Jesus refer to these twelve hours?*

It is a figurative way of answering His disciples concerning the security of His own life. The disciples wondered that He should return to Judea, when so recently He had to flee from their rage. His reply was, the day has its twelve hours, and the night will not come on until they are past. So with my life, I have my work, and my allotted time to do it, and till then the darkness of this age will not settle over Me. In this confidence, Jesus fearlessly enters the scene to work the works of God. It is a striking example to all workers for God, and should encourage them to work and fear not.

17–32. *Why did the arrival of Jesus not remove the sorrow of these sisters?*

Because they knew not at first what He intended to do. Lazarus was dead, and their grief was intense, for they had no hope of his return to life. Even when He said to Martha, "Thy brother shall rise again," His words were met with, "I know that he shall rise again at the resurrection of the last day," and in this truth alone they found consolation. They knew that Jesus could raise him if He only chose to do so, but they did not expect that He would. So they wept on, although Jesus was with them.

33. *Why did Jesus groan in spirit when He saw Mary weeping?*

Because He did expect that His presence would have brought, at least to her heart, the relief it should have inspired. But in this He was disappointed. Hence He groaned in spirit, and also wept at the unbelief, not only of the multitude, but of her who had sat at His feet.

39. *"Lord, by this time he stinketh." Why did Martha say this?*

Because Jesus had ordered the removal of the stone from the cave or sepulchre, and she thought possibly only of the loathsome form being exposed, not even then expecting that he would be raised from the dead. Death had quenched her hope, and his decomposition, which she thought was going on, rendered exposure an offence. She therefore hastily intercepted His action, but was rebuked for her unbelief.

42. *Jesus generally expected faith ere He showed His power. Why did He manifest it on this occasion, against the unbelief of all?*

It was in order that they might believe that God had sent Him. He manifested His power in the face of their unbelief, and thus sought to assist them to learn the truth needful for their salvation. The evidence furnished on this occasion was like that of His own resurrection, not dependent on faith, but provided in grace that they might believe.

45. *Did this miracle convince them that He was the Son of God?*

Only some of those who witnessed it. There was in the minds of the Pharisees such a deep-laid prejudice against Him that no sign was allowed by them to remove it.

47. *Why were they so prejudiced against Him?*

Because of their selfishness. If His influence prevailed over the people, theirs would be destroyed, and this they clearly saw, and resolved if possible to prevent it. They had, however, only one way in which it could be prevented, as they thought, and that was to put Him to death, and from that time they determined to take His life.

54. *Was it their wicked plot that led Him to withdraw?*

Yes, until the passover, when six days before it He returned to Bethany, in order that all things written of Him by the prophets might be fulfilled.

CHAPTER XII.

1. *Why did Jesus return to Bethany six days before the passover?*

That He might fulfil the Scriptures, an object ever kept before Him. The lamb that was killed at the passover was taken up on the tenth day of the month, and was a type of Himself. He came there that He might be ready, and every day entered into Jerusalem; thus showing that He was in their hands if they wished to make Him their victim.

2–8. *At the feast held in Bethany, Martha served, while Mary anointed His feet? Did these acts indicate conditions of mind?*

Actions, when free, always indicate the true state of those who perform them. It became evident that these two women had very different estimates of Jesus. The serving of Martha at this supper was her highest respect to Him as a dear friend, while the anointing of Mary was her act of faith in His purpose to suffer and die. Between this act of the flesh, and this act of faith, there was a striking difference. Jesus acknowledged the latter, while the former passed unnoticed.

Mary anointed the feet of Jesus with her costly ointment. Was it done on the spur of the moment?

"Against the day of my burying hath she kept this" (ointment). From the time she understood that Jesus would be crucified, her purpose to anoint him was formed, and this opportunity occurring, she embraced it.

What was there so notable in this anointing of Jesus?

Her faith in His testimony that He would be delivered into the hands of wicked men and be crucified, which none of His disciples seem to have credited. The anointing of His feet on this occasion proved her faith, beyond all question, and must have been very refreshing to His heart to find that she understood and believed His word.

Judas Iscariot is said to have murmured at the seeming waste of the ointment, but why did John call him a thief?

Judas is said to have kept the bag, and have what was put therein; and, as he mentally reckoned the worth of the pound of ointment, he was annoyed at missing the three hundred pence which should have fallen to his custody. His very anxiety about it is enough to make one suspicious, though not sufficient to sustain John's charge. The Revised Version, however, has made John's statement a proof for the charge, "Having the bag, he took away what was put therein." This is in keeping with Luke's statement, that he purchased a field with the reward of iniquity, that is by unjust appropriations from this bag.

10. *Why did the chief priests consult to put Lazarus to death, when they knew that Jesus could raise him again?*

Yes, but their purpose was, first of all, to put Jesus to death, and then Lazarus, and so hinder the people from believing on Jesus.

12. *This scene of triumph, in the shout of hosannas and waving of palm branches by exulting disciples, is a striking contrast to these plots against His life. Were they the same persons who did both?*

There were evidently two classes; for Christ had friends as well as foes. Some would have made Him a king, while others sought to take His life. We do not think that those who shouted "Hosanna" were those who shouted "Crucify Him, crucify Him." There were those that bewailed Him, as well as those that derided Him; and it is needful to discern between the two, in order to understand much that is written of Him.

20. *Were these Greeks, so-called, Jews or Gentiles?*

We judge that they were Gentile proselytes, who, though they had come to worship, were limited in privilege. Their desire to see Jesus indicated the yearning that was manifesting itself in Gentile minds, and though God intended to satisfy it, they had to wait the times and seasons marked out for them as Gentiles.

24. *"Except a corn of wheat fall into the ground and die, it abideth alone." Why refer to this corn of wheat?*

It was a reference to Himself, the true corn of wheat, who must die ere there could be fruit for others. The enquiry of these anxious Greeks is before His mind, and He knew that before He could satisfy their yearning desires He must suffer and die; hence His allusion to this well-known law in nature, and the results from death to those related to it, "If it die, it bringeth forth much fruit."

27. *"Now is My soul troubled." What was it that so troubled Him?*

We can only think of two things at all likely to give Him trouble, viz., His own sufferings and death, and the unbelief of those He came to save and bless. Now His own sufferings were no cause of trouble to Him, and He never shrank from them. "What shall I say? Father, save Me from this hour; but for this cause came I unto this hour," was His ready response. The blindness, the prejudice, and unbelief of the nation was more trouble to Him than all the weight of woe which hung over Him. Over their persistent rejection of His miracles and testimony He both groaned and wept.

28. *"Father, glorify Thy name." What did He mean?*

The response from the Father was, *I have glorified, and will again glorify.* Or, as given by the prophet, "Though Israel be not gathered, yet shall I be glorified, and my God shall be my strength" (Isa. xlix. 5). His mission was being rejected, but He is assured that others will receive it, and that while His death would be the crime and stumbling of the one, it would be the glory and triumph of the other.

31. *"Now is the judgment of this world: now shall the prince of this world be cast out." To what does He refer.*

In seeking an answer to this question we must keep before us the people who had rejected His testimony and were seeking to take His life. This was the world whose judgment or crisis had come, and whose ruler or prince was about to be removed. It was once a beautiful *kosmos* or arranged system, but through sin it had become a chaos, and judgment rested upon it, and its ruler or high priest was about to be removed from his position. They may put Me to shame by lifting Me up to the cross, but I shall yet draw the people by my love in dying for them.

32. *"And I, if I be lifted up from the earth, will draw all men unto Me." Why does He say this?*

These enquiring Greeks are still before His mind, and He speaks prophetically of their future. His ministry while on earth was limited to the Jews, but the proclamation of the Gospel would be free to the

Gentiles, and they would then be drawn to Him.

34. *" Who is this Son of man ?" Why did they ask this question ?*

They had understood from the teaching of Moses, that the anointed who was to come should abide for ever, but when Jesus spoke of dying they could not reconcile His teaching with that of their lawgiver. Had they received the teaching of Jesus concerning his resurrection they would have had no difficulty, but they rejected this truth, and so were blinded, and believed not.

40. *" He hath blinded their eyes and hardened their hearts." How can this be reconciled with the benevolent aspect of the Gospel ?*

The Gospel is to be preached to all for their acceptance and salvation, but condemnation is threatened upon those who reject it. This blinding of their eyes, and hardening of their hearts, followed their not believing the report, and could not have preceded its proclamation. God sought to bless them through Jesus, but when they refused to accept of Him, His glory and greatness were hidden from them; and this is what He declared by the prophet He would do.

CHAPTER XIII.

1. *" Jesus knew that His hour was come." Why is " hour " named ?*

It is symbolic of that brief period, marked off in the arrangement of God, in which Jesus should suffer and die. Up to this time His hour was future, now He knows that it has come, and calmly prepares for it. That hour was the most eventful in His whole life, both to Himself and all concerned. It is also called their hour, and the power of darkness— His to yield to all their desire, theirs to inflict upon Him all their evil hearts could devise. Up to that period He is under divine protection,

after that, until His death, neither God nor angels interfere. The wild blast of human wrath sweeps over Him in pitiless fury, and until His life is given up to their rage, and the sad fact is revealed, that men have nailed to the cross the Son of God, it never ceases. Two things are manifest in this deed of blood—the depth of human depravity, and the greatness of divine love. We may stand aghast at the one, and marvel at the other ; but the dire hatred of man, and the love of God will remain facts for ever.

" He loved them [His disciples] unto the end." How was this love manifested ?

By comforting and instructing them for their approaching trial, and then, while passing through death, specially committing them to the protection of His Father.

2. *How did Satan get the evil thought of the betrayal of Jesus into the heart of Judas ?*

Through the medium of the money that could be got by betraying Him. Judas had indulged in covetousness, and thus made ready the soil of his own heart, into which the evil seed entered and brought forth evil fruit. It would no doubt appear as a good stroke of business to make thirty pieces of silver so easily ; but it was evil, and therefore of the evil one. There is a moral lesson in it that all may study with profit. The terrible wind-up of many a life startles us with its awful disclosures, but it had its beginning in some small departure from right, but for which the sad end never would have occurred. Just as there is an inseparable connection between the spark on the train of gunpowder and the rending explosion, so is there between the first evil action and the crime that shocks the world. Had Judas never stolen from the bag, he would never have taken the thirty pieces of silver.

Let us beware of the first evil act, or if wrong has been done, let it be confessed and forsaken. Whenever we become servants of evil, Satan is practically our master, and we may have work to do we never dreamt of.

3–10. Is there any connection between the Saviour's knowledge that all things were given into His hand, and His act of washing His disciples' feet ?

The majesty of His claim as heir of all things, and His humility in this menial act, form a most striking contrast. He into whose hands the sceptre of the universe was given, condescended to wash the feet of His disciples, and thus practically illustrated what must be their feeling and action toward each other. " If I then, your Lord and Master, have washed your feet ; ye also ought to wash one another's feet."

Was this example of humility and service all that Jesus intended to teach by it ?

I think not. There were moral lessons which He wished them also to learn. Peter at first refused to humble His Master by such a lowly act; but when Jesus said to him, " If I wash thee not, thou hast no part with Me," we get at least a hint about spiritual cleansing. When Peter understood that without this washing he would forfeit a privilege, he rushed to the other extreme, and asked that feet, and head, and hands might all be washed ; but was then instructed that " he that is washed needeth not save to wash his feet."

" Save to wash his feet." What did Jesus mean ?

We read in the margin of the Revised Version, that some ancient authorities omit *save* and *his feet.* The Sinaitic MS. does not contain them, and, according to Tischendorf, they are omitted by Origen, who quotes the verse not less than six times. It is also wanting in some copies of the old Italic. If we therefore omit these doubtful words and read : " He that is washed needeth not to wash, but is clean every whit," we certainly set aside a difficulty, and also make plain the truth taught by Jesus.

11. " For He knew who should betray Him." Why choose such a man for a disciple ?

To place Judas in such a position was a most gracious act, and one by which he should have profited. But all example and teaching failed to subdue that spirit of covetousness which he cherished, and at last he made merchandise of Jesus. It was to His great favour that Judas owed such a position, and it was base ingratitude to abuse such favour.

26. Was Judas present at the institution of the memorial feast ?

No. He was present at the passover, and received the sop from Jesus, which was looked upon as a pledge of favour ; but John, who does not even name the memorial feast, says, that after the sop Satan entered into him, and he went immediately out, and did not wait for anything further.

What is meant by " Satan entered into him " ?

One would judge that up to this time Judas had wavered, but after the Saviour's words his decision was made, and he left that room ready to do the work of the evil one.

CHAPTER XIV.

Was the consolatory instruction given by Jesus in these three chapters delivered on the night of His betrayal ?

This rather lengthened address was most likely delivered between the close of the passover feast and their entrance into the garden of Gethsemane, and was most appropriate to their need.

1. *"Let not your heart be troubled."*
Why were they troubled?

Because He had told them He was about to leave them, and go where for the present they could not follow Him. This intimation filled their hearts with sorrow, and specially called for the consolation imparted.

Jesus acknowledged their faith in God. Why had He to say, "Believe also in Me"?

They had been trained by the writings of Moses and the prophets to trust in God, and by His teaching and miracles He had matured that trust; but now He asks them to believe in Himself, and the claim must have startled them. To give to one called the Son of man the honour and trust which had been given to God would seem to a Jew a direct violation of the first command given to them by God, and must have been difficult to accept. But here they learned, as afterwards more fully, that He who claimed this undivided honour by Moses as the one Jehovah, now claimed it as the Word made flesh. It is in His new standing as the Son of God that He asks for their trust, and ultimately receives it.

2. *What does He mean by "In My Father's house are many mansions"?*

It was not only an affirmation that His Father had a home, but an assurance that they were to dwell there, the many mansions implying no more than that there were abiding places for all, and that He was going to prepare a place for them, and would come again for them, that they might be with Him.

3. *Does the language of Jesus define the future home of His disciples sufficiently clear?*

Most certainly, and no words could more clearly show that the home of God, to which He would shortly depart, was also to be their abode.

L

He said that He was going to His Father's house to prepare a place for them, and would come again, and receive them unto Himself.

5, 6. *The way to the Father was to them a great difficulty. Does His statement that He was the way remove their difficulty?*

It was, doubtless, sufficient; but, like many other words spoken by Jesus, it required appropriate illustration to understand it, and this was afterwards amply supplied. When He died and rose again, and ascended to the Father, not only was the way really opened, but these facts became the means by which they also might ascend to be with God.

16. *What was the nature of the help promised to the disciples through the Comforter?*

It will be better to read Advocate than Comforter, as He was given to help them in their work, by the bestowal of gifts which should prove the truth of their proclamation, by bringing to their remembrance all the teaching of Jesus, and by fitting them to be qualified as apostles, prophets, evangelists, pastors, and teachers—the gift of Christ to His church. They were also empowered by the Spirit to bestow gifts on others, which they could not do during His ministry, being the greater things which they were to do, because He had gone to the Father, and which also confirmed all the words He had spoken and the works He had done.

"Another Comforter." What does Jesus mean by another?

He had been their Advocate or helper by His teaching, but was now about to leave them, and the Holy Spirit was promised to fill His place. He should guide them into all truth, and should abide with them for ever.

17. *"Even the Spirit of truth, whom the world cannot receive." Why not the world?*

When Jesus said the world could not receive the Holy Spirit, we must understand the restriction to apply to those who rejected Himself. This was most marked at the first bestowal. The Spirit rested not upon the priesthood in any of its divisions; nor upon the Pharisees, the straitest of the Jewish sects; nor upon the scribes, the writers of the law of God; but upon those who received Him as the exalted Son of God. The baptism of the Spirit, or the bestowal of any of His gracious gifts, was only to believers, and never preceded their faith in Christ. It is an inversion of the divine order even to pray for the Spirit instead of first hearing and obeying His testimony, and all who are doing this should pause and learn God's plan.

18. *What did Jesus mean when He said, "I will not leave you comfortless: I will come to you"?*

The margin more correctly reads, "Orphans," or, as Wiclif translates, "Faderless," *i.e.*, with no one to care for you. The Father would specially care for them during His crucifixion and death, and then the Spirit, His Advocate, would be to them during their labours all they would need.

22. *Why was Judas, not Iscariot, so puzzled about this manifestation which should be to them, and not to the world?*

Because he was looking for a public display, and by reasoning thus he was encouraging a vain expectation. The promised privilege was spiritual, and was to be confined to the obedient, and by such alone could be fully known to be of God.

26. *The Saviour seems to have fully instructed His disciples for their future work. Why, then, did they need the Spirit?*

To preserve from any human mixture the truth taught by Jesus during His ministry, as well as to prove to the world that He was the Christ.

This arrangement has secured for all time the perfect teaching of Jesus, and rendered their testimony worthy of all acceptance. Jesus was their teacher, the Spirit their helper to reproduce His teaching.

27. *What does He mean by "My peace I leave with you"?*

He evidently refers to the spirit in which He left them when leaving the world, and for which He was gradually preparing their sorrowful spirits by this sweet declaration. It was not in anger or reproach for unfaithfulness that He parted from them, but with the benediction of peace. Those uplifted hands and that parting blessing must have hallowed all their toilsome life.

28. *"My Father is greater than I." Is not this a plain assertion of His own inferiority?*

Yes, of position, for He became a servant; but not in nature, for He "was God." What He was, when in glory, and what He became to dwell on earth, must not be lost sight of, or we shall pervert His words, and dishonour Him who is now Lord of all.

CHAPTER XV.

1. *Why does Jesus call Himself the "true vine"?*

To those who are familiar with the teaching of the prophets, it is a symbol full of suggestive truth. The nation of Israel had been the vine of God :—"Thou hast brought a vine out of Egypt: thou hast cast out the heathen, and planted it" (Ps. lxxx. 8). "Yet I had planted thee a noble vine, wholly a right seed: how then art thou turned into the degenerate plant of a strange vine unto Me?" (Jer. ii. 21). "Israel is an empty vine, he bringeth forth fruit unto himself" (Hosea x. 1). The vine, a symbol of Israel, was cultivated only for its fruit, and if this was lacking, it was fit only for the fire. (See Ezekiel, chap. xv.) Such was the condition of the nation when Jesus said, "I am the true vine,"—i.e., the one bringing forth fruit for God the husbandman. And, as He here teaches, the branches of this vine must either be fruitful or be taken away.

2. *How could a branch be in Christ the vine, and bear no fruit?*

The arrangement by which union with Christ is effected is one thing, but fruit-bearing, the result of faithfulness to Him, is another and very different thing. We read in the life of Jesus that men believed in Him as the Messiah, and so became His disciples, but when tested by further claims to obedience, they refused to accept them, and walked no more with Him. Union with Christ is effected by faith in Him and obedience to His claims as given in His commission ; but this union is maintained only by continued obedience. If His claims are refused, there will be no fruit for God, and then follows, " Every branch in Me that beareth not fruit, He taketh away."

" Every branch in Me that beareth fruit, He purgeth it." How does God purge these branches?

An illustration may help us to understand it. On the vine, when there are straggling useless branches, these must be pruned away, or they will weaken the fruit-bearing ones. So in Christian life ; if the strength of mind and body are expended in worldly lusts and speculations, and if the flesh is indulged beyond prescribed bounds, there is little left for God. He therefore forbids all useless growth, that there may be fruit for Himself. To allow this heavenly pruning of all useless practices, is to yield to the heavenly husbandman, and fruit for God will follow ; but to resist His claims is to bring forth fruit to ourselves.

4. *Jesus said there could be no*

fruit except through abiding in Him. *How do men abide in Him?*

By abiding in His truth, which alone unites and preserves in Christ. The truth of the Gospel received into the heart is the connecting link between Christ and men ; hence obedience in faith and love unites to Jesus, while persistent disobedience separates those who have been united.

6. *Why does Jesus refer to the burning of fruitless branches?*

He is teaching the sad doom of fruitless disciples, but this allusion to the burning of fruitless branches is borrowed from Ezekiel xv., where the prophet teaches a most solemn lesson to the house of Israel, by asking them to consider the vine tree, which, unless it bore fruit, its wood was worthless. Not even a pin, on which to hang a vessel, could be made of it : it was fit only for the fire. Jesus simply repeats the prophet's conclusion, " men gather them, and cast them into the fire, and they are burned," and left the truth to do its own work. Jesus does not say that fruitless disciples will be burned, but judgment is certainly implied in the illustration, and was intended as a warning to all who assumed to be His disciples.

9, 10. *What does Jesus intend to teach by referring to the love of the Father to Himself?*

A very practical lesson, in which He affirms a rather startling truth, viz., that the continued approving love of the Father was enjoyed by continued obedience, and when asking them to continue in His love He shows them that it must be by keeping His commandments.

Had Jesus to win for Himself the position He occupied?

Most certainly. Every position He occupied was the fruit of conquest, every point gained was through self-denial. His life of obedience was not only a vindication of God's righteous claims, so completely ignored by the disobedient Jews, but a proof that His favour can be enjoyed only through obedience. It was a demonstration that God ought to be trusted and obeyed without a single reserve. By His obedient life, the Saviour proved that God was worthy of all it could yield to Him ; and then, as their Lord, He claimed from them a corresponding obedience to Himself.

11. *That My joy might remain in you." What is the nature of this joy ?*

It is the joy of obedience, and this joy He desires for them.

13. *Why does Jesus speak of a man laying down his life for his friends ?*

He had asked them to love one another, and this would involve much self-denying action toward each other. How far this might be carried needed a word of illustration, and this He furnished in His own action, in surrendering His life for His friends. He had asked from them a manifestation of His own spirit, and they would prove that they were His friends if they carried out His request.

19. *" I have chosen you out of the world." Was this choice for personal salvation or for service ?*

Election or choice in Christ is of God, but the election of the disciples by Christ was, that they might be witnesses of His resurrection, and proclaim salvation to the world in His name. As the Saviour of men, and having the promise of universal authority, it was in keeping with His great mission to choose those who should be His co-workers. They had not chosen Him, He was God's choice, as said Isaiah (xliii. 10), Behold " My servant whom I have chosen," but it was His work to ordain others and send them into the world. Hence His word, " I have chosen you."

20. *Why did He tell them of persecution ?*

That they might not be surprised when trials came over them. They were to share His throne, and they must also share His cross.

26. *" But when the Comforter is come . . . He shall testify of Me." How would the Spirit testify ?*

Through the apostles, whose Spirit-guided testimony concerning Jesus was sustained by signs, wonders, and gifts of the Holy Spirit, and which were all done in the name of Jesus.

CHAPTER XVI.

Is this chapter a continuance of the discourse commenced in the previous chapter ?

The last words of chap. xiv. are, " Arise, let us go hence." The company then left the upper room where much consolatory instruction had been given, and some other privacy was sought, and the unbroken discourse of chaps. xv. and xvi. was delivered, and where He offered His intercessory prayer (chap. xvii.). After this Jesus and the eleven passed over the brook Cedron to the garden of Gethsemane, to prepare for His surrender to His foes.

1, 2. *" That ye should not be offended." What was likely to offend them ?*

It will be better to read *ensnared*, that is, with the people, who, not having shown any sympathy to Jesus, were not likely to show it towards them. To expect their friendship would only be disappointing to themselves, and they were directed to be faithful, and expect persecution.

7. *Why was it necessary that Jesus should go away before the Spirit, the Advocate, could come ?*

While Jesus was with them, His presence supplied all need, but as the work of redemption was to go on by means of testimony, and the obedience of faith, His departure was needful, that the testimony might be made.

8–11. *How was the coming of the Spirit to reprove the world of sin, righteousness, and judgment ?*

The united powers of the world put Jesus to death as an impostor, but when the Spirit came, and with signs and wonders demonstrated that He was the Son of God, they stood convicted of sin before God. They might neither feel nor own the crime. but, as in courts of law evidence decides the case against the person charged, and judgment righteously follows, it would be so with them. When the Holy Spirit, by signs and wonders, proved that Jesus was the Son of God, they stood convicted of putting to death a righteous person: In that testimony their sin and His righteousness became openly manifest.

" *The prince of this world is judged." Who is this prince ?*

It is—*lit., the ruler of this world has been judged*—*i.e.,* he who condemned Jesus to be crucified will then be convicted of guilt. Pilate, the representative of Roman authority in Judea, not only involved his own nation by crucifying Jesus, but also the Jews, at whose behest it was done. By the Spirit's testimony on behalf of Jesus, the united forces of the world were brought under the judgment of heaven, *i.e.,* under deserved condemnation. The verdict of the Jews was, " He is guilty of death," and·Pilate executed the sentence, and thereby involved the world in judgment.

13. *Why is the Spirit called " the Spirit of truth " ?*

Because all truth is revealed from Him, whether by prophets, or Christ, or apostles. It is that part of the great work of redemption over which He presides, and all that we know

of God and His great purposes of redeeming love has been made known by Him. From the first recorded promise of grace announcing the woman's seed, to the last sentence, " The grace of our Lord Jesus Christ be with you all," we have one continuous stream of revelation under His gracious presidency. He who by holy men of God in past ages, revealed so much concerning the coming One, was then coming to the apostles that He might guide them into all the truth which the ascended Jesus had taught them. One peculiarity of the Spirit's mission was, that Jesus should be the great theme of His ministry. " He shall take of Mine and show it unto you," an example that should stir all hearts, and lead all workers in the heavenly vineyard to understand that Jesus is to be the one great object of Christian ministry. Not self, but Christ. Not human philosophy and science falsely so called, but Christ. It is Christ the sinner needs to save and bless him, and nothing else can meet the yearning of his spirit. It is Christ the saint needs to cheer and help in this trying pilgrimage, and no theme however interesting can fill His place. The Holy Spirit in His ministry provided the true bread for the hungry, and it is sad when professed helpers give stones instead. He has provided fish for the feast, and none should offer scorpions in their place. It is a cruel mockery to do so, and all workers and feeders of the flock should watch against such a perversion.

16–22. *The disciples appear to have been perplexed about the Saviour's departure and return to them. Were the explanations given to them by Jesus sufficient to remove their difficulty on these matters ?*

His whole teaching on this occasion was intended to remove their difficulty, but He gently hints that the fulfilment of His gracious plan was necessary in order to their full apprehension of it. In a " little while " He was going away to the Father, but He would return to them in the ministry of the Spirit, who should fill His place, and abide with them all through the age. This is what He means by going from them and returning to them. The world would rejoice, and they should have sorrow, but their sorrow should be turned into joy. Their trial, between these two events, should be as the pangs of a woman in travail, that ended with the birth of her son. The birth - pangs of a new state were felt by them when Jesus hung on the cross, and lay in the tomb, and went away to the Father; but when the Spirit descended, and power to testify was given, they were filled with joy and with the Holy Spirit—Jesus having been glorified. It is true that Jesus did return to them a little while after His resurrection, teaching and preparing them for their work, and trial, and joy; but soon He would leave them and go to the Father, and then they should have joy in possessing the promised Comforter, which none should take from them.

CHAPTER XVII.

Was this intercessory prayer offered in the hearing of all the disciples ?

It is most likely that all were present except Judas, as, at its close, Jesus, with the eleven, went across the brook Cedron on their way to Gethsemane. To have listened to that prayer, as it fell from His lips, was no ordinary privilege; but, although few were so favoured, yet, through this record of John, millions have felt the throbbing of His loving heart towards them.

1. *" Father, the hour is come."* *What hour was this ?*

The hour of His sufferings and death. The hour when the serpent should bruise His heel. The eventful hour that had been the subject of prophecy during four thousand years had arrived, and Jesus stood upon the threshold of this eventful period, and awaited all its issues.

What did He mean by " Glorify Thy Son " ?

It is a reference to His resurrection, which, although promised, was within the range of faith and prayer. To raise Jesus from the dead was to glorify Him, and this was in order that He might save men, and thus God would be glorified.

2. *" As Thou hast given Him power — lit., authority — over all flesh."* *Why was it given to Jesus ?*

That He might give eternal life to those given to Him, and for its bestowal as a personal gift this authority was required. The gift of life belonged to God, and this great prerogative was bestowed on Him who gave His life a ransom for the guilty.

" As many as Thou hast given Him." *Do these words not teach an arbitrary giving of men to Christ ?*

The words " as many as " have no corresponding words in the Greek of this verse, and must therefore be left out of the text, and for this simple reason, that they do not belong to it. Thousands of times these words have been used to prove that some persons were eternally given to Christ, to receive eternal life through Him, while others, not so given, were left in their ruin, and yet, it turns out, that these words were never uttered by Him. The words which He did utter—and they form a part of His prayer to the Father, and were answered in His resurrection—are most simple, and should inspire with confidence the hearts of all who are looking to Him for salvation and life. Leaving out, then, these three words, which are found in no other translation that I possess, we shall give a simple rendering of this beginning of His prayer, in which He so earnestly expresses His desire to be fitted to carry out the loving purpose of His Father. The division into verses, as in our common version, has made the second verse to read as a distinct petition, and has thus obscured the thought expressed by Jesus, and this we must carefully avoid. The section must be read in its unbroken connection, and then we may observe its beautiful harmony. *These words spake Jesus* (the words of the preceding chapter), *and lifted up His eyes to heaven, and said, Father, the hour is come ; glorify Thy Son (by raising Him from the dead), that Thy Son also may glorify Thee : according as Thou gavest to Him authority over all flesh, so that* (of) *all Thou hast given to Him, He might give to them* (even) *eternal life.* Now we think there is no difficulty in understanding this first part of the prayer of Jesus. As the Christ who should come into the world, He had received the promise of universal authority, and now that the Jews were about to put Him to death, He asks that God would glorify Him by raising Him from death, so that He also might glorify God, by giving life to all those who believe in Him, who are also given to Him to form His church and His bride. And as no one is restricted from believing in Christ as made known in the Gospel, so Christ is now pledged in that Gospel proclamation to do all that is needed by ruined man.

For what objects did Jesus specially pray on this occasion ?

His prayer was for persons, and included Himself, the apostles, those who should believe on Him through their word, and through the united testimony of His ambassadors, for which He specially prayed—that the world might believe in Him as the Son of God.

5. *What petition did He offer for Himself ?*

A request for glorification, and this petition included His resurrection, exaltation, and also possession of power for the purpose of saving and redeeming men.

What petitions did He offer for His disciples ?

There were not less than four distinct petitions which He offered to the Father on their behalf :—(1.) Their preservation from the evil of the world. (2.) Their sanctification by the truth. (3.) Their oneness of testimony. (4.) Their introduction into glory when their work was done.

9. *" I pray for them : I pray not for the world."* Why pray not for the world ?

If any suppose that it was the salvation of the world for which He would not pray, they have certainly made a mistake. The context of truth and facts must here be weighed, and we shall then better understand, and possibly approve of the omission. Jesus was about to begin a new dispensation, to build a new temple, to form a new priesthood, etc., which necessarily involved the entire destruction of the old economy. The hearts of its friends might cling around it, and even disciples might plead for its continuance, but its doom was fixed, and its end was drawing nigh. It was the upholding of this old system, and not the salvation of the world, for which He would not pray. We could not harmonise the two statements (1.) that He is the propitiation for the world, and (2.) that He would not pray for it, if they referred to the one object. We must therefore conclude that world— lit., *kosmos*—is not only applied to the whole human family for whom He gave His life, but also to that Jewish system, for the sustaining of which He would not pray.

Is it a correct application of kosmos, *to apply it to the Jewish economy with its people and institutions?*

The Saviour so uses it in ver. 14, and other places. " The world hath hated them," must apply to their own brethren, who were set upon upholding the system which was so soon to fall. These men, so closely allied to Jesus, had to bear a measure of the scorn which fell upon Himself.

Why did Jesus require to pray to the Father for His disciples?

Jesus had been their special guardian and teacher during His ministry, but with His arrest that must cease for a " little while," hence they are specially commended to God during the trying period of His crucifixion. " Holy Father, keep through Thine own name (during this period) those whom thou hast given Me."

15. *The first petition of Jesus for His disciples was their preservation from evil. What kind of evil did Jesus refer to?*

Both physical and moral evil, for they were to be exposed to both. They would have enemies both to their message and themselves; and from these protection was needed and supplicated.

17. *His second petition was for their sanctification through the truth. How does truth sanctify?*

By obedience to it, separation from all impurity is effected. Much had been done already in them by the teaching of Jesus, and by the truth that work was still to go on. There is no other method of sanctification, than of accepting and obeying the truth which separates from all evil.

21. *In praying for their oneness, what did He mean?*

Their oneness of testimony as the ambassadors of His truth; and His prayer for this object was fulfilled to the very letter. Their proclamations and teaching were uniform, and have become the basis on which all disciples may unite. To accept their teaching union must follow, to refuse it, schism and condemnation.

24. *In praying that they might be with Him, and behold His glory, what did this imply, seeing that all believers will ultimately enjoy this privilege?*

Yes, but at death believers enter paradise, where Jesus Himself went after death, but the special request of Jesus was, that these disciples, who had witnessed His shame, should be with Him when ascended and honoured in glory, prior to the glorification of all; and this was to them a special privilege.

20. " *Neither pray I for these alone, but for all them which shall believe on Me through their word.*" *Why must it be*, through their word?

Because they are His appointed ambassadors, and no other have been sent out by Him. Their testimony therefore must be received, or there can be no claim to His promises. True, the apostles are dead, but their testimony, which is no less than the testimony of Christ, through the Holy Spirit, must remain authoritative to the end. " Lo, I am with you alway, even unto the end of the world,"—lit., the age. It is therefore by the acceptance or rejection of their word, that men are to be blessed or condemned. It is by acceptance of their testimony that we become one with the apostles, whose fellowship is with the Father and with His Son Jesus Christ. To accept of human arrangements, on mere ecclesiastical or any other authority, must leave outside of assured blessing all who do so. Men are in special danger of being tempted aside from those God-given arrangements which have come into the world through the apostles of Jesus, and require to be reminded that the truth by which man is to be saved and purified in spirit can be derived from no other source. " He that heareth you heareth Me," etc. (Luke x. 16).

CHAPTER XVIII.

1. *" When Jesus had spoken these words, He went forth with His disciples." Was this from the upper room ?*

No, that appears to have been left earlier in the evening, and some other place selected, where further instruction was given and His prayer offered for them. Then they passed out of Jerusalem, down into the valley, and across the Cedron, and ascending the slope of Olivet, they entered the garden of Gethsemane.

2. *"Judas knew the place." Knew it in what sense ?*

As the prayer-place or closet of Jesus, for he ofttimes (when at Jerusalem) resorted thither. Judas knew where and when to find Him alone, *i.e.*, absent from the multitude, and was not disappointed.

3. *Why did Judas obtain a band of men and officers ?*

This band of men, with officers to direct them, went with Judas, simply to arrest Jesus when pointed out by him. The arrest was no part of his work ; that belonged to them. His part in the solemn tragedy was to betray Him into their hands with a kiss ; theirs to seize and take Him away.

4–6. *Is it not strange that Jesus should meet this band, and challenge their purpose. Might He not rather have escaped ?*

Yes, He might have escaped, or rather He might have gone out of

their reach altogether. But in coming into the world, He came to be God's lamb, to meet the world's great necessity, and yield His life a ransom for them ; so that we need not wonder at this, or any other voluntary act of His life.

John alone mentions the falling to the ground of the band. Were they overawed by His bold challenge, " whom seek ye ? "

We must remember that this was a small band of Roman soldiers, who were simply on duty by order of the priests whose interests they had to watch. The challenge of Jesus was a very searching one, Who are *you* seeking ? or, What do *you* want with Jesus of Nazareth ? and for the moment this had a paralysing effect upon them, and they fell back to the ground. But, having a duty to perform, and being aroused to do their work, the panic was overcome, and He was bound and led away ; but at the same time requesting that the three disciples that were with Him might not be arrested, and were therefore let go away.

10. *Why did Peter cut off the man's ear ?*

It was an impulsive act in defence of Jesus, which he would not have done had he only believed his Master's teaching. His mild reproof contains a lesson, both for Peter and all others, viz., that it is better to drink the cup God gives us, though it may lead to our death, than to set it aside, though we may have power to do so.

13. *Why did the officers take Jesus to Annas first ?*

Annas had been the high priest, and though at the time deposed from office, was recognised and sought unto in civil matters. Hence his judgment was first obtained, and afterward that of Caiaphas.

14. *Why does John name the prophecy by Caiaphas ?*

Possibly to show the effort made to reconcile the minds of many to the proposed death of Jesus, to which many were likely to object. The prophecy was used for a political purpose, and the people were led by it to believe that His death would effect their national deliverance from the Roman yoke, and thereby the consent of many was secured.

15, 16. *"And Simon Peter followed Jesus, and so did another disciple." Who was he?*

As John does not give us his name, but says that he was known to the high priest, and even spoke to her that kept the door and brought in Peter, we can think of none who could be so likely to have influence there as Judas. He had covenanted with them, and must have been well known to all engaged in the trial. That Judas would be interested in the issue of it we cannot for a moment doubt, and Matthew states that he watched it until he saw that Jesus was condemned. Judas, therefore, was most likely that other disciple.

Why should Judas be so interested, seeing he had betrayed Him?

It was the interest of fear, not of love; he had betrayed Him for money, but did not expect that His condemnation would be effected thereby. He had access into the palace, etc., as an associate, and through his influence Peter was admitted to witness the trial. He could not but feel anxious about its termination, and when the sentence of death was past, he returned the money, confessed the innocence of Jesus, and died by his own hands.

25–27. *When Peter denied that he was a disciple of Jesus, was it through fear?*

Not through cowardice, but fear lest his faith had been misplaced. Peter had not believed the word of

Jesus respecting His end, and this caused his perplexity when he saw Him in the hands of sinners. He looked for honour, not shame; for triumph, and not defeat; and was staggered when he saw Him led as a lamb to the slaughter.

28. *The "hall of judgment" was the third place to which they took Jesus. Why take Him there?*

It was the place where the Roman governor gave judgment in all criminal cases, and without his sentence of condemnation they could not put Jesus to death. Pilate, therefore, was called early into the judgment hall, to do what they so earnestly desired.

Had Pilate any personal spite against Jesus?

None whatever, and at first declined to have anything to do with the case.

31. *Why did he say "take ye Him, and judge Him according to your law"?*

He must have looked upon the charge against Jesus as an offence in something pertaining to their religion, and not a criminal offence, and therefore urged them to dispose of it, according to the power still possessed by them of settling their own disputes. But when they claimed that He should be put to death, he re-entered the judgment hall, in order to try the case, and test their charge against Him.

33. *Why did Pilate ask Him, "Art Thou the king of the Jews?"*

The reply of Jesus furnishes the reason. "Sayest thou this thing of thyself, or did others tell it thee of Me?" *i.e.*, have you seen anything in My action that could prompt such a question? and was at once informed that His own nation had delivered Him up on this charge, and he wished to know what He had done.

Why did Jesus speak of the nature of His kingdom?

In order to let him know that He was a king, and had a kingdom, but that it would present no opposition to him, because His servants would not fight with carnal weapons. This explanation, though imperfectly understood by Pilate, so far satisfied him, that he resolved to release Jesus, but offered to do it according to the custom of releasing a political prisoner every year at the passover. To have done so would have implied the truth of their charge, but this they refused to accept, and cried, saying, " Not this man, but Barabbas."

CHAPTER XIX.

1. *Why did Pilate scourge Jesus ?*
Either to extort confession of guilt, a once common method of dealing with criminals ; or else to punish Him in order to prevent the heavier sentence of death, thinking the Jews would be satisfied with this ; but he found that he was mistaken.

2. *Why did the soldiers put the crown of thorns upon His head ?*
To insult and mock their victim. He had claimed to be a king, and upon this claim their insolent mockery was based. These Roman soldiers were just influenced by circumstances, and ignorantly lent themselves as tools for the occasion.

7. *" We have a law, and by our law He ought to die." What law was this ?*
The law against blasphemy. He assumed to be the Son of God : they judged Him to be only a man.

Would Pilate know any thing of Jesus prior to this meeting with Him ?
As the Roman governor he dwelt at Cæsarea, and knew little beyond what rumour might convey, and though he had heard now from His own lips that He is a king, he saw nothing serious in the claim. But

when he heard that the prisoner claimed to be the Son of God, he was afraid, and at once demanded an account of His origin ; but to this demand Jesus gave no reply.

10. *Why did Pilate appeal to his power ?*
It would seem that his pride was touched. " Speakest Thou not to me ? knowest Thou not that I have power to crucify Thee, and power to release Thee ? " It was the appeal of might against weakness, of a judge against his prisoner ; but he understood not who that prisoner was.

11. *Why did Jesus remind him of the source of his power ?*
Because it was derived, and for the right use of it he was responsible.

12. *Pilate was anxious to release Jesus ; why did he not do so ?*
Because of the pressure brought to bear upon him by the leading men of the nation : "If thou let this man go, thou art not Cæsar's friend." This charge was too much for his time-serving policy, and he granted all their request, and commanded Him to be crucified.

Was crucifixion a Jewish mode of punishment ?
No. It was strictly Roman ; but the Jews on this occasion ceased to press their first charge, that Jesus was a blasphemer, the penalty of which was death by stoning, and pressed the alternate charge that He was an usurper against Cæsar, the penalty of which was crucifixion.

19. *Why did Pilate put such a title on the cross as " Jesus of Nazareth, the king of the Jews " ?*
It was the charge under which His conviction had been secured, and though the Jews would not own Him as their king, and loudly protested against it, he would not alter the inscription.

Why write it in three languages ?
In order that it might be read by both Jews, Greeks, and Romans,

many of them being then at Jerusalem. Besides, these languages were representative of the three great forces of the world—the Hebrew of religion, the Greek of philosophy, and the Latin of Roman law. Pilate thus involved the world in the condemnation of Jesus, and made each of its marked divisions to share the crime of His death.

23, 24. *Were the clothes of criminals the perquisites of the executioners ?*

This seems to have been the case ; but how sad to think that possession of that seamless robe of Jesus should rest upon a throw of the dice ! The soldiers raffling at the foot of the cross, to decide who should have His garment, shocks every feeling of modesty, and yet these were the wicked hands the Jews used to crucify Jesus.

25. *Were there three or four women standing by the cross of Jesus ?*

If we conclude there were but three, then there were two Marys in one family, which is not likely. The Peshito Syriac Version of the second century has *and* after sister, which shows they understood that four were present.

26. *Was the committing of His mother to the beloved disciple His last act ?*

It appears so, and is a striking illustration of what an unselfish sympathising heart will do—turning aside from its own need to care for the need of others. The prophecy of Simeon was then being fulfilled, " a sword shall pierce through thine own soul also ! " but He who caused those pangs sought to soothe them by His sympathy.

30. *" It is finished," were His last words on the cross. What was finished ?*

In His intercessory prayer He said, " I have finished the work which Thou gavest Me to do." It was not the work of salvation consequent upon the faith and obedience of those who receive Him, as that would be going on till His return from heaven ; nor His work of rule and intercession which He would take up when seated on the throne at God's right hand, but His work and suffering here. Nothing was left undone which had been marked out for Him to do or suffer ; but neither work nor blessing consequent upon His own service can be included in this cry, " It is finished." Indeed, John has made the true application of the words in ver. 28, " After this, Jesus knowing that all things were now accomplished—*lit.* finished—that the Scriptures might be fulfilled, saith, I thirst."

31. *What does John mean by "for that sabbath day was an high day" ?*

It was the passover sabbath, which, assuming that Jesus was crucified on Thursday, would be the day preceding the weekly sabbath, and was thus a high day, a day having special claims on their regard.

34. *Why does John refer to the blood and water that came from the side of Jesus ?*

It was an evidence that He was truly dead, although not a bone was broken.

CHAPTER XX.

1. *If Jesus was three nights and two full days in the sepulchre, why did Mary Magdalene not visit it sooner than the first of the week ?*

There were several reasons which we presume would prevent her doing so. (1.) There was a guard of soldiers who kept watch till that day. (2.) The two days that intervened were both sabbath days, during which no servile work, not even anointing the body, could be done. The visit, therefore, for these reasons was delayed.

Did she expect to find Him risen from the dead ?

No ; she, and other women that went with her, took spices to anoint Him, but were surprised to find the tomb empty, and judged His body had been removed.

2. *"Then she runneth and cometh to Simon Peter." Was it to tell him that Jesus was risen ?*

No ; but to tell him that the body was removed, and they knew not where it had been laid.

8. *" Then went in also that other disciple . . . and he saw and believed." Believed what ?*

The report of the women that the body was taken away, and not that He was risen.

11–16. *Why did Mary linger at the sepulchre when the body of Jesus was gone ?*

She felt assured the body was gone, but she could not tear herself away from the spot where she thought it should have been. And, as she ventured to take one more gaze at the empty sepulchre, she then saw two angels in white sitting, the one at the head and the other at the feet, where the body of Jesus had lain. These angels asked Mary why she wept, and as she told them the cause, and turned round, another person stood before her, who also asked her why she wept, and in a few moments she knew that it was Jesus.

17. *Why did Jesus forbid Mary to touch Him, when His disciples were pressed to examine His body ?*

They were to be His witnesses to the world, Mary was not. She required only to believe for herself that He was risen, and His voice assured her of that. They had to be satisfied in order to affirm it, and every opportunity was given them to do so. They not only saw and heard, but felt and handled the Word of life. This may account for the difference.

19. *The disciples assembled on the* *evening of that first day of the week. Why did they do so ?*

I presume it was to commemorate the death of their Master and friend, according to His direction when instituting the memorial feast. It was the first Lord's day meeting, for the breaking of the loaf, under the new economy, and was to continue "till He come." It is interesting to note that Jesus entered while they were thus together, and breathed on them His peaceful benediction.

How did He enter that room ?

Miraculously, I have no doubt ; and though they were at first affrighted at the manner of His appearance, yet when He showed them His hands and His side, they were satisfied that He was their risen Lord and Master. It was a blessed recompense for their first act of obedience, that Jesus should enter their midst.

21. *"As My Father hath sent Me, even so send I you." What idea would this convey to them ?*

I presume they would understand, that as He was the Father's apostle, and had brought messages from God, so they were to be His apostles, to carry forth messages from Him to the world.

22. *" He breathed on them, and said, receive ye the Holy Spirit." Did this take place just then ?*

Facts are the best exponents of this declaration, and on these we must rely in seeking an answer. There is nothing to indicate that they did then receive the Holy Spirit ; but at Pentecost His illustrative action of breathing on them was fulfilled.

23. *"Whosoever sins ye remit, they are remitted unto them," etc. How did they exercise this high prerogative ?*

Their action after Pentecost must guide our understanding of it. On that memorable day they began to use the power granted to them, but it was by announcing "remission of sins" to immersed penitents upon (their confession of) the name of Jesus. Their power to remit sins was by their proclamation of Christ's law, and that law He has never changed. The apostles never assumed this power in any other form. The remission of sins is an act of divine sovereignty, but it was made known to the world by the apostles of Christ, and can be obtained now according to their testimony, and no one can be certain of obtaining it in any other way.

26. *Why did John say, "after eight days" they were again assembled, instead of the first day of the week?*

The eighth day was the first day, but it was in Jewish style to so term it.

Why did they meet again on the first day?

To remember the death of Jesus, as they had done on the previous first day, according to His direction. It was their first recognition of His authority, and may be counted as an authorised precedent for the worship and honour of Jesus. His repeated presence in their midst gave to their assembly a divine sanction, and the seal of His approval still rests upon it.

27. *Was this uncovering of His wounded hands and side to unbelieving Thomas, a gratuitous act on the part of Jesus?*

He was not compelled to do this, but was anxious to remove every doubt from the mind of His chosen witness ; and having shown to the ten His wounds, He meets Thomas on his own terms. "Reach hither thy finger, and behold My hands ; and reach hither thy hand, and thrust it into My side, and be not faithless, but believing." It was enough for him to gaze upon that spear-pierced side and exclaim, "My Lord and my God."

31. *What is the special purpose for which John records these signs?*

To induce conviction that Jesus the Nazarene was indeed the Son of God, and that believing they might have life in His name.

What is the nature of the life here promised?

It is the favour of God as made known in the Gospel, and received only through Jesus. Those who believe with their heart the Gospel of Jesus, receive the life-giving truth, and by His directions are born into the family of God.

CHAPTER XXI.

1–14. *John has already recorded three manifestations of Christ, once to Mary Magdalene, and twice to His disciples. Why does he record this fourth appearance?*

The former were manifestations of His person; this was a manifestation of power, timely and wisely shown to them. The apostles had become weary of the inactive life they were called to lead during that intervening period, and it became a snare to them. Simon Peter could wait no longer, and said to five of his fellow-disciples, "I go a-fishing," who said, "We also go with thee." Boats and nets were soon obtained, and that night they were toiling on the Sea of Galilee. It was an unsuccessful toil, and, weary and dispirited, they turned to the shore. A stranger was walking near to the place they were putting in, and asked about their success, and learning their failure, in a friendly manner suggested where they might cast the net. His direction was followed, and at once a great multitude of fishes were enclosed. To draw it to land became a most exciting effort, but when it was whispered to Peter by him who first perceived it, "it is the Lord," he at once girt on his coat and made for the shore. The rest slowly dragged the net to land, and all found a meal of bread and fish provided for them.

15–17. *"Lovest thou Me?" Why did Jesus make this thrice-repeated appeal to Peter alone?*

There are several reasons why Jesus should make this searching and repeated enquiry, and these are closely related to the great work to which he had been called. The mission with which he had been entrusted would demand loving firmness, and in these qualities he has just shown a wavering spirit. Then the character of his work had to be again pointed out in the hearing of his fellow-disciples, that all might know what he had personally to do. And again, he was shown that personal love to Jesus would be required for its faithful discharge. Thus he had to endure this thrice-repeated appeal.

"Lovest thou Me more than these?" To what did Jesus refer?

The word "these" evidently requires to be supplemented by either persons or things, and it is only when the proper affix is made that the force of His question becomes apparent. It would hardly seem appropriate for Jesus to say to Peter, "Lovest thou Me more than these" disciples? How could he answer such a question? But, as His finger, possibly pointed to the large shoal of fish lying on the beach, and also in relation to the great work to which he had been called, it would be most appropriate for Jesus to say, "Lovest thou Me more than these" fish? That is, would you rather spend your life in catching fish, than in doing My work? To this Peter could and did reply as often as the question was repeated, "Thou knowest that I love Thee?"

"Feed My lambs," etc. This appears like a commission in addition to his ambassadorship. How shall we designate it?

It is the pastor added to the ambassador, and shows how wisely and efficiently the great Shepherd, who gave His life for the sheep, arranged for their necessary spiritual provision. It was His purpose that not only should they hear the jubilee message of life and pardon from his lips as at Pentecost, but that from his pen also, they should receive that fully digested system of truth, promises, precepts, directions, cautions, and assurances which are given in his epistles, to be used by the saints in all the ever-varying necessities of their life. Thus did Jesus arrange, and thus was His will carried out, that Peter should feed the lambs and sheep of His flock.

Why is "feed" thrice repeated?

It is only proper to notice here that Jesus uses two words, while our version has but one. He said *boske* —lit., "feed" with the truth "my lambs;" then *poimaine*—lit., *shepherd* or tend "my sheep." Then again, *boske*, "feed" with the truth "my sheep." These two words, indicating the nature of the work which Jesus would have done for His flock, both being necessary to express His will, ought to have a place in our version. The New Revision has met this need, and supplied the word "tend," which shows what further would be needed, than simply feeding.

A brief extract from Trench's "Synonyms of the New Testament" will enable us to discern more clearly the meaning and necessity of the two words used by Jesus. Trench says, "*Bosko*, the same word as the Latin '*pasco*,' is simply 'to feed;' but *poimano* involves much more,— the whole office of the shepherd, the entire leading, guiding, guarding, folding of the flock, as well as the finding of nourishment for it."

Jesus then begins with *boske*, " feed ; " then He uses *poimaine*, " tend;" and then closes with *boske*, the simple direction to feed with the truth. Why He should do this is no doubt instructive, if we can only take up the lesson. Upon the reason for this repetition of *boske* Trench further adds : " Still, it may be asked, if *poimainein* be thus the higher word (this is assumed), and if *poimaine* was therefore superadded upon *boske*, because it was so, and implied so many further ministries of care and tendance, why does it not appear in the last, which must be also the most solemn commission given to Peter? How are we to account, if this be true, for His returning to *boske* again ?" This question is then answered by Trench, by a quotation from Stanley's "Sermons and Essays on the Apostolic Age," p. 138, who writes :—" The lesson, in fact, which we learn from this, His coming back to the *boske* with which He had begun, is a most important one, which the Church, and all that bear rule in the Church, have need diligently to lay to heart —this, namely, that whatever else of discipline and rule may be superadded thereto, still, the feeding of the flock, the finding for them of spiritual nourishment, is the first and last. Nothing else will supply the room of this, nor may be allowed to put this out of its foremost and most important place. How often, in a false ecclesiastical system, the preach-ing of the word loses its pre-eminence ; the *boskein* falls into the background, is swallowed up in the *poimainein*, which presently becomes no true *poimainein*, because it is not a *boskein* as well, but rather such a ' shepherding ' as God's Word, by the prophet Ezekiel, has denounced " (xxxiv. 2, 3, 8–10; Zech. xi. 15–17; Matt. xxiii).

18, 19. *What was indicated by this prophetic announcement concerning the last days of Peter ?*

His death for the truth, but the manner of it is not given to us. This alone is certain to us, that his days were to be cut short by martyrdom.

20–23. *Why is he so concerned about the fate of John ?*

Possibly he was curious to know what would befall one who he expected would have a similar fate to himself.

What did the answer of Jesus reveal concerning him ?

Nothing definite, but a wrong conclusion was formed out of it, and the brethren judged that John would not die, because Jesus said, " If I will that he tarry till I come, what is that to thee ?"

" *Till I come.*" *Did He refer to His second advent ?*

Not to His advent in person, I presume, for that is not so probable, but to His advent in power, which John was no doubt permitted to see. With this longer survival than himself Peter had nothing to do, but was urged to show his personal faithfulness by following Jesus in all His appointed ways.

THE ACTS OF THE APOSTLES.

Is " Acts of the Apostles" a proper title to give to this book ?

Not if we intend it to apply to all the apostles, because it is a record of the labours of only two of them.

Acts of Peter and Paul might have been more definite, but as they are representative men, it is truly " The Acts of the Apostles:"

Why have we not a record

of the labours of all the apostles?

It would have been most interesting if we had been so favoured, but possibly of no further benefit than what we may derive from that which is given to us. It was evidently the design of the Spirit, by a very full record of the labours of Peter and Paul, to fully illustrate God's gracious purpose in a new administration by His Son Jesus Christ. At that time the world was divided into three great sections—viz., Jews, Samaritans, and Gentiles, or the nations—each having a peculiar relation to God, and all needing His mercy and grace. Now, from the recorded labours of these two men, and also of Philip, who went down to Samaria, we get a full account of the provision which God has made for His fallen creatures, and how that provision can be realised. The proclamation of acceptance and remission of sins, upon their repentance and immersion in the name of Jesus, was first made known among the Jews by Peter, and this long-looked for privilege was then realised by all who accepted Jesus as thus made known to them by this apostle of the ascended Christ. A thousand cases selected from the after labours of the twelve apostles could not have made it plainer how Jews were to obtain the remission of past sins, than this one pentecostal scene. After this we are furnished with an account of the visit of Philip to Samaria, and may learn how, by faith and obedience to Christ Jesus, these Samaritans were accepted of God, and received the gift of the Holy Spirit. Then we have a further record of Peter being called to minister of the grace of God to the Gentiles, to open the door of faith to them; and by the bestowal of the Holy Spirit it was manifest that they might be baptised into the name of Jesus, and enjoy every gracious privilege as well as Samaritans and Jews. Then for this new field we have a new labourer raised up, and sent forth by the Lord to extend the work among all the nations of the earth. Thus through the labours of these men the arrangements of God for the salvation of all who will be saved in God's way, are fully made known, and may safely assume, that in order to show how men could be saved, nothing further was required.

What period of time does the " Acts of Apostles" embrace?

About thirty years. The first record is of the ascension of Christ, A.D. 33, and the last at the close of the second year of Paul's imprisonment in Rome, A.D. 63.

CHAPTER I.

1. *The author's name is not appended to this book. How can we know who wrote it?*

By noting that the person who wrote this book of "Act of Apostles" to Theophilus had previously written to the same person a detailed account of the birth, life, death, and resurrection of Jesus, and in that book or treatise we have the subscription "Luke," who is thus proved to be the author of this book. He was a companion of Paul in many of his travels, and was therefore an eye-witness of many things recorded.

Does this book fill any special place in the New Testament?

Yes; it is the second of the four notable divisions of this inspired volume, and its contents are indispensable to a correct understanding of the administration of the Son of God. In the four Gospels, which form the first division of the New Testament, we have a fourfold testimony to prove that Jesus is the Christ, while "The Acts" is a book of proclamations in His name, and of conversions to Him. In this

M

book we get the last commission of Jesus practically worked out. Here we see it preached both among Jews and Gentiles, and see it accepted and enjoyed in fulness of blessing. It is the divinely-given standard of preaching and conversion, and we can only be sure that these are right when carried out in accordance with this book. The book of "The Acts," therefore, fills a most important place in the Christian economy.

Had Theophilus any reason to expect such a treatise as this?

In his "former treatise" Luke told him that a proclamation of repentance and remission of sins was to begin at Jerusalem, the place of the shame and death of Jesus, and extend outward among the nations of the earth (Luke xxiv. 47); and it is quite natural that he would feel anxious to know the result of this great mission among these nations, and might possibly crave an account of the undertaking from him who had already furnished so much information about Christ.

Was Theophilus a Gentile?

It is very likely that he was a Roman official, because in his gospel Luke addresses him by the title "Most Excellent," being the same as given by Paul to Felix (Acts xxiii. 26). We judge, therefore, that he was a Gentile, and filling some position under the Cæsar administration.

What do you note in Luke's Gospel to indicate the Gentile standing of Theophilus?

His very many references to the bearing of the work of Christ upon man as man, in which aspects Theophilus would take a deep interest. For instance, the message which the angels brought to the shepherds, and which was called "tidings of great joy," was to be "to all people." Then the genealogy of Christ is traced up to Adam, as if to show

His relation to the whole of humanity. Then the preaching of the Gospel was to be "among all nations," with scores of other instances, which clearly indicate the world-wide bearing of the mission of Christ. These instances seem to point out that it is the mind of a Gentile that is being instructed by Luke.

Does "The Acts" confirm this thought?

While the preaching of the Gospel among the Jews is fully reported, the labours of Paul, the specially elected apostle to the nations, are much more largely given; and by this report Theophilus was enabled to see that the salvation of Jesus had been made known in every province in Asia, even in Rome itself, and that its reception by Gentile converts had been sealed by the Holy Spirit.

Do you look upon Luke simply as a reporter of conversions as they actually occurred under the preaching of Jesus by the apostles?

Yes; and it will help us very much in reading this book, to remember that Luke is reporting to one person all through, as this will account for many peculiarities in the record, especially in the details of conversions. For instance, in one place we have the way in which men were converted to Christ very fully given, while in another, the account is very limited; and we should not conclude that some things required and attended to in the one case were not attended to in the other. The writer certainly expects that the reader will keep in mind that those things which are shown first of all to form an integral part of conversion, though not always named as having occurred, yet were always present. Indeed, to name the occurrence of a single act of submission, was intended to suggest that all the rest had been attended to. To say that a person had been immersed in the name of Jesus, Theophilus would know that that person had also believed in and confessed Jesus to be Christ the Son of God. Or to say that a person had believed or had been added to the Church, he would understand that all that was required by Christ for discipleship had been faithfully attended to. We shall require to note this again and again, as we go over these cases of conversion.

In writing again to Theophilus, why does Luke refer to the "former treatise"?

This was quite proper, especially as the matters contained in each are so closely related. The reference is brief but comprehensive. Luke had written of "all that Jesus began to do and teach, until the day in which He was taken up," and to these a few more facts are added. The forty days' sojourn with His disciples, the necessary instruction concerning the kingdom, the appearance of two in white apparel after His ascension, the election of one to fill the place of the apostate Judas, are all briefly noticed, and thus the mind of Theophilus is prepared for the grand inauguration of the new dispensation. Luke's account of all necessary things is most orderly, and with due attention a satisfactory knowledge of them may be obtained.

3. *"Showed Himself alive after His passion." What does this mean?*

That after His sufferings, which terminated in His death, He showed Himself alive to His disciples by many proofs.

4. *What was this promise of the Father?*

The promise of the Holy Spirit, which was first announced by the prophets, then declared by John, and here they are assured that the promise would be fulfilled in a few days.

6. *What does the question of the disciples about the restoration of the kingdom to Israel indicate?*

Two things at least—a great unwillingness to believe that the rule of the nation had come to an end, and also a misconception of the nature of the rule about to be established. The answer of Jesus gently indicated that if they would only wait a while, they should understand all about it. It is you who will receive power as My ambassadors, and not the nation for which you are pleading, does seem to be implied in His answer.

9–11. *" The disciples were assured by the two men in white apparel that Jesus would return in like manner as they had seen Him go into heaven." Will the descent be in all respects like the ascent?*

There will be a great difference, if Paul is to be heard in this matter. He says that Jesus will come in flaming fire, but He did not go away in a fiery cloud. He also says, that He will come with angels of His might, but none were seen to go away with Him. We therefore presume that they referred to one thing only which in His return would be like His going away, viz., His return in person. Or, as these heavenly visitants affirm, that it would be " this same Jesus."

18, 19. *Luke states here that Judas "purchased a field with the reward of iniquity," while Matthew (xxvii. 7) says, that the chief priests bought a field with the thirty pieces of silver which he cast down in the temple. How do you reconcile these statements?*

I do not try to reconcile them as diverse statements, but accept them as separate facts. Judas did purchase a field with money taken from the bag which he bare, and which contained the joint-stock of the disciples, and for which base act John calls him a thief (xii. 6). In this field he perished by his own hands. The chief priests also purchased a field with the money Judas returned to them, and it was set apart as a burying place for strangers. Both fields might appropriately be called "Aceldama, that is to say, The field of blood."

20–26. *Was it proper for the eleven to choose one to fill the place of Judas?*

The one elected could not be an apostle of Christ, *i.e.*, one sent out by Him, but he did become an elected witness of His resurrection, and took his place with them in this important work. Peter does not say that he was chosen to be an apostle, but "a witness with us of His resurrection." A twelfth apostle was in due time chosen, but it was by Christ Himself.

CHAPTER II.

1. *What is the meaning of "Pentecost"?*

Pentecost means fiftieth, being that number of days after the waving of the sheaf of first fruits before the Lord (Lev. xxiii. 10). It was called by Moses the "feast of harvest," and also the "feast of weeks," but Luke calls it "Pentecost," its Greek name, and by which it was then known. It was one of the three notable feasts of the Lord, at which all the males of the nation were required to appear at Jerusalem.

What does "fully come" mean?

The day commenced at sunset, but had not fully come till sunrise ; and just then, on that pentecostal morn, the promised immersion by the Holy Spirit took place.

2. *Was the sound they heard, and the cloven tongues which they saw, necessary for the immersion in the Holy Spirit?*

Not necessary for the immersion, but important for themselves. The sound "as of a rushing mighty wind," arrested their attention, and

also that of many others in Jerusalem, while the divided tongues as of fire that sat upon each of the apostles, indicated the kind of help to be afforded them on that occasion.

If what was heard and seen by them formed no part of the immersion in the Spirit, in what did it consist?

In their being filled with the Spirit, which was the promised immersion, and their speaking with tongues the proof of it.

3. *Were these divided tongues that rested upon them, really fire?*

Not fire, but "as of fire"—more correctly, they were flame-like in appearance.

4. *Why was this gift of tongues bestowed upon the apostles at this time?*

It was in order to meet an existing difficulty. When the descendents of Noah began to build the tower of Babel, they were all of one speech, but because of their ambition God confounded their speech, and to restrain them divided their language, or broke it up into many different forms, so that they could not generally understand one another, and were compelled by this division to separate and form the various colonies and nations which were afterwards found throughout the world. Now the state of things at Pentecost was simply this : a great number of Jews during the oft-disturbed state of Palestine had left it, and settled in almost every part of the Roman and Grecian empires, and learned the language of the nation among whom they sojourned. These Jews, who soon became foreigners to their own country, would still occasionally visit Jerusalem to pay their tithes, offer their sacrifice, and receive the priest's benediction ; and at the solemn feasts a great number of them would always be found there. Some of these remained for a longer, others for a shorter period, and it is just this condition of things that Luke refers to here in this chapter. A great multitude of Jews and proselytes from every nation were assembled at Jerusalem, each speaking the language or dialect in which he had been born, while the apostles who had to preach the Gospel of Jesus to them all, could only speak one. Now it was to meet this common difficulty or necessity of the people to understand their language, that this gift of tongues, or power to speak so that all could understand them, was bestowed upon the apostles.

11, 12. How was this strange ministry received, and what brought the multitude out to hear it ?

Luke is made to say, " when this was noised abroad the multitude came together," but in the margin we read, " when this voice was made," etc., which would lead us to understand that what was heard was " the sound from heaven, as of a rushing mighty wind," and this voice or sound brought them out to learn the cause. It was, however, soon manifest that there were two classes in the multitude—scoffers and enquirers—and both spake according to their minds. The scoffers said, these men are drunk, therefore not worth attending to; while the enquirers said, what does all this mean? and Peter begins at once to answer them. The scoffers are dismissed in one sentence, their objection being too trivial for further notice, while the enquirers receive a full exposition of the whole matter.

16–21. In replying to these enquirers, why does Peter refer to the prophecy of Joel ?

In order to show them that, strange as these occurrences might appear, they were only what their own prophet had said should come to pass, and then quotes this remarkable prophecy that they might be compared together, and thus this out-pouring of the Spirit might be seen to be according to the Scriptures.

But Joel speaks not only of the pouring out of the Spirit, but also of wonders in heaven, and signs on the earth, of the sun turned into darkness, and the moon into blood. When did these things take place, and why did Peter quote them ?

These wonders and calamities did not take place till near forty years after the outpouring of the Spirit, but the prophecy foretells both the mercy and the judgment. The mercy came first, and the judgment only followed rejected testimony. Peter quotes the prophecy of coming judgment in order to warn against trifling with provided privileges.

Is it to the literal sun and moon, etc., that Peter refers ?

No; it is the nation of Israel to whom he applied these things. Not only Joel but all the prophets had used this planetary system as symbols of the nation. They had been made light-bearers by the revelations of God, but as they had been unfaithful, an eclipse by darkness, trouble, and confusion was to take place; and the after experience and position of the nation proved the truth of this prophecy.

When was this great and notable day of the Lord ?

It was the day of His judgment and overthrow of the nation, and which is rendered in Joel " the great and the terrible day of the Lord," and ere it closed all these wonders and signs were manifest.

Why did Peter quote the " whosoever shall call upon the name of the Lord shall be saved " ?

Because there was grace as well as wrath, and on that very day it was made known in connection with Jesus, the exalted one—a salvation not for the Jew alone, but also for the Gentile; not for one nation, but every individual man of all nations who would call upon the name of the Lord.

What did Peter mean by "calling upon the name of the Lord"?

Confessing Him to be the Son of God; this being required of all who believe the Gospel testimony, and precedes the putting on of the Lord Jesus. To all who do so, the promise of salvation has been made.

22. *Why does Peter refer to the death of Jesus?*

In order to bring forward and sustain the fact of His resurrection. The fact of His death was known to all in Jerusalem, and though He had led a blameless life,—a life approved of God by signs and wonders,—yet they put Him to death by wicked hands.

23. *Peter says, "Being delivered by the determinate counsel and foreknowledge of God." Should not this palliate their crime?*

By no means. God's plan to give up His Son and His foreknowledge —*i.e.,* foreshowing that He would do so—is indeed a wondrous act of grace; but to put that Son to death was a crime of immeasurable magnitude. They put Him to death, but God raised Him from the dead.

24–28. *Why does Peter appeal to the Scriptures to sustain the resurrection of Christ?*

He is evidently sustaining three great facts—viz., the descent of the Holy Spirit, the resurrection, and the exaltation of Jesus—by an induction of prophecies, all of which were in their hands, and the fulfilment of which the twelve were prepared to prove. And, having sustained the first from Joel, he next quotes from David, and shows that some one was not to be left " in hell "—*lit.,* hades—nor to see corruption, but who this would be was a matter to be proved, and Peter is at once ready with the proof.

Is there anything in Psalm xvi.

from which Peter quotes, that will positively settle who this person should be?

Peter quotes the Psalm to show that a resurrection of some one was foretold, and claims that it was fulfilled in Jesus, who was raised from the dead, and saw no corruption. That David was not risen from the dead they were able to prove; for his sepulchre, holding, I presume, his embalmed body, was with them, and was an object of interest to the whole nation. That Jesus was raised from the dead they could bear witness, as also the Holy Spirit whom God had given unto them, and therefore Jesus was the person spoken of in the Psalm.

33. *What evidence could they give to the people in proof of His resurrection?*

The evidence of signs, tongues, and other miracles, which were done in His name, and therefore proofs of His living authority.

Would this evidence prove His ascension also?

It was adduced to prove both resurrection and exaltation. Every man in his own tongue, wherein he was born, heard the wonderful works of God from these Galilean fishermen; and there was not only something marvellous about it, but they declared it was from that Jesus who had been crucified by them, and was then at God's right hand.

The Messiah was promised to David as a son to sit on his throne. Did David expect that He would reign in Jerusalem?

David was God's elected king over Israel, and received a promise that the Christ should be his son and successor, but it was also revealed to him where the seat of His government should be, and the nature of His rule. David had written down the promise given to him :—" The Jehovah said to my *Adonai,* sit thou at my right hand, until I make thy foes thy footstool" (Ps. cx.); and Peter quotes this prophetic promise as literally fulfilled in the exaltation of Christ as then declared by them. David's joyous ambition was, not in having a son to reign in Jerusalem, for he had many successors there, but to have a son who should sit at God's right hand, and should reign over those who were willing—*lit.*, free offerings—in the day of His power. It was neither over an earthly people, nor in an earthly sphere that David expected his promised Lord and son to rule, and if we should be looking for this, we are far behind David.

If Peter delivered this address to the whole multitude of foreign Jews and proselytes, how could all understand it?

Though spoken by Peter in one language every man heard it in his own tongue. It was miraculous, but intelligible to all present, and both startled, instructed, and convicted them of sin and danger.

36. *What part of the address produced that painful conviction manifest in their anxious cry?*

His argument, which had been grandly cumulative, reached its climax in that final charge:— "Therefore let all the house of Israel know assuredly, that God hath made that same Jesus, whom ye have crucified, both Lord and Christ." This declaration was so keenly felt by them that they cried out, "Men, brethren, what shall we do?"

38. *Do you not think the answer Peter gave to them very brief?*

Yes, very brief, but very complete. What they really required to know concerning Jesus, in order to faith in Him, was made known in his previous proclamation, and what He required from them, in order to remission of sins, was fully declared in this first authoritative reply to their question.

How many things were required?

Only three things are named in this reply, viz., repentance, confession, and immersion; but faith is implied, having been produced by his testimony, and in their deep anxiety they ask what they are to do—*i.e.*, how they may obtain forgiveness. These directions were, of course, necessary, because they had not previously been published; and here we learn distinctly what they were.

Four things, then, were evidently required prior to the enjoyment of remission. Is the order in which they are to be done of any importance?

The order is as fixed as the things to be done. Faith must precede repentance, confession, and immersion, for "How shall they call on Him in whom they have not believed?" and Peter's directions as to the order of the other three are plain enough, "Repent, and be baptised every one of you in"—*lit.*, upon (your confession of) "the name of Jesus (as Lord of all) for the remission of sins," etc. But apart from these special directions there is order —*i.e.*, one thing properly preceding another,—arising out of the nature of the things required, and to change these must produce confusion. For instance, to put baptism before faith, is to make it a mere bodily act, or to attend to it without confession of Christ with the mouth, is to ignore His specific claim, and prevent that voluntary acknowledging of Christ which He positively demands. The order, then, of the requirements of Christ for remissions of sins, is (1) Faith in Christ as the exalted Son of God; (2) Repentance—*i.e.*, a fixed purpose to serve Him, which is in all who do so, a change of mind, or as a true *metanoia*, with the mind;

(3) Confession with the mouth of the faith which is in the heart; and (4) Baptism—*lit.*, immersion in water—which, by the plan of God, is into "the name of the Father, and of the Son, and of the Holy Spirit." This order should be thoroughly understood by all who seek to help enquirers in their desire to obey Christ, and obtain His promise; and also by enquirers for themselves, that they may know when they have yielded obedience unto Christ. It is manifest unfaithfulness and disloyalty to Him who is Lord of all, to change, diminish, or add to His arrangements; and it is also unjust to those who are willing to obey Him to the very letter, to be hindered or misdirected by unfaithful time-serving men. The example of these first proclaimers and enquirers is an example and guide for all time. Peter opened the kingdom by this first authoritative announcement of the gracious laws of the exalted king: and "they that gladly received his word were immersed, and the same day there were added to them about three thousand souls."

Was it possible for three thousand persons to have been immersed on that day?

I could not doubt the possibility of such a thing, had there only been so many candidates for immersion; but I am inclined to think that many of those added to the apostles, were already immersed believers in Jesus, and were eligible by their faith and immersion as disciples of Jesus, to be united with the newly-animated body of Christ. Luke says that there were a hundred and twenty, named by Peter, waiting for this event, and Paul speaks of five hundred brethren who were permitted to see Christ before He ascended. Many of these would possibly be at Jerusalem, anxiously waiting to see the promise fulfilled to the twelve, and would take their places along with the newly immersed; and on the first day, the list swelled up to three thousand souls.

Did Peter's first proclamation form a constitutional law of the kingdom of God, never to be changed, or was it only for the time being?

It remained in force all through their ministry, and, according to Christ (Matt. xxviii. 20), it was to continue to the end of the age. Under this law sinners did receive remission of sins, and the arrangement has neither been cancelled, nor any other given by divine authority. It must therefore remain an integral part of the administration of Christ, which all must either accept or reject.

Did the immersion of these Jews change their relation to Moses, or did it remain as before?

In confessing Jesus to be the Son of God, and being immersed into Him by the command of His apostles, they accepted Him as their leader, Saviour, and Lord, and thus their relation to Moses terminated, being then not under the law, but under grace.

"Ye shall receive the gift of the Holy Spirit." Was this some gift from the Spirit, or the Holy Spirit Himself?

We shall best understand what was intended by what was done. The Holy Spirit rested upon the apostles, and likewise upon the house of Cornelius, without a human medium, but only upon others by the laying on of the apostles' hands; and which became manifest in the form of a gift of supernatural power. The power of bestowing gifts upon those who believed, was granted to the apostles, and we presume that it was to this bestowal that Peter referred when he said "ye shall receive the gift of the Holy Spirit."

39. *"For the promise is to you,*

and to your children." Could the children enjoy it through the parents?

No; it could be enjoyed only through faith and obedience to Christ, as then proclaimed to them. But it was most important for them to learn that it was the beginning of a gracious dispensation, and that what was free to them, was free also to their posterity, nay even to all that were afar off.

Why say "as many as the Lord our God shall call"?

It would be more correct to read "as many as shall call unto Him."

40. *What did Peter mean by "save yourselves from this untoward generation"?*

It is *lit. crooked generation*, and refers to their spirit, action, unbelief, rejection of Jesus, and their judgment. Save yourselves from it all by a full acceptance of Christ, and thus come out from it.

42. *What did Luke mean by "the apostles' doctrine," in which "they continued stedfastly"?*

The *teaching* of the apostles, which they unhesitatingly accepted and obeyed. They had accepted their message as apostles of Christ, and now they accept them as teachers.

And what by "fellowship"?

It is *lit.* "the fellowship"—the joint communion of all that believed, the caring one for another in things temporal, in which the poor share with the rich, and that which was needed by one was as freely bestowed by the other. It was a manifestation of love to each other, a fruit of the love of Christ to all. The fellowship in which all, as they desired and had means, communicated, and in which all as they had need received.

" And the breaking of bread," but in ver. 46 *we read, " breaking bread from house to house." Were both these the memorial institution?*

No. The first of these was the memorial feast, attended to by the whole assembly ; the second was that private demonstration of unselfishness, in which love triumphed over caste, selfish prejudice, and synagogue separations, which had so largely prevailed in Jerusalem. They ate meat one with another in gladness and singleness of heart, which they would not before have done.

47. *" The Lord added to the Church." How did the Lord add them"?*

By their submission to Him in the apostle's proclamation.

" Such as should be saved." Were they first added, then saved?

It is *lit. those being saved*. They were saved by accepting Jesus, and, as saved ones, were added to the saved.

Is " the Church" the name given to this new gathering of disciples?

According to our Authorised Version this new assembly was called the church, but the weight of MSS. is against this reading. We have therefore to read, *And the Lord added daily those who were being saved*. But if church is not named, it is certainly implied.

CHAPTER III.

1. *Did Peter and John, who went together into the temple at the hour of prayer, go there to worship?*

I judge they went there to preach to those who had not been hitherto reached by their efforts. It was on purpose to extend the mission so triumphantly begun, and was attended with great results. They knew that many pious worshippers would be at the temple to offer their evening sacrifice, and the opportunity was embraced to bear witness for Jesus.

2–11. *Why did they heal the poor cripple?*

To show the power of Jesus, who had been crucified by these very worshippers, and though the cure was effected in a few minutes, the cured man could not restrain himself on finding that he possessed the power of his limbs, and very soon gathered round the apostles a large crowd, who gazed in wonder at the men who cured the cripple, who had been lame from his mother's womb.

12. *What led Peter to commence his appeal ?*

It was rather an explanation of what they yet required to understand. He saw their wonder, and knew that the source of the miracle had been misunderstood, and therefore said, Why do you look at us ? it is not our power that has made this man to walk,—it is the power of that Jesus who has been glorified by the God of Abraham, the God of our fathers, but whom you delivered up, and denied in the presence of Pilate, when he was determined to let Him go.

16. *"And His name, through faith in His name, hath made this man strong." Had the cripple himself faith in Jesus ?*

I should judge there was faith in the man who was bid to rise and walk, and whose responding effort to do so was assisted by Peter taking hold of his hand, and immediately strength to walk passed into his withered limbs. It was in the name of Jesus that the miracle was done, and the man praised God for the healing done in His name.

17. *Does not Peter somewhat palliate their crime ?*

He allows that in ignorance of the true character of Christ they had put Him to death, though their unbelief was the cause ; but as God had shown by the prophets that He would so suffer, and as He had raised Him from the dead, in order to bless them, they were urged to avail themselves of this marvellous grace now brought nigh.

19. *They were called upon to " repent, and be converted." Why did he not say, " be immersed," as at Pentecost ?*

We feel certain that Peter would make the requirements of the new covenant plain to them, or how could they become obedient to the will of Jesus ? But we should remember that Luke is simply a reporter to Theophilus, and having fully stated, in chapter ii., the laws of the new administration, there was no necessity to repeat these in chapter iii. Theophilus would know at once, and we ought to know, that " repent, and be converted " could be nothing less than his first command, " repent, and be baptised." Peter could add nothing to the first proclamation, which we must assume to have been a perfect one, and he could diminish nothing from it on a second proclamation.

Is " be converted " a proper rendering ?

No. " Be converted " implies passivity, but the Greek word is *lit.* " turn "—implying personal action that would prove their change of mind. In their immersion they would show their repentance, and would thus reach the promise.

" That your sins may be blotted out." Is not this a strange expression ?

It may be to us, but not to those Jews addressed by Peter. The trial of jealousy was familiar to them, with the blotting out of the curses written in the book, and drinking the bitter water that was death to the transgressor. They had made Jesus drink the bitter water of death, and now the blotting out of their own sins was freely made known in His name.

Were the " times of refreshing," of which Peter spoke, future to that

*time or consequent upon their re-
pentance ?*

The " times of refreshing " had
come to those who had already received Christ, and the enjoyment
was consequent upon personal acceptance of Him in all others. Besides,
the word *opos*, here rendered *when,*
should be*, so that* the times of refreshing may come from the presence
of the Lord.

*What does Peter mean by the
" presence of the Lord " ?*

It is *lit.* the face, *i.e.* the countenance, which, by metonomy, indicated
favour. In the Gospel the smile of
Jesus was to be seen, and they were
urged to turn to that gracious One
and be saved.

20. *" And He shall send Jesus."
What does this mean ?*

Its meaning is best learned from
the context. Jesus had been made
known by the prophets, and these
prophecies had been fulfilled, and
Jesus had ascended into the heavens,
and would remain there till all that
had been spoken was fulfilled.

21. *Was " times of restitution of
all things " a present or future state ?*

We might read, " times of restoration," or the introduction of a better
era, a period which began with the
proclamation of the Gospel, and is
still going on. During these *times*
God is making good all that was
spoken by the prophets. Indeed
Peter distinctly says that all the
prophets from Samuel had foretold
of these days.

*Does " since the world began " re-
fer to the creation of the world ?*

It is *lit.* from an age, and as Peter
specially names Moses, and Samuel,
and the prophets that followed, we
judge that it was that Jewish age
during which so much was written
of the coming dispensation, or administration of the Lord, that was
referred to.

22. *Why did Peter refer to this*

*prophecy by Moses about the coming
prophet ?*

Because Jesus was that prophet,
and in Him we get the " restoration " or filling up of the prophetic
word. Christ fully answered to
the prophecy. (1.) He was of His
brethren. (2.) He was a lawgiver
as Moses was. (3.) He had put
forth His claims to be heard by
signs, as Moses had done, and had
also declared that judgment would
fall upon the disobedient. The discourse then closes with a powerful
appeal by Peter to their Jewish
standing, their relation to Abraham
and the covenant, and then urges,
that as God had raised up His Son
Jesus, and sent Him to bless them,
they should avail themselves of this
gracious overture by turning away
from their iniquities. To turn them
from their sins was the great object
of His mission, and in no other way
could they be blessed by Him.

CHAPTER IV.

1. *The discourse of Peter seems to
have been broken off by the sudden
advance of priests, Sadducees, and
the captain of the temple ? Why did
they interfere ?*

The priests were doubtless annoyed by the interruption of worship, for the thousands that should
have been engaged with them were
listening to Peter. Then the Sadducees were annoyed by the teaching
of the resurrection, which they denied,
while the captain of the temple was a
military official, set over a band of
men to preserve order and protect the
priests and worshippers.

3, 4. *Peter and John were put in
prison that evening. Why did Luke
refer to the large number who believed ?*

His object was to report success,
and he could not therefore overlook
the striking fact, that Peter's dis-

course, which followed the miracle, led five thousand to believe in Jesus. This would surely gladden the heart of Theophilus, and also show the progress of the truth in Jerusalem:

5–10. *The council assembled on the morrow. What charge did they bring against Peter and John?*

Their first question related to the man that was healed: "By what power, or by what name have ye done this?" To this question Peter was ready to declare, that by the name of Jesus the Nazarene, whom they had crucified, but who was raised from the dead, the man was made whole.

Was the man that had been healed present with them at this trial?

The man was doubtless present, as Peter in his defence could say, "By Him doth this man stand here before you whole."

11. *"This is the stone which was set at nought of you builders, which is become the head of the corner." Why did Peter quote this prophecy?*

In order to present Christ Jesus in three very gracious aspects. (1.) As a stone—a God-laid foundation—on which men may rest securely. (2.) As a corner-stone, *i.e.* a stone uniting in one living temple the varied sections of humanity, as Jews, Samaritans, and Gentiles, who believed in Him. (3.) As head of the corner, *i.e.* having power to bless and save all who accept Him as their Lord, and also power to dishonour the rebellious.

13. *"They perceived that they were unlearned and ignorant men." What does this mean?*

That they had not been educated under the accredited teachers of the law, would be apparent to all the council; but from their ready references to Jesus they knew that they had been with Him. Their standard of learning was the teaching of Rabbis, and by this the apostles were untaught men; but

with the facts of the resurrection and power of Jesus they were familiar, as was seen by all present.

18, 19. *"And they called them, and commanded them not to speak at all nor teach in the name of Jesus." Why prohibit them from speaking?*

Their speaking was seriously offensive to the council, who had united to condemn and crucify Jesus, because they affirmed that He was alive again, and exalted to the right hand of power. Such teaching made the council guilty of a terrible crime, and they sought by their authority to cause the apostles to cease. Christ, however, had commanded them to speak, and they had no hesitation in deciding whether God or man should be regarded.

23–31. *"And being let go, they went to their own company." In what light did they view this first arrest?*

It was a clear intimation that a severe contest would soon follow. The council had commanded them not to speak at all in the name, or by the authority of Jesus, and this command they were resolved not to heed. To go on with their work was to openly defy the power of the great council, and a conflict would most assuredly follow. This was clearly perceived by the company to whom Peter and John reported the interdict of the rulers, and for threatened opposition they must now prepare themselves. They had no other purpose than to preach Jesus, and no resource but His promised help, and this they now unite to seek. They were weak in themselves, and their enemies were the combined forces of the nation, upheld by imperial Rome. But He who had said by the mouth of David, "Why did the heathen rage, and the people imagine vain things?" He who had made the heavens and the earth, was on their side, and in His strength they purposed to go forward. All they ask for the occasion is boldness to speak the Word, and signs from Him to prove it true; the rest they are content to leave with Him. Nor did they ask in vain, for the place was shaken, they were filled with the Holy Spirit, and the needed boldness was thus imparted. The course pursued by these devoted workers is very suggestive to all who are placed in trial in their service for Christ. They first of all seek the company of fellow-helpers in the truth, and then all unite in supplications and prayers to Him who alone could help them.

27, 28. " Both Herod and Pontius Pilate, with the Gentiles and the people of Israel, were gathered together, for to do whatsover Thy hand and Thy council determined before to be done." If they were doing what God determined to be done, how could their action be a crime?

We should read the verses so as to understand that it was Jesus, whom God anointed to do whatever His hand and council marked out beforehand to be done, against whom both Herod, and Pontius Pilate, with the Gentiles, and the people of Israel, were gathered together; and not that they were doing God's purpose, but opposing it, and even had put Jesus to death. And not only so, but they were opposing His apostles, who now in prayer were asking God for the necessary courage to go on with their testimony, however terrible the opposition might be.

29, 30. The apostles asked that signs and wonders might be done in the name of Jesus. Would it be right to present such petitions now?

Prayer should always be in harmony with promises made to us, and it is needful to discern what was given exclusively to apostles, and what is common to all saints. Christ bestowed on them the gift of healing, etc., and they very properly ask that

it might be fulfilled in order to confirm their testimony. They saw that suffering would have to be endured in the work, and they ask for boldness to go on with it in the face of all opposition. It was a noble spirit, and deserves to be emulated, but we should not pray for things not promised to us.

32. It is here said of these first disciples of Christ that " they had all things common." Does this establish communism as a part of Christianity?

Christianity does not give one person an absolute claim over the goods of another, but it does claim that if a man love God, that he love his brother also, and this love will show itself in caring for his need. But still the act is voluntary, and there is not a single case in which compulsion was ever used by the apostles. We read of them naming cases of need, and asking the saints to remember these on the first day of the week, but beyond this they never insisted. Even Peter said to Ananias, " While it remained (unsold), was it not thine own? and after it was sold, was it not in thine own power?" The need of many of the first converts, poor Jews and proselytes from the provinces, was very great, and nobly did the brethren who had means respond to it. They did so, however, by creating a fund, towards which all who desired contributed, and from this resource the wants of the needy were supplied.

36. " And Barnabas (which means son of consolation) having land, sold it." Why did Luke name this sale of his land?

It was such a disinterested act as to be worthy of record. He was from Cyprus, but had acquired a little property in Jerusalem, and to meet the need of his poor brethren he voluntarily turned it into money to supply what was lacking. For "son of consolation," we had better read, *son of exhortation,* and in this very simple but important gift he seems to have excelled. The apostles taught, and Barnabas urged the people to practise the teaching, and in this he was a most useful co-worker.

CHAPTER V.

1. *The case of Ananias and Saphira his wife was one of deliberate hypocrisy; but why does Luke record it?*

There may have been several reasons for putting on record this bold act of hypocrisy: (1.) Their mean deception formed a striking contrast to the many noble acts of disinterested benevolence which he had named. (2.) It was a striking illustration of the power which Jesus had given to His apostles to inflict judgment upon opposers of His truth. And (3.) to show Theophilus how a deep-laid plot had been formed to bring into discredit the work of the Holy Spirit. Ananias and Sapphira were the chief actors in this plot, and after the signal judgment with which they were visited, Luke adds, " And of the rest durst no man join himself to them, but the people magnified them,"—*i.e.*, the apostles (ver. 13).

3, 4. *Peter asked Ananias, " Why hath Satan filled thine heart?" and again, " Why hast thou conceived this thing in thine heart?" How do you reconcile these statements?*

The statements are not contrary to each other, but simply mark the stages of this process of evil. Satan suggests through the circumstances this evil course, and Ananias receives and perfects the plot to deceive the Holy Spirit; or, in other words, Satan sowed the evil seed which Ananias received into his heart, and when finished in the act, it brought forth death.

Why was the penalty against this so severe?

As the blasphemy against the Holy Spirit could not be forgiven, because His power in Christ was ignored, so this denial of His indwelling in the apostles was visited by death. Ananias was evidently leading a faction who dared to treat the man who had opened the kingdom of heaven, as if he had received no such authority, and his daring was most signally visited.

18. *" And they laid hands on them,"*—i.e., *the apostles,—" and put them in the common prison." Why were all arrested?*

The rulers were evidently annoyed at the increased influence of the apostles, whose power over the people was greatly increased. Some hypocrites were smitten with death, diseases fled with a touch, and many began to flock from the surrounding cities with their sick folk, and all were healed, and by these things the fact of the resurrection of Jesus, in whose name these things were done, was more firmly established. It was no doubt the Sadducees, whose denial of resurrection was practically overthrown, that were the chief movers in this second arrest, which seems to have included all the apostles.

19–21. *Why did the angel release them, and bid them go on with their testimony?*

It was a very important stage in their work; many had been convinced of the truth of their testimony by the miracles which had been wrought, but yet required to hear the Gospel, *i.e.*, the words of this life, in order to learn the special purpose of these manifestations. It was not to astonish people that they wrought miracles, but to prepare them to receive the truth, without which they could not be saved. Now the first part of this work had been done, and they were busy instructing them, in order to their conversion, when this sudden arrest was made, and the whole of the apostles were put into the common prison. It would be to them a rather perplexing thing, but ere the officers arrived in the morning to conduct them into court, an angel had come and set them free, and directed them to go on with their proclamation.

What was meant by the "words of this life"?

The resurrection of Jesus had disclosed a new life, which the Sadducees denied, and, as was understood by them, it was not merely that life was manifested in Him, but that His resurrection was a pledge of the life of others, and this they were to continue to make known.

21–28. *How did this matter end?*

Luke tells us the apostles were soon found by the officers, and quietly led by them before the assembled council, who preferred three charges against them :—(1.) That they continued to teach when forbidden to do so. (2.) By so doing they had filled Jerusalem with their doctrine. And (3.) they were bringing the blood of Jesus upon the city, as having slain an innocent person.

What reply did they make to these charges?

Peter, who is the chief speaker, admits the charges, but gives reasons why they persisted in this course. His defence is very forcible. You bid us be silent; God has bid us speak. You put Jesus to death; God has given Him life. In nailing Jesus to a tree, you have brought His blood upon yourselves; but God having exalted Him, He is able to bestow forgiveness of sin.

31. *How could God, by the exaltation of Jesus, give repentance to Israel and forgiveness of sins?*

Repentance is a change of mind; and, admitting that they were sincere in putting Jesus to death as an impostor, yet, when God raised Him from the dead, and exalted Him to princely power, it should have induced this needful change. Peter affirms that Jesus was exalted to bestow remission of sins upon all who accepted Him, and for those who rejected Him there could be no hope. A change of mind in these Jews could only be effected by their reception of the apostles' witness of the resurrection of Jesus, but refusing to do this they could only be hardened in their sin.

32. *"We are witnesses of these things, and so is also the Holy Spirit." How did they bear joint witness?*

The apostles witnessed orally that Jesus was raised from the dead, and exalted to power at God's right hand, and the Spirit bore witness by the gifts bestowed in His name. This was amply sufficient to induce repentance in all hearts, except where a fixed determined rejection of Jesus prevailed. Here it was powerless, and ever will be. These rulers and priests rejected this double evidence, and hardened themselves in their unbelief.

Peter said that the Holy Spirit was given to them that obey Christ. Was this a general or special statement?

I presume that he refers to gifts bestowed on that occasion, as evidences of the power of an ascended Christ, and not to a general bestowal of the Holy Spirit. It is of extraordinary manifestations in some that Peter is speaking here, and not of the indwelling of the Spirit by the truth, which is true of all believers. This is very marked in the brief history of the Church as given in the New Testament. Some did receive miraculous gifts of the Spirit, for the profit and confirmation of all, while all who received Christ in faith and love had the abiding communion of the Holy Spirit.

34–39. *Why did Gamaliel interpose for the apostles?*

He saw that the authorities were going to act unreasonably towards them, and therefore offered some sound advice, based upon the fact of two notorious impostors, with whose actions, and the result, they seem to have been familiar. Let them alone, said he, for if it be of men it will come to nought, but if of God, ye cannot overthrow it. His advice was taken, and with some stripes and threats the affair terminated.

41, 42. *The apostles rejoiced, and went on with their work; but why does Luke use the two words " teach and preach Jesus Christ " ?*

The words simply indicate the two classes to whom they were daily ministering. To the unconverted they preached, and to this class this word is strictly applicable ; while believers were taught all things needful for life and godliness. To the former it is, and must always be, proclamation—*i.e.*, preaching—while to the latter it must always be instruction concerning the Lord's will.

CHAPTER VI.

1. *What was this " daily ministration " ?*

The daily supply of the poor saints, from the liberality of those who had given money to meet their need.

Why were they neglected ?

It was possibly an oversight, through want of proper arrangement. We cannot for a moment think the neglect was through partiality. It may have been that these Grecian widows were strangers in Jerusalem, and so were overlooked, and this led the more wealthy Grecians to murmur against the Hebrews.

2. *What had the apostles to do with this matter ?*

They had the provisional oversight of the whole Church, and had to meet this first difficulty in the true spirit and wisdom of their Lord and Master. Indeed the plan proposed by them showed a deal of good common sense. They did not contend with those that murmured, but at once met the difficulty by proposing the election of seven men of honest report, who should have the special charge of this business, and thus leave the apostles free to labour in word and doctrine.

5. *Were the seven that were chosen to this service Grecian Jews, or Hebrews ?*

It is most likely they were nearly all Grecians, as the names are said to be Greek, and were chosen by the whole multitude of disciples. They were a noble band, and, in addition to table-serving, two of them became distinguished for their faithfulness in proclaiming and defending the truth.

Was this the first appointment to special service in the church ?

We do not read of any preceding this, and it forms, we think, a precedent for similar election in all churches. The brethren elected the men, and the apostles recognised their choice by prayer and the laying on of hands.

7. *What does Luke mean by " the word of God increased " ?*

An increased proclamation of the truth, as the context proves. Others besides the apostles came to the front, and by proclamation and confirming signs, did good service, so that disciples were multiplied, and even priests became obedient to the faith. It was a most signal triumph of the truth over great opposition.

8–12. *How was it that Stephen and these Libertines, Cyrenians, etc., entered into such a serious controversy ?*

Stephen, himself a Grecian Jew, had possibly made a special effort to win these provincial Jews to the faith in Christ. It was a new field into which this bold and zealous labourer entered, and a fierce discussion followed, in which he proved himself their superior. Not being able to cope with him in argument, they resorted to ignoble means, and at last brought him to the council, and made false charges against him, in order to defeat him.

13. *What charges did they bring against him?*

They affirmed that he said that Jesus of Nazareth—*lit.*, the Nazarene —would destroy that place, and change the customs which Moses delivered unto them.

Did he really say these things?

I presume he did, or words equivalent to them, as time proved their fulfilment. But they were most offensive to these people, and enabled them to prefer a charge against him before the Sanhedrin. Hence the trial that followed, and his thrilling defence, in the hearing of this august council, of what he had previously uttered.

CHAPTER VII.

1. *"And the high priest said, Are these things so?" Was this a proper question to propose?*

It was not improper to ask the question, when charges had been made against him. In our courts of justice the question is always put, "guilty, or not guilty?" and this was what the high priest really meant. The question gave Stephen an opportunity to reply, and this chapter is Luke's record of his defence. It seems to have been listened to with almost breathless attention to the close, and never was nail driven and clinched with greater precision, than was this historical argument by Stephen. It should have humbled them into contrition, but instead of this it awakened a spirit of murderous revenge.

N

Why did Stephen introduce what we might call a history of the chief men of the nation?

It was a reply to the charges made by his accusers; but the point of his argument in connection with Abraham, Jacob, Joseph, Moses, David, and Solomon, unless carefully noted, may not be seen. It is possible that some other feature of these brief narratives may arrest attention, instead of that one object for which all were selected. His brief allusions to these men, like a thickly-barbed spear, was intended to pierce and fill them with penitence, but instead of this, it led to his death.

Did he intend to irritate them?

I think not. He rather wished to show them where others had failed, and thus he warned them not to pursue a similar course. If they did, it was plainly intimated in these examples that they would lose the God-provided salvation, as these men by disobedience had forfeited promises made to them, and others would enjoy what they refused. This is the great practical lesson of his appeal, and this must be noted.

2–9. *Abraham is the first on Stephen's programme. Did he fail in his obedience?*

Yes, most certainly, and this is the reason why he notes that though God promised to give him the land, yet He gave him no inheritance in it, no, not so much as to set his foot on.

Why did God fail to fulfil His promise?

Because he failed in prompt obedience, as Stephen distinctly notes. "Brethren and fathers, hearken; The God of glory appeared unto our father, Abraham, when he was in Mesopotamia, *before* he dwelt in Charran, and said unto him, Get thee out of thy country, and from thy kindred, and come into the land which I shall show thee." Instead of doing this, he went along with his father to Charran or Harun, and remained there till his father died. For this act of disobedience he lost his personal right in the land, and even his seed had to go into bondage, and be deprived of the promise four hundred years. This fact Stephen wishes them to notice, and though Abraham, after his father's death, acted upon the old command, and went into Canaan, yet he soon found that his own right to the land was lost, and the promise renewed only to his seed through him.

Was failure the only thing noticed by Stephen in respect to Abraham?

No. He marks as distinctly the grace of God; for though his seed would be afflicted and oppressed, yet they should be brought out and serve Him in that place, and by the covenant of circumcision a seed was secured to Him after the flesh, through whom Christ should come to save and bless mankind.

9–13. *Joseph is the next upon the list. Why is he introduced?*

To show how their fathers, the patriarchs of the nation, rejected God's chosen deliverer.

How could they have known that Joseph was to be a ruler and a saviour?

His dreams, which were given of God, were a testimony unto them, but God's plan required both faith, patience, and submission, ere the favour could be realised, and instead of accepting their brother to rule over them, as his dreams so plainly intimated, they sold him into Egypt in order to defeat the self-humbling plan of God.

It could not have been pleasant to the Sanhedrin to have this fact so plainly brought before them; but was this all that Stephen wished to show them?

It would not have savoured of the spirit of his Master had he simply marked the sins of their fathers, but he wished also to show them the goodness of God, who made that brother, whom they sold into slavery, and whose feet were hurt with fetters, their friend and saviour in the great famine that afflicted all lands. Stephen then shows, that after Joseph revealed himself to them, they wisely accepted his help, and father, and brothers, and their families went into Egypt, where they were nourished all through the famine.

14. *In relation to the number of souls that went into Egypt, Moses says (Gen. xlvi. 27) that there were threescore and ten, including Joseph's family; while Stephen says there were threescore and fifteen. How may this difference be adjusted?*

Stephen quotes from the Septuagint, which gives this number; they adding five surviving wives of Jacob's sons, which Moses distinctly states he omitted.

15. *How do you account for the statement here that Abraham bought the sepulchre of the sons of Emmor, when Moses says that Jacob bought it?*

There is confusion in the present reading, which I would not impute to Stephen, but to some copyist who has omitted the name of Joseph, and given the name of Abraham, instead of Jacob, which Stephen would not have done, being familiar with all the facts. The present reading makes Stephen say that Jacob was buried in the sepulchre bought of the sons of Emmor, when it was Joseph that was buried there, and that Abraham bought it, when it was Jacob. Jacob was buried in Machpelah, which was purchased by Abraham of Ephron the Hittite.

16. *Then how would you read this verse?*

We may read, " And (Joseph) was carried over into Sychem, and laid in the sepulchre that Jacob bought," etc. (Josh. xxiv. 32), as being the facts recorded in Gen. xxxiii. 19.

20. *Why did Stephen introduce Moses ?*

To show the action of the nation toward God's appointed deliverer. The people were at that time in a most helpless condition as bond-slaves in Egypt; but God having promised to bring them out, provided a deliverer in the person of Moses, who surrendered every earthly privilege in order to carry out God's purpose. But this provided deliverer they thrust away, and refused to accept him whom God appointed.

It must have been annoying to the council to have this fact brought before them, but was this all he wished to show them ?

No; he showed that after forty years God brought back this rejected Moses, to deliver them from their still deeper subjection, and by signs and wonders, and by a mighty outstretched hand, they were all brought up out of Egypt. These facts should have been thoughtfully pondered by the Sanhedrin, as they were not only serious charges against the nation, but striking proofs of the compassion of God.

37. *Why did Stephen quote the prophecy by Moses about another prophet, who was to be heard in all things ?*

It forms his reply to the first charge brought against him, that in preaching Christ as a law-giver he had spoken against Moses. This charge is proved to be false by this prophecy of One who was to be heard in all things. The place which Moses filled was thus shown to be only for a season, when he should be succeeded by another prophet whom God should raise up.

38. *Stephen had spoken of the rejection of Moses in Egypt. Why*

does he also refer to this rejection of him at Sinai ?

Because this second rejection was more to be condemned than the former. Moses had led them out of bondage, and through the Red Sea; and at Sinai he had formed them into an assembly by means of the lively—*lit.*, living—oracles.

What is meant by living oracles ?

Words spoken by the living God. The ten commands were orally delivered by God, and voluntarily received by them.

39. *Did the nation reject Moses when they made a golden calf ?*

They rejected him during his lengthened stay on the mount, before they made a calf. They first turned back in their hearts to Egypt, and then the calf was made to lead them back again.

This sad fact in the history of their fathers must have been very annoying to the council, but was the grace of God manifested at Sinai ?

Stephen distinctly notes the favour of God on that occasion, but not until he had named another sad fact in their sojourn, by a quotation from Amos v. 26, in which it is shown that during their forty years' sojourn in the wilderness the nation itself offered no sacrifices to God, and even became idolatrous, worshipping the host of heaven in their desire to have a visible God. The sacrificial service in the wilderness was sustained by the tribe of Levi, who, having refused to take part in the worship of the calf, were selected by God to serve before Him instead of the nation, who might have been a kingdom of priests. Amos also refers to the idolatry of the ten tribes, with their threatened captivity beyond Babylon, which Stephen quotes, and in these instances God himself is the rejected one.

" Beyond Babylon." Where was that ?

Assyria, whither Shalmaneser the king carried the ten tribes, and placed them in the cities of the Gentiles.

You have referred to three instances of failure, the golden calf, the forty years' failure, and the idolatry of the ten tribes. Was favour shown in all these cases of apostacy?

Stephen only names one, the tabernacle of witness, but there was grace in connection with the others, and although Stephen does not name them, they either were or should have been familiar to all.

What were the unnamed instances of favour?

The first is a very striking one, viz., that their lives were spared at Sinai by the intercession of that Moses, who in heart they had put from them; and though afterwards thrown upon their own responsibility for obedience to God, yet on that occasion they were saved from being set aside as a nation, entirely through his intercession for them. That was certainly a special favour. Then the ten tribes had been released from their Assyrian captivity, or at least as many of them as accepted the universal proclamation of Cyrus, which extended over Assyria. Even this deliverance should be counted as a favour.

The cases referred to by Stephen at the close of his address are more briefly stated than at the beginning, with apparent omissions of important matters. How do you account for this?

It is not difficult to account for his hurried manner; there were frowns possibly gathering on the faces of his accusers, and rising murmurs warned him to be brief.

46. *What further subjects does he advance?*

Just four, and these close his defence and his life. The first was the tabernacle of David, a place of special privilege, and a type of Gentile ac- ceptance, which in the days of Amos had fallen into ruin, but the promise of its antitype was given, and should have been accepted. The second was the house which Solomon built, but of which he asks by quoting Isaiah (lxvi. 1, 2), "Where is the place of my rest?" which is a reply to them about destroying the temple, as if the temple was to stand for ever. The unfinished quotation really said, It is in the contrite heart that I will rest, and not in this house made with hands. And so Stephen would be understood to say, Of what use is your temple, when God will not dwell in it?

51. *You have named but two. What are the remaining?*

The resisting of the Holy Spirit, and putting to death Him of whom the prophets wrote. This last charge hastened the crisis, for though it was true, it aroused their rage to a murderous pitch, and began to show itself in the gnashing of their teeth.

Both their fathers and themselves resisted the Holy Spirit. How did they do this?

By resisting His testimony in those who made it known. So Nehemiah explains it (see chap. ix. 30), and in this way the Spirit is still resisted by those who do not obey apostolic testimony.

53. *"Who received the law by the disposition of angels." What does this mean?*

If we read *who received the law through ranks of messengers*, it will be easier to understand the circumstances to which Stephen so briefly alludes. Moses received the law from God, but the people were instructed in it by appointed messengers, possibly the elders of Israel; and yet, though so fully instructed in the law, they did not keep it.

Was there anything further added by him which they would not endure?

An unexpected event occurred just

at the close—a vision of the Son of man in heaven, to which he at once bore testimony, " Behold, I see the heavens opened, and the Son of man standing at the right hand of God." This was to them a crowning provocation, and the whole council raised a shout of indignation, stopped their ears, and hurried him outside the city, where witnesses, those who distinctly heard his words, stoned him to death. He evidently counted upon his doom, because he kneeled down to offer his dying request, " Lord, lay not this sin to their charge," having just before said, " Lord Jesus, receive my spirit."

How would Luke obtain the facts of this case ?

From a young man whose name was Saul, at whose feet the garments of the murderers were laid.

59. *Is the word " God " a proper addition ?*

It is an addition without authority, and should be left out.

CHAPTER VIII.

1. *Why does Luke give so brief an account of Saul as a persecutor ?*

It was quite sufficient to enable Theophilus to see what a terrible enemy the Church had in this young man, who though he did not directly take part in the stoning of Stephen, yet as he held their clothes, he would no doubt spur them on in their deed of blood, and take a very active part in the great persecution that followed. From that day Saul became a leader in the furious onslaught that followed, against the disciples, and many had to flee to escape from suffering. It is to these scattered ones that Peter wrote his First Epistle, in order to encourage and help them in their trial.

" They were all scattered abroad except the apostles." Why not the apostles ?

The persecution was chiefly directed against foreign Jews, who having no proper citizenship there, were legally expelled from Jerusalem, while the apostles, as native-born Jews, could not be so thrust out. Persecution they might have to endure, but they were not to be chased away as if they had no right to be there.

2. *" And devout men carried Stephen," etc. Were these fellow-disciples ?*

I think not. Stephen was a good man, and his death, so lawlessly effected,—for the charges were not proved against him,—was a blot upon the whole community, with which act these men had no sympathy. They therefore washed their hands of this deed of blood by assisting at his burial, and let the crime rest upon those concerned.

3. *" Saul made havoc of the Church." Was this the cause of the dispersion ?*

So Luke intimates. These saints had to flee for liberty and life, each choosing the way and place as seemed best to him, but though driven from Jerusalem, they preached the Word in every place they entered. Thus others heard the Gospel of Jesus, and this heavy trial became a general good.

Why did Luke narrate the mission of Philip to Samaria, in preference to many others which might have been selected ?

The reason, if I apprehend it aright, is a deeply interesting one; preaching among the Gentiles had not then commenced, so that the preaching was only to the Jews. But Philip entered a new field, one specially named by the Master, and his success was most striking. The Samaritans held a distinct place between Jews and Gentiles; they lived on Jewish territory, and had a system of worship chiefly fashioned from the law of Moses, and had a very ancient copy of the five books of Moses. It was among these that Philip opened his mission, and Luke records the success. To Theophilus this section of his report must have been very interesting. The river of the water of life, which had risen from under the sanctuary, was widening and deepening in its onward flow, and he would eagerly follow its course on toward the great sea of nations, healing and blessing wherever it came (Ezekiel xlvii. 1–12).

5. *Would you think Samaria a likely place at which to open a mission?*

Just as likely as Jerusalem, which was not a very favourable place for publishing the authority of Jesus. In Jerusalem, the people were under the influence of the priests, and in Samaria they were under the influence of a sorcerer,—in fact, man ruled where God alone should have ruled, and the subjection was a most degrading one; and ere any good could be done, this rule must be reversed. It is instructive to notice how Philip began to change this wicked rule. "Then Philip went down to the city of Samaria, and preached Christ unto them." This had been done at Jerusalem, and the result was most marked, and in Samaria it was tried with astonishing success. It was the claims of a loving and exalted Jesus against the claims of a priesthood and a wonder-working sorcerer, and produced a great change. This message concerning Jesus is the only one God has provided in this world to effect all the change that is needed. Men may be turned to churches, creeds, etc., instead of Christ, but the turning will be short of the heavenly goal. To stop anywhere short of Jesus as a Saviour is outside of life and salvation. Every one therefore who will be a co-worker with God, must be guided by these first workers in the great harvest field.

6–8. *Philip worked miracles among the people as well as preached Christ unto them. How did he obtain this power?*

From the same source the believing Samaritans received it, viz., by the laying on of the apostles' hands. This gift of power to heal, etc., he had received in Jerusalem from their hands, but could not confer it on others. The apostles alone could do this, and for this purpose, by advice of the other apostles, Peter and John made a special visit to Samaria, to confer spiritual or miraculous gifts on those who had believed. This case illustrates, as fully as we could desire, both the source and the medium of spiritual gifts. The Holy Spirit was the source, while the apostles were the medium, through whom the gifts were imparted; and at their death, the bestowal of these gifts ceased. This result is in perfect harmony with the whole arrangement. The twelve apostles were the only Christ-elected witnesses of His resurrection; and to them alone was given this peculiar power to confirm it. Hence Paul could say of the saints at Corinth, who were distinguished for spiritual gifts, "The seal of mine apostleship are ye in the Lord." It is therefore important to understand that the truth of the resurrection and exaltation of Jesus, as well as the commands and promises of the Gospel, rests exclusively upon the confirmed testimony of the twelve apostles of Christ, and that to all who receive their testimony He is responsible for the correctness of every direction, and for the fulfilment of every promise uttered by them; and that He is responsible for the dicta of no other. We may also see why it was necessary that Peter and John should visit Samaria, and why Luke has recorded the visit. The Samaritans were a new class of subjects, as marked down by Christ in His commission (chap. i. 8), and the truths believed, and the ordinances obeyed, by them, required and received apostolic confirmation. Philip could work miracles in confirmation of the Gospel he preached, having received this gift from the apostles, but the power to bestow such gifts rested only with them : hence the required visit of Peter and John, that the Samaritans also might receive gifts, and be confirmed as the disciples of Christ. This confirmation was only once, and was for all time. This bestowal of gifts upon Samaritans by the apostles never required repetition, either for these or any other Samaritans, in order to believing the truth of the Gospel. Any Samaritan, believing, confessing, and obeying the testimony of the apostles this very day, should see his place in the Saviour's prayer, as recorded by John (xvii. 20), " Neither pray I for these alone, but for *them also who shall believe on Me through their word.*" And so of the other two divisions of the human family—believing Jews and Gentiles,—whose acceptance has been confirmed by gifts bestowed upon them by the apostles, once and for ever ; " That the world may believe Thou hast sent Me."

12. *In reporting to Theophilus the result of the preaching of Philip at Samaria, why does Luke record the precise form of it, when it is similar to that recorded in chapter ii. ?*

The result of the work at Samaria is similar to that in Jerusalem at Pentecost, the form of their obedience being precisely the same. In chapter ii., Luke states that, " They who gladly received his word were baptised ; " and here he states, " When they believed Philip preaching," etc., " they were baptised," only adding, " both men and wo-

men." Now, the reason for this repetition is a very striking one. Here we get a new class of subjects, among whom a co-worker with Christ is called to labour. Would the same glad message be proclaimed to them which had been proclaimed to the Jews ? Would the same form of obedience be required and rendered as required before ? A clear statement relating to these matters would not only greatly interest Theophilus, but should interest us all. We see from this record that there was no change in anything. There was the same grace in the proclamation, the same form of obedience rendered, and the same privileges enjoyed by these persons of mixed blood, as by those of the fleshly seed of Abraham ; and this will help us in our future study of all the cases that may come before us in this book. Where the persons occupy a new relation, there is more detail, and where they happen to be persons whose class has been fully dealt with, it is noticed in the briefest manner possible. These omissions and changes have often been perverted, but it shows a sadly perverted mind to so treat a historian whose records should be studied as a whole, and whose teaching has to do with our eternal welfare.

13–21. " *Then Simon himself believed also : and when he was baptised,*" etc. *Is there not some difficulty as to whether or not his faith was of the right kind ?*

There is no difficulty in Luke's report of the case ; it is a straightforward account of what Simon did, both of what was right and what was wrong. He saw the miracles, heard the proclamation, believed on Jesus, confessed Him as the Son of God, and was immersed on a confession of his faith. Now, all this was perfectly right, being done under Philip's teaching and direction.

Simon started well, and if he had not yielded to temptation, he would have held on the course begun. But he had to be tested, as all confessors of Jesus must be. It may be a day, or a week, or a month, or a year, before the testing period comes, but sooner or later it is sure to come to all. To Simon it came very soon, and proved too much for him. The visit of Peter and John revealed to him a source of power in connection with the faith, and it became a snare too great for him to resist, and he vainly offered a price to possess the same, and was condemned for his daring sin. Now this coveting of power was wrong, both in act and motive, because it was sought to exalt himself, and not Christ. The state of his heart was faithfully pointed out by Peter, and he was urged to repent of his wickedness, and pray to God that the thought of his heart might be forgiven.

Did Peter look upon the case as absolutely hopeless ?

Certainly not. The man had done wrong, but he had the privilege of asking forgiveness, and if sincerely sought it would have been granted. Peter earnestly urged him to avail himself of this provided forgiveness, which, by repentance and confession in prayer, might be obtained.

22. *Is this direction to Simon, to repent and seek forgiveness, a guide to all failing believers ?*

The whole case fully reveals the law of God, both for the returning sinner and those who have put themselves under the administration of Christ. Simon was called upon with others to believe in Christ, and to be immersed into Him, and according to the commission of Jesus, this is the divine law for a returning sinner. When Simon did wrong he was directed to repent —*i.e.*, change his mind—and pray for forgiveness, and this is the law

of God for the failing believer. (See 1 John i. 9.)

24. *" Then answered Simon, and said, Pray ye to the Lord for me,"* etc. Why ask Peter and John to pray for impending consequences to be removed ?

This request seems to indicate that the sin of Simon had involved him in judicial punishment, which his own prayers would not remove. This is indicated in Peter's words, " I perceive that thou art in the gall of bitterness," etc. The apostles are asked by him to do what, in after days, James directs that one so involved should ask the elders of the Church to do (v. 14, 15). If it was a sin unto death, John afterwards writes (1 John v. 16), " I do not say that he shall pray for it." " If not unto death, he shall ask," etc. Simon had sinned against the prerogative of the apostles, and was judged. This appears evident, but the final issue is not revealed.

26. *Was this angel that spoke to Philip a celestial messenger ?*

He was simply a messenger of the Lord, but whether from earth or heaven the context does not help us to decide, nor does it matter anything to us from whence he came. The Lord sent a message by an accredited agent, and Philip received the message, and obeyed the command of the Lord. It is very suggestive to notice the prompt obedience of this servant of the Lord. He was called to leave a populous city for an almost uninhabited district, and to leave a crowd to instruct a solitary individual; but his Master sent him, and he promptly obeyed.

27. *Was this eunuch a Jew ?*

From his going up to Jerusalem to worship, it may be fairly implied that he was either a Jew or a proselyte. Every year thousands of Jews travelled from the provincial cities to keep one or other of the great feasts that had been appointed of God, many of them possibly only once in a lifetime.

This happy meeting of Philip and the eunuch was by a special arrangement of God. May we expect such interpositions now ?

God is exceedingly anxious that men should hear the truth and be saved, and I have no doubt there are many more gracious providences that would lead to this result, if improved, than people either use or even notice. Still, we are called to see, in the case of the eunuch, that whatever means God may use to bring His truth near to us, it must be learned and obeyed, or we shall be no better for it. Philip was sent to meet the eunuch by God, but he had to hear, and learn, and obey, ere he could rejoice in God's salvation. Now, there are multitudes who, through God's good providence in possessing the New Testament, can hear the same preacher, and have, through him, the terms of blessing made known to them, and yet do not obey them. Many are really tempting God in asking Him day by day to enlighten their minds, and yet do not receive His word, which is given for enlightenment. To plead with God to bless them, while refusing the Bible terms of blessing, is what many, alas, are doing ; but it is a course of disobedience which should be at once abandoned.

32. *This portion of the 53rd of Isaiah which the eunuch was reading differs from our version. How is this accounted for ?*

The eunuch was reading from a Greek version of the prophet, now called the Septuagint, which in some instances differs from the Hebrew, from which our version is rendered. It is the version which was then in common use.

34. " *Of whom speaketh the prophet this ? " Ought not the eunuch to* have known the purport of this prophecy ?

This could hardly be expected. When Philip said, " Understandest thou what thou readest ? " he very properly replied, "How can I, except some man should guide me ? " Both Jews and proselytes were more occupied with traditional precepts, than with the coming Messiah, and this prophecy is possibly the first that had been perused by him. His question therefore was a very natural one, and received a full and instructive reply.

35. " *Philip . . . . preached unto him Jesus." Why did Luke not give more of his exposition ?*

Theophilus did not require to be told what was implied in preaching Jesus ; Luke's previously reported discourses had made this sufficiently plain, so that here he has only to make known the result, and this is done in the plainest manner.

36. *The eunuch said, " What doth hinder me to be baptised ? " Why did he ask such a question ?*

It was the teaching which he had just received, that prompted such a question. Philip had spoken of the life, death, resurrection, commission, and ascension to power of the very person he was reading about ; and as the promise of salvation which that commission contained was then clearly set before him, he at once exclaimed upon reaching some way-side pool, " See, water ; what doth hinder me to be baptised ? " His hearty response to the question of Philip, was all that could be desired, and in this appointed ordinance of immersion, he surrendered himself to Christ.

Why do enquirers so seldom put the same question now ?

Because they do not receive the same teaching. If they did, the result would be the same. It is the teaching that shapes the result.

37. " *If thou believest with all thine heart," etc. Why is it that*

nearly all recent translators omit this verse?

Because it is wanting in all ancient MSS., except E. Laudianus, and on this account it is rejected by all critical editors ; the weight of evidence being against its retention. There is, however, some evidence in its favour, because it is found in writings earlier than these MSS. According to Scrivener, this answer was cited by Irenæus (A.D. 196), without the least misgiving. He also says that Acts viii. 37 was known to Cyprian, Jerome, Augustine, and others, who lived earlier than these MSS. which do not contain it. This much does certainly prove its early existence. I will not say that Luke wrote the verse, but to me the narrative appears defective without it, but possibly not so to Theophilus. Luke was recording results, and had already made him familiar with what was required in order to Christian immersion. He knew that Philip would not immerse any one without faith in Jesus the Christ, and this could not be known without confession with the mouth. There was therefore no need to supply him with the information that the eunuch confessed his faith previous to this required act of obedience. If Luke did not write this, some other hand very early supplied what he knew was always given by every applicant for immersion, viz., a confession of faith in the anointed Jesus.

38. *Some people say that there was not sufficient water in this desert to immerse him ; and others say that, granting that there was sufficient, they only went to and from the water. How do you settle these conflicting theories ?*

To me there is no difficulty ; the word itself settles the whole matter. Luke says that Philip immersed him, and the word *ebaptisen* cannot be made to indicate any other action.

Every honest expositor will give to the word its full value, and this will regulate all necessary requirements.

39. *" The Spirit of the Lord caught away Philip." Why was this done ?*

It was a miracle to confirm the testimony delivered. The eunuch had heard from Philip words of life and blessing, but how could he know that these were true ? The word was confirmed by a sign of power in taking away the man who delivered them, " and he went on his way rejoicing."

CHAPTER IX.

1. *" And Saul, yet breathing out threatenings," etc. Why does Luke again refer to Saul ?*

It was in order to note his conversion, which commenced while he was following the saints to Damascus, with intent to bring them bound unto Jerusalem. The word " yet " indicates that, from the death of Stephen to the time that he started from Jerusalem, he had pursued this persecuting career, and had become more like a wild beast panting for its prey than a human being.

2. *" And desired of him letters to Damascus." How could the high priest empower Saul to arrest the citizens of this Syrian city ?*

It is not likely that he could do this, but Saul expected to find there some who had been chased out of Jerusalem, and were members of the synagogues, over which the high priest held rule. It was these refugees which Saul was empowered to arrest and bring back to Jerusalem, and the escort which he had received were to enable him to do his work effectually.

Why are the circumstances of the appearance of Jesus to Saul given so minutely ?

The principal reason is to show that Saul received his commission direct from Jesus, and that by His appearing and charge, he became a witness of His resurrection, and His apostle to the nations of the earth. Without these details the book would be defective. Then how much this account of the appearing of Jesus would confirm the faith and hope of Gentile believers to learn, that the man who had led them to trust in the Lord Jesus for acceptance and immortality, had been sent to them by that Lord Himself. From the start of Saul from Jerusalem with letters of authority, until he preached Christ at Damascus, Luke has recorded the principal facts of this interesting event; and thus Theophilus is prepared for the account of his labours among the Gentiles, to whom Jesus sent him. The opening of the door of faith to them by Peter, and the sending forth of Saul and Barnabas by the church at Antioch, are also duly recorded, and then follows the grand successful labours of his life.

6–18. Saul asked Jesus what he should do, and was told that he should have an answer in Damascus. To what did Jesus refer ?

We must follow him to Damascus to learn the answer. We read that Ananias directed him to yield himself up to Christ in immersion, and in that act he separated himself from his former standing as a Jew, and stood committed to any course his new Master might dictate.

The conversion of Saul was preceded by extraordinary circumstances. Were these absolutely necessary for conversion ?

No. Neither for his conversion nor that of others did these extraordinary things occur. The gift of tongues at Pentecost, the signs and wonders done by the apostles, and the appearing of Jesus to Saul, had each their specific object, and should not lead others to expect the same things as necessary for their conversion. Conversion to Christ is by the truth concerning Him, while these signs were given to prove the truth of the Gospel they were urged to receive. In the record of these conversions, we must discern between what is gratuitous, extraordinary, and therefore temporary, and what is binding in the commission of Jesus all through the dispensation. The miraculous was extraordinary and after a while ceased; while the preaching, hearing, faith, and obedience, must continue to the end.

19. After the visit of Ananias, we find Saul with the disciples. How were they led to have confidence in him ?

Ananias would acquaint them with the appearing of Jesus to him, and his immersion into Him would remove all fear of deception. They would doubtless visit him and cheer him in his new position, and soon had the pleasure of hearing him witness for Christ.

Though Saul had seen Jesus in the way, yet during the three days of blindness he appears to have been unhappy, since he did neither eat nor drink. How do you account for the great change by the visit of Ananias?

Although he had seen Jesus, and was convinced that he had been spoken to by Him who was put to death, yet by this appearing his guilt became manifest, because he was persecuting this very Jesus in persecuting His disciples; and as Jesus said nothing to him of forgiveness, but had smitten him with blindness, his anxiety as to what would follow must have been very great. It is no wonder that he could neither eat nor drink. But when Ananias went to him by the command of the Lord, to restore his sight, and to announce the bestowal of the Holy Spirit, and directed him to be immersed, in which act of submission forgiveness was received, and acceptance by Christ was realised, all his difficulties were removed, and joy filled his heart. He could then receive meat, and was ready for Christian fellowship and labour.

32. *From this statement that "Peter passed throughout all quarters" we learn that he had left Jerusalem. Why did he do so?*

No reason is assigned by Luke for this journey through all quarters, meaning possibly a visit through the churches, but it is not difficult to judge why he did so. (1.) The bitter persecution which prevailed at Jerusalem, made it desirable for him to leave it. (2.) The churches in these places required to be confirmed in their faith in Christ, and his visit was both timely and helpful to the saints. (3.) The miracles performed on Eneas and Dorcas, were useful in leading many others to turn to the Lord. And (4.) then, taking up his abode at Joppa, he was prepared for his further work of introducing the Gentiles into the one body of Christ.

CHAPTER X.

1. *Was Cornelius the centurion a Gentile?*

There is no doubt of this, and his conversion, along with others of his Gentile associates, forms a most important era in the new administration.

What are the peculiar features of this new section of " The Acts"?

In the preceding nine chapters, we have an account of the preaching of Christ the Lord among the Jews; the opening of the kingdom, by the admission of penitent immersed believing Jews into it; and the formation of the Church, upon which its exalted head bestowed the many rich gifts designed and prepared for it. In the church thus formed out of these believing Jews—the remnant according to the election of grace—we have a grand demonstration of the grace and power of the ascended Jesus, and a fulfilment of many things spoken by the prophets. But outside of these were the nations—the teeming population of the world, unto whom, up to this time, the Gospel had not been preached. Seven years had passed away since Peter made his first proclamation of remission of sins at Jerusalem, and Philip had preached among the Samaritans the name of Jesus; and yet no apostle or preacher had ventured into the third division named by Christ (Acts i. 8), to make known to them His salvation. It was pleasing to Him, by whom are all things, that Peter, who had opened the kingdom to the believing seed of Abraham, should now by preaching, faith, and immersion, lead into the fold these outcasts of the earth. In this chapter Luke records the circumstances connected with this remarkable event.

Does Luke's report of Gospel work among the Gentiles begin with the conversion of Cornelius?

We do not read of a single Gentile convert prior to this gracious visitation. Cornelius and his house were the first to whom the door of faith was opened, and from this time we see the Gentiles become special objects of interest and labour. The thing was seen to be of God, and even Peter, though reproved for what he had done, said that he could not withstand God. We would here observe that Luke's report of Pentecost is very full, while conversions after Pentecost among the Jews are but briefly narrated; so here, at the induction of the Gentiles, we get a full report of the circumstances—the discourse, the baptism of the Spirit, and their baptism in water; while conversions which follow are but briefly described. This should not be forgotten in our notice of these cases.

Why did God select Cornelius as the person to whom this display of grace should be shown?

There is no doubt but that God looked upon him as a proper person for this gracious demonstration of His favour. He was a pious God-fearing man, and both prayerful and benevolent, but withal he was a Gentile, and to such the good news had not then been proclaimed. As a centurion he would be familiar with the Jewish feasts, having to be in Jerusalem on these occasions, and he would also be acquainted with the facts of the Saviour's life. How often he might have conversed with disciples of Jesus we cannot tell, but as an uncircumcised man he was still outside, and had to learn the meaning of that promise to Abraham, "In thy seed shall all the families of the earth be blessed." That he was ready to enter the fold of Christ if God could admit him is evident, and here we have God preparing for his admission through the door which was never more to be closed upon the race.

Why was Peter selected to introduce the Gentiles into the faith?

Because to him Jesus had given the keys of the kingdom, and as he, by a proclamation to the house of Israel, and immersion of those who received his word, introduced them into the reign of the Messiah; so it was divinely arranged that he should in like manner lead the Gentiles into the same kingdom and covenant, that had been formed of the believing seed of Abraham. Cornelius and his collected friends heard from Peter the somewhat startling words, "I perceive that God is no respecter of persons." And again, "Whosoever believeth in Him shall receive remission of sins." In selecting Cornelius as the first fruit of this grace, and Peter as the instrument of the work, God acted wisely.

Both Peter and Cornelius were prepared by God for the interview. Why was preparation needed?

In Peter there was strong Jewish prejudice against the Gentiles, which had to be overcome, hence the training needful for his work; while Cornelius needed instruction, and had to be prepared to receive God's appointed messenger. God prepared both, and then brought them together.

25. *Was it not strange that Cornelius should fall down in worshipping attitude before Peter?*

It does appear strange to us, in our present knowledge of what is right, but when we think how largely veneration was cultivated in Roman soldiers, trained to prostrate themselves before superior officers, we need not wonder at the grateful act of this centurion, when a messenger of God stood before him. It was well that Peter refused the homage which this grateful man would gladly have rendered. Had his pretended successors only acted as faithfully in this matter of homage, it would have been well for the church.

30–33. *When Peter heard that Cornelius expected a message from God by him, would the apostle know what it was?*

Yes; he knew that he had to deliver the message of peace by Jesus Christ to these Gentiles. Nor did he hesitate to declare the glad tidings of remission of sins by Him, whose life, death, and resurrection, were briefly set before them.

The effect of this discourse upon their minds is not stated. Why omit this?

The effect is assumed by what followed. They were evidently ready to hear this glad message, and at once believed it, and then the Holy Spirit fell on all them which heard the word.

43. *What did Peter mean by "through His name"?*

By His authority, which included not only His promise, but also their union with Him through the Gospel arrangement by which it was secured.

Why did Peter use the word "repent," when speaking to the Jews at Pentecost, and "believing," when speaking to these Gentiles?

The reason must be sought for in their different conditions. The minds of those who slew Jesus required to be changed, and they were called upon to repent, and prove their repentance by submission ; but these Gentiles had no such feelings towards Jesus, and were called upon to trust Him. A difference in condition or state of mind when it exists, ought always to be noticed in Gospel work.

44. *"The Holy Spirit fell on all them which heard the word." Would this not interrupt the discourse of Peter?*

It is possible that he would have said more if this event had not occurred just at that moment, and which became a grand demonstration of God's purpose to accept them, which none present could mistake. The proof was indeed afterward accepted at Jerusalem by the whole convocation of apostles and elders.

How did Peter know that the Spirit rested upon them?

By the gift of tongues to Cornelius and his friends, as at Pentecost to the apostles. But we should notice, that at Pentecost it was the preachers who received the immersion in the Spirit and the gift of tongues, in order to reach and convince the hearers, while here it is the hearers who receive the Spirit, in order to convince the preacher and those with him, that God was ready to receive them. Thus Luke carefully reports to Theophilus the preaching of the Gospel in these three divisions of the human race, viz., to Jews, Samaritans, and Gentiles, and that

its confirmation was as signal in the latter as it had been 'in the former. True, this was but the beginning of a great work in this new field, and though both Peter and his friends were astonished " that on the Gentiles also was poured out the gift of the Holy Spirit," yet the fact was undisputed by all, " For they heard them speak with tongues, and magnify God. Then answered Peter, Can any man forbid water, that these should not be baptised, which have received the Holy Spirit as well as we? And he commanded them to be baptised in the name of the Lord."

Luke does not even name their belief or confession before their immersion in water. Why does he omit these requirements?

Because Theophilus knew that these would be attended to, as the commission required these things, and the report is not burdened with detailing what he knew would precede their immersion. He is careful to note that Peter said, " Whosoever believeth in Him shall receive remission of sins." When he reads of their immersion in the name of Jesus, he knows they have both believed in, and confessed their faith in the Lord Jesus.

Does the promise, " He shall baptise you in the Holy Spirit," which was fulfilled at Pentecost, and in the house of Cornelius, encourage any and every believer to expect its fulfilment now?

The baptism—*lit.,* immersion—on both occasions, were manifestations of the grace of the ascended Jesus, and have never been repeated, and, we may presume, never will. They were given to prove God's willingness to accept both Jews and Gentiles in Christ Jesus, and do not require to be repeated, but accepted as evidence of this all-important truth.

CHAPTER XI.

1, 2. *The news of the Gentiles receiving the Word of God reached Jerusalem before Peter. Why did the upholders of circumcision object to their reception into the family?*

They do not seem to have understood that it was God's plan to give to them a like admission into the new covenant; and having been so long possessors of the privileges of the old covenant, they had become selfish, and objected to their participation in these higher privileges. They should have considered that their own admission into the Church of Christ was by means of a new covenant, and that He who in mercy had admitted them could also admit others. This, however, they did not think of, and so objected to their introduction by Peter into the body of Christ.

3. *Was it because he did eat with the uncircumcised that they contended with him?*

This was their direct charge, and his doing this was a violation of the law of Moses, and by that law he was to be blamed. But then he had immersed them into Christ, and thus a new relationship was formed under a new covenant, in which Peter stood no higher than Cornelius. To eat together was a recognition of this oneness in the body, and to have refused to do so he would have denied this great truth.

4–18. *Why does Luke record Peter's rehearsal of this matter before the apostles and brethren in Judea?*

In order to convey to Theophilus a deeply important fact—viz., that this act of Peter's was sanctioned by the apostles and leading brethren in Jerusalem, and could not, therefore, be properly questioned again. Their exclamation, "Then hath God also to the Gentiles granted repentance unto life," was an acknowledgment which holds good through the entire dispensation.

19–21. *Why does Luke refer to the labours of the dispersed by the persecution that arose about Stephen?*

It was in order to notice that at first their labours were confined to Jews; but when some of them, men of Cyprus and Cyrene, came to Antioch, and hearing the news about Peter and Cornelius, which it is here supposed they did, they began to speak unto the Grecians (the best MSS. read Greeks), and the hand of the Lord was with them, and a great number believed and turned to the Lord. These men saw the grace of God toward the Gentiles, and began to preach to them salvation by Jesus, and their testimony being confirmed by signs, it was an unmistakable confirmation of the grace they had heard of in Cæsarea.

22. *Why did the Church at Jerusalem send Barnabas to Antioch?*

In order that they might learn the full particulars of this gracious work among the Greeks or Gentiles.

23. *What is meant by Barnabas seeing the grace of God?*

He evidently witnessed signs of their acceptance, which left no doubt upon his mind that God had received them into favour, and upon this his earnest exhortation was based.

25. *Why did he go to seek Saul?*

He had heard of his special call to preach to the Gentiles, and thought he would be the right man to sustain the work so graciously begun in Antioch. In Saul he found a prepared vessel for the work, and for a whole year they instructed the saints, and confirmed them in the faith.

26. *"And the disciples were called Christians first in Antioch." Was this name given in taunt, or by the Spirit?*

It was by the Spirit, through Paul and Barnabas, that this name was given to these disciples. A more literal rendering of the verse will, I think, make this plain to all. *And it came to pass that they*—(i.e., *Paul and Barnabas*)—*assembled during the whole year in the church, and taught much people, and called the disciples Christians first in Antioch.* Even the word *chrematisai*, rendered " called," shows that it was done by divine authority, and was afterwards endorsed by Peter (1 Pet. iv. 16).

Are denominational names, as Moravian, Lutheran, Presbyterian, Baptist, etc., etc., improper?

Since the name " Christian " is a God-given name, it must be right to wear it, and wrong to take any humanly-imposed name. In our relation to God as a Father, we are " children ; " to Christ, as our Teacher, we are " disciples ; " to one another we are brothers and sisters, and in character we are " saints ; " while to Christ, as our head, we are Christians, and should not allow ourselves to be called by any other name. It is a family name, and by it we are to be distinguished, not from others who love Jesus, but from the world who neither love nor serve Him.

CHAPTER XII.

1–4. What Herod was this who dared to kill one of the apostles of Christ?

Herod Agrippa, a grandson of Herod the Great. He received the rule of Judea and Syria from the Emperor Caligula.

What was the character of Herod?

Cruel, despotic, and time-serving. We are not told directly why he killed James, but to do so made him a murderer ; and, because this act pleased the Jews, he arrested Peter also, and shut him up in prison.

Why did the days of unleavened bread prevent Herod carrying out his purpose?

During the seven days of the feast both civil and criminal courts were closed ; whatever, therefore, Herod intended to do had to be postponed till after the feast.

Is " Easter " a proper term to use here?

It is strictly the " passover," and should be so rendered. It is sad to think that men should substitute the name of a Romish festival for an appointed ordinance of God.

What is a quaternion of soldiers?

Four soldiers formed a quaternion ; so that there were sixteen soldiers appointed to watch Peter. Each quaternion kept watch for three hours, two soldiers being chained to the prisoner, and two outside the cell. No prisoner could have been more closely guarded, and yet God set him free.

5–17. " Prayer was made without ceasing of the Church unto God for him." Was it for his release?

Possibly not; for they were greatly startled when they heard that he was standing at the door. No doubt they would plead with God that he might be sustained in the trial through which he was called to pass, but for his actual release they were hardly prepared. Their prayers, however, were more than answered in his deliverance out of prison, and Peter's enemies were frustrated in this purpose by such a timely interposition.

18, 19. How was Peter's escape accounted for by Herod?

He accused the keepers of aiding him to escape, and commanded that they should be put to death. It was a cruel and most unrighteous sentence, but he would rather accuse them than believe that God set him free.

23. The death of Herod was a most fearful one, and resulted from divine judgment. Does retribution follow in all cases?

Not in all; but there is often a striking connection between the life and the death of the enemies of truth and righteousness. Herod was an enemy of the Lord, and much long-suffering was shown unto him. His self-appropriation of divine glory was his crowning sin, and the angel of the Lord smote him.

What lessons may we learn from this brief episode upon Herod's persecution and death?

In this brief reference to him we see the fearful opposition the Church had to meet, and the signal triumphs which God gave to them over their enemies. Kings were against them, but God was on their side. They could not fight, but they could pray, and in their greatest extremity God could deliver, and so recompense those who trusted in Him. It is an encouragement to all the tried followers of the Lord

" To pray and wait ;
Jesus never comes too late."

Herod, the cruel opponent of the Lord Jesus, was eaten of worms, and gave up the ghost ; but the word of the Lord grew and multiplied. Such was the triumphant testimony Luke could narrate to Theophilus.

CHAPTER XIII.

1. *Were they chiefly Gentiles that formed this church at Antioch?*

A great number of the saints in it were Gentiles, but there were also Jews, as indicated by their names. Paul, and Barnabas, and Simeon were Jews, but the bond of fellowship was their faith in Christ. It was not as Jews or Gentiles that they were to be known, but as Christians, *i.e.*, as belonging to Christ ; and for their confirmation in the faith, both prophets and teachers were given.

o

In what things were the church at Antioch distinguished?

They were distinguished as the first assembly of God that was formed of both Jews and Greeks, which was a new thing in the earth. Then they were the first to receive the new and divinely-imposed name of Christian, the name which the disciples of Christ was ever afterwards to wear. And in this chapter Luke shows that they were the first church to send out evangelists to preach the Gospel to every creature they could reach. Jerusalem was the centre from which the Gospel was carried to Jews and Samaritans, but Antioch was the first centre for missionary efforts among the nations. Paul and Barnabas, the chosen evangelists of the church, had no restriction laid upon them. This would be deeply interesting to Theophilus.

2, 3. *Why did the Holy Spirit make known the will of God concerning these two labourers through the church?*

The case is deeply instructive, and claims the special notice of the Church of Christ. This church in Antioch, composed of believers out of the nations, and upon whom gifts were bestowed by the Spirit, were here reminded of their responsibility to send on the Gospel to others. The way in which they respond is suggestive of the way in which the Church should still act. They select of their brethren fitted for this work, and even an apostle becomes for a while a servant of that church in the Lord.

4. *If Saul and Barnabas were sent on a mission to the Gentiles, why did they first of all visit a Jewish synagogue?*

It was not to Gentiles merely that they were to preach, but to men as men, whether Jews or Gentiles. They acted according to God's order, " to the Jew first, and also to the

Greek." So in this town of Salamis, in Cyprus, they enter the synagogue, and tell of Jesus; but before they left the isle we read of them preaching before the deputy, or Roman governor of the country, who is said to have become a believer in the Lord.

6. *Why did Elymas oppose Paul and Barnabas when seeking to instruct Sergius Paulus?*

To prevent him from receiving their testimony, assuming that if he did so it might injure his own influence. Elymas, though a Jew, was a bad man, a deceiver, and opposed to the truth, and suffered a most humiliating reproof, in being struck with blindness for a season.

9. *Why was the name of Saul changed to Paul?*

The name Saul was strictly its Hebrew form, while Paul was Roman, and, after being sent to the nations, he was ever afterward called by this latter name.

14, 15. *In Antioch, in Pisidia, they again enter a synagogue of the Jews. Would this be their first effort in that place?*

It is most likely they would first visit those who had the Word of God in their hands, and, through the courtesy of the rulers, a most favourable opportunity was given them to deliver their message.

16. *"Men of Israel, and ye that fear God." Who are these last persons referred to?*

There were evidently two classes in the synagogue, Jews and pious Gentiles, who went in to hear the Scriptures read, and who were also invited to listen to Paul's address.

17-22. *Why does Paul give the history of the Jewish nation?*

In order to lead their minds along this line of accomplished facts, which none doubted, to other facts very closely connected with them, and which they required to have pressed upon their attention, and for the first time this is done by Paul. He narrated briefly how God chose their fathers, delivered them out of Egypt, and led them into Canaan; how He gave them judges and a king, even Saul, and then raised up David, to whom the promise of a Son, who should also be his Lord, was given. "Of this man's seed," said he, "hath God, according to His promise, raised unto Israel a Saviour, Jesus."

Why does Paul connect Jesus with David when there is such a large space of time between them?

From David, the king of Israel, to Jesus, there were more than a thousand years; but the son promised to David, and whose reign was to be age-enduring, had not appeared until Jesus, the Son of Mary, came into the world, and became, through Joseph His reputed father, the heir to David's throne. It was therefore proper to announce to these Jews at Antioch that this long-looked for promise had been fulfilled.

24-26. *Why does he refer to John?*

Because John had borne witness to the appearing of Jesus to the nation of Israel, and as Jews they ought to have had some knowledge of this fact, and without further detail of these things, he announces the glad tidings that both to the stock of Abraham, and to others that feared God, the word of salvation was sent.

27-33. *Why does Paul announce to them the death and resurrection of Jesus?*

Because upon these facts the salvation he declared to them was based. In their ignorance of Jesus, although revealed in the prophets which were read by them every sabbath day, the people and rulers of Jerusalem, through the power of Pilate, had put Him to death. "But," said Paul, "God raised Him from the dead," and of His resurrection there are now living witnesses.

The Galilean witnesses were not there to testify. How were these people in Antioch to be satisfied that Jesus was risen?

Paul adopted a method of proof which was applicable not only to the Jews in Antioch, but in every other place, viz., that the prophets had written of one who should rise from the dead, and of God's holy one who should not see corruption, and then affirmed that this had been fulfilled in Jesus, who as a Saviour he then made known to them.

"Thou art My Son," etc. How did Jesus derive this title?

By His birth from the grave by the power of God. Jesus was thrice born, and thus entered into a three-fold relationship. He was born of the flesh, and became the "Son of man." He was also born out of water at His baptism, and thus became spiritually the "Son of God." And He was also born out of the grave, having been begotten into life by the power of God, and thus became the "Son of God with power, according to the spirit of holiness, by the resurrection from the dead."

34. *What were these "sure mercies of David"?*

According to Paul, they were an ever-living Christ. All the previous successors of David had, like himself, "fell on sleep . . . . and saw corruption," but he looked for one who should not see corruption, and in this risen and exalted Jesus his hope was fulfilled.

38. *Would they not be startled when Paul made known to them forgiveness of sins through a man?*

Possibly they might think it blasphemous, to be turned from the rites of the law of God to trust in the man Christ Jesus, but the proclamation met a need which the law of Moses could not meet.

I have heard a preacher affirm from this passage that "forgiveness of sins" is already effected in Jesus for all who believe in Him. Is this what Paul teaches here?

No; because such a statement would contradict the first proclamation of Peter at Pentecost, and also his declaration in Solomon's porch, when he announced, "Repent, and turn, that your sins may be blotted out." According to this preacher, and many others who believe with him, this statement should have been "Repent, and turn," because your sins are blotted out in Christ. But this was not true, therefore he did not say so. To tell a sinner that his sins are forgiven in Christ and urge him to believe it, is to lead him to believe a lie, and beget a false peace. The first proclamation was, "Repent, and be immersed each one of you in the name of Jesus Christ for the remission of sins." This was God's way, and those who obeyed it were forgiven according to the promise. Sin is charged upon every sinner until he submits to Christ, and in his act of submission he obtains the promise. The terms of forgiveness being publicly proclaimed, sin could not be forgiven until the sinner yields to them. To say that sin was forgiven at the cross is to deceive. Jesus was wounded and bruised there, that sinners might be healed. He bore the curse, that sin might be forgiven.

40. *Did Paul expect that they would receive his message?*

There must have been something that led him to fear they would not, because he warns them to beware lest the judgment spoken of by the prophets come upon them.

44. *What was it that on the following sabbath brought almost the whole city together?*

The proclamation of salvation to any that feared God. This awakened the interest of nearly the whole city, and brought them to hear what might further be said upon this matter, which to them was deeply important.

45. *Was it the gathering of the multitude that brought out the bitter opposition of the Jews?*

Yes. When they understood that the Gentiles were invited by Paul to share with them the blessings of salvation, " they were filled with envy, and spake against those things which were spoken by Paul, contradicting and blaspheming." Thus they rejected eternal life, and led Paul to quote a beautiful prophecy, in which the salvation of the Gentiles was fully declared.

48. *Luke writes of these Gentiles, " As many as were ordained to eternal life believed." Do these words express his meaning?*

I think not. The word ordain implies the action or appointment of another, while Luke is writing of their own decision. If we rendered the sentence, " As many as were disposed or set towards eternal life, believed," we should see his meaning, and scholars so render it. The words of Paul made it plain to these Gentiles that God had provided salvation for them, and those who were determined to possess it, yielded to the terms on which it was to be enjoyed.

CHAPTER XIV.

1. *Paul and Barnabas were expelled from Antioch through the opposing Jews. Is it not strange that in the first city they enter they should again seek the synagogue of the Jews?*

If they had thought only of persecution they might not have done so, but they had a message of life for them, and wished to deliver it, whatever the result might be. There were, however, gracious results of their first

proclamation, as a number both of Jews and Greeks believed.

Were these Greeks Hellenistic or Greek Jews, or were they Gentiles?

The word is *Hellenes*, by which Luke designates Gentiles, and not *Hellenists*, Greek Jews or Grecians, as in chap. vi. 1.

2–5. *" But the unbelieving Jews stirred up the Gentiles." Did they doubt Paul's testimony?*

It is more strictly *the disobedient Jews*, which shows that while they could not overturn his testimony, which a great number both of Jews and Greeks believed, they were determined not to receive it, and stirred up otherwise peaceable Gentile citizens to join in an assault against the apostles. So fierce were they in this unrighteous onslaught, that Paul and Barnabas were compelled to leave the town, and seek another field of labour.

6. *From Iconium they fled to Lystra and Derbe. Why did they not again enter the synagogue?*

There was no synagogue there; the people were idolatrous Gentiles, worshippers of Zeus, and Hermes, here rendered Jupiter and Mercurius, and had to be addressed upon nature and providence, and the works of God the Creator of all.

8. *Why did they heal the poor cripple?*

In order to arrest attention, and prepare them to receive their testimony.

Did any conversions follow this effort?

According to ver. 21, disciples were made, and a church formed, and on their return journey were confirmed in the faith. The success, however, was limited by two causes : (1.) the apostles were believed to be gods who had come down to them in the likeness of men, and (2.) that persecuting Jews from Antioch and Iconium followed them, and stoned

Paul, who for a time seemed to be dead. He, however, revived, and then left for Derbe.

16. *" Who in times past suffered all nations to walk in their own ways."* *What did Paul mean by this ?*

He refers to the fact that, while God put the Jews under special training and oversight, giving them the law and the prophets to mould their lives according to His will, He left the nations without these laws, literally allowing them to walk as they listed. True, they had those revelations which had previously been given, and the good providences of God which were never taken from them, but no restraints were added beyond those which God first imposed upon the nations of the earth through Noah.

Why did they return from Derbe, and revisit those towns where they had been so ill treated ?

They had made disciples of Jesus in nearly all these towns, and it was to confirm in the faith, and set them in order, that they revisited these places, and not to visit synagogues, or encounter disobedient Jews. Against some of these they had had to shake off the dust of their feet.

22. *Does "confirming" here sustain Episcopal confirmation ?*

Not any further than the sound of a word may sustain it. But the difference between Paul confirming the souls or minds of these disciples, by further teaching the truth, and a bishop releasing sponsors from their solemn vows, by laying his hands on the youths on whose account these vows had been taken, is as wide as the poles. The action of the apostle was a wise and necessary one, but the action of both sponsors and bishop is a solemn mockery.

23. *Does "when they had ordained them elders in every church " suggest anything as to how it was done ?*

During the absence of Paul and Barnabas the faith and spirit of all had been tested. Some had grown in grace and knowledge of Jesus, and had shown their fitness to take oversight of the Church. The word *cheirotonesantes* seems to express both the action of the church, in showing who were fitted for this work by the uplifted hand, and the action of the evangelists in appointing them to the required oversight.

27. *The return of the evangelists to Antioch would be hailed by the church. Would their report establish anything of importance ?*

Yes ; Luke is careful to show to Theophilus, and it must have afforded him intense pleasure, that the door of faith which had been opened to the Gentiles was being entered by some of them in every place visited by these faithful labourers, and it would also afford great joy to the church which had sent them out on this evangelistic tour.

CHAPTER XV.

1. *" And certain men which came down from Judea taught the brethren,"* *etc. Was this before or after the return of Paul and Barnabas ?*

It is *lit., and were teaching the brethren.* So that they were busy teaching the brethren that they must be circumcised in order to be saved, when the evangelists returned from their first missionary tour.

Would you not look upon this new mission from Jerusalem as a daring attack upon the truth and grace of the Lord Jesus ?

It was an attempt to make the Gentiles pass through the gates of Judaism ere they could enter the city of God—in fact, to unite Moses and Christ, the Law and the Gospel —in order to effect their salvation. It was a soul-ruining scheme, and worked sad results among the churches. We may wonder why God did not stay them in their work by visible judgment, but in not doing so He has taught us that error must only be met with truth, not by physical force. Paul and Barnabas did not seek for judgment to rest upon these opposers, but disputed with them in order to convince them of their error, and establish the truth. Ultimately the church decided that they should go to Jerusalem, and lay the whole matter before the apostles and elders.

Did both parties agree to this way of settling the dispute?

Possibly not. These men who went from Judea were hired agents, sent to frustrate the gracious work of God. They were mere timeservers, and had to push on their mission, whatever decision the apostles might come to. The apostles and elders decided against them, but this did not stop their evil work. They went through Galatia after Paul had planted churches there, and did great harm. They were men of no principle or piety, as the character given them by Paul in his letters fully show (see Phil. iii. 19). Still the decision of that Jerusalem convocation would be of immense advantage to both labourers and churches, so it was sought and obtained.

3. *Why did Luke name Phenice and Samaria being visited on their route to Jerusalem?*

Because the churches planted by Philip in these districts, and which still held their faith and obedience to Christ, were not of Jewish birth and blood, and when they heard of the conversion of the Gentiles it caused great joy unto all these brethren.

4. *At Jerusalem Paul and Barnabas declared to the church what things God had done by them. I suppose this refers to the conversion of Gentiles?*

Yes, and a most interesting report it must have been, especially as it would not only contain many interesting items of persons and places, but also of many signs and wonders wrought among them by the power of the Holy Spirit, in which their acceptance was thus divinely sealed.

5. *"But there rose up certain of the sect of the Pharisees," etc. Was it in the conference at Jerusalem that this opposition occurred?*

No. This opposition occurred in the church at Antioch, and was the reason why Paul and Barnabas went up to Jerusalem to consult with the apostles and elders respecting it. The two evangelists are here simply narrating to the church respecting the opposition which had taken place. "Then the apostles and elders came together to consider of this matter."

Who may be considered to have the first claim to speak at this conference?

The man who first opened the door by preaching to the Gentiles, and commanding them to be immersed in the name of the Lord Jesus. In common courtesy, he should be heard before any others in defence of God's grace to the Gentiles. But before he was permitted to deliver his conclusive speech there had been a good deal of disputing. Luke, however, has recorded only those addresses which were really to the point.

What were the conclusive points in Peter's address?

He refers to three facts in the conversion of Cornelius and his company, which were unanswerable. (1.) That it was God's will that the Gentiles by his mouth should hear the word of the Gospel, and believe. (2.) That God gave them the Holy Spirit, as He had first done to the apostles. And (3.), that He had purified their hearts by the truths believed. He then asks, Since God has done this so freely, why do you put upon the neck of the disciples a yoke which neither we nor our fathers were able to bear?

12. "*Then all the multitude kept silence.*" *Why did they do so?*

In order to give Barnabas and Paul an opportunity of speaking; and after Peter's effective appeal to facts, it was only proper that they should be heard. They had worked out the mission which he so signally began, and on this occasion they appeal to the miracles and wonders which God had wrought in confirmation of it.

13–17. *The previous speakers had all appealed to facts. Why did James, who gave the closing address of this conference, appeal to prophecy?*

It was in order to show that, while the conversion of the Gentiles was begun and confirmed by the Holy Spirit, it had also been shadowed forth in the prophetic types of the old dispensation. James selected the prophecy by Amos. "After this I will return, and will build again the tabernacle of David, which is fallen down," etc. (ix. 11.)

What is this tabernacle to which Amos refers?

It will be well to note here that it was not the fallen house of David to which reference is made, nor to the tabernacle of Moses that had been set up at Shiloh, and afterwards at Gibeon, where the nation worshipped; but to the tabernacle or tent made by David expressly for the ark of the covenant. This ark, which had been carried out of Shiloh by Hophni and Phinehas to the war with the Philistines, was captured by them, and was never restored to the old tabernacle; and after remaining many years in the house of Abinadab in Gibeah, it was ultimately brought up to Jerusalem by David. The ark was evidently understood by David to be a type of Him that was to come, and in

this tabernacle of curtains in which it was placed he was permitted to sit and worship, girded with a linen ephod, a garment which priests or Levites alone had been permitted to wear. In this new service sacrificial offerings had no place, but a service of praise was instituted, which, day and night (Ps. cxxxiv. 1), was sustained by Asaph and the Kohathites, and for whose use many of his most beautiful psalms were composed. Indeed, the force and beauty of many of these psalms can only be understood in relation to this curtain-tabernacle; and to sit in it, a posture never allowed in the old tabernacle, was to sit before the Lord (2 Sam. vii. 18). The whole of this service was evidently typical of a new order of things—a shadowing forth of service and access to God, altogether separate from the law, and from the people under it. After the death of David, and the ark of the covenant had been removed to the newly-built temple, this tabernacle fell into decay. Many years after, when God was revealing by Amos some things that would happen to the nation, we have him writing, as quoted by James from the Septuagint, "After this I will return, and will build again the tabernacle of David that is fallen down; and I will build again the ruins thereof, and I will set it up: that the residue of men might seek after the Lord, and all the Gentiles, upon whom My name is called, saith the Lord, who doeth all these things." Now, James applied this prophecy to the case before them, and urged the brotherhood to accept these believing Gentiles with all confidence, and at once to give directions for their future guidance.

18. *What does he mean by "known unto God are all His works, from the beginning of the world"?*

It is, *lit., from the beginning of an*

age. That is, God knew that He should call the Gentiles to share His grace, and therefore gave the type in David's priestly access to Himself in this tabernacle, and the prophecy by Amos, of Gentile acceptance. This closing address by James settled the matter in that assembly, and not a dissenting voice was raised against it.

I suppose that this would be a most important decision for Luke to report ?

This matter of Gentile acceptance through faith in Jesus, without having to pass through the gates of the law of Moses, had become the question of the period, and this decision was a most important one. The evidence of God's will concerning the Gentiles was well presented and sustained ; fact and prophecy were most efficiently applied, and the question was settled for ever.

19, 20. *Why does James suggest that they should be urged to abstain from fornication, from blood, etc., when he had shown that they were not under the law of Moses for acceptance ?*

The things insisted upon had been imposed upon the nations by God, through Noah, as well as upon the Jew. They had, therefore, to be instructed in these divine requirements, and, as accepted ones, to become obedient to God.

Is it wrong for us to eat blood, and animals that have been strangled ?

Most certainly. Because, though not under the law of Moses, we are under the law of God. It would be as wrong for us to eat blood, or partake of a creature that had been strangled, as it would have been for the saints in any of the churches visited by Paul and Barnabas.

21. *What did James mean by, "For Moses of old time hath in every city," etc. ?*

It is simply to show that the Jews who had learned these things

from Moses did not need to be instructed in them, but only the churches of the Gentiles.

22–33. *Why did the apostles send Judas and Silas with Paul and Barnabas ?*

They were sent with them to give additional confirmation to the decision of the apostles and elders, and place the message above all suspicion. They were received with joy in every place, and the churches were established in the faith.

36. *The separation of Paul and Barnabas, after such a long service together, seems to have been unfortunate. Did the circumstance justify the separation ?*

We are not able to judge in this matter, but must leave it with God. When John Mark left them in Pamphylia and returned to Jerusalem, Paul looked upon him as shirking the work, and would not forgive his apparently cowardly act. He may have had a proper reason for what he did, as he afterward proved himself to be a faithful labourer and not a coward. Years after, Paul acknowledged his value, and directed Timothy to bring him with him. We feel sorry that Barnabas should have left Paul, as it is the last record we have of this good man. From that time Silas became Paul's companion, and shared with him the trials of his arduous life.

CHAPTER XVI.

1. *We have here Paul revisiting, with Silas, the churches he and Barnabas had planted. What was their object on this occasion ?*

It was to deliver the decrees which had been ordained by the apostles, and at Lystra they met with Timothy, who afterward became a most valuable fellow-labourer in preaching the Gospel.

3. *Why did Paul circumcise this*

Grecian Jew, when he had made such a noble stand against the circumcising of Gentiles ?

It was not that he might obtain salvation through it—that question was settled for both Jew and Greek —but in order to soften down strong Jewish prejudice against him as being uncircumcised, and thus to open his way for more acceptable labour among them.

8, 9. Up to this period Paul does not seem to have had any special direction as to places to be visited. Why does he now receive special guidance ?

Up to this time he had laboured in Asia, and when this man appeared to him in a vision, and called him into Macedonia, he was in the small seaport of Troas, where the Ægean Sea divided Europe from Asia. It was the will of God that he should cross over and preach the Gospel in this new quarter of the world. He was at the time uncertain where to go, but that vision was accepted as a call from God to visit Macedonia. Then, as it is the first time in the joint travels of Paul and Luke that we meet with the pronoun *we*—so frequently met with after this—we presume that it was at Troas that Paul met with the " beloved physician" and the historian of his life. From Troas, therefore, the company sailed over into Macedonia, and soon arrived at Philippi.

12. We read that there was a colony at Philippi. What does this mean ?

That a colony of Jews were residing in Philippi, who had also their place of worship by " a river side," and at their first meeting after the arrival of Paul and his company, the missionary band were present with them, and in that Jewish prayer-place their mission in Europe was opened.

13. It is said that they " spake unto the women which resorted

thither." Why did Luke not tell Theophilus what was said ?

Because he knew what would be said from the accounts already given. It is results which are now recorded rather than the truths which produce them.

14. It is said of Lydia " whose heart the Lord opened." How was this effected ?

By the instruction given to her by Paul. Lydia was a pious Jewess, who had often read about the coming Messiah, and was no doubt looking for His appearing. But she had never heard that the prophecies concerning Him had been fulfilled until these missionaries came to Philippi to make known His coming into the world. Paul would no doubt approach the mind of Lydia and others through the Scriptures, and while he recounted the wonderful story of His life, death, resurrection, and gracious power, the words fell upon her mind, like the rays of the sun upon a closed flower, which soon opened to receive them. The effect was produced by this adequate cause, for as she heard and understood the testimony about Jesus the ascended Lord, she began to love Him, and was ready to yield obedience to Him. Or, as Luke states, " she attended to the things which were spoken by Paul."

Luke does not so much as name her faith, or repentance, or confession of Jesus as the Son of God. Are these things implied in her attending to the things spoken by Paul ?

Theophilus would know that ere she could be buried with Christ in baptism, the preceding requirements would all be met. He does, however, record one noble act of her faith and love : " If ye have judged me to be faithful to the Lord, come into my house, and abide there. And she constrained us."

Do you suppose that this result would be effected in one day ?

It is more likely to have been the result of oft-repeated instruction upon the great themes of the Gospel. Paul and his company visited this *proseuche*, or place of prayer, many days, instructing not only Lydia but many others, until a church was formed in Philippi.

16–23. This damsel with a spirit of divination is a very strange affair. How do you account for it ?

I do not account for it, but simply receive it as reported. That this damsel did possess a spirit of divination, which was used by her masters for base purposes, is beyond all question. This spirit was cast out by Paul, after which she either could not, or would not, deceive any longer, and this expulsion of the spirit led to the imprisonment of Paul and Silas.

24. Would you not think the jailer into whose charge they were given, a cruel man ?

Well, he was a stern, rough man, no doubt, and a measure of such sternness was needed for his position ; but his treatment of Paul and Silas was certainly harsh and unfeeling. It is said that he "thrust them into the inner prison, and made their feet fast in the stocks." And although their backs were lacerated with the many stripes laid upon them, and their garments stiffened with blood, and they even requiring food, he does not seem to have shown any sympathy towards them. He had received a charge to keep them safe, and beyond this duty he does not seem to have had a thought about these prisoners. The stern jailer forms a very striking contrast to the gentle, truth-seeking Lydia, and yet both alike needed the salvation of God. She had doubtless been searching the Scriptures for years, and had not found the pearl of great price ; he possibly had never read them at all, and required

to learn by the earthquake that "verily there is a God that judgeth the earth." The Christ-saving truth was required by both, in order to their enlightenment, and while Paul's gentle reasoning out of the Scriptures about Jesus was sufficient to open her heart to receive Him as her Lord, the jailer had to be aroused and learn from the Gospel that Jesus alone could save him.

25. "At midnight Paul and Silas prayed and sang praises to God." One cannot but regret that Luke did not record the song they were singing when God's earthquake chorus followed their anthem. What do you think it might be ?

To guess is useless, though I feel sure it would be appropriate to their condition, and most likely one of the Psalms. Think of the 46th Psalm ringing through the jail at midnight :

"God is our refuge and strength,
    A very present help in trouble.
Therefore will we not fear though the
        earth be removed,
And though the mountains be carried
        into the midst of the sea."

No wonder the prisoners heard—*lit.*, were listening to—them. They would think them strange men to be singing in their bonds.

26. Would this earthquake be a local one ?

Possibly ; but we know not the extent of its force. It was sufficient for its work, and that was enough. It opened doors, loosed bonds, awoke and alarmed the jailer, and must have been a solemn time to all concerned. It not only set free the apostles, but furnished them with blessed work, in directing the jailer to the Saviour of sinners.

31. Was their simple direction to him to believe on the Lord Jesus Christ sufficient to guide him to assured salvation ?

If nothing further had been said

to him he would have been left in perplexity. The direction was an important one, as it brought before him a person who could do all he needed. How he could do this, and how he could be assured of it, he had still to learn, and this instruction they at once supplied ; or, as Luke records, "they spake unto him the word of the Lord, and to all that were in his house."

What is meant by the word of the Lord ?

The previous part of Luke's record must supply the answer. Theophilus understood it, I have no doubt, hence the results alone are recorded, and these show us how thoroughly the truth had taken hold of his heart. (1.) He washed their stripes ; (2.) he and all his house were immersed straightway ; and (3.) he set meat before them, and rejoiced in God with all his house ; a most signal and blessed triumph of the Gospel.

> " His doctrine is almighty love,
>   There's virtue in His name,
> To turn the raven to a dove,
>   The lion to a lamb."

37. *What did Paul mean by " being Romans" ?*

That they were Roman citizens, and as such had protection against the degrading and unjust punishment which the magistrates had inflicted on them through the instigation of a lawless mob. Paul therefore claimed and obtained, by virtue of this right, an honourable dismissal.

CHAPTER XVII.

1. *Why did Paul go to Thessalonica ?*

Thessalonica, now called Salonica, was the capital of one of the pretorial districts of Macedonia, and was therefore an important place to which the Gospel might be introduced. Here Paul found a syna-

gogue of Jews, and among these he opened his mission.

Did Luke accompany him on this tour ?

Silas and Timothy appear to have been his associates, while Luke most likely remained at Philippi to take charge of the newly formed church. Its future upbuilding in the faith of Jesus would largely devolve upon him, and through him, they would keep up that loving fellowship with Paul for which they were so distinguished. Luke afterward met Paul at Troas (Acts xx. 6).

2. *Paul reasoned with the Jews at Thessalonica out of the Scriptures. Why did he prefer this method to the proclamation he had to make ?*

I judge that he did proclaim the facts of the Gospel message, but as a wise master builder, he goes first to their own prophets, read by them every sabbath, and upon these the facts of Jesus suffering and rising again from the dead are based. He placed the prophecies concerning the Messiah, and the facts concerning Jesus of Nazareth, side by side, and then boldly affirmed, "this Jesus, whom I preach unto you, is the Anointed."

4. *Paul's success seems to have been the greatest among the Greek or Gentile population. How do you account for their large acceptance of his message, while the Jews as largely rejected it ?*

There were several reasons for this both pleasing and painful result, which we may note. (1.) Paul spoke to the Jews, and proved from their Scriptures that Jesus whom he preached to them was the Messiah of the prophets, but their prejudice against Him whom their nation had crucified was so great that they refused to believed in Him, excepting a very few, and in great anger rejected both the messenger and his message. (2.) That Paul so preached

Jesus that the Greeks, both men and women, understood that they were welcome to receive Jesus as their Lord, and become partakers of His salvation, and most readily embraced this gracious offer. We attribute the difference between the few Jews, and the many Gentiles receiving Christ, to arise entirely from the national antipathy of the former, which had spread by rumour from Jerusalem to the provinces; and the absence of it in the latter, many of whom were already devotional and waiting for the salvation of God.

5-9. *Why did the lawless mob of Jews and Gentiles assault Jason?*

Jason appears to have lodged Paul and his companions, and was the first to suffer from the brutish attack of these disturbers of peace and order. The visitants were charged with treasonable purposes, so that even the rulers of the city became alarmed, and had to demand security from Jason lest serious results should follow the visit of those persons received by him. The visit, however, was not in vain: some received Christ Jesus the Lord and were formed into a church, and afterward received valuable help in the letters written to them by Paul.

10. *Why did they send him and Silas away?*

Because prejudice against them was running so high that their lives were in danger, and it was hoped that their removal would quell the tumult. So they are sent off to Berea, an adjoining city, while the new converts are left to brave the furious storm of persecution which the Christ-rejecting Jews raised against them.

11. *Were these more noble Bereans Jews?*

Yes, for it was into their synagogue that Paul entered, and to their Scriptures he appealed, and it was their daily personal reference to these Scriptures that led to their believing recognition of Jesus the Christ. It may be well to note here that these Jews at Berea are not compared with Gentile converts in Thessalonica, who, after believing on Christ, suffered so much for Him; but with the Jews who, in ignorance, opposed the truth in that city. In the one place the Jews disregarded the Scriptures, while in the other they searched them daily: "therefore many of them believed." To these there were also added "of the devout Greeks a great multitude, and of the chief women not a few." This successful service was, however, soon interrupted, and the labourers had to be sent away to some other field.

15. *Why did Paul go to Athens?*

He seems to have had no choice in the matter, but was taken there by his guides, that he might get free from his pursuers. There they left him, a lonely man in the capital of Attica in Greece, a city wholly given to idolatry.

17. *Were these "devout persons" met with in this synagogue in Athens, Jews?*

I judge they were Greeks who attended synagogue worship, which had then become common throughout the provinces, but were ignorant of God's salvation. To these Paul stated the Gospel, and reasoned with them to prove its truth.

18. *Who were these philosophers that encountered Paul?*

They were either teachers or scholars of that system of so-called philosophy, of which Epicurus and Zeno were the founders. These two men each having framed a system of their own, opened their schools in Athens about 300 years before the Christian era, and taught those principles, which at the time of Paul's visit there, were popular throughout Greece. Their scholars were distinguished as Epicureans, from the name of their teacher, and Stoics, from the Stoa, or painted porch at the entrance of the school of Zeno. They were trained to reason out the theorems of their masters as settled truths, and were skilful in dispute with any that opposed their notions.

Why did they encounter Paul ?

Because he brought before them a person of whom they had not heard, and a fact which in all their range of speculative thought they had never conceived. It became therefore a matter for dispute, and that a fair hearing might be secured, Paul was taken to Areopagus, and an opportunity given him for a full exposition of the new doctrine he had brought to their ears.

What was this Areopagus ?

It was the supreme court of Athens, the place where the judges, or Areopagites, sat for the trial of all cases in which the interests of the city, both civil and religious, were concerned. The word means "Mars' hill," and is so rendered in ver. 22. It was the top of a rock, out of which the seats of the judges and others were hewn. Whether a trial was intended, Luke does not state, but nothing like a trial followed his discourse, although great objections were made to it.

22–25. *"I perceive that in all things ye are too superstitious." Did he speak this in respect or censure ?*

His words strictly rendered would read, *I perceive you are very reverent to demons*—*i.e.*, hero or god worship—and would be looked upon by them as an acknowledgment of that in which they were distinguished, and not in any way disrespectful. They worshipped many gods, each having its name and supposed work or charge; but as Paul passed by and beheld their devotions, he saw an altar with this strange inscription, "to an unknown god"; and as they

here acknowledged that there was a God of whom they were ignorant, he at once began to make Him known as the living Creator and upholder of the world and all its creatures. Their fathers had known and worshipped this God, but as their children sought out and fashioned to themselves idols, or visible gods, the knowledge of the true God faded away from them entirely, except, as this altar testified to their shame, that there was such a God, although He had become to them "unknown."

26. *Is Paul's testimony to the unity of the human race to be accepted as decisive ?*

It is in harmony with the testimony of Moses, which no one is able to disprove, viz., that Adam was the head of all humanity. In reading Paul's statement here, we should omit the word "blood," and read, *and hath made out of one all nations of men*, etc.

28. *Why did Paul refer to their "own poets" since they were heathens ?*

Though Aratus, Cleanthus, and Pindar, the poets to whom Paul refers, were heathen, yet their ancestors had the knowledge of God; and though strangely mixed up with their own reasonings, yet Paul discerned and recognised the truth which they had sung, viz., that they were the offspring of this great Creator of all things, and ought not to fashion Him in gold, or silver, or stone, as in so doing they were reducing Him to their own level.

30. *What is meant by God winking at the times of their ignorance ?*

Simply that He did not bring to judgment the nations whom He left walking in their own ways. The revelations concerning Christ, given from Abraham onward, had not been given to them; they were therefore not responsible, as were the Jews. But as the Gospel had been sent to all men through the apostles, God commanded all men everywhere to repent, because at the appointed day all would be judged by Christ.

31. *"He hath given assurance to all men." Is this of the day of judgment or of their own resurrection?*

Of both, we presume. That God will judge the world righteously is a testimony by the prophets; that He will do so by Christ, whom He raised from the dead, is also testified by apostles; and in raising Christ He has assured all others that they will be raised, and stand before Him.

Why did they mock on hearing about the resurrection of the dead?

Because it was a truth which their philosophy had never evolved, and instead of receiving the message they derisively trifled with it.

CHAPTER XVIII.

1. *How long did Paul remain in Athens?*

The exact time is not stated, but some circumstances are referred to which may help us a little in forming our judgment upon this matter. (1.) We learn that those who conducted him to Athens left him there alone, but carried back a message to Timothy to come to him with all speed. (2.) We learn from his first letter to the Thessalonians that Timothy did visit him, but his anxiety about them became so great that he could not rest, and sent him back to Thessalonica to learn how they behaved amid the terrible persecutions which raged against them. Then (3.) we have the return of Timothy with cheering news of their steadfastness, after which he left for Corinth. The time, therefore, that he remained there was the time occupied in these journeys, which in those days were not performed very speedily.

2. *When Aquila and Priscilla left Rome by order of Claudius, no apostle had visited Rome. How did they become disciples of Christ?*

There is no evidence that they were disciples of Christ when they left the Imperial city. They had to depart from Rome, not because they were Christians, but because they were Jews; and Paul's location with them in Corinth was because they were tent-makers, and agreed to work together. That Christ Jesus would be the great theme of their fellow-workman one feels sure about, and from his earnest conversation and instruction these two noble hearts would be led to accept of Jesus. That Paul the apostle should have been compelled to labour with his hands one almost regrets, but with such results we feel more than satisfied that he had to seek their abode.

5–7. *When Silas and Timothy arrived at Corinth they found Paul "pressed in spirit." What does this mean?*

Paul had discovered that his quiet sabbath day reasonings in the synagogue was producing no effect upon the Jews, and when he was constrained to an open testimony that Jesus was the Christ, it was met with such frenzied opposition that he was led to shake his raiment, and free himself from their blood, declaring that from henceforth he would go unto the Gentiles.

Did Paul revoke this solemn decision?

He saw that the Jews were unitedly determined to oppose his testimony, and while intensely anxious to labour for the salvation of both Jews and Gentiles, the opposition of the former made this impossible. His heart, therefore, was filled with grief at having to leave them to ripen for judgment, and from this time we read of but few conversions among them. The work went on, and churches were formed in all the principal cities of Asia, but they were from the Gentiles who gladly welcomed the Gospel of Christ. For instance, in this city of Corinth, there were only two Jewish converts, Crispus and Justus, while many of the Corinthians hearing believed, and were baptised.

9. *When the Lord told Paul to remain in the city and speak, He said, " for I have much people in this city." Did He refer to the converted or the unconverted ?*

It is strictly, "Because there is much people for Me in this city," *i.e.*, towards Me, or wishing to hear of Me : therefore remain and be speaking, that they may hear. Possibly both classes are included—the converted needed instruction, and the anxious needed the Gospel, so the Master said, *Fear not, but speak, and be not silent ;* and he continued there a year and six months, teaching the Word of God among them.

12–17. *What was the purpose of this insurrection against Paul under the deputy rule of Gallio ?*

Their object was to obtain from Gallio, the Roman procurator of Achaia, judgment against Paul, but signally failed to do so. Gallio saw at once that as a judge he had nothing to do with their charge against Paul, and so drove them from the judgment seat.

Luke states, " Then all the Greeks took Sosthenes, the chief ruler of the synagogue, and beat him before the judgment seat. And Gallio cared for none of those things." What does this mean ?

The best readings now omit " Greeks." It was the Jews who did this, because Sosthenes favoured Paul, and not being able to obtain judgment against him, they vented their spite against this ruler, even before Gallio. When Luke says he " cared for none of those things," he simply means that he could not be moved from his purpose not to act judicially in this case.

18–23. *Paul after this tarried there a good while. May we presume that he obtained protection ?*

As a Roman citizen he would have protection, and would thus be enabled to instruct the disciples, until he saw fit to remove. After this he sailed to Ephesus, taking with him Aquila and Priscilla ; and leaving them in Ephesus, he sailed for Jerusalem by Cæsarea, and then went to Antioch, and Galatia, and Phrygia, and possibly returned to Ephesus.

24–28. *Why does Luke introduce this case of Apollos ?*

It is one of more than ordinary interest. Apollos was a Jew from Alexandria, and having been instructed by one of John's disciples that Jesus was coming, and being baptised into the expectant theory, he became a most zealous and earnest preacher of this old faith. On coming to Ephesus, he pleaded boldly in the synagogue that all should expect the Messiah, which, when Aquila and Priscilla heard, they saw at once his mistake, took him unto them, and expounded to him the way of God more perfectly. With a childlike spirit Apollos sat at their feet, heard their teaching, accepted the truth that Jesus had come, and then became a helper, both of the saints who had believed and of Paul in his labours.

CHAPTER XIX.

1. *Had Apollos been to Ephesus previous to Paul's visit there ?*

It is most likely that he came there between Paul's first visit, when he left Aquila and Priscilla, and his return by the upper coasts, where he found these disciples, who had been converted, either by Apollos or some one, to John's baptism. The work, however, had to be undone, whoever the worker had been.

2. *Was it not a strange question for Paul to ask : " Have ye received the Holy Spirit since ye believed ? "*

Not at all strange, as he specially referred to the gifts of the Spirit, and as these were only conferred by apostles in confirmation of the truth they preached, it was natural for him to ask this question.

I presume their answer would startle him ?

Yes ; and at once awakened his suspicion, and led to further enquiry. " Unto what, then, were ye baptised ? And they said, Unto John's baptism." This at once revealed their position, and led him to give them all necessary instruction in the truth, and these twelve men were baptised, or immersed, into the name of the Lord Jesus.

4. *Would Paul not instruct in the Gospel of Christ before he immersed them ?*

We may be sure of that. The order was preaching, belief, and obedience, and when guided by the apostles, this was always the way in which men were led to accept of Christ.

If the immersion of John was right during his ministry, how was it wrong to these twelve ?

John's immersion was right in his day, because God sent him to proclaim the Coming One, and immerse all who, believing his testimony, confessed their sins and need of a Saviour. But when Jesus was crucified, and risen, and ascended, and a new administration was going on in His name, it was surely wrong, though in ignorance, to ignore all this, and act as if it had never been done. This is what these twelve men had been doing, by the direction of some ignorant teacher, and was wrong, because out of date. We may learn some important lessons from this circumstance. We see (1.) that old arrangements cannot be accepted when new ones have been divinely introduced ; and (2.) that one plan cannot be a substitute for another, however sincerely performed. We may presume that these men were as sincere as possible, and yet their immersion was not valid, because Christ was not accepted as a present Saviour.

6. *After their immersion into the name of Jesus, these men received the gift of tongues and prophecy. What purpose did these serve ?*

They were the seal of the Spirit to the truth believed and obeyed ; and to this fact Paul refers when he wrote, " After that ye believed, ye were sealed with that holy Spirit of promise " (Eph. i. 13).

Does the sealing of the Spirit still take place on those that believe ?

The seal of the Spirit, according to New Testament evidence, was an external attestation on all who received it, and one to which others could bear witness. Whether it was Christ or His apostles, the house of Cornelius or these Ephesians, the seal of the Spirit—in signs, tongues, and prophecy—was manifested for the profit of others, and not for personal advantage. That such a seal as this is not now affixed to any believer is evident, because no one can show it ; and to ask us to believe that the fruit of the Spirit, as seen in the life of the child of God, is the seal of the Spirit, as was given by Him to confirm the truth, is to confound things that differ. But few received the seal ; all must bear fruit to the glory of the name of Jesus.

8. *When Paul shook his raiment in the synagogue of Corinth, he seemed to have done with the Jews. Why did he enter the synagogue at Ephesus ?*

He was unwilling to give them up, for his bowels yearned over them. He knew the consequences of their rejection would be fearful, so another effort is made—a most persistent one. Even for the space of three months did he dispute and persuade in the things concerning the kingdom of God.

9–12. Why did Paul remove to the school of Tyrannus ?

In order to get the disciples away from the influence of these disputatious Jews, and in this room they had protection, which the synagogue did not afford. It will be more correct to read *discoursing daily,* and not " disputing," as it was for the more quiet instruction of disciples that Paul selected this place. No doubt many visitors to Ephesus would likewise avail themselves of this lengthened opportunity of hearing the Apostle of the Gentiles. Here, also, many miracles were done by Paul, and the word of his preaching was confirmed by the signs that followed.

13–20. Why did these seven Jews, who were professional exorcists, attempt to cast out an evil spirit in the name of Jesus ?

Their object was to neutralise the influence of Paul by using the name of Jesus, whom Paul preached, vainly thinking the same result would follow with them as with him. In this, however, they were disappointed, as a scene followed not easily described. Their clothes were torn off by the demonised man, and wounds were inflicted upon them, which shows that they but narrowly escaped with life. The event could not be hid, and many that used curious arts confessed their evil deeds, burned their books, and thus owned the truth of the Gospel of Jesus.

Should not such a demonstration to the truth have turned the whole of Ephesus to Christ ?

If conviction of the truth was all that was needed, this might have been done, but conversion to Christ is at urning from sin, and this many were not willing to do. Most people

P

understand that to become a Christian is to lead a new life, and for this they are not ready. The people in Ephesus were astonished at the power of Jesus, but many still held on their evil way.

23–41. Were the bad times that came to Demetrius, the silversmith, and his workmen, occasioned by the labours of Paul ?

Demetrius made silver shrines for the worshippers of " the great goddess Diana," and as many of these were converted, and drawn away from her worship, his trade decreased, and his income was becoming more and more limited. He knew the cause very well, and determined an attack, not by pointing out his own loss, as in truth he should have done, but the dishonour the city would sustain, not only in all Asia, but also the world. The city was therefore aroused to defend their time-honoured goddess, some associates of Paul were seized and hurried into the theatre, and but for the timely interference of the town clerk, a very serious riot would have followed. He very wisely suggested, that if Demetrius and the craftsmen had sustained any damage, they ought to seek redress in a court of law, and not in a lawless assembly. His advice had a most tranquillising effect on the people, and the assembly quietly dispersed.

What is the meaning of " silver shrines" ?

A shrine means a temple, and we judge that the shrines made by Demetrius were miniature silver models of the goddess and her temple ; and these were purchased, and held sacred by all her worshippers.

CHAPTER XX.

1–3. Paul's visit into Macedonia would, I suppose, include Thessalonica and Philippi ?

These places are not named, but as they had become important mission stations, they would not be overlooked. Then we get notice of a visit to Greece, which occupied three months, and, if he had not been hindered, he would have sailed direct in Syria, and then gone up to Jerusalem.

What hindered him ?

The discovery of a plot to take his life, which led him at once to change his course, and thus frustrate their wicked purpose.

What was Paul's purpose in going up to Jerusalem ?

He had been entrusted with offerings from the churches of the Gentiles, for the poor saints at Jerusalem, and we find him here arranging to fulfil this trust.

4–6. How was it that so many distinguished brethren met at Troas ?

They had evidently arranged to go with Paul, and Troas being fixed as the place of embarkation, they met there in order to accompany him. There were at least seven brethren with Paul, and as they were expecting Luke from Philippi, they waited for his arrival, possibly intending to sail into Syria by that vessel.

Why did the party remain seven days at Troas ?

Most likely waiting until the vessel was ready to start.

7. Was there a church at Troas ?

We do not read of one, but it is instructive to note that though on travel these disciples did not neglect the memorial feast. It is a most impressive instance of their faithfulness and estimate of this divine institution, and may be the reason why Luke has recorded it.

How was it that their meeting took place in the night, and yet is said to have been on the first day of the week ?

We judge that they had received notice that the ship would sail on the first of the week, and therefore decided to spend their last night in Troas in happy fellowship with Paul, and break the loaf in the morning before starting on their journey. They met on what we now call Saturday evening, and the time till midnight was occupied by Paul preaching to them, or *lit.*, discoursing with them ; they most likely asking questions, or making enquiries, to which Paul would reply. His discourse, which was continued till midnight, was interrupted by the fall of Eutychus, and this event for a while changed the character of their meeting.

Was Eutychus a disciple ?

Possibly not, and his interest in the discourse was evidently not sufficient to keep him awake. It might have cost him his life, and but for the power of God, manifest through the speaker, he would have slept in death. It was a joy to all to see him restored to life, and must have deeply impressed the minds of all present.

It is said that " the disciples came together to break bread." Why was there so much discoursing before they did so ?

It was upon the first of the week that the commemorative loaf was broken, and for this they were waiting, and were profitably spending the time till it arrived. After the restoration of the young man, and quiet was obtained, they broke the loaf, continued their conversation till break of day, and then departed.

13. The company went to the ship, but Paul decided to walk to Assos, at which port the ship was to call. Why did he choose to walk there ?

We cannot say. The distance was about twenty-four miles, and he would possibly travel alone. He was leaving scenes of more than ordinary interest, and was setting his face toward Jerusalem, and knew not what would befall him there. Possibly he wanted time for thought and prayer, and this solitary walk would be most fitting for this object.

We learn from 2 Timothy that he left his cloak at Troas with one Carpus, also some books and parchments. Why did he do so?

We presume that it was not on this occasion that he did so, but on his return from Rome into Asia, after his release by Nero. It was not from his prison in Rome that he sent his request to Timothy to bring them, but possibly from Nicopolis, where he had arranged to winter. These things had been left by him in Troas, and as he requested Timothy to go to him before winter, he was to bring with him the things named.

14–16. Luke has noted the places at which the vessel called from Troas to Miletus. Why stop at so many ports?

It was a trading vessel in which they sailed, and as it called at these places for passengers and merchandise, it gave them an opportunity of seeing brethren, on their journey. At Miletus, the Ephesian elders met him by request, to whom this ever-memorable address was delivered.

18–35. Why was he so anxious to see them?

That he might prepare them to resist the apostacy which he knew would sorely test the faithfulness of the Church.

Did he believe it possible to prevent these departures from the truth?

He believed it was possible to be faithful to Christ, and warned and urged them to fulfil the intention of the Spirit, who had placed them in such a responsible position.

What are the principal lessons taught in this address to these elders?

The most impressive of all was the fact that the Church of God had been purchased with precious blood; and that Paul's own life, and labours, and sufferings were in harmony with this hallowed purchase. To feed the Church which had been thus purchased, and on whose behalf so much suffering had been endured, was an obligation that ought not to be trifled with.

Is "Church of God" a correct reading?

Some ancient MSS. read, *The Church of the Lord, which He acquired with His own blood.* And this reading is now generally accepted by scholars as the one to be preferred.

How was the Church to be preserved from this apostacy?

Paul suggests two things, which, if faithfully sustained, would preserve from apostacy: (1.) to be faithful themselves to the truth made known to them; and (2.) to feed the Church with the same truth.

"The flock, over which the Holy Spirit made you overseers." How did He do this?

By instructing and revealing the qualifications necessary for this work, as afterwards committed to writing in the letters to Timothy and Titus.

If "overseers" are unfaithful to their trust, has the Church any remedy against it?

Yes. "I commend you to God, and to the word of His grace, which is able to build you up, and to give you an inheritance among all them that are sanctified." As long as any believer has the Word of God in his hand, he can be faithful to God, whoever may prove unfaithful.

CHAPTER XXI.

1–8. I suppose we may designate this journey, a part of which has been already given, as Paul's journey to Jerusalem?

In chap. xix. 21, we read, that just about the close of the tumult in Ephesus, "Paul purposed in the

Spirit, when he had passed through Macedonia and Achaia, to go to Jerusalem." The journey, therefore, was arranged at Ephesus, and after going into Macedonia and Greece, he purposed to sail direct for Syria, and thus reach Jerusalem. After hearing that the Jews plotted to take his life, he separated from his friends and returned through Macedonia, and met with them at Troas, where, after a few days, they embarked and sailed from port to port until they reached Patara, which possibly might be the destination of the ship. Here they found a ship that was going to Phœnicia and went aboard, and after calling at Tyre, where disciples were found, and also Ptolemais, they reached Cæsarea in safety, and became the guests of Philip the evangelist.

9-14. *Why did Paul dare to go up to Jerusalem, when by the Spirit Agabus and the daughters of Philip protested against him doing so ?*

I think we must understand it as a conditional protest, for it was in this light that Paul viewed it. He would not have dared to go up if God had positively forbade. The revelation seems to have been, that he must not go up unless prepared to suffer, and the nature of the trial to which he would be subject if he went was plainly illustrated by Agabus, when he took Paul's girdle and bound his own hands and feet and said, "So shall the Jews at Jerusalem bind the man who owneth this girdle." The Holy Spirit would have spared him the suffering if he only chose to accept the release, and his friends tried to persuade him to do so, but all in vain. His noble response to their entreaties revealed a firmness of purpose that no amount of suffering could shake. "What mean ye to weep and to break my heart? for I am ready not

to be bound only, but also to die at Jerusalem for the name of the Lord Jesus." The Holy Spirit made it plain to all of them that if he went forward a great trial awaited him, and his friends intreated him not to become a voluntary sufferer. But it was the path of service to carry those alms to the poor saints, which loving hearts from among the Gentiles had entrusted to his care, and he would not turn aside though bonds looked him .in the face. "And when he would not be persuaded, we ceased, saying, The will of the Lord be done."

15. *"We took up our carriages." Were these the vehicles that conveyed them up to Jerusalem ?*

We should read *baggage* or luggage, for this is what is meant.

16. *This verse reads as if Mnason of Cyprus went up with them from Cæsarea. Was it so ?*

If we read the verse—There went up with us also of the disciples of Cæsarea, bringing (us) to a certain Mnason, a Cyprian, an old disciple, with whom we should lodge—we shall see what Luke really intended.

17. *The reception of Paul by James and the elders seems to have been most cordial. Was it not a violation of the principle of his teaching among the Gentiles, to accept their proposal to unite with the four men with the Nazarite vow on them ?*

Paul taught among the Gentiles that a sinner could be accepted of God through the faith of Jesus, without circumcision; Nazarite vows, or anything else commanded by the law, and what he did on this occasion, was no violation of his teaching. It was a false report which the disciples had received, that he taught the Jews in the provinces to forsake Moses, and not to circumcise their children, and it was to undo this report that he was urged to join these four men in the rites of purification. There was nothing in the law of the Nazarite to which Paul as a Jew could not consistently yield. To be a Nazarite was to be separated to God, and this vow he fulfilled sincerely and truly. Indeed, on his former visit he went up to Jerusalem as a Nazarite, and as we might term him, a Christian Nazarite—one separated unto the Gospel of God. The tumult which followed arose out of a mistake, the Jews having seen with him Trophimus an Ephesian, and supposed he had brought him into the temple and so polluted it. Paul never taught the Jews to forsake Moses, but urged them to accept of Christ, and when this was sincerely and honestly done everything else fell into its proper place. We have however to remember that there was even among the religious Jews at Jerusalem a deep-rooted prejudice against Paul, and they were ready to seize upon any pretext by which they might accuse him of wrong. Upon seeing him in the temple, they at once cried out that he had " polluted this holy place," and as soon as possible they ejected him from the temple.

Why did the Roman soldiers interfere with Paul?

The chief captain of the band was responsible for any disturbance that might occur, and for the protection of all subjects under Roman rule. The news of the uproar soon brought them into the scene, and Paul was arrested and bound with chains, until they could learn the nature of the charge against him. After considerable tumult and some rather harsh treatment by the captain, Paul was permitted to address the infuriated assembly, and explain matters involved in his own peculiar course of action.

CHAPTER XXII.

1. *" Men, brethren, and fathers, hear ye my defence." Why did Paul narrate his conversion to Christ before this multitude ?*

The story of his conversion is his defence or apology for the course he had pursued, and although it had proved most objectionable to them, he hoped, by showing that he had acted in obedience to a heavenly vision, to have removed their hostility.

2. *Why did speaking in the Hebrew tongue procure greater attention than if he had spoken in Greek ?*

It was sacred to them being the dialect of their religion, and was sure to obtain profound respect. It was held then, and is still held, that their religion would be dishonoured by being spoken in a foreign tongue. Paul knew their strong feeling on this subject, and availed himself of this resource.

3–5. *Why did he refer to his former zeal in defence of the law ?*

It was in order to prepare them for the change that had taken place. It was not defective education that led him to act as he had done, because he had sat at the feet of Gamaliel, a doctor of the law ; nor any lack of zeal in its defence, as the high priest and the elders could bear him witness ; it was a higher authority than all these that had led him to change his course of life, and to that authority he must now appeal.

6–15. *Did Paul wish them to understand that the change in his life and labours was owing entirely to the unexpected appearance of that Jesus whom he persecuted ?*

This is the distinct object he has in view, and this is the reason why he is so definite in his statements about the letters from the high priest, the journey, the time of the appearance, the great light, the voice, and the fear that seized the whole party that were with him. He also further refers to the challenge of Jesus, and his own enquiry; the direction to go into Damascus, and the visit of Ananias, the pious Jew; and being assured that he had been chosen to see the just One, to hear His voice, and to be His witness to all of what he had seen and heard; he had obeyed the command to be baptised, and wash away his sins, calling on the name of the Lord. These reasons are assigned by him for the course he had pursued.

16. *Is the direction given to Saul, about washing away his sins, in harmony with apostolic teaching in general?*

It must be in harmony with all directions proceeding from the one Spirit; but in this counsel of Ananias there is a distinct and very important aspect of the ordinance of immersion, which is not always stated, though it may be implied— viz., the relation which it bears to life. The life of Saul, up to that time, had been a life of opposition and blasphemy against Christ and His disciples, and now he is called upon, not only to identify himself with Christ in this ordinance, but as it strictly reads, *bathe away from thyself thy sins—i.e.,* the sinful actions of thy past life.

Did Ananias mean that he should wash away the guilt of sin?

He could not mean that, because, though every one, in submitting to Christ in this ordinance, receives the promise of remission, God alone, in Christ, forgives sins. The immersed are called upon to put from them all the evil of a past life, and to become new creatures in Christ Jesus; and this was what Saul was called upon to do in his baptism.

What did Ananias mean by "calling upon the name of the Lord"?

It is, *lit., Thyself calling upon His name.* Or, according to Paul's teaching in Rom. x. 9 :—" Confess with thy mouth the Lord Jesus." It was the "good confession" he was called upon to make, prior to to being immersed.

17–21. *Why did Paul refer to the trance, or vision, in which, on his first visit to Jerusalem, he had received directions for his future labours?*

It was in order to show them that his mission to the Gentiles was not of his own seeking, but that he would much rather have laboured for the conversion of his own people. In this vision, he says that this person who first appeared to him commanded him to quickly leave Jerusalem, and he had pleaded to remain, but was again told to depart. "For," said He, "I will send thee far hence unto the Gentiles."

22–29. *Why did this word "Gentiles" so enrage them?*

Because it was on account of this mission they could not endure him, and his reasons for it they would not hear. They were as much opposed to Christ as to His mission, and sought to crush Paul as His chief agent.

Why did the chief captain desist from scourging Paul when he heard that he was a Roman?

Because he knew it was a violation of Roman law to punish a Roman citizen without a trial before a judge; and when informed of it by the centurion, he eagerly enquired how the privilege had been obtained.

What did Paul mean by "I was free born"?

As Paul derived his citizenship through his birth, it had most likely been obtained by his father from the state, for some service done for it, and descended to his son, who now claims protection on account of it.

CHAPTER XXIII.

1. *" And Paul earnestly beholding the council." What council was this ?*

The Sanhedrin of the Jews, which had been hastily summoned by the chief captain, with Ananias as the president of the council.

Why did he call them together ?

That he might learn what Paul had done to cause such a tumult; for the public peace was broken, and for that he was responsible.

2. *Why did Ananias command Paul to be smitten ?*

Because he counted his declaration of having lived a conscientious life an insult to the assembly.

Was Paul's reply becoming ?

Paul was stung with the injustice done to him as an uncondemned man, but afterwards apologised for undue disrespect to the high priest, but at the same time declared that he did not know that he was the high priest.

3. *" God shall smite thee, thou whited wall." Was this a prophecy ?*

It was most certainly a revelation of his sad end, and history shows that he died through violence. According to Josephus, he was slain during an assault which was made upon Jerusalem, and, according to Paul's statement, his death was a judgment from God.

6–10. *The council was composed of Pharisees and Sadducees. Was it right in Paul to take advantage of this diversity of faith by declaring himself a Pharisee ?*

There is certainly a show of stratagem in the course pursued by Paul, and although not responsible for the discussion of the council, the issue of their doctrinal contest was to him a most favourable one, as he was taken altogether out of their hands—indeed, by disagreeing among themselves, they became disqualified

as judges in his case, and the abrupt interference of Claudias Lysias was very proper. When Paul said that he was a Pharisee, he intended it to apply only to their common faith in resurrection; but having affirmed that it was proved in the resurrection of Christ, and the Jews denying this, it became the fact about which he was called in question. Instead, however, of trying him on this question, they began a most clamorous dispute among themselves, and the affair terminated in Paul's rescue, by the chief captain taking him out of their hands, and he was never again delivered over to their will.

11. *" And the night following the Lord stood by him." Why was Paul favoured with this vision ?*

It was pleasing to the Lord to give to him this new revelation of his future work; a work possibly never contemplated by His willing servant. It had been revealed through Ananias that Paul should "bear His name before the Gentiles, and kings, and the children of Israel;" but here it is revealed to himself: " As thou hast testified of Me in Jerusalem, so must thou bear witness also at Rome." This was the last part of the revealed programme of his life as a witness, and right nobly did he fulfil it in the presence of Cæsar.

12–16. *Why did these Jews put themselves under oath to kill Paul ?*

It is evident that they had purposed to take his life on the previous day, and were much enraged by the unexpected rescue of Paul by the Roman guard. It was this frustration of their purpose that led to this desperate conspiracy, and but for the overruling hand of God his life would have been sacrificed to their rage. The captain, however, was informed of their plot, and at once arranged to prevent it; and while they were waiting to execute their evil purpose, Paul, under a military escort, was on his way to Cæsarea, and was safely delivered over to Felix, the governor.

CHAPTER XXIV.

1-6. *" And after five days Ananias the high priest descended with the elders, and a certain orator Tertullus," etc. Would this be an official deputation of accusers ?*

No doubt they were sent by the council officially and in due form, as an advocate had been elected to represent the case before the governor, and though Cæsarea was over sixty miles from Jerusalem, yet if they could only obtain Paul's condemnation, it would repay all trouble and expense of the prosecution, and as he was arrested and under Roman jurisdiction they felt certain of success. The charges against Paul by Tertullus, were very orderly and efficiently presented before Felix, and as these were serious, it appeared very proper to claim protection against one who was a mover of sedition among the people, and had also profaned the temple.

7-9. *How did Felix refuse to examine these charges ?*

He did not refuse to try the case, but as Tertullus had stated that Lysias came upon them and took Paul out of their hands, when they would have judged him according to their law, Felix demanded that the trial should be postponed till Lysias could be present, and after hearing Paul's defence, he closed the trial for that occasion.

10-22. *Did Paul in his defence give a fair exposition of the case ?*

After expressing his entire satisfaction at having Felix for a judge, on account of his experience, he states his own case for his judgment, in a most orderly manner. First he tells him that it was only twelve days since he went up to Jerusalem, and that neither in the temple, nor the synagogue, nor in the city had he been found disputing with any man, and defied them to prove their accusation.

I suppose he might have closed his defence with this denial, and left Tertullus to prove his charges ?

He might have done so, but he rather wished to inform Felix how the matter fully stood. He had been charged with sedition, when it was only their interpretation of his manner of worshipping the God of his fathers, and when charged before the council, he was only accused of declaring his faith in the resurrection of the dead.

I suppose that Paul's defence would enable Felix to fully understand the case ?

He evidently saw through the whole matter, and was satisfied that Paul was no enemy to Roman rule, but was persecuted on account of his religion. He therefore determined to defend Paul, and frustrate the purpose of his enemies.

24. *Some days after this trial Felix with his wife Drusilla sent for Paul to hear him concerning the faith in Christ. Was it curiosity, or a desire to receive it ?*

From Luke's report of what was said to him by Paul, we judge that he looked upon Felix as a man of evil and intemperate habits of life, and, like a faithful servant of Christ, instead of gratifying his desire by talking about the faith, he began to reason with him about righteousness, temperance, and judgment to come. Only think of Felix coming to hear about the faith in Christ, with the wife of another man sitting by his side. He might trifle with the truth : not so the man who was his prisoner, who faithfully set before him that solemn future, when he would have to answer for his sins before God. Paul's honest testimony was felt by Felix, for he trembled, but instead of at once turning from his sins, he spoke only of seeing Paul again at some convenient season.

Did he see him again ?

Yes. He sent for him a number of times, and conversed with him, and if Luke had not told us of his base motive, we might have put a favourable construction upon his action. But when we read that it was for money that he so acted, we are startled at his trifling. Paul knew that he was in his power, and the governor let him know that a bribe, if only forthcoming, would open his prison doors ; but while he doubtless yearned for liberty, he could not stoop to accept it on such ignoble terms, and so he waits till other help arrives. Two years pass by, and to please the Jews, on retiring from the procuratorship, he handed him over to his successor, Porcius Festus.

CHAPTER XXV.

Was there a second trial in Cæsarea during the rule of Felix ?

We have none recorded. Felix preserved Paul from further annoyance, but the Jews still retained their ill feeling towards him, and as soon as Festus came into the province, and ascended to Jerusalem as the newly-elected procurator, they renewed their suit against him, and desired Festus to bring him to Jerusalem, purposing, if he did so, to kill him in the way. Festus, however, refused to do this, but promised a trial on his return. After ten days he left Jerusalem for Cæsarea, and the next day sat on the judgment-seat, and commanded Paul to be brought before him. His accusers also, being notified of his purpose, were present, and the trial was duly opened.

7–12. I suppose they would present their charges ?

As accusers they were bound to do this, but Luke finding nothing special to record simply states that they " laid many and grievous complaints against Paul, which they could not prove." The recorded answer of Paul is as brief as the charge, " Neither against the law of the Jews, neither against the temple, nor yet against Cæsar, have I offended anything at all."

Was it not strange that Festus should ask Paul to go and be judged at Jerusalem, when he had denied the Jews a trial there ?

There seems to have been an over-ruling hand in that question. With Festus it was a stroke of time-serving policy, but to Paul it opened a way of deliverance. He had been charged with sedition, and conscious of his innocence, he appealed to Cæsar, and on his right of Roman citizenship this could not be denied him. Besides, it was a relief to Festus, who was perplexed with the case, and at once he replied, " Hast thou appealed unto Cæsar? unto Cæsar shalt thou go."

I suppose this visit of Agrippa and Bernice was a formal recognition of the new procurator ?

Yes. Both Agrippa and Festus were serving under Cæsar, and this recognition was a matter of courtesy between them. The case of Paul, being made known to Agrippa, he expressed a desire to hear him, and it was arranged that on the morrow this request should be granted. The interview was to be a public one, and the chief captains and principal men of the city were gathered to the place of hearing, where Festus, Agrippa, and Bernice joined them in great pomp. The reasons for assembling were then briefly stated by Festus, and Paul was allowed to state his case, in order that those present might be able to judge.

CHAPTER XXVI.

1. *Should we call this hearing before Agrippa a trial?*

No. Paul was simply asked to speak for himself, and nearly all that were present were at least friendly towards him.

2. *Why was he so happy to speak for himself before Agrippa?*

Because Agrippa, though of Idumean descent through Herod the Great, had become familiar with the history and religion of the Jewish nation, and was better prepared to understand Paul's reasons for the changes in his faith and practice than either Felix or Festus.

4. *How is it that the account of Paul's conversion is again given, Luke having twice previously recorded it?*

Each of these narrations are connected with important events, and were therefore specially called for in these relations. In chapter ix. we have Luke's own account of it, possibly obtained from Paul himself, which was intended to show Theophilus how this persecutor of the saints became a witness and an apostle of the glorified Christ. To him and to all the churches of the saints this would be a most important record. Then, in chapter xxii., we get Paul's own account of the appearance of Jesus to him, as given before the Sanhedrin, which was intended to show them the reason for the course he had pursued as an apostle of the Gentiles. This was his public testimony to the nation at Jerusalem. Then, in the present chapter, we have Paul standing before the representatives of Cæsar, and proving, at least to one of these, that the course he had pursued was in harmony both with fact and prophecy, and to the knowledge of Agrippa Paul could appeal. Indeed, we cannot but feel thankful that Luke has given to us Paul's grand appeal to his deeply-interested judge, who is compelled to wince under his "words of truth and soberness," and who has to parry the keen thrusts that are made upon his consciousness of the truth of these things. "King Agrippa, believest thou the prophets? I know that thou believest." Thus nobly "before the Gentiles, and kings, and the children of Israel," did Paul witness for Christ.

6, 7. *"And now I stand and am judged for the hope of the promise made of God," etc. What hope was this?*

The hope of the Messiah, whom God had promised to send to the nation of Israel, and for its fulfilment they were anxiously looking. "And now," said Paul, "I stand and am judged for the hope of the promise," i.e., for its fulfilment in a risen Christ.

8. *"Why should it be thought incredible with you that God should raise the dead?" To whom does he refer?*

To Christ, who was raised from the dead, and whose appearance to him was brighter than the sun at mid-day, a fact which those who were with him could not deny.

16–23. *Why did Paul refer to his mission to the nations before Agrippa?*

Because this was the matter in dispute between him and the Jews. He was witnessing both to small and great, both at Jerusalem and among the nations, the things which Moses and the prophets did say should come, and for this they were going about to kill him.

In saying that he was sent to "open their eyes," and that they might receive "forgiveness of sins," why did Paul omit to show how these things were to be done?

Paul is simply referring to his commission, and this version of it is in general terms. Theophilus did not require to learn, at this stage of Luke's treatise, how the Gentiles were to be enlightened, nor how forgiveness was to be enjoyed; and Agrippa was not prepared for the detail of these things.

"An inheritance among them which are sanctified." To whom does this refer?

To Jewish believers who "first trusted in Christ," and were seated by Him in the heavenlies, and with whom Gentiles were called to share through the Gospel which was preached unto them.

28, 29. "Almost thou persuadest me to be a Christian." Was Agrippa almost persuaded?

It was in a taunting spirit that he spoke about becoming a Christian, which a more correct rendering of his words will enable us to perceive. We give Dean Alford's rendering of these verses, as fairly expressing Agrippa's meaning in his reply to Paul, "Then Agrippa said unto Paul, Lightly art thou persuading thyself that thou canst make me a Christian. And Paul said, I would to God, that whether lightly or with pains, not only thou, but also all that hear me this day, might become such as I am, except these bonds." Agrippa had no desire to become a Christian, and was rather disposed to mock Paul's effort to make him one than otherwise. However, after this pointed appeal by the prisoner, the meeting closed; and, while Agrippa and Festus decided that he had done nothing worthy of death or of bonds, yet, having appealed to Cæsar, his appeal must be complied with.

CHAPTER XXVII.

1. Paul had often prayed that he might be able to visit the saints in Rome. Would he not feel humbled to go as a prisoner?

Not as a prisoner for the Gentiles, on whose account he had been apprehended and tried, and as his way thither had been thus strangely opened, he no doubt gladly accepted of it.

2. "And entering into a ship of Adramyttium, we launched." Did Luke accompany him?

From the frequent use of this pronoun "we," it is plain that Luke was a companion on this perilous voyage.

Aristarchus, a Christian brother, is said to have been with them. Was it as a friend or as a prisoner?

We could not tell from what is here said of him, but in Colossians iv. 10 he is said to be a "fellow-prisoner," but how he became so we are not told.

3. "And Julius courteously entreated Paul, and gave him liberty to go unto his friends at Sidon." Why should an officer treat a prisoner so favourably?

It shows the estimate in which Paul was held by the centurion. There was no fear of Paul running away.

4–13. Can we trace this voyage on the map?

Very easily, and especially one on which Paul's travels are marked. Suppose now you take a Biblical atlas, and run your finger on the line of travel from Cæsarea to Rome, it will certainly give you more interest in reading about this voyage.

The map indicates that the route of the ship was circuitous. Why go round by Cyprus when they might have gone direct to Crete?

If the vessel had been intended for the whole voyage they might have sailed direct, but it was a ship of Adramyttium, and was obliged to go by Cyprus on account of contrary winds, and then over the sea of Cilicia and Pamphylia, until they reached Myra, a city of Lycia.

At Myra they embark in a ship of Alexandria. What was she doing at Myra?

We judge she was one of the many vessels that carried wheat from Alexandria to Puteoli, and had been driven out of her course by the same wind that sent Paul and his company round by Cyprus.

At Crete Paul besought them to remain through the winter. Did he do this by revelation?

Paul would never have delayed a vessel by a mere thought of danger if it had not been revealed to him as the best thing for all concerned, and it would have been if they had attended to his advice. In leaving a place of safety they not only suffered great hardships, but lost their vessel, though God preserved their lives.

14–20. What is the meaning of Euroclydon?

It was a great wave or waves, caused by a strong wind peculiar to that sea, and would be understood then very much as would be understood now by a "sou'-wester." It was so fearful a storm that they were obliged to let the ship drive on the sea without being able to control her. It must have been a sad sight on board that ship during that terrible storm. Nearly all were keeping a self-imposed fast, the sailors and prisoners were casting overboard the tackling of the ship, while the darkness and tempest must have caused trouble to all hearts—to all indeed except Paul, who alone seems to have been able to cheer others.

22–25. How was it that Paul could be so cheerful?

God gave to him a vision, in which not only his own safety was promised, but that of all with him. It was just like God to mingle some drops of comfort in their cup of sorrow. The storm blew on in all its fury, but the few words spoken to Paul in the night by an angel of God became as oil on the troubled waters to that tempest-tossed crew. The word of Paul was believed, and though the ship was to perish, they were to be cast upon a certain island, and thus escape from their danger.

33. On that memorable morning, when Paul urged them all to take meat, it is said they had fasted thirteen days. How do you understand this long fast?

They had simply fasted each day till evening, and then taken food, and would have done so on the fourteenth, had not Paul urged them on that morning to take food. "For," said he, "there shall not a hair fall from the head of any of you." This form of fasting was common among the Jews and other nations. See Judges xx. 26, 1 Sam. xiv. 24, and was the mode of fasting during two weeks in this storm.

CHAPTER XXVIII.

1. The island upon which they were driven and escaped from the wreck was called Melita. What is it now called?

It is almost universally conceded that the island now called Malta is the place upon which Paul and his company were cast. Some have contended that Meleda, an island in gulf of Venice, was the scene of this shipwreck, but it has little to support it except the name.

2. The people on this island were called "barbarous." Does that mean savage?

It would be better to read *barbarians*, a term used by the Jews and Greeks to denote those nations that were less cultured than themselves. The people were exceedingly kind and hospitable, and kindled a fire because of the cold.

3. Was it not strange that Paul should gather sticks for the fire?

Not at all. He was ready for any service that time and occasion called for. The barbarians kindled a fire, and Paul was ready to do his part to keep it burning. This stick-gathering spirit is very much needed, both in the Church and in the world, in the shop and in the family, and each of these departments would be in a better state than they are, if each one would gather up the daily-needed bundle of smiles, and helps, and cheers, to keep the kindled fire burning. Let each feel their own personal responsibility as Paul felt his.

That viper springing out of the heat was a serious-looking affair. Did it really bite Paul?

Yes, I suppose this is what Luke means by "fastened on his hand." There was the bite, and the barbarians expected death to follow.

4. These people must have been superstitious in thinking that fate or vengeance followed murder, but is there not some truth mixed up with this belief?

Yes. God's truth, that sin will not go unpunished. Still there are many calamities endured that are not visitations for crime. Paul was not a murderer though the serpent bit him, neither did he suffer, because he was preserved in accordance with the promise of Jesus (Mark xvi. 18).

7–9. Luke names some miracles done by Paul on the island, but does not say whether or not he preached the Gospel to them. Is this not strange?

That Paul would preach Christ there we cannot for a moment doubt, but to record this was not Luke's object, and his report must be studied in harmony with his direct purpose. There are two aspects of Paul's life, which, like two strands of a rope closely twisted together, have an inseparable connection—the one, his testimony for Christ as a Saviour of all who trust in Him;

and the other, the care of Christ over his life while doing this work. His journey from Cæsarea to Rome is recorded, not so much as a matter of witness-bearing for Christ, as life-caring by Christ. Paul had preached to the Jews and to the Gentiles, he had borne witness before the Sanhedrin at Jerusalem, and the representatives of Cæsar at Cæsarea, and now he has once more to bear witness, and then his work would be nearly over. "Fear not, Paul, thou must be brought before Cæsar." Hence what we get here is, Paul's remarkable preservation from many dangers until he is brought into the imperial city.

13. At Puteoli, where they disembarked from the ship that brought them from Melita, they found brethren who desired him to remain with them seven days. Was his doing so by permission of the centurion?

As a prisoner he could not have remained a day without permission, but as the centurion was deeply indebted to Paul, as being a means of his own preservation on that voyage, he most generously granted the request, and for a few days these brethren enjoyed the fellowship of this distinguished man.

15. Why did Paul thank God and take courage when he met the brethren from Rome?

He was going to Rome as a prisoner of Jesus Christ, for preaching Him among the Gentiles. What kind of a reception he should meet with in that city, and especially from Jewish brethren, as possibly most of them were, was a serious question. This unexpected meeting of brethren, who had heard of his coming, and travelled thirty-three miles to meet him, was a loving demonstration of their approval of his work, and called forth his special thanksgiving, and cheered him on in his strange path.

16. *Why was Paul permitted to have a hired room of his own, though watched by a soldier?*

This would arise partly from the peculiar nature of the charges against him, and partly from the favour he had found in the eyes of the centurion. How could he have witnessed all those striking instances of Christ being with Paul from Cæsarea to Rome, and not be impressed with the power of a holy and God-guarded life! As a prisoner Paul must be under guard, and his hand must be fastened to the soldier that kept watch over him; but he was permitted to hire a room for himself, where he could keep an open door for all who would visit him.

17-22. *Who were the first to visit him?*

The first invited were the chief of the Jews, who, responding to his invitation, heard from him the causes which had led to his removal to Rome, and his being bound with a chain. They tell him, what is rather strange, that no ill report of him had ever reached them. They desire, however, to know his mind upon the sect everywhere spoken against.

What sect was this?

It was what Tertullus called the "Sect of the Nazarenes,"—the disciples of Jesus, those who owned Him as their Law-giver, Lord, and Saviour. They appeared anxious to hear his mind upon this matter, *i.e.*, whether or not Christianity was of God, and for this purpose a day was appointed.

Were those whom Paul invited Christian Jews?

No, but they were his brethren in the flesh, men of standing and influence, and whose minds were unsettled as to whether Jesus of Nazareth was or was not the Messiah. From morning to evening therefore he expounded to them the truth, and though it was a most gracious op-portunity, they made a very sad use of it.

Why have we no report of his exposition to the Jews?

For this special reason, that it would only be a repetition of the facts of former reports, and from which Theophilus had learned the sum of apostolic testimony; and from which all others may learn the same. Any person who will fully master Peter's expositions and proclamation, as reported by Luke, will have the key to the whole question of God's provision for man's salvation, and the way to enjoy it; but if these are overlooked, and every new case of testimony and conversion is treated without reference to these, there will be sure to arise uncertainty and confusion.

Paul preached salvation to the Gentiles. Was the proclamation of Peter as wide as the testimony of Paul?

Most certainly, for even at Pentecost, his quotation from Joel was, "Whosoever shall call upon the name of the Lord shall be saved."

23. *Luke says that Paul testified the kingdom of God, and persuaded them concerning Jesus. Was it a fact or a prophecy that he was speaking about?*

The word "testified" indicated its existence, as there could be no testimony of that which did not exist. Before Christ the kingdom was a matter of prophecy; after Christ it was a matter of testimony, because it was a reality.

30. *"And Paul dwelt two whole years in his own hired house." Where shall we learn about what he did during those two years?*

Luke tells us in his last record of him, that he was preaching and teaching all who came in to him; and the epistles written to the churches from that hired room will show us what incessant labours and what blessed results were crowded into those two years of continued prison life. In Asia his life was filled up with arduous toil and travel, and in Rome, although it was comparative rest, yet who can say whether preach-ing sermons, or writing epistles, have produced the most efficient results? Both were needed, and opportunities for both were furnished and filled up, that God in all things might be glorified.

ROMANS.

CHAPTER I.

Why did Paul write this epistle ?

In order to prove that the salvation provided by God for man, and preached by him among the nations, was not only called for by the need of the whole human family, but was also in harmony with His purpose, as made known to Abraham, and through the prophets, and might be enjoyed, through Jesus, by all who believe in Him.

Paul was serving under a special commission from the Lord Jesus. Was it a new commission ?

Not a new one, as that given by Jesus to the eleven embodied all that Paul preached; but he was a new agent, and was raised up and sent to carry out the commission in one part of the field of the world, which, up to that time, had received very little attention. The commission of Jesus to His apostles was as definite as possible :—*Go, make disciples of all the nations.* And, according to Luke, they were to begin at Jerusalem, and also to be His witnesses in Judæa, and Samaria, and unto the *uttermost parts of the earth.* Now, in three of the places named by Luke, the directions of Jesus had been fulfilled to the very letter; but in the fourth place mentioned no well-sustained effort had been made. True, God had opened the door of faith among the Gentiles by accepting Cornelius and his friends; and "men of Cyprus and Cyrene" had preached to Greeks at Antioch; but it was only when this new labourer was sent out that the work commenced by Peter received the attention which it really claimed.

If Paul, in preaching to the Gentiles, was only carrying out the commission given to the apostles, why is he called upon, as in this epistle, to defend his work ?

Because there had arisen among those first converted by the apostles a sad heresy, the very first, I presume, of the many that followed— viz., that of confederating Moses with Christ and the law with the faith. Luke's account of it is as follows :—" And certain men which came down from Judæa taught the brethren, and said, Except ye be circumcised, after the manner of Moses, ye cannot be saved." The opposition of these "certain men" was soon found to be a strongly organised effort to neutralise the testimony of Paul, and, being vigorously sustained by them, necessarily called out this most elaborate defence of the grace of God, as shown in His accepting of Gentiles apart from the law of Moses. This had been done in Jerusalem before apostles and elders, and also in many of the churches, but this Epistle to the Romans is an exhaustive refutation of the whole heresy.

Had the saints in Rome any sympathy with this heresy ?

The writing of this epistle is at least suggestive of this thought, or else, Why does he write to them in defence of the Gospel he preached?

1. *Why does he begin with " Paul, a servant of Jesus Christ "?*

It was in order to mark the special relation which he sustained to this great and gracious scheme of Heaven. He was not its author, but a helper. He did not form the plan, but was only a servant carrying out the will of God under the Lord Jesus. In this first sentence, Paul states his true relation to the Gospel of Christ, and with this humble position his whole life and labour accords.

What does he mean by " called to be an apostle "?

It is *lit., a called apostle,* and points distinctly to the fact that he was not a self-sent preacher, but called and sent by the Lord Jesus. It was well known that Paul was not one of that chosen band of apostles to whom Jesus gave His final commission, just before He ascended to His throne ; but his apostleship was nevertheless from the same Jesus, who appeared to him, and sent him to preach to the nations. It is to this special induction into his work that he undoubtedly referred when he wrote : " Called to be an apostle, separated unto the Gospel of God."

What does he mean by the " Gospel of God "?

It is a definitely formulated expression, and one which underlies the argument of the epistle, and, unless clearly understood, we cannot follow him intelligently. That Paul looked upon his mission as a special one is evident from his many peculiar references, both to its sphere and his theme, as,—" My gospel," " Our gospel," " Gospel of the uncircumcision committed unto me," " Gospel of God, to which I am separated," etc. We must, there-fore, pause over this sentence, " Gospel of God," before we proceed further. We must see clearly to what he is pointing, that we may go along with him to the close. We must ponder it attentively, until it becomes to us like a well-sounded key-note that is heard through the whole melody. We may very properly term this " Gospel of God" the *thesis* of the epistle—the great revealed purpose of God, which Paul afterwards explains, illustrates, and establishes—viz., the blessing of the nations through Jesus Christ, as He had promised afore by His prophets in the Holy Scriptures.

Is this " Gospel of God" something different from the facts of the death, burial, and resurrection of Jesus, generally called the Gospel of Christ ?

Yes ; these facts were the provision which God in His love had made for man, but this Gospel, or glad tidings of God, to which Paul was separated, concerned the subjects of this provision, as God Himself had made known before to Abraham, saying, " In thee shall all nations be blessed." This was the " Gospel of God," even the promise of blessing to all the families of the earth, and to fulfil this promise, Paul was separated as a servant of Jesus Christ.

Were the nations to be blessed absolutely or conditionally ?

The " grace and apostleship " conferred on Paul, as a preacher and teacher of the Gentiles, was for the " obedience of faith "—*i.e.,* the enjoyment of life and salvation by the nations was to be through their obedience to Christ ; and Paul rejoiced that he was sent to make this known to them.

"Concerning His Son Jesus Christ." What connection has this with the " Gospel of God "?

It is simply to show that the blessing of the nations was to be through Christ, who was the "seed" through whom the promise should be realised. And, being "made of the seed of David according to the flesh," the promise made to David was fulfilled; and by His resurrection out from among dead ones, He was declared by the "spirit of holiness," in signs and wonders wrought on His behalf, to be the Son of God in power; and therefore empowered, not only to send Paul on this gracious mission, but was also fitted to do for the nations all that God had before promised.

17. *Is "Beloved of God" expressive of the apostle's affection towards them?*

It is the application of a prophetic announcement, as quoted by Paul in chap. ix. 25, "I will call her beloved, which was not beloved." Paul could therefore write to these saints in Rome, "Beloved of God."

Has "called saints" any correspondence with a "called apostle"?

The calling of both are in one respect similar. Paul was called to the apostleship long after the twelve were chosen, and these Gentile believers at Rome were called long after the beginning of salvation among the Jews. The word "called," therefore, is alike applied to both.

8–11. *Why was the faith of these saints in Rome, for which Paul gave thanks, so marked as to arrest attention wherever known?*

In nearly every other place the truth had been received upon miraculous evidence, but in Rome, the simple testimony had been received without visible demonstration to sustain it. This simple acceptance of the truth gave Paul special joy, and led him constantly to plead in his prayers that God would open his way to them, that he might impart to them some spiritual gift, to the end they might be established and he comforted by this confirmation.

Q

14. *How was Paul "a debtor both to the Greeks and barbarians, both to the wise and the unwise"?*

Because he was sent by Christ with a gospel message to all these distinct classes, and also with power to confirm its truth, and thus prove that it was of God.

If the Gospel had been made known and believed by these saints in Rome, why was Paul so ready and even anxious to preach there also?

In order to demonstrate the truth, that salvation was provided in Christ for believing sinners of the Gentiles, and it was important to prove this even in imperial Rome by those signs which attended his ministry among them, in every other place.

16. *What does Paul mean by saying, "I am not ashamed of the Gospel of Christ"?*

Scholars now omit "of Christ," and read, "I am not ashamed of the Gospel, for it is a power of God to salvation, to every one that believes." The reason why Paul was not ashamed of it was, because everywhere, when believed, there was deliverance from sin, and fruit unto holiness, both among Jews and Greeks. It was not of the Gospel itself that Paul here speaks, but of its results when received. With these he was perfectly satisfied, and was ready to test it in any place, being confident of fruit unto holiness. It was a settled question with Paul, that whoever received the Gospel, would be purified by its soul-purifying truth.

17. *What does he mean by "For therein is the righteousness of God revealed"?*

He had just said that he was not ashamed of the Gospel, because of its heart and life purifying power, in all who really received it; and here he asserts that what he now calls the "righteousness of God" is revealed in it, and therefore to be expected from all who received it, and in this he had not been disappointed. Paul is not showing here how God pardons or even justifies sinners who believe in Jesus, as that is not called for in writing to saints, but what He expects from those who have been forgiven. These righteous claims of God are therefore revealed in the Gospel which brings to men the message of His love.

What is meant by " revealed from faith to faith" ?

It is *lit., of faith, into faith ;* and while the style is peculiar to this epistle, the truth taught here is very simple. The *of faith* is, by metonymy, the prophetic testimony concerning salvation by Christ ; whilst the *into faith* is the believing reception of this testimony as made known by the apostles. Or, " as it is written," *the just by faith* (in the testimony) *shall live.*

18-25. *Does the apostle give this long catalogue of crime and uncleanness to show how guilty and debased the Gentiles were ?*

Not that alone ; it was rather to show from how deep a depth of vanity, and folly, and crime, the Gospel could raise and purify those alienated nations of the earth.

" For the wrath of God is revealed from heaven against all ungodliness and unrighteousness of men." How was this done ?

By His Spirit in the prophets, who revealed the wrath of God against all manner of evil, just as He had revealed His righteous claims in His testimonies. It is not the execution of His wrath that Paul is speaking of here, for, as he said to the Athenians, " The times of this ignorance God winked at,"—*i.e.*, He did not bring the transgressors to judgment ; but it is the revelation of His displeasure against iniquity, and this made the repentance of the Gentiles so absolutely necessary. The proclamation of the Gospel is not merely

that man might be forgiven, but that he might also repent or turn from his transgressions, and in righteousness and holiness serve God all the days of his life.

19-25. *Does Paul teach here that God may be known from His work in creation ?*

Not Himself personally, but something about Him, " even His eternal power and Godhead," *i.e.*, His divinity. The personal God could only be known by a revelation of Himself, and whatever revelation these persons had of Him they had lost by exchanging the truth for a lie. Still, in creation everywhere, men could see that which was above the power of man—something that man could not do ; therefore, in fashioning the maker of these things in the form of a man, or bird, or beast, they were without excuse, *i.e.*, in so doing they were to be blamed.

26-31. *What is meant by " God gave them up" ?*

" God gave them up to uncleanness ;" " gave them up to vile affections ;" " gave them over to a reprobate mind ;"—that is, He did not check them on this downward course of evil to which they had committed themselves, by any prohibitory revelations, even from the time of Noah to the preaching of the Gospel by the apostles ; and as those first claims of God were set aside for their own vain reasonings, we have as a result the long list of crimes which Paul has here given. The lesson is a most suggestive one, and full of instruction to all who will regard it. If we walk in the light of truth, our life will be pleasing to God ; but if we walk in our own reasonings, a sad catalogue of evil is sure to close the scene. God must judge evil in all who practise it ; but His judgment is never irrespective of previously neglected or despised claims. Now we must not overlook that it was to such as those referred to here that Paul was sent by the Lord Jesus —sent to open their eyes, to turn them from darkness to light, and from the power of Satan unto God; and so wondrous was the change effected by his proclamation among them that he could say, " I am not ashamed of the Gospel : for it is the power of God unto salvation to every one that believeth." In writing to the Corinthians (chap. vi. 9, 10), he is led to give a most striking illustration of its power to change the heart and life of all who receive it; which will also show how carefully those results were marked by him. In giving, on that occasion, a list of crimes which he declared would disqualify for the kingdom of God, he immediately adds, " And such were some of you : but ye are washed, but ye are sanctified," etc. The nations had indeed become debasingly immoral in character, and unclean in their practice ; but through the Gospel many of them had " turned to God from idols to serve the living and true God ; and to wait for His Son from heaven."

CHAPTER II.

Why does Paul in this second chapter make a direct appeal to the Jew ?

His appeal to the Jew, and all who were trusting in the law of Moses, as included in this specific case, was in order to show that the law in which he rested had been broken by him, and he was therefore condemned by it, and was even more guilty than the Gentiles who had it not. God had but one method of deliverance for all, and the despisers of His grace had no alternative but ruin; and of this danger Paul desired to convince them.

Where does his appeal to the Jew commence ?

In the last verse of chap. i., the first word being evidently introductory to his charge against them, and, if supplemented, this will be at once apparent. (But there are some) " who knowing the judgment of God, that they who commit such things are worthy of death, not only do the same, but have pleasure in them that do them. Therefore thou art inexcusable, O man," etc.

On what ground does Paul rest his charges against the Jew ?

On the ground that they knew the law or claims of God, while they approved and practised the evil condemned by it.

1. *Paul's charge against the Jew is a very serious one. Can his charge be sustained ?*

His quotations from their own scriptures are quite sufficient to sustain it, and with him these scriptures were decisive.

2, 3. *Why does he speak of God judging according to truth ?*

To show them that truth being God's standard of judgment, if the truth of God was violated they could not escape it, no matter what their standing might be.

4–6. *Does Paul refer to judgment and repentance as alternatives possible to the Jew ?*

There were two courses open to him, one of which he must choose. The riches of God's goodness in the gift of His Son was designed to lead to repentance and salvation, but if despised, then he must meet the ever-accumulating wrath of God.

What does he mean by " treasurest up unto thyself wrath against a day of wrath " ?

It is *lit.*, wrath *in* a day of wrath, and presents a sad fact in the condition of the Jew, which truth and honesty will not allow him to hide. It was then a day of wrath, for the threatenings of heaven rested upon them, and in due time must be executed. God, in the riches of His goodness, granted a space for repentance, but how they would use it remained to be seen.

7–11. *In speaking of rewards and punishment, why does he not refer to Christ?*

He does not name Christ, but Christ is implied in "well doing," and "obeying the truth," and "worketh good," for there is no attainment of glory and immortality apart from Him. What Paul seeks to express is, that those who seek for these things in the way in which they are to be obtained, will obtain life, whether Jew or Gentile; but the evil-doer, whoever he may be, will be visited with the wrath of God. "For there is no respect of persons with God."

What does he mean by "to the Jew first," both in tribulation and peace?

Paul is speaking according to fact and testimony. There was priority both in privilege and judgment. It so pleased Him, who is the source of both, that the Jew should be the first to hear the Gospel, and upon his rejection of it judgment should follow. His privileges date from the call of Abraham, and were perfected in the proclamation of the Gospel; those who accepted peace by Jesus Christ were honoured, but upon the nation that rejected Him the wrath of God came upon them to the uttermost.

12. *"For as many as have sinned without law." How could men sin without law?*

Men could not sin against a law under which they had never been placed, and the law of Moses was not given to the Gentiles; but men could sin against the claims of God as made known to Adam and Noah, and through them to all their posterity, and it is to this that Paul refers. Revelations concerning the Coming One were given to Adam for his descendants, and faith and appropriate obedience could be rendered, as witnessed in Abel and Noah at the altar; but the claims of God could be set aside, as done by Cain and the idolatrous children of Noah, and thus they sinned against God, and suffered for their sin. Let us not understand Paul to mean that the Gentiles, by the mere promptings of their own minds, apart from previous revelations, could do the things contained in the law; because in chapter i. he had stated that revelations of God were once possessed by them, and had been exchanged for their own vain reasonings: but where these revelations had been retained and obeyed, God would approve of all who did so, even though not under the law.

16. *"In the day when God shall judge the secrets of men by Jesus Christ." What day and what judgment is this?*

It is the day appointed for the judgment of the whole world, of which Christ, who was revealed both in prophecy and the Gospel, will be the judge. There was a dispensational judgment which came upon the Jew for his open violations of God's law; but in that day to which Paul refers, the secret—*lit.*, hidden things—of those without (outside) the law of Moses, and of those who in the law sinned against God, will be judged.

17–27. *Why does Paul bring forward these very serious charges against the Jew?*

In order to show the folly of mere profession. The Jew made his boast of having received the law, and of a superior intellectual discernment, but by breaking the law given to him God was dishonoured, and even his circumcision was made null by his disobedience. The apostle could charge them with violating their own teaching, and in the following

chapter he brings forward undeni-
able proofs of it.

*To be a circumcised Jew was no
doubt a privilege, but did this involve
him in any special obligation?*

Of course it did. To be a Jew
demanded a corresponding character;
and being circumcised, a man was a
" debtor to do the whole law."

28, 29. *"For he is not a Jew,
which is one outwardly; neither is
that circumcision, which is outward
in the flesh." What does Paul
mean?*

To be a Jew, and to be circumcised, evidently belonged to the
typical dispensation, and when the
new or Christian economy was set
up, they were no longer required, or
even accepted. To be an accepted
Jew then, according to Paul, a man
must be a Christian: and "we (only)
are the circumcision, who worship
God in the spirit, and rejoice in
Christ Jesus, and have no confidence
in the flesh."

*Is a fleshly relation to Abraham of
no advantage under the new covenant?*

None whatever, except we add a
higher obligation to accept Christ
Jesus, who was the hope of Abraham,
and whose coming was entwined with
the whole of that Jewish dispensation. To be related to Abraham
after the flesh is of no value now,
and, as the old covenant has been
done away, there is not a single promise which a descendant of Abraham
can now claim on the ground of that
fleshly relationship.

CHAPTER III.

1, 2. *In the preceding chapter
Paul condemns the assumption of the
Jew. Why does he own the advan-
tage and profit of his position here?*

Let us not misunderstand him,
or we shall miss the truth and the
instruction he is trying to impart.
What he really condemned in the
Jew was a foolish resting in the
law which he had broken, and
rejecting a God-provided Saviour,
without whom he could never be
justified. In showing the advantages of their position, etc., he really
still further condemns them, because
the greatest of all the advantages
acknowledged was, "that unto them
were committed the oracles of God,"
and these oracles or teachings of
God they had not followed.

3, 4. *"For what if some did not
believe? shall their unbelief make the
faith of God without effect?" Why
ask these questions?*

They are very important questions,
and full of spiritual teaching. Paul
had to accept the fact that some had
failed to believe, and he has to reply
by asking, "Shall their unbelief
make the faith of God,"—*i.e.*, the
testimony of God concerning Christ
and life through Him,—"of none
effect?" His reply is the triumph
of truth and confidence, "God forbid,"—*lit.*, Let it not be. "Let God
be true," etc. Or, as he really seems
to mean, God is true, though man is
false, or refuses to believe His word,
and it will be fulfilled in all who do
believe it.

5. *"But if our unrighteousness
commend the righteousness of God?"
What does this mean?*

This " unrighteousness " which
was manifest in the Jew, a failure
caused by the weakness of the flesh,
only showed that something else was
really needed; while the "righteousness of God" is that which is
" through the faith of Christ," and
has been provided for those who
do accept Him. If God has to take
vengeance on the Jew, it is not
because he failed under the law, but
because he despised the provision
made under the Gospel; and in doing this Paul affirms that He is not
unrighteous.

6. *" God forbid, for then how shall*

God judge the world?" *For what purpose does Paul say this?*

Read, " Let it not be," instead of " God forbid." That is, if God did not judge the Jew for his rejection of His Son, how will He judge the world for its rejection of His grace? But He will judge both, for all rejectors of His grace must stand before the judgment-seat of Christ.

7, 8. *"For if the truth of God hath more abounded through my lie unto His glory."* *To what does he refer?*

Possibly to his own experience. He had chosen a false position and denied the Christ of God, but this only brought out that abounding grace in which mercy was shown to him with faith and love ; and why should he be counted a sinner in accepting of this mercy? It was not designedly but ignorantly that he had set himself against God, and not, as some affirmed, that he said, " Let us do evil that good may come." Such persons deserved condemnation, but he had neither thought nor acted in such a spirit.

9. *When Paul says, " What then, are we better than they?"* *Does he include himself?*

Yes; he did not wish to be thought better than any Gentile, since what he had proved against the Jew, he had proved against himself ; nay, he even counted himself worse than many of his brethren, calling himself the chief of sinners : but, in submitting to Jesus, he obtained mercy.

10–18. *I do not find this long quotation in my Bible; why does Paul say " it is written"?* *Where is it written?*

It is taken from the 14th Psalm, but the greatest part of this section is only found in the Septuagint or Greek version of the Psalms, and these were in common use in the time of the apostles. Why it has been omitted in the Hebrew we cannot say. It is a sad picture of the Jews' degeneracy, but is accepted by the apostle as the truth of God. Paul uses it to show that the Jew was guilty before God, and was condemned by the very law of which he made his boast.

" Therefore by the deeds of the law there shall no flesh be justified in His sight." *Why does Paul make this statement?*

It is a simple conclusion from the facts previously proved, viz., that those who were under the law had become transgressors without a single exception, and could not therefore be justified or made righteous by that which only condemned them. The faith of Jesus could alone effect this desirable object.

21. *" But now the righteousness of God without the law is manifested,"* etc. *Where was it manifested?*

In those saved by the Gospel which Paul preached. He could triumphantly turn to the faith, and love, and obedience of Gentile converts, to prove that men to whom the law had never been preached, and who had never been put under it, were bringing forth the fruits of righteousness, which were by Jesus Christ, to the glory and praise of God. Nay more, even the law and the prophets were witnesses that such lives were in harmony with the spirit of their claims. Neither law nor prophets could condemn the lives of loving disciples of Jesus, and it was of such that Paul was not ashamed.

22–24. *Why does he say, " Even the righteousness which is by faith of Jesus Christ"?*

It is explanatory of what he means by the "righteousness of God." It is that which is by His Son—by the faith in Him through the Gospel which had been preached. Paul is careful to show, not only what had been effected, but the cause of this gracious result.

In speaking of the " righteousness of God which is by faith " Paul says, it is " unto all, and upon all them that believe." Does not this imply a reception of favour, as well as holiness of heart and life ?

Yes; both are included, not only what God claims and receives from the believer, but also what He does for him. Hence Paul distinctly states that it is " by faith of Jesus Christ," and the faith of Christ includes both the testimony of God's love in the gift of Jesus, and trust and obedience to Him.

What does he mean by " unto all and upon all them that believe " ?

Scholars now omit " and upon all," leaving " unto all them that believe " as a simple sentence, and easily understood. God made " no difference,"—*lit., no distinction*—in the showing of His favour. " For all sinned," and all who believe are justified freely through the redemption which is in Christ Jesus.

25. What is the meaning of " propitiation " ?

The word should be *propitiatory,* or mercy-seat, which, as a part of the tabernacle arrangement, was familiar to every Jew. The apostle uses the type as an illustration to reach the understanding of the Jew, and show him that what the mercy-seat was to a worshipper in that old economy, Christ is to the believer under the new. The mercy-seat was sprinkled with blood, and then God could speak graciously to the worshippers, and since Christ has died, He can now accept all who draw near through Him. This blessed truth is fully stated by the apostle, but will, I think, be more easily apprehended when read in the following somewhat transposed form :—*Being made righteous, freely, through that redemption which is in*

Christ Jesus: whom God before-appointed, in His blood or death a propitiatory, and through the faith declaring His righteousness for the remission of past sins, through the forbearance of God.

" The remission of sins that are past." To whom does Paul refer?

To those who believe in Christ, both Jews and Gentiles. God was righteous in forgiving sin through Christ, and His forbearance was largely manifested to both classes. The Jews killed His Son, and cast Him out of the vineyard ; yet, though the crime deserved destruction, He would not destroy them until His pardoning mercy was made known in Jesus. The Gentiles walked in their own way, but " God was in Christ, reconciling the world unto Himself, not imputing their trespasses unto them." That is, both Jews and Gentiles, each in his own way, had previously sinned against God, but, in great forbearance with them, passing by their former transgressions in not visiting with deserved judgment, as He might justly have done, He thus sought to have mercy upon all, through the Lord Jesus Christ.

27. Why does he refer to boasting? Who were likely to do so ?

The Jew boasted in his superior position, but as it could not save him, it was useless to boast in it; and as salvation was by Christ, through the faith, all merit was excluded. The law of faith excluded all boasting, because salvation was through Christ.

30. " Seeing it is one God, who will justify the circumcision by faith, and uncircumcision through faith." Has God two ways of dealing with these two classes ?

No ; but there are two ways of reaching the knowledge of His grace. The Jew had the *ek pisteos* —*i.e.,* the testimony concerning

Christ in the prophets—and through these he might have been led to Christ ; while the Gentile had the *dia tes pisteos*, the Gospel, which led him to Christ, through whom alone both could be justified by God.

CHAPTER IV.

1–3. *Why does Paul refer to Abraham and his justification before God ?*

In order to sustain what must have been a rather startling declaration, both to the Jew and any circumcised Gentile—viz., " that a man is justified by faith without the deeds of the law." The fact of Abraham's acceptance by God was known to the whole nation, but the ground of his acceptance had scarcely been noticed by them, so Paul has to quote the sentence : " Abraham believed God, and it was counted unto him for righteousness," to show to them how even Abraham, their father, had been accepted of God.

Is Paul's quotation from Gen. xv. 6 given correctly ?

Having quoted from the Septuagint version, he has varied the sentence a little, which it will be instructive to notice. In the Greek version we read, " Abraham believed God "—*i.e.*, a testimony of God—while in the Hebrew we read, " And he believed in the Lord "—*lit.*, the Jehovah—*i.e.*, the Coming One ; and, therefore, through faith in this Coming One, he obtained blessing, and not through works of law. Both statements are correct, but one is explanatory, while the other is not. When Abraham saw the burning lamp, which passed with consuming flame among the provided victims (Gen. xv. 17), he saw in a figure the way in which the promised blessing was to be obtained :—" And he be-

lieved in the Lord "—*lit.*, Jehovah— " and He counted it to him for righteousness " (Gen. xv. 6).

6–8. *" Blessed are they whose iniquities are forgiven, and whose sins are covered." Why does Paul quote this testimony of David ?*

To illustrate the nature of the blessedness enjoyed by Abraham through the Messiah, even the forgiveness of his sins, which he received, " not in circumcision, but in uncircumcision." Paul, therefore, quotes two witnesses, Moses and David, to prove that before either circumcision or the law, Abraham obtained " the blessedness " of the forgiven man.

11, 12. *Why was Abraham circumcised ? and what was its purpose to him and his seed ?*

He was circumcised by the command of God, and its purpose was twofold—to him, a seal of the righteousness which he had by faith ; and to his seed, a sign of the covenant which God made with him, " till the seed should come to whom " (or concerning whom) " the promise was made." The circumcision of Abraham should always have reminded them that their father obtained blessing through believing in the promised Messiah ; while their own circumcision was an assurance that from them, as a people, the Messiah should come.

Why does Paul refer to Abraham being the father, both of the circumcised and the uncircumcised ?

Not father of them merely as circumcised or uncircumcised, but " the father of all them which believe," though they be not circumcised, that righteousness might be imputed to them also ; and the father of circumcision to them who are not of the circumcision only, but who also walk in the steps of that faith of our father Abraham, which he had, being yet uncircumcised.

Can the fleshly seed of Abraham now claim him as their father ?

Not unless they have received Christ. In a lengthened discussion between Christ and the Jews on this very question, He assured them, " It is the Spirit that quickeneth "—*i.e.*, by the truth—" the flesh profiteth nothing " (John vi. 63). Hence, as unbelievers, they have no God-allowed claim on Abraham, and to have descended from him through the flesh is now of no value.

13–18. *What is meant by Abraham being " heir of the world " ?*

Having for his children all believers in Christ, whether circumcised or uncircumcised, whether under the law or outside of it ; and the promise that he should be a father of many nations, and should have a seed as numerous as the stars upon which he was told to look, was to be through the faith, and not through either law or circumcision. Both of these had their distinct typical purposes, and when these were reached they were set aside. Abraham being " heir of the world " is not being heir of land, property, or worldly estate, but of that which is far higher, even believers, the purchased possession of Jesus, through whom the promise made to Abraham is fulfilled.

19–22. *Was there any difficulty in Abraham believing that he should be the father of a believing family ?*

There were two very difficult things, which nothing but the gracious power of God could overcome. The more remote of these was Jehovah coming of his seed, and then, through death, becoming a deliverer of all trusting in Him. The nearer difficulty was having a son when he was past age, and then to believe that he would be his heir, although commanded to offer him up. The faith of Abraham, that God could overcome these first difficulties, was

accepted as evidence of his faith in the remoter difficulties—viz., that God would send His Son, and after being offered up in death, He would be raised, and become the medium of a seed, of whom Abraham should be a father.

23–25. *" Now it was not written for his sake alone, ... but for us also." How can the record of these things be for us ?*

Paul was writing to Jews, who questioned the bestowal of blessing through Him who was crucified, and here affirms that the record of Abraham obtaining blessing through believing in God was not made for him alone, but for those also who should believe concerning Jesus. It was to be held as certain that blessing would follow in the latter case, as it had done in the former.

CHAPTER V.

" Therefore being justified by faith" is often quoted to prove that men are justified by *" faith alone." Is this what Paul means ?*

If by " faith alone," repentance, confession, and immersion, which Christ claims from all who will be His disciples, are set aside, then we say that Paul never used faith in that sense of being alone ; but if such persons mean that believers are justified through Christ without the deeds of the law of Moses, then we say yes. We should, however, say that Paul never uses the sentence " faith alone " in any of his letters. He does write of being " justified by faith,"—*i.e.*, through the testimony concerning Jesus, of being the " children of God, by faith of Christ Jesus," etc. But in these places he does not use the word faith, to indicate mere belief, but the testimony believed.

Is " being justified" here an act

of God, or a result in man through " *the faith* " *?*

The literal meaning of the word must be kept before us, and this indicates result in those who have believed, through the testimony, rather than God's action towards them. The verse *lit.* reads, *Having been declared righteous out of faith, we have peace with God through our Lord Jesus Christ.* Paul is not writing here of pardon of sins, which the believing receive through Christ, but of the effect of faith in the life of those who have believed the testimony concerning Him; and when the result is reached through Christ, which the Jew in vain sought to attain through the law, there is intelligent abiding peace with God.

The Revised Version reads, " Let us have peace with God." Is this reading to be accepted as the true one?

It is only right to say that the weight of evidence is in its favour, and by the majority of MSS. the Revisers and others have been ruled. Dr Scrivener, however, says, " Had the scales been equally poised, no one would hesitate to prefer " we have" to " let us have," for the closer the context is examined, the clearer it will appear that *inference* not *exhortation* is the apostle's purpose; hence those who most regard " ancient evidence " (Tischendorf and Tregelles, Westcott and Hort), have struggled long before they would admit " let us have" into the text. We much prefer the reading of the Authorised Version, because it is not a matter of exhortation with Paul, but of positive enjoyment. " Therefore, being justified by faith, we have peace with God through our Lord Jesus Christ." He has given it to us in His promise, and we possess it without doubt or fear.

2. " *By whom also we have access by faith into this grace wherein we stand." What does this mean?*

Access to God was a privilege connected with priestly service, and was obtained by sprinklings of blood, and washing in water; but the worshipper thus fitted to approach could not abide there, but had to renew his medium of access, and only when permitted to do so. But, said Paul, we have not only access, but abide in His presence, and rejoice in hope of the glory of God.

3. " *We glory in tribulation also." Why does Paul say this?*

Because, as between the promise made to Abraham of a son and its fulfilment, there was the deadness of his body, which set aside all hope from nature, and also the scoff of those who held his cherished hope in derision, all of which he had to endure ; so between the promise of the glory of God and its fulfilment, they had to endure affliction and trial consequent upon this delay; yet, said Paul, we glory in it, or rather in our God while passing through it. In looking beyond our tribulation we rejoice, and though called to pass through it, we know that an important end is to be accomplished by our doing so.

What end did this tribulation serve?

It worked out what is ever pleasing to God, " patience"—*lit.*, endurance. The tribulation tested their faith, and their patience or endurance proved their confidence in the promise of God. As the faith of Abraham was put to the test or proof in delaying to do what He had said, so delay, trial, etc., is the putting to the test the faith of those who receive the promise.

4. " *And patience, experience." What is meant by experience?*

It is *lit.* proof. Those who have endured trial for the truth are proved, *i.e.*, tested. They have been put to the test, and have endured it. It is no·longer a question of what they are, the trial has made it manifest.

It is a thing known to all concerned with it.

"*And experience hope.*" *What is this hope?*

It is the hope of glory, the possession of which hope the believer has reached in Christ. Hope is not a mere wish or expectation, but both combined. There are many who wish to share the promised glory, but being out of Christ can have no proper ground for expecting it; while the believer not only desires it, but has a ground for expecting it through the Lord Jesus. This is the hope of the believer, and does not shame those that possess it.

5. *How does the Holy Spirit shed abroad in the heart the love of God?*

By revealing and manifesting it, both by signs which were an evidence of it, and by revelation or testimony concerning it. It was thus confirmed to them as a reality, and in this undoubted assurance their hearts overflowed with joy.

By "the Holy Spirit given to us," does he refer to the immersion in the Spirit? or the gifts of the Spirit?

Possibly both, for both were evidences of His favour and love. The former beginning, the latter sustaining, the proofs of that love.

6–9. *Why does he refer to Christ dying for the ungodly?*

In order to confirm his previous statements concerning justification, and the hope of glory given to the believer. For, admitting the facts of man's guilt, ruin, and inability to remove the consequence, we have another wonderful fact, even Christ dying for ungodly helpless sinners, and from this fact he is prepared to affirm, " Much more then, being now justified in His death, we shall be saved from wrath through Him." As if he had said, God having met our difficulty, in Christ dying for us, when we were without strength, we

fully count upon Him meeting all the rest of our need.

7, 8. *What is the difference between a righteous man and a good man? and why refer to these distinctions?*

A " righteous man " is one against whom no charge can be brought, while a " good man " is one whose goodness has laid others under obligation. The fact of Christ's death for men is brought forward to prove that men are guilty. A good man might be involved, and require and find a loving substitute, but a righteous man does not need one because there is no charge against him. What Paul is evidently teaching in these verses which are parenthetical is, that the death of Christ for man, is a demonstration both of man's guilt and of God's love to him in his sin. This love he sets forth in a most striking manner. Friend may suffer for friend, but Jesus was given up to die for man when in positive rebellion against God.

10. "*For if, when we were enemies, we were reconciled to God,*" etc. *What is reconciliation?*

A bringing together in friendship or oneness parties that had been separated, or hostile to each other. Man by his sin was alienated from God, but by the death of His Son believers have become reconciled, and "being reconciled," he adds "we shall be saved by—*lit.*, in—His life," etc., His life has become to us a new way in which we walk in obedience to God.

11. *Why "joy in God"?*

Because Jesus, who is the means of this atonement—*lit.*, reconciliation—had been given by God, therefore, instead of being afraid of God, we joy in Him through our Lord Jesus Christ.

12. " *By one man sin entered into the world, and death by sin.*" *Why refer to these sad facts?*

The facts referred to are sad indeed, but as they are to form a very important part of his argument, they are for this end introduced. Paul was writing to instruct those who were resting in the law, and were making their boast in God through Moses; and here he wishes to show them that the great difficulty in which all are involved was introduced before either Moses or the law came into force, and that the Deliverer must be one superior to Moses. And, as by one, Adam, sin entered into the world, and death by sin, which has passed upon all men; so by one, Christ Jesus, the free gift came upon all men unto justification of life.

13. *"For until the law sin was in the world." Why does Paul make this statement?*

It will be well to notice that this section, from verse 13 to 17, is parenthetical, and explanatory of his argument, and should by no means be allowed to interrupt it. The matters introduced are important, but we should still read verses 12 and 18 together, so that the "Therefore" of verse 18 may closely follow the "Wherefore" of verse 12. In this parenthesis the apostle begins by saying that sin and death preceded the law, and that a remedy was required for those who were outside of it. This remedy God provided in the *Coming One*, of whom Adam was a figure or type.

14. *"Them that had not sinned after the similitude of Adam's transgression." Who were these?*

All those who lived from Adam to Moses, who, though death was not the penalty of their own sin, neither were under the law, yet were under the universal reign of death, thus proving that death followed Adam's sin, and not their own transgression. *"Who is the figure of Him that was to come." What does this mean?* It is—*lit., Who is a type of the*

Coming One—Christ Jesus being evidently referred to. Paul wishes to teach here that in some respects Adam was a type of Christ, while in some other things they widely differed, and what these were must be carefully noted. Indeed, Paul has not failed to show in what they are alike as type and antitype, and in what they are dissimilar.

15. *"But not as the offence, so also is the free gift." What does this mean?*

If we read, *But the offence is not as the free gift*, we shall see that Paul is speaking of things in which Adam and Christ form a striking contrast. Through the offence of the one the many died, while through the other, the gift of God's grace, life abounded unto many, *i.e.*, unto all who receive Him.

16. *"And not as it was by one that sinned, so is the gift." Is this a further contrast?*

Yes, it is another aspect in which the gift differs in its effects from the sin. "The judgment was by one (offence) to condemnation (of many), but the free gift is of many offences to justification" (of those who believe).

17. *"For if by one man's offence death reigned by one," etc. Is this a further contrast?*

It is rather an explanation of things that differ, and is a most important one. By the one offence of one man death reigned over all, and it is by the one, Jesus Christ, that the privilege of reigning in life is bestowed; but this is only enjoyed by those who receive the gift of righteousness. Life through Jesus is received by faith, and here we get solemn responsibility.

18. *"Therefore as by the offence of one." Is the contrast continued in this verse?*

Yes, but it will be better to read, as rendered by Alford, "Therefore as through one trespass (the issue was) unto all men to condemnation; even so through one righteous act (the issue was) unto all men to justification of life." It is one offence or trespass that brought condemnation to all in Adam, and it is one act of righteousness that brought blessing to all in Christ.

Why does he add "For as by one man's disobedience," etc. ?

It is explanatory of the reason why these results follow through Adam and Christ. The many in Adam were made or constituted sinners through his disobedience, and so suffer death; and the many in Christ are made or constituted righteous through His obedience, and so obtain blessing and life.

20, 21. *"Moreover the law entered, that the offence might abound." What does this mean ?*

The abounding of the offence or trespass was not the direct object of the law of Moses, since it was given to restrain transgression. This restraint, however, was refused, and through the unsubjectedness of their hearts they became worse than even the Gentiles. " But where sin abounded (in those who were under law), grace did much more abound" (in providing for them a Saviour).

CHAPTER VI.

1. *" Shall we continue in sin that grace may abound ? " Why does Paul ask this question ?*

In order to show that continuance in sin was contrary to the purpose of God in the great scheme of redemption, and that righteousness unto holiness must be rendered by all who accept it. The Gentiles sinned against the revealed claims of God, and their vice and uncleanness were manifest to all; the Jews apostatised from His law, and were guilty in His sight; but in the plenitude of His grace both were met in the rich provision of the Gospel, and both were invited to share it freely. But, said Paul, now that we are forgiven, "shall we continue in sin," etc.? and this question he now proceeds to answer.

2. *Is his first reply " God forbid " a correct rendering ?*

It should be rendered " Let it not be," which implies not only that such a course would be highly improper, but should not be allowed by any who are the subjects of this abounding grace. The answer is not " God forbid," but we, to whom such marvellous grace has been shown, should forbid it.

" How shall we that are dead to sin live any longer therein ? " Does this part of his reply indicate that it is improbable or impossible to do so ?

Not impossible, for they would be again tempted to sin, but improbable when the result of past sin was considered. It will be better to read, *How shall we who died by the sin* (not " that are dead to sin") *live any longer in it ?* How shall we return to live in that which has already taken our life ?

Why does he refer to their baptism into Christ ?

Because their baptism, *i.e.* their immersion into Him, was into His death, *i.e.* into Him, as having been crucified on account of sin. They died to that which caused both His death and their own, and were buried with Him in their immersion, and were raised with Him to walk in newness of life. How could they continue in sin when they had accepted another position ?

What connection is there between the raising up of Christ from death and the raising up of the believer from the grave of immersion ?

Christ was raised to live a new life, *i.e.* a life separate from sin, He being no longer under its imputation, so believers were to be free from its practice, being raised to live a life of holiness.

5. *"For if we have been planted together in the likeness of His death."* What does this mean?

A more literal rendering of this sentence will help us to better understand Paul's meaning. Hence we read, *For if we have become conjoined in the likeness of His death, so also shall we be of His resurrection.* That is, Christ died on account of sin, was buried, and raised from the dead; so we died to sin, and were buried with Him in our immersion, and were raised to a new life and walk before God. Thus are we conjoined with Christ in the likeness or purpose of His death, and this is a further reason why we must not continue in sin. This is the righteousness of God revealed in the Gospel, and accepted in faith and love by the believer.

6. *" Knowing this, that our old man is crucified with Him."* What does Paul mean by this " old man"?

The "old man" was the "body of sin," which was formed out of the vices and evil practices of the old life, and was animated by the lusts and passions of the flesh. This old man, says Paul, we crucified, that the body of sin might be destroyed, that henceforth we should not serve sin. Christ was crucified through sin, and we crucified the old man, the body of sin; that henceforth we should not serve it, but Him who is raised from the dead.

7, 8. *" For he that is dead, is freed from sin."* Is literal death referred to here?

The verse *lit.* reads, *For he that died is made righteous from sin.* It is the death which the believer dies in relation to sin, and not to literal death that Paul refers. In literal death, a man is not only dead to sin but to everything else; but Paul is speaking here only of dying to sin,

while to righteousness he lives. In ver. 8, this thought is made plain, and though expressed hypothetically really means, *We died with Christ, and we live with Christ.*

9–11. *Why does he repeat the well-known fact of Christ being raised from the dead?*

It is — *lit.,* raised from among, or out of (the) dead,—leaving the dead and the realms of death behind, never to enter it again. We know that death will never reign over Him again. He is set free for ever and now lives to God; and here we note Paul's application of this fact, "Likewise reckon ye also yourselves to be dead indeed unto sin, but alive unto God through Jesus Christ our Lord." That is, be like Christ free from sin and serving God. We may also see the bearing of these references to his question, "Shall we continue in sin?" and the force of his reply, No; we have done with it, for we died to it, and as our Lord dies no more on account of sin, so we have died to it once and for ever.

12. *" Let not sin therefore reign in your mortal body."* Is this the body of flesh?

Yes; but through sin, the sin of the one man, it is rendered mortal, dying, and will die. But while living, it has its lusts and passions, which if obeyed, will enslave the mind; so he exhorts, "Let not sin therefore reign in your mortal body, that ye should obey it in the lusts thereof."

13. *Since the body has become mortal through the sentence against sin, is subjection to sin an absolute necessity?*

No. The mind is above the body, and can control its actions : hence our responsibility. We *may* yield our members as instruments of unrighteousness; or, being made alive through Christ, we *may* yield them to God, to do His will and serve Him. So Paul exhorts, do not obey its desires, nor yield your members to do evil, but "yield yourselves to God, as those who are alive from the dead."

14. *Why should being "under grace" and not law, prevent the lordship of sin?*

To be "under grace," is to be under Christ, and to have all the benefit of His work, and love, and promises, etc., and these are all-sufficient for those that trustingly obey Christ, for their complete victory over sin and temptation. Sin is not an absolute master to the believer, it is only so to those who yield to it. There is no fated necessity to be its slave, since the truth shall make free all who become obedient to it.

15. *" What then? shall we sin, because we are not under the law, but under grace?" Why ask this question again?*

You will observe that the question is not the same as asked in the first verse. There it is, "Shall we continue in sin, that grace may abound?" here, "Shall we sin because not under law, but under grace?" The reply is the same as before, "Let it not be." Or, it must not be, and for these solemn reasons, that to whom they yielded themselves servants to obey, his servants they were, whether of sin unto death, or obedience unto righteousness.

17. *Is it not strange that Paul should say, " God be thanked that ye were the servants of sin"?*

Yes, it would be strange indeed if he thanked God for their past sinful life, but he does not do this. The construction of this verse is peculiar to Paul, and his letters furnish many instances in which the first part of the sentence is clearly connected with the last and must be joined to it to get its true application. The verse contains a statement of two facts, both of which were true of these saints at Rome. (1.) They had been the servants of sin, which was a cause of grief, but is not expressed here. (2.) They had obeyed from the heart that form of doctrine which had been delivered to them, and for this he could say, "God be thanked."

What does Paul refer to in this "form of doctrine" delivered to them?

It was the death, burial, and resurrection of Jesus, which became a form or mould into which they had been cast. That is, they had died with Him to sin, they had been buried with Him in their immersion, and had been raised to walk in newness of life, and for this Paul was thankful.

19–22. *In exhorting to continued faithfulness, why does he refer to their past life of sin?*

Because the contrast between the fruit of sin and the fruit of holiness was so marked, that the appeal could be thoroughly felt. In the fruit of sin there was only shame, in the fruit of holiness there was everlasting life.

CHAPTER VII.

Who are the persons addressed in this chapter?

I presume they are Jewish saints, who knew the law, and could feel the force of the apostle's teaching respecting its power and lordship over all who were under it.

2. *Why does he refer to the law of marriage?*

Because it presents a striking illustration of the life-long power of law, which they well understood. The woman who had a husband was bound by the law of marriage to her husband as long as he lived, and she could only be released from it by his death. Then, and then only, could she be married to another man.

4. *" Wherefore, my brethren, ye also are become dead to the law by the body of Christ." How could the body of Christ set them free?*

Christ died under the curse of the law, and in death exhausted its full penalty, as it could follow Him no further. But when God raised him from the dead, and made Him the head of a new creation, all who became united with Him were set free from their first subjection. Death and burial with Christ preceded their rising, and in that act their marriage-union took place. They were then married to Him that was raised from the dead, that they might bring forth fruit unto God. Thus were they set free from the law by the body of Christ, that they might henceforth serve Him.

Then is the law dead?

The law is not dead, it cannot die, but the believer dies, and rises to live in a new relation to a new and living head.

5. *" When we were in the flesh." What does Paul mean by this?*

Being ruled by the flesh, its desires and passions obeyed instead of Christ. Being "in the flesh" is put in contrast by Paul with being "in the Spirit"—the one a definition of the flesh-ruled man, the other of the Spirit-ruled man.

What had the law of God to do with exciting the motions or passions of sins?

The law did not excite them, but only restrained from sin those that were under it; but being "in the flesh," as well as under "the law," its restraints were unheeded, and lusts and passions gratified in the very face of its prohibitions. The law of God, under which the Jew was placed, was like a glass that reflected the beauty or deformity of the onlooker, but did not make either. Sin became manifest in disobedience to the law, the fruit of which was death.

6. *" But now being delivered from the law, that being dead wherein we were held." Is not this deliverance from the law by its death?*

Yes, if this was a correct rendering of the sentence. But we should read, *Having died to that in which we were held.* The law did not die, but we believers did, and now, being united with Christ, we serve in newness of spirit, and not in oldness of letter.

What is meant by " oldness of the letter"?

" The letter " is used by Paul for the law of Moses, which had become old by the introduction of a new institution under Christ—an institution in which He was served in spirit and in truth.

7. *Why does he ask, " Is the law sin?"*

It was needful to ask this question in order to defend the law from any wrong imputation. The law was not sin, but a sin revealer, and made manifest how contrary he was to God. He did not know the evil desires of his own heart, until these became manifest by the prohibitions of God.

8. *What is this concupiscence which sin wrought in him?*

It is simply coveting, or over desire. When he tested his own heart by God's law, he saw that he desired what God had forbidden. " I had not known lust," or coveting, " except the law had said, 'Thou shalt not covet.'" The coveting was in full operation before he observed it. The command did not make him covet or desire, but only revealed that he did so.

9. *" For I was alive without the law once." What does this mean?*

He refers to his own conscious standing before God, when, as a Pharisee, he blamelessly attended to the traditions of the fathers. Then he was alive in his own estimation, but when compelled to look at himself in the light of God's pure law, all this fancied life expired ; or, as he states, " Sin revived, and I died." He saw that in the light of God's law ; his only standing before Him was that of a condemned sinner.

When did he get this alarming view of himself?

In Damascus, where he was left three days without sight, and had to look inwardly to learn his true state before God. It is quite possible that when he wrote that sentence, " Sin revived, and I died," his mind was glancing over that ever-memorable struggle in the house of Judas, in the street called Straight. No wonder that in the discovery which he then made of his state before God he should neither " eat nor drink." Ananias found him slain by the law—dead before God, and ready for a new life. When the God-sent messenger came to him, and said, " And now, why tarriest thou? Arise, and be baptised, and wash away thy sins, calling on the name of the Lord,"—he found Saul ready to obey, and at once he confessed the ascended Jesus.

10. " *The commandment, which [was ordained] to life, I found [to be] unto death.*" *Was Paul writing this from experience?*

Yes ; from painful experience. He had judged his state from tradition, and was satisfied, but when obliged to judge himself in the light of God's claims, and the mission of Jesus, his hope expired. God's estimate differed from his own, and when Jesus appeared to him, he was led to accept that true estimate of his state.

14–23. " *I am carnal, sold under*

sin." *Is this spoken of Paul the saint, or Saul the flesh-ruled sinner?*

It is Saul under the dominion of the flesh, and not Paul the saint,—walking, " not after the flesh, but after the Spirit," that is here referred to. And though most expositors refer the whole paragraph to Paul's Christian life, it will not harmonise with his teaching in other places to do so.

But why introduce it as his experience?

It was his experience when simply a Pharisee, or, as he had already stated, "when we were in the flesh," or walking after the flesh. Then he was carnal, a slave to sin ; and though enlightened by the law under which he lived, and even approving in his conscience this divine rule, yet found that he was a slave to evil desire, and under the dominion of passions which struggled within for gratification. But what the law could not do through the weakness of the flesh, the love of Christ could and did effect. To suppose that his words, " I am carnal, sold under sin," and " what I do, I approve not," and " what I hate, that do I," was Paul's Christian experience, is to mistake the object for which it is given. Paul had served under two masters or lords, and he gives his experience under both. He had served under the law, and inwardly approved of all its claims, but the flesh ruled him, and brought forth fruit unto death ; and he had also served under Christ, and found in Him deliverance from the law of sin and death. While under the one we hear him cry, " O wretched man, who shall deliver me?" and under the other, " I thank God through Christ Jesus." In this twofold sketch we may clearly perceive (1.) Paul the Jew without Christ, and so in bonds to sin ; and (2.) Paul the Christian set free, and rejoicing in Him. To

R

assume that he is describing a man with two natures in operation at the same time, is to make him teach what he never intended, and introduces confusion of thought in all who receive it.

Why does he introduce these matters to these saints in Rome ?

In order to show that while the law could manifest sin and convict of guilt, it could never justify or induce the spirit of obedience ; and that to urge conformity to it instead of to Christ, which Judaising teachers were everywhere doing, was a vital mistake. The Gospel of God, concerning His Son Jesus Christ, could alone meet man's need, and bring the heart into loving obedience to Him.

"I see another law in my members." What is this law that brings into captivity ?

A tendency or proneness to selfish gratification, which is always contrary to God's will or law, and which ruled in the members with the power of an impelling law. The law of God was approved by his inward man, or mind, but he saw, what was to him a matter of conscious experience, another law in his members, which ruled over him, and which led him to cry out, " Oh wretched man, who shall deliver me from the body of this death ? "

24. *What does he mean by the " body of this death" ?*

Not his mortal body I presume, but what he terms in another place " the old man," which, before he received Jesus as his deliverer, he dragged about with him, and from which he could not free himself. This " old man, which is corrupt according to the deceitful lusts," was under condemnation, and was therefore fitly termed the " body of this death."

25. *Is Christ a perfect deliverer from it ?*

Yes. " Thou shalt call His name Jesus, for He shall save His people *from* their sins." " If ye walk in the Spirit," *i.e.*, according to His teaching, " ye shall not fulfil the lusts of the flesh." If the "new man " is put on, then righteousness and true holiness will clothe the believer.

" So then with the mind I myself serve the law of God ; but with the flesh the law of sin." Does not this indicate two natures or two services existing and going on together ?

No. It is simply Paul's statement of his condition when living as a flesh-ruled man. With his mind, he even then approved the law of God ; but with his flesh, he yielded to the law of sin.

CHAPTER VIII.

1. *" There is therefore now no condemnation to those in Christ Jesus." Is this true of all believers ?*

Yes. All who are in Christ are free from judgment, whether Jew or Greek, bond or free ; a freedom the law could never effect.

2. *" The law of the Spirit of life," and " The law of sin and death." What are these two laws ? and how does the one set free from the other ?*

The "law of the Spirit " is the truth, or testimony, which being revealed by Him, and received by those who have life in Christ through faith in Him, it becomes a law or ruling power in all such, and delivers them from the " law of sin and death," *i.e.*, the law in the members, which, through unchecked desire, leads on to sin, and results in death, *i.e.*, condemnation.

3. *" For what the law could not do, in that it was weak through the flesh." Is this a different law from those already mentioned ?*

Yes. This is the law given by God through Moses, and was holy, and just, and good ; but the obedience required by it was not effected through the condition of the flesh of those to whom it was given, the mind being subjected by it.

Did God intend man's restoration by this law ? and if not, why was it given ?

God never intended the law for man's salvation, because He had promised a deliverer long before it was given. The law was added because of transgression, *i.e.* to restrain it, until the promised Deliverer should appear. It was an embodiment of His authority, and a test of man's heart, and showed out fully his true condition before God ; but it was only by Jesus that man could be restored, and for this purpose He sent His own Son in the likeness of sinful flesh.

" In the likeness of sinful flesh." What does this mean ?

It is *lit. in the likeness of the flesh of sin, i.e.,* like those who were to be redeemed ; for the "Word was made flesh," only not sinful flesh, because He was holy, and undefiled, and separate from sinners. Christ was not from Adam, or He must have been like his posterity, but He was conceived by the Holy Spirit, and became the woman's seed. And being made flesh, and having a prepared body, He could and did suffer in it the condemnation of God against sin.

4. *" How is the " righteousness of the law" fulfilled in believers ?*

The law demands obedience, and this is effected by the love begotten in them by the Gospel. Those who accept of Jesus, who in love died for them, do walk in loving obedience to His will,—not according to the flesh with its sinful desires, but according to the teaching of the Spirit, who guides them into truth and righteousness.

5. *How are these diverse states to be distinguished from each other ?*

By the action appropriate to each. If we mind the things of the flesh, we are *lit., according to the flesh ;* if we mind the things of the Spirit, we are *according to the Spirit.* Each one can test his own action by the Word of God, and so learn his standing before God.

6. *What is meant by " carnally minded " and " spiritually minded" ?*

It should be rendered, the *mind of the flesh,* and the *mind of the Spirit.* It is not mere fleshly tendencies that Paul refers to, but to the mind of the flesh, which as a lord rules over and provides for its gratification, according as its lusts may incline. So the mind of the Spirit is not mere wishing for or approving of good, but having the body and the life ruled by His controlling truth.

7. *When he says that the mind of the flesh cannot be subject to God's law, does he mean that such cannot be converted ?*

No. He means that two opposite rules cannot be acknowledged at the same time. If the flesh rules the man, God does not rule him ; and if the Spirit rules him by the truth which He has given, then the dominion of the flesh is set aside.

10. *" And if Christ be in you, the body is dead because of sin." What body is this ?*

It is what he terms, in chap. vi. 6, the " body of sin," the " old man." This " old man," he says, " was crucified with Him, that the body of sin might be destroyed "—*i.e.,* rendered powerless. Here he adds, " If Christ be in you, the body is dead because of sin "—*lit.,* through sin. It is a body which sin has formed, and that dies when Christ lives in you ; " and the Spirit is life because of "—*lit.,* through—"righteousness "—*i.e.,* a righteous life, through the indwelling of the Spirit by the truth.

11. *" Shall also quicken your*

mortal bodies." Does this refer to resurrection ?

I think not. Paul had been speaking of the death of the body of sin, *i.e.*, the old man, and here he is speaking of the quickening of the mortal body, for the service of Christ, by the indwelling Spirit ; or, as in chap. vi. 12, "Let not sin reign in your mortal body, ... but yield yourselves unto God."

12. *" Therefore, brethren, we are debtors." To whom were they debtors ?*

He affirms that it was "not to the flesh to live after the flesh," but it is implied that it was to Him who had redeemed them by giving up His own life. The debt they owed to Him was, to mortify—*lit.*, to put to death—the deeds of the body through the Spirit which He had given them ; and if they did this, the life He had given them would be sustained, but if not it should expire.

14. *Why does Paul connect being " sons of God " with being " led by the Spirit " ?*

In allowing themselves to be guided by the Spirit of God there was evidence that they were God's children. Their submission to Him proved their relationship.

15. *Why does Paul refer to the " spirit of bondage " and the " spirit of adoption " ?*

In order to show the contrast between the fear engendered by the one and the spirit of adoption—*lit.*, sonship—begotten by the other. In Moses and Paul we have a true representation of the spirit of the two institutions. Moses said, " I exceedingly fear and quake" (Heb. xii. 21); while Paul could say, " Alway rejoicing " (2 Cor. vi. 10).

What is this " spirit of adoption"?

It is *lit.*, the spirit of sonship—the spirit which is begotten in the believer by the knowledge of the relationship which God has established with him through Christ.

What is meant by " Abba, father " ?

Abba is the Chaldee word for father, which was first written in this form, and then translated for the benefit of those to whom it was not familiar.

16. *" The Spirit itself beareth witness with our spirit." How did He do this ?*

If by " our spirit " we understand Paul to mean *our testimony*, as the apostles of Christ, we shall then see what Paul meant. The apostles had declared that believers in Christ, whether Jews or Gentiles, became the children of God ; and to the truth of their testimony the Holy Spirit was bearing witness, or confirming it with signs following.

17. *Does being " heirs " necessarily follow being children ?*

So Paul reasons : " If children, then heirs." The possessions of the father strictly descend to the children. If there is but little to receive, still it is theirs ; if there is much, they are enriched by it. Believers are heirs of a kingdom, which God has promised to them that love him (James ii. 5). It is said of Abraham that he gave all he had unto Isaac, his only Isaac, and the family enjoyed his possessions in and through him. So God has given all to Jesus, His only begotten Son, and the family, being joint-heirs with Him, enjoy all through Him.

Does that which is inherited by Jesus already indicate the nature of the portion which the heirs shall inherit ?

Most certainly. A joint-heir shares with the heir his portion, and, as Jesus has been glorified, if we suffer with Him, we shall also be glorified with Him.

18. *How could Paul balance glory against suffering when the glory was not revealed ?*

Not in the saints, but it was in

Christ, and He is both their fore-runner and their security. "If we suffer with Him, we shall also reign with Him."

19–21. *"For the earnest expecta-tion of the creature waiteth,"* etc. *What does Paul refer to in this word "creature"?*

The word *ktisis,* rendered "crea-ture" three times in this section, and "creation" once, should be *crea-tion* in each instance. But, admit-ting that the word should be so rendered, its proper application should also be carefully considered. The word *ktisis*—creation—while doubtless including the act of the Creator, is, in the New Testament, specially applied to that which is created, whether the material uni-verse, or man, or the saints, or human institutions; and its appli-cation must in every instance be learnt from the context. Some per-sons do apply this groaning and ex-pectation of creation to the material earth on which the curse rests, and to the lower animals which suffer on account of man's sin; but I think the context here does not furnish sufficient ground for such a thought. Paul is writing of the saints, of their sufferings and hope, and not of animals. When God promised full deliverance to His people, His new creation, He promised the li-berty of the glory of the children of God, and for this they wait and sigh, as in travail or birth pangs, and will do so until delivered by a faithful God.

What is this "manifestation of the sons of God"?

It is their manifestation in glory, which, though promised to them, is at present deferred. A poet has ex-pressed it thus:

" The saints are here unknown,
  Are princes in disguise,
Nor shall their glories be reveal'd
Till Christ shall leave the skies.

" Then shall they see His face,
  And in His blissful sight,
Shall with His image be adorn'd,
And shine divinely bright."

This is the hope which they see not, but for which they patiently wait.

22, 23. *" The whole creation groaneth and travaileth in pain to-gether." Is it not the whole material universe to which Paul refers?*

We must be careful not to make him say so, if he did not intend his words to be so applied; and as all Scripture is from one Spirit, a sen-tence in one part may help us to understand a like sentence in an-other part, and of this help we should be ready to avail ourselves. In Mark (xvi. 15) we read that the apostles were to preach the Gospel, *lit., to all the creation.* Now, we have no difficulty in deciding that they understood Christ to mean the people that dwelt on all the earth—*i.e.,* all the nationalities of the world; and Paul uses precisely the same words when he wrote, " The whole creation "—*lit., all the creation*—" groaneth and travaileth." If, there-fore, Mark refers to men and women, and nothing outside of these, we may conclude that Paul refers to no-thing else than those who among the Gentiles had heard, through the Gospel, of God's promised deliver-ance ; and from these the " pantings of hope," as one expresses it, were continually ascending to God for the fulfilment of His promise. " And not only they (these Gentile be-lievers), but ourselves also (the apos-tles), who have the first fruits "—*lit.,* the first fruit—" of the Spirit," *i.e.,* gifts bestowed by the Spirit, " even we ourselves groan within ourselves, waiting for the adoption." Thus we learn that these apostles, even though specially endowed with the power of the Spirit, were not exempt from suffering, and, along with other believers, were groaning for deliverance.

What is this "adoption" for which the saints are waiting ?

It is *lit.* sonship, *i.e.*, the privilege of sons, which Paul explains to be "the redemption of our body."

24. *"For we are saved by hope." How does hope save ?*

If we read, *For in hope were we saved, i.e.,* the hope of redemption, we shall see what Paul means. It is as if he had said, In saving us, Jesus gave us this hope of deliverance, and though we see it not, yet with patience we wait for it.

26. *"Likewise the Spirit also helpeth our infirmities." What previous help does Paul refer to ?*

To the hope begotten by the promise of redemption, which hope was strengthened by all the Spirit had done in them and for them. It was by His revelations that they were able to pray and intercede aright before God, and thus their own infirmities and deficiencies were assisted.

28. *"The called according to His purpose." What is meant by "His purpose"?*

His set-forth plan to save men by Jesus ; and all who have accepted Him as their Saviour, love God, and all things that God does is working for their ultimate good. To be called according to His purpose, is to be called by Jesus to salvation and glory, and He alone is the way.

29. *"For whom He did foreknow," etc. What is foreknowledge ? and who are those foreknown by God ?*

Foreknowledge is, by metonymy, forerevelation, and specially relates to the saints and their privileges, as made known by the prophets. The favours predetermined of God under the Messiah, were largely revealed by the prophets, and it was distinctly announced that the righteous or obedient should enjoy them. It is to this fore-revealing of the privileges of

the saints, under the Gospel economy, and especially of glorification, that Paul refers when he wrote, "For whom He did foreknow, He also did predestinate," etc.

What is the meaning of "predestinate" ?

To mark out beforehand to privilege specially designed for those to whom it appertains. The privilege of resurrection glory is not an afterthought with God, but was predetermined in the divine plan, for all who are prepared for it by Jesus. Jesus the Son of God having been raised from the dead and glorified, has become the type or image to which the saints will be conformed.

Did this "foreknowledge" and "predestinating" take place in a past eternity ?

If to "foreknow" and "predestinate" be the fore-revealing and declaration of God by the prophets, as it most assuredly is, then it is confined to time, and was prophetically unfolded by them, and then made known in the "due time," by preaching. When Peter was preaching at Pentecost, he quoted from Joel, that "Whosoever shall call upon," *i.e.,* confess, "the name of the Lord Jesus, shall be saved." Here from this prophet it was foreknown, because pre-revealed, who should be saved. And so it is of all else that is revealed by them.

30. *"Moreover whom He did predestinate," etc. Who are these ?*

They are believers, whether Jews or Gentiles, and to both the Gospel was preached, and their calling, justification, and glorification followed their acceptance of Christ.

How can they be said to be "glorified," since glorification is yet future ?

Yes, future to the saints, but not to Christ, and they are one with Him. Their calling, justification, and glorification are all in and through Him. They had been called and justified, for these things are true of every believer ; and in due time their glorification will follow. We might assume that by "glorified" the apostle intended to express the honour given to the saints, even on earth, by their acceptance of Christ Jesus ; but it is most likely that he refers to their glorification when Jesus shall return.

32. *" He that spared not His own Son." Why does Paul refer to this blessed fact ?*

It was in order to meet an objection which might have been made against such high expectations as those which Paul had raised in their minds ; so he turns to what God has already done, and asks, " How shall He not with Him also freely give us all things?" The difficulties are met with facts which are unanswerable, " If God be for us?" If Christ died for us? and is our Intercessor at God's right hand, then as chosen in Him we have nothing to fear.

35. *" Who shall separate us from the love of Christ." Did he mean Christ's love to them, or their love to Christ ?*

Their love to Christ. Paul had been viewing in all its marvellous manifestations the love of Jesus, and here we have his bold defiance of all testing circumstances. He had already suffered much for Christ. " For thy sake we are killed all the day long," and he was ready to suffer more. " In all these things we are more than conquerors through Him who loved us." " Distress and persecution, peril and sword, had all been endured for Christ."

38. *Are death and life, angels and principalities, still further difficulties ?*

A higher class of difficulties. Elements of the perilous times that would sorely test their faith, but which Paul, in the strength of his faith and love to Jesus, defies.

CHAPTER IX.

Does Paul commence a new subject in this chapter ?

It might rather be called an explanatory defence arising out of his previous argument. He had "before proved both Jews and Gentiles, that they were all under sin," and therefore under the condemnation of God ; and that from this condemnation, the law of Moses, under which the Jew was placed, could not save him, but left him as hopeless as the Gentile whom he despised. He then goes on to show that God by a new arrangement, though old in promise and prophecy, could accept of sinners, even through His Son Jesus who had died for all, and could save all who would believe in Him, whether Jew or Gentile. Now this newly-manifested plan of God, not only set aside the law, the bond of the covenant which God had made with the Israelites, at Sinai, but also their peculiar privilege of being the seed of Abraham. Instead of electing in Abraham their father, He began to elect in Christ ; and instead of calling those who were born after the flesh His children, He acknowledged only those who were born from above. This new arrangement of God, which had been fully opened under the seal of the Holy Spirit, dispossessed the Jew, who still clung to the law, of every privilege enjoyed under it, and this necessarily prompted the question, " Is there unrighteousness with God?" This question the apostle endeavours to answer in this and the two following chapters ; and not only vindicates the action of God in saving men through His Son, but shows the consequences that will follow to all who reject Him.

1. *Why does Paul open this section with such strong declarations of sympathy with his brethren in the flesh ?*

In order to show them that he was

not writing in a vindictive spirit, nor resenting the cruel treatment which he had received from many of the Jews. His affection towards them was unabated, and he could solemnly affirm, as in the sight of God, that he had "great heaviness and continual sorrow in his heart" on their account.

3. *"For I could wish that myself were accursed from Christ for my brethren."* What does he mean ?

This rendering would lead one to suppose that the love of the apostle was so strong towards his brethren that he was willing, even then, to be accursed on their behalf. Now I confess that I cannot see the wisdom of such a desire, or what could possibly be effected by it even if possible. If he had said that he was willing to labour for their spiritual good, to suffer pain, persecution, or loss, in seeking to lead them to Christ, one would have felt how true such utterances were ; but to be accursed from Christ for them he could not be, and therefore would not desire an impossibility.

There is, however, another rendering of these words, and that part of this verse to which grammatical criticism has been applied, doubtless required alteration. *Eukomen*, which in our version is rendered "I could wish," is in the imperfect tense, and should be rendered *I wished* or *was wishing*, and evidently expresses what Paul had once done, and not what he was then wishing to do. James Morison, in his very elaborate and critical exposition of this chapter, has proved most conclusively by the renderings given to this tense in many other parts of the New Testament, that it should be so rendered here ; but in seeking for the time when Paul was really wishing to be "accursed from Christ," he has gone back to that sad period of his life when he was madly persecuting the

saints that believed Jesus of Nazareth to be the Son of God, to show that "virtually, and by consequence, and in its ultimate issues and bearings, that was his wish." Now to this forced application, *For I myself was wishing to be accursed from Christ*, we must object, and shall show it to be wrong by giving another rendering of *anathema*, here rendered "accursed." There are two forms of this word differing only in a single letter, which Trench (see his "Synonyms of the New Testament") regards, "as having been at first only different pronunciations of one and the same word ;" one of these being applied to whatever was set apart to sacred or religious purposes. Among the Jews, whatever was devoted to God was *anathema*, whether for His service, or for His judgment and destruction ; and among the Greeks, according to Trench, *anatheema* was "the technical word by which all such costly offerings as were presented to the gods and placed in their temples, were called, and thus were separated for ever from all common and profane uses." Now I think it is not difficult for us to see what Paul meant when he used *anathema*. He did not wish to be accursed, *i.e.*, devoted to destruction, but he was wishing to be separated for service among his brethren, and here says that he had desired from Christ Himself to be so separated. This desire, however, Christ did not gratify, but sent him into another field of service. Now it so happens, that we have Paul, when addressing the Sanhedrin in Jerusalem (Acts xxii. 17–21), referring to this very desire, and shows that he even pleaded with Christ that he might labour among his own brethren, but his request was refused, being told to depart, "For," said Jesus, "I will send thee far hence unto the Gentiles." This "depart," though contrary to his desire, decided Paul's future line of service, and left him no alternative than to commit himself to the great work of preaching among the nations, to which work Christ had separated him. We may therefore safely render this section in harmony with this expressed idea, that Paul's desire was not to be " accursed," but to be separated to the work of testifying the Lord Jesus to his brethren the Jews. *I say the truth in Christ,—I lie not, my conscience also bearing me witness in the Holy Spirit,—that I have great heaviness and continual sorrow in my heart. For I earnestly desired from Christ myself to be separated for my brethren* (for service on their behalf), *my kinsmen according to the flesh.* Now Paul here evidently appeals to the fact,—that he had once even desired Christ to appoint him for service among his brethren,—as strong presumptive evidence that his grief on account of their rejection of Christ ought not to be questioned. He could indeed appeal to his conscience before God, that in this matter he did not lie.

4, 5. In these two verses, the apostle enumerates nine distinct favours that were conferred upon the seed of Abraham after the flesh. What is the import of each? and why does Paul refer to them?

Each of the favours named suggest to us that they had been very highly distinguished by God, and were doubtless intended to instruct and prepare them for higher service and blessing, even that of His dear Son. A mere notice of each of these specially named privileges will show this. (1.) " *Who are Israelites,*" *i.e.*, they were not only descended from Abraham, who was distinguished for his faith, but also from Jacob, who as a prince, had power with God and prevailed, and had his name changed to Israel, *i.e.*, one who has power

with God. As his children, this name Israel became their patronymic possession, and being named Israelites, they were most impressively reminded that blessing had been personally obtained by their father Jacob, and could also be obtained by them, above and beyond mere fleshly claims. (2.) " *To whom pertaineth the adoption,*"—*lit.*, the sonship. Being nationally begotten in Egypt, and born out of the cloud in the sea, they became the children of God, having been delivered by His power, and placed under Himself by the law which they received. And though not spiritually His children, this privilege being obtained only through the faith in Jesus, yet, having a typical sonship, they were thus brought into a relationship with God, which should have prepared them for that higher relationship which is perfected in Christ. (3.) " *And the glory.*" This glory was, I apprehend, that visible manifestation of the presence of God which guided them out of Egypt, which appeared on Mount Sinai, which rested on the tabernacle and over the mercy-seat, and afterwards filled the temple of Solomon. It was an accredited token of Jehovah's presence with them, and in it God was brought very near to them. To them and to no other people did this glory belong. By this visible manifestation they should have been prepared to receive the Messiah—the antitype of this symbol of God's presence. Paul was grieved that they should have had the former and rejected the latter. (4.) " *And the covenants.*" The covenant made with Abraham, and confirmed to Isaac and Jacob; the covenant made with their fathers at Sinai and sealed with the blood of animals; the new covenant made known through Jeremiah (xxxi. 31–34), and which embraced a coming Saviour and life through Him—were all intended for their benefit. But alas! all were despised, and even when salvation through Christ was proclaimed to them, they refused to accept of it. It was their refusal of such manifold favours, that caused continual sorrow in the heart of Paul. (5.) "*And the giving of the law.*" That is, the law was given to them to restrain them from transgression, and to prepare them for obedience to the Gospel of Christ. (6.) "*And the service,*" *i.e.,* the service of the tabernacle and the temple, so rich in spiritual teaching, was specially committed into their hands. (7.) "And the promises," *i.e.,* the all-inclusive promises concerning the Christ, which they should have been ready to receive. (8.) "*Whose are the fathers.*" It was their privilege to have a descent from those noble great-grand-sires of the nation, whose faith in the coming Messiah formed such a striking example, and of whom they should have been close imitators. (9.) "*And of whom as concerning the flesh Christ came,*" *i.e.,* He was "son of David, son of Abraham, and therefore, as concerning the flesh, He was born of them." This nearness of relation should have induced a joyous reception of Him in all the purpose of His loving and gracious mission, but alas, instead of this, He had to quote as applicable to many of them, the sad words of Isaiah, "All day long I have stretched forth my hands unto a disobedient and gainsaying people."

Does the closing doxology of this section belong to Christ?

Yes; and it forms a striking contrast between the estimate of Paul and of those who rejected Jesus. To them He was as a root out of a dry ground, a base impostor; while to him He was "God blessed for ever. Amen."

6. "*Not as though the Word of God hath taken none effect.*" What

does Paul mean by this statement?

He simply means that although the Jews, who rejected the Messiah, failed to obtain the privileges provided in Him, the Word of God had not failed or "taken none effect," because the promise was never intended to be realised on the ground of a mere fleshly claim. Even Abraham received the promise through believing in the Lord—*lit.,* the Jehovah—and those who were to be his seed, "through the righteousness of faith," must also obtain it by believing in Jesus. This gracious plan was no afterthought of God, but had been fully declared both in the psalms and in the prophets. David had written : "But know that the Lord hath set apart him that is godly for Himself" (Ps. iii.)—*i.e.,* in the new dispensation the godly alone would be recognised by Him ; and this truth is repeated in nearly every prophetic psalm. The prophet Isaiah had declared, "The holy seed shall be the substance thereof," or the stem of the nation (chap. vi. 13); and every other prophet, in one form or other, had reiterated this declaration. In forming, therefore, believers in Jesus into "a chosen generation, a royal priesthood, an holy nation," instead of Abraham's fleshly seed, there was no deception on the part of God, and there should have been no mistake on the part of the people. But, in accepting the type for the antitype, the shadow for the substance, the externalisms of the law and tradition, for the faith of the Gospel, they exposed themselves to a most humbling disappointment. Paul's reply in this sixth verse is very suggestive, but as our translators neglected to render the Greek particle *de,* generally translated "but," and which should have commenced this verse, the bearing of his explanatory statement is somewhat obscured. We must, however, restore this omitted " but," which was evidently used as a recoil from a possible thought, which the apostle assumes may have been caused by his statement of the many privileges enjoyed by those who were Israelites —viz., that as God bestowed upon them so many privileges, in that past dispensation, He may also have intended their absolute enjoyment of the higher privileges under the Messiah. So he immediately adds, But (although they have enjoyed all these typical favours, it is) " not as though the Word of God had taken none effect," or had been set aside; since the " Word of God "— the promise concerning the nations through Christ—preceded the adoption, the glory, etc., which the Jews were permitted to enjoy. The same thought is given in Galatians iii. 17, only differently expressed: " And this I say, that the covenant, that was confirmed before of God in Christ, the law, which was four hundred and thirty years after, cannot disannul, that it should make the promise of none effect."

" *For they are not all Israel, which are of Israel.*" *What is the import of this statement?*

It is intended to show that mere descent from Jacob did not insure a Jacob-like spirit, and this was essential to enjoying God's promise. The privileges of the new covenant could not be possessed by those who were only " of Israel," but by those who, like him, prevail with God, and obtain life through the kingly-mediator, Jesus. God's word of promise had not failed, for " the election hath obtained it, and the rest [unbelievers] were blinded."

7. " *In Isaac shall thy seed be called.*" *Why refer to descent according to Isaac?*

It is important to keep before us, that Paul is reasoning upon the fact

of a new administration, and that the Jews occupied a very different relation to Abraham, now that it was in force, from that which they held prior to its introduction. Under the old economy, Abraham was the father of every one lineally descended from him, but when the new covenant was brought in all fleshly relation to him terminated, and he was no longer the father of any one after the flesh. This is why Paul states at the beginning of this verse, " Neither because they are the seed of Abraham [after the flesh], are they all [his] children: but in Isaac shall thy seed be called." When Isaac, the child of promise and of faith, was born, Ishmael ceased to be the son and heir of Abraham in relation to the Messiah; so, when Christ opened the new economy, the seed of Abraham after the flesh had to give place to the seed who were after the faith; or, as Paul gives his conclusion on this matter in his Epistle to the Galatians (chap. iv.), the son of the bondwoman, type of Jerusalem or the Jew, who was then in his bondage, was cast out, while the son of the freewoman, type of believers in Jesus, became the heir of the promises.

8. " *That is, They which are the children of the flesh, these are not the children of God,*" etc. *Is this a conclusion from his previous statements?*

Yes; and one we should very carefully notice. Paul's introductory statements in the two previous verses are here formulated into a well-defined proposition, viz., *That the children of the flesh are not the children of God, but the children of the promise are counted for the seed.* To overlook this proposition, or to fail in giving it the attention it demands, is sure to prevent us from feeling the force of his references to Sarah, Rebecca, Esau, Pharaoh, the Jews, etc. In all these cases we have God setting aside the flesh as a ground of choice, and thus illustrating the great principles upon which He would save men by Jesus Christ. To read these cases in the light of the Gospel, they will be found to be as simple as truth can make them ; but to read them, as is too frequently done, as illustrations of God's choice of men, without a revealed reason, is only to bewilder all who do so.

9. *"And Sarah shall have a son."* *Why refer to this word of promise ?*

It is simply to show that Ishmael, the child of the flesh, had to be set aside for Isaac, the child of promise. Abraham was at first unwilling to accept of God's arrangement, and pleaded, " O that Ishmael might live before Thee ! " but his prayer could not change the purpose of God, and he wisely bowed to the " word of promise. At this time "— *lit.*, season — " will I come, and Sarah shall have a son." The season at which God was to give them a son was when Abraham was a hundred years old, and when the " deadness of Sarah's womb" excluded all hope of nature's fitness for its fulfilment. But God had spoken, " Sarah shall have a son," and Abraham rested upon His power to accomplish His own will. Paul wished the Jews to understand from this allegorical illustration that, as a fleshly seed, they must, like Ishmael, be set aside, and could only become heirs of life through Him who died and rose again. It is sad to learn that, because they were not allowed to inherit spiritual blessing through the law, they would not accept it through the faith, and this caused Paul great heaviness and continual sorrow of heart.

10–13. *" For the children being not yet born, neither having done any good or evil," etc. " It was said unto her, Jacob have I loved, but*

Esau have I hated." Does not this seem like eternal election and reprobation ?

To quote Scripture in this way, is to confound things that differ. There are two statements here which are very distinct, and widely separated from each other, and both must have our attention. The first is a revelation made by God concerning Jacob and Esau before they were born ; the other is a declaration by Malachi respecting their posterity, long after their fathers had passed away. Now, it is important to understand that this declaration by Malachi, and which evidently refers to manifest conduct and character, was not spoken to Rebecca ; while that which was spoken to her was about the relation which her twin sons should bear to each other when formed into nations. When Rebecca accepted Isaac as her husband, it was with the distinct understanding that he was heir to the promises concerning the Messiah, and in faith she yielded herself to be the mother of the Messianic people. For a long time Rebecca was barren, but when, in answer to prayer, conception did take place, she was soon astonished to find that twins were in her womb. She expected only one son, and was perplexed to find that she must give birth to two. God's answer to her enquiry was, " Two nations are in thy womb, and two manner of people shall be separated from thy bowels ; and the one people shall be stronger than the other people, and the elder shall serve the younger" (Gen. xxv. 23). Now these revelations to Rebecca had, doubtless, a literal fulfilment in the two nations that sprung from her twin sons, Jacob and Esau, viz., the Edomites, who rapidly increased, and soon became a powerful nation ; and the Israelites, who, for a long time, were a weak and enslaved people, and often stood in awe of their brethren. The lesser people, however, were early called to sustain and develop a divinely arranged system of spiritual types, and, after becoming a powerful and distinguished nation, ultimately gave birth to the Messiah; while the stronger, and at one time the more powerful nation, were subjected and made to serve them, and, at last, their standing as a nation was completely broken up. Now, the existence and destiny of these two nations, so very closely related to each other, are evidently more to Paul than what seems to lie upon the surface. He sees in the history of Jacob and Esau what he also sees in Sarah and Hagar, viz., an allegory, and the instruction he conveys by means of it is most solemn and important. The Jew, after his birth out of Egypt, had grown into a powerful nation, and continued to hold his position until a brother nation was born, and, under divine direction, claimed the promises. The eventful history of Jacob and Esau is evidently repeated in the Jewish and Christian nations, and the conflict between them is easily traced. The elder brother, the Jew, is a cunning hunter for spoil and position, a man of the field of the world; but the craving is not good, and in his carnal hunger he sells his birthright for a mess of pottage. The younger brother, the Christian, through faith in Jesus, obtains the promised blessing, and is confirmed as a joint-heir with Him who had received all the promises. Now Paul wished them to understand that, outside of the promises in Christ, they could no more succeed than did Esau, and are thus urged to abandon their natural trust, and seek life in a risen and exalted Saviour.

Why does Paul quote from Malachi, " Jacob have I loved, but Esau have I hated."

His argument is conducted on the assumption that Israel, as a nation, were cast off by God, and that believers in Jesus, not only of Jews but also of Gentiles, were beloved of Him. The reason why God does this is, as plainly shown, the rejection of Christ by the one, and the acceptance of Him by the other. The words of God by Malachi, " I loved Jacob," does not apply to the man Jacob, either before or after his birth, but to the people called by his name; and to that period of their history as declared by Hosea, " When Israel was a child, then I loved him, and called my son out of Egypt" (chap. xi. 1). The same period is also referred to by Jeremiah, " Thus saith the Lord; I remember thee, the kindness of thy youth, the love of thine espousals," etc. (chap. ii. 2). Their noble surrender and trust on that occasion did call forth God's loving approval. So, likewise, the declaration "I hated Esau," did not apply to the man Esau, but to his posterity, and to that period when they were called by Malachi, " The border of wickedness, and the people against whom the Lord hath indignation for ever." In approving what is right, and condemning what is wrong, there is no unrighteousness with God. He has always done this, and, as the unchanging God, he always will. Paul is most earnestly seeking to show the Jews that, in rejecting Christ, they were justly exposing themselves to an Esau-like doom; and this caused him great heaviness and continual sorrow of heart.

14, 15. *" For he saith to Moses, I will have mercy on whom I will have mercy." Why does Paul quote this saying?*

These words were uttered by God on the occasion of the Sinaitic apostacy, and are quoted by Paul to show the position in which the Jews stood as a people. At Sinai, the newly-formed nation voluntarily accepted God as their leader, and in reply to His claims through Moses said, "All the words which the Lord hath said will we do" (Exod. xxiv. 3). The covenant, which God uttered in the hearing of all the people, was written and sealed with blood, and both the book and all the people were sprinkled with it, and thus a covenant agreement was secured. But when Moses came down from the mount with the tables of the covenant in his hands, he found that they had made a molten calf, and declared it to be their deliverer and leader. By this act of idolatry, their accepted relation to God was forfeited and never regained. Moses, indeed, pleaded for their lives when threatened with national extinction, and his prayer was heard; but, though they were allowed to continue as a nation, the threatened judgment was never withdrawn. Moses became their mediator, and was commanded to lead them on, with the promise of the angel or guiding cloud to go before them. "Nevertheless," said God, "in the day when I visit, I will visit their sin upon them" (Exod. xxxii. 34). Now Paul had to remind the Jews, and all persons inclined to Judaism, that that Sinai judgment had still to be executed upon the nation, and though so long delayed, it must ultimately descend on all connected with and abiding in the old institution, which had to be broken up, root and branch. There was one way of escape, and only one, "I will have mercy on whom I will have mercy," etc.

To whom then will God show mercy?

To those who accept of His Son, whatever their former position or character may have been. So the declaration by Peter runs, "Unto you first God, having raised up His Son Jesus, sent Him to bless you, in turning away every one of you from his iniquities" (Acts iii. 26). And also in his 1st epistle, "According to His abundant mercy He hath begotten us again," etc., "by the resurrection of Jesus Christ from the dead."

16. *Something here is said to be "not of him that willeth, nor of him that runneth." What is it?*

The passage is evidently elliptical, but the ellipsis, or omitted words, as supplied by expositors, seem to have been according to preconceived ideas, rather than what Paul had previously stated. It is indeed amusing to note how variously the supposed deficiency has been made up, each one supplying that idea which he thought to have been intended. Our translators have ventured to supply "it is," but this gives us no light whatever as to what is "of God." The word "is" rather forming a peg on which each expositor or reader is invited to hang whatever he or she might think best, and the deposit of thought has been exceedingly varied. One supplies faith, as not of him that willeth, etc., another election, another repentance, another regeneration, another mercy, etc. But if Paul himself has not supplied the required thought, it is not very likely that we shall supply the right one. In carefully noting the argument, we perceive that the question is about who are the "children of God"? or who are "the children of the promise counted for the seed"? and Paul having shown that Isaac, the child of promise supplanted Ishmael, the child of flesh; and as Jacob the lesser supplanted Esau the greater; so believers became the children of God, instead of fleshly-descended Jews. To this aspect of the matter he applies his conclusive, "So then" (omit "it is") "not of him that willeth, nor of him that runneth" (is this position or privilege),

" but of God that showeth mercy,"— i.e., to those who are brought nigh through Christ Jesus.

17. *Why does Paul bring forward the case of Pharaoh?*

To show the sad results that followed his rejection of the claims of God—viz., hardness of heart and utter destruction. Moses was sent to him by God with a most reasonable claim, " Let my people go that they may serve me," but the claim was refused. Again and again the claim was renewed, but with no better result ; judgment followed judgment consequent upon his refusal, until his life was in danger through his obstinate rejection of the claims of God. From the justly deserved doom of death, which even then had fallen upon him, God, however, raised him up, that His power might be shown in him, and that His name might be declared through all the earth. This effect did indeed follow, as afterward shown by Rahab to the spies, " As soon as we had heard these things, our hearts did melt," etc., " for the Lord your God, He is God in heaven above, and in earth beneath." It may seem strange that God should harden the heart of Pharaoh, but this hardening was consequent upon the position he occupied in opposing God, and enslaving His people. The opposition of Pharaoh to God's claims did not begin with the visit of Moses to bring them out of Egypt ; it had been continued during the forty years that Moses was in Midian, and his tyranny towards Israel was so oppressive that it had become necessary for God to interfere. Now this interference was not only for the deliverance of Israel, but also for the judgment of Pharaoh and his people ; and is here referred to for the purpose of showing the Jews that, in resisting Christ the Moses-like prophet, they were preparing themselves for a Pharaoh-like doom of hardening and destruction. Indeed, the hardening of heart had already begun, and the overthrow was not far off. The case of Pharaoh was given as a warning to them. Therefore hath He mercy on whom He will (those who receive Christ) and whom He will (those who reject Christ) He hardeneth.

God is said to have hardened the heart of Pharaoh. What does this mean?

To harden the heart is to render it insensible to that by which it should be easily impressed. First we have Pharaoh hardening his own heart, i.e., refusing either to yield to God or accept His claims ; then we have God in righteous judgment hardening his heart, i.e., rendering him insensible to the danger or wrath that He saw fit to bring upon him ; that so, others might be warned by his doom, and might avoid his daring hostility against God.

19. *What is the force of " Why doth He yet find fault? For who hath resisted His will?"*

From God's words at Sinai, a part of which Paul quotes, we learn that there were unfulfilled judgments which had yet to fall upon the nation, and though so long delayed, they would not slumber much longer. Nor was this a new truth, for Jesus had said when denouncing with terrible woes the truth-rejecting scribes and Pharisees, " That upon you may come all the righteous blood shed upon the earth," etc. (Matt. xxiii. 35). And as these woes were about to fall upon the people who had been more highly favoured than all their ancestors, the heart of the apostle was filled with poignant grief on their account. So, if possibly he may affect their minds by informing their judgment, he allows their question, " Why doth He yet find fault?" and answers it by asking another, " Who hath resisted His will?" The reader will please note that I have followed the Elzevir edition of 1624, and omitted "For." Paul's question is a most instructive reply to their ignorance. It is a word of sober reasoning about the folly of such a course as pursued by them. They ask why God continues to find fault, and his reply is, because you are resisting His will, and in such opposition it is a folly to reply against God acting in righteousness.

21. *Why does he ask about the potter's power over the clay?*

It is in order to vindicate God's course of action toward them, and the circumstance, as given by one of their own prophets, is used for the illustration. Jeremiah was sent to the potter's house, to learn a word for Israel, and found the potter at work upon a piece of clay. He was evidently working after a pre-arranged plan, and was intending to form it into a certain kind of vessel; but while at work upon it, it was marred in his hand, and instead of throwing it aside, he fashioned it into another vessel, as it seemed good to the potter to make it (Jer. xviii. 1–4). Now, it is with this illustration before them that Paul asks the question, "Hath not the potter power over the clay, of the same lump to make one vessel unto honour, and another unto dishonour?"—*i.e.*, hath not God, the great Potter, authority to honour those who receive His Son, and to dishonour those who reject Him, even though they may have descended from Abraham? It is therefore not to show God's power to create men to honour or dishonour that led Paul to bring forward the case of the potter and his clay, but to show what God would do to the house of Israel in their rejection of His first and most gracious purpose to bless and honour them by the

gift of His Son; even to dishonour them by casting them off.

22. *"Vessels of wrath fitted for destruction." Who are these?*

Christ-rejecting Jews, of whom three things are here affirmed by Paul: (1.) that they were fitted for destruction by their persistent rejection of God's will; (2.) that God was willing, or purposed to show His wrath against those who did so; and (3.) that, although determined to manifest His wrath, He had delayed the execution of it with much long-suffering. Now this "much long-suffering" is very emphatic, and calls for special notice. In putting a golden calf in the place of God, as was done by the nation at Sinai, they forfeited their standing as His people; but, through the mediation of Moses, their nationality was continued. Instead, however, of profiting by the forbearance of God, they became worse in their journeying in the wilderness, and still worse in Canaan under the judges. God, however, preserved them, and sent His prophets to instruct them concerning the coming Saviour, but they only went deeper into sin, and in the end they killed the "Prince of Life." And though God raised Him from the dead, and sent a message of peace in His name, the entire nation, a few thousands excepted, deliberately and persistently resisted God's will or purpose to save them. So here Paul has to write, and there is nothing else that he can write, than "vessels of wrath fitted to destruction."

23, 24. *"Vessels of mercy." Who are these?*

Paul's reply is, "Even us whom He called," *i.e.* believers, for God has called no other to glory, "not of Jews only, but also of Gentiles." The preparation for glory is by the Gospel, its reception and influence over the heart is therefore an absolute necessity.

25–29. *" I will call them My people, which were not My people." Why does Paul quote this statement from Hosea ?*

It is a very important quotation, and is intended to show the end of God's dealings with the nation of Israel, and the outflow of His mercy to those, and only those, who became obedient through Christ. By his marriage with Gomer, the daughter of Diblaim, and the God-given names of his three children, Hosea has to learn the final history of the kingdoms of Israel and Judah, and also of the acceptance and establishment of another people. Their history is written in symbols, but that none may err, the prophet expounds them plainly. The name Jezreel (I will visit, *i.e.*, with judgment), given to his firstborn, was prophetic of the doom of the kingdom of Israel, which in a little while was to cease for ever. Lo-ruhamah (the unpitied) was the name given to his second child, and excluded any possible hope for the restoration of the nation. "For I will no more have mercy upon the house of Israel; but I will utterly take them away." The kingdom of Judah was to remain until Shiloh should appear, and the name given to Hosea's third child (Lo-ammi, ye are not my people) was prophetic of the doom of Judah after that event. Then the prophet adds, as quoted by Paul, "And it shall come to pass," etc. "The children of the living God" are then, doubtless, believers in Jesus, and to them, and to them alone, these privileges belong.

What does Paul mean by " A remnant shall be saved" ?

His quotation from Isaiah is to prove that it is not the nation that will be saved, although numerous as the sand of the sea, but a remnant, *i.e.*, believers in the Lord Jesus. But for this "chosen generation," this "royal priesthood," the nation would

s

have become as Sodom and Gomorrah, *i.e.*, totally extinct.

CHAPTER X.

1–4. *Why did Paul's earnest prayer to God, and his intense anxiety for the salvation of his brethren, fail to secure it ?*

Not only was he anxious for this object, but he also accepts the fact that they were very zealous too, and yet both failed to secure it. The reason assigned for this failure is one which should be deeply pondered by all, whether seeking their own salvation or the salvation of others. If the salvation of men was effected by the mere decree of God, then He would only have to will and it would be done; but as salvation is a joint result of His grace and of man's acceptance of Christ, the refusal to accept of Jesus must prevent its enjoyment. God does indeed will all men to be saved, but it must be by coming to the knowledge of the truth. He has made all needful provision for man's salvation, and has sent the proclamation of it through the world; but when that message has been despised, and God's long-suffering goodness trampled under foot, then the dread alternative of judgment must follow. God wished the Jews to be saved, so did Jesus, and the Holy Spirit, and the apostles, but a selfish insubordination hindered the result. Paul has marked the cause of failure, and it should prove a warning to all others. They had zeal, but not according to knowledge, *i.e.*, the revealed will of God; they sought to establish their own righteousness, and did not submit to the righteousness of God, *i.e.*, to the Lord Jesus. For, said Jeremiah, "this is the name whereby He shall be called, The Lord our Righteousness" (xxiii. 6).

5–8. How was Christ the end of the law for righteousness?

The law was a pedagogue or child-conductor to Christ. Every ordinance, every sacrifice, pointed forward to Him, through whom alone its object could be realised. The law was but a shadow, Christ was its substance; the law was a type, He its antitype, and the hope of those who looked for redemption in Israel.

What is the difference between the righteousness of law and the righteousness of faith?

The righteousness of the law was obedience to the testimony of God by Moses, and secured only those promises relative to the present life, while the righteousness of faith was acceptance of Christ, which secured to those who did so the salvation which He alone could bestow.

9. Is faith in Jesus as the Son of God, and confession of Him with the mouth, required of all who will be disciples of Jesus?

Both are appointed by Him, and therefore necessary steps in discipleship. The Word of faith, *i.e.*, the Gospel, is given to induce trust in Him for salvation and righteousness, which could not be reached by the law of Moses; and confession of that faith with the mouth is claimed by Him, in order to the salvation which He alone can bestow.

Faith in Christ is certainly necessary, but is not confession with the mouth an arbitrary law?

It is a question whether anything appointed by Christ is purely arbitrary. There is a reason for every requirement in His law of love, and generally it is not far to seek. Everything appointed by Him stands related to something else, and must be considered in its relation. For instance, Christ has appointed that all who believe in Him shall be immersed into Him, but how could

this faith be known unless confessed, which is to be done by the mouth— a personal, voluntary confession of Him as the Son of God. Thus do we receive Him, and He receives us into blessed saving union with Himself.

12. " For there is no difference between Jew and Greek." Is not this contrary to his previous statements?

If we read, *There is no distinction between the Jew and the Greek, i.e.*, God showing mercy alike to both through Jesus, we shall better understand his meaning. There was a difference in their standing, but salvation was freely made known to both.

17. " So then faith cometh by hearing, and hearing by the Word of God." Why does Paul reason to this conclusion?

His conclusion, as here stated, is very instructive. From ver. 12–16, and indeed to the end of the chapter, he is speaking of two classes who form a very striking contrast. There were the Jews, to whom the Gospel had been preached, but who had not obeyed it, as Isaiah in his prophecy declared, "Lord, who hath believed our report?" and there were Greeks or Gentiles, to whom it had been preached, and who had believed and called on the name of the Lord; and Paul asks how this latter result had been brought about. They had called on the name of the Lord; they must therefore have believed in Him; and how could they believe in Him without first hearing of Him, or being invited to do so by a proclamation? and how could this be done unless it was sent of God? In this 17th verse he concludes thus, "So then faith cometh by hearing, and hearing by the Word of God,"— *lit.*, of Christ,—that is, their believing had followed a divine proclamation to them, and this had been made by the authority of Christ.

Paul is not here answering a very oft-proposed question, How is faith as an act of the mind produced? but is simply showing that Gentiles trusted in and confessed Christ for righteousness and salvation, by the authority of His appointed messengers.

CHAPTER XI.

1. *"Hath God cast away His people?" Why did Paul ask this question?*

In order to explain a very important aspect of his argument. He had proved in the preceding chapters, both by his grief over his kinsmen according to the flesh, and his illustrations from Ishmael, Esau, Pharaoh, and the dishonoured vessel of the potter, that they stood in this position, and were therefore cut off or cast away. It was a most solemn fact to prove, but in faithfulness he had no alternative, and as other issues were involved, he had to notice and explain them. In casting away Jews as the seed of Abraham after the flesh, had God cast away His people? This question he now proceeds to answer. The answer is given in part in the previous illustrations, and these only require to be noticed in order to feel the force of his present instructive reply. Had God cast away the child of promise when Ishmael was set aside from being the heir of Abraham? No. Had God changed His purpose when the birthright-rejecting Esau was denied the blessing which had just fallen upon Jacob? By no means. When God led Israel safely through the Red Sea, and destroyed Pharaoh and his rebellious host, was He unrighteous? No. Now it is in the light of this fact that, God having cast away the unbelieving seed of Abraham from being the heirs of the promises which were to be enjoyed only through the Messiah, we are prepared to hear Paul ask, "Hath God cast away His people?" and also to hear him reply, "God hath not cast away His people whom He foreknew."

2–5. *"Whom He foreknew." What does this mean?*

Had Paul said, God has not cast away those who have received the Messiah as revealed by the prophets, one could scarcely fail to perceive his meaning, and this is what is intended by "Whom He foreknew." Both in testimony and allegory God had revealed the heirs of the promise of His grace, and the apostles speak of them as foreknown or fore-revealed by God. Ishmael, as the bondwoman's son, was cast out, while Isaac, the child of promise, was honoured as the heir. "Now we (believers), as Isaac was, are the children of promise" (Gal. iv. 28). The prophets had declared, "The just shall live by faith," and "Whosoever shall call upon the name of the Lord shall be saved." These persons were not cast away, but the mere fleshly seed of Abraham were set aside.

Why does he refer to Elias or Elijah?

To illustrate the position he had stated, and the reference is a very forcible one. Elijah had to denounce the house of Israel for their idolatry, and to refuse their claim to be the people of God; but when he declared that as a witness for God he stood alone, the answer of God to him, "I have reserved to myself seven thousand men who have not bowed the knee to Baal," must have been a pleasing surprise. The nation were disowned for their idolatry, but the seven thousand faithful ones were accepted instead of them. "Even so then at this present time also there is a remnant according to the election of grace." Or,—and the apostle seems to be giving the sum of previous statements—as Isaac, the child of promise, had been elected heir of the Messianic promises, instead of Ishmael, the child of the flesh; and as Jacob, the lesser people, had been elected to enjoy these privileges instead of Esau, the greater people; and as the seven thousand were reserved for God instead of the ten tribes, even so had He elected believers in Christ to be heirs of life and glory, although but a remnant, instead of the nation, who might be as numerous as the sand of the sea.

Do not some people think that " Whom He foreknew " refers to those who from eternity He elected to be saved ?

Yes, some people do think so ; but then it is only their thought and not Paul's teaching. Paul is teaching of what God revealed in time by the prophets, and not what He did before time began.

What is this " election of grace " ?

Election, or choosing in Christ, in whom alone God chooses to salvation and life.

6. *" And if by grace, then is it no more of works." What works are set aside by grace ?*

Works of law, which by some were being done to merit God's favour. We must, however, beware of presuming that the obedience of faith is also set aside by grace. Christ claims obedience from all who will be His disciples, and bestows His favour not for their obedience but through it. In our obedience we are permitted to claim and enjoy His promise, and joy in the gracious Giver.

7. *" The election hath obtained it, and the rest were blinded." Who caused this blinding ?*

We should read " hardened," and the context assures us that it was God who hardened them. " According as it is written, God hath given

them the spirit of slumber (or stupor), eyes that they should not see," etc.

8. *If God was really seeking their salvation, is it not passing strange that He should harden them ? How could they find it when hardened into stupor ?*

God was really and earnestly seeking their salvation, as the ministry of prophets, of Christ Himself, and of apostles must prove beyond a doubt ; but this threefold ministry was persistingly rejected, and though professing to worship God, it was done in selfish hypocrisy. Hence the prophet Isaiah (chaps. xxviii. and xxix.) distinctly states that two things preceded this sad insensibility to coming wrath, viz., God laying a foundation on which all might rest in eternal security, and their defiant challenge of His right to punish them when refusing to accept of this provision. God did not harden them that they could not find salvation, but to confound them in their arrogant schemes to overthrow His purpose. This hardening into stupor, and insensibility to wrath, be it noted, was at a certain stage in the divine programme. God sent His Son to save the lost sheep of the house of Israel, but His ministry soon disclosed a formidable combination of the nation to prevent His gracious work, " The kings of the earth stood up, and the rulers were gathered together against the Lord, and against His Christ " (Acts iv. 26). Their success at first was fearful, for they succeeded in crucifying the Lord of life and glory; and when God set His king upon His holy hill of Zion, and a message of peace came from His throne, they again renewed their diabolical plot to extinguish the work so graciously begun. A crisis was inevitable : either they should frustrate God's purpose in seeking the salvation of all who would accept of it, or God must crush their power in judgment. To make all see that it is an evil and bitter thing to sin against God, He determined to bring against them the abominations of the desolator ; and this hardening into insensibility is the first stage of divine judgment. It is just that course which it was right in God to pursue, because His efforts to save them had all been rendered abortive by their unbelief.

9. *What does he mean by " Let their table become a snare and a trap " ?*

A table is a symbol of provision, and this God did not fail to supply, even though they were disobedient. Now this did become a snare to them, for the language is prophetic, because instead of seeing the goodness of God toward them in the face of all their transgression, they rather accepted it as a sanction of their evil state, and thus it became a stumbling-block, instead of humbling them before God. Their eyes were darkened, and in this blindness they stumbled and fell under a perpetual yoke, and have never been set free.

11, 12. *" Have they stumbled that they should fall ? " What is meant by these things ?*

The stumbling was their unbelieving rejection of Jesus as the Messiah, after He had been preached to them for salvation. " For they stumbled at that stumbling-stone ; " while their " fall " was their deposition from the position they had so long occupied as God's people under the old covenant. It will be well, however, to notice that the " fall "—*lit.*, offence —through which salvation is come unto the Gentiles, and is also the riches of the world,—is a very different word from the former. The fall which followed their stumbling was their ejection from their dispensational standing ; while their fall or offence, which became the riches of the Gentiles, was the crucifixion of

Jesus. Paul here asserts, that as salvation and the fulness of privilege was proclaimed to Gentiles through this Jesus whom they put to death, it should have provoked them to jealousy, *i.e.*, it should have aroused the Jews to seek the same privileges through the same source.

" How much more their fulness ? " Does Paul refer to their conversion or future return ?

No, but to the result of it when first they repented and turned to the Lord. Of their first standing when brought out of Egypt, Moses could write, " Happy art thou, O Israel : who is like unto thee ! " etc. (Deut. xxxiii. 29) ; but when they accepted of Jesus, Peter could write of them, " But ye are a chosen generation," etc. (1 Peter ii. 9). In accepting of Christ they became " His body, the fulness of Him who filleth all in all " (Eph. i. 23). To them, the special honour of being the Church of Christ was first given ; while the Gentiles only became sharers of this grace. Their fulness under Christ was far greater than their standing under Moses, is what Paul wishes to express.

15. *Paul here speaks of the casting away of the Jews, and the receiving of them again. What is the meaning of this " life from the dead " ?*

It is simply their new standing before God when Christ is received, which this expression " life from the dead " fitly describes. Their former standing had been broken up by the bringing in of a new covenant and a new seed ; and as Ishmael, though in the house of Abraham, was cast out when Isaac was established, so these Jews, though in the house of God, were cast off or cast away, when the new heir was established, their old relation being no longer acknowledged. Yet, the casting away of them by this change of administration opened the door of faith to the nations, and the world, *i.e.*, those of the nations who believed in Christ were reconciled to God. For the Jew, cast away from his fleshly relation to Abraham and to God, to enter by this new and living way into the family, was indeed " life from the dead,"—*lit.*, from among dead ones. It was only by being born again, that he could enter the kingdom of God.

16. *The " first fruit " and the "root " are here referred to. What are they, and why does Paul refer to them ?*

Abraham was the root of the Jewish nation, and it had its rise in him; but as he obtained acceptance through faith in the promised Messiah, this was a plain indication that the branches must be like the root, or that they, to form a part of this symbolic tree, must become, like him, believers in Christ. Then the first fruit was that portion of the harvest which was presented to God, and being accepted by Him, was called holy, and through this acceptance the consecration of the mass or lump was secured. Both root and first fruit when accepted of God were intended to illustrate what kind of persons could be accepted under the Gospel. To be God's accepted people they must be Abraham-like in faith.

17. *Paul speaks of a good olive tree and a wild olive tree. What do these represent ?*

The good olive tree was a symbol of Abraham, to whom—by means of two covenants which God made with him—two seeds were secured, each in its own time and place. One covenant secured to him a seed after the flesh, with Canaan and its privileges for their portion; the other secured to him the Christ as his seed, in whom all nations should be blessed. Now his seed after the flesh were the natural branches, but these were broken off when the second covenant came into force, and a reunion can never be effected by nature. They may be grafted in by faith in Christ, but there is now no other way of union. The wild olive tree represents the Gentiles, who, through faith in Christ, became branches of the good olive tree, and partakers of the promises with believing Jews.

In referring to Abraham and the Gentiles, why does Paul select the olive tree in preference to any other ?

Because the Holy Spirit selected the olive, and its oil or fatness, as a symbol of divine communications under former dispensations; he is therefore only transferring the selected symbol to his own teaching. Even the Gentiles, through Adam, Enoch, and Noah, received revelations from God; but as these were exchanged for their own vain reasonings, they grew up as an untrained tree, and are most fitly described as a wild olive. Abraham also received revelations concerning the Messiah, and believed them, and brought his life into harmony with them; and after showing his faith in offering up his son, all these promises are joined with his name, and believers partake of the root and fatness of this good olive tree.

20. *The natural branches were broken off. What is the security of the grafted branches ?*

" Thou standest by faith : be not high-minded, but fear." God has broken off the Jews, the natural branches, but is able to graft them in again, and will, if they abide not in unbelief. He has grafted you in, said Paul, but your standing is secured only by obedience to the Lord Jesus.

25. *What is this mystery or secret of which he would not have them ignorant ?*

This secret seems to include at least two things. (1.) That the blindness—*lit.*, hardness—was not universal. Some of the Jews had believed, and thus proved that God could graft in again the broken-off branches ; and that those who, through their unbelief, were hardened, were not yet under the judgment, for God endured with much long-suffering, even the vessels of wrath, fitted to destruction, and if not despised they might yet escape. And (2.) that this deserved judgment would be held back "until the fulness of the Gentiles be come in."

What is this "fulness of the Gentiles"?

It is not the enjoyment of privileges by Gentile believers for a certain period of time, but the completion or fulness of the blessing of the Gospel of Christ, which consisted of the gifts of the Spirit, and the perfected teaching of the apostles, and the revelations of Jesus, given to John in Patmos, when the canon of revelation was closed by Jesus saying, "I am Alpha and Omega, the beginning and the ending, the first and the last" (Rev. xxii. 13). With these words the fulness of gift and prophecy to the churches, then largely composed of Gentile believers, was completed, and the judgment on the Christ-rejecting people of Israel descended shortly after.

26. *What is meant by "so all Israel shall be saved"?*

It is a very important statement, because it is explanatory of Paul's argument. Too often it is read without noticing either the qualifying "so," or the quotation from Isaiah, and when read as an absolute declaration of the salvation of all Israel, a totally different idea from that of Paul is introduced. In chapter ix. he affirms that "they are not all Israel who are of Israel," and in chapter x. he states that it is those who believe with the heart, and confess with the mouth, that Jesus is the Christ, that will be saved. Now,

this affirmation must be read in the light of these and kindred statements, and then we shall understand what Paul means by "And so," *i.e.,* in this way or manner, "all Israel shall be saved ; " as it is written, "There shall come out of Sion the Deliverer, and shall turn away ungodliness from Jacob," *i.e.,* the people who are represented by His name, "For this is My covenant unto them, when I shall take away their sins." In the prophecy quoted from Isaiah the mission of the Messiah was to turn Jacob, *i.e.,* the people, from their ungodliness, and Paul assumes that where this is not done it is because the Messiah is rejected. So also in the condensed quotation from Jer. xxxi., the promise pledged to them was the removal of sins, and that when sins are not removed, it is because the covenant is refused, or its conditions of enjoyment are violated. It is, therefore, not the absolute salvation of the nation that he is here affirming, but he is disputing the claim of those who rested upon their fleshly relation to Abraham. As long as the Jews refused to accept the conditions of the new covenant, which included faith in Jesus, Paul refused to acknowledge their right to the promises of God.

28. "*As concerning the Gospel, they are enemies for your sakes : but as touching the Gospel, they are beloved for the fathers' sakes." What do these statements mean?*

Our translators, by adding and repeating the words "they are," as shown in italics, have made both parts of this verse to apply to the Jews, whereas Paul in the first part is referring to the hostility of the Jews upon God's reception of believing Gentiles, while in the last part he is referring to these Gentiles who he affirms are "beloved for the fathers' sakes." Now it must not be overlooked that God promised to

Abraham that in him, that is in his seed the Christ, all the families of the earth should be blessed, and also confirmed the same to Isaac and Jacob, and these are the fathers to whom Paul refers. What Paul is really teaching here is, that God having promised to these fathers Messianic blessings for the nations through the Christ, they are to be looked upon as "beloved for the fathers' sakes." And though the Jews became hostile on account of their reception, yet as "the gifts and calling of God are without repentance"—*lit.*, regret—the calling of these Gentiles and the gifts bestowed on them by the Spirit are unregretted by Him.

30–32. *The Gentiles believed not, yet obtained mercy. How was this?*

They were *lit.*, disobedient, but when, in the mercy of God, the Gospel was preached to them, they, believing in Christ, were accepted. So, writes Paul, may the disobedient Jews receive mercy through this Saviour, through whom mercy has been shown to you. God has concluded all in disobedience, that He might have mercy upon all who would receive it through His Son. Well might Paul exclaim, "O the depth of the riches both of the wisdom and knowledge of God! How unsearchable are His judgments, and His ways past finding out!"

CHAPTER XII.

1. *What does Paul mean by the "mercies of God"?*

It is, *lit.*, the *compassions of God*, which were so largely shown to both Jews and Gentiles who had accepted of Jesus. He had been compassionate to both—to the Jew, who, as a prodigal son, had wandered from his father's house until all his resources were exhausted; and to the Gentile,

whose vice and crime, like heated brands, had burned deep into his whole being. To both, now made partakers of His grace, Paul could say, "I beseech you by the compassions of God, that ye present your bodies."

Why does he say "present your bodies"?

He had shown in his vivid picture of their past lives, how by lust and passion, by vice and crime, they had degraded their bodies in yielding their members as instruments of unrighteousness unto sin. So here he exhorts, "present your bodies," *i.e.*, your whole being, to God, as those who are alive from the dead.

Why does he say "a living sacrifice"?

A Jew would best feel the force of the sentence, "a living sacrifice." Their sacrificial victims were given up to die. Present yourselves to God to live to Him.

"Be not conformed to this world." What does this mean?

It is, *lit.*, And fashion not yourselves to this age, which, in Gal. i. 4, he calls an "evil age." The world is not evil, for God made it, but the habits, principles, etc., of those who are led by the god of this age are evil. So he exhorts, Do not be like them.

2. *What had the renewing of the mind to do with transformation?*

To have a renewed mind is the only way to have a life according to godliness. When truth rules the mind, the mind will rule the body, and preserve it from surrounding evils. And it was only by a renewed mind that they would be able to prove or test the good, and acceptable, and perfect will of God.

3. *What is meant by the "measure of faith"?*

It is the portion or gift which each had received, not for personal ends, but for the good of the body.

6. In referring to their gifts, he names only one which may be called supernatural. How is it that these saints at Rome possessed so few, while the church at Corinth possessed so many ?

Because spiritual gifts were received through the apostles ; and as no one had then visited Rome, they were without those gifts which might have been conferred by them. In the opening of this epistle Paul expresses an ardent desire that he might see them, and impart some spiritual gift to their confirmation.

If no apostle had visited them, and according to Paul they had the gift of prophecy, how did they obtain it ?

Prophecy was not specially a gift of the Christian economy, as it was bestowed in every age. Either it had been received at Pentecost by the strangers of Rome, or given by the will of God.

8. " He that giveth, let him do it with simplicity." What is this ?

Another reading is "liberally," and this is very likely to be the true reading.

9. What is dissimulation ?

Hypocrisy, guile. Love must be real, not feigned.

11. " Not slothful in business." Does Paul refer to worldly business ?

No. It is, *lit.*, In diligence not slothful, and rather applies to every God-imposed duty, which should be vigorously pursued, *i.e.*, be earnest in doing all He requires from you.

12. " Rejoicing in hope." Is this hope in general ?

It is, *lit.*, In the hope rejoicing, in the tribulation enduring. It is the hope of the Gospel, which is to be the source of joy, but which also brings trial consequent upon fellowship with Jesus.

13. " Distributing to the necessity of saints, given to hospitality." Both are acts of benevolence ; what is the difference between them ?

The difference is in the objects, and not in the spirit which ministers to them. There were the needy in the family of God, and these were to have their need attended to ; and there were also persecuted saints who, when on travel, must be received into their houses, for Christ's sake.

18. " Live peaceably with all men." Is this possible ?

We cannot be responsible for what others may or will do ; but we must so act, that if there is not peace, the fault will not be ours.

19. What is avenging ourselves ?

Saying, doing, or thinking anything in retaliation for some wrong done to us. God claims the right to avenge, and we should not use His prerogative. We should bless and pray for them, and then leave every wrong that others may do to us with Him who will act wisely towards all His creatures.

20. Would refusing food to an enemy when hungry be avenging ourselves ?

Most certainly ; hence we need to watch against negative as well as positive vengeance.

CHAPTER XIII.

1. What are the " higher powers " to which the saints are to be subject ?

Rulers and authorities in the state ; indeed, all whose rule is God-appointed.

Why was it needful to exhort to this obligation ?

Because many of these rulers were persecuting and cruel, and this might cause the saints to fail in their God-imposed duties.

2. The saints were called upon to obey both God and rulers, but if rulers imposed laws contrary to God what were they to do ?

There is strictly but one authority, for there is no authority but of God;

for the authorities that be are ordained of God, and when kings and magistrates are obeyed, then God is obeyed. But if the claims of the inferior are contrary to the claims of the superior, they must not be obeyed. Nebuchadnezzar commanded the three Hebrew children to bow down to his image, but, though their king, they properly refused, and God defended their noble resistance.

4. *In urging obedience to magistrates or rulers, why does he refer to the sword ?*

The sword was an ancient symbol of magisterial authority, just as a crown was a symbol of kingly rule.

5. *Why does he say, " be subject, not only for wrath, but for conscience' sake " ?*

It was not merely to avoid suffering that they were to be obedient, but to please God. The highest form of service is that in which God is served, and not circumstances. This is obeying, not through fear or reward, but for conscience' sake.

7. *What was the difference between tribute and custom ?*

Tribute I judge to be the tax imposed on conquered subjects by the government under which they lived. Christ Himself paid this tax to the Romans, and met the claim on one occasion by the fish which Peter caught, and found in its mouth the required sum ; while custom was imposed on merchandise. Matthew was sitting at the receipt of custom when Jesus called him to the apostleship. There were, and still are, temptations to avoid these imposed dues. " Render to all their dues " is the direction of Paul. Christians should have as much pleasure in paying what is right as in receiving what is right. To please God in all things should be their daily joy.

8. *Does " Owe no man anything " prohibit debts in money ?*

I do not think that Paul is teaching here that they should not go into debt, or incur any obligation, but that every obligation should be met. The incurring of obligation is a matter that calls for prudence, and even the spirit of honesty is involved in it. It is easy to incur debts which there is no reasonable prospect of discharging, and self-denial would be a far safer and more honourable course. The believer should be just before God in all these things, and strictly " owe no man anything."

Why does he say, " but to love one another " ?

We owe this to all for the Lord's sake, and must never free ourselves from this obligation.

9, 10. *Why does he name the prohibitions of the law of Moses ?*

Because he had spoken of their obligation to love one another, and then affirms that when love reigned in the believer there would be neither adultery nor murder, dishonesty nor slander ; indeed, every evil thing would be ruled out of the life, because not in the heart, where love reigned. " For love worketh no ill to his neighbour ; therefore, love fulfils law.

11–13. *" And that knowing the time, that now it is high time to awake out of sleep," etc. To what does he refer ?*

The figure is a simple one, but we shall have to use the context of the epistle to make the proper application. The figure is of one who has slept through the night, but the morning watch has sounded, the dawn is approaching, and slumber must be shaken off, because an eventful day is at hand. We have seen in the epistle that a Pharaoh-like doom rested over a Pharaoh-like people. It had been spoken of by the prophets, but was specially detailed by Jesus, and the sentence rested like the darkness of night over all who by their sin would be involved in it. But the day of deliverance was at hand also, and the pure and obedient would escape the crushing doom. Hence the exhortation : " Let us walk honestly, as in the day "—*i.e.*, as those who have been enlightened, that we may share the deliverance.

14. *" But put ye on the Lord Jesus." If believers put on Christ in their immersion, why exhort them to put Him on again ?*

He does not exhort them to put Him on again, but to be invested with Jesus, instead of that sad immoral covering of a dissipated life. To put on Jesus in immersion is to put ourselves under His authority ; to be clothed with Him is to have on the fine linen, which is the righteousness of saints.

CHAPTER XIV.

1-4. *What does Paul mean by, " Him that is weak in the faith " ?*

He refers to one who, in fear of being defiled with Gentile preparations of flesh, confines himself entirely to herbs or vegetables. It is a Jew, we presume, who, from his former training under the law in relation to what was clean and unclean, would take this decided stand, and refuse to join his Gentile brethren in their ordinary meals. Had he believed the teaching of Jesus, that " there is nothing from without a man that entering in can defile him," he could have had no scruple about the kind of food prepared, but here he was weak, and Paul claims for him the forbearance of his brethren, who are cautioned not to reject him on this account. As a Jew, Paul could feel for his brethren in the flesh, having felt the difficulties connected with becoming a Christian. The weakness referred to,

therefore, is not of faith in Christ, but as to whether they were set free from that Jewish yoke. One who was accepted of God was not to be despised for his peculiarity in food. Hence he warns against judging one another, or, as he puts it, " judging another man's servant."

5. *" Let every man be fully persuaded in his own mind." Is sincere conviction of being right in our doing or not doing things sufficient to make them acceptable to God ?*

No. God's revealed will must decide their acceptability. It is not a man's esteem for a certain day or thing that will make it right before God. A man must be fully persuaded that he is guided by the will of God in all that he does.

6. *What does Paul wish to teach by referring to the different estimate in which days and food were held ?*

He wishes them to respect the conscientious scruples of each other. A Jew, even in Rome, might regard certain feast-days, and select certain meats, while a Gentile might be indifferent to both, but each was sincere in so doing ; and Paul claims that this sincerity should be respected, and not to judge each other.

10. *" We shall all stand before the judgment seat of Christ." Will believers have to stand there as well as the ungodly ?*

Paul makes no exception. Jesus will have to confess those who confessed Him, and deny those who denied Him. He is the Judge, and does not allow us to judge one another.

12. *Is this, " Every knee shall bow to Me, and every tongue confess to God," a proof of universal homage being rendered to Christ ?*

Paul has not quoted this writing to prove universal homage, but to prove that all men must receive their destiny from this Christ, as the context clearly proves. Very few even of the God-fearing Jews in the days of Paul would own Jesus of Nazareth as the risen and ascended Lord ; but all will have to bow before Him when seated on His judgment-seat. This solemn truth was to check their judgment of each other, as each would have to give an account of himself.

13, 14. *What is the stumbling-block to which he refers?*

The eating of meat by one enlightened to know his liberty to do so, but which grieves his brother who has not yet been delivered from the yoke of legal ceremonies. I know by the Lord, said Paul, that no food is unclean of itself, but if your brother is grieved with your liberty, consider him, and walk in love towards him, lest he stumble and fall through your liberty.

15–18. *How could one man be destroyed by the food of another?*

It is to its indirect results that Paul refers, and his allusion to these things claim our special consideration. It is true that the religion of Jesus makes no difference between one kind of flesh and another, but a Jew uninstructed in this liberty might count the system itself unclean, and so be driven from the Church and from Christ. The evil began with the food, but ended with apostacy; therefore the strong should bear with the weak, and not merely seek to please themselves. If eating and drinking were strictly required by the kingdom of God, then they must obey, whatever the result might be ; but as it was " righteousness, and peace, and joy in the Holy Spirit," they could yield their personal enjoyment of certain foods for their brothers' sake, and for Christ, who was pleased to accept such service when rendered to Him.

22. *Does " Hast thou faith? have it to thyself before God," apply to faith in general?*

I presume it applies to the matter before us. If it was faith in Christ, or anything commanded by Him, then it would be wrong to make it a private thing ; but when it related to food, it would be better not to insist upon even their own right, " For meat commendeth not to God." It would be far better to deny themselves that which is lawful, if a brother was thereby benefited.

22, 23. *" Happy is he that condemneth not himself in that thing which he alloweth." To what does this refer?*

In these closing verses he is speaking both to the strong and to the weak—to the strong who in his enlightened liberty disregards his weaker brother, and to the weak who act contrary to their faith. Both are warned and urged to act conscientiously.

CHAPTER XV.

1. *How does Paul prove that the " strong ought to bear the infirmities of the weak"?*

By presenting the example of Christ, who voluntarily suffered for others. In Him this principle was fully manifest, and He is an example to all.

3. *How did the reproaches of God fall on Jesus?*

Jesus came into the very scene where God was disobeyed, dishonoured, and set at naught ; and by His firm defence of God's claims, He endured all the reproach which had been heaped upon God.

4. *Is " Whatsoever things were written aforetime were written for our learning," a general statement?*

Yes, with a special application that if we endure as those who are given as examples of patience, we may have the hope and comfort of the promised reward. The Scriptures furnish the example, and when we have copied it into our life, we may be assured of sharing the prize with those who first won the promise. The Scriptures were written for our instruction, even in the matter of not pleasing ourselves.

5. *Is Christ the chief-example?*

Paul desires that they might all be like Jesus, and in His blessed spirit, helping each other, bearing with each other, self-denying for the sake of each other, they might with one mind and one mouth glorify God.

7. *Their own reception by Jesus is presented as an example. How were they to apply it?*

If we read *you* instead of "us," a reading now generally accepted, we shall be better able to see the force of his exhortation, "Wherefore receive ye one another," although there are these differences in eating and drinking, "as Christ received you," irrespective of your Gentile standing, "to the glory of God."

I have heard this verse quoted to prove that the immersed ought to receive the unimmersed at the Lord's Table. Is this a proper application of this text?

I should rather call it a perversion of the text. Paul is not teaching them to ignore the commands of Jesus, but to set aside their own appointed laws of exclusion, and to receive those who had received Christ, though still weak, *lit.*, powerless to break up old Jewish forms.

8. *"Christ Jesus was a minister of the circumcision." Does not this prove the higher claim of the Jew over the Gentile?*

Paul mentions the fact to show that it was not because they were superior to Gentiles that Christ became specially a servant to them, but because of a promise made to their fathers; but God, who promised them that the Messiah should come of their fleshly seed, also promised to Abraham that in his seed, the Mes-

siah, all the nations of the earth should be blessed.

9–12. *Why did Paul make these four quotations from the prophets about the Gentiles?*

In order to show that there should be fellowship in Christ of all those who believe in Him; hence in all these quotations both Jews and Gentiles are either named or implied, and called upon to rejoice together, the Gentiles with His people.

19. *Why does he refer to his very extensive circuit from Jerusalem to Illyricum?*

Because his mission among the Gentiles in all these places had been confirmed by mighty signs and wonders of the Holy Spirit, and to him it was an unanswerable proof that the believing among the nations were accepted of God.

20. *Why was he so anxious to preach Christ where He had not been named?*

That he might fully prove the truth of his great mission among the Gentiles: (1.) by the signs that accompanied his preaching, (2.) by the fruit that followed it, and (3.) to fulfil the prophets who had so largely spoken of this work, one being specially quoted by him, "To whom He was not spoken of, they shall see: and they that have not heard shall understand."

25–27. *Why does he refer to the contribution for the poor saints in Jerusalem made by the Gentiles, and given to him to carry to them?*

It was a very telling proof of their love in Christ, that Gentiles should so act towards Jews. True, he does not here urge them to so feel towards each other, but the fact is left to do its own work.

29. *"When I come to you, I shall come in the fulness of the blessing of the Gospel of Christ." What was this fulness?*

The gifts of the Spirit, which were

received by the laying on of the hands of the apostle, and which confirmed his testimony that Jesus had sent him to call the Gentiles into His favour. Paul knew that even in Rome this seal would be given, and this was one reason why he so anxiously desired to visit the imperial city.

CHAPTER XVI.

Does this chapter belong to the epistle?

It is an epistle itself, a commendatory letter, written by Paul on behalf of certain saints, and reveals to us by its brief statements the high Christian character which these early saints maintained; and also that, when passing from place to place, they carried with them letters of commendation to the brethren among whom they went to sojourn.

Were the saints named in this chapter living in Rome, or going to Rome?

They appear to be a company of believers who were returning to Rome from Corinth and its neighbourhood, where Paul wrote this letter, and he might possibly be stirred up to do so by having this opportunity of sending it to the saints in that place. In Acts xviii. 2, we read that Claudius commanded all Jews to depart from Rome, and that Priscilla and Aquila had found their way to Corinth, when after their conversion they became very helpful to the cause of Christ in that place. Here we have them named among the returning band, the edict having been cancelled, and they and other fugitives were again seeking the place of their adoption. The apostle is able to certify, that while in Asia they had lived noble lives, and done many noble deeds for Christ and truth, and he earnestly

commends them to the loving greeting of saints in Rome.

1. *Phebe, who is commended by Paul to the saints in Rome, is said to have been a servant of the church in Cenchrea. Was this an official position?*

It is, *lit., a deaconess of the church,* and whether officially appointed or the service lovingly taken up is not stated. She was doubtless a person of worldly means, for she had succoured many in their need, and even the apostle himself. Her love to Christ constrained her to labour for His Church, the apostle approving her noble service, and here claims for her any help she might need in her business in Rome.

4. *What does Paul mean by Priscilla and Aquila " laying down their own necks"?*

It is upon the neck of the beast that the yoke is put for service, hence it is used as a symbol of service. These two saints had willingly laboured to sustain Paul in his time of need at Corinth, and enabled him to preach without making any claim for his service. For their noble loving service on my account, said Paul, not only I give thanks, but also all the churches of the Gentiles.

5. *" Likewise greet the church that is in their house." Were these going along with them?*

Our translators in adding the word " greet," have given another meaning to Paul's words. We therefore leave it out and read, "Unto whom not only I give thanks, but also all the churches of the Gentiles, and the church in their house." Here we have three parties specially indebted to Aquila and Priscilla. (1.) Paul himself; (2.) the churches of the Gentiles universally; and (3.) the church that met in their house. Well might he say to these saints in Rome, " salute them," they are worthy of your love.

Epænetus is said to have been a firstfruit in Achaia for Christ. Is there anything in this calling for special notice?

Yes. It shows that Epænetus did not wait till others became Christians, but nobly yielded himself to Christ. He counted Christ worthy of his love, whatever others might do, and so became a first-fruit to Him. This early decision was highly appreciated by Paul, when commending him to their loving greeting.

7. *Andronicus and Junia are said to have been in Christ before him. How could this be if all saints are chosen in eternity?*

But men are not chosen in eternity but in time, and when they are united to Christ. Possibly these men were converted at Pentecost, and if so, before Paul. They had stood firm through all trial, and he asks for them a loving greeting.

16. *In urging the saints to salute one another with a kiss of love, does he make it a church ordinance?*

Not for the church when met together, but for the saints wherever they might meet. The kiss of love is not a church ordinance, but a saint ordinance.

17. *Who were those who caused divisions and offences?*

Most likely the teachers of Judaism, who, by insisting upon submission to its rites in order to salvation, caused divisions in the Church, and laid a stumbling-block in the way of many. The apostles had taught no such doctrine, and these saints are entreated to mark those who do so, and avoid them.

25. *"Now to Him who is able to establish you according to my Gospel." Why does he call it "my Gospel"?*

It is well to notice this peculiar designation. In chap. i. 1, he calls it the "Gospel of God," meaning by the sentence, the glad message which God made known to Abraham concerning the nations of the earth, who, on believing on Christ, should be blessed. Now Paul being sent by Jesus according to the will of God, to make known this message to the nations, here terms it "my Gospel," *i.e.*, that which I preach, as before he had termed it "the Gospel of God," *i.e.*, that which He preached to Abraham. These glad tidings, which Paul had made known from Jerusalem to Illyricum, had been confirmed by the Holy Spirit, and he earnestly desires that he might visit Rome that it might be confirmed there also.

"The preaching of Jesus Christ, according to the revelation of the mystery." What does this mean?

The mystery, — *lit.*, secret — was "that the Gentiles should be joint-heirs, and a joint-body, and joint-partners in the promise in Christ Jesus through the Gospel," and the preaching was in harmony with this revealed secret, *i.e.*, those who were to form the body, were called to it by the proclamation of a full and free salvation by Jesus Christ, and altogether irrespective of their former state.

"The mystery kept secret since the world began." Was this the beginning of time?

It is strictly *a secret which was concealed during the times of the ages,* *i.e.*, during the Jewish dispensation. And, although much was revealed in type and prophecy, yet this great purpose of God, that believing Gentiles with believing Jews should form the body of Christ, was concealed even from the prophets during the prophetic ages.

26. *"Kept secret since the world or ages began," and yet Paul says, "and by the Scriptures of the prophets . . . made known to all nations," etc. How can this be?*

It was the preaching of the Gospel of Jesus, which according to, or by, the scriptures of the prophets, was to be made known to all nations for their obedience to Him, and not the secret of the one body which was afterwards revealed to Paul.

THE FIRST EPISTLE OF PAUL THE APOSTLE TO THE

CORINTHIANS.

CHAPTER I.

Why did Paul write this letter to the Church at Corinth?

To deliver and preserve it from errors to which it was exposed, and which even then had led some to question the truth of the Gospel, and to turn aside after the devices of Satan.

To what errors do you refer?

To three very prominent forms of error—viz., Paganism, Grecian philosophy, and Judaism. Paganism, with its corrupting system of idolatry, was popular in Corinth, and the people generally were slaves to the vices it produced. Its influence affected many domestic arrangements, and even the depôts of food were under the control of idol priests. To maintain their liberty, and yet disown idolatry, required at times much wisdom and firmness, and Paul supplies in this epistle much necessary instruction for this end. Then there were schools of philosophy, both Platonic and Epicureans, and into one or other of these speculative systems the youths of the upper classes of society were trained. The speculations of these philosophers were often pitted against the facts of Christianity, and had on the minds of many a most damaging influence. The saints in Corinth had also to suffer from Judaising teachers, who sought to weaken the authority of Christ. The fruit of holiness was undeniably manifest among the saints, and yet this fruit was greatly imperilled by one or other of these prevailing systems. These evils are all distinctly dealt with in this epistle, and most valuable lessons are thus given, not only to them, but also to us, as far as these evils are repeated in our day.

1. *Would Paul be understood by the Corinthians in styling himself "a called apostle"?*

I do not think that Paul would use a word in any of his letters which those to whom he wrote would not understand; and when we recollect that he was there a year and six months, we feel sure they would have become familiar with his application of this word " called " to himself, as indicating that he had been specially visited, and sent on his great mission to the nations by the Lord Jesus.

2. *Why does he apply the term " called " to them also?*

Because their position was in some respects similar to his own. They had been called into the fellowship of the saints by a special visitation, and sealing of the Holy Spirit in spiritual gifts; and though Jewish brethren in the house of Cornelius were astonished when they saw this baptism of the Spirit, and the church in Jerusalem was excited by these strange reports, yet all had to own that God had to the Gentiles granted repentance unto life. This term " called," therefore, is applied to this peculiar aspect of their introduction into the grace of God.

4. Paul thanked God for the grace given to them. What favour does he specially refer to ?

To the large measure of spiritual gifts they had received, which, though they did not confer salvation upon the receivers, yet were powerful confirmations of the truth of the Gospel.

5, 6. What does he mean by "ye are enriched by Him in all utterance and in all knowledge" ?

The gift of tongues and of prophecy, which confirmed Paul's testimony concerning Christ.

7. Does Paul say that they were waiting for the return of Jesus from heaven ?

His words transposed would read, so that in waiting for the apocalypse —*lit.*, the manifestation of Christ— ye came behind in no gift. That is, you have not been disappointed in your trust, but have been largely enriched by Him, who shall also confirm you unto (omit "the," and read) an end, *i.e.*, until blamelessness in the day of our Lord Jesus Christ is attained.

10–13. Why does Paul urge them to maintain unity of mind, testimony, and judgment ?

Because divisions and contentions were rising among them, to their shame.

In what things did Cephas, and Paul, and Apollos present such diverging aspects as to make them the heads of parties which Paul condemns ?

Paul preached salvation through Christ for all, without the deeds of the law, while Peter placed himself on one occasion at the head of those who demanded that Gentiles should pass into the new covenant through the gates of Judaism (Gal. ii. 12). Apollos was an eloquent exponent of the expectant theory of John the Baptist, although the Messiah had

T

actually appeared long before the former delivered his orations in Ephesus and Corinth. Thus we have three distinct positions taken up by these men, two of them in opposition to the truth ; and though it was afterwards renounced, yet its effect is here showing itself in the church in Corinth, and has to be rebuked by Paul.

Was Paul wrong in his position, since he also is made the head of a party ?

The wrong was not in his preaching, but in their practice. It was a wrong both to Christ and to themselves to make Paul the head of a faction, and it is sternly rebuked by him. "Is Christ divided ? Was Paul crucified for you ? Or were ye baptised into the name of Paul ?" To ask these questions is to make apparent the folly of the course pursued by them. Christ is the head of His people, the shepherd of His flock, the husband of His bride, and the saviour of the body ; and for any one to be distinguished by the name of a human leader, or some appointed ordinance, or some principle of church polity, etc., is a dishonour to Him who alone rightfully claims to be our head. Paul rebuked this first act of schism in the Church as a dishonour to Christ, and if wrong then, it is so still. Let all beware of being led into this ruinous and Christ-dishonouring position.

14. "I thank God that I baptised none of you but Crispus and Gaius." Why did Paul say this ?

Because of the improper use they were about to make of his services ; or, as he states, "Lest any should say that I had baptised into my own name." As he had only baptised in Corinth the persons named by him, their desire to make him their leader was so far frustrated.

May we not judge from Paul thanking God that he had baptised so few, that he but lightly esteemed the ordinance of baptism?

Paul is not speaking here of the importance of baptism, but the non-importance of the baptiser, and it is unjust to charge him with doing one thing when he is really speaking of another.

17. *"For Christ sent me not to baptise but to preach the Gospel." Might he not have set aside the ordinance altogether, when it was not in his commission?*

No. For although sent with the glad message that Christ died for the Gentiles, and that through Him they might be saved, he had no power either to set aside or alter any part of the general commission. This commission was to continue to the end of the age, and therefore every disciple of Jesus must submit to it. Paul himself had been baptised, not by the special direction of Jesus, but according to this previous enactment of Christ. And while not compelled to personally baptise any of the converts led by him to Christ, he had to see that the commission was fully carried out.

"To preach the Gospel: not with wisdom of words." What does this imply?

The Corinthians would understand him to refer to the disputers of that age, whose oratory, though exceedingly attractive, was of no value to those who heard them. The message that "Christ died for our sins" concerned every man in Corinth, and not only revealed the guilt of all, but made known a remedy for that guilt. Paul was more disposed to instruct than to charm, to save the sinner than amuse him on his way to destruction.

18. *"Them that perish." What is this?*

It is, *lit.*, those who are perishing, *i.e.*, those who are loosing themselves away from the salvation which is in

Christ through their rejection of God's glad message.

How is the cross the power of God to the saved?

By delivering them from the guilt and practice of evil. It is by Jesus, who died upon the cross, that God is setting free from the bondage of sin those who have been its slaves. Through Jesus they are forgiven, and cease to love and practise that which caused His death.

Why does he refer to God's challenge of the wise, and the scribe, and the disputer of this age?

To show how their systems had failed to effect what the Gospel had really done. Philosophy had never turned men from vice and idolatry; but the Gospel, foolish as it might seem to them, had reached men's hearts, and reformed their lives, and thus had God made foolish the wisdom of this world, and proved its vaunted philosophy to be an empty boast.

22. *Why did the Jew seek for signs?*

He had been trained to expect them, for his religion was founded upon signs; but unfortunately he looked for demonstrations of power, rather than the light of truth. True, the religion of Jesus was not without its manifest tokens of power, as even these Corinthians, by a large reception of spiritual gifts could bear witness. But the grandest display of its power was in renewing the heart, and producing a new life, and for these priceless results the Jew never looked, and therefore the cross that produced them was foolishness to him. He would rather have seen the sea made dry by Omnipotent power than floods of vice dried up by penitent grief; or water flowing from a flinty rock, than tears of regret for a life of sin. So he stumbled at the stumbling-stone.

26–29. *I observe that the words*

"*are called,*" *at the close of this verse, are in italics.   Is this addition by our translators a proper one ?*

It is a very improper addition, and makes Paul to say, what he never intended,—viz., that not many wise men after the flesh, not many mighty, not many noble (are called by God). Now Paul is speaking of those whom God chose to carry His message of love, and not of those who were called by it.   The two words should be erased from every Bible, for thousands already have been misled by them.   Had they added *call you*, the truth would have been stated, but this is not required, as Paul's meaning is plain enough without it.   *For you see the calling of you, brethren, that not many wise according to flesh, not many powerful, not many high born ; . . . . that no flesh should glory in His presence.*   There had indeed been great changes effected in themselves, but they were indebted, not to philosophers but to Christ, not even to the messengers, but to the message which they brought of a once-crucified Jesus.

30. *Are "righteousness, sanctification, and redemption," fruits of faith in Jesus ?*

Yes, and also of the wisdom of God ; because His wisdom is manifest in these results.

What is "righteousness" ?

That holy life which is a fruit of faith in Jesus—the investment of the new man, when Christ is put on.

What is "sanctification" ?

Separation to God—holiness of heart and life.

What is "redemption" ?

Freedom from the evils which sin has entailed upon us, both in its practice and consequences, by the death of Christ Jesus.   To Him therefore we owe all these gracious results, and to Him belongs the glory of our redemption.

CHAPTER II.

1–3. *When Paul went with the testimony of God to Corinth, he says it was in fear and much trembling. Why did he tremble ?*

Lest they should refuse the testimony on account of the unfavourable circumstances attending its delivery.

What were these unfavourable things ?

His own infirmity, and persistent proclamation of Gospel facts, rather than the "enticing words of man's wisdom."   His preaching of the Anointed having been crucified, must have formed a striking contrast to the polished declamations of their accomplished orators.   He was therefore afraid lest they should be influenced by mere sound, and so reject his life-giving message.

If there was much to hinder their reception of the message, was there nothing to commend it ?

Two things at least which claimed their attention—(1.) Their own individual need of the pardon and peace proclaimed through Jesus.   (2.) The demonstration of the Spirit, which was given to prove its truth ; and which furnished a far more reliable basis than the wisdom or philosophy of man could supply.

6–8. "*Howbeit we speak wisdom among them that are perfect.*"   *What wisdom was this ; and who were these perfect ones ?*

The "wisdom of God" which Paul taught these saints, was God's perfected system of grace and privilege among believing Gentiles, and, although arranged beforehand, it was hidden even from prophets during the preceding Jewish ages.   They were called "perfect," because they had received the full complement of gifts which were bestowed through Jesus.

"*But we speak the wisdom of God in a mystery, even the hidden wis-*

dom," etc.   What is this hidden mystery ?

It is, *lit.,* the hidden secret, or the secret, which, although " ordained before the world,"—*lit.,* the (Jewish) ages — " unto our glory," yet was concealed during that period. The secret itself is, " That the Gentiles should be fellow-heirs, and of the same body, and partakers of His promise in Christ by the Gospel." So Paul explains in Ephesians iii. 6.

What was it that the " princes of this world " did not know ?

They are, *lit.,* the rulers of this age, *i.e.,* those who combined to put Jesus to death. What they did not know was the exaltation of the Gentiles. They put Him to death to prevent a class outside of themselves from gathering to Christ, but in so doing they enabled God to extend His grace from Jewish harlots and publicans, to sinners of the Gentiles. Had they known this, said Paul, they would not have crucified the Lord of Glory. And when it was known, for Paul did not hesitate to announce it to opposing Jews, they were the more intensely provoked by it.

9, 10. Is Paul's quotation from Isaiah, to show that these great things are hid from Christians, or from men in the prophetic age ?

To show that it was not revealed either to eye, or ear, or thought during that prophetic period ; but, said he, it is now revealed to us by His Spirit, and through us to all believers.

11–13. Why was Paul so certain that there was no mistake in his teaching ?

Because, said he, as the spirit of a man knows the things which are within him, so the Spirit of God knows the things of God, and having received this Spirit, we know the things that are freely given to us of God.

What does he mean by " comparing spiritual things with spiritual " ?

I presume he means, that as he spoke by the Spirit of God, and thus revealed the things freely given to them of God, he compared or judged who were spiritual by their reception of spiritual things, *i.e.,* the things revealed by the Spirit.

14. What does he mean by a " natural man " ?

One who refused to receive the revelations of the Spirit, through the appointed agents, and counted it foolishness because he judged all by his own reason. This error was the fruit of pagan philosophy or rationalism.

15. " He that is spiritual."   To whom does he refer ?

To one who practically received the revelations given, and whose life and spirit were conformed to those revelations.   Such a one decerned and received the truth, and was above the judgment of the mere rationalist who refused these divine communications.

CHAPTER III.

1. Why was it that Paul could not speak to these Corinthians as spiritual, but as carnal ?

Because they were not obedient to the truth, but had become flesh-ruled instead of truth-ruled. Their strife, envying, and disregard one for another, had made this abundantly manifest, and it is with much pain of heart that he has at once to condemn their carnality, instead of instructing them in the privileges of saints.

2. " I have fed you with milk." What was this milk ? and why were they not able to receive meat ?

Milk for babes, both in their natural and spiritual state is proper food, since even Peter wrote to Jewish believers, " As new-born babes desire ye the sincere milk of the word, that ye may grow thereby "

(1 Peter ii. 2.) But, as the babes for whom Peter prescribed milk as a proper diet to begin with, continued so long in their babyhood, that even Paul in his epistle to them as Hebrews, years afterward, had to reprove them for want of proper development; so here at Corinth, although they had been fed with milk even by an apostle, they had not grown in grace and had to receive a like rebuke. The milk— here used as a symbol of the truths he taught them—was the needful instruction derived from those life-begetting facts which he had "first of all" delivered unto them. The life and spiritual strength which might have been developed from a reception of these facts of Christ's death for sins, etc., should have matured into a life of holiness by separation from all evil, and this was the end which he had in view. He had indeed shown in chap. i. 8, that Christ was able to confirm them by the truth, until this end—blameless-ness—should be attained, and for this end the milk had been supplied by himself. His effort, however, had so far failed, because nearly every chapter in this epistle contains, either a direct charge of evil practised by them, or their association with it is implied. Instead of being prepared to receive his inspired teaching upon their standing and privileges, such, for instance, as that given to the Ephesians, he has to point to their glorying in leaders of their own selection; to their tendency to depreciate apostolic authority; to their being puffed up with a fornicator; to their going to law with brethren; to their dissolving the marriage bond without a God-given reason, etc. The list of charges is indeed very serious, and one does not wonder that he should write, "And I, brethren, could not speak unto you as unto spiritual."

4. *"For while one saith, I am of Paul, etc., are ye not carnal?"* *Is it wrong to wear party names?*

Most certainly. It is wrong in principle and condemnable in practice, for any person or persons to profess to have Christ as their leader or Lord, and at the same time to be moving under the banner of some human leader, or principle, or doctrine, or nation, that must more or less determine the action of those who do so. The man may be a good man, and the distinguishing doctrine divine, but if he was as good as Paul or Peter, and the doctrine from heaven, we should have neither one nor the other inscribed on our banner. Let us have no master but Christ, no head but Him who bought us with His blood.

6. *Some persons say that Paul may plant and Apollos may water, but all will be unavailing unless God gives the increase. Is this what Paul teaches here?*

There is a wide difference between Paul's statement and theirs. He affirmed a fact, they utter a notion. In a very simple figure, he shows the servant position they occupied,— *I planted, Apollos watered, and God gave growth,*—in order that God might be honoured as the Lord of the field. But to teach that a person may work in God's field, and no good follow, unless God may happen to bless the effort, is confusion.

7. *"But God that giveth the increase."* *Why give prominence to this fact?*

To show the folly of giving honour to the servant when the Master alone should be honoured. The field was God's, the Gospel seed was His also. Even the servants, Paul and Apollos, were from Him, and were both working for one Master. To say I am for Paul, and I for Apollos, was to misjudge the whole matter.

10. *Why does Paul refer to the foundation ?*

Because he had spoken of God's building, and His building must have a right foundation, and upon that foundation the right material must be laid, or shame and loss would follow to all concerned.

How could Paul say, " I laid the foundation," when, according to prophecy, it must be God-laid ?

So it was. God raised Jesus from the dead, and so, according to Isaiah, laid it in Zion; but Paul was the first to announce in Corinth that Jesus was the Christ, and now he affirms that there is no other foundation or sure resting-place for man ; and warns all to beware, in building upon it, that they build the right material.

12. *Paul speaks about building on the foundation, wood, hay, stubble, gold, silver, and precious stones. Are persons or doctrines intended by these symbols ?*

Persons, I presume. The foundation is a person, and the material must be in harmony with the foundation. You may build persons upon Christ as a foundation, but not doctrines. You may associate doctrine or teaching with the persons, because either truth or error must be used in giving position. If the truth was used and accepted, then the material would be fitly termed gold, silver, or precious stones; but if error or false teaching, then the result would be wood, hay, stubble,—all of which apply to different classes. Paul preached Christ Jesus, the once crucified, but then risen and ascended Lord ; and, according to Luke, " Many of the Corinthians, hearing, believed, and were baptised " (Acts xviii. 8). Others followed, preaching Judaism and philosophy, which could never unite to Christ. The one might cut the flesh in circumcision, and the other puff it up with vain thoughts, but neither gave it up to death; and without dying the true life could not be reached. The material could be only wood, hay, stubble, and would be burned up. And even if the builder himself was saved, yet it would be as by fire.

15. *How could he be saved by fire ?*

By himself enduring the same test that would be applied to his work. Fire, as a symbol, is in appropriate harmony with those already employed. Wood, etc., would be consumed ; gold and silver would abide the test. Neither Judaism nor philosophy could prepare men for the day when God shall judge the secrets of men's hearts by Jesus Christ. The Gospel of Christ alone can do that.

16. *Why does he remind them that they were God's temple, and must be fitted for the Spirit to dwell in.*

To awaken in them a sense of responsibility, and to show the need of purity of heart and life. The tendency of the doctrines, against which he seeks to guard them, was to produce evil, and God's temple must be holy or He would not dwell there. He wished them to know that a mere form of religion would avail nothing.

" The Spirit of God dwelleth in you." How did He dwell in them ?

By the truth, the practical reception of which became the medium of His access to their minds, and the refusal of which the cause of His departure.

" If any man defile the temple, him shall God destroy." How destroy him ?

For one word in Greek our translators have given us " defile " and " destroy." There should have been uniformity in rendering, because what they would do to God's temple He would do to them. If they marred or corrupted it, He would mar or corrupt them. Destroy is too strong a word, and they have not used it in rendering this Greek word in any other place.

21. *Why does he say, " Therefore let no man glory in men. For all are your's " ?*

To reprove their folly in selecting one servant when God had graciously given them so many ; but the bearing of their choice they had not perceived. If Paul was their choice, then Cephas was ignored ; or, if Apollos was the selected leader of a party, then both Peter and Paul were set aside. All were God's servants, and were given for their need, and if Christ was theirs, all was theirs.

22. *If the selection of one servant of God was the rejection of another, would not a selection of one truth be a rejection of others ?*

So Paul seems to teach, and since Christ, as God's heir, inherits all things, so they, being heirs with Christ, possessed all in Him. "Whether Paul, or Apollos, or Cephas, or the world, or life, or death, or things present, or things to come ; all are your's."

CHAPTER IV.

1. *When Paul says, " Let a man so account of us as the ministers of Christ,"—does he refer to some one specially ?*

I think so, because, as in chapter xv., he refers to one who questioned the doctrine of the resurrection which he preached, so here is one who questioned the position he occupied. He therefore asks for himself and others to be allowed to stand in their true place. They did not assume to be more in their joint labours than ministers—*lit.*, underrowers—*i.e.*, persons acting under the command of a superior—and

stewards—*lit.*, house-distributors of the mysteries—*lit.*, secrets—of God. And having been called and entrusted with a knowledge of His will, they were simply working with and for Him.

3–5. *Had his motives and action been judged by these Corinthians ?*

It would appear so. Possibly first by an individual and then by the Church, who foolishly yielded to the snare. We see, however, how nobly he rises above their judgment in relation to his high trust. "But with me it is a very small matter that I should be judged of you, or of man's judgment "— *lit.*, man's day ; and asks that their judgment should be suspended till the Lord should come, and then all who deserved it would have praise of God.

6. " *And these things I have in a figure transferred to myself and Apollos for your sakes," etc. What does this mean ?*

It is a simple reference to himself and Apollos, as an example of oneness in labour, and was intended as a reproof. Paul was not envious or puffed up against Apollos, nor Apollos against Paul, and he wished their example to be copied by them, and not to be puffed up one against another.

7. *Why were they puffed up ?*

Through their gifts, which, though bestowed in grace for the glory of Christ, were being used for self-exaltation. Paul's appeal to them is a grave charge upon their moral honesty, "If thou didst receive, why dost thou glory as if thou hadst not received ? "

" *For who maketh thee to differ from another ? " is applied by some to conversion. Is it a proper application ?*

No. It is a perversion of the word to so apply it. Paul is speaking of the difference made by the Spirit in the bestowal of gifts, and not of conversion. To turn to Christ was the privilege of all, but gifts given to those who had turned were according to His own will, and for the profit of all others.

8. *"Now ye are full, now ye are rich,"* etc. *Is not this strange language?*

Yes, very strange indeed; but I judge it to be an ironical repetition of their own false estimate of their state. The Saviour similarly repeated the false estimate of the Laodiceans, " Thou sayest I am rich," etc., but only to warn them of their delusion. These Corinthians were being misled by false teachers, who opened out to them a far easier path than the cross which Paul preached. To him it plainly taught that glory could only be reached through suffering, and to teach otherwise was only a snare. Most graciously indeed did Christ accept all who received Him as their leader and Saviour, forgiving all their sins without any previous merit, but the first step involved self-denial in taking up the cross. To offer any easier course was only like Bunyan's bye-path meadow, which tempted the pilgrims into a wrong position.

9–14. *Why does Paul refer to his own sufferings and shame?*

In order to furnish a practical reply to the delusive thought that they had found an easier path than their first teachers, and reigned as kings without them. His reply intimates : If you reign, we do not; if you are full, we are hungry. " Even unto this present hour we both hunger and thirst, and are naked, etc. I write not these things to shame you, but as my beloved sons I warn you," *i.e.,* of the snare into which false teachers have led you.

" Naked." *Was Paul really naked?*

Not stark-naked, but often destitute of sufficient clothing through the violence of his foes. In 2 Cor. xi. 27 he refers to the same, but uses the terms "cold and nakedness."

16, 17. *Why does he say " be ye followers of me"?*

It is, *lit.,* "be imitators of me," *i.e.,* as I have set aside everything to bring to you the Gospel for your conversion, so do you set aside everything that would hinder your Christian life. And to help you to do this, " I have sent Timothy, who is my beloved son, and faithful in the Lord, who shall bring you into remembrance of my ways which be in Christ, as I teach everywhere in every church."

18. *Why were some puffed up with the thought that Paul would not return to Corinth?*

Because he had power to punish transgressors, and if he went, these perverters would be in danger. But he assures them that he would come and test their boastful speech.

20. *" For the kingdom of God is not in word, but in power."* *Why does Paul say this?*

To remind those Judaising teachers at Corinth, who were setting him at defiance, that there was more than testimony in connection with the kingdom of Christ—there was power, and though the reference to it is as gentle as possible, it would one day crush their system out of existence.

CHAPTER V.

1. *" It is reported commonly that there is fornication among you."* *Why does Paul refer to this manifestation of evil in the church?*

For several reasons I judge, each of which it would be well to ponder. (1.) They had been puffed up with their newly-accepted philosophy, and here was the sad fruit of it, that one in the church should have his father's wife, a sin not practised even among the Gentiles. This fruit of their philosophy showed their folly rather than wisdom, and to have mourned instead of being puffed up would have shown a better spirit. (2.) It was needful to remove the evil if possible, and this must be done by their removal of the offender, and thus refusing any longer participation with the evil. He therefore tells them what they are under obligation to do as the body of Christ, and what would be the result if they did not.

3. *" For I verily, as absent in body, but present in spirit, have judged already." What does he mean ?*

That he had already delivered his testimony as an apostle, and under it they were called to act as by the authority of Jesus.

4. *What does he mean by " and my spirit, with the power of our Lord Jesus Christ" ?*

My testimony, spirit being used for the judgment declared, which, as an apostle, Christ would endorse.

5. *Paul commanded that the fornicator should be delivered to Satan for the destruction of the flesh. Can the Church do so still ?*

The Church does not require to do this, as an apostle has done it already. The Church must separate from her fellowship all such evil doers, lest they become partakers of their sins, but the declared doom of the fornicator must be inflicted by God. To take the members of Christ, and make them the members of an harlot is a sin that God will judge with physical judgment. It may require the remainder of life to prove it, but in the end this will be manifest.

6. *Why does he refer to the well known effect of leaven in the lump ?*

To warn them what the end would be. They had allowed evil in their midst, and the corruption of the whole assembly would certainly follow. The only way to avoid this would be the removing of the evil,

that they might be a new or purged lump.

7. *It is the old passover arrangement that is here referred to. Why use it to a Gentile assembly ?*

But there were Jews in that assembly, and these would feel at once the force of his allusion to the passover. Besides, the Gentiles were instructed both about its typical purpose and the lesson applied in the exhortation that followed. They could scarcely have failed to learn that on the fourteenth day of the first month, ere the passover was killed, all the Jews put from their habitations all leaven, and for seven days remained strictly free from it. Thus were they prepared for Paul's exhortation—"Purge out therefore the old leaven, that ye may be a new lump, as ye are unleavened, for even Christ our passover is sacrificed for us." Then he exhorts, let the feast be kept, not with the leaven of malice and wickedness, but with sincerity and truth unleavened. In the old Jewish feast all leaven was to be put away, so in the feast which is to continue through the Christian's life all evil must be put away.

8. *"Therefore let us keep the feast, not with old leaven," etc. Is leavened bread forbidden at the Lord's table ?*

It is not against the use of leavened bread at the table of the Lord that he is exhorting, for this would not defile, but against the practice of evil, which defiles the doer of it. It is not leavened bread that was to be put away, but malice and wickedness.

" Malice and wickedness." Why name these two forms of evil ?

Because it was intended to reach two classes—the Jew, who was most in danger of inward evil, as malice, guile, hypocrisy, and envy ; and the Gentile, who was most in danger of external vice, through old associations with heathenism. But both the inward and the outward evil must be put away, for the feast of the Christian's life must be kept in purity.

9–11. "*I wrote unto you in an epistle,*" etc. *Had Paul written a former epistle to these Corinthians?* .

It would appear so, but having served its special purpose it is now lost to us.

Why does he again refer to this subject of association with fornicators?

To make more plain the course to be pursued by them. Their intercourse in trading was a necessity which was not forbidden; but if a brother became a fornicator, or a drunkard, with him they were not even to eat.

12, 13. *Why did Paul refuse to judge those who were outside the church?*

Because the judgment of those outside belonged to God, and with the judgment of all such he would have nothing to do.

"*Do not ye judge them that are within.*" *How could they do this?*

By separating the ungodly from the assembly, according to God's direction; and thus evil-doers were judged.

CHAPTER VI.

1. *In challenging their prosecutions of each other, why does Paul say, "Dare any of you?"*

Because they were doing what had been forbidden by Jesus, and therefore asks, How dare you do this? How can you so violate the spirit of Christianity by prosecuting your brethren?

2. "*Do ye not know that the saints shall judge the world?*" *What judgment is this?*

It is not the judgment of persons, because that prerogative belongs to God alone, as stated in chap. v. 13, "Them that are without," *i.e.,* the world, "God judgeth"; but of things

of the world, or, as stated in ver. 4, "Ye have judgments of things pertaining to this life." If, then, this prerogative is given to you in the church, why do you go to law, and that before unbelievers?

3. "*Know ye not that we shall judge angels?*" *Are these celestial beings?*

No, there is nothing either in the context, or even in the Bible, to indicate that saints shall judge celestial beings. The word "angels" here is *lit.* messengers, and refers to those who visited the churches professing to bring divine messages. Such persons were subject to the test or judgment of those who were gifted by the Spirit to try them. It is to these that John refers when he says (1 John iv. 1), "Beloved, believe not every spirit,"—*i.e.,* prophet or messenger, — "but try the spirits whether they be of God, because many false prophets are gone out into the world." The gift of "discerning of spirits" was bestowed upon some in the church, that it might be preserved from false messengers. So Paul adds, If such judgment is given to us, how much more things that pertain to this life?

4–6. "*Set them to judge who are least esteemed in the church.*" *Who are these?*

It will be better to read as in the Revised Version, "Do ye set them to judge who are of no account in the church?" referring doubtless to heathen magistrates; and, because Christ had given them power to judge their own differences, of which they had not availed themselves, Paul had to condemn their unkind practice. To go to him with their brethren before unbelievers was a dishonour to Christ, their common head.

7. *What course does Paul commend?*

That the judgment of wise brethren

be obtained in all matters of dispute, and where decisions could not be obtained, to rather take wrong and be defrauded, than go to law before unbelievers.

9, 10. *"Be not deceived, neither fornicators nor idolators," etc. Why does he give such a sad list of crimes?*

Paul's statements in relation to these debasing sins are general, but they are intended to have a special application to the Corinthian church. They had already tolerated fornication in a brother, and this act was in Paul's judgment as leaven, which, unless removed, would soon leaven the whole lump. He has therefore to warn them of separation from the kingdom of God, by declaring God's judgment against these sins.

11. *"And such were some of you: but ye are washed." What does this mean?*

It is *lit.*, "And these things some of you were, but ye bathed away"— *i.e.*, washed from you these vile practices, or, in other words, they had voluntarily set themselves free from these vices in their baptism, not from the guilt, but from the practice. This is what is meant in the words of Ananias to Saul, "Arise, and be immersed, and bathe from thee thy sins." True, immersion is done by an immerser, but the surrender is the voluntary act of the subject. And, as the putting away was expressed in immersion, it was fitly termed a "bathing away."

"But ye are sanctified." What is this?

It is *lit.*, "Ye *were* sanctified,"— *i.e.*, separated to God, set apart to Him and to His service, instead of the service of sin. There was not only a severance from the sins and vices of the old life, but devotedness to God in a new life most forcibly expressed.

"But ye are justified." What is this?

Lit., ye *were* made righteous. It was a complete contrast to their former state, and was effected by their loving reception of the precepts of the Spirit of God through the apostles.

If these gracious results followed their acceptance of Christ, why has Paul to bring so many charges against them?

Because they had become unfaithful in their new life. Or, after abandoning those gross vices of their former state, they had allowed themselves to be ensnared into the sins charged against them; and he has now to show that these were inconsistent and evil.

12. *"All things are lawful unto me, but all things are not expedient." Why does he make these statements?*

It is a fine illustration of an unselfish spirit, and is worthy of being copied by every saint. Paul had his rights as a man, and might have insisted upon them, but we see him even refusing to use the liberty he possessed if self-denial would better serve the cause of Christ. But his own course of action is presented for imitation, so he adds, "Now the body is not for fornication, but for the Lord,"— *i.e.*, your body as well as your spirit belongs to Christ, and to use it contrary to His will is to sin against Him.

18. *Paul distinguishes between fornication, which is against a man's own body, and other sins which are without the body. Do other Scriptures sustain this view?*

Yes; and in their general testimony we can better see his meaning. As a sin, fornication stands alone, both in its criminality and its judgment. This is the reason why Paul delivered this fornicator over to Satan for the destruction of the flesh, and is most likely the "sin unto death" to which John alludes (1 John v. 16).

If the fornicator forsake his sin, will he not be forgiven ?

Yes, and his "spirit will be saved in the day of the Lord Jesus," but judgment may rest on the flesh even though grace may be thus shown to the repentant one. John writes, respecting this sin unto death, "I do not say that he shall pray for it," —*i.e.*, for deliverance from the affixed doom. It is, indeed, well when the sin is forsaken, and forgiveness from the guilt of it obtained, but the guilty will have to endure consequences which God may never set aside. David obtained forgiveness for his sin in the matter of the wife of Uriah, but the sentence, "the sword shall never depart from thine house," was never withdrawn.

CHAPTER VII.

"It is good for a man not to touch a woman." What does Paul mean by this answer to their question ?

That it was not good to enter into the married state ; but this restriction applied only to saints, and was enjoined as best for the then existing distress.

2–4. Here he says, "Let every man have his own wife," etc. Why does he say this ?

To show that where the union did exist, it must be maintained in all purity and faithfulness, in order to avoid possible temptations. There was no liberty to set aside mutual claims, but all must be rendered as in the sight of God, and what was just to each other.

6. "I speak this by permission, not of commandment." Would it not then be uninspired ?

Not uninspired when he had the Spirit of God, but was given as advice under the circumstances, and not by express command.

10. Why has he to forbid the separation of those who were married ?

Some misunderstanding seems to have arisen among them, chiefly through Judaising teachers, who still held to the command of God, as given through Moses, forbidding alliance with the nations. Paul had to show them that Christianity did not dissolve the marriage bond when formed, but left its obligations in full force.

14. What does he mean by the unbelieving wife being sanctified by her believing husband ? Does not sanctification mean holiness ?

Yes ; but as being "sanctified" may apply to things, states, and persons, we have always to learn to what it should be applied. A vessel, a lamb, or a man sanctified, or set apart for God, would be fitted for its position by such a consecration. Now, marriage is an appointment of God, and the fruit of it in children is accepted or approved of by Him, whatever their spiritual relation to Him individually may be. It is on this ground that Paul forbids separation when one became a Christian. It is as if he had said, You must not leave each other, because marriage is of God, and you are sanctified in each other to the end for which it was appointed, "else were your children unclean, but now are they holy."

Would the faith of one of the parents be a proper qualification for the baptism of their children, as is now asserted by some ?

By no means, unless God had so appointed, which He has not. It is not because children are born of one or both believing parents that they are qualified for baptism, since personal faith is the qualification appointed by Jesus. Besides, this verse does not refer to baptism at all, and it is an unjust application of it to use it in support of baby baptism.

18–23. *Why does he exhort, not only the married to abide in the union formed, but also the circumcised and the slave to abide in their calling?*

From his teaching we learn that Christianity does not break up any civil relation, and that every relation should be so used that Christ may be honoured. It may appear strange that Paul should urge a slave to be more anxious to honour Christ than seek deliverance from his slavery; but when rewarded by Christ with eternal freedom, it would more than counterbalance all the trials of slavery.

24. *" Let every man therein abide with God." What does this mean?*

Associate God with your position, your trials, and duties, and this will enable you to do or suffer whatever may fall to your lot.

CHAPTER VIII.

1. *What had these Christians to do with " things offered to idols" that Paul should specially refer to it?*

They had nothing to do with them directly, but they were in danger of indirectly conceding what would not be true—viz., that the idol was something when it was nothing. From the context we gather that sacrifices were offered to idols by their worshippers, and that these sacrifices were afterwards sold as food for the people, and counted by them as better than food not so offered. Many of those who had been led by the preaching of the apostles to a knowledge of the living and true God could eat this food without any regard to the idol, but there were others, whose conscience or power of judgment being weak was defiled, being emboldened by the action of their brethren. He therefore urges a due regard for the weak brother, and bids them beware lest their liberty should become a stumbling-block to those who were weak.

Why does he say, " Knowledge puffeth up, but love edifieth"?

Possibly the first part of it is used as a general statement, but intended to have a special application to them. Their superior knowledge in respect to idols had induced vanity of mind, as if they knew everything, when it was manifest that of many things they knew very little, and especially of love to their brethren.

3. *" If any man love God, the same is known of Him." What does this mean?*

John may help us to see the meaning when he says, " He that loveth God will love his brother also" (1 John iv. 21). If any one love God, He has been made known or manifested by loving action.

6. *" To us there is one God ;" but why does he add, and " One Lord Jesus Christ"?*

Because some who believed the former did not understand and receive the latter, and this was the cause of their want of humility and love.

11. *How could the weak brother perish through the action of another?*

By being confirmed in the delusion that an idol was a reality. In thus confessing to it, Jesus, as the one Lord, was ignored, and to perish, or be loosed away from His salvation, was the only alternative.

CHAPTER IX.

1–6. *Why does Paul refer to his apostleship?*

Because, having been questioned in Corinth, it had become necessary to defend both his calling as an apostle and his liberties as a servant of Christ.

" *Have I not seen Jesus Christ our Lord ?* " *Did this constitute his proof of being an apostle ?*

No. These Corinthians were the seal of his apostleship, for the gifts they possessed were bestowed through him. It is strange this evidence should have been overlooked by them.

On what ground does he claim to be supported as a servant of Christ ?

On the simple ground that they had not only accepted him, but had been benefited by his labours. He therefore claims a right to be supported in his labour, or, as he states it, to have power to eat and drink, to lead about a sister, a wife, etc., and to forbear working while labouring on their behalf.

7. *Why does he refer to the soldier, the husbandman, and the shepherd ?*

Because each of these cases furnish an illustration which serves to prove that his claim was not an unreasonable one. The soldier did not fight at his own cost, nor the shepherd tend his flock without partaking of the milk of the flock. This was counted reasonable, and he applies it to himself and other labourers without hesitation.

8–10. *From reason Paul advances to Scripture ; but is not his plea from the law concerning oxen a questionable one ?*

If we believe Paul was writing by the Holy Spirit, we must hold, when God commanded the Jew not to muzzle the mouth of his ox while treading out the corn, that in that merciful precept He was teaching about the return which those should receive who should afterward preach the Gospel of Christ. Such use of this precept of the law may at first sight appear strange, but when we remember that times, and seasons, and days, and moons, and lambs, and garments, and metals, and colours, etc., were all used by God

as shadows of heavenly things, we shall cease to wonder at Paul's application of this precept of the unmuzzled ox to himself and other labourers in the Gospel.

12. *Paul's defence of his rights seems to be unanswerable. Why did he not avail himself of them ?*

His reasons will show how deeply he partook of the spirit of his Master. "Nevertheless, we have not used this power, lest we should hinder the Gospel of Christ."

13, 14. *Paul here speaks of those who minister in holy things, and those who serve at the altar. Were there two classes serving and sustained by the worshippers of the temple ?*

There were the Levites who served in the more external work of temple rites, while the priests alone served at the altar, yet both were sustained by the gifts of worshippers.

Had he any special object in referring to these two classes ?

It is very likely that he wished to show that not only apostles who were sent with a direct message from Christ were entitled to be supported in their service, but also such men as Barnabas and Apollos, who watered and encouraged the saints, and thus helped on the work of the Gospel.

16. *Why does he say " Woe unto me if I preach not the Gospel " ?*

Because he was sent by the Lord Jesus to preach it, and therefore, whether sustained or not, he went forward in his great work, looking not to men but to Christ for reward. Paul did not wait for engagements or even invitations, but wherever there was an open door, if it was possible, he entered it with the glad message of the salvation of God.

18. " *That I abuse not my power in the Gospel.*" *What is the meaning of this twofold reference ?*

His power in the Gospel was his right to be sustained whilst preaching it, but in Corinth he had purposely restrained himself from using this power. In this way he had set himself free from all claim, but having received a stewardship from Christ to preach to all, he had made himself servant to all, that none might be overlooked.

20–22. *There are four classes named here—"the Jews," and those "under the law;" then, "those without law," and "the weak." What is the precise position of each of these classes?*

The "Jews" were the fleshly descended seed of Abraham, through Isaac and Jacob; while those "under law" were Gentile proselytes, who by being circumcised had put themselves under the law. Those without law were the Gentiles who had never been put under the law of Moses; while "the weak" were those who through fear of being defiled by flesh ate only herbs.

How could Paul adapt himself to their varied positions?

His writings will best explain how he did so. (1.) "To the Jews he became as a Jew." Here we must note that Paul was a Jew, and when he entered into a synagogue we see him opening their Scriptures, reading the promises made to them through their fathers, and sharing with them the soul-exulting hope of the Messiah, for whom all were looking, taking up the prophecies of His sufferings, death, and resurrection, and then closing with "This Jesus whom I preach unto you is the Christ." Thus we see him as a Jew, with the Jews. (2.) "To them that are under the law, as under the law," *not being myself under the law* (this last sentence is now added by scholars as part of the text), "that I might gain them that are under the law." Having himself obtained deliverance from the galling yoke of the law, how feelingly he could now urge upon others in a like position to

seek this blessed freedom. (3.) "Them that are without law, as without law," *i.e.*, the Gentiles. To these Paul could preach the Gospel of salvation, even the law of Christ, under which every sinner could put himself and be saved. (4.) "To the weak I became as weak." Paul could take his place alongside of the weak one, and give up flesh, or wine, or anything that would stumble his brother. In this way he was made all things to all, that he might by all means save some.

24. *Why does he refer to the race?*

Because the contests known as the Olympic games, and the laws which governed defeat or victory, and the severe training to which men subjected themselves, furnished a most impressive illustration and example to all Christians. It is as if he had said, shall the believer who is looking for an incorruptible crown be less earnest, less self-denying, than those who are striving for a corruptible crown? Let it not be: "so run that ye may obtain."

27. *Could Paul be a "castaway," or lose the prize?*

Paul counted upon no special favour being shown to himself more than others, or contrary to the arrangements of Christ which he had made known. His appeal to these Corinthians is an appeal to his own heart. His warning to them is heeded by himself. I keep under my body, lest after preaching to others I myself should be a castaway. Paul expected to be approved by Christ, only on the ground of having been faithful to Him.

CHAPTER X.

1, 2. *Why does Paul refer to the privileges and failures of the children of Israel?*

In order to warn the Corinthians that even a sincere acceptance of

Christ, and present standing in Him, would not secure freedom from judgment, should they become unfaithful to Christ. The fathers of the Jewish nation were all under the cloud, and all passed through the sea; they ate of the manna which God gave them, and drank of the water from the smitten rock; and yet they were overthrown in the wilderness, because of their unfaithfulness.

" Now these things were our examples." Does this apply to the judgments as well as privileges?

It is, *lit., but these things became types to us,* applicable to both privileges and judgments. In their baptism into Moses their accepted leader, they became types of believers who are baptised into Jesus, in whom all spiritual privileges are enjoyed; and in the judgments which followed their disobedience, God has shown that He will judge those who are unfaithful.

How were they baptised unto Moses?

It is, *lit., and all into Moses immersed themselves, in the cloud, and in the sea.* It is well to note that up to this time they had been under Pharaoh as their Lord; but, under the guidance of Moses, who had been commended to them by signs and wonders in Egypt, they marched into the cloud, and were thus immersed into him, by voluntarily accepting him as their deliverer.

How could they be immersed in a cloud?

Just as really as in water, since covering is the root-idea of immersion. The Israelites went voluntarily into the cloud, and thus were covered; and by going into the cloud they went into the sea, and in this strange pathway found deliverance.

3, 4. What does he mean by " spiritual meat," and " spiritual drink," and a " spiritual rock"?

Meat and drink which shadow forth spiritual truth. Their manna was a type of the living bread, even Christ, on which believers feed; and who is also the living water which flows down in the truth into every believing heart.

7–10. Paul names four transgressions of the Israelites, viz., idolatry, fornication, tempting of God, and murmuring. Why refer to these four?

He had convicted them of four similar transgressions, and he wished them to reflect upon their sins in the light of the judgments which followed those typical transgressions. Some of them had made concessions to idols, by eating of meat offered to them; and the Church had also fellowship with fornicators. They had also tempted Christ by choosing party leaders, and had murmured at the restraint which Paul had laid upon their carnal ambition. Their condition therefore was perilous, and they were urged to profit by these examples.

11. He says, the " ends of the world" had come upon them. What was that?

It is, *lit., the ends of the ages.* The ends of the jubilees or periods into which the dispensation was divided had arrived, or rather had culminated in the precious fulfilment of its types and shadows. This harvest of ripened grain, which had been growing through all these periods, was ready for their reaping, and involved grave responsibility. It has all been written, said he, for our admonition or instruction.

12. " Let him that thinketh he standeth take heed lest he fall." Does Paul here question their sincerity?

If we read, *Let him who thinks to stand, take heed,* etc., we shall see both the bearing and wisdom of the caution. He had just told them how the fathers of the Jewish nation had fallen and perished, by their disobedience, and if they wished to stand, it could be only by taking heed in careful obedience to God.

14. *"Flee from idolatry." Was Paul afraid they might become idolators?*

No. It was participation that he feared. In partaking of food offered to idols, there was danger in thereby owning its power. This must be jealously watched against, even in their food, and from the illustrations that follow, we are led to judge that Paul counted even the eating of food that had been offered to idols a participation with them. The principle of indirect participation with evil is a matter to be carefully guarded against by all Christians.

16. *What does he mean by "the cup of blessing which we bless"?*

It is the cup on the table of the Lord, for which praise or thanks is given.

What is the "communion" of the blood of Christ, and of the body of Christ?

It is, *lit.*, fellowship, *i.e.*, the joint-participation of believers, who are the body of Christ, in all the privileges secured to them by His death, and these are represented by the cup of which all partake.

"The bread which we break." What does this signify?

It is, *lit.*, the loaf, which in itself is a symbol of the oneness of those who partake of it, and also of Him who is their life. The breaking of the loaf, or each breaking a piece from it for the purpose of eating, is their voluntary reception of His life to be embodied and reproduced in their own.

18–21. *Why does Paul refer to the priests of Israel partaking of the sacrifices?*

In order to illustrate the nature of participation in evil things. The altar on which sacrifices were offered was God's altar, and all that was offered up on it belonged to Him; but in some offerings a portion was given to the priests for their sustenance, and thus they became partakers of the altar with God. Now though an idol was nothing in itself beyond the material of which it was made, yet as every idol was made to represent a demon, or departed one, a hero or person who was deified, to eat of things offered to them was to become partakers with the worshippers in the object for which sacrifices were made. Now, said Paul, "I would not that ye should have fellowship with devils," —*lit.*, demons. "You cannot drink the cup of the Lord, and the cup of demons: you cannot be partakers of the Lord's table and the table of demons." Therefore beware lest you arouse the jealousy of God.

Can this matter of participation be extended to other things?

Doubtless it can; and this is what should make believers so careful in their associations with anything that is wrong. To give even a penny to an institution that is not approved by Christ, is to be identified with wrong. To say we have no sympathy with it, and so think ourselves free from responsibility, while by presence or means we support it, is to deceive ourselves. So in all good things. Our presence, our means, our prayers, identify us with them, just as Paul counts the Philippians as having fellowship with him in the Gospel, because they supported him while preaching and suffering for it.

23. *Why does he contrast what is lawful with what is not expedient?*

Because he was exhorting to brotherly consideration. Personal rights ought to be set aside, if by so doing a brother could be built up. He who gave Himself for our sins, has set us an example, which in spirit must be imitated.

24. *"But every man another's*

U

wealth." I observe that wealth is added by the translators; is it a proper addition?

No ; because it limits the end to be sought to one object only, when it is intended to apply to anything that may be required. It will be far better to leave the statement in its own direct appeal to the heart, and learn from the context what Paul claims from each on behalf of his brother, instead of personal gratification.

25. *Why were they not to ask questions, either about food sold in the market, or at the table of a friend?*

Because the food so provided was neither better nor worse even though it had been first offered to an idol. It was only when the conscience of another was involved, that they should refuse to purchase or to eat it. By their knowledge of God they were to rise above all superstition in themselves, and also refuse to encourage it in others.

31–33. *How could they eat and drink to the glory of God?*

By specially regarding others in their food and actions, "Giving none offence, neither to the Jews nor to the Gentiles, nor to the Church of God." Such a self-denying life Paul led, being more anxious for the salvation of his fellow-men, than for his own personal gratification.

The Jews, the Gentiles, and the Church of God. Why does Paul note this division?

It is, *lit.*, *"Without offence be ye, both to Jews and to Greeks, and to the Church of God,"* and each division required attention to its peculiarities, so that offence might be given to none.

Do these divisions still continue?

Not exactly as they were, and those which continue depend on circumstances for their continuance. If every Jew became a Christian,

this division would cease, being maintained only by his rejection of Christ. The idolatrous Greek can scarcely be counted as a division, being now merged among the nations. The Church of God does exist, but only so long as she remains obedient to Christ. An assembly governed by its own laws would cease to be the Church of God. Paul's advice, however, is still important. It is as if he had said, Do not cause any to stumble by any improper action on your part, and this advice we should carefully follow.

CHAPTER XI.

1. *" Be ye followers of me." What does this mean?*

It is, *lit.*, Be imitators of me. Do unto each other as I have been doing to all, after the spirit and example of Christ.

2. *" Ye keep the ordinances as I delivered them to you." What were these?*

It is, *lit.*, *traditions*, or things delivered to them at the beginning by Paul, and not things delivered from former times as now understood by the word.

3. *Why does he introduce this matter of headship to the Church in Corinth?*

In order to meet the irregularity and insubordination that was being manifested in the assembly of God. The instruction is valuable, not only as meeting their need, but also supplying the direction needful for every age. The man is the head of the woman, and this authority must be acknowledged by her ; and Christ is the head of the Church, and to Him it must be obedient in all things, as Christ was to the Father.

4. *Why was the woman when praying or prophesying to cover her head?*

As a token of her subjection, being a type of the Church ; while the man must be uncovered, as he is the image of God, and a type of His authority.

5. *In 1 Tim. ii. 12 we read, " I suffer not a woman to teach . . . but to be in silence ; " while here they are allowed with covered head to pray or prophesy. How do these things agree ?*

There is no disagreement between the two directions. " I suffer not a woman to teach," is a word of authority, but if God should send a message even by the woman, the time and place for its delivery should be afforded. She might pray or prophesy if anything was revealed to her by the Spirit, but with covered head. What was the rule and what the exception, is thus plainly taught.

10. *" For this cause ought the woman to have power over her head." What power was this ?*

From the context we judge it to have been her veil, which, being the sign of her subjection, Paul insists that it should be on her in the assembly. Young renders this verse thus, " Because of this (her being created because of the man) the woman ought to have a *token* of (his) authority upon the head."

" Because of the angels." Are these celestial beings ?

No. The word should have been rendered messengers, and doubtless refers to "messengers of the churches" before whom Paul desires that becoming order should be manifest.

13. *" Is it comely that a woman pray unto God uncovered ?" Did women pray in the Church ?*

Yes ; but with their heads covered or veiled. Paul does not forbid them either to pray or prophesy, but directs that the veil be upon them when they do so.

20. *Is " Lord's supper " a proper designation for the " breaking of bread " ?*

I do not think that Paul uses this term as a name for that institution. These Corinthians had introduced in connection with the assembly a supper or feast which corresponded to the passover supper of which Jesus and His disciples partook before they attended to the feast which was given for the commemoration of His own death. It was at this supper that the irregularities of which Paul speaks prevailed, and which he affirms was not " the Lord's supper,"—*lit.,—a lordly supper,—i.e.,* a supper worthy of a lord. It was their own supper—a ministering to their own appetites ; " and as a result, one is hungry and another is drunken."

21. *" Drunken." Were these Corinthian Christians really intoxicated in the assembly ?*

Drunken is a literal rendering of *methuei*, but in contrast with hungry, it is most likely to have been used here in a figurative sense, viz., as meaning, to be full, repletion, or as rendered by Dr King (Imperial Dictionary, Principal Fairbairn's, 1870), "One was famished while another was *surfeited*." The rich brought of their abundance, while the poor had nothing, and so they were divided, and thus the union of the body was sacrificed in seeking carnal enjoyment.

23-26. *" For I received of the Lord that which I also delivered unto you," etc. Does Paul refer to the breaking of bread, to remind them of the Lord's authority for attending to it ?*

No ; but to remind them of the purpose for which the revelation had been given to him, and which, though he had made known to them, they had evidently not understood, or else had disregarded his instruction.

What was this purpose ?

The unity of the body of Christ, which He had formed of all those who believed in Him, both Jews and Gentiles, rich and poor, bond and free, and who were made one in Him. A more literal rendering of verses 23–26 will make his meaning sufficiently plain. *For I received of the Lord that which I also delivered unto you, that the Lord Jesus in the night in which He was betrayed took a loaf*—[Note, one loaf, a symbol of unity]:—*and when He had given thanks, He brake it, and said, This is My body, which is for you: this do in remembrance of Me. After the same manner also He took the cup* —[Note, one cup],—*when He had supped, saying, This cup is the New Testament in My blood: this do ye, as oft as ye drink it, in remembrance of Me. For as often as ye eat this bread, and drink this cup, ye do show the Lord's death* [for all] *till He come.* This unity of the body had been revealed to Paul in connection with the one loaf and the one cup, but was completely ignored by the carnal idea which ruled their *agapai*, or love feasts. Paul wished them to understand that it was not mere eating and drinking that fulfilled the intention of their Lord, but their joint participation in the symbols of His life and death, and for this a crumb eaten from the one loaf, and a sip from the one cup, sufficed.

27. *Does "unworthily" refer to state of mind or to the object of eating and drinking?*

Possibly to the object which the participant may have before him in partaking of the loaf and cup. Indeed this is so stated in ver. 29, "not discerning the Lord's body." Paul is not writing so much about personal fitness, although that is necessary, as the unworthy object of the partaker. To eat and drink for bodily gratification was to pervert the institution and bring judgment upon themselves.

29. *"Not discerning the Lord's body." What does this mean?*

"Lord's" is omitted by many scholars, although it may be implied. They did not discern the one body—*i.e.*, the Church, which is His body—even though the loaf and the cup were symbols of this truth.

30. *"For this cause many are weak and sickly among you." Was this physical or spiritual weakness?*

It was physical, I judge, although their spiritual condition would also be involved. There was the "sin unto death," which followed transgression, and to this class of offenders Paul refers.

31. *How would they escape being condemned with the world by self-judgment?*

Because, by judging themselves in the light of God's Word, they would bring themselves under discipline, and so reform and escape the judgment, which will come on the world of the ungodly.

CHAPTER XII.

1. *Why does Paul seek to enlighten them about spiritual gifts?*

Because, while they were endowed with a large measure of the gifts of the Spirit, which were bestowed in confirmation of the Gospel of Christ, they were using them for personal exaltation. The gifts had been conveyed to them by the hands of Paul, but the purpose had been entirely overlooked.

2. *Why does he refer to their former idolatry?*

To impress two manifest truths upon their minds, viz., that the dumb idols they had served conferred no gifts and made no revelations. This should have been noted by them, that, instead of being puffed up one against another, Jesus might have been honoured by them.

3. *Were there some persons known to them that called Jesus accursed ?*

No doubt the unbelieving Jews, with whom Paul had no small contention, did this, but such, he affirms, could not speak by the Spirit of God.

How did it require the Holy Spirit to say that Jesus is the Lord ?

It did require the Holy Spirit to prove it, and this is what Paul means. The proofs which he furnished neither babbling, idle priests, nor scoffing Jews could deny. The proofs were with themselves, and might be fully tested.

4–6. *Why does he refer to the diversity of gifts, administrations, and operations of God, of the Lord, and of the Spirit ?*

To show the oneness of the body of Christ, since all this diversity was for the one body.

Why are diversities of gifts connected with the Spirit, while differences of administrations are connected with the Lord, and diversities of operations with God ?

All gifts, whether wisdom, prophecy, or healing, were by the one Spirit ; while all administrations— *lit.*, services—were done for Christ the Lord, whether planting, or watering, or suffering. Then all operations were according to the will of God, who worketh all in all. Would that all teachers were as careful as Paul in assigning to each their manifested place in the great scheme of redemption.

7. *" But the manifestation of the Spirit is given to every one to profit withal." Does he mean that each had received a gift ?*

No. He simply means that where bestowed the gift or gifts were not for personal ends, but for the profit of all. As they were one body, each one must minister to its general need.

8–11. *Had they no choice of gifts ?*

None whatever. The Spirit, who bestowed them, divided to every man severally as He willed.

13. *" For by one Spirit are we all baptised into one body, whether Jews or Gentiles." What does this mean ?*

The Spirit was given at Pentecost to the apostles prior to the immersion of believing Jews, and the same Spirit fell upon the Gentiles in the house of Cornelius, which also led to their immersion. Now, the one Spirit given to both led to this declared oneness. So Paul writes, " For in [the reception of] one Spirit, we all into one body were immersed, whether Jews or Greeks, whether bond or free."

" And were all made to drink into one Spirit." What does this mean ?

According to Tischendorf, the Alexandrian MS. has instead, " And are all one body." This reading is certainly in harmony with the context, and commends itself as a true reading.

14–26. *" For the body is not one member, but many." Does Paul here refer to the natural body ?*

Yes, and his reference to it is very appropriate and instructive. They had failed to apprehend the purpose for which God had made one those who believe in Jesus, and this simple reference to the natural body, and the very close relation of all its members, was intended to help them to see the divinely-imposed obligation to feel and care for each other. As the members of the natural body were in full sympathy with each other, so in like manner should be the members of the body of Christ.

How could this very desirable object be secured ?

On the same principle that the

hand ministers to the foot, and the eye to both, in obedience to the head, which cares alike for all; and which in every recurring necessity calls upon them to assist each other. Jesus, the great head of His spiritual body, cares very specially for every member of it, and in return He calls upon them to specially care for each other. Nor should they be guided, in discharging this obligation, by mere natural affection, but always in response to the Spirit, who says, "By love serve one another." Then again, the head does not assist the hand but through the eye, and the foot; and Jesus the head of His body does not carry the cup of cold water to a disciple, but through disciples, who become His hands and feet to minister to their need. He is in heaven, doing what they cannot do; and they are on the earth, to do what He wishes to be done here. It is indeed a blessed mission to fill the Master's place, and minister in His stead. "Ye call me Master and Lord: and ye say well; for so I am. If I then, your Lord and Master, have washed your feet; ye also ought to wash one another's feet. For I have given you an example, that ye should do as I have done to you."

27–30. Why does he speak here of apostles, prophets, etc., etc., and not of elders and deacons?

Because he is speaking of the Church when under the training of Spirit-endowed apostles, prophets, evangelists, pastors, and teachers (Eph. iv. 11–13); and not of the Church when left under overseers and deacons, who were instructed and perfected by them. This twofold provision for the Church—so distinctly marked by the apostle—should be as carefully noted by us; and our failure to do this is sure to lead to confusion and apostacy. The Church at the beginning—when inspired instruction was so absolutely necessary for her perfect initiation into the will of God—was placed under men, who by the Holy Spirit were endowed as apostles, prophets, and teachers; and as their preaching and teaching is recorded for our learning, so it remains the only authoritative standard of preaching and teaching for the age. Then the order of the gifts bestowed upon them is instructive, "First apostles," etc.; "after that miracles," etc. The former being for the need of the Church, the latter to confirm the truth of the apostles' work.

31. Why does Paul say, "Covet earnestly the best gifts"?

It will be better to read, *Ye covet earnestly the best gifts; but I will show you a more excellent way:* which in the following chapter is most impressively done.

CHAPTER XIII.

1–3. Is Paul showing the more excellent way in this chapter?

He begins to show them what is better than tongues, or the gift of prophecy, or the power to remove mountains; even the love that endureth all things, and rejoiceth in the truth.

Why show this to the Church?

Because of their vain ambition in seeking the gifts, which were only temporary, and in neglecting those traits of character and spirit which were to abide for ever.

Could they have gifts without grace?

The gifts possessed by these Corinthians were grace, *i.e.*, they were favours conferred on them through the ascended Messiah. They were gracious gifts, evidences of His power and wealth, but which did not insure to the possessor spirituality of mind. The gifts did not make them more gentle, or humble, or holy; the Spirit of Jesus in them alone could do this. It was no doubt a grand thing to be selected to do anything for Christ—to herald His coming as did John; to heal the sick and cast out demons in His name as did the twelve; to go up to the third heavens as did Paul; to speak with tongues, and prophesy, as these Corinthians did; but the work was dangerous to the bearer of the gift, as he might seek to share the glory which belonged only to the Master. Indeed, these people had yielded to this snare, and were puffed up one against another.

4–7. *Is the word " charity," so often used in this chapter, a proper rendering ?*

As charity nearly always indicates almsgiving, it must fail to convey the idea intended by Paul. Love is a correct rendering of *agape*, and without love men will never do what Christ requires.

Were there any special reasons why Paul names the things that love will do ?

These beautiful sketches of Christian character, which the apostle as a spiritual artist has here given, were most likely intended to reflect upon the behaviour of these Corinthians towards each other, because it was far from what it should have been. Their envying and divisions were the reverse of love, and he wished them to look, first on this picture and observe what love could do, and then on that and see what the flesh could do; in order that they might repent, and do works meet for repentance.

8. *" Charity never faileth ; " while prophecies and tongues were to cease. Why should the latter be removed, while the former must continue ?*

Prophecies and tongues were given to prove the truth of the apostles' words, and having done this were no longer required, and therefore ceased with them : but the former, being a fruit of faith, must abide to the end.

Have there been no signs or miracles since the apostles passed away ?

Not a single sign has been given to prove the truth of Christianity, or to establish the requirements of the Lord Jesus since they left the world; and if signs or miracles have been given, they have been for some other purpose. To accept of any other evidence of its truth, or even to seek after any other, is only to destroy the power of that already given; and must result either in deception or confusion, or both together. That men have turned from the Scriptures, to seek internal or external evidences of divine assurance, is everywhere manifest; and that confusion and uncertainty prevail in the minds of all such is equally plain.

10. *" When that which is perfect is come." To what does this perfection apply ?*

To the perfected administration of Christ by His apostles. It was needful for them to know that tongues and prophecies would cease; and being only like the scaffolding of a building which would be removed when the building was completed, because no longer needed, so would these external evidences terminate. Now Paul wished them to think more highly of the building, than of the scaffolding that surrounded it; of the testimony delivered, than of the signs which supported it; the former would abide, the latter would pass away.

11. *Is the illustration about the child and the man intended to confirm this view ?*

Yes, and is a very apt illustration. The action of the child and the man, are in striking contrast. When I was a child—*lit.*, a babe, or one under manhood,—as a child I spoke, as a child I thought, as a child I reasoned, but when I became a man

I put away the things of a child. So with this administration. You have been treated as children in these gifts conferred upon you, and you must be prepared to let them go as things of the child-state, and not intended to remain, when you grow to be men.

13. *" But now we see through a glass darkly, but then face to face." Is not this a contrast of earth with heaven ?*

No ; it is rather intended as a reproof, although it may serve as an illustration. Paul wished to show the difference between depending upon signs for continued confirmation of the truth, and the perfect testimony of the apostles. Their testimony gave a full, clear view of the grace and power of the ascended Christ, and left nothing more to be desired ; while signs, which were for those who believed not, were only for a season.

14. *" The greatest of these is charity." Why is charity or love greater than faith and hope ?*

Love is less selfish than faith and hope. It is pleasant to believe gracious testimonies ; it is cheering to hope for the fulfilment of promises ; but love is self-emptying for the good of others. Love cares for others, acts for others, covers the faults of others, etc. " These three ; but the greatest of these is charity."

CHAPTER XIV.

1–5. *" Follow after charity." How were they to do this ?*

By doing those things which were lovely.

Why is prophecy commended more than other gifts ?

Because of its practical value to the Church. Tongues, which are here specially named, were inferior to prophecy, because they were for a sign to unbelievers, while prophecies

were divine revealings of things needful for believers.

What is meant by a tongue ?

A language in which some communications were made, but unknown to those present except through an interpreter or translator, and when such were not present, tongues were to be restrained. The gift of tongues was not a mere babble or sounds without meaning, as the Spirit of God did not make displays of that useless character ; but even when such communications were made, they were useful to the Church only when understood through an interpreter.

6. *What is the difference between revelation and knowledge ?*

Revelation was that which was communicated directly by the Spirit to him who had to make it known, while knowledge was that which had been learned from previous revelations or teaching, whether by prophets or apostles.

7–14. *Why does Paul refer to the pipe or harp giving distinction in the sounds ?*

On purpose to show that the pipe or harp when played upon, and the trumpet when sounded, would be useless unless the sounds were so distinctly arranged as that the melody or signal could be understood. Who could be sorrowful or joyous, unless the harp produced its corresponding tune ? or how could soldiers arm for war unless the signal was definite ? So in the Church, whether revelation or tongue, whether doctrine or interpretation, all must be intelligible if the Church is to be benefited.

I suppose that Paul's advice about uttering " words easy to be understood " is just as needful now as then ?

Just as needful. It is of vital importance to convey God's message in the plainest terms. Too often, alas, some who wish to blow the

Gospel trumpet, do not themselves understand what God wishes to be made known. They are like Ahimaaz the son of Zadok, ready to run, but have no definite tidings ready. They may be eloquent as Apollos, who, knowing only the baptism of John, hindered rather than helped the cause of truth. It is well for all such when some well-instructed Priscilla and Aquila happen to meet with them, to teach them the truth as it is in Jesus; and it is well when they are ready to receive it. No person need remain uninstructed, since God's truth is sent into the world; and if there should be no teachers outside His book, there is instruction there, plain and simple for all.

15. *" I will pray with the Spirit,"* and *" I will sing with the Spirit."* *What does this mean ?*

Simply that instruction, both in prayer and praise, was given by the Holy Spirit. Divine guidance was specially required for their infant state, and was thus most graciously and efficiently supplied. How could heathens know how to pray or praise the living God when just turned from dumb idols, except as instructed by an inspired teacher, or directly by the Spirit Himself. This necessary direction was therefore given to some for the benefit of all, and until it could be received in the ordinary way of teaching and learning. It was like the setting up of the tabernacle of which Moses had received the necessary patterns in the Mount, and then God inspired Bezaleel and Aholiab with all wisdom and skill for the work; while they instructed others to aid in its completion.

Can we now obtain the guidance of the Spirit in worship, prayer, and praise ?

Yes, through apostles and prophets, by whom He has been pleased to give all necessary direction in these things, and this is the only source of instruction available to us. Our brethren and sisters who are instructed in the truth, may help us by teaching us with it, but let us beware of tempting God to enlighten either saint or sinner by any other than His own selected method. Nothing is more common in the present day than for anxious persons to pray and wait for the Spirit to make known to them in some imaginary way of their own the way of salvation, when He has again and again by the apostles in the New Testament revealed the very things they wish to know, but of which they do not, and some will not, avail themselves. I was once trying to help a woman whose disappointed anxieties and prayers had nearly extinguished all hope of being saved. In vain I made known to her the Gospel she was invited to believe and obey. At last I said, " Suppose that God should send an angel from heaven to tell you He would forgive all your sins, would that satisfy you ? " " Yes," she replied, " I would ask no more." I then opened the Testament and read a few portions and said, " Here is what God by His servants speaks to you, will this not satisfy ? " " No," she replied, " I would rather have the angel." It may appear harsh to say to those who seek signs from heaven other than God has given in His Word, that He will not help them further; and if such persons persist in their self-chosen plan, there is no assurance that such will ever be saved. We have no ground to expect that God will ever change His arrangements even to save His creatures, since His plans are laid in infinite wisdom and love; and since He has been pleased to reveal them by apostles and prophets, it is man's obligation to learn and obey them.

*" With the understanding also."
What does this mean ?*

Paul meant that he would sing
and pray intelligently, so that those
who were listening might be benefited, and that even those who were
previously uninstructed could add the
" Amen " when thanks were given.

16. *What did this Amen indicate?*

It was the confiding acceptance
of the truth by those who did not
possess spiritual gifts.

19. *What do you think of Paul
speaking "five words" that might
instruct, in contrast with ten thousand
that could not be understood ?*

I think it is a very wise utterance,
and one that might be studied with
profit by many who attempt to teach
in the Church. If, instead of profitless addresses, to which at times
the Church is compelled to listen,
a few timely and instructive words
were spoken, it would be well.
If the Church demanded a more
extensive application of Paul's plan
of " five words,"—*i.e.*, a few wisely
selected thoughts that could not fail
to profit, there are those who might
be led to speak who seldom open
their lips, while others who wander
recklessly on would have to be
limited, because they will never limit
themselves.

26. *" Every one of you hath a
psalm, hath a doctrine," etc. Does
Paul condemn this variety of service?*

No, he only suggests that whatever was done in the Church, should
be for its upbuilding ; and, that this
object might be accomplished, these
things should be in order.

27. *"If any man speak in a tongue,
let it be by two, or at the most by
three." Two or three what ?*

Two or three sentences at once,
and then these were to be inter-
preted ; but if there was no interpreter in the Church, then " let him
keep silence."

29. *The prophets were revealers of*
things to come. *Why were they to
be restricted to two or three ?*

Because prophecy in the Church,
judging from the "Acts of Apostles,"
was chiefly about temporal things ;
and, although these prophecies were
important to those concerned, they
were not to occupy the time that
should be devoted to prayer, praise,
and teaching.

34. *" Let your women keep silence
in the churches." Why are they not
permitted to speak ?*

The woman is a symbol of the
Church, while man is a representative
of the Church's head. The silence
imposed upon the woman is full of
instruction to the Church, and is
designed to teach her own subjection
to her Lord.

38. *"But if any man be ignorant,
let him be ignorant." What does
Paul mean ?*

In ver. 37 the apostle demanded
that the prophets should testify that
he had spoken the commandments
of God, which, by their possession
of this gift, they were able to do.
He then adds, " But if any man be
ignorant [through the lack of this
gift], let him be ignorant," that is,
let him not be regarded whatever
else he may happen to say.

CHAPTER XV.

*This chapter is upon the resurrec-
tion of the dead. Why had Paul to
defend this doctrine ?*

The resurrection of the dead had
been denied by some in Corinth ;
and, as the saints were in danger
from the baneful influence of this
denial, it had become necessary to
refute it by the evidence which he
was able to produce.

*From what source was this error
derived ?*

The error was not a new one,
although we cannot tell who introduced it into the church at Corinth.
The Sadducees defended it in opposi-

tion to Christ, and when declared by Paul in Athens, the philosophers of that city scoffed at the idea of a resurrection of the dead. It is most likely that some of the disciples of this ancient school, though they had united with the Church, still held the error, and by teaching it to the brethren, had disturbed the faith of the assembly. The matter had evidently been referred to the apostle; and in the facts, illustrations, and revelations, which are brought forward in this chapter, the abettors of this error have had a most crushing defeat. In this masterly argument we get, not only the truth of resurrection established, but of our glorification also, and in the latter privilege our redemption will be completed.

1. *Why does Paul commence his argument with the facts of the Gospel?*

Because one of these is a fact of resurrection, and was amongst the first things he had made known to them. By faith in Jesus who died for their sins, and who had been raised from the dead, they had been saved, and are here encouraged to be faithful to the end.

2. *Why does he add, " Unless ye have believed in vain"?*

That is, unless the proclamation be a falsehood, and in that case you are yet in your sins.

3–8. *Why does he bring forward all this evidence to prove the resurrection of Jesus?*

In proving the resurrection of Jesus, the denial of the doctrine was completely refuted; and, as the testimony of it was based upon the evidence of those who saw Jesus after He was risen, it was necessary to thus briefly state the facts of the case. Hence, he affirms that Cephas and the twelve, and James, saw Jesus after He was raised from the dead; and then he adds, "And last of all, he was seen of me also, as of one born out of due time."

" One born out of due time." What does this mean?

One born after the proper time for seeing Him was past. Still, though prevented from seeing Him at that time, yet, by His appearing to Him on his way to Damascus, he did actually see Jesus; and through this appearing Paul became a witness of His resurrection.

9–11. *" For I am the least of the apostles." Does he refer to Christian character and standing?*

No, but to the place he held as a witness. In bearing witness to the resurrection of Christ they stood first. They had not only seen but handled Him, they ate and drank with Him, and then saw Him ascend to His throne; they were, therefore, His greatest witnesses. And, though Paul could add his testimony to theirs, yet he is pleased to call himself the "least of the apostles," nay, even unworthy of the honour, having been a persecutor of the Church of God.

12–19. *" How say some among you that there is no resurrection of the dead?" Why this challenge?*

It was to enable him to push the consequences of such a denial to their just issue. If there is no resurrection, then Christ is not raised, our preaching is vain, ye are yet in your sins, and we are found false witnesses of God. And not only are these sad consequences attached to this denial, assuming that it is true, but even those who have fallen asleep in Christ are perished. The sad issues of such an alternative he can endure no longer to contemplate, and sets them aside by not only affirming the resurrection of Christ, but the bearing of that resurrection on the future of all believers.

20. *Why does he term Christ "the first fruits"?*

It is, *lit., a first fruit,* and stands related to others who also will be raised from the dead. The Jews, before they reaped the harvest, presented a sheaf of it to God, which, being waved before Him, was accepted, and the harvest could in due time be reaped with acceptance. So Christ was cut down by the sickle of death, and then became the wave-sheaf in resurrection, and is now the pledge of the resurrection of all believers, who, in due time, will be presented for God's acceptance in life and immortality.

How could Christ be a first fruit, *when others were raised from death before Him?*

He was the first to be raised from death to immortality, while others, after being raised, returned to corruption.

21. *Is the resurrection of the saints a natural sequence of Christ's resurrection?*

No, it is a gracious one, and, being promised in Jesus, it has become a part of their blessed hope. As it pleased God to allow death to reign over all in Adam, so in Christ shall all be made alive.

22. *Does "all" here apply to every human being?*

Yes, but only according to their relation with their head. "In Adam all die," *i.e.*, as every human being, Christ excepted, is from Adam, having his nature, so all are under the sentence of death, "even so in Christ shall all be made alive": the "all" here being those who are "in Christ." It is only those who are *in Christ* that have the promise of resurrection. Not that those out of Christ will not be raised, because it is affirmed by Christ that all "that are in their graves shall come forth," etc., but Paul is speaking here only of the "dead in Christ," who have in His resurrection a pledge and assurance of their own.

23. *"But every man in his own order." How many orders will there be?*

It is, *lit.*, each one in his own rank or band, and Paul names but two; *Christ a first fruit, after that those of Christ in His presence.* The sheaf of first fruits was first presented to God, and then the harvest, which in due time would be reaped, was sanctified in it.

24–28. *"Then cometh the end." What end is this?*

It is strictly, *then the end, i.e.,* the end of the reign of Jesus. The great object of His reign, viz., the putting down of all opposing rule, and the salvation of all who have received Him, will then be an accomplished fact. The manifestation of saints and the judgment of the ungodly will then take place, and the kingdom will be delivered up to God, even the Father. This is the end of which Paul is speaking.

29–32. *"Else what shall they do which are baptised for the dead, if the dead rise not at all?" What does this mean? and what has it to do with his argument?*

Believers are not only associated with Christ by their immersion into His death, but being raised they are associated with Him, and His resurrection has become their hope and pledge. It is as if he had said, What is the use of all this if there is no living Redeemer? "Why are they then baptised for"—*lit.* over—"the dead." Is it for a dead Christ? That would be useless, and so would be the sufferings we endure on His behalf.

33. *Why does he add "Be not deceived"?*

It is a solemn warning against the immoral consequences that would follow a denial of this vital doctrine, and the consequences to themselves in being associated with those who do so.

"Evil communications corrupt good manners." Is this a quotation?

It is said to be found in the writings of Menander, an Athenian poet, and was possibly well known to these Corinthians. It is very appropriate to them, and was none the less so in being familiar to them. The quotation should indeed be heeded by us all. It may seem but a small matter to listen to vain conversation, to read profitless books, and to be associated with questionable practices; but the result of these things no one can calculate. "A little leaven leaveneth the whole lump," therefore "be not deceived."

35. *"How are the dead raised up? and with what body do they come?" Were these questions asked by some at Corinth?*

Yes, and were proposed as difficulties not easily met. Paul, however, does answer them, and the answer has opened to us the purpose of God in relation to all believers. The dead will be raised by the power of God, and will be reclothed as seen fit by Him.

36. *Why does he say "fool"?*

It might be better to render it *foolish one, i.e.,* thoughtless, inconsiderate one. Paul terms this person, or party, foolish, because they had overlooked simple facts of nature —facts which might have helped them to a more reasonable conclusion than to question the truth of resurrection. They might have learned from nature that a new life follows death, and that while every seed has its own body, the body raised is not the body sown, whether of wheat or any other grain. This they should have considered, but did not, and so deserved a rebuke.

37. *"Thou sowest not that body that shall be." Does Paul intend this to illustrate the resurrection body of believers?*

Most certainly, or why should he bring it forward. The body that springs from the earth is not that naked grain that was sown in it, neither is the body that is sown in corruption the same that is raised in incorruption.

How can it be called a resurrection if it is not the same body?

It is not a resurrection of the body that turns to dust, but a standing up again that is promised, while the body, the house that is to be tenanted, is to be from heaven, or heavenly. This is the teaching of the revelation of the Spirit.

39. *"All flesh is not the same flesh." Why does he refer to this difference of flesh?*

Simply to show that God is not limited in His power to produce whatever He thinks fit. Already there is considerable manifest variety in the flesh of men, and beasts, and birds, and fishes; there are also celestial bodies, and bodies terrestrial. In this way Paul answers the question, "With what body do they come?" a question which sounds very much like the taunt of Grecian philosophy, a science which had no hope in the presence of death. His reference even to creation and nature is a triumphant reply to their sceptical taunt.

42–44. *"It is sown;" "It is raised." Does this not indicate that the body sown is the body that will be raised?*

No. It is very clearly shown that as "star differeth from star in glory, so also is the resurrection of the dead." And again, "Thou sowest not that body that shall be, but bare grain . . . but God giveth it a body as it hath pleased Him." As then that which rises from the earth differs from the naked grain that was sown in it, so also will the body that is to be raised in incorruption, glory, and power, differ from that which was sown in corruption, dishonour, and weakness. That which is sown or buried is a natural or animal body, while that which is raised is a spiritual body.

45–47. Why does Paul change his statements respecting Adam and Christ from first and last to first and second?

In speaking of Christ as the "Last Adam" and the "Second man," Paul is revealing very important truth. The first man failed, both as head and ruler in creation, and God raised up a second man to meet the failure. Then, in order to show the importance of looking to this second man, he declares Him to be the last Adam; and that if men will enjoy God's salvation it can only be through this Redeemer.

" The first man Adam was made a living soul; the last Adam a quickening spirit." What does Paul mean to show by this contrast?

That the one simply received life, and was therefore dependent upon God; while the other was a giver of life to those who are dead.

50. " Flesh and blood cannot inherit the kingdom of God." Why does he state this?

To illustrate the following statement, "Neither doth corruption inherit incorruption." That just as the kingdom of God cannot be entered by any right of the flesh, but only by faith in Christ Jesus; so incorruptibility is not a growth or right of corruption, but a gift of God through this second man.

51. " Behold, I show you a mystery; we shall not all sleep." What does this mean?

Behold, I tell you a secret, we shall not all die; for when Jesus returns, the living will be changed "in a moment, in the twinkling of an eye." Up to that moment death will reign, but after that death will cease; his reign being ended by the victorious triumph of Jesus.

55. Why is death said to have a sting?

Death is spoken of as a serpent whose poisonous bite extinguishes life, and but for the balm of the Gospel of Jesus, would have been eternally fatal. Through Him believers have life, and will have glory and immortality. The grave—*lit., Hades*—receives us all, but at the command of Him who now holds the keys it must restore its prey; and with glorification, mortality will cease. So now we sing, "Thanks be unto God who giveth us the victory, through our Lord Jesus Christ." And so sure is Paul of this ultimate triumph of the saints, through Christ, that he can urge, "Therefore, my beloved brethren, be ye stedfast, unmoveable, always abounding in the work of the Lord, forasmuch as ye know that your labour is not in vain in the Lord."

CHAPTER XVI.

1. " Now concerning the collection for the saints." What saints were these? and why collect for them?

They were the poor saints at Jerusalem, who through the dearth foretold by Agabus (Acts xi. 28), were in great need. We learn here that the Gentile saints in Galatia and Corinth, were stirred up by Paul to contribute towards their relief, and this contribution was, to his heart, a most fragrant offering.

Why did Paul command this collection to be made on the first of the week?

It was on this day that the Church met for the breaking of the loaf; for prayer, praise, and teaching; and we conceive of no place, or time, more fitted for their benevolence, than when seated at the table of the Lord. Paul has assigned no reason for the direction he has given, but it may be received as the teaching of the Holy Spirit, and furnishes a precedent for all the churches of the saints.

5–12. *Why does he refer to the visit of himself, Timothy, and Apollos, to Corinth ?*

To show them the deep interest which all felt in their welfare, and to urge a worthy reception of these noble co-workers in the truth.

13. *Why urge them to steadfast watching in the faith ?*

To remind them, that while it would be a privilege to have these servants of the Lord ministering among them, the contest against evil must be carried on by themselves. If they would be victorious, personal watchfulness, and determined fortitude must be maintained to the end.

20. *Was the " holy kiss " appointed as an ordinance in the Church ?*

Not in the Church, but was called for as an expression of Christian love whenever appropriate. The saints that accompanied Paul to the sea shore, fell upon his neck and kissed him, and thus gave him their affectionate adieu. The meeting and parting of brethren is a fitting occasion for this expression of their love to each other.

22. *" If any man love not the Lord Jesus Christ, let him be Anathema Maran-atha." What do these words imply ?*

Anathema means accursed, *i.e.*, devoted to judgment by the command of God, while Maran-atha should be rendered, *the Lord has come.* This is the reason why a curse is so justly deserved by all who love Him not. To refuse to love this Jesus, is man's highest crime, and destruction must follow to all who refuse His salvation.

THE SECOND EPISTLE OF PAUL THE APOSTLE TO THE

CORINTHIANS.

CHAPTER I.

Why did Paul write this second letter to the church at Corinth ?

His most direct object seems to have been to express his joy at the result of his first letter, and then to defend his special mission against these Judaising teachers, whose influence was still felt in Corinth. And further, to exhort them to purity of heart and life, as becometh the children of God.

1. *" Paul, an apostle of Jesus Christ by the will of God." Was it needful to make this known to them ?*

It was needful to show that his mission was by the conjoint will of the Father, with the appointment of His Son. And as his authority had been questioned, it was important to give prominence to this combined arrangement in sending him to preach the Gospel.

2. *" Grace to you and peace." What is the import of this statement ?*

It is a divinely authorised assurance that every favour provided by God, and ministered by His Son, was for their enjoyment. This was a matter never to be questioned.

3–10. *Why does he refer to some great trial that he had passed through ?*

To assure them that great as that trial had been the assurance of their faithfulness had more than compensated for all he had endured. Possibly this danger may have arisen through his labours for them, and had called forth their earnest prayers for his deliverance; and now they are invited to share with him the consolation flowing from this divine interposition, and to join him in the praise so justly due to God.

11. *Paul mentions their prayers as contributing to his deliverance. How is prayer a means of help?*

Prayer is one of the conditions associated with God's help in our trouble. God is the source of help, and He has said, " Call upon Me in the day of trouble, and I will deliver thee, and thou shalt glorify Me." Here we have God opening up to His children the vast resources of His power; and if there were nothing to lead Him to act otherwise, He would certainly set them free. His help must be sought if blessing is to be obtained, but it should always be sought in deference to His will. Thus, the children of God, in their prayers, take hold of His promised help, and, if for their good and His glory, they will prove His gracious interposition, and thus prayer is a means of help.

12. *" For our rejoicing is this." In what does this differ from the mutual comfort and consolation he had before referred to?*

This joy or rejoicing, was his personal experience as the fruit of their godly behaviour, while the comfort or consolation in their trials was imparted to them by the God of comfort.

14. *" Ye have acknowledged us in part." What does he mean by this?*

That only some of them had acknowledged him as an apostle of Christ. Some of them were for Peter, and others for Apollos, while these hailed him as a messenger of life; and he trusted that by their faithfulness to the end they would be his rejoicing in the day of the Lord Jesus.

15. *What does he mean by a*

" second benefit," which his purposed visit would confer?

A renewed confirmation of the truth, by the signs which would be manifest, should he again visit them; and this he had solemnly purposed to do.

17. *When he speaks of coming to them on his way to Judea, why does he speak of " lightness" and " purposing according to the flesh"?*

To meet a false charge that he was moved by mere personal considerations. Paul had a far higher motive, and he assured them that his purpose was in harmony with a true God and a true Gospel.

19. *What does he mean by " Yea and nay"?*

Making statements and then failing to meet them. Neither Paul nor his co-workers could be charged with such a course. They had preached the Gospel of Christ, and the signs following proved it to be true.

20. *" For all the promises of God in Him [Christ] are yea, and in Him Amen." What does this mean?*

In Him yea—*i.e.,* affirmed or declared—*and in Him Amen*—*i.e.,* confirmed or fulfilled. Just as there was no uncertainty in the proclamation, so there was none in the fulfilment.

21, 22. *To whom does this anointing, sealing, and the earnest of the Spirit apply?*

To Paul and other chosen witnesses for Christ. They were anointed, for the Holy Spirit rested upon them. They were also sealed, for the signs of power were visible to all, and in their hearts this became an earnest of their future bliss.

CHAPTER II.

1–5. *" But I determined this with myself, that I would not come to you again in heaviness." Why does he say this?*

As intimated at the close of his first letter, he had intended to visit them; but after reflecting upon their condition, which he knew would call for much reproof, or, as he terms it, "a rod" (1 Cor. iv. 21), he determined not to do so, but rather to wait the result of his letter. But on the return of Titus from Corinth, with the cheering news of the penitence of many of them, the separation of the fornicator from their assembly, and his ultimate restoration, he at once decided to write this second letter. In much anguish of heart, and with many tears he had reproved their evil ways; and now that he hears of reformation, he is resolved to further instruct them in righteousness, and by the truth enable them to perfect holiness in the fear of God.

6–10. "*Sufficient to such a man is this punishment.*" *What does this mean?*

Paul refers to the excommunicated fornicator, whose manifest penitence called for restoration, comfort, and forgiveness, in which all should unite. His exclusion from the Church should be counted a sufficient punishment, and now, on the ground of his penitence, his restoration must be sought.

11. *Why would Satan get an advantage if they did not restore this man?*

His being delivered over to Satan for the destruction of the flesh was a judicial act of terrible import, and to have refused to restore him when repentant would have been confusion. It would have been a device of Satan to have been vindictive, but this they are urged to avoid by restoring him in love, and not to be overreached by Satan.

14–16. "*For we are unto God a sweet savour in Christ, in them that are saved, and in them that perish.*" *How could he be sweet savour to both?*

The salvation of all who believed in Jesus was indeed fragrant to God, and it was also fragrant to him, that all that was possible had been done for those who madly perished in their unbelief.

Who were these perishing ones?

From the following chapter, I should judge them to be the Christ-rejecting Jews; who, like Moses, who put a vail over his face, had put a vail over their hearts, and so were blinded by their unbelief, and were perishing or loosing themselves away from the only God-provided Saviour.

17. *How did some corrupt the Word of God?*

By mixing or adulterating it with the traditions of Judaism, and the problems of philosophy, against which ruinous deceptions Paul held forth the unmixed glad-tidings of Christ and of God.

CHAPTER III.

1, 2. *Why does Paul speak of epistles of commendation, to and from the Corinthians?*

Paul is contrasting himself with some whom he afterwards calls "false apostles, deceitful workers," and whose only commendation was the letters they had brought from Judea. To allude to these letters was no doubt a reflection upon their own weakness. They had accepted these written documents, instead of the signs of an apostle which had been wrought among them, and so they deserved to feel the rebuke. It was a matter of life and death, and if they could only be brought to see the folly of their course, it would be a blessed thing for themselves, though it should be effected by a taunt. These deceivers required letters to commend them; but you, said he, are our letters, which all can know and read.

X

3. *Why does he call them " the epistles of Christ " ?*

It is, *lit.*, *an epistle of Christ*, and is used as a fitting contrast to the letters used by these deceitful workers, who were only servants of a disturbing faction in Jerusalem. They have their letters of commendation, written with ink, but you are an epistle of Christ, written by the Holy Spirit ministered by us.

Why does he add, " not in tables of stone, but in fleshy tables of the heart " ?

It is an apt allusion to what was the basis of the ministry of these teachers of the law. It might have an imposing effect, to show that God wrote the very law of the ten commandments with His own finger, and that therefore it should be received. But, said Paul, you are " the epistle of Christ, ... written not with ink, but with the Spirit of the living God."

4, 5. *" And such trust have we." Was it concerning them ?*

Yes. He had spoken of the Spirit having written the truth on their hearts, and he sincerely expressed this as his confidence. And though it was by himself and others that God had worked in them, yet the sufficiency was of Himself and not of them.

6. *Why does he refer to the new covenant, of which he was made a minister ?*

To show that the law was out of date, and as God had brought in a new covenant, it must be wrong to enforce the covenant of death.

What is intended by the " letter," and the " Spirit " ?

By the *letter* the law of Moses is referred to, which upon its first introduction killed three thousand ; and by the *Spirit*, the Gospel or testimony, which upon its first proclamation quickened a like number.

Some persons apply " the letter killeth " to the whole Bible, and say that unless the Word is quickened by the Spirit, it can only be a minister of death. *Is this a true application of it ?*

No. Those who say so, understand neither what they say, nor whereof they affirm. It is confusion to use the Scriptures so. The law did kill transgressors, but the Gospel is the life-giving message of the Spirit to all who receive it, and needs no further quickening to make it so, but only to be received.

13. *A glory rested upon the face of Moses when he came down from the mount. What did it indicate ?*

The presence and authority of God.

When did Moses vail his face ?

When he had done speaking the words of God. In the presence of God, and when speaking His words, he was unvailed, as we should read Exod. xxxiv. 33–35, " And when " (not till) " he had done speaking, he put a vail over his face. And the children of Israel saw the face of Moses, that the skin of his face shone."

What does the covering of this glory indicate ?

To Paul it was a type of their condition of mind, in not seeing that it was a fading glory ; and also a contrast to his own plainness of speech in the proclamation of the Gospel.

14. *What should they have seen when reading the Old Testament ?*

The Messiah or Jesus, of whom Moses wrote so much. But, alas ! through unbelief, they saw Him not, because " the vail was upon their heart."

16. *Can the vail be removed ?*

Yes, by believing the testimony concerning Jesus, and we know of no other way.

17. *What is this Spirit of the Lord that gives liberty ?*

It is the testimony or the Gospel

of the Lord Jesus. The Spirit gave forth the testimony through the apostles, and Christ who is proclaimed gives liberty to all who receive Him.

CHAPTER IV.

1. *" Therefore seeing we have this ministry." What is the import of Paul's frequent use of this word ministry, minister, etc. ?*

The word minister, ministry, etc., might be appropriate enough, were it not that a minister is now a clergyman, and ministry his vocation ; but if we thus apply Paul's *diakonia* exclusively to such a one, we do him an injustice. In the Bible a minister is simply a servant, and ministry service,—whether preaching the Gospel or serving tables, or any work for either God or man. It would only have been right for our translators to have rendered *diakonia* uniformly by either ministry or service, as it might have prevented a misapplication of the term.

To what service does Paul refer, and in which he did not faint ?

To the proclamation of the glad tidings of the covenant to the nations of the earth. He had preached it to Jew and Gentile, Greek and barbarian, bond and free, with unflagging zeal ; and it grieved him, that either the Jew should introduce circumcision, or the philosopher his speculations, or the sinner his unworthiness, to obstruct the freeness of the grace of God.

Is " faint not " a proper rendering?

Dean Alford says that most of the oldest MSS. read, " we shrink not back," instead of " we faint not." That is, in spite of all our difficulties, and they are many, we still go forward in our work. And in the service of such a Master, who had shown so much love and mercy, Paul would neither shrink back nor be unfaithful.

2. *Why does he refer to " dishonesty " and " handling the Word of God deceitfully " ?*

We should judge that there had been some very crafty proceedings in order to pervert the Gospel of Christ, especially by those Jews who set up a counter mission against Paul, and by an ignoble and time-serving policy turned the people from the Word of God to " old wives' fables." With such a dishonest system, Paul compared his own open, honest service in the Gospel.

3. *Why does he say, " If our Gospel be hid," etc. ?*

Because he knew it was hid or vailed to some who were lost—*lit.,* perishing,—but he had not hid it. He had held up the illuminating message of the glory of the exalted Jesus, and if this light was vailed to any mind, it was through the vailed testimony of the *god of this age,* which blinded the minds of those who believed it.

What might be the things used to cover over the Gospel of Christ?

Possibly the elements of the former dispensation, or the reasonings of the philosophers of that age, or both combined, which being put forward by deceitful workers, effectually hid the light of the truth of the soul-saving message of Christ.

5–7. *Why does Paul say, " For we preach not ourselves, but Christ Jesus " ?*

Simply to show the relation which they sustained to Him. They were only as the casket, He the jewel. He was the light, they the light-bearers. He the Master, they were His servants. It was not to exalt themselves that they preached, but Jesus, whom God had exalted.

7–9. *Why does he refer to their twofold experience in the service of Christ ?*

To show (1.) what man could do

—trouble, perplex, and persecute; and (2.) to show what God could do in sustaining and encouraging them in their work.

10. " *Always bearing about in the body the dying of the Lord Jesus.*" *What was this?*

Sufferings endured on account of the sufferings and death of Jesus. In Gal. vi. 17, he calls them the *stigmata, i.e.,* the brand-marks of the Lord Jesus.

" *That the life also of Jesus might be made manifest in our body.*" *What does this mean?*

His wonderful preservations from death while preaching the Gospel were to him so many evidences of a living and all-powerful Jesus. For, though always delivered unto death, always exposed to the murderous spirit of his enemies, yet marvellously preserved.

16. *What does he mean by the outward and the inward man?*

The *outward man* was the body, which day by day was dissolving; while the *inward* was the mind, which by the truth was renewed in the faith and hope of immortality. And while looking at these unseen things, these eternal realities, the afflictions endured were but for a moment, and working out a glorious issue.

CHAPTER V.

1. *How did Paul get to know about this heavenly and eternal house?*

By revelation, by promise, and by illustration in the glorified Jesus.

Why does he refer to it?

To show how he could triumph over sorrow, suffering, and death. Why should he fear any of these things when such a happy issue awaited him?

If the body is to be raised and re-inhabited at the resurrection, why does he speak of two houses?

Paul does not say that he will have to reinhabit the old house, but that he is to have a new one; and the contrast between the two is clearly put. The old house is of the earth, hand-made and dissolving; the new house is " of God, not made with hands, eternal in the heavens." The heavens being the sphere of the latter, as the earth is the sphere of the former, each is located according to its nature.

2. " *In this we groan.*" *Does not this indicate impatience?*

It might be better to use the word *sigh* than *groan,* as better indicating aspiration than impatience. There was great pressure on the body, not easy to endure, but there was hope that awakened aspiration—a sighing for that which was to come. Or as one expresses it, the pantings of hope—the strong yearnings for that which had been promised.

4. *What does he mean by wishing not to be unclothed, but clothed upon?*

It was revealed to him that when Christ should appear, the living would not die but would be changed in a moment, and mortality would be swallowed up by immortality; so Paul expresses his desire to be over-clothed rather than unclothed, to have the body changed rather than dissolved. Paul did not obtain his desire, but now waits for the manifestation of the children of God in glory.

5, 6. *What has the " earnest of the Spirit" to do with his confidence?*

Every manifestation of the Spirit, both in the Church and in the apostles, was to Paul an evidence of the truth of His testimony, and an earnest of future glory.

8. " *Absent from the body, and present with the Lord.*" *Is being present with the Lord, after death, a general privilege of all believers, or was it special to Paul as an apostle?*

It may have been special to him

with other apostles, through the special request of Christ, " Father, I will that they (the apostles) be with Me where I am, that they may behold My glory " (John xvii. 24). Nor should we think it strange that all saints do not share it at death, since even Christ when disembodied did not ascend to the Father, but went to paradise. It is at His coming that the saints receive their immortal bodies, and will then be "ever with the Lord." It is at resurrection that this glorious hope will be consummated.

9. *In Eph. i. 6 Paul says they were "accepted in the beloved." Why should he say here, " Wherefore we labour . . . . to be accepted of Him"?*

Paul used two words. That in Ephesians shows what God in grace had done, "accepted (or graced) in the beloved," and here what the accepted were doing. *We labour to be well-pleasing to Him.* Our translators, having used only one word, have somewhat hidden Paul's meaning.

10. *" We must all appear before the judgment-seat of Christ." Did Paul expect to stand there?*

Yes, though not to be judged but approved by Christ, and for this end he says, "we labour." The word *appear* should be rendered *be made manifest*, and for this approval Paul was waiting. His actions and motives had been challenged, but Christ would then manifest his sincerity, and for this blessed manifestation he would patiently wait.

14, 15. *" For the love of Christ constraineth us." Constraineth to what?*

To unwearied service in the great mission to which Christ had appointed him. So earnestly, indeed, did he labour, that some had even said that he was beside himself.

Was it the love of Christ to sinners, or Paul's love to Christ, that constrained him so to labour?

It was the love of Christ, as shown in His death for a ruined world, that constrained him to labour for their enlightenment and salvation. Since Christ, in his love, died for all, he would labour, in the face of suffering and death, to make it known to all for their redemption. Hence, he says, for the love of Christ constraineth us, having judged this, that if one (Adam) died for or in relation to all, then all died (through him). And for all He (Christ) died, that they who live (through faith in Him) should no longer live to themselves, but to Him who died for them and was raised again. This brief allusion to the results which follow the relation to Adam and Christ, through the flesh and through the faith, is more fully expanded in Rom. v. 12–21, and may be profitably consulted by the reader.

16. *" We know no man after the flesh." What did Paul mean by this statement?*

It was not as Jew or Gentile, circumcised or uncircumcised, that Paul looked upon men, but as having become involved in one common ruin, and for whom God in His love had provided one all-sufficient Saviour.

Why did Paul cease to value Christ's fleshly relation?

Because, after His death, fleshly relation to Christ was of no value. Christ was a Jew after the flesh, and during His life in the flesh every Jew had a claim upon Him as a brother, and right nobly did He respond to this tie; but when they put Him to death this fleshly tie was severed. The union possible to man after His resurrection was only through faith, and this was possible to all alike because so proclaimed, and not through the flesh.

17. *To what part of his teaching*

here does Paul connect, "Therefore, if any man be in Christ, he is a new creature"?

It is, *lit.*, a *new creation*, and stands connected with *all died*, through the first Adam, and is intended to show that the standing and relation of the believer to God is through a new source. The relation is now through a new creation, or, as he states it in Eph. ii. 10, "For we are His workmanship, created in Christ Jesus unto good works." So here, "Old things are passed away; behold, all are become new."

18–20. *"And all things are of God." To what things does Paul refer?*

To the things of redemption, and in these verses he has given an epitome of the whole scheme. Here is God who loved the world, and gave His Son for its redemption; here is Christ who died for all, and sent a message of peace to it through the apostles whom He had chosen; and here is the ministry,—*lit.*, service of reconciliation,—which includes preaching, hearing, believing, immersion, and salvation, as made known by the apostles in the name of Jesus, —the Holy Spirit guiding and perfecting the whole arrangement.

Is it God or man that needs to be reconciled?

It is man, the alien, who needed to be reconciled, and this reconciliation God is seeking to effect by the death of His Son.

"Reconciling the world unto Himself, not imputing their trespasses unto them." What does this mean?

By the world, here, Paul refers to the nations of the earth, to whom he had been sent with the Gospel of the grace of God; and by not imputing their trespasses unto them he means, not that God did not hold them responsible for their trespasses, but that instead of visiting them with judgment, as their vile abominations

deserved, He sent to them the sin-forgiving and heart-purifying message of His grace. Indeed, God did not bring His great judgment upon the Jews until the gospel preached by the apostles had been deliberately rejected by them.

What is the "word of reconciliation"?

The Gospel of Christ, by which He is seeking to reconcile men to God.

What is an ambassador?

One sent to act in the place of a king.

Paul says, "We are ambassadors for Christ." Are all preachers ambassadors?

No one can be an ambassador for Christ, unless personally sent by Him. Others may carry forward their message, but the ambassadors alone have authority.

"We pray you." Is you *a proper addition here?*

Our translators have added *you* twice in this verse, and both should be erased. It was not saints but sinners that Paul besought to be reconciled to God. He had once prayed them to be reconciled to God, but, having yielded to His grace, he now beseeches them not to receive it in vain (vi. 1).

21. *How could Christ be made sin?*

Christ could not be made a sinner, but He could be treated as a sinner, and to this end He gave up Himself to death. Just as the clean bullock was burned to ashes, when made a sin-offering under the law; so Christ, by His death on the cross, was made a curse for us, that we might become the righteousness of God in Him.

CHAPTER VI.

1. *Paul here beseeches them not to receive the grace of God in vain. What grace was this?*

The grace which had brought them, though Gentiles, into the previously-promised salvation of God; and in which blessed standing the fruit of holiness was required.

2. *Why does he quote this ancient prophecy about the " day of salvation ? "*

To show them that the prophecy was fulfilled, and that the promised day had come.

Is it right to tell the sinner that the day may soon close?

The day of salvation, of which Isaiah wrote (xlix. 8), and is here quoted by Paul, was applied to the whole dispensation, and this will not close till Jesus comes. The sinner by his delay may lose his opportunity, and can only be sure of provided privileges by at once embracing them; but the day has come, whether he use it or not. Blessed are they who accept of Jesus, and are saved by Him.

3–6. *" Giving no offence in anything." Was this intended for the Corinthians, or does Paul affirm this of himself and his co-workers in the Gospel?*

He is speaking of what he and they had done to prevent any failure in its desired results; and though the list of things endured is a striking one, yet both afflictions and necessities, stripes and imprisonments, had been patiently borne, that so the cause of failure should not rest with those who had preached it to them. And not only were these things endured, but many Christian virtues, as pureness, patience, kindness, and sincere love, were nobly manifested by these first workers in God's field, in order that His gracious purpose might be fully accomplished.

Why does Paul put the "Holy Ghost" in the list of their Christian virtues?

It is our translators who have done this, and not Paul. It is better to read *a holy spirit,* and this internal state accounts for much that was external in their behaviour.

11. *Why does he say " our mouth is open to you" ?*

Because he had suffered so much on their account that he could speak with the utmost freedom.

13. *" Now for a recompense in the same." What is this?*

A claim for a noble and generous return in self-denial for Christ and holiness.

14. *" Be ye not unequally yoked together with unbelievers." Why use this term yoked ?*

God had commanded under the law, " Thou shalt not plough with an ox and an ass together" (Deut. xxii. 10); and quite likely this prohibitory type was before his mind when he gave this exhortation. The ox was a clean animal, a type of regenerate man, and was fitted by his separation both for service and sacrifice, while the ass was an unclean animal, and was allowed to live only by virtue of its redemption with a lamb, being a type of unregenerate man. God forbade the yoking together of these beasts in service, and Paul applies it to these Corinthians. They had been separated for God, by their faith in Jesus, and are warned against uniting themselves with unbelievers. Already some of them had done this evil thing. One had committed fornication, others had fellowship with idols, and others had become schismatics; and Paul has to warn those who feared God, that unless they avoided this unholy fellowship they would have to forfeit the fellowship of a holy God. The only safe course open to them was separation from all manifest evil, that God might " dwell in them and walk in them."

CHAPTER VII.

1. *In telling over again these precious words of God, "I will be a father unto you,"* etc. *Why does he include himself in the exhortation, "Let us cleanse ourselves,"* etc.?

Because he had to do himself what he called upon them to do. His flesh was naturally no better than theirs, and had to be restrained by the truth, or it could not be held in obedience to God. It was therefore appropriate to include himself in the exhortation.

What is holiness, which he says must be perfected?

Holiness is separation from evil, and perfecting it is the same as cleansing ourselves from all filthiness of flesh and spirit. Consecration to Christ is the first step, and when every forbidden thing is put away holiness is perfected.

Why does he name spirit as well as flesh?

To cleanse the flesh from ceremonial defilement was demanded by the law, and Judaising teachers, who everywhere crossed the path of the apostle, sought no higher standard. God, however, demanded a clean heart, as well as clean hands, hence this earnest exhortation.

2. *"Receive us."* *What does he mean?*

Receive us as teachers, as apostles, and servants of Christ. Receive our example and spirit as worthy of your imitation.

4–6. *"I am exceeding joyful in all our tribulation."* *What gave him this special joy?*

The news which Titus brought him into Macedonia. He had written them a letter in which he condemned their unholy associations and failures, and he became intensely anxious to know whether or not they would heed his counsel. He had told them by the authority of Jesus what they ought to do, and waited with deeply excited feelings to know what the issue would be. Would they own him as a servant of Christ, or would his labour be all in vain? The return of Titus hushed all his fears. They had sorrowed to repentance, and with carefulness and zeal they had cleared themselves of the charge against them.

8. *"I do not repent, though I did repent."* *How do you explain this?*

It is, *lit.*, I do not regret, though I did regret. His letter had caused grief, and this grieved him—a fine example to all who may have to rebuke. To feel a portion of the smart which our hand has caused is indeed to weep with those that weep. But then his rebuke had worked salutary good, and this he did not regret.

9. *What is repentance?*

Not sorrow for sin, but a change of mind, issuing in action. Or in other words, Gospel repentance is an inward purpose to serve Christ. The sorrow of these Corinthians led to repentance, or a purpose to do what Paul required them to do, which course he said they would never regret.

What is godly sorrow?

It is sorrow or grief according to God. It is looking at sin and wrong as God looks at it. Such a view leads to putting it away, not from its consequences merely, but from its nature.

CHAPTER VIII.

1–3. *"We do you to wit of the grace of God."* *What does this mean?*

It is, *lit.*, But we make known to you of the grace of God bestowed or given to the churches, etc.

What was this grace bestowed?

A spirit of liberality in the midst of deep poverty, and shows how largely they drank into the benevolent spirit of Jesus, in caring for others.

Who were the special objects of their liberal collections?

The poor saints in Jerusalem, who were suffering from the dearth that prevailed in that district. Paul in his first letter had asked the saints in Corinth to remember them on the first of every week, and now he brings before them this striking instance of the generous spirit of these Macedonians.

4–6. "*And this they did, not as we hoped.*" *What did he hope or wish?*

That the fellowship of their ministering to the saints should have been given to Titus, who was the first to stir up their liberality; but being asked to minister it himself, he afterward saw it to be the will of God that he should do so. His journey to Jerusalem was indeed the first step towards Rome.

"*They first gave themselves to the Lord.*" *Was this their persons or their gifts?*

Their gifts, no doubt, and their example is worthy of imitation. They gave what they had to give, "first to the Lord," and then the distribution of it to Paul. If all believers could understand the principle upon which they acted, and would follow it, Christian giving would be a happy and efficient thing.

Should all that is given be first given to the Lord? And should it be a fixed sum?

I think that giving should be to the Lord, just as much as singing, praying, working, or any other form of Christian service, and the sum given to the Lord should be fixed, according to Paul, in whom we must hear the Holy Spirit speaking to the saints. "Let each one of you lay by him in store, *as God hath prospered him.*" This then is the standard which Paul gives, and is nothing short of positive tithing. It is a man giving according to his income,

be it little or much. It is not a man putting his hand into his pocket to see if there be anything when a claim is made, and possibly saying, I cannot afford anything to-day. If the object is worthy, then the question will be, How much is there in the Lord's store? For if I first of all give to the Lord according to that I have received from Him, then there will always be a sum for disbursement, and wisdom will be required in acting as almoner for God. It is not a question with God as to whether we have little or much to give, but of faithfulness in what we have. If we decide upon a tenth of our income, the standard fixed by Jehovah for the Jews, then week by week, or month by month, this portion will be separated for the Lord. The giving to the Lord will be as regular as our own supply; the disbursement will be governed by the varied claims which may be made upon us, or as we may decide to meet them. In giving first to the Lord a fixed sum, and then wisely using what has thus become His portion, we shall deliver ourselves from the mere impulses of our nature, and shall have both freedom and pleasure in this service of love. If we are guided by the Lord's will, we shall give to Him as conscientiously as we shall pay for our purchases; and when given to Him, we shall no more dare to use it for ourselves than to put our hand into our neighbour's purse. We have all need to beware of taking our own way, instead of yielding to the Lord.

7–9. *Why does Paul bring forward the amazing grace of Jesus?*

He had asked them to abound in the grace of giving, and from their store to enrich those that were in need, and to show them that he was not asking too much, he refers them to the example of Jesus. He was rich, rich in glory—immeasurably rich, but all was laid aside that they might become rich through His deep poverty. It is well also to notice God's standard of acceptance. It is not much or little, but "according to that a man hath," and "a willing mind."

14, 15. *"He that gathered much had nothing over, and he that gathered little had no lack." Why does he refer to the gathering and supply of manna?*

He is teaching them that the family of God should feel for each other; that the abundance of some should supply the need of others; and that in this supply of the saints in Jerusalem, the churches in Corinth and those in Macedonia should so co-operate, that there should be enough for their supply. He did not wish all the burden to fall upon one Church, but that there should be equality. The churches in Macedonia had done much even in their poverty, and he wished the Church in Corinth to do in its abundance what was still further needed. Paul's quotation about the manna, and the homer which each person received, no more, no less (Exod. xvi.), is suggestive of the thought, that there was an arrangement by which mutual labour and supply was regulated. The appointed portion for each Israelite was a homer; all that were able were gatherers, possibly into a common stock, but each took only his portion. Some might gather more than others, but could take no more, while others, less successful, gathered less, but each had a full portion. The supply was by the gracious power of God—the fixed allotment was also from Him.

18. *Who was "the brother whose praise was in the Gospel throughout all the churches"?*

Most probably Luke is intended, and, by the Gospel which he wrote, he must have been well known to most of the churches of the Gentiles. His writings, which became the common property of the saints; his travels with Paul, in which he often shared his trials; and his general interest in the cause of Christ everywhere, must have endeared him to many hearts. To have a visit from such a man, along with Titus, was no ordinary privilege, and Paul expected good results from their joint visit to Corinth. Would that we had brethren who would take upon them such a voluntary service, and go from church to church to stir them up in holy zeal and service for the Lord. That there is room for such a work as this will not be questioned, and that good results would follow is almost certain. "Who, then, is willing to consecrate his service this day unto the Lord?" (1 Chron. xxix. 5.)

CHAPTER IX.

1–4. *If Paul knew of their forwardness to minister to the saints, why did he send brethren to stir them up?*

He knew their readiness for this good work, for he had boasted of them in Macedonia; but he also knew that the flesh is weak, and required to be kept down, lest it should prevail over the spirit. Paul himself had once needed the "thorn in the flesh," and these Corinthians required the visit of Titus and Luke to help them to perfect their contributions for the poor saints.

5. *If their service must be willing—i.e., voluntary—to be accepted, was it right in Paul to bring such a pressure to bear upon them?*

We must discern between the efforts to instruct and stir up to duty, and the results which may follow. They are perfectly conformable with each other. It was not to *make* them act that Paul sent Titus and the brother, but to *prepare* in them a willing mind. And this is the character of all divinely-appointed service. " Knowing, therefore, the terror of the Lord, we *persuade* men," said Paul, and " we *beseech* also that ye receive not the grace of God in vain."

7–10. Is Paul teaching here that a liberal heart will never have a lack of means to distribute?

He is teaching something very like it. It is as if he said, If you will be a channel of blessing to others, God will use you; and He is testing you by what you have already in seeing how you use it.

11–14. Is Paul here anticipating the results of their contributions?

Yes; and it is very striking to note how much he expects to flow out of this collection for the poor saints. (1.) It would supply the need of those who were suffering from the dearth. (2.) It would call out much thanksgiving to God from those relieved. (3.) It would manifest the power of the Gospel, and help to unite Jew and Gentile in one loving brotherhood. Then (4.) it would be in them an act of grace, and would manifest the spirit of Jesus.

15. What is this unspeakable gift for which he gives thanks to God?

His well-beloved Son, through whom all grace abounds, all sympathy arises, and all blessings flow.

CHAPTER X.

1. Why does he say, " Now I, Paul myself, beseech you"?

He had sent Titus, and with him " the brother," to exhort them to be faithful to the claims made upon them; but now he has to exhort them upon an important matter that concerns himself. His position had been challenged, and though it was

needful that he should reply for the sake of others, yet he wishes to do so in the spirit of his meek and gentle Master.

What was the nature of this challenge?

His apostleship had been called in question, and his defence, which begins with this chapter, is carried on to the close of the epistle; and not only is his defence most complete, but he has also given some important facts connected with his own life, which we cannot fail to ponder with peculiar interest. And while we regret that any should question that he was an apostle of Christ, we are pleased that he has written such a noble defence.

2–5. Why did they reckon that he walked according to the flesh?

It was a false insinuation, yet he condescends to reply to it. " We do walk in the flesh," it is true, " but we do not war after the flesh." The flesh seeks only for itself, but we seek all for Christ. The weapons we use are not for self-exaltation, but to bring even every thought into obedience to Christ.

Why does he use military terms?

In order to help them to better understand the matters he wished to illustrate. Doubtless, they were familiar with fortresses which had been stormed by the legions of the Roman army, who were in that day the terror of all opposing forces; and with the power of the mighty Cæsar, in whose name every conquest was made. It was not with carnal weapons that Paul and his fellow-helpers were fighting, but they were " casting down imaginations, ... and bringing into captivity every thought to the obedience of Christ;" and these were the conquests in which he could glory, and which he was ever seeking to accomplish.

6–11. " And having in a readiness to revenge all disobedience when your obedience is fulfilled." What does this mean ?

His aptly-chosen military metaphors are continued. The directions given to Roman officials were, not to destroy, but to add all willing forces to the imperial sway. They might destroy fortresses and towers, for there the opposers were entrenched, but persons never, if they would yield. Destruction was only for the obstinate. So Paul reminds them that, while the authority given to him was for upbuilding, the disobedient must beware. They might deride his appearance and denounce his address, but they would find him armed with the power of Jesus.

12. *" Some that commend themselves," and "measuring themselves by themselves." Who are these ?*

As the apostle was writing specially to these Corinthian Christians, we assume that they would understand who were referred to, while we can only judge from his many and varied references to them. These persons had their " letters of commendation " from Jerusalem, we presume, and upon these their measure or line of authority was based. It came from their own party, and was of no value, but only a cause of trouble in the churches among the Gentiles. Paul and his co-workers had also their measure or line of action, but it was to preach the Gospel among the nations, and by this rule they had reached even to Corinth ; and if the Church was but faithful they should be able to go further, even to the "regions beyond."

CHAPTER XI.

2, 3. *" I am jealous over you." Why this jealousy ?*

Because he had espoused them to Christ, and he had become afraid they would yield to seducers, and be led aside from the simplicity that is in—*lit.*, for—Christ. It was not truth or argument that he feared, but that seductive measure by which the serpent beguiled Eve, in persuading her to seek fancied good by disobedience. It was the old snare, and would end in ruin.

4. *"For if he that cometh preacheth another Jesus," etc. Why does he say this ?*

If these men had even made known another Saviour, and bestowed another spirit, and preached another gospel, there would have been some excuse for listening to them. But, instead of this, they had nothing to present but a mixture of Judaism and philosophy, which could neither save nor enlighten any one.

5. *" I was not a whit behind the very chiefest apostles." Is Paul contrasting himself with the apostles of Christ ?*

No, but with false apostles—with those sent by men, but to whom he was nothing inferior, even on literary grounds. He had been in Corinth a year and six months, and his capabilities were well-known to them.

6. *Does he admit that he was " rude in speech " ?*

Possibly, he did admit that when contrasted with Grecian orators he would fall short of their standard ; but, if inferior in oratory, he far surpassed them in knowledge. Their speeches were mere empty declamations, his proclamation was a message of life.

Why did he preach the Gospel in Corinth without charge ? and why refer to it here ?

That he might prove by so doing what he afterwards states, " For I seek not yours, but you," and thus remove a possible hindrance to their reception of the gospel. Then his unselfish course formed a striking contrast to those who had made a gain of them.

8. *" I robbed other churches."* *What does he mean ?*

He means that, while labouring in Corinth, he received help from other churches who might justly have claimed his services, but, instead of giving them their just due, he had spent his time there.

14. *What does he mean by "for Satan himself is transformed into an angel of light"?*

I presume that he refers to what is common to Satan in all temptations, viz., to assume a better purpose than his intentions really are. Take the first temptation on record as an illustration. He professed to Eve that he was really seeking her advancement, when he purposely sought her ruin. He appeared as a friend, but was a deadly enemy. So in the temptation of Christ, he professedly sought His relief and elevation, when he really sought His overthrow. So with these false apostles at Corinth, they professedly sought their welfare, but were " deceitful workers."

I suppose we have still to beware of this satanic feature of deception ?

We should beware of everything that is not after Christ. We should not only beware of others, but also of our own reasonings. We may trust in Jesus with all confidence, but in ourselves or others never.

18–22. *Why does Paul challenge the fleshly position of these opposers ?*

His object seems to be to shame those who had been deluded by them. They had evidently boasted of their fleshly standing, and these Corinthians had been taken in this snare. They had been deceived in supposing that these things of the flesh, which he afterwards names, were of great importance, and that Paul was destitute of them. So he goes over these items of supposed value one by one, until they cannot fail to see that he stood at least upon a level with them. " Are they

Hebrews? so am I. Are they Israelites? so am I. Are they the seed of Abraham? so am I." What do they boast of that I can not boast of?

23–28. *" Are they ministers of Christ ?"* *Why does he ask this question ?*

The recital of his own experience will best show why he does so. That they were Hebrews, and Israelites, and the seed of Abraham after the flesh, he does not deny. But he goes further than this, and asks, "Are they ministers of Christ?" and the appended catalogue of the trials, and sufferings, and calamities, endured by himself, suggests the answer that ought to be returned. It is as if he had said, you acknowledge me as a minister of Christ; well, these are the things I have had to endure, and, if these Hebrews have endured anything like this, I shall be more disposed to own their claim. But no, these "false apostles," these "deceitful workers," had so mixed the law and the gospel, had so united Moses and Christ, as to cause the offence of the cross to cease; and thus they escaped all persecution. In preaching salvation through a once-crucified Jesus,—salvation for all who believe in him,—Paul had proved that it neither suited Jewish nature nor human nature, and yet it was the only remedy a God of love could provide.

29. *" Who is weak, and I am not weak? who is offended, and I burn not ?"* *What does he mean ?*

Who is weak, and I do not feel it? who stumbles, and I am not pained by it?

32. *Why does he refer to his escape from Damascus? since it must have been a trivial affair compared with after hostilities.*

Yes, but it was his first experience of the hostility of the human heart against the testimony of Christ; and that hostility had never ceased, and to him it never did.

CHAPTER XII.

1. "*I will come to visions and revelations of the Lord.*" *Why does Paul refer to these visions?*

In order to still further meet the assumptions of Judaising teachers, whose pretentious claims to be heard, rather than an apostle of Christ, had been already more than met; he had asked, "Are they Hebrews? so am I," etc., and then asks, "Are they ministers of Christ?" and only feels how foolish it was to ask such a question. His voluntary service on behalf of these Corinthians, and his unparalleled sufferings on behalf of the truth, was a reflection upon these "deceitful workers,"—whose god was their belly, and whose glory (in their circumcision) was their shame,— that should have carried conviction to all minds. And now he says, "I will come to visions and revelations" (on behalf of the cause of Christ), although it should even reveal how much more I have had to endure for Him whose servant I am.

2. "*I knew a man in Christ . . . caught up to the third heaven.*" *Does he refer to himself? and what is the third heaven?*

That he refers to himself is certain. "Of such a one will I glory;" and by the "third heaven" he means in Hebrew style, the present abode of saints who have passed away from earth. In verse 4 he calls it "paradise," a place into which Jesus entered at death, and also the penitent thief who died with Him. Into this paradise Paul was permitted to enter, and heard what it was not lawful for a man to utter.

"*Whether in the body I cannot tell, or out of the body I cannot tell.*" *Why did Paul say this?*

I cannot say. This much, however, is certain. Paul must have believed that consciousness was possible to the unclothed spirit. He was self-conscious of being there, but of his condition he was not conscious. God knew, but he did not.

4. *Of what use were these unutterable words, if he was not permitted to speak them?*

I think we should understand him to mean that he could not use these revelations or visions for his own glory; but it is very likely that many of the revelations of the future state, afterward given to the Church, were obtained on this occasion.

7. "*There was given to me a thorn in the flesh.*" *Was this a figure or a reality?*

We presume that it was both. It was a figure of a severe trial through which he was called to pass, but it was in reality a messenger of Satan, who, in some way not stated, was permitted to sorely harass him. It was some person who was a tool of the evil one, and the trial was most keenly felt.

Why did God allow the trial?

Lest he should be exalted above measure through the abundance of the revelations. It was a balance against this special favour, and was doubtless required by him.

What lesson may we learn from Paul's trial for ourselves?

We may learn that gifts may endanger our humility, and when we desire them, we should either expect some counter trial, or we shall be imperilled by our natural tendency to vanity.

8. *Why did the Lord not remove his trial when so perseveringly entreated?*

Because Paul was asking a foolish thing. The Lord had sent that trial for his safety, and he asked Him to take it away. The trial was doubtless painful, but pride would have been destructive. The Master knew better than his servant, and for a while prolonged the trial.

9. *When the Lord said, "My grace is sufficient for thee," was not that an indication of its removal?*

No; he was only reminded of what he already possessed, and which should more than have balanced against the trial. It was not even a promise, but a gentle hint of what he had overlooked. The words of his Lord, *lit.*, was, *Sufficient for thee is My favour,* "for My strength is made perfect in weakness." This should have been sufficient for him.

Did not Paul know this before?

Yes; but in his trial he had overlooked it, and now when his Lord has brought it so fully before him, he as fully accepts it, and declares that he is able to rise over all his difficulties.

10. "*Therefore I take pleasure in infirmities." Is not this a strange experience?*

Yes, but very instructive. It shows what the assurances of Christ can do for the man who believes them.

12. *What were the signs of an apostle?*

Not only the possession of gifts themselves, as specially promised by Jesus (Mark xvi. 17, 18), but the power to bestow them on others. To this Paul refers when he asks, "For what is it, wherein ye were inferior to other churches?"

14. *Why does he refer to a third visit?*

He had twice before been in Corinth, and had not been dependent upon them, and was going again, and was resolved to pursue the same course. "For I seek not yours, but you."

CHAPTER XIII.

1, 2. "*This is the third time I am coming to you." Why does Paul refer to the law of Moses concerning witnesses?*

The reference is very appropriate to his determined course of action respecting offenders. He had been twice to Corinth, and had declared the truth with the authority of Jesus, but some had ignored his proclamation. So now he reminds them, that on his third visit, he would make good his word against all such. "If I come again, I will not spare."

3, 4. *Why does Paul illustrate his own case by the crucifixion of Christ?*

There is a striking parallel between them. Christ was crucified through weakness, but was exalted to power by God; so he intimates, although we are weak, we shall live in you by the same power.

How could Christ become weak?

He voluntarily gave up His life for the guilty, and thus became weak; and having placed Himself under the Father's judgment, His protection was withdrawn; so there was nothing left to withstand their purpose, and in weakness He was crucified. In this aspect Christ was like Samson, who could never have been overcome by the Philistines had he not voluntarily yielded the secret of his strength; but having done so, he became as another man. Christ willingly yielded His right over His life, and so became weak.

5. *Why does he say "Examine yourselves"?*

They had asked a proof of Christ speaking in Him, and his reply is a severe but deserved reproof. "Examine yourselves, whether ye be in the faith; prove your own selves;" and then you will have the proof for which you are seeking. The very gifts over which some of them had been puffed up one against another were bestowed through his own hand, "know ye not your own selves, how that Jesus Christ is in you (by His power), except ye be reprobates?" or cannot abide this test.

7. "*Now I pray God that ye do*

no evil." How do you view this desire ?

As the greatest possible proof of his own disinterestedness. It is as if he had said, no matter what becomes of our claims, I pray that you may do no evil. Be right yourselves, and then it will be well with you. Not that we may appear approved, but that ye may do that which is honest, though we be as reprobates. What I desire is your perfection, for the truth cannot be changed by us.

11. This final charge is of a most practical character. Is it really possible to so live as he directs ?

I do not think that Paul would ask impossibilities. He only asks what Christ claimed from all His disciples, nor should one of them desire to render less. To profess to be a disciple without rendering obedience would be a mockery. Let us rather strive to do as Paul directs, and honestly obey his precepts. "Be perfect," *i.e.*, walking along the straight line that Jesus has marked out ; "Be of good comfort," for He is faithful ; "Be of one mind," by your conformity to His will ; "Live in peace," by having the spirit of peace, "and the God of love and peace shall be with you."

14. Is this apostolic benediction a mere benevolent wish for their spiritual welfare ?

It is far more than that. As a good man, Paul would doubtless desire for them all it includes. But the "Amen" was a divine assurance that grace, love, and communion of the triune Deity was theirs through the faith of Jesus. Not something to be prayed for, but truly possessed by the grace of God. When this benediction is pronounced at the close of the meetings of the saints, it should be understood by all that this is their common privilege, and in the assurance of it they should go on their way rejoicing.

THE EPISTLE OF PAUL THE APOSTLE TO THE

GALATIANS.

CHAPTER I.

Why did Paul write this epistle to the churches of Galatia ?

To prevent their reception of the error which Judaisers had introduced among them, and which they were evidently disposed to accept.

What was this error ?

That, in order to their being saved, they must be circumcised, and keep the law of Moses—a demand which God never imposed on the Gentiles.

Is this epistle a refutation of that error ?

It was designed to be so ; and in his masterly induction of facts, principles, prophecies, and illustrations, Paul has unanswerably proved that salvation from sin might be obtained through Christ Jesus, apart from either the law or circumcision. Whether his conclusive argument was received by them or not, the error was triumphantly refuted.

In what way did this doctrine affect the mission of Paul ?

It was an indirect impeachment of his apostleship. It charged him with proclaiming salvation through a false medium, and of setting aside what they held necessary for its enjoyment. It was needful therefore to oppose the error, and to show the consequences that would follow the acceptance of such teaching, and this the apostle has most fully done. In this epistle not only is the death of Christ for sins declared, but also his own calling as an apostle to proclaim Him as a Saviour, the promise of God given to Abraham concerning the nations, the temporary character of the law given by Moses, and the consequent rejection of grace by all who attach the law to the Gospel for salvation, and these things are all fully stated and proved in a most convincing manner. The argument, which begins with the first sentence and is continued to the last, is full of valuable instruction, and all who desire a knowledge of the way of salvation may study it with much profit.

1. *" Paul an apostle, not of men, neither by man, but by Jesus Christ." Why does Paul make these statements ?*

In order to show that he was sent on his great mission by the Lord Himself, and was therefore His apostle, and delivered His testimony, and not like those who had been sent from Jerusalem, who were only apostles of men. His claim to be heard was based upon the fact that he was an apostle of Christ, and serving by the will of God, who had raised Jesus from the dead, *lit., out from among the dead ones.*

2. *" And all the brethren which are with me." Why join the brethren with himself when appealing to authority ?*

Not that he derived any authority from them, because as an apostle of Christ he was independent of all other authority, even of those who were apostles before him; but it was pleasant to him, that not only had these brethren received him as an apostle of Christ, but joined him in his appeal to the churches of Galatia on behalf of the Gospel he had preached.

Y

3, 4. *" Grace to you, and peace from God," etc. Why does he use this salutation to the Galatians ?*

He is simply reminding them of a very blessed fact, viz., that grace had been shown to them, though they were Gentiles, and that in the preaching of the Gospel peace had been brought unto those who were once " afar off." It was indeed marvellous grace that had been displayed, and as Christ Jesus had given Himself for their sins, he marvels that they should now turn to Moses and seek in him what Jesus alone could bestow.

" That He might deliver us from this present evil world." Is the world really evil ?

It is, *lit., age,* not world. The material world is not evil, for God is its creator and upholder ; but age, a word which denotes the course or flow of time, is, by metonymy, used to represent the spirit or character of those who rule it. The outcome, both of Judaism and heathenism, was evil, and so Paul calls it an *evil age,* from the evil of which Christ came to deliver.

" To whom be glory for ever and ever. Amen." What glory is this ?

It is, *lit., the glory, i.e.,* the glory of their deliverance. It was not to Moses or the law that glory or praise was to be ascribed, but to Him who died for their sins ; and no action or rite that would deface this great truth could be for a moment allowed. To renew the observances of the law, which was only a shadow of good things to come, was to deny that the substance had appeared, and into this error these churches were being ensnared.

" For ever and ever." Does this mean eternity ?

It is, *lit., into the ages of the ages,* and ages certainly belong to time, not eternity. The Jewish dispensation had its ages or jubilee periods, and the Christian has likewise its marked divisions, and, from its superiority over the former, it is fitly termed *the ages of the ages.* The work of Christ began in shame, and principalities and powers frowned upon Him; but God glorified Him in raising Him from death, and will glorify Him by subjecting all rule and all authority to Him. To whom be the glory into the ages of the ages, is not only expressive of the deep obligation under which Paul felt himself to be laid, but is prophetic of the grand consummation that will follow when every knee shall bow, and every tongue confess that He is Lord, to the glory of God the Father.

6. *"I marvel that ye are so soon removed from him that called you into the grace of Christ." Why did he marvel?*

Because the Gospel preached by him had been confirmed by miracles, while the false teachers had no divine attestations whatever. It will be better to read, as in the Revised Version: I marvel that ye are so quickly removing from him that called you in the grace of Christ, etc.

" Him that called you." To whom does he refer?

To himself. He had been sent in the grace of Christ to call these idolatrous Gentiles to salvation, and now they are turning away from him to false teachers. Well might he marvel at them.

Why does he call it "another Gospel, which is not another"?

It is better to read, *a different glad tidings, which is not another.* That is, the message they brought was that salvation could be obtained through the law of Moses, and was very different from the message of salvation through Him who was crucified. There was no glad tidings for the sinner in their message. They were only troubling the churches and perverting the Gospel of Christ.

8. *" But though we, or an angel from heaven, preach any other Gospel, etc., let him be accursed." Is it right for an apostle to use such language?*

We might object to man's anathema, but Paul is speaking by the Spirit of God, and in the name of Jesus, so that it is not man but God that speaks. Besides, he puts himself along with the angel, and affirms that both would be accursed if unfaithful to the God-appointed message. God declared to Abraham that in his seed—the Christ—the nations should be blessed; and having given His Son to die, and He being exalted to power, and having sent forth Paul to declare salvation to the nations, woe must betide the man or angel that would change or pervert this message of life and peace.

10–12. *" For do I now persuade men or God?" What does this mean?*

If we read, Do I now *obey* God or man? we shall better perceive his meaning. It was not man but God that he was serving, as he adds, "If man I was pleasing, I should not be the servant of Christ." For the mission on which I am sent is not after man, "For I neither *received* it of man, neither was I *taught* it, but by the revelation of Jesus Christ."

"By the revelation of Jesus Christ." Why does he make this statement?

To show that he had received the message directly from the Lord Himself, and was specially instructed by Him in the work he had to do. Paul was not prepared for his work among the nations by a Priscilla and Aquila, nor even by the twelve who were apostles before him, but by Jesus; who, having sent him directly and personally to the Gentiles, he ever afterward claimed to be "an apostle of Jesus Christ."

13, 14. *Why did he refer to his former conversation or behaviour in the Jews' religion?*

Simply to show what he had been when advancing beyond many in Judaism, and what he had become by the grace of God, even a preacher of the Gospel to the Gentiles. The contrast is most striking, and his reference to it was designed to impress their minds and lead them to see the folly of taking up this very Judaism which he had laid down, and of abandoning the Gospel which, by the will of God, he had preached to them. His former life was no secret, for even these Galatians knew of his zeal in upholding the traditions of his fathers; and but for the will of God and the revelation of Jesus, he would never have preached the Gospel of salvation to the heathen.

15–24. *"But when it pleased God, who separated me from my mother's womb." Why does he refer to his birth?*

Not merely to show that God was the author of his life, although a truth in itself, but to show that from his birth God separated or designed him to be a messenger of His grace to the nations,—according to His promise made to Abraham,—and which also accounts for the extraordinary appearing of Jesus to him, and thus making him an eye-witness of His resurrection on behalf of these nations—and also a joint-witness with those who had seen Him prior to His glorification.

"I conferred not with flesh and blood." Does he refer to himself or others?

To others, doubtless; in fact, having been sent by Jesus, he did not seek any other authority. He did not even go to Jerusalem to consult the apostles, and for a long time he was known to the churches in Judea only by report. His reason for naming his visit into Arabia, and returning to Damascus, and then going into the regions of Syria and Cilicia, all of these being Gentile cities, was evidently to show that, after receiving a commission from Christ, he had no need to seek any other sanction, but had simply to go on with his work. He does, indeed, say that three years after his conversion he went up to Jerusalem to see Peter, but the visit was strictly a fraternal one, and not to obtain either his direction or authority.

CHAPTER II.

1–9. *Why does Paul name his going up to Jerusalem fourteen years after his former visit? and what has it to do with his argument?*

There were at least four notable things connected with this visit which he deems important to bring forward: (1.) That he was allowed to place before Jews of repute at Jerusalem the same glad tidings which he had preached among the Gentiles, and which these Jews accepted. (2.) Titus, a Greek convert who went up with Paul, was allowed to fellowship with the saints in Jerusalem without having been circumcised. (3.) The clamour and influence of false brethren (Judaising teachers) was fully set aside. (4.) The giving of the right hand of fellowship to Paul and Barnabas by James, Cephas, and John; and even sending them away to fulfil their mission among the heathen. And to these we may add the confirmation of Paul's glad tidings, by signs which were equal to those given to Peter. Now, all these things occurred on the occasion of Paul's visit, and are worthy of being repeated in this argument.

Was this visit to Jerusalem the same as that recorded in Acts xv.?

Yes; it is almost certain that Luke in the Acts and Paul in this epistle refer to the same event. True, there are matters in each which the other has not recorded, but these only give us a fuller view of that important visit. The result was all that Paul and Barnabas and others with them could have desired, and in this letter he most triumphantly refers to it.

Does the Gospel of the circumcision committed to Peter differ in anything from the Gospel of the uncircumcision committed to Paul ?

In nothing except the sphere of labour in which each was called to serve. Peter laboured chiefly among the Jews, though occasionally among the Gentiles ; while Paul laboured among Gentiles, but also among Jews when opportunity served him. A very careful examination of the preaching and teaching of both will fail to reveal any difference between them. Nor could it be otherwise, unless they had been unfaithful. When both were sent by one Master, and both guided by one Spirit, how could their testimony differ ? It was the class among whom they ministered that differed, and not the Gospel they preached.

10. *" Only they would that we should remember the poor." What poor were these ?*

The poor saints at Jerusalem, who, on account of their faith in Christ, were called to suffer much, even the " spoiling of their goods." But Paul was ever mindful of them, even stirring up the Gentiles to this work, and at one time he took a large collection to Jerusalem for their benefit.

11–13. *Paul had to reprove Peter at Antioch for his unfaithful action. Was this after the conference at Jerusalem ?*

It is most likely to have occurred some time after, and when there had been considerable change in the leading brethren in Jerusalem. James—who understood the truth thoroughly at that conference, and by a very ap-

propriate application of the prophecy by Amos (ix. 11), closed it in Paul's favour — had evidently fraternised with Judaising teachers, and his influence was being felt even by Peter. When Peter went down to Antioch, his fellowship with Gentile believers was all that could be desired,—he ate with them, and thus showed openly that meat commendeth not to God, and should make no difference among brethren,—but when certain came from James, he separated himself, fearing them who were of the circumcision. His separation from the tables of Gentiles—evidently through fear of being reported to James—led other Jews to dissemble with him, and even the simple-minded Barnabas was carried away with their dissimulation or double-dealing.

Was Peter's dissimulation damaging to the truth ?

Not to the truth, which by the Holy Spirit he had proclaimed ; but those who respected his action rather than his proclamation, must have been greatly confused by it. The faith had been delivered to the saints once for all, which even Peter's wavering could not change, and had they held to his testimony, in spite of his swerving spirit, he would have stood alone in his shame. As it was, he carried others with him, and had to be reproved before all.

Is it not strange for one apostle to have to blame another ?

Yes ; but we must remember that it was not for his testimony, but for his unfaithfulness to his own testimony which he had before delivered and acted upon. He knew God's will respecting these things, but did not do it. The sheet let down from heaven, with symbols of cleansed Gentiles, could not have been forgotten, but his cringing fear of man was a snare and a blot upon his otherwise valuable life. And though it was only a changing from one table to another, it was a cause of stumbling to many guileless souls. The truth remained the same, but his failure in practice was injurious to many. All believers should feel the solemn responsibility for good or evil in relation to others, which attends every step in life. No one can tell the result of a wrong step, eternity alone will reveal it. It may injure but one solitary heart, or it may affect millions. We should be exceedingly careful to act in harmony with truth, so that if others do wrong they may not have us to blame for what they do. It is, indeed, strange to read of Paul reproving Peter, but the reproof was needed, and very effective. I do not think he repeated the offence.

14–21. *How far does Paul's address to Peter extend?*

To the close of the chapter, I presume, and while his appeal is specially to him, the truths are adapted to the general argument, and embrace several important aspects of the case. —(1.) He asks Peter why he a Jew, who had actually lived as a Gentile, should by this change compel Gentiles to reverse their position, and live as Jews, *lit.*, to Judaise. (2.) "Knowing" (Peter, Paul, and others) "that a man is not justified by the works of the law, but by the faith of Jesus Christ, even we have believed in Jesus Christ, that we might be justified by the faith of Christ." Then (3.) if, while we have sought this privilege, we also are found sinners,— *i.e.*, in reversing this plan,—is Christ chargeable with this? By no means : "For if I build again the things which I destroyed or loosed down, I make myself a transgressor." It is I who have changed, not Christ. (4.) For I through law died to law, that to God I might live, and now shall I go back to that to which I died? Again, I (the old man) have been crucified with Christ, yet I (the new man) live, no longer I (the old

man), but Christ lives in me; and the (holy obedient) life which I now live in the flesh I live by the faith of the Son of God, who loved me, and gave Himself for me. Under such reasoning Peter must have felt reproved, and did not attempt a reply.

CHAPTER III.

1. *" O foolish Galatians." Why call them foolish?*

It is, *lit.*, thoughtless,—*i.e.*, without thought,—and this was strikingly manifest in the course they had pursued. They had allowed these false teachers to induce them to add Moses to Christ, the law to the Gospel, circumcision to baptism, the shadow to the substance ; and nothing could have been more foolish. Indeed, they had been so fascinated by them, that they accepted the bond of the old institution, and Christ was thus virtually abandoned.

Why does the Revised Version omit, " that ye should not obey the truth" ?

According to Alford, this sentence is omitted by nearly all the oldest authorities, and is supposed to have been a gloss inserted from the margin into the text. It is on this account omitted by the Revised Version.

2–5. *In these four verses the apostle asks four questions, but gives no answer. Why is this?*

The first of these questions was about the gifts of the Spirit, which they had consciously received through him ; and he is now led to ask whether this was done through the works of the law or through the hearing of faith?—*i.e.*, through their obedience to Christ or the teachers of the law. They were all conscious that false teachers conferred no gift, and worked no miracles ; but Paul the apostle of Christ had done both. The other questions refer to their going back from spirit to flesh, and to their suffering for Christ in vain, that is, said he, " if it be yet in vain." To even ask these questions was to manifest their folly.

" Received ye the Spirit," " begun in the Spirit," " ministereth to you the Spirit." What do these statements mean ?

It is to the gifts of the Spirit, manifestly bestowed or ministered to them, and which were associated with their first reception of Christ, that Paul refers. They were evidential proofs of the truth of Christianity, and should have been held by them as unanswerable proofs of its reality.

6. *" Even as Abraham believed God," etc. Why refer to him in his appeal to Gentiles ?*

To show that he received the promise through faith in the coming Messiah when in uncircumcision and before the law was given, and that all those who are now accounted as his children can only be so through faith in Jesus. To seek this position through the law or the flesh was absolute folly.

8. *" And the Scripture, foreseeing," etc. How do the Scriptures foresee ?*

It is by metonymy that the Scriptures are said to foresee, because it is in them that we read that God announced the glad tidings to Abraham : " In thee shall all nations be blessed." In this figurative manner, therefore, Paul is showing the folly of seeking blessing in any other way than that which had been previously written.

10. *" For as many as are of the works of the law are under the curse." Why should the curse of the law rest on all who are under it ?*

Because of disobedience ; of which all who were placed under it were proved to be guilty. The law, which consisted of wise and needful commands and prohibitions, was not in-

tended to curse—*i.e.*, condemn—but to restrain wrong doing ; but without love, which it could never produce, its penalties were unheeded, and so judgment rested upon wrong-doers. It was indeed foolish for these Galatians to add such a system to the Gospel of Christ.

11. *" The just shall live by faith." Why does he quote this statement ?*

He is again appealing to the Scriptures, and as they affirm that the just or righteous become so by faith, the possibility of being made so by the law is altogether set aside. And this still further confirmed the folly of these Galatians in turning back to the law.

13. *"Christ hath redeemed us from the curse of the law." To whom does this apply ?*

To those who received Him, and only to such, these blessed words apply. True, " He gave Himself a ransom for all, to be testified in due time ; " but it is only in the acceptance of this testimony that redemption from condemnation is realised.

14. *" That the blessing of Abraham might come on the Gentiles," etc. What blessing was this ?*

The blessing promised to him for the nations through the Messiah, his seed. It is, *lit.*, the good word of Abraham, or that which was spoken to him concerning the nations being blessed through the Messiah. To fulfil this promise of the Spirit Christ was made a curse, and now, through Him, this promise of the Spirit is fulfilled in all who believe in Him.

15–17. *Why does he refer to covenants to illustrate his statement about God blessing Gentiles ?*

To show that God's covenant, which He had made with Abraham concerning Christ, was unchangeable. Just as a man's covenant, when confirmed, could not be altered, so neither could the covenant of God. Even the law, which was given 430 years after, could not make the promise of none effect. When Abraham offered up Isaac, God swore to him : " In blessing I will bless thee, and in multiplying I will multiply thy seed [believers] as stars of heaven. . . . . And in thy seed [Christ] shall all the nations of the earth be blessed " (Gen. xxii. 17).

" *He saith not, and to seeds, as of many ; but as of one* " (*seed*). *Why this discrimination of singular and plural in relation to this promise ?*

It is a fine illustration of Paul's critical exegesis upon a word, and shows how important it is that every Word of God should have its full value—no more, no less than God intended. The reason why Paul is so critical is, because there were other seeds about which God had spoken to Abraham. There were his fleshly seed, of which, according to the flesh, he was father and head,— " I know," said Jesus to the Jews, " that ye are Abraham's seed, but ye seek to kill Me because My word hath no place in you" (John viii. 37), —and there was also his seed through Christ, of which he was to be the father, because of his own faith in the promise of the Coming One. Now, Paul is very careful—for the benefit of these foolish Galatians—to discriminate between the seeds referred to as to which of them the promise really appertained. By being circumcised these Galatians were being put among his fleshly seeds, to which, as such, the promise of spiritual blessing did not belong. So he reasons : " Now to Abraham and his seed were the promises made. He saith not, and to seeds, as of many," and the seed of Hagar, Sarah, and Keturah are here included ; "but as of one, and to thy seed, which is [through] Christ."

18. *What was this inheritance* which was not of the law, but of promise ?

That which was to be enjoyed through Christ ; or, as he puts it in his letter to the Ephesians, " All spiritual blessings in heavenly places in Christ ; " or, as Peter puts it, " All that pertains to life and godliness." It could not be the land of Canaan, for though promised to Abraham for his seed by Sarah, it was inherited through the law. The nation in the wilderness lost it through breaking the law, and their children were put out of it for their violation of it. Besides, Paul never once mentions the land of Canaan in his argument. The possession and retention of the land, and obedience to the law went together, while faith in Christ never put any man in possession of it, and never was intended to do so. The land, as an inheritance, was only a type for the time then present, as were many other things, and not the very image or substance of the things. We must therefore look for the antitypical inheritance in the Gospel, and there we find it to be the rest, and pardon, and peace, and ultimate glorification through Christ. This met all man's need, and was worthy of the God who provided, in His Son, that which alone could satisfy. God could use the material to typify the spiritual ; a rest in Canaan, for the rest of faith ; circumcision of the flesh, for holiness of heart and life ; but we must advance from the flesh to the Spirit, from the carnal to the spiritual, and never the reverse.

19. *Why does Paul ask, " Wherefore then the law ?" or, Why was it given ?*

In order to meet a difficulty which would be sure to be felt— viz., of what use is the law if we may not put ourselves under it ? So he gives the true purpose of its imposition. "It was *added* because of transgression"—*i.e.*, to restrain it until the seed should come to whom the promise was made. It was a city of refuge in which they were preserved from the avenger of blood, until the death of the high priest, when liberty could be granted, even to the man-slayer. Now, it would have been very foolish for a man-slayer to prefer to remain in the city when, through this official death, he might be free; and it was more foolish still for a Gentile, charged with his own peculiar crimes, through which he was worthy of death, to be induced to enter this provisional refuge when he might enjoy a full and free forgiveness of his sins. Yet this was what these Galatians were really doing.

"The law . . . was ordained by angels in the hand of a mediator." What does this mean?

Paul is speaking here not of celestial beings, but of messengers, through whom the law was transmitted from Moses, after God permitted him to become their mediator. Their right to national existence had been forfeited by worshipping the golden calf, but by granting a mediator they were allowed to continue till the seed should come. It was, therefore, but a temporary arrangement.

How could Moses be both the lawgiver and a mediator?

He is in this matter a type of the prophet that was to be like him. Jesus was the lawgiver of the new covenant, and also its mediator, and both have officiated from the necessity of the parties who stood related to them. When Moses came down from the mount with the law in his hands, which the children of Israel had promised to accept, he found they had broken it, and soon learned that God could righteously destroy them from being a nation. Moses at once began to plead for them, and

was allowed to become their mediator. God heard him on their behalf, and spared them from death. It is to this fact that Paul here refers, and a most solemn reference it is,—viz., that the mediation for their national preservation was only allowed to be in force till the seed should come, and that it should then terminate. With the introduction of another mediator the official position of the former ceased, and their treatment must then rest upon their acceptance or rejection of the Messiah. For the Jews to remain under Moses, who could no longer fill the office of mediator; or, for the Galatians to put themselves under him, after Christ had been accepted, was absolute folly.

20. *"Now a mediator is not of one, but God is one." What does this mean?*

If we read, a mediator of *oneness* or *unity*, it might help us to see his meaning. A mediator implies a state of hostility or failure, a condition of things in which there is a call for interposition to prevent just consequences. Now, this could not be charged upon God, but upon the people, and through the law under which they had placed themselves. God did not force the fiery law upon Israel; it was proposed and accepted, but not kept, and then the mediator had to interfere to save from death.

21. *"Is the law then against the promises of God?" Why does he ask this?*

Simply to show that instead of being against them it rather manifested their need. The law could never meet man's condition, and God having promised life through a Saviour, this provision should be accepted.

23–26. *"But before faith came." Does he mean before we believed?*

No; it is, *lit., the faith,*—*i.e.*, the Gospel administration, with its full, gracious provision. Before that came the Jews were kept under law,—*i.e.*, guarded by it,—and shut up under it, until the deliverer should come to open their prison door.

"*Wherefore the law was our schoolmaster unto Christ.*" *Does he refer to its severity?*

No, but to its office. The law was our *paidagogue*, *lit.*, a child-leader, —*i.e.*, one taking charge of minors until the teacher appeared and the school was opened. It was their privilege then to enter for instruction —to be trained by the lessons of the Master, and perfected in all heavenly wisdom. To remain under the law or child-conductor when the teacher had appeared,—and the Jews were doing this,—or to go from the teacher to the law-guarded condition of a child, as these Galatians were doing, was an act of great folly. "For ye (who have believed) are all the children of God by faith in Christ Jesus;" and this liberty and instruction is your privilege as children.

27. *Why does he refer to their baptism?*

Because in their immersion they put on Christ; just as in marriage, a bride puts on her husband, and from henceforth is one with him. All that Christ possessed became theirs when made one with Him. To put on Christ in their baptism was to put off all former distinctions, and they were no longer to be looked at as Jew or Greek, bond or free, male or female, but to be seen only in Him. And having put on Christ, why should they put on Moses?

29. "*And if ye be Christ's, then are ye Abraham's seed, and heirs according to the promise.*" *Is this a conclusion of his argument?*

Yes; the argument proper terminates with this conclusive statement. What follows may be considered as illustration and application of his argument, and contains most valu-able instruction. He had stated (ver. 16), "Now to Abraham and his seed (in the one great seed) were the promises made," and to show who these were was his special aim in this chapter, and here we have his conclusion, "If ye be Christ's, then are ye Abraham's seed, and heirs according to the promise," or the heirs for whom the promise was intended. If you are not Christ's, you are not Abraham's seed, even though you may be Jews; nor can any claim the promise, even though they may be circumcised. It is only the new-created in Christ Jesus that become the heirs of the promise of God.

CHAPTER IV.

1, 2. *Why does Paul bring forward the case of a minor or heir under age?*

The case itself is very simple. That no minor or infant could legally inherit property was well known. Tutors might direct its studies, and overseers manage its affairs, and like a servant it must yield to control until the time appointed of the father. Now Paul intended this illustration to apply to these Galatians. They were believers in Christ, and were therefore children of God and heirs of the inheritance. But having put themselves under law, they were in the condition of children under age, and as long as they remained in that state could not inherit even what might otherwise be their proper right. The application of this illustration is made in verses 8, 9.

3. "*Even so we, when we were children.*" *To whom does he apply this?*

To pious Jews who lived before the coming of Christ.

What were these elements of the world under which they were in bondage?

I suppose they are what in the epistle to the Hebrews he calls "meats and drinks, and divers washings; carnal ordinances imposed on them till the time of reformation" (ix. 10). Or, as in this epistle (v. 1), what he terms "a yoke of bondage."

4. *What does "fulness of the time" imply?*

The completion of the period which preceded the coming of Jesus. The time of His coming had been marked on the prophetic scroll, and when it was completed, "God sent forth His Son, made of a woman," and therefore her seed, and the Saviour of her ruined children.

5. *" The adoption of sons." What process does this involve?*

The word *adoption*, as we now understand that term, rather hides than opens the apostle's meaning. An adopted child is not truly the child of those who adopt it, but a child of God is begotten by His word of truth, and born into His family, and is truly His child by regeneration. It would be better to read *sonship* than adoption of sons, as comprising not only the fact itself, but all associated privileges.

What is the meaning of " Abba, Father"?

Abba is a Syro-Chaldaic word, which means father, and here Paul has first transferred the word, and then translated it, that they might understand its meaning.

7. *Is "servant" and "son" used here to indicate spiritual standing?*

Yes; and the contrast should be specially noticed. Moses was but a servant, and the law could not raise him to a higher rank; but Paul and other believers were sons through Christ Jesus. True, a son may be also a servant, but a servant is not necessarily a son. Sonship had been conferred on them through Jesus, and it was great folly to renounce their sonship and go back to the standing of a servant.

8, 9. *Why does he refer to their former service of idols?*

It was in order to ask a question concerning their conduct, and his own reply reveals their very deep folly. " But now, after that ye have known God," by the revelations made to you, " or rather are known of God," by His gracious gifts bestowed upon you, "how turn ye again to the weak and beggarly elements, whereunto ye desire again to be in bondage?"

Why does he call circumcision and the service of the law weak and beggarly elements?

Because these things could not meet man's deep spiritual need. Christ alone could do that; and from Him they were turning away.

10, 11. *" Ye observe days, and months, and times, and years." What did this indicate to Paul?*

A manifest proof that they were giving up Christianity for Judaism. These days, and moons, and times, all pointed to Christ and the new covenant, and were all right and good while His coming was future; but to attend to them, when fulfilled in a present Saviour, was to ignore the fact and proclaim Christianity to be a lie. It is no wonder that he should exclaim, " I am afraid of you, lest I have bestowed upon you labour in vain." John, who I presume refers to the same error, counts the action a denial of both the Father and Son. "Who is a liar but he that denieth that Jesus is the Christ? He is antichrist that denieth the Father and the Son" (1 John ii. 22).

12. *" Brethren, I beseech you, be as I am; for I am as ye are." What does he mean?*

Our translators have tried to express Paul's briefly-stated exhortation by adding a few words, but have failed to reveal what he means. Possibly further supplements are required, and when in harmony with facts, we may safely append them. The following may help a little in understanding the import of his appeal, "Brethren, I beseech you, be as I" (now am, free from these rites); "for I" (was once) "as ye are" (now, in bondage to Jewish ceremonies). And, as if he had said, let my example have weight with you, for it is not me ye are injuring, but yourselves, by going back to the law.

13–15. *"Ye know how through infirmity of the flesh I preached the Gospel unto you at the first." To what does he allude?*

That there was some bodily infirmity in connection with his preaching to them is very plain, but why he should allude to it is not so evident; or why their reception of the facts of the Gospel at a time when he was suffering should be such a praiseworthy matter is not so easily perceived. He may, however, refer to his detention in Galatia, on account of the maltreatment he had previously received; and, being obliged to remain for a time to recover from this abuse, he preached the Gospel to them, and in the face of all this rejection and cruelty inflicted by the Jews, they received him as a messenger of God. Dr Howson suggests that this first visit occurred on his second missionary tour, and when he was not intending to remain, but was obliged to do so from his condition of body. It was not through natural but inflicted infirmity that he was detained and preached to them, and the cordial reception of his message under the circumstances forms a striking contrast to their behaviour afterward, and is here used as a reproof.

19. *What does he mean by "little children"?*

The present accepted reading is, *my children*, and it will be better to so read it.

Is "travail in birth again" appropiate to them?

They had left their standing as children, and his effort to replace them in the family was as the pangs of a travailing spirit.

21–31. *Why does he introduce this allegory about Agar and Sarah, when the events recorded took place many years before the law was given?*

Yes; but it was written by Moses, and as these two women were types of the two covenants on which the two dispensations were founded, it is a very appropriate illustration of the result of being under the one or the other.

Is it not strange that God should select two women and their seed to represent two covenants?

Yes, very strange to us, but very full of instruction; and as God was giving "shadows of good things to come," we ought not to be surprised at the somewhat strange forms these are made to take. God had promised a son to Abraham, and for its fulfilment he was anxiously looking; but as conception by Sarah was delayed, an expedient was proposed, and Agar, the bondmaid, was given to him to wife, by whom Ishmael was born. But Ishmael was a child of Abraham's flesh, and God made that mother to represent the covenant of the flesh, which He made at Sinai, and her son to be a type of Abraham's fleshly seed by Isaac. And as Ishmael, the child of the flesh, was cast out of Abraham's family, and not allowed to be heir with Isaac, the child of promise, so the Jews, the fleshly seed of Abraham, were not allowed to be heirs with the children of promise, but were cast out, according to the word of Sarah:—"Cast out the bondwoman and her son." How foolish these Galatians must have appeared to Paul, in putting themselves among the bondwoman's children, as the fleshly seed of Abraham had then become.

"*Rejoice, thou barren that bearest not.*" *To whom does this quotation apply ?*

To her represented by Sarah, the once barren woman, or, as Paul terms her, Jerusalem, the city of God, which is above or superior to Sinai ; or, in other words, the Church, the mother of believers, according to the prophet. For a long time she was barren, having nothing to comfort her but the promise of God. At last the child of hope was born, and in due time a numerous progeny has been given to her, and the long-desolate one hath many children—not children of the flesh, but of the faith.

CHAPTER V.

1. *What liberty is this in which they are exhorted to stand ?*

The liberty of which Sarah and her son were a type,—a liberty to remain in the house, when the bond-woman and her son must be cast out. This verse is the conclusion of his instructive allegory, and should not have been separated from it.

"*Be not entangled again.*" *What does this imply ?*

A former state of bondage under sin and idolatry, and he warns them against being entangled with bondage under law.

2–4. "*If ye be circumcised, Christ shall profit you nothing.*" *How do you reconcile this with Paul circumcising Timothy ?*

The two cases differ widely. Timothy was circumcised to open a door of access to the Jews in preaching and teaching; while these Galatians were being circumcised in order to be saved. In the one case it was a mere matter of acceptability, in the other a denial of Christ as a perfect Saviour. In accepting Moses

they put themselves under obligation to do the whole law, and thus renounced grace.

5. "*For we through the Spirit wait,*" etc. *Is waiting the present attitude of believers ?*

Not for righteousness, since that is provided in and through Jesus, and is for present attainment. Paul is speaking, as is common to him in his teaching on Christian privileges, about the expectations of believers, as viewed through the inspired teaching of the prophets. They declare that certain things are to be realised when the Christ shall come, and He having come, the promise is attainable. Now we are not seeking righteousness by law, but righteousness by faith, as directed by the Spirit in the prophets.

6. "*For in Jesus Christ neither circumcision availeth anything,*" etc. *Did it never avail ?*

Yes, for some things, but not for salvation. Circumcision under the law was a great privilege, but when Jesus began His administration it secured no privilege under Him. Faith, leading to loving obedience, was what He asked from both Jew and Greek, and from each it was alike acceptable.

11. *What was the "offence of the cross" ?*

Salvation through a crucified and risen Jesus, which was so offensive to the Jews, and for which they persecuted Paul in every place. It is as if he said, If I preach circumcision (as some say I do), why then am I persecuted?

"*I would they were even cut off which trouble you.*" *Why does he say this ?*

It is, *lit.*, *I wish they who trouble you would cut themselves off.*

13–15. *Why does he warn them against licentiousness ?*

If his statement respecting false teachers, as recorded in Phil. iii. 19, and also that by Peter, second epistle, chap. ii., and Jude, be carefully pondered, we shall find them guilty of very vile practices ; and Paul well knew what the result would be to their disciples. If the teachers lived after the flesh, their followers would be sure to imitate them.

16. *" Walk in the Spirit." How could they do this ?*

By obeying all His precepts, and this is the only security against yielding to the lusts of the flesh. The Spirit has made known all that is necessary for life and godliness, and to walk in these directions is to walk in Him.

17. *" For the flesh lusteth against the Spirit," etc. What is the meaning of this verse ?*

The flesh has its own tendencies and desires, and these are contrary to the directions of the Holy Spirit, so that those who walk in the flesh cannot do the things they ought to do. Verses 16 and 17 should be read together.

19–21. *Why has Paul given this long catalogue of the works of the flesh ?*

To enable them to understand that these evil practices, the works of the flesh, would disqualify for the kingdom of God. To name these vices was far better than any general statement about sin, because when named they were known by all. What they did require to know was, that if these vices were practised they were walking contrary to the Spirit of God. Idolators might allow their indulgence, and even Judaising teachers might sanction them, but God condemned them, and this should suffice.

Do the terms given by our translators sufficiently indicate what Paul meant ?

Yes, with the exception of a few terms, which might be more clearly expressed. For instance, for "hatred" we might read *enmities ;* for "variance," *strife ;* for "emulation," *jealousy ;* for " wrath," *self-seeking ;* for " seditions," *divisions* or *factions ;* and for "heresies," *sects.* According to scholars, the first term *adultery* is not found in the most ancient MSS.

22–24. *Are these fruits of the Spirit expected from all the disciples of Christ ?*

They are not only expected, but are sure to follow the putting on of Christ, and walking in the Spirit. " They that are Christ's have crucified the flesh with its affections and lusts."

25. *What is the difference between " live in the Spirit" and " walk in the Spirit " ?*

It is, *lit., by spirit* in both clauses. The former refers to what is received, the latter to what is to be done. In the one we get the grace, and in the other the responsibility, both of which are revealed by the Spirit.

CHAPTER VI.

1. *" If a man be overtaken in a fault." Does* fault *express what Paul means ?*

It would be better to read *offence* —a falling away from a right course ; a result of sudden temptation.

Is " overtaken" correct ?

It might be better to read *surprised,* as Paul does not seem to refer to wilful transgression, but to those who were led astray unawares by false teachers, and whose offence called for sympathy rather than condemnation. The restoration of all such should be sought in meekness, ever remembering that we may be tempted or tried beyond what we have yet conceived. Believers should never have sympathy with wrong-doing, but should always seek to lead the wrong-doer away from evil.

2. *" So fulfil the law of Christ." What is this ?*

Loving one another as He gave commandment, and it is a proof of love to help to bear another's burden.

Is it poverty or bodily necessity that is the burden to be shared?

Possibly neither. There are burdens which some have to bear that are far worse than poverty—burdens which crush the heart, and which loving sympathy alone can help. Jesus never possessed Himself of worldly means, and yet who ever helped the broken-hearted like Him?

4. *Why did he call upon each to prove his own work? and how were they to do this?*

By obeying the Spirit, who, through the apostles, had made known the truth; and that there might be no deception in their profession, he calls upon each to prove himself, because every one would bear his own burden,—*i.e.*, his own freight or responsibility. Burden here is not the same word in Greek as in verse 2.

6. *Does Paul teach here that the taught in the word should help the teacher?*

Yes, if his need so require. Some who were gifted to teach had to deny themselves the ordinary means of supplying their own need, and for such the saints were to care, or to communicate, *lit., share ye in all good things.*

7, 8. *Why does he refer to sowing aud reaping?*

Because it is a fit illustration of human life. Men sow and reap, but the reaping and the sowing will correspond with each other. To the observant eye this is fulfilled every day.

What is sowing to the flesh?

Yielding to its lusts or desires, so that our actions are controlled by it.

What is sowing to the Spirit?

Walking according to His teach-

ing; heart and life being in conformity to His will.

What is " corruption "?

That which does not abide but perishes, and so fails to serve in time of need.

What is " life everlasting "?

The favour of God in Christ, which abides in all the believing and survives all perishable things.

9. *What is the nature of this " well-doing," in which he urges them to fail not?*

Obedience to Christ, and, as the full recompense will not be realised till He comes, to have to wait is a test that too often discloses weariness, or, *lit., losing heart in the service.* Do not lose heart, said he, for in due season we shall reap, if we faint not.

10. *What is the distinction between " all men " to whom we are to do good, and the " household of faith "?*

All men here are the world, to whom, as opportunity opens, good must be done; but the household of faith are believers, who have a special claim, arising out of relationship. To believers, every believer is a brother or sister, and they must feel for each other; to the world they must be as good Samaritans, to sympathise and help as opportunity shall serve.

12. *" They constrain you to be circumcised, only lest they should suffer persecution." How could circumcision keep them from persecution?*

It must be noted that up to that time the Jews were the chief persecutors of the disciples of Christ, not in Judea alone, but in every place in which they existed in sufficient numbers. The representatives of Roman authority did not at first interfere with Christians, except as compelled by Jews. The union of Judaism with Christianity was a wretched expedient to prevent persecution, and was carried on with untiring zeal until God by His sore judgment destroyed their nationality.

To accept of circumcision protected the subject of it from persecution, while to refuse to be circumcised was to set aside the whole institution, and exposed all who did so to the most bitter persecution.

14. *How was the world crucified to Paul by the cross?*

It is, *lit., a world,* and refers specially to the old dispensation—the Jews' religion. Paul's course formed a striking contrast to these false teachers. They, to avoid persecution, upheld the law of Moses; while he accepted the cross, the synonym of the death of Jesus for sin, and by it became separated from his former standing, fleshly, tribal, and ceremonial, painful though it must have been. But what things were gain to me, those I counted loss for Christ.

What does he mean by " the Israel of God"?

He refers to those who Jacob-like prevailed with God, and through Jesus found acceptance; in contrast with those who were " Israel after the flesh" (1 Cor. x. 18).

17. *What does he mean by the "marks of the Lord Jesus"?*

In Greek it is *stigmata,* a well-known term for the brand which a master burned into his slave, and by which mark he was everywhere known. I bear the stigmata,—*i.e.,* the brandmarks of the Lord Jesus,—and by these scars in my flesh it is known that I belong to Him. These scars in my flesh have been affixed by persecuting brethren, on account of my preaching salvation to the Gentiles, apart from the law. Therefore " let no man trouble me" by joining hands with these opposers of the grace of God.

THE EPISTLE OF PAUL THE APOSTLE TO THE

EPHESIANS.

CHAPTER I.

What is the special character of this epistle, and why was it written?

The epistle is directly addressed to " saints at Ephesus," although the words " at Ephesus " are omitted in some MSS., nor is there any internal evidence of any special relation which it may bear to them above that of any other church of Gentile believers. Some have suggested that it is a general letter with a local address, and would be circulated among all the churches of the saints. Admitting then that this epistle had written upon it, " to the saints which are at Ephesus," and was carried there first of all by Tychicus; yet, as it contains a double address, being (1.)

" to the saints which are at Ephesus, and (2.) to the faithful in Christ Jesus " (in every other place), it would be circulated among all the churches, as specially designed to be.

We look upon this epistle to the Ephesians as a full exposition of the standing of believers, and should be understood to be the great charter of their privileges in Christ, and from which they may obtain the divine assurance of present possessions in Christ Jesus. As an exposition and revelation of the believer's standing and responsibility, this epistle stands alone, and no other of the epistles written by Paul can be a substitute for it. It bears to believing Gentiles a relation similar to that which the 1st Epistle of Peter bears to believing

Jews, and in these two letters the instruction of both, as respects Christian standing, is complete. Every convert, from the very first day of surrender to Christ, under a well-instructed guide, should begin an exhaustive study of this epistle, and thus obtain a full knowledge of all that God in His grace has granted to His children. The epistle was written under the guidance of the Holy Spirit, to assure believing Gentiles of their acceptance, election, and heavenly standing in Christ; of their possession of all the privileges first granted to believing Jews; and to urge them to walk worthy of their heavenly calling; and the instruction afforded to them is afforded to all others who since that time have received Jesus as their Saviour and Lord. In the commission, as given in Mark xvi. 15, 16, the promise to the obedient disciple is, "shall be saved," and in this epistle we have the divine exposition of what being saved implies. It is important that all disciples should be promptly led from the one to the other; that a knowledge of position may give strength for service and conflict.

2. " *Grace be to you, and peace from God,*" etc. *Is there anything special in this apostolic benediction?*

Yes. Coming as it does from an ambassador of Christ, it is a divine assurance that every privilege provided in Jesus was given them to possess.

3. " *Blessed the God and Father . . . who hath blessed us.*" *To whom does he refer?*

To believing Jews "who first trusted in Christ," and who were sealed by the Spirit with the miraculous gifts bestowed on behalf of the Christ. To feel the force of the apostle's illustration, it will be needful to note the frequent use of "we" and "us," especially from verses 3–12, in which we may clearly discern the prior enjoyment of these privileges by them. Then in verse 13 we have the "ye,"—ye heard, ye believed, ye were sealed, which as clearly points out the believing Gentiles, who were afterwards united with them, and together they formed the one body of Christ.

If the object of this letter was to assure saints from among the Gentiles of their acceptance with God, why does Paul make any reference to believing Jews?

Because the election and sealing of believing Jews was an unquestioned fact, and their enjoyment of spiritual blessings was fully established. But while he is careful to note that they were the first to enjoy all spiritual blessings, he is as careful to show that it was all in and through Jesus. They were " chosen," but it was "in Christ;" "predestinated to Sonship," but it was "by Jesus Christ;" "accepted," but "in the beloved;" and to all these things the Spirit had borne witness. Now upon the believing of Gentiles, and upon their being also sealed by the same Spirit, in the like gifts bestowed on them, he is authorised to affirm their gracious induction into the same standing and privileges as those who " first trusted,"—*lit.,* fore-hoped— " in Christ."

4. " *According as He hath chosen us in Him.*" *To whom does this apply?*

To Jewish believers specially, as their introduction into privilege was so definitely marked, being sealed by the Holy Spirit with signs and gifts from Pentecost onward.

This text is often quoted to prove " *eternal election.*" *Does it sustain that view.*

It is, *lit., according as He chose us in Him,* and therefore Paul only states what God actually did upon their believing in Christ. He does not even refer to God's purpose, but to His actual selection for the reason named. Persons who had no existence could not be elected to office, privilege, or indeed to anything, as this could only be done upon their fitness for the position or privilege intended. Paul here says of God, "Who blessed us with all spiritual blessings in heavenly places in Christ: according as He chose us in Him;" referring most distinctly to the preaching of the Gospel, and the bestowal of spiritual gifts upon those who believed in Christ, which to Paul was a demonstration of their election of God.

Then why does he say "before the foundation of the world"? Is not this in eternity?

This sentence must be understood in harmony with its context; and as Paul states that there was an actual choice by God upon their believing reception of Jesus, then it cannot refer to what He did in a past eternity. This *pro kataboles kosmou,* here rendered "before the foundation of the world," must be understood to refer to God choosing Jewish believers before the union of Jews and Gentiles in one body took place, and thus making in Jesus of two one new man. It may be well, however, to state here that *kosmos*—meaning order, arrangement, embellishment, etc., and is applied to men, things, and even institutions—is never applied to the material substance of the universe, and is only used, by metonymy, of one or other of these things; at least my own researches into its use have led me to this conclusion. When we read that God so loved the *world,* we understand that the people who are in it are intended. When Jesus said, "Go into all the *world,*" we know that it was to the people in it, wherever they might be, that they were to carry the glad tidings. *Kosmos,* it is said, was first applied to the world

z

by Pythagoras, B.C. 550 years, to express the orderly arrangement of the universe, and from that time it became a symbolic word.

5. *What is "predestinated"?*

It is, *lit.,* marking out beforehand, and has special reference to the privileges of believers. It does not make believers, but is a pre-arrangement that all who are such shall enjoy sonship, with all its associated blessings.

6. *"Wherein he hath made us accepted in the beloved." What does this mean? and to whom does it apply?*

It would be more correct to read, *Wherewith He graced us in the beloved.* It is not a question of acceptance here, but of His grace to the accepted. It is the Father bestowing upon the bride of His beloved Son all the riches of His favour. Those to whom Paul is applying these heavenly privileges are the seed of Abraham, and must be so understood from verse 3–12, where he speaks of them as having first trusted in Christ. They were indeed the first who, like their father Abraham, took hold of the higher promise of God through the promised Messiah. And, even in verse 9, where Paul speaks of the mystery, which is the union of Gentiles with them, it is as His "purpose" "made known to us."

"The dispensation of the fulness of times." What is this?

It is, *lit., an administration of the fulness of the seasons,* a gathering together for Himself under-one-head, all things in the Christ—the things in the heavens (the Jewish state) and the things upon the earth (the nations) even in Him. There were promises made by God to the nations, through Abraham, and there were types and shadows in the law which were given to the Jews, and both were to be fulfilled in Christ. We might liken them to streams, rising in different places, and flowing on separately it may be for a while, but at last converging together to supply the need of some famishing city. Or, like the rain-clouds of the sky, which for a while float hither and thither, but at last unite, and pour their refreshing showers upon the thirsty earth beneath. But in the grace of God, the Jews were the first to drink from the fountain of the water of life, and to receive the early rain, after which the Gentiles shared with them the marvellous grace of God.

13. "*In whom ye also, after that ye heard the word of truth.*" *Does Paul here refer to these Ephesian saints?*

Yes, and the contrast between the two parties is clearly marked; and his letter cannot be intelligently read without noting, first the "*we*" and "*us*," and then the "*ye*," "*ye also,*" "*ye heard,*" "*ye believed,*" "*ye were sealed with that Holy Spirit of promise, which is the earnest of *our* inheritance.*" That is, you have got the same seal, and the same earnest that was given to us; therefore the two are made one in Christ, "For through Him we both have access by one Spirit unto the Father" (chap. ii. 18).

Have we any historical evidence of the sealing and earnest of the Spirit given to Gentiles?

Yes, Luke has recorded what took place in the house of Cornelius (Acts x.); and also of these Ephesians, who, on Paul's first visit, received through him the gift of tongues and prophecy (Acts xix.). And even Peter said of the first of these, "God gave them the like gift, as He did unto us, who believed on the Lord Jesus" (Acts xi. 17). Thus these Ephesian saints, though Gentiles, received the earnest and sealing of the Spirit, which to Paul was an un-answerable proof of their being fellow-heirs, and of the same body.

14. "*The earnest of our inheritance until the redemption of the purchased possession.*" *What does this mean?*

Believers are the purchased or acquired possession of Jesus, who in due time will bring them into the promised inheritance by His redeeming power, to the praise of His glory; while the Holy Spirit which He has given, is the earnest or pledge that all will be fulfilled.

15–19. *What is the purport of Paul's prayer for these Ephesians?*

That they might know the riches of the grace that was treasured for themselves in Christ; and what they as His newly-acquired possession as saints had become to Him; and also the exceeding greatness of His power towards all believers.

20. *How were they to know all this?*

By knowing Christ, who was God's illustration of all He desired for them. God had raised up Jesus from the dead, and was to raise them also from the dead. God had exalted Jesus into the heavenly places—*lit.,* the heavenlies—and to a like position they had been called. Christ was God's great pattern for the saints, and to Him they were to be conformed. And while Paul desired that these newly-converted ones might know all this, he is permitted to make known to them the revelation of these grand secrets.

22. *Christ was to fill the Church, His body. How was He to do this?*

By bestowing upon her gifts, standing, exaltation, etc. The Church in her reception of these has fully illustrated the power and grace of her exalted head, and has thus become His fulness, who filleth all of them with the riches of His grace and power.

CHAPTER II.

1. *These Ephesians are said by Paul to have been dead in trespasses and sins. What is the nature of this death ?*

It is simply a separation from the holiness and favour of God by a life of transgression, in which they were counted as dead.

Is there anything in the Scriptures to illustrate this kind of death ?

Yes. The case of Miriam (Num. xii.) furnishes an illustration. When she joined with Aaron in speaking against Moses, she was struck with leprosy, and had to be separated from the congregation. Her separation was to her as death, because she could enjoy no privilege ; and Moses prayed for her as one dead (ver. 12). Then the prodigal son (Luke xv.) is also an illustration. When in the far country his father counted him as one dead, being by his separation outside the family circle.

I have heard persons say that sinners are as dead as Lazarus in his grave, and that nothing short of Almighty power could awaken them. Is it so ?

It is confusion to declare that moral death is the same as physical death, because to so understand it compels one to look for the same agency to effect a change in one as the other. But as the deaths are not the same, we must look for the agency divinely adapted to both. The omnipotence of God was used to raise Lazarus, while the Gospel was used to bring to life these Ephesians who were said to be dead in trespasses and sins. By their sins they were separated from the enjoyment of His favour, fitly termed death, but by the Gospel of His Son, they were called into life.

2. *These Ephesians once walked according to " the course of this world." What does this mean ?*

It is, *lit., the age of this world, i.e.,* the moral fashion of the character of the people, as seen in the covetings and reasonings of their foolish hearts and lives ; and thus being under the prince of the power of the air, the spirit that now worketh in the children of disobedience.

What does " power of the air " mean ?

Air, I presume, is used by Paul as a symbol of the atmosphere of thoughts, reasonings, and imaginations of their hearts. These were the breathings of their minds, and in this sphere Satan rules, and is the prince or ruler of it. It is not in the material air that Satan rules, but in the minds of those who live in carnal reasoning instead of truth.

3. *" Among whom also we all had our conversation." Does he refer to Jews here ?*

Yes, for though they had the law of God in their hands, they had been ruled in their minds by fleshly covetings, and a disobedient spirit.

" And were by nature the children of wrath, even as others." What does this mean ?

Paul is still speaking of Jews, and of himself among them, as being " children of wrath even as others " (not God's wrath), but that they were like the Gentiles, children of a passionate, wicked disposition. " Children of wrath," *i.e.,* wrathful children, is similar in construction to " children of disobedience " of ver. 2, *i.e.,* disobedient children.

4. *" But God, who is rich in mercy, for His great love," etc. What is the difference between love and mercy ?*

Love is the fountain from which, through Jesus, mercy flows down to the guilty. The mercy shown to the guilty proves the great love of God. Even when dead in sins, He prepared for their quickening.

5. *" Quickened us together." Who are intended by this word " together,"*

which is thrice repeated in this chapter?

It is the quickening, raising, and seating together of believing Jews and Gentiles, of whom he has been speaking alternately from the beginning of the epistle. Some persons understand Paul to say, When Christ died, I died; and when He rose from the dead, I rose with Him. But it is not common sense, much less Scripture, to say that we died and rose from the dead before we had existence. In writing to the Romans (vi. 3), Paul says they were immersed *into His death,* and that *like* as Christ was raised from the dead, even so they (being also raised from death) were to walk in a new life. To this privilege both Jews and Gentiles were unitedly called in one body, in Christ their living head.

6. *" In heavenly places." What does this mean?*

The Greek word *epouraniois* is a word peculiar to Paul and to this epistle, and is correctly rendered by *heavenlies.* Twice he speaks of it as a gracious position, and one into which believers, both Jews and Gentiles, were raised in Christ (i. 3 ; ii. 6). Once he speaks of it as a position in which Christ has been invested with all authority (i. 20) ; and again he speaks of it as a position in which the saints have to contend against combined forces of evil (vi. 12) ; and is rendered in the Authorised Version, " high places." From what we read of the combined opposition of governments against Christ and the saints, we have no difficulty in concluding that Paul refers to the heavenly state in which God placed the Church, and in which a strife had to be maintained against principalities and powers of the world. The Church of Christ is not of earth, yet upon it ; and it is not in heaven, yet is of it. The word *heavenlies* is therefore a most fitting

word to denote the exalted position she is called to occupy.

7. *" That in the ages to come He might show," etc. What ages are these?*

The Christian economy, in which the wealth of His grace is manifest, and which in the Jewish ages was the subject of prophecy.

8. *" For by grace are ye saved" was addressed to believing Gentiles. Why does he in ver. 4 speak of mercy when addressing Jews?*

" Mercy " has special reference to the Jews, who had God's Word but sinned against it ; while " grace " was shown to Gentiles, in saving them through Christ, though dead in trespasses and sins.

" It is the gift of God." Does Paul refer to salvation or faith?

Not faith, as some say, but salvation by grace through the faith. This salvation is " not of works " (of law), but God's gift to the obedient in Christ.

11–13. *Why does he refer to their godless and hopeless condition in the past?*

To make more manifest to them the marvellous grace of God. Through Jesus He could meet all their need, forgive all their sins, and bring them nigh through His precious blood.

14. *" Who hath made both one." To whom does this apply?*

To believing Jews and Gentiles, who, being both indebted to Jesus for their salvation, are united in one family, of which God is their Father, and in one body, of which Jesus is their head.

15. *" And hath broken down the middle wall of partition." To what does he allude?*

Literally to that " balustrade of stone" which, according to Josephus, separated the court of the Gentiles from the holier portion of the temple, and beyond which no foreigner was allowed to pass ; but figuratively to "the law of commandments contained in (Jewish) ordinances," which by His death was set aside, and a new and living way opened, in which the Gentile had the same liberty as the Jew.

17. *"To you that were afar off, and to them that were nigh." Who are referred to here ?*

The Jew, who was ceremonially nigh, and the Gentile, who had no such access. To both peace was proclaimed by the Gospel. And thus, after showing what God in grace had done for the Gentiles — removing their hindrances, and providing for their need—he is now prepared to affirm what follows their acceptance of Christ. " Now therefore ye are no more strangers," etc.

20. *What does " foundation of the apostles and prophets " mean ?*

The foundation is Christ, who was foretold by prophets (Isaiah xxviii. 16), and proclaimed by apostles ; and on this foundation the Church was built.

What does " corner stone " mean ?

The term *corner* is borrowed from the prophecy, but the term is derived from the corner boards of the tabernacle. These corner boards united the walls of boards, and so formed one tabernacle. Christ the corner-foundation received upon Himself the separated sections of Jews and Gentiles, and being united by faith in Him, they were builded together for an habitation of God through the Spirit.

How " through the Spirit " ?

By the one Spirit baptising the representatives of both Jews and Gentiles, and thus marking out the temple of God.

CHAPTER III.

1. *How was Paul " the prisoner of Jesus Christ " for these Gentiles ?*

By his faithfulness in carrying out the commission of Jesus, and thus proclaiming salvation to the nations irrespective of the law of Moses, he had so irritated his brethren in the flesh, that when at Jerusalem he was assailed by them, and but for the timely interposition of the Roman guard he might have been torn in pieces. And, though delivered from their fury, he was detained a prisoner, first in Cæsarea, and then at Rome, not much short of five years. Well might he write, " the prisoner of Jesus Christ for you Gentiles."

2. *" If ye have heard of the dispensation of the grace of God which is given me to you-ward." To what does he refer ?*

To his special mission among the Gentiles, being sent to open their eyes, etc. And though some would understand his mission very well, yet many others required to learn respecting it, that they also might have confidence in his testimony. So, in this parenthesis, extending from verse 2 to the end of the chapter, he enters into an explanation of his great work.

What is the meaning of dispensation ?

The word *oikonomia* is variously rendered economy, stewardship, dispensation, and administration ; possibly the latter word best expresses its meaning. It is formed from " house " and " law," and is shown by Paul to be an arrangement for securing the privileges of Gentile believers, and was entrusted to him that he might reveal and perfect this gracious plan of God, in order that the Church might know His grace and manifold wisdom.

3–5. *" He made known to me the mystery." Is mystery a proper rendering ?*

It should be *the secret*, as it was not a mystery, because it is plain enough when revealed. But it was a secret, because it was hidden during the ages—*lit.*, the generations previous to its revelation to Paul.

6. *What was this revealed secret ?*

That the Gentiles should be, *lit.*, joint-heirs, and a joint-body, and joint-partakers in the promise of Christ Jesus, through the Gospel, of which, said he, I became a servant.

" Joint-partakers " with whom ?

With Jewish believers, who, being the first to own the Christ, were the first to enjoy that to which the Gentiles were admitted, when God in grace opened the door of faith to them.

But Paul quotes very largely in his letters from the prophets about blessing to the Gentiles. Were not these revelations ?

Yes, but not the revelation of which he is speaking here. The prophets spoke very much of salvation and blessing to the nations through the Messiah, but where do they speak of the saints unitedly forming His body ? The day was to declare it, and in due time this was done by the apostle of the nations.

Did the first Jewish believers understand the new institution to be distinct from the old ?

I think not ; although distinctly announced as the new covenant. These converts were very much like the disciples in relation to the kingdom : it was plainly enough described, but an idea of their own hindered their perception of it. As these blessings of the new covenant were spoken of by their prophets, they judged them to be only as the latter rain that followed the old harvest,—a larger crop of fruit only from the old tree, and under new pruning. They judged that these blessings belonged to them as the children of Abraham after the flesh, and when Gentiles were called to share with them through the Christ, they saw their mistake, and fiercely resented the intrusion. The special

mission of Paul to the Gentiles only widened the breach which has never been healed. Being compelled to choose between Christ and Moses, they chose the latter, and continued as we find them to-day, determined either to have another Messiah than Jesus or none at all. Paul, however, writes to instruct the Gentiles to claim their privileges, and to walk worthy of them.

8. *" The unsearchable riches of Christ." What does this mean ?*

It is, *lit., the untraced wealth of the Christ.* The prophets saw a little of His grace and mercy, and searched diligently to know more. The saints who first believed could trace it in pardon and peace, and gifts of the Spirit ; but the full wealth of His glory was yet untraced until proclaimed to the Gentiles, and became their hope. For its final development in resurrection and glorification all must wait.

How could Paul be less than the least of all saints ?

I suppose he means that he was the least worthy of this honour, because of his former persecuting spirit.

11. *" According to the eternal purpose." Is not this a plan formed in eternity ?*

It is, *lit., according to a plan of the ages,* which shows that Paul refers to something that God was doing or arranging in time. It is the same truth that we get in Hebrews i. 2, and xi. 3, in which we are taught that God formed or arranged the ages on account of Jesus His Son. We may, for instance, look at the seven feasts of the Lord, as arranged in Leviticus xxiii., to see an illustration of this plan. In these feasts, beginning with the passover, and closing with the feast of tabernacles, we get a plan of the great scheme of redemption. So again we might refer to the jubilee, and many other parts of that great institution of shadows of good things to come, to learn that the Christian administration was not an afterthought with God, but according to a purpose of the ages.

13. *Is it not strange for him to desire that they might not faint at his tribulation for them ?*

The present rendering completely hides Paul's meaning. He was suffering on their account, and here says, *Wherefore I desire not to faint at my tribulation for you, which is your glory.* In fact, he asks, in his noble unselfishness, for strength to suffer in confirmation of the truth he preached.

14, 15. *" The Father . . . of whom the whole family in heaven and earth is named." What are we to understand by this ?*

He was just going to tell these Gentile saints of the great things he had supplicated on their behalf; but before he does so, he makes this apt though incidental reference to the purpose and provision of God, as embracing the entire family—not only those in heaven, alluding to Jewish saints, but also those on earth, even Gentile saints : heaven and earth being used as symbols of their former relative conditions. His prayer, therefore, was in harmony with God's purpose to bless them all.

16. *" Strengthened with might by His Spirit in the inner man." How could this be done ?*

The inner man is the mind, which receives strength through revelation of the truth, a large measure of which Paul desired on their behalf.

17. *" That Christ may dwell in your hearts by faith." How by faith ?*

It is, *lit., by the faith, i.e.,* the entire circle of facts, truths, and ordinances as delivered to the saints by the apostles. It is by the acceptance of these that Christ is received, and by continuance in them He dwells in the heart. The same truth

is expressed by Christ (John xiv. 23), " If a man love Me, he will keep My words : and My Father will love him, and We will come unto him, and make Our abode with him."

19. *" And to know the love of Christ which passeth knowledge." How could they know what surpassed knowledge ?*

Paul uses the word knowledge for revelation, and refers to the revelations of the prophets. The manifestation of that love by Jesus far exceeded all that they had said about it, and it is this manifested love he wishes them to know.

21. *The Church by Christ Jesus was to give the glory to God, throughout all ages, world without end. Amen. But what does this mean ?*

It is a strange rendering which our Authorised Version has given to Paul's words, and from which we could scarcely know what he intended to convey. It is, *lit., into all the generations of the age of the ages, Amen.* Here we see that Paul names both people and periods—the age, the ages, and the generations. The ages were those periods of the law, in which, according to ver. 11, God had a purpose which continued till Jesus came in the fulness of the times, and opened what he now calls *the age* of these ages, *i.e.,* the Christian age. The *generations* are those who live along this period, and who are to give God the glory. The word *Amen,* so shall it be, is here prophetic. The glory shall be given to God, all along this age of the ages, by those who received Christ as God's gift of love.

CHAPTER IV.

1. *In commencing this section Paul repeats, " I therefore, the prisoner of the Lord." Why does he do so ?*

He was evidently beginning to exhort them at the opening of chap. iii., when a thought of the possible ignorance of some of his special mission to Gentiles came before him, and at once he begins a deeply instructive detail of the trust or deposit of revelation which had been given to him on their behalf. And this full account of his own work brings more fully to view their great and gracious privileges, so that he is stirred up more earnestly to beseech them to walk worthy of the calling to which they had been called. And though he repeats, "I therefore, the prisoner of the Lord, beseech you," it is not as a prisoner suffering for them that he now appeals to them, but, *lit., in the Lord, I beseech you that ye walk worthy*, etc. It is not his sufferings, but the grace of Christ that is the ground of appeal.

2. *Walk . . . "with all lowliness and meekness, with long-suffering,"* etc. *Why did they need this exhortation?*

Temptations mostly arise out of circumstances, and these were before his mind in relation to them. They had been lifted out of their deeply-degraded position into the heavenlies, from being outcasts, and far off, to union with the body of Christ and the temple of God; and now it was needful for him to say, "Be *lowly* and *meek*, and *bear patiently* with your brethren; God has shown much grace towards you, therefore be humble before Him.

3. *In what way were they responsible for the unity of the Spirit?*

It devolved upon them to uphold the institution by which this unity had been secured. The uncircumcised and the circumcised had been made one body, they had received the one Spirit in gifts and sealing, they had received the one hope of glory through Christ the one Lord, they had embraced the one faith by the apostles, and the one immersion into Christ, and one Father by their birth from above, and this unity was to be kept unbroken. Judaising teachers were even then busy in laying another foundation, even the rites of Moses; and they are urged to beware and accept of no other ground of unity than that laid by the apostles of Jesus.

Is the exhortation of Paul required now?

It is possible to propose and accept of other bonds of union than that proposed by the apostles, and we have need to beware of being party to them. Men have proposed many other arrangements or constitutions on which to unite, but we must avoid every thing which has not a "thus saith the Lord."

7–9. *Why does he refer to the diversity of gifts in the one body?*

To prepare them not only to accept that diversity, but to appropriate all its advantages. Jesus, according to Ps. lxviii., had ascended like a triumphant conqueror, and then upon those set free He bestowed gifts, according to His wisdom and the munificence of His wealth.

"He led captivity captive." *What does this mean?*

It is quoted by Paul from Ps. lxviii. 18, a psalm which was written by David when the ark of the covenant was removed to Mount Zion, and the quotation should be studied in the light of that deeply interesting event. The ark had long been in captivity, but when carried by David, as his captive, up to the place prepared for it, the ascent was a most jubilant occasion; and even gifts of bread, flesh, and wine, were bestowed by the king upon the people. Now Paul, by the Spirit, evidently read the event as a type of Christ. He, as the true ark of the covenant, had been in captivity; and when He became God's captive, He was carried in triumph to His throne, and, from the munificence of His wealth, appropriate gifts were bestowed on those who rejoiced in His ascent.

" He also descended first into the lower parts of the earth." To what does this apply ?

To His incarnation, doubtless. Ps. cxxxix. 15 will best explain to what Paul refers.

11–13. *" And he gave some apostles," etc. Are these the gifts referred to by Paul ?*

Yes ; these apostles, prophets, evangelists, pastors, and teachers, were given by Christ " for the perfecting of the saints " (the comma omitted) " for the work of the ministry " (*i.e.*, for service), " for the edifying of the body of Christ, till we all come in the unity of the faith," etc.

Were the gifts bestowed miraculous ?

Yes ; those who were thus endowed received them as the gifts of Christ, through the Spirit, and were thus fitted to meet the need both of the world and the Church. Through the Spirit-endowed apostles and evangelists the world could hear, with absolute certainty, the way of pardon and life ; and through pastors and teachers, who were gifted in like manner, the Church could learn all that was required of them as disciples of Christ. In this way, Jesus provided that there should be neither error nor mistake in the truths preached and taught.

Why are these special gifts not continued to the Church ?

They have never been taken away. That is to say, the writings of the apostles contain all that is necessary for life and godliness ; and it is under these apostles and pastors that the world and the Church are now called to put themselves, and thus be saved by Christ. The world, *i.e.*, the unsaved, must hear the proclamations of the apostles, for there is no other message to them from the ascended Jesus than by these ambassadors ; while the Church must hear them as pastors and teachers, and thus " come in the unity of the faith, and of the knowledge of the Son of God."

" Unto a perfect man." What does this imply ?

A physically healthy man is a symbol of unity, as the members of his body act in harmony with the head that rules them all. So when the Church " continues stedfastly in the apostles' doctrine and fellowship," she will then be, according to this symbol, a perfect man, and manifest the fulness of her exalted head. For this perfected growth or manhood she is now responsible, as all that is needful for it has been provided in the apostles' teaching.

22. *What is the " old man " ?*

The sins of the old life, which, singly, are members of this so-called man or body of sin ; and which is to be put off.

24. *What is the " new man " ?*

That which is created in righteousness and holiness by the truth. It is being invested with the Lord Jesus, whose truth, and love, and grace, and kindness, adorns the life of the believer.

25–31. *Are the sins which Paul names here the members of the old man ?*

Yes ; lying, anger, theft, and impurity, are all his members, and must be put off.

" Be ye angry and sin not." How is this possible ?

We do not see how it could be, as anger must be sin. It is more likely that he said, *sin not in being angry ;* and this is in keeping with all the other injunctions, as *lie not, steal not, speak not corruptly, grieve not the Spirit,* with many other things which must have no place in the Christian's life. Christ died for our sins, and we must die to them.

32. *They were to forgive each other in the remembrance of their own forgiveness. Is it for the sake of Christ that God forgives?*

It is, *lit.*, " in Christ," and should be so read. The administration of mercy as well as judgment is in the hands of Jesus, and He is Lord of all. This is a truth we need to fully understand, that we may "honour the Son."

CHAPTER V.

1. *Is not this chapter a continuation of the exhortations of chapter iv.?*

Yes, and the first precept of this chapter ought not to be separated from it. There he says, God has been kind to you, He has forgiven you, " Be ye therefore followers,"— *lit.*, imitators—of God, as beloved children.

2. *What is the purport of his reference to Christ offering Himself?*

To impress upon their mind three very important things—(1.) That in imitating God, they would have to make sacrifices, but that Jesus had even offered Himself. (2.) That the offering of Christ was fragrant to God, being in fact the antitype of the burnt-offering, one of the sweet-savour offerings, in which all was consumed on the altar. (3.) That every Christ-like act was also fragrant to God, being a sweet-smelling savour.

3–6. *In addition to the sins named in the previous chapter, Paul gives a new list here. Why does he do so?*

Because these sins were commonly practised among the people of the world, being the outcome of the old life of sin and idolatry, and they were in danger of imitating them; it was needful therefore to warn against them. Besides, the apostle adds very

solemn reasons against such practices, viz., that such persons would be cut off from any inheritance in the kingdom of Christ and of God, and not only deprived of this privilege, but also exposed to the awful wrath of God.

Fornication and sins of this class are not common among professors of religion now; but is not foolish talking and jesting frequently practised?

Too frequently, alas, do we hear it! Some people can naturally make fun; they are clever at witticism, and display their gift in the circle where profitable and wise remarks would be more seemly. To hear a brother preaching or praying with seeming earnestness, and then as soon after as possible using vain and jesting words is very unseemly. Such ought to remember that the condemnation of God rests on such behaviour. It is better, said Paul, to give thanks than to jest.

Why is covetousness called idolatry?

Because it is a lusting of the heart, and is applied not to gold exclusively, but to any forbidden object which is allowed to occupy the place of God. It is the adoration of a seen object, and is as idolatry.

8–11. *What is darkness?*

Error, ignorance of what is right, vice, and every form of evil. It is a self-chosen separation from the truth.

What is light?

Goodness, righteousness, truth, and holiness; and being enlightened by the truth, they were to walk as children of light.

Are the precepts given in this chapter sufficient to form a holy life?

They are given for this express purpose, so that what saints were to do, and what to avoid, are fully stated.

16. *What is redeeming the time?*

Buying up the opportunity—*lit.*, the season—at the cost of self-denial. God will give the season, but wisdom and promptness will be required to use it well.

18–20. *Why does he warn these Christians against drunkenness ?*

Because there was danger of being overcome by this too common sin. Christians require to watch against this forbidden gratification of the flesh, the temptation to which abounds on every hand. But while he warns them against being drunk with wine, in which is dissoluteness, he urges them to be " filled with the Spirit."

How were they to be filled with the Spirit ?

By being filled with the truth which has been revealed by Him, the manifestation of which will form a striking contrast to being filled with wine. In the one case, the tongue and passions are excited only to show the folly of those who indulge in it ; while in the other, under the guidance of the Spirit, it will show itself in psalms and hymns and spiritual songs —a spiritual exercise in which thanksgiving also will be largely practised.

21–24. *Why does he refer to the relative duties which husband and wife owe to each other ?*

Because they are types of Christ and His Church ; and when He is accepted by them, they are under obligation to manifest this mutual relation to each other, according to the direction of the Spirit. " The husband is the head of the wife, even as Christ is the head of the Church :" and as Jesus is the saviour or preserver of His body, the Church, so must the husband maintain and cherish his wife, which has become his body. Then the wife is to be in subjection to her own husband, because she is a type of the Church which is to be subject to Christ in all things.

25. " *Husbands, love your wives.*" *Is there any moral purpose in this obligation to love ?*

If we are to be guided in our understanding of the purpose of love, as revealed concerning Christ, we shall see that purity of heart and life is the purpose and fruit of love. Christ gave Himself for the Church, that He might sanctify and cleanse it ; and love in the husband, and subjection in the wife in the Spirit of Jesus, will secure this desirable result.

26. " *That he might sanctify and cleanse it with the washing of water by the word.*" *How could this be ?*

It is important to note the peculiar construction of the passage in order to understand it. There are two things which Christ was to do for His Church, viz., to sanctify and cleanse ; and two agencies were to be used to effect this result—water and the word, each of these being appropriate to the result desired. The first sentence must be joined to the last, and then we may read, " Christ also loved the Church, and gave Himself for it," *that He might sanctify it by the Word, having cleansed it in a bath of water.*

How does He cleanse it in a bath of water ?

The bath of water—or immersion as appointed by Jesus—is a separating ordinance, and should be attended to with this object. So that as Noah was separated by the flood from the old world, and as Israel was separated from Egypt by their immersion in the cloud and in the sea, so the believer—by his immersion into Christ —is separated from all his past life, and putting himself under the guidance of Christ, is sanctified by His word, and made meet to stand before Him, without spot or wrinkle or any such thing. It is a bridal purification that is intended, and the arrangement is most appropriate to a loving chastity of life and spirit.

Is the Church without spot now ?

I fear it has too many spots and blemishes, but this is to the grief of the bridegroom, who has made a full provision for her cleansing; and it will be her loss and shame if she does not avail herself of it. Still it is well to remember that the Church being composed of many members, and as these spots, etc., are on unfaithful ones only, the faithful will not have to bear their sin. In His letters to the churches, Jesus had to threaten the unfaithful with extinction, but promised an eternal reward to every faithful disciple. We should all hear His word, " Hold that fast which thou hast, that no man take thy crown."

30. *"We are members of His body, of His flesh, and of His bones." Is this the reason why He so cares for us ?*

Yes, and from this union we are very dear to Him. As Eve was dear to Adam, because taken from his side, and as the wife should be loved by her husband, because made one with him, so Christ loves His church because she is His body, and is, therefore, dear to Him. We must, however, omit the words, " of His flesh, and of His bones," as they are not found in MSS. of highest authority.

Some persons say of Christ that " He is bone of our bone, and flesh of our flesh." Is this a quotation ?

It is a quotation of words, but a misapplication of persons. Adam did say of Eve, " This is now bone of my bones, and flesh of my flesh;" but we have no right to say this of Christ, as if He had descended from us.

31, 32. *In Genesis ii. 24, God said of the two united in marriage, " they shall be one flesh." Why does Paul say this is a great mystery ?*

It is, *lit.,* a *great secret;* and had remained so during four thousand years. The reason why God made

two to be one flesh is now opened by Paul. Christ and His Church are one, and marriage is an illustration of this wondrous union.

CHAPTER VI.

1-3. *" Children, obey your parents in the Lord : for this is right." But if parents should command some wrong thing, what should they do ?*

They should refuse, for this is not in the Lord. A parent's authority should be in harmony with the will of Jesus, or it cannot be lawfully enforced.

" Honour thy father," etc., is a command of the law uttered on Sinai. Why enforce it on Christians ?

Because it is re-issued by the Spirit, and therefore binding on believers. This must be our guide in relation to all things given under the law ; they are only in force when re-enacted, or implied from the spiritual principle embodied in them.

Will obedience to parents secure the promise of lengthened life and blessing now ?

Most certainly, and Paul quotes this promise to show that it will be so. The result of obedience and of disobedience may be seen every day, by those who will take the trouble to trace it.

4. *" And, ye fathers, provoke not your children to wrath." Why is this obligation imposed ?*

Because as God requires the obedience of children, so He requires wisdom and prudence in training ; and as children are to show, in their obedience to parents, the proper action of all towards God, so must parents show in their action toward their children, the true rule of God over all.

5-8. *Are servants promised a divine reward for their faithfulness to earthly masters ?*

Yes, when it is done for the Lord's sake, which only a believer can do ; and as the most menial service, when faithfully done as to the Lord, will win His approval, so all should be careful to let this principle rule their service.

9. *Why remind masters of their obligations ?*

Because, while they were masters over others, they also had a Master, even the Lord. Some MSS. read, *Knowing that the Master of you and of them is in the heavens,* and there is no respect of persons with Him. It is well to be reminded of these things.

10–12. *What was the nature of the opposition brought to bear against the saints ?*

Paul says it was not against flesh and blood they were called to wrestle, *i.e.,* he speaks not here of that which was within, but of that which was without. Principalities, authorities, world-rulers of the darkness of this age, etc., were all in opposition to the followers of Jesus ; and this more literal rendering of these terms will enable us to understand something of its nature. The official rulers of the age were so opposed to the truth, and to Christ, that it was no easy matter to stand against them.

What are we to understand by "spiritual wickedness in highplaces" ?

It is, *lit., spiritual things (i.e.* powers or forces) *of evil in the heavenlies ;* and as this word *heavenlies,* indicates the exalted position into which the Church had been raised, it is very clear that the mystery of iniquity was even then beginning to show itself in some places, and had to be resisted by those who would obey Jesus. The forms of evil were varied, and the forces of wickedness were powerful, but when resisted with the panoply of heaven, victory was certain to all who did so.

13-18. *Does the armour provided by God indicate the nature of the contest ?*

Yes, and if we only strip each part of its military relation, we shall clearly understand the nature of the opposition. *Truth* had to be maintained against error, *righteousness* against wickedness, *peace* against unholy strife, *salvation* against *condemnation,* and *faith* in God against unbelief. And as faith was to be over all, so prayer must be mixed with all ; " and having done all "— *lit., having overcome—*" to stand."

19, 20. *In directing them to pray and supplicate, he asks as a personal favour to be remembered by them as "an ambassador in bonds." What does he mean ?*

It is a very touching aspect of his condition. He had been sent by the King of kings with an embassage to the nations ; he had received the message from His own lips, and never was hindered from going whither he would ; and he now asks them to remember him in their prayers. But his petition only shows how unselfish he is. He does not ask to be set free, but to be bold in his testimony for Jesus—to be faithful in speaking as he ought to speak.

How is it that in this epistle to the Ephesians there is not a single charge of wrong-doing brought against them ; whilst in epistles to other churches so many failings are dealt with ?

It is important to note this peculiar feature of this epistle, which evidently holds a distinct place among the epistles of Paul to the churches. In this epistle we have the heavenly bridegroom instructing His bride, and revealing all that appertained to her as accepted in the beloved. It is a bridal endowment of all that He has made over for her enjoyment in Himself ; and to have brought a charge against her in this inventory of her privileges, would have been as unseemly as for a bridegroom to upbraid his bride upon her wedding day. It is when the spirit and life had been fairly tested, and conduct had shown unfaithfulness, that such matters are dealt with, and the letters to the Corinthians and Galatians are illustrations on this point. There the bride is proved unfaithful, and has to be reproved. These Ephesians became unfaithful afterwards, as is shown in the letter written to them by John (Rev. ii.

1–7), which is a sad sequel to this written by Paul. "He who had invested His bride with such exalted privileges had to mark the waning of her affections, and had to warn her that unless she repented, her candlestick would be removed. It would be well to study both epistles, and profit by the revelations of Him who loved us, and gave Himself for us.

THE EPISTLE OF PAUL THE APOSTLE TO THE

PHILIPPIANS.

CHAPTER I.

What were the circumstances which led Paul to write this letter to the saints at Philippi?

Their practical sympathy with him during his imprisonment at Rome. Having sent relief by Epaphroditus, which was no doubt most providential, both for the rent of his own hired house and other required comforts, this letter was written as an acknowledgment of their sympathy.

Should we look upon his imprisonment as a calamity, or as an overruling providence to attain more blessed results?

His arrest, and consequent imprisonment, was not only a wrong done to himself, but was an unrighteous attempt to frustrate his great work. We may, however, rejoice that God is able to bring good out of evil; and that when Paul could no longer preach in market-places and reason in synagogues, he could talk with Roman citizens in his own hired house, and write letters to churches the value of which no man can calculate.

1. *In some epistles Paul writes as an apostle, but in this he simply joins himself with Timothy as a servant. Why does he make this change?*

In many of the churches, through false teachers, the truth was called in question, and Paul had to urge its acceptance with the authority given to him as an apostle of the Lord Jesus. But in Philippi the truth was held fast, and was bringing forth fruit in their practical fellowship with him in his labours, and there was no desire on his part to make a mere parade of his authority. To them he presents himself on the simple ground of a servant of Jesus Christ.

Is "bishops and deacons" a proper rendering?

It would be more literal to render *overseers and servants*, and then we should better understand their relation to the Church.

Is "grace and peace to you" a simple benevolent desire for their good?

It is an assurance that all that is implied in these words belonged to them as believers in Jesus, although they were Gentiles.

5. *"Your fellowship in the Gospel."
What is this?*

Their joint contributions to sustain him in his witness for the truth of Christ, as preached by him among the Gentiles, was their fellowship with him in the Gospel. It commenced while he was in Philippi, and when in Thessalonica they had sent once and again unto his necessity ; and now that he is in Rome, and more than ever in need, their fellowship is renewed. His joy in their fellowship shows how he was enabled to rise above all the distressing circumstances of his condition, because the truth had triumphed in these Philippians.

6. *What was this " good work " begun in them?   And who commenced it?*

It was the fellowship to which he here refers, and involved a great deal more than the giving of their money. It was the expression of their faith in the Gospel he had preached to them, and was an effort to uphold him while suffering for the truth. It had been begun most likely by Luke, who was left at Philippi, and who aided and guided them in this holy work.

" Will perform it until the day of Jesus Christ." What is his meaning?

If we read, will perfect or complete it *against* a day of Christ, we shall, I think, better see his meaning. That is, the work being faithfully done, will then stand over for His approval in the day of His manifestation.   But if *achris* will not allow of being rendered *against,* then he must refer to the day of his own deliverance, when their help would be no longer required.

7. *" Because I have you in my heart." What does he mean?*

We should read, *because you have me in your heart.* They had given unmistakable proof of this, which

he felt bound to acknowledge, and he counted upon their faithfulness to the end.

9–11. *Are the things for which he here prays necessary for their continued faithfulness?*

Yes.   He knew that mere zeal would soon fail unless sustained by " knowledge,"—*i.e.,* revelation and " judgment," *i.e.,* understanding of revelation,—hence he prays that they might be able to distinguish good from evil by the knowledge and understanding thus received, and that their sincerity and blamelessness might continue till—*lit.,* for or into—a day of Christ.

12–14. *Paul here reminds them that his bonds had furthered the Gospel.   Were they not afraid that it would be otherwise?*

It was quite natural to think that his bonds would prove unfavourable to the work, and possibly they were somewhat cast down on that account. This is why he so specially reminds them, that, instead of hindering the work, his bonds had rather helped it forward.   As Paul had appealed to Cæsar, it could not fail to be a matter of inquiry, not only among the chief of the Jews, but also among the Prætorian soldiers and guards, into whose custody he was committed, as to the nature of his offence.   It would also soon become known that he was not an offender against Cæsar, but had been charged by his own people with affirming that the Messiah of the prophets had come, and that Jesus whom they had crucified had been raised from death and made Lord of all, and that from the furious onslaught they had made upon his life he had simply sought the protection of Cæsar.   The matter could not fail to interest even the common soldiers, for the one to whom he was chained every day would surely understand that the Gospel of Christ was for all men, even for soldiers as well as civilians. And so the truth spread in Rome, and the love of Jesus became known and was felt, even by some in Cæsar's household; and by his patient suffering for the truth, many of the brethren in the Lord were emboldened to speak the Word without fear. So the truth triumphed in Rome, even though its ambassador was in bonds.

15. *"Some indeed preach Christ even of envy and strife." How could they preach in such a spirit ?*

We must understand that these were enemies, both to Paul and to the Gospel he preached, because their making known of Christ was in order " to add affliction to his bonds." They affirmed the facts that Paul preached, but insinuated that he preached Jesus as another king, in opposition to Cæsar, and thus sought to bias the public mind. The scheme, however, was to them a failure, but by it Christ became more widely known, and Paul adds, " I therein do rejoice ; yea, and will rejoice."

19–21. *What does he mean by " this shall turn to my salvation " ?*

The words are found in Job xiii. 16 (Septuagint Version), and are evidently quoted verbatim by Paul. The quotation is a striking one, for the position of Paul and Job was in some respects similar. Both were misjudged, and evil spoken of, and both were confidently expecting God's deliverance. And, as Paul intimates respecting himself, even should it be otherwise, " according to my earnest expectation and my hope, that in nothing I shall be ashamed, but that with all boldness, as always, so now also Christ shall be magnified in my body, whether it be by life or by death."

" For to me to live is Christ, and to die is gain." Does he mean a gain to himself ?

No ; self is not even thought of by Paul, except so far as his preaching, suffering, or dying might serve the cause of Christ. The one great thought of his heart was, how to further the interests of his Lord and Saviour. Paul had no other end to seek, no other purpose to serve, than this all-engrossing work. For years he had laboured to bring souls to Christ, and now his suffering, and even his imprisonment, is a gain to Christ, because by them some are led to believe in Him, even in Cæsar's household. So that he could say, " For me to live [is for] Christ, and to die gain " for the cause of Christ.

22–24. *" For I am in a strait betwixt two." Why in a strait ?*

Alford's rendering of ver. 22 will help us to better understand why he was in a strait. " But if to live in the flesh, this be to me fruit of my labour, then what I shall choose I know not." That is to say, if my bonds bring so much fruit for Christ —in the emboldening of the saints, and in the conversion of sinners— and, also, having a desire to depart and be with Him, then I do not know what to choose. He desired to depart and be with Christ, which was far better than suffering ; and he also wished to remain and help on the work, although he should have to suffer ; and so he was in a strait betwixt the two.

" And to be with Christ." Is this privilege common to all believers after death ? or was it special to the apostles ?

Christ prayed for the apostles that they might be with Him, and behold His glory, and was therefore for them a special request—a request in which Paul expected to share. Jesus Himself went to paradise after death, and only ascended to the Father forty days after His resurrection. We judge, therefore, that the saints at death—like their Lord and Master

—depart to paradise, and will only ascend to be with Him for ever when re-clothed at their resurrection.

CHAPTER II.

1-4. " If there be, therefore, any consolation in Christ." Four times in this verse " if" is repeated ; what is its special bearing here ?

If we use an improved rendering of the verse, and note the claim which he makes in the following verse, we may then see the force of his earnest appeal. It may be well, however, to note here that there was one thing in the church at Philippi which hindered the full joy of the apostle, and this evil he now seeks to remove. We only get a hint here that there was dissension in the church, but in chap. iv. 2 he names two women who were at strife with each other, and most likely there were partisans who supported the cause of each. In the light of these sad facts, I now give Howson and Conybeare's rendering of the first four verses of this chapter. " If, then, you can be entreated in Christ, if you can be persuaded by love, if you have any fellowship in the Spirit, if you have any tenderness or compassion, I pray you make my joy full, be of one accord, filled with the same love, of one soul, of one mind. Do nothing in a spirit of intrigue or vanity, but in lowliness of mind let each account others above himself. Seek not your private ends alone, but let every man seek likewise his neighbour's good." From this rendering, which I think can be proved correct, we shall see that Paul's appeal is to themselves. It is not about as to whether there is any consolation in Christ, but would they, in their self-seeking, be entreated by the example of the love and humility of Christ, and this ex-

2 A

ample he is now going to set before them.

5-8. When Paul urges that they should have the mind of Jesus, does he refer to the self-sacrifice He made in becoming a Saviour ?

Yes, this is distinctly before his mind, and he wishes it to be felt by those whom he addresses. Jesus had laid aside all He previously possessed, and having taken upon Himself the form of a servant, He submitted even to the death of the cross.

" Who, being in the form of God, thought it not robbery to be equal with God." Is not this strange language concerning Christ ?

What he really said was far more incisive and rebuking to these Philippians than as rendered in our Authorised Version. It will be better to read, *Christ Jesus was in the form of God, but deemed not His equality with God a thing to be grasped at, i.e.*, as if afraid to lose it ; *but emptied Himself, and became a servant.* Some of them were contending for their rights, but their Lord laid all His own aside.

9. " Wherefore, God also highly exalted Him." What is this intended to teach ?

That he who humbles himself shall be exalted. That God's way of ascending is by descending. *What is this highest name which God gave to Him ?*

The name of " Lord." The name to which universal supremacy is attached, or as Jesus puts it, " All authority is given unto Me in heaven, and on earth," to which Paul adds, " and under the earth."

10. And " under the earth." What does this mean ?

When Jesus appeared to John, He told him to fear not, for He had the keys of hades, *i.e.*, the unseen world, and to this Paul refers, as being under Him.

11. All are to confess that Jesus

is Lord, is it to be done lovingly or reluctantly ?

Both, I presume. Some, through the preaching of the Gospel confess Jesus to be Lord, but others will do it unwillingly only when He is manifested. The former will be honoured by Him, the latter dishonoured.

12, 13. *" Work out your own salvation with fear and trembling ; for it is God that worketh in you,"* etc. *How are these texts to be harmonised ?*

There is no want of harmony between them, but when separated from their context, as is generally done, the commendation and instruction given by Paul in the entire paragraph is not perceived ; and what is worse, by so doing, these directions have been perverted to serve purposes which Paul never intended. The wrangling of Calvinists and Arminians over these texts, have been caused by first making them independent propositions, and then each selecting the one which seemed to favour his adopted system, and thus they have set the Word of God against itself. The proof text of the Arminian, who held the free-agency of man, was, " Work out your own salvation with fear and trembling ; " while the proof text of the Calvinist, who held the absolute sovereignty of God, was, " It is God which worketh in you both to will and to do of His good pleasure." For centuries the champions of these separate schools, whilst advocating their opposing theories, have most unmercifully pelted each other with these broken fragments of the rock of truth ; and, not only showing at times a very bad spirit, but also sadly perverting the perfect teaching of the Holy Spirit. What Paul really does say in these verses is, Wherefore, beloved, as ye always obeyed my directions when I was with you, now, that I am taken from you, much more earnestly work out your own salvation ; for, though I am taken from you, you have God to work in you by His truth, both to will and do, both in your choice and action, and (thus being obedient), you will please Him. Now it is impossible to separate any part of this beautiful and encouraging teaching, without injury to the whole. First, they are commended for their noble-hearted obedience while Paul was in Philippi ; then, though deprived of his presence, they are urged to maintain their obedience to God in all things, being assured that He was with them, and would help them in all their need ; and such teaching should also be helpful to us. Teachers may be removed, circumstances may seem unfavourable, but God is ever nigh to help and direct us. It may be well to state that " your own salvation," does not refer to pardon of sin, or deliverance from guilt through Christ, but to their deliverance from the evils, vices, etc., by which they were surrounded. Hence they are urged to patience, blamelessness, and a godly life.

CHAPTER III.

Why does Paul introduce the matter of his fleshly relation to the stock of Israel and the law of Moses, when writing to Gentile saints ?

It is to warn them against Judaising teachers, who were seeking to bring Gentile believers under the law. Possibly he could not have used a more powerful argument than to show them that he had laid down as useless for salvation the very things they were urged to take up.

1. *Why does Paul write, " Finally, my brethren," in the middle of his letter ?*

It will be better to read, As to the rest, or, what remains to be said,

"Rejoice in the Lord." Let Him be your joy, not Moses. It is safe that I remind you of these things, and warn you of impending dangers.

2. *In warning them against certain persons, he uses the term " dogs," and " evil-workers," and " the concision." What do these terms imply ?*

The dog was an unclean animal under the law, and was held as such by the nation. It was even unclean in its habits and, according to the proverb, returned to its own vomit. It was therefore a fit symbol of these Judaisers, whose god was their belly. Beware of them, for they will lead you into uncleanness. They are " evil workers," therefore shun them. Concision is a term which Paul applies to these men. They circumcised those who submitted to their teaching, but Paul will not allow their work to be called by this typical rite, now that its day was past, but terms it " the concision," *i.e.*, a mutilation. " For we are the circumcision, which worship God in the spirit, and rejoice in Christ Jesus," and not they who merely cut the flesh, that they may glory in it.

3–8. *Some had confidence in the flesh. What did they hope to attain by it ?*

The promise and favour of God, but in this they had made a great mistake. He had more to count upon than most of them, yet he had given it all up for Christ.

" *That I may win Christ.*" *Had he not won Christ ?*

Yes, but he is speaking here of what he had given up that he might do so. Both Judaism and circumcision, tribe and law, were all abandoned as refuse for this end, and he wishes them to see the folly of picking up what he had cast away.

9. *What does he mean by " the righteousness which is of the law," in contrast with " that which is through the faith of Christ" ?*

The righteousness of the law was that obedience which it claimed, but the promises secured by it were only temporal, and could not meet man's need as a sinner against God ; but the righteousness of faith was that obedience to Christ, which, commencing in pardon, led to purity both of heart and life, through the truth of the Gospel. To obey the law secured the " promise of the life that now is," but to obey the Gospel secured both that which is, and " that which is to come." No wonder that Paul having learnt this, should desire only to be found in Him, and possess that righteousness which is of God by faith in Jesus.

10. *What does he mean by " that I may know Him," etc. ?*

This is explanatory of what he means by *the faith of Christ*, the fruit of which was the righteousness in which he desired to be found. Faith was not some undefinable gift, or feeling, or experience, but loving confidence in the facts of the sufferings, death, and resurrection of the Lord Jesus ; and he had completely stripped himself of all his former religious habiliment, that he might be in all things conformed to the death of Christ, by being obedient to Him.

What does he mean by " that I might attain unto the resurrection of the dead" ?

The rendering of a now approved reading of this clause reads, *the resurrection from among the dead, i.e.,* leaving the dead behind, and doubtless refers to Jesus ; and not " of the dead," as rendered from the Textus Receptus. This change is a very important one, as we are now able to make a correct application of these words of Paul, which as read in our Authorised Version, have been a source of difficulty to many. It may be well to note that both these aspects of resurrection are given us in the

New Testament, viz., the resurrection *out from among the dead*, and the resurrection *of the dead*; the former being strictly applied to Jesus, the latter to the saints, and to the resurrection in general. Now the reading of this 10th verse being proved by conclusive evidence, we can see that Paul was speaking of the resurrection of Christ, and not of his own, and that as Christ by His resurrection was separated from all the past, so Paul desired and determined to be separated from all the dead things of the old dispensation. For the attaining of this out-resurrection state he had been buried with Christ in baptism, and had been raised to walk in newness of life,—in fact to be one with Him.

12. *" Not as though I had already attained, either were already perfect." Does he refer to his spiritual attainments, or to his hope?*

To his hope of glory doubtless, for this is distinctly stated in verse 14, " I press towards the mark for the prize." There are two things which he is speaking about in this chapter, viz., present attainments through Christ, for which all else had been renounced; and future glory which he had not yet attained; and, as he passes abruptly from the one to the other, unless we are careful we may fail to rightly apply his words. Paul had won Christ, for he was " in Him"; he had attained to a new life through His resurrection, for he could say " I live," but to the glory he had not attained, but was following on that he might apprehend that for which he had been apprehended of Christ Jesus.

15. *In verse 12, Paul says that he was not perfect, but here he assumes that he and some others were perfect. How is this?*

Although it is the same word that is used, we must not suppose that he would contradict himself, but that he is referring to two distinct matters. In this verse he refers to their being perfected or matured in the knowledge of the will of Christ, and should therefore be like-minded with Him in self-sacrifice. In the former he is speaking of being perfected by complete redemption towards which he was pressing, and in the anticipation of which he was forgetting that which was behind.

18. *There are some persons of whom he warns them to beware. Who are these?*

They the Judaisers of whom he speaks in verse 2, who by circumcision set aside the cross of Christ. Their walk was carnal, their belly was their God, and their end destruction. Well might he warn against their unholy influence. Their earthly tendencies form a striking contrast to the apostle, and others like him, whose heavenward aspirations were worthy of imitation.

20. *" For our conversation is in heaven." What does this mean?*

From the many different renderings given to *politeuma*, there must be some difficulty in expressing what the apostle really meant. Rotherham renders it " commonwealth," Alford " country," Young " citizenship," Conybeare " life," Le Clerc " city," and Ellicott " citizens." Paul's idea is no doubt definite enough, but the term employed is possibly one of contrast, and so presents a difficulty. Judaisers may have boasted of Jerusalem and its time-honoured associations, but Paul and those like-minded had turned away from this doomed city, and were seeking something more satisfying and abiding, even the home of God; and to this higher portion he evidently now refers. There is, however, another rendering of *politeuma* which I much prefer to all these, viz., *our home. Our home is in the heavens;* " from whence also we look for the Saviour, the Lord

Jesus Christ : who shall change our vile body," etc. The institution to which these false teachers were seeking to lead them, was perishing in every part of it ; and by showing them the higher privileges of the new institution he thus sought to prevent what would be both their folly and their ruin.

21. *Why does he say " our vile body " ?*

It is, *lit.*, the body of our humiliation ; because through sin it has been subjected to suffering and death, and must return to dust. God's purpose, however, is to transform it, and fashion that future body like to the body of the glorified Christ. For this they waited in hope, and when Jesus returns will be partakers of this hope, and dwell in this heavenly home for ever.

CHAPTER IV.

1. *" So stand fast in the Lord " implies an example. To whom does he refer ?*

To himself, as in chap. iii., where he tells them that all had been laid aside for Christ—all connected with Jewish standing, and the flesh had been laid aside.

What was the special ground of complaint against Euodias and Syntyche ?

Self-seeking, which led to disunion, and strife, and trouble, in the church. Paul urges them all to unite in doing Christ's will instead of their own.

3. *" True yoke-fellow."*⸴ *Who was this ?*

Possibly Epaphroditus, who was sent by Paul to minister among them, and who here is specially exhorted to this work.

" Help those women who laboured with me in the Gospel." Who were these ?

We should read, *these* (women, Euodias and Syntyche) who strove together with me in the Gospel, but are now striving against each other.

" The book of life." What is this?

The record which Jesus keeps of His disciples, whose names, according to Paul (Heb. xii. 23), are wrttten in heaven, and which record John calls the " book of life of the Lamb " (Rev. xiii. 8).

4. *Is joy the privilege of all believers ?*

Joy is a fruit of possession of Christ, and without Him there can be no true joy. Joy is the heart exulting in its attained object, and here the apostle urges them to let Christ be that object. He had said in chap. iii. 1, "Rejoice in the Lord," and here he says, "Again I say, rejoice."

5. *" Let your moderation be known unto all." How were they to show it?*

It is, *lit.*, gentleness, or forbearance towards each other, because their Lord was near. There had been contention among them, and this exhortation was needful.

6. *" Be careful for nothing." What does this exhortation imply ?*

A tendency to over-anxiety, which he wishes them to avoid. His exhortation is in view of approaching trial, which he knew would overtake them in the service of Christ. They were not to fear, but to pray ; not to be divided in mind, but to supplicate and trust in God ; and His peace should guard their hearts and thoughts in Christ Jesus.

If it is wrong to be over-anxious, and equally so to be careless, how can we avoid both evils ?

By obedience to God. He has given full directions for our guidance in all things, and true obedience will preserve from both anxiety and indifference. To do all that God commands we shall not be careless, and to tell Him all our need, believing that He will supply, will preserve from anxious fear.

10–14. *Their liberality had given him special joy. Why did it do so?*

Not because it relieved his want, for he had learned to be hungry as well as full; but in relieving his affliction they identified themselves with his work, on account of which he was suffering, and this greatly cheered his heart. Twice in Thessalonica, and now again in Rome, they had ministered to his need, and he now assures them that he has enough. Only one desire remained —" I desire fruit that may abound to your account."

The epistle to the Ephesians contains a full detail of their privileges as believers, but no charge of wrong-doing, whilst this epistle is entirely the reverse. How is this to be accounted for?

On the simple principle that the church at Philippi had to avail themselves of the authoritative declarations of the epistle to the Ephesians, which was also written to all the faithful in Christ Jesus; whilst this epistle to the church at Philippi, and that sent to Colosse, etc., were to be read by other churches, and thus they might learn how evil is reproved and denounced. We may also learn from this, and it is important that we should note it, that while every epistle is perfect as respects the matter upon which it treats, it is yet only a part of a divine structure or plan for the instruction and perfecting of the saints in righteousness. And that what Paul affirmed of the Old Testament writings is true also of the New, viz., that " All scripture is given by inspiration of God, and is profitable for doctrine, for reproof, for correction, for instruction in righteousness: that the man of God may be perfect, thoroughly furnished unto all good works." It will be therefore necessary to read them according to this pre-arranged plan of the Spirit, that the end for which this provision is made may be accomplished in us.

THE EPISTLE OF PAUL THE APOSTLE TO THE
COLOSSIANS.

CHAPTER I.

What was the object of Paul in writing this epistle?

It was written chiefly to uphold the authority of the Lord Jesus, and thus to counteract the doctrines of Judaism and Grecian philosophy, by which they were being ensnared. They had received Christ, and this had given great joy to the heart of Paul; but having heard that they were in danger of being spoiled through philosophy and vain deceit, he most earnestly seeks to prevent it.

What is the difference betwixt this epistle and the epistle to the Ephesians?

The epistle to the Ephesians contains an authoritative exposition of the privileges and standing of the believer in Christ; but as these Colossians had been instructed in these matters by Epaphras, Paul is chiefly concerned to prevent if possible their apostacy from Christ, and his declarations of their privileges have more or less some relation to the errors to which they were exposed.

3. " *We give thanks to God and the Father.*" *Why does Paul say,* " *God* and *the Father*"?

"And" is omitted by the best MSS. We should therefore read, *God the Father*, etc.

4. *Why did he give thanks upon hearing of their faith and love?*

Their faith in Christ, and their love to all the saints, were striking evidences of the transforming power of the Gospel which he preached. These Colossians had been the slaves of vice, and had now become the loving disciples of Jesus. Well might he give thanks upon hearing of their faith and love.

5. "*For the hope which is laid up for you.*" *What was this hope?*

Christ Jesus was their hope, but glory and immortality also awaited them in Christ; and for the possession of this glory they were called upon to be faithful.

Why did he say "laid up for you in heaven"?

Because glory and immortality is not to be enjoyed here but in heaven, and this revelation should guide and settle the faith of all believers.

Paul says, they had heard of it in the Gospel. How did the Gospel reveal it?

The resurrection of Jesus was one of the great facts of the Gospel, and that fact was an illustration of their privilege, and the foundation of their hope. The resurrection of Jesus is the assurance of our own, and in Him the life and incorruptibility of the saints is brought to light.

6. *What was the fruit brought forth by the Gospel?*

Faith, love, holiness, peace, and other kindred graces; to which some MSS. versions and fathers add, "and increasing," or growing. That is, not only did the Gospel bring forth fruit in their own hearts and lives, but it was being preached to others, that they also might be saved.

9, 10. *In verse 6 he had spoken of their knowledge of His grace, but here he desires their knowledge of His will. What is the difference between them?*

The grace of God revealed in the Gospel was concerning His pardoning mercy in Christ Jesus, but the will of God was in relation to their walk as believers. Paul desires that, as they had known God's love, so they might know His will, and might walk worthy of the Lord unto all pleasing. Epaphras, or some other disciple, had made known to them the former, and in this epistle Paul makes known the latter.

11–13. "*Giving thanks to the Father.*" *Is it Paul that gave thanks, or were they to do so?*

It is these Colossians who are called to thankfulness, because they had been fitted to share the portion of the saints; and in this indebtedness to God Paul unites himself with them.

What does he mean by the "power of darkness," from which they had been delivered?

It is, *lit., the authority of darkness, i.e.,* the domination of evil under which they had served in their former state. Darkness is a symbol of disobedience and error, as light is of truth and holiness.

"*Translated us into the kingdom of His dear Son.*" *Were these Colossians really in the kingdom of Jesus?*

Most certainly, or Paul would not have said so. The reign of Jesus was by means of the laws of the New Covenant; and as they had yielded to His claims, they had become the subjects of His gracious rule.

How could He reign when not visibly present?

As Jehovah—through the laws, statutes, etc., published by Moses—reigned over Israel, though not visibly present; so Jesus—through the laws published by the apostles, one of them having opened the kingdom—

reigns over all who yield obedience to His claims.

15–18. *How was Christ "the image of God"?*

As an image is a representation of some person or thing, so Christ is a manifestation of God in all things necessary for man to know.

What does he mean by "the first-born of every creature"?

It is, *lit., a first-born of all creation*, and refers not to birth merely, but to the rank, dignity, etc., possessed by a first-born son. By His resurrection from the dead, and His exaltation in the heavenlies, Jesus has not only become the head of the Church, but is also the head of all creation, which, as Jehovah or the Word, came from His hand — for "all things were made by Him: and without Him was not anything made that was made." Paul's reference to thrones, dominions, principalities, etc., was to show how foolish it must be to accept of created authorities, instead of Him who had become Lord and head of all things.

19. *"For it pleased the Father that in Him should all fulness dwell." What is meant by this fulness?*

It is simply the manifestation of God, whose spirit, character, power, grace, and love, are all displayed in Him. The word *pleroma*, here rendered fulness, is used in the New Testament in connection with quite a number of things, as fulness of the earth, fulness of God, etc., and from these references we may learn its meaning. That which the earth produces is its fulness; and that which is manifest in Christ is the fulness of God; while the gifts and graces of the Church are the fulness of Christ.

20. *"And having made peace through the blood of His cross." To whom does Paul refer?*

To Jews and Gentiles; the enmity of the former against the latter, through supposed superiority, being very great. Jesus, however, died for the sin of both, and those who accepted of Him as their Saviour, irrespective of their former standing, were not only saved but reconciled both to God and to each other; and "so making peace."

"Whether things in earth or things in heaven." What are these?

Both earth and heaven are used here as symbols of Jews and Gentiles in contrast with each other. The former from their exaltation were as heaven, while the latter from their debasement are fitly symbolised as earth.

23. *Why does he say "If ye continue in the faith?"*

He had said in the previous verse that the object of Christ was to present them unblameable and unreprovable, and then stated that if they were not faithful His object would be frustrated.

26. *"The mystery which hath been hid from ages and from generations." What was this mystery?*

It is, *lit., the secret*, viz., that believers, Jews and Gentiles together, should form the body of Christ. This highest of all the privileges of the saints had not been revealed in the ages by types, nor during the generations by the prophets, nor even to Peter, although honoured to open the kingdom; but its unveiling was reserved for Paul, who was made a steward of this secret of God on behalf of the Gentiles. So highly, indeed, did Paul estimate this special mission, that all suffering endured in connection with it was counted a privilege rather than a trial.

CHAPTER II.

1. *Was this conflict, which Paul had for these Colossians and others, mental or physical?*

It was an inward conflict, I presume—a painful exercise of heart, *lit.*, an agony, lest they should yield to the pressure brought to bear upon them by false teachers, and so apostatise from the Christ on whom they had believed.

2–4. *How did he expect to prevent this possible apostacy?*

By warning them of beguiling teachers, and then instructing them further in the knowledge of Christ.

Is this "mystery of God, and of the Father, and of Christ," the same as referred to in the preceding chapter?

Yes; but it will be better to read, *the secret of God;* (and) *Christ in whom are stored* (not hidden) *all the treasures of wisdom and knowledge.* There were the purposes of God respecting the one body, which was kept secret during the ages, and was strictly God's secret; and there were riches of His grace which, being stored in Jesus, were even for believing Gentiles. Of the truth of these things Paul wished them to be fully assured.

5. *" For though I be absent in the flesh, yet am I with you in the spirit." What does this mean?*

Spirit is doubtless used for the testimony or truth delivered to them; and though spoken by Epaphras, who had been instructed by Paul, or in this epistle sent from Rome, the testimony had all the authority of Christ the Lord. Paul evidently seems to fear that false teachers would take advantage of the circumstance, that as they had not had personal intercourse with him, they were free to act independently of his control, or else could not claim the promises and assurances declared by him. His reference to this matter is of very great moment, because, if the testimony of Christ by him was valid in churches which had never seen him at that time, it is valid still to all who receive it, and will condemn those who reject it. It is this which makes his letters so valuable to all the churches. They are the testimony of Christ by His chosen apostle, and should be received with all confidence by all the saints.

8. *" Beware lest any man spoil you through philosophy and vain deceit, after the tradition of men." Does Paul refer to two distinct systems?*

Yes, he refers to philosophy and Judaism, both of which were used to ensnare the disciples of Christ. The teachings of Plato and other philosophers were well-defined systems of thought, constantly taught in their schools, and in the days of Paul their philosophy ruled the minds of millions throughout Greece and Asia. Judaism, or more strictly Rabbinical theology, was more limited in its influence than philosophy, but at the same time more injurious, as through its paid agents almost all the churches of the Gentiles were visited, in order to draw away disciples after them. The teachers of philosophy with its empty deceit, and those of tradition with its worldly elements, had both become impatient in the presence of a new system that promised far better things than either; and most vigorous efforts were made to drag away as spoil those who had accepted the religion of the Lord Jesus. Paul had therefore to caution the saints at Colosse against these men, who were of the world, and not after Christ.

Do the snares against which Paul warns the Colossians exist in the present day?

Not exactly in the same form, because as systems they were broken up, and only fragments of them remain. But as these fragments have become entwined with the religion of Jesus, it is only as they are tested by the Scriptures that they can be proved to be not of God but of man. Romanism has fashioned for itself a splendid robe, but the material and colours have all been collected from these ancient looms of Judaism and Pagan philosophy; and Ritualism is now busy copying this gaudy dress. Then the so-called evangelical religion of the present day is largely tinctured with Platonism, which was introduced by philosophers who were won over to Christianity in the second century. It is evidently present in the minds of those who wait for some influx of power to prove them favourites of heaven, rather than render prompt obedience to the Saviour's commands, and so obtain His promise. Some are waiting for Christ to bless and sanctify them in some arbitrary manner, rather than learn His will and accept His blessing on the terms He has so graciously proposed. This is after men, and not after Christ; and of these snares we need to beware.

9. *What is meant by " Godhead," the fulness of which dwelt in Christ?*

The word occurs only here and in Romans i. 20 ; but though rendered Godhead in both places, yet in Greek the words are different, and present different aspects of Him whom they represent. The context may guide us to see that *Theiotes* in Romans denotes the manifestation of divine power, as seen in creation ; while *Theotes* in Colossians denotes the divine nature as manifest in Christ, "in whom dwelleth all the fulness of the Godhead bodily," *i.e.*, in His humanity. For love and grace, power and deity, were all manifest in the man Christ Jesus.

10. *Why does he add, " And ye are complete in Him"?*

It is strictly, *ye are filled up in Him, i.e.*, you do not require either Judiasm or philosophy to meet your need. There is in Christ Jesus all that you require. It is not to cha-

racter that Paul refers, but to the fulness of provision that is stored in Christ for those who receive Him.

11. *" In whom also ye are circumcised with the circumcision made without hands." What does this mean?*

Circumcision of the flesh, as instituted in the family of Abraham, was the cutting off the foreskin of every man child ; while the circumcision of believers was the " putting off the body [of the sins, omit] of the flesh by the circumcision of Christ," *i.e.*, by the sacrifice of Christ, the whole fleshly or Jewish institution was set aside. In His death the whole of the sacrificial types were fulfilled, and were therefore no longer required. In fact, to continue their use, was to ignore the work of Christ. The Holy Spirit, by the truth concerning Jesus, circumcised believers, by separating from them all uncleanness of the flesh, a striking contrast to the hand-made circumcision of the old institution.

12. *" Buried with Him in baptism." Why refer to this ordinance?*

The burial which takes place in this ordinance is very significant, both as respects Christ, and the believer who is buried with Him. Every relation to the past terminates at the grave, and with a new life new obligations take the place of the old. This was true as respects Christ, who, at His death, had done with the old covenant; and being only a shadow of Himself it ceased also. When Jesus was raised from the dead it was not to go up to Jerusalem to keep feasts, etc., but to enter upon a higher state. So with the believer in Jesus ; having risen from a grave of water in which he was buried with Christ, he has not only done with the sins of a past life, but with all that remains of the old economy. The same truth is taught by Paul in his letter to the Corinthians,— " Therefore if any man be in Christ, he is a new creature : old things are passed away ; behold, all things are become new." And being risen with Christ, and having through Him a new life, the believer has only to serve his newly-accepted Lord and life-giver.

"*Through faith in the operation of God." What does this mean ?*

The resurrection of Jesus was the operation or work of God. Jesus accepted death and the grave, and God raised Him into life ; and these Colossians believing this were buried with Him in baptism, and were raised into a new life with Him. It was a strange pathway into life in both cases, but being God's way the end was secured.

Some persons say that baptism came in the room of circumcision, and that as infants were circumcised in order to enter the Old Covenant, they also have a claim to be baptised, and thus enter the New. Is this correct ?

If such persons only understood the teaching of Moses, they would never so affirm. A Jewish child entered into the covenant by its birth, and its circumcision was in order to the enjoyment of its privileges, and both are striking types of God's arrangements for the enjoyment of all the privileges of the New Covenant. It is by a birth out of water and the Spirit that the believing enter into the family of God, and then are circumcised or made holy, in order to enjoy all its covenanted blessings. Persons who overlook the truth that faith is first required by Jesus before baptism, and then bring children to it, who, from their incapacity cannot believe, make a very serious mistake. They not only deceive themselves if they presume that they have obeyed Christ, but in very many instances it becomes a deception to the child when willing to become a disciple of Jesus. We would like to say to all persons who reason in this manner, that to misunderstand and then misapply the types of the Old Covenant, is not only to confuse their own minds, but is sure to lead them to disobey God. There is always some analogy between type and antitype, and this should not be lost sight of in our enquiry after the meaning of anything really typical.

14. "*The handwriting of ordinances that was against us." To what does Paul refer ?*

To the ordinances of the law which were written by Moses, and which continued in force until the death of Christ. When Paul speaks of blotting out the handwriting of ordinances, and of nailing them to the cross, he is evidently referring to the effects of that death upon the whole Jewish institution. For centuries, through those writings, God had claimed sacrifices in order to access to Himself—a privilege which the Jew alone could enjoy ; but when the blood of Christ was shed upon the cross, those claims were by metonymy blotted out, and God never allowed them to be presented again. The nails that fastened Jesus to the cross were driven through those long-standing claims, and, according to an ancient custom, when a nail was driven through a written claim, it could never again be presented. In putting Jesus to death, the Jews did what they never intended to do ; they put to death the privileges of the old institution. God raised up Jesus to life again, but gave no life to these, and unless they accepted of Him nothing but judgment remained. To those who would accept Him a new way of access was opened.

15. *What were these principalities and powers which Christ spoiled and triumphed over ?*

The divinely appointed officials of that age, who as rulers, teachers, priests, etc., were all set aside when God raised Jesus from the dead, and exalted Him to power. It was not Moses that could rule, nor Aaron that could minister for the worshippers when God said to Jesus, "Thou art a priest for ever after the order of Melchisedec." Jesus stripped them all of their official authority, and though set at nought by them He was made the head of the corner.

16. *Why should meats, and feasts, new moons, and sabbaths, be set aside by a new institution?*

Because they were but shadows of good things to come, and when the substance appeared, the shadows were no longer needed, and the saints were not to be judged for neglecting them.

Was the sabbath a shadow? and should it not be kept holy as commanded?

Sabbath means rest, and was a shadow of the rest which believers have in Christ. "For we which have believed do enter into rest" (Heb. iv. 3). The seventh day was the sabbath or rest of God in creation, and was afterwards given to the Jews, and formed part of their economy of types. But since Christ has come, this typical rest cannot be kept without ignoring Him as our rest. The Jewish sabbath is past, and the first day of the week has begun in life and liberty. It is not physical rest that is to be sought, but praise and adoration to Him who has brought life and immortality to light. On the first of the week the believer ceases his daily labour, but it is that he may honour Christ by His spiritual service. The first of the week should never be called a sabbath, because it is neither true nor appropriate to so name this resurrection day.

18–22. *"Let no man beguile you of your reward."* *What does Paul seek to prevent?*

Their acceptance of Judaism, which in its varied forms was being imposed upon them. His plain advice is, have nothing to do with them, they are all to perish.

23. *What is " will worship"?*

It is worship or service according to human choice. It is man having his own way instead of God's.

CHAPTER III.

1. *" If ye then be risen with Christ."* *Does Paul express a doubt as to their state?*

Not a doubt, but a recognition, because in chap. ii. 12 he declared they were raised through the risen Christ. If we read, *Since then ye were jointly raised with Christ,* we should see his meaning more clearly, and should feel the force of his exhortation to seek the things above.

Would you say it was their duty or responsibility to do so?

That is a very low aspect of the matter. If I have a father who has an inheritance for me in some distant land, it would be strange for any one to say, It is your duty to seek after it. It would be my privilege to do so; but if not appreciated, then I might require to be stirred up to a proper estimate of it.

2. *How could they set their affections on unseen things?*

To be called upon to have affection for things, the nature of which we cannot fully understand, must present a difficulty to most minds, and lead them to regret the coldness of their hearts. But if we read the exhortation, *Mind ye the things which are above, not the things on the earth,* we shall see that the exhortation is of a far more practical character than merely having affection for them. Being made heirs of the glory into which Jesus, the forerunner, has entered, he now claims that our walk shall correspond with our high destiny. Hence the walk and spirit of the believer in going through this world must be in harmony with the will of God.

3, 4. *" For ye are dead, and your life is hid with Christ in God." What is meant by the present death and hidden life of these Colossians ?*

It is, *lit.*, *For ye died,* which death was their voluntary separation from their past state, whilst their hidden life was the glory into which Christ entered, and will only be manifested in His manifestation. Christ in glory is the believer's security, and also His life ; and Christ, who is the head, and believers, who are the members of His body, will be manifested together.

5–7. *Mortify therefore your members which are upon the earth. What does this exhortation mean ?*

The members of the body, which Paul calls the "old man," are the sins specially named, as fornication, etc. These, he says, you must mortify—*lit.*, put to death—because on account of these the wrath of God cometh on the children of disobedience ; and if you give life to these vile passions, you will bring upon yourselves this same wrath.

8–11. *These Colossians had put off malice, anger, wrath, etc. Why does he require to specially urge them to " lie not one to another " ?*

Lying, or falsehood, was a practice more common to heathens than any other sin, and was no doubt more difficult to put away than other more flagrant vices. Special and repeated exhortations were needed to lead them to continue truthful ; and since they had put off the old man with his deeds, they must not again, by renewed practice, give form and life to that which by the truth had been put to death.

What does he mean by saying,

" Where there is neither Greek nor Jew " ?

He means that when the new man is formed by a knowledge of Jesus these fleshly distinctions are all set aside. Both Greek and Jew, barbarian and Scythian, bond and free, had each his peculiar distinction and standing in life, according to nation, circumstance, and training, and by these things, which were of no moment, they were separated from each other. But when buried with Christ in their baptism, and risen to form one holy brotherhood, all these distinctions vanished, and Christ alone, instead of these national distinctions, was to be seen in all.

12. *How were they to be clothed with Christ ?*

By being clothed with kindness, meekness, forbearance, and love ; by which traits of character they resembled Him.

15. *In exhorting them as individuals, why does he refer to the body ?*

Because of the relation which, as individual members, they sustained to it. The peace of God was to rule them individually, that the body might be benefited thereby. There is a very close connection between the individual life and the whole assembly. The influence of a worldly-minded person in the church may be immensely injurious to it, while the presence of an earnest, devoted, and loving spirit may do a great deal of good ; and the more these are multiplied the more must be.

16. *" Let the Word of Christ dwell in you richly in all wisdom." Should the pause be put after wisdom ?*

The punctuation of this sentence would be better as follows : " Let the Word of Christ dwell in you richly ; in all wisdom teaching and admonishing each other ; with psalms hymns, and spiritual songs, with grace or thanksgiving in your hearts singing to the Lord "—the Word of the Lord being the source of both the teaching, the song, and the admonishing.

Are sentimental and patriotic songs proper for the Christian ?

The songs are to be spiritual, and the singing must be to the Lord, and this must guide us in all that we sing. The believer must refrain from every song that he cannot sing to his Master. As one redeemed from sin by precious blood, the praise of his Lord should continually be in his mouth. When this course is pursued, there will be neither room nor time for creature pleasing.

18–25. *Is it not strange that Paul should give directions about wives and husbands, children and parents, servants and masters ?*

Not when the behaviour of each will either honour or dishonour their Father in heaven. We should study His will in whatever relation we stand, that in doing it we may obtain His reward.

CHAPTER IV.

In exhorting masters to be "just and equal" to their servants, why does Paul remind them that they also " have a Master in heaven" ?

Because from Him they must receive praise or blame at the last solemn reckoning day, according as they may have been just or unjust.

Do not circumstances influence masters and servants now, much more than justice and equity ?

The relation between master and servant in the present day is sustained in a spirit much to be deplored. The combinations of both servants and masters to compel submission to terms of their own arrangement, is destructive of the principle upon which both service and payment should be based. Christian masters and servants have great need to watch and pray, lest, instead of being ruled by the Word of God, their actions are governed by mere selfishness and worldly policy. God expects servants to be faithful, and masters to be just, and has given instruction to both how to be so.

2. *" Continue in prayer," etc. Does he refer to general or special supplications ?*

Prayer should always be special, that is, we should pray for the things we need. Paul was exhorting wives and husbands, parents and children, masters and servants, to fulfil all required obligations as in the sight of God, and to do this unto all pleasing would not be an easy task, and to overcome selfishness divine aid must be sought. It is to this end that he urges them, not only to pray, but to continue in prayer; not only to watch lest they should be overcome in temptation, but to record with thankfulness every attained victory over self and sin.

3. *Paul desired that himself and fellow-labourers and sufferers should be remembered by them in prayer, in relation to their work. Why does God require to be importuned to help on the work of conversion ?*

I do not think that all the prayers of all the saints in the world will ever make God more willing to save and bless men than He really is; but as God's method of conversion is by men hearing, believing, and obeying the truth, these things must always precede true conversion to Christ. It is instructive to note the request which Paul here desires them to make. It was not that God would convert sinners, or put forth His power and awaken them, or touch their hearts and make them feel their need ; Paul could not have mocked God with such petitions, or asked others to do so. Both he and Aristarchus were fellow-prisoners, and he asks these Colossians to pray that God would open a door for the word, that they might speak the mystery of Christ, and thus by the Gospel men might be led to accept of the Lord Jesus.

5. *" Walk in wisdom toward them that are without." What does this imply ?*

Christian behaviour before the world. Many who do not read the Bible, will read the actions of those who profess to take it as their guide, and will be the better or the worse for the life they live.

What is redeeming the time ?

Buying up the seasons as they come into our hands, and using them as gracious opportunities that must be seized at once, or lost for ever.

6. *What is " salt " with which all speech must be seasoned ?*

Truth, of which salt was a symbol under the Old Covenant. The typical offerings were never to lack the salt of the covenant, and the speech of the believer must be seasoned with truth, that those who hear may be benefited thereby.

7–9. *Why did Paul send these two messengers, Tychicus and Onesimus to Colosse ?*

Tychicus was the bearer of several letters to the churches in Asia, and was specially charged with communications respecting the state of the apostle, which he desired them to fully understand. Onesimus was returning to his master at Colosse, and was also instructed to assist in making known the state of the apostle.

11. *Why had Paul so few helpers among those who were of the circumcision ?*

The reason is a very sad one, and caused Paul much grief of heart. He was preaching salvation to men irrespective of the law of Moses, and but few of the Jews assisted him in this grand and God-like mission. There were other helpers, as Aristarchus, and Epaphras, and Luke, but these were Gentiles. The Jews had heard him in his own hired house, and had great reasonings about the truth, but nearly all failed to receive it.

14. *Is this Demas, who sends greeting to the saints, the one who in 2 Timothy is said to have forsaken him ?*

The same I have no doubt. His apostacy from Christ was through love of the world, and the simple record of it should be a warning to all.

THE FIRST EPISTLE OF PAUL THE APOSTLE TO THE

THESSALONIANS.

CHAPTER I.

Why did Paul write this letter ?

This letter, the first written by him as an apostle of Christ, was prompted by his deep anxiety for the church in Thessalonica, after he had been so hastily driven from their midst. His efforts to lead them to accept of Christ began in the Jewish synagogue, where only a few believed in Him as the Messiah ; while his proclamation among the Greeks was accepted by a great many. This so enraged the unbelieving Jews, that a most furious assault was made by them against those who had embraced the new faith, and it was deemed advisable to send Paul away. The apostle yielded to the advice of the new converts, and was taken by them first to Berea, where they were followed by the persecuting mob, from which he had again to escape, and was ultimately conducted to Athens. Here the apostle became so anxious about the converts left behind, that he could not rest until he had sent Timothy to enquire about their state, and when assured of their firmness in the faith, he wrote this letter to encourage and instruct them in their new life. After some details respecting his first preaching of the Gospel to them, he is led to give them most valuable instruction respecting their spirit and life in the world. This preceptive teaching of the apostle was not only valuable to them, but also to the saints in every generation, and should be studied by them in order to obedience in all the will of God. But not only has the apostle instructed believers how to walk and how to please God, but he has also given most valuable revelations concerning the return of the Lord, with the attendant circumstances that will usher in the final and glorious destiny of His saints. In this brief section the apostle has so clearly made known what is to take place when Jesus shall return, that we can now look forward with intelligent apprehension of our future glorious destiny, and with these words should exhort one another.

1. *Why does Paul join Silvanus and Timotheus in this salutation ?*

Because they were joint-labourers with him in their conversion and upbuilding, and were equally solicitous about their steadfastness.

2. *Paul prayed definitely for these saints. Is definiteness in prayer absolutely required ?*

It is very important to be definite

in our prayers, and to tell God what we want and for whom we supplicate. The example of Paul in simplicity and definiteness, is worthy of imitation by all the saints.

3-5. *" Knowing, brethren beloved, your election of God." How did Paul know this ?*

By the gifts of the Spirit which followed their reception of Christ; for the preaching of the Gospel was followed by signs and wonders among those who believed. The acceptance of Gentiles was at that time a disputed matter, but the signs proved that God was no respecter of persons, and gave assurance to those who had believed through grace, even though of Gentile birth.

These Thessalonian saints are here highly commended by Paul for their faith and labour. How does this agree with Luke (Acts xvii. 11), who says they were not so noble as those in Berea ?

Those to whom Luke refers were Jews, who refused to examine their own Scriptures, and were therefore guided by their own thoughts; but these were believing Gentiles, a noble band of witnesses for the truth, and whose example was for good throughout all the churches of Macedonia. It is sad to think that those who had the prophecies concerning Christ, should refuse to search the rolls which contained them, even when their fulfilment was declared; while the Gentiles, to whom no direct revelation was given, should, on the first proclamation of the Gospel, so eagerly embrace it, yet this was the case at Thessalonica. The Jews refused the message, and drove away the man who brought it; the Greeks believed, and accepted Christ as their Lord and Saviour.

6-10. *What are the proofs that they had really accepted Christ ?*

The apostle furnishes several which are unmistakable. (1.) They turned from idols to serve the living and true God. (2.) Believing that what was good for them would be good for others, they became missionaries of the Gospel they had received, and sent it through Macedonia and Achaia. (3.) They became imitators of Paul and of Christ, in leading holy lives. And (4.) they were waiting for Jesus to return and fulfil His promise of glory and immortality. To turn from evil to good, from vice to virtue, and from an impure to a holy life, is an evidence of conversion that none will question.

CHAPTER II.

1–6. *What was the purpose of Paul in reviewing his early labours in Thessalonica ?*

It was in order to impress them with the importance of the truth, which, after severe suffering at Philippi, he had preached to them ; and, having under such painful trials sought their salvation, apart from every carnal motive, he now desires that they might stand against all temptation.

Of what use is this narration of his labours and sufferings to us ?

It will be a noble use of Paul's reference to himself, if we only learn to labour and suffer for Christ as he did. When persecuted and forced out of Philippi, he went to Thessalonica, and when the Word was rejected by Jews, he preached it to Gentiles. In the morning, when all was bright with hope, he sowed the seed, and in the evening, when darkness and evil gathered on his path, he held not back the truth, that from some part of it there might be fruit for Christ.

What may we learn from his plain and faithful presentation of the truth to all ?

We should learn to make known

2 B

the truth, however unfavourable the circumstances, never to use flattery when the truth should be spoken, to do good without being hired to do it, and to embrace every opportunity of service from love to Christ and precious souls.

7–9. *" But we were gentle among you," etc. What may we learn from his spirit ?*

We should learn to be like him. The figure used by him to express his care towards them, that of a nurse towards her children, is a very homely one, but if we restore an omitted word, it will be far more impressive. *We were gentle in your midst, as a nurse would cherish her own children.* The tenderness of a mother is now before us, and we can see the gentle yearnings of the apostle's heart over these converts at Thessalonica. Here is a lesson for all to imitate. True, the children may not be of our begetting by the Gospel, but when they are a part of our heavenly Father's family, they should have a brother's sympathy and a sister's care. Paul not only gave to them the Gospel, but had it been needful he would have given for them his life.

10–12. *What is the purpose of Paul's reference to his own blameless life among them ?*

It is recorded for imitation. He wished them to be what he had been —holy and blameless in their midst. And it would be well if we could all say to the church to which we have been joined, and in which we have laboured, " Ye are witnesses, and God also, how holily and justly we behaved ourselves among you that believe." Every believer in Christ should be His servant, and every servant should set an example worthy of imitation by others.

13. *" The Word of God, which effectually worketh in you that believe." Is this the same as the doctrine of " effectual calling " ?*

Not as that doctrine is generally understood. It is presumed to be a call that is not resisted, but which issues in the faith of the person called; but here Paul affirms that their work proved their faith in the Word of God, or, as he states it, their faith led them to endure affliction for the truth.

16. *" The wrath is come upon them to the uttermost." To whom does he refer ?*

To the Jews, the bitter opponents of the truth. They had killed the Lord Jesus, and the prophets who spoke of His coming; they had persecuted Paul, and forbade him to preach to the Gentiles, lest they should be saved, and through a Gentile mob had raised up persecution against them; thus they filled up the measure of their sins, and wrath had come upon them to the uttermost— *lit.*, for an end.

18. *Paul would have visited them " once and again," but Satan hindered. How did he do this ?*

By some willing tool of his evil purpose. It is, *lit., the adversary,* but human agents were found ready to carry out his design. He is the master of all evil workers, who become by the service they perform his accredited servants.

CHAPTER III.

1–5. *Why does he refer to the sending of Timothy ?*

To show them his yearning desire to have them established in the truth, and fitted to meet the ever-varying forms of temptation with which they might be assailed. That the tempter would assail them he very well knew, but in what way he could not tell. But he knew that by the truth they would be prepared for every emergency; and so, when he could not go himself, Timothy was sent to instruct and prepare them for the conflict.

6–9. *Why did Timothy return so speedily to Athens ?*

He found them so firmly established in the truth, and so nobly contending against opposition, that he thought it best to return and inform Paul of their faith and love, and desire to see him again. These joyful news more than balanced all the affliction he was called to endure, and his prayers and supplications on their behalf were presented to God night and day.

10–13. *Why did he wish to return ?*

To confer on them further gifts and instruction, and to perfect what might still be lacking in their faith. But lest he should not be permitted to see them again, the remainder of the epistle is filled with valuable instruction concerning their walk, and with revelations of future glory, and union with the Lord; and as these revelations set forth the privileges of all the saints, we should ponder them with special interest.

CHAPTER IV.

1. *What is the first thing to which Paul exhorts in this chapter ?*

To abound in the things in which they had been instructed, that in all things they might please God.

3. *Why has he to exhort them to abstain from fornication ?*

Fornication and its associate vices were, alas! too common in Thessalonica, and indeed in every place where idolatry prevailed. The gods they formed and worshipped were according to their evil passions, and Christians had to learn that these evil things were displeasing to God. It was needful to instruct them that, as their bodies were temples or dwelling-places for the Holy Spirit, every organ and passion must be subjected in harmony with His will. The instructions respecting these matters are also necessary for us, lest we should yield to fleshly gratification instead of being controlled by the will of God. Every member of our bodies should be subject to Christ, so that each may minister to His glory. So Paul taught the Romans (vi. 13), " Yield yourselves unto God, as those that are alive from the dead, and your members instruments of righteousness unto God."

6 – 8. Is the defrauding which Paul here forbids connected with the ordinary affairs of life ?

To defraud in anything is wrong, but he is here speaking of fornication, or the taking of another man's wife. God not only forbade this, but would punish those who did so. The sin was not against man only, but against God.

13. How do you account for this sudden change from exhortation about Christian life to revelations about those who had fallen asleep ?

It is very likely that Timothy had brought the tidings of their anxiety respecting some who had already fallen victims to their persecutors, and from their unwarranted thought that all must be alive to share the glory of the promised return of Jesus, they had begun to mourn on behalf of those who had died, believing that they would not enjoy it. Hence the apostle has to correct their notion by revealing the purpose of God respecting both living and sleeping ones, and thus relieved their sorrow by instructing their minds.

14. Why does he refer to the death and resurrection of Jesus ?

To illustrate and assure them that all who die shall rise again. " For if we believe that Jesus died and rose again, even so them also which sleep in Jesus will God bring with Him."

" Bring with Him." Is it from heaven ?

No ; but from the grave. As Christ was brought from the dead by the power of God, so are believers to be brought also, or, as stated in ver. 16, " the dead in Christ shall rise."

15–17. " We which are alive and remain unto the coming of the Lord shall not prevent them which are asleep." What does this mean ?

Paul means that the saints who are living when Christ shall return shall not precede or enter into glory before the saints who had fallen asleep. " For the Lord Himself shall descend, . . . and the dead in Christ shall rise first." That is, those who are in their graves shall be raised from death before the living, who will be changed, shall ascend, and both shall be caught up together to meet the Lord in the air, and will ascend with Him to the promised glory.

Why are the saints taken up from the earth?

Because, according to Peter, the earth and its works shall be burned up, and the promised home of believers is in the Father's house, where Christ now is. " Wherefore comfort "—*lit.*, exhort—" one another with these words."

CHAPTER V.

1. What does Paul mean by " times and seasons" ?

Times are periods, in which certain things appointed of God happen or come to pass ; while *seasons* are opportunities afforded in those periods. The former are of God's arranging for His own special purpose, while the latter are for man's advantage, and involve his responsibility. For instance, the " day of the Lord "

—*i.e.,* the day of His manifestation —belongs to the *times* which are in God's hand; while the *seasons— i.e.,* the opportunities for faith and love, sobriety and watchfulness—are granted for improvement during His delay.

2. *Why does he illustrate the coming of the Lord by a " thief in the night " ?*

The thief enters and carries away property while its possessor is asleep, who awakens only to find it gone; so will it be with those who do not use their opportunities, they will awake in the day of the Lord to find them gone for ever. For when He comes destruction will come upon all the neglectors of His salvation.

Does Paul refer to the judgment at the end of the world ?

" Times and seasons " may indicate dispensational judgment, which came first upon the nation of Israel, who failed to improve the seasons which God in kindness gave to them; but may also apply to the end of the present dispensation.

4 – 7. *What does he mean by " darkness " and " light " ?*

Darkness is *ignorance,* the condition of those who, in their sinful neglect of the truth, were saying, " peace and safety ; " while light is *knowledge,* which these Thessalonians had received, and by which their new life was being modelled.

8. *Why does he refer to the armour of soldiers when illustrating the means of spiritual defence ?*

The illustration would be a familiar one, as every city under Roman rule would have its garrison, and with soldiers armed with helmets on their heads and cuirass or breastplate on their bodies, suggestive both of danger and means of defence. So by this fact Paul reminds them that there were spiritual foes, against which they must be pro-

tected by the breastplate of faith and love, and by the hope of salvation as their helmet.

12. *Were these persons that were said to be over them in the Lord, overseers ?*

Yes, and were justly entitled to be so called. They toiled among them, and admonished them in the Lord; so that they were a good type of overseers even if not called such.

14, 15. " *Warn them that are unruly,*" etc. *Are these precepts binding on all disciples ?*

Most certainly, and there is nothing required here but what every disciple should seek to fulfil.

16. " *Rejoice evermore.*" *Is this possible ?*

Yes, when Christ is our joy ; because, as a reason for joy to the believer, He never fails and never changes.

17, 18. *Both prayer and thanksgiving require to be unceasing. How can two different acts be continuously performed ?*

Prayer and praise are like the alternate motions of the chest; the air is first received and then breathed out, and thus the natural life is sustained ; while in prayer we inhale heavenly blessing, and in praise we breathe out thanks to God, and thus our spiritual life continues.

19. " *Quench not the Spirit.*" *How could this be done ?*

By restraining the exercise of those gifts bestowed by Him for the confirmation of the truth.

20. " *Despise not prophesyings.*" *How could they despise them ?*

By not regarding them because of the agents who might deliver them. Important directions from the Spirit might be sent by humble messengers, and the danger of despising His message through them might easily arise.

21. *How could they prove all things ?*

It is prophesying which they are here called upon to prove ; or to try all (which the prophets utter) ; and this they were able to do by the gift of discerning of spirits bestowed upon them.

22. *"Abstain from all appearance of evil." Does Paul mean by appearance that which is not strictly evil ?*

It will be better to read, *every form of evil.* It is evil they were to shun, whatever form it might assume.

" Your whole spirit and soul and body." Does man possess a triune nature ?

Most certainly. He has a body which is from the dust ; and he has a soul, his conscious personal self ; and also a God-given spirit, which for a while inhabits the body. Paul desired that all might be preserved blameless for Christ.

THE SECOND EPISTLE OF PAUL THE APOSTLE TO THE

THESSALONIANS.

CHAPTER I.

1–4. *Why did Paul write this second epistle to the Thessalonians ?*

To express (1.) his thankfulness on account of their growing faith in the truth first received, and in the abounding of their manifest love to each other, and for their patience under severe and prolonged persecutions. (2.) To correct a false report which had been circulated among them respecting the coming of the Lord, and which was causing great trouble of mind on account of their disappointed expectation in relation to Him.

5. *" Which is a manifest token of the righteous judgment of God." To what does this apply ?*

To the righteous decision of God, that by their sufferings for Christ they were deemed worthy subjects of His reign. Paul's thought is more clearly expressed in Conybeare's rendering of this verse. " And these things are a token that the righteous judgment of God will count you worthy of His kingdom, for which you are even now suffering."

6–10. *When would this infliction of tribulation upon their adversaries take place ?*

" When the Lord Jesus shall be revealed from heaven," and for this interposition they were to rest, or quietly wait until delivered by Him.

" Glorified in His saints." How will this be ?

By their deliverance from corruption, and all the evils of the present life, then will Jesus be glorified in having fulfilled His word, and will also be admired by all who are the happy partakers of His gracious power.

Their persecutors were to be punished with everlasting destruction. *What does this imply ?*

Everlasting separation from the presence and glory of the Lord ; and, whatever else may be involved, even this will be a most terrible doom.

CHAPTER II.

"*Now we beseech you, brethren, by the coming of the Lord Jesus Christ.*" *Why beseech them* by *His coming?*

It is rather *concerning* His coming, as it was their trouble of mind, caused by misrepresentation respecting it, that led him to write this second letter.

"*And by our gathering together unto Him.*" *Does he refer to a present or future gathering?*

To their ordinary Lord's Day gathering at His table, I presume. Their assembling was so identified with His return that Paul wishes them to understand that Jesus could not return without recognising their faith and obedience. This is his first assurance to them that His coming had not taken place.

2. "*Neither by spirit, nor by word, nor by letter as from us, as that the day of Christ is at hand.*" *What was the nature and design of these disturbing efforts?*

The design of these efforts, which were doubtless put forth by Judaising teachers, was to induce these saints at Thessalonica to believe that the day of the Lord had really come, and thus to break their confidence in Paul as a teacher. Three things are distinctly named by him as having been done to accomplish their purpose, viz., (1.) "by spirit," *i.e.*, by prophecies, either feigned or perverted, which were equally deceptive; (2.) "by word," *i.e.*, a rumour or false report; and (3.) "by letter" as from us, *i.e.*, a letter, said to be from Paul and his friends, sustaining this report. Paul has, therefore, to denounce the whole effort, and to fortify their minds by further revelations respecting the coming of Jesus.

Why should this rumour so disturb them?

Because if it was true Paul was false, and they had been deceived. When Christ did return in glory, they—according to the word of Paul —were to be glorified, and this had not taken place. No wonder, then, that they were troubled.

3–7. *Does Paul give any data from which they might know when the Lord would come?*

No; he only assures them that the Lord would not come until the *apostacy*, which even then was showing itself, was matured by the manifestation of the *man of sin*.

Can we know from Paul's description of him who he is?

He has drawn a portrait of a peculiar kind, and shown clearly what the man of sin would be and do. In the light of this characteristic sketch we are able to search for the person intended, until the one answering to it is clearly before us.

What are the chief characteristics of this man of sin?

Those named here are—(1.) Opposition to what ought to be in the Church of Christ, viz., His own pure rule. (2.) Self-exaltation above all authority appointed by God, even seating himself as a god in God's temple. (3.) Using signs and deceptive wonders to further his ambitious object.

Was this temple a material one?

No; God inhabits no material temple on earth now. The tabernacle of Moses was His dwelling-place, and the temple of Solomon His abode; but it was in symbol and type that He inhabited those places, and only until the "time of reformation," when through Christ He could dwell in the contrite heart. Since then He "dwelleth not in temples made with hands, as saith the prophet." It was in the Church as a temple the man of sin sought a place of supremacy.

Have these things been done, or are we to wait for their fulfilment?

We believe that history supplies every item named by the apostle, as having been fulfilled in him who assumed to be an overseer over divinely-appointed overseers—a bishop over all churches; and, at last, claiming authority over all human authority, commanded even kings to bow at his feet.

How was this daring assumption effected?

The beginning of this evil was in the Church itself—a repetition of the Sinaitic apostasy, when the people said to Aaron, " Up, make us gods, which shall go before us "; and soon a calf was put in the place of the living God. We see it rising in the church at Corinth, when in their carnality they elected human leaders in the place of Christ. Had Paul or Apollos been as foolish as Aaron, we should have had a much earlier display of the apostacy; but Paul wisely crushed the hateful demon by asking, " was Paul crucified for you? or were ye baptised into the name of Paul?" Then, in 3 John 9, we get a brief glance at the aspirant whose beginning, though small, in the latter end greatly increased. " I wrote unto the church: but Diotrephes, who loveth to have the pre-eminence among them, receiveth us not." Here we have one, possibly an elder, claiming supremacy over the church, and setting aside even the authority of an apostle. In Rome, amid the fluctuations of imperial influence, the bishop of the church gradually rose into power and influence among the people; and when the seat of royalty was removed from Rome to Constantinople, the advice of the bishop was frequently sought by the citizens in their disputes with each other. These frequent arbitrations in their difficulties made him popular among them, and paved the way for uniting secular with spiritual rule. The propositions that the church was higher than the state, and the bishop greater than kings and emperors, were pleaded for the specific purpose of making the bishop a ruler of states as well as of the church; and after pursuing it with unwearied zeal for centuries, this coveted supremacy and seat of power was at last obtained. From that time the prerogatives of Christ were usurped by a man; and as a god, he sat down in the Church, the temple of God, showing himself as a god. " Remember ye not, that when I was yet with you," said Paul, " I told you these things?" "For the mystery [or secret] of iniquity doth already work : only he who now letteth will let, until he be taken out of the way."

" He who letteth will let." *What is the meaning of this sentence?*

He who hinders or restrains, will better express Paul's meaning. The mystery of iniquity—*lit.*, the secret of lawlessness—*i.e.*, the assumption of personal power, was even then secretly working. There was the bud of that which eventually became a flower. It would have become full blown much earlier, but the season was delayed through one who hindered.

Who was it that hindered?

The aspirant to supremacy was the metropolitan bishop of Rome, but against this assumption both emperors and states combined, which was at first an effectual hindrance. Hence there must be revolutions to check both. In due time these took place, and in his season the " man of sin " was revealed.

Some say the Holy Spirit is the hinderer, and others the Church, and that both must be removed ere that wicked or lawless one be revealed. Is there any Scripture for these statements?

No; and to assert these things is to deny Scripture facts. Both the Holy Spirit and the Church were manifestly here when Paul wrote, and yet the lawlessness was working even then. It is an attempt to set aside two historically developed facts, viz., that there has been a perfected apostacy from the faith once delivered to the saints, and that its civil and tyrannical rule has been arrested. To assume that these prophecies are yet to be fulfilled is a mistake, and a striking proof of the victorious power of Jesus is thereby overlooked.

8. *" Whom the Lord shall consume with the spirit of His mouth, and shall destroy with the brightness of His coming." What does this mean ?*

We must carefully note that there are two stages in these operations against the wicked or lawless one : (1.) There is consuming with the spirit of His mouth, and (2.) destruction with the brightness of His coming. Now the spirit of His mouth evidently refers to His Word, the prophetic utterances which He has given forth in the book of " Revelation," which is specially His book of prophecy. Contrast the two periods : 1514, when there was announced during the session of the council of Lateran, " The whole body of Christendom is subject to its head,"— *i.e.,* to the Pope ; and 1870, when the Italians claimed Rome, and wrested the last fragment of civil power from his hand ; and say if there has not been a consuming of his power, which is truly marvellous. This was declared in " The Revelation of Jesus Christ," and we see His Word fulfilled in these historical facts. The withering word of Jesus has rested upon the head of the " wicked." The power which he has so long used, and in which he exulted, has been wrested from his hand through Jesus, who is now at God's right hand. Or, as stated here by Paul, " whom the Lord . . . shall destroy with the brightness of His coming."

9, 10. *" Even him, whose coming is after the working of Satan." What does this mean ?*

The coming or presence is that of the Lord, and this is to be according to the working of Satan in this wicked one. The usurper would seek to sustain his assumption by means of falsehood, but these would be met and overturned so manifestly, that all, except those who believe the lie, will see the power of the mighty and exalted Jesus.

11, 12. *What is "the truth" which some refused to believe ?*

That Jesus, the Son of God, possesses all authority in heaven and on earth, and is the anointed Lord of all.

And what is " the lie " the belief of which is the delusion ?

Putting a man in the place of Christ, and thus investing a creature with the authority of God, in opposition to His testimony. This lawlessness has been manifested, and must be judged according to His word.

13–15. *What " beginning " was this from which God chose them to salvation ?*

I am inclined to think that Paul does not refer to any period of time, but to a fact in their history, viz., their acceptance of Christ Jesus, from which beginning their personal enjoyment of blessing is dated. If he referred to them in their Gentile standing, then he would have before him the first manifestation of grace to them in the house of Cornelius, but if to them personally, then it would be to their personal faith in Christ, and when they were elected to salvation.

Was God's choice of them to salvation the pardon of their sins ?

No, but the choice of them " to the obtaining of the glory of our Lord Jesus Christ," and which was to follow sanctification of spirit and belief of truth, *i.e.,* the truth concerning Christ, which these apostates from the faith would ignore. The life of these saints was a life of obedience to Christ, and would issue in eternal glory. "Therefore, brethren, stand fast, and hold the traditions which ye have been taught, whether by word, or our epistle."

What does he mean by "traditions" which they were to hold ?

The instructions which they received from himself and Timothy when with them, and the epistle which he had written to them. Both were to be remembered and used for the sustaining and guiding of their new life.

16, 17. *Is there anything special in this benediction ?*

There is a joyous acknowledgment of the love of God, and the age-lasting encouragement which he and other believing Jews had received, and he now desires for these Thessalonians the same comfort and stability in every good word and work.

CHAPTER III.

1–3. *Paul had given to these saints much instruction, and even " revelations of the Lord." Is it not strange that he should ask them to pray for help in his work ?*

Not strange when we think of the relation which prayer sustains to the work of Christ. But in order to pray intelligently and with acceptance, we should understand what God must do, and what man must do, ere conversion can be an accomplished fact in the case of any sinner; and in this matter Paul's request will guide us. He does not ask them to pray that God would shake sinners over hell, or that He would send the Spirit in power, or send conviction to

their hearts, etc. Such prayers, which are often presented now, are only the fruit of misdirected thought. Paul knew that sinners would have to hear the Gospel, believe upon, and obey Christ, ere they could be saved, but the Gospel must first be preached to them, and there were many hindrances in the way of this being done. Now Paul asks them to pray that the Word of the Lord might have free course, that they might have an open field in which they might publish the glad tidings, and be delivered from wicked men, *i.e.*, persecuting Jews who had not the faith. The narrative of his sojourn at Corinth (Acts xviii. 9–11) will show that these prayers were not in vain.

6. *" Withdraw yourselves from every brother that walketh disorderly." Is this direction for the Church, or for individual believers ?*

If individual believers were faithful to this direction, the disorderly brother would be left alone, and his influence for evil would be so far prevented. The assembly has doubtless its own responsibility in relation to disorderly brethren, but Paul is not writing of that here, but of personal relation to those who practise evil. The warning is similar to that given by Hosea (iv. 17), " Ephraim is joined to idols, let him alone," *i.e.*, keep away from him, lest you be contaminated with his evil ways.

Should all efforts to restore a disorderly brother cease with his exclusion from the Church ?

By no means. To seek his repentance and restoration is a God-like work, and may always be put forth without association with his evil ways.

THE FIRST EPISTLE OF PAUL THE APOSTLE TO

TIMOTHY.

CHAPTER I.

Why did Paul write this epistle?

To instruct Timothy how to behave himself in the house of God, and also how he might carry on the warfare against false teachers, who were seeking to corrupt and lead away from the truth ; as well as the up-building of the saints in their holy faith.

1. *In stating that he was an apostle of Christ by God's commandment, why does he add " Jesus Christ our hope"?*

The Judaisers whose errors he directs Timothy to oppose, made the law their hope ; and against this he presents the centre truth of faith and holiness, " Jesus Christ our hope."

2. *" Unto Timothy, my own son in the faith." Does this imply that he was converted by Paul?*

We should read, *a true or genuine child in faith;* in which he refers not to him being his son by the Gospel he had preached, but to the spirit in which he had instructed and confirmed Gentile converts in the faith. So that Paul could write of him to the Philippians (ii. 22), " But ye know the proof of him, that, as a son with the father, he hath served with me in the Gospel."

3. *Why was Timothy left in Ephesus when Paul departed from it?*

Paul left Ephesus to preach the Gospel elsewhere, but on account of false teachers, who were urging the law and tradition upon the new converts, it was necessary to leave Timothy there to counteract this ruinous effort.

" *As I besought thee to abide still at Ephesus." Why does he refer to this previous charge?*

The reason is no doubt implied but is not fully stated by Paul. Our Authorised Version has attempted to supply the reason, by adding at the close of verse 4, " *so do."* This bare hint, however, being thought defective, the Revised Version has improved upon it by adding two more words, " *so do I now,"* and possibly by these supplemented words, we get to see why Paul referred to his former charge. It is as if he had said, As I urged you then to oppose this dangerous error, so I urge you now, as the promoters of it are still active.

4. *What does he mean by " godly edifying which is in faith"?*

This rendering, which is according to the Elzevir edition of 1624, and is, *lit.,* the *upbuilding of God which is in faith,* is now set aside by scholars for, *administration of God,* etc., which is the reading of many MSS. I am inclined, however, to think that Paul refers here not to the dispensation, but to the result of it. Fables and genealogies pulled down, the faith of God built up, therefore Timothy is urged to oppose the former and support the latter.

8. *When Paul affirms, as he does here, that the " law is good," why does he condemn those who urged its acceptance?*

Their objects were very different. Paul knew that the law was good for morals, *i.e.,* to restrain men from the vices to which they were prone, but they enforced it for salvation, which it could not even help to secure, and this was a fatal error.

11. " *According to the glorious*

Gospel of the blessed God, which was committed to my trust." This does not seem to follow verse 10 ; *with what part is it connected ?*

It properly follows ver. 5, the verses between forming a parenthesis. So that when we have read, " Now the end of the charge is love out of a pure heart and a good conscience and faith unfeigned," we may connect with it, " according to the glorious Gospel," etc.

Why does he say " the law is not made for a righteous man " ?

Paul here assumes that men are made righteous or obedient by the Gospel which he preached, and did not require the law of Moses to make them so. The spring of all that is good and right was fixed in their hearts by their reception of Jesus, and His example and teaching ruled within them.

12–16. Why does Paul refer to his former life as a persecutor ?

It is no doubt with humbled mind that he glances over that sad portion of his life ; but having been sent by the Lord Jesus to make known His grace among the Gentiles, he cannot but refer to its wondrous manifestation to himself. He had been a most violent opposer of Christ, but instead of being punished—as he most justly deserved—he had been forgiven, and then, as a pattern of the long-suffering and grace of Jesus, he had been sent among the Gentiles to tell them of His marvellous grace.

" Sinners, of whom I am chief." Did Paul count himself the greatest of all sinners ?

Not greater than many of his brethren in the flesh, but he is speaking here of sinners among the Gentiles, who however deeply defiled they might have become, yet when his own highly favoured position was compared with their neglected state, he felt that he was as a chief of

sinners—as one standing in the first rank, and more guilty than they.

" I did it ignorantly in unbelief." If ignorant, how could he be so guilty ?

It was unbelief which kept him in ignorance, and for this he was responsible. The evidence of a living and exalted Jesus was furnished in the signs and wonders done by the apostles in His name, and these he should have examined. His failure in this kept him in unbelief, and his neglect was his guilt. Men are responsible not only for what they know, but for what they might know of the claims of Christ.

17. *" Now unto the King eternal, immortal, invisible." Who is this ?*

The only God (" wise " is omitted by the best MSS.), who out of the riches of His grace was saving men by Jesus Christ.

Why is He called " the King eternal " ?

It is, lit.,—*the King of the ages—i.e.,* the One who ruled in past dispensations, and is still ruling among men. He who said to Abraham, " In thy seed shall all the nations of the earth be blessed," is now blessing according to His promise.

" Immortal." Why does he apply this term to God ?

It is strictly *incorruptible,* the root idea of this word being *unchangeableness,* and in this aspect Paul uses the word in this verse. It is not of His strict absolute nature that Paul is writing, but of the manifestation of Himself as a merciful God—a God showing mercy to the guilty—because in this He is unchangeable. That God who showed mercy to Adam and Eve and clothed them with the skins of beasts that had been offered in sacrifice, instead of the fig leaves of their own providing, thus pointing them to the coming Redeemer, was by Paul making known His mercy through that Saviour. Yes, God is indeed the unchanging One, a most fitting aspect in which to make Him known.

"Invisible." Why refer to His invisibility ?

There is an important reason no doubt for every word used by the Spirit in teaching, whether by Christ, or prophets, or apostles ; and it will aid us very much in making a right application of either words or illustrations, to note the connection in which they stand. Now Paul is writing about God's mercy as made known in the *"faithful saying,"* and as it is by testimony concerning Christ that He is seeking to rebind man to Himself, His invisibility is a special necessity in the carrying out of His gracious plan. Hence this word is but a condensed echo of the teaching of Jesus, "No man hath seen God at any time ; the only begotten Son, who is in the bosom of the Father, He hath declared Him" (John i. 18). Now this declared testimony, as sent to men from an unchangeable and invisible God, must either be rejected or accepted by them, and on this their salvation or judgment depended.

18. *What was the charge committed to Timothy ?*

The work in which Paul had laboured so devotedly, and which Timothy is urged to defend against false teachers, and by the truth to war a good warfare.

To what prophecies respecting Timothy does Paul here refer ?

We judge that prophets in the Church had prophesied of his work, and he is now urged to equip himself for the contest.

19. *What had Hymeneus and Alexander done ?*

They had made shipwreck of the faith, *i.e.*, they had denied the resurrection of Jesus, and in that denial the foundation truth of the Gospel had been set aside.

CHAPTER II.

1. *Why did Paul exhort to prayer and supplication for all men ?*

Because, surrounded as they were in Ephesus by false teachers and violent opposers of the truth, and also of themselves, they would not naturally invoke blessing upon their enemies ; and yet to do so was one of the special injunctions of Christ. To this Christ-like act, therefore, Paul desires them to give themselves.

2. *What is the object to be sought in praying for kings and all in authority ?*

The privilege of serving God without magisterial hindrance ; a right so long denied to the disciples of Christ.

Why did God allow the fiendish cruelty of rulers to prevent the enjoyment of this right so long ?

If God ruled by absolute force instead of by truth, He would have hindered many things which have continued, but as He wishes all men to be saved by the truth, He therefore respects the liberties of all. Many of those who became the friends of Christ were once His bitter opponents, but through His forbearance they have been won to serve Him. God's forbearance with tyrants has no doubt prolonged and increased the sufferings of the oppressed, but by their sufferings they have won the plaudit of their Lord. God is wise and gracious in all His ways.

"Who will have all men to be saved." Some persons argue from this statement that either all men will be saved, or God must fail to effect His own will. How will you meet this difficulty ?

If such persons would accept all God has to say on these matters, they might be preserved from such blunders. He does indeed will all men to be saved, but it is by coming to a knowledge of the truth. When Christ the truth is not received, then He wills their condemnation.

Since protection and liberty to worship and serve God has been granted to the saints, should they now pray for kings and all in authority ?

They could not intelligently pray for that which has been secured, but they should be thankful for the favours bestowed. Deliverance from kingly and priestly thraldom—under which the saints suffered so long— has been effected, and for this they should be daily thankful. To overlook this would indicate ignorance of what God has wrought.

5. *" For there is one God and one mediator between God and men."* *Why does Paul state this ?*

Simply to show that these great truths were in full harmony with his mission to all men. Since there was but one God the creator of all men, the interests of all of them, both Jews and Gentiles, must be alike considered by Him; and as there is but one mediator for the saints, the man Christ Jesus, so all believers are alike the subject of His mediation.

9. *Should the sisterhood comply with Paul's teaching about dress ?*

Yes, if they wish to please God. If the Holy Spirit has been pleased to give directions about the clothing of the body, it must be important to them to conform to His will. Indeed, it will be a test as to whether self or God shall be pleased.

Is it not of greater moment to have the heart right before Him than to be so particular about the body ?

A right state of heart is so closely associated with obedience that it cannot be right if God is disobeyed. When He says the hair should not be plaited, and gold and pearls should not be worn, there is no alternative but obedience or insubordination.

Is it not difficult in some cases how to act in regard to dress ?

It may be difficult, but a fixed purpose to obey God will overcome every difficulty. To render herself attractive by dress is woman's snare since the fall, but to render herself attractive by her good works is God's desire, and between these she has now to choose.

11–15. *Why has the woman to be in subjection, and learn in silence ?*

The answer is both instructive and humbling. She has been made a type of the Church which has to learn of Him, and this is no ordinary privilege; but as she allowed herself to be deceived by the serpent, God wishes her to take a lowly place. By the grace of God she has been made the bearer of a seed, through whom also she shall be saved, if she continue in faith and love and holiness, with sobriety; and upon her obedience to these terms her personal salvation depends.

CHAPTER III.

" This is a true saying." Was this spoken of what precedes or what follows ?

I think it closes the preceding section, and should be read with it. Three times in this epistle Paul appends to important teaching, " This is a true or faithful saying."

Is " the office of a bishop " correctly rendered ?

There is but one word in Greek for this sentence, and *episkopes* should be rendered *oversight*. It is not of office but work that Paul is speaking, and if a man desires oversight, he desires a good work.

2–7. In this section Paul gives the qualifications necessary for this work. Why does he do this?

In order to help Timothy to understand, and through him the Church, what manner of persons ought to have charge of it. If there were such, the Church could bear witness, and he could appoint to the service; but if there were none, the Church must remain as before.

Were any of the required qualifications for oversight special gifts of the Spirit?

It is somewhat striking that not one miraculous gift was required to fit men for this work, but only those traits of character and spirit which are produced by loving obedience to the Spirit's teaching, along with those domestic qualifications He has seen fit to demand.

Are these named qualifications plain enough to be understood by persons of ordinary judgment?

If sufficient attention is given to them, scarcely any one could fail to understand what manner of persons the Holy Spirit wishes to be set over the assembly of Christ, or how could they be called upon to judge of the fitness of any brother to undertake this important charge? If, however, there should be any one requiring instruction in these things, there should be some in the assembly who are able to impart it.

Will you classify these qualifications for oversight, and add any further explanation that some words may possibly require?

The requirements are both positive and negative, and may·be arranged as follows:

I. What the elder or overseer must be. He must be—

1. "Blameless,"—*i.e.*, according to the truth.

2. "The husband of one wife,"— *i.e.*, not a polygamist.

3. "Vigilant," — *i.e.*, watchful and active in the service of Christ.

4. "Sober,"—*i.e.*, self-controlled by the truth.

5. "Of good behaviour,"—*i.e.*, living becomingly.

6. "Given to hospitality,"—*i.e.*, willing to entertain, if necessary, strange brethren.

7. "Apt to teach,"—*i.e.*, skilful in teaching the truth.

8. "Patient,"—*i.e.*, not rash, but gentle and forbearing.

9. "Ruling well his own house," —*i.e.*, in wisdom, prudence, and in the fear of God.

10. "He must have a good report of those who are without."

II. What the overseers must not be.

1. "Not given to wine," — *i.e.*, not indulging in intoxicating liquor.

2. "No striker,"—*i.e.*, not quarrelsome.

3. "Not greedy of filthy lucre,"— *i.e.*, not using improper methods of obtaining money.

4. "Not a brawler,"—*i.e.*, not contentious.

5. "Not covetous,"—*i.e.*, not lusting after improper things.

6. "Not a novice,"—*i.e.*, a new convert.

How is it that age is not named among these qualifications?

Whenever the above-named qualifications are present, the age required for oversight will be sufficient; but when these are lacking, no amount of years will suffice.

What is a church to do that has no such qualified persons?

They must obey Christ and His apostles, just as they would be directed to do by efficient overseers. When a church conforms to the teaching of the Holy Spirit, it will be pure and happy and useful, and fitted for the glory to which Christ has called it.

Some persons say that neither evangelists nor the Church has power to elect overseers, since an apostle is not here to direct them to do so. How would you meet this objection?

To allow this objection to set aside Paul's teaching to Timothy here, we must set aside all other teaching given to the churches through him and others. But the Saviour's commission, "Lo, I am with you alway, even unto the end of the world, Amen," would set aside such an objection, and direct us to receive all they have written for the churches.

8–10. "*Likewise the deacons.*" *What is a deacon?*

In the New Testament a deacon is one who simply serves the church as its need may require. Every church that was formed according to the "apostles' doctrine" not only contributed to supply its own temporal need, but also selected from its number those who were counted fit to take charge of these temporalities. When the Grecian widows, in the church at Jerusalem, were neglected in the daily ministration, the apostles directed that seven men of honest report, etc., should be appointed to this business, and accordingly they were chosen and appointed to this work. The nature of this service was doubtless well understood by Timothy, hence the spiritual qualifications for this service are alone stated here.

"*Holding the mystery of the faith.*" *What does this mean?*

Holding the secret of the faith as declared by Paul, viz., that the Gentiles, through faith in Jesus, should be joined to the body. The deacon who did not hold this was not fitted to serve the church.

Why are such high qualifications required for deacons?

"Be ye clean that bear the vessels of the Lord," said the Spirit by Isaiah (lii. 11), and "I will be sanctified in them that come nigh me," said God to Moses (Lev. x. 3). This will help us to know that God will have all who do the Master's work to possess the Master's Spirit. So the deacons must be grave, sincere, temperate, benevolent, and sound in the faith. And having been first proved, then let them serve, being unimpeachable.

11. *Why must the wives of deacons have special qualifications?*

Our translators by adding a few words have made Paul say "their wives," but, correctly rendered, he says, "Women in like manner grave, not slanderers, sober, faithful in all things," showing that he is writing not of wives but of deaconesses who were called to serve the church in some required service, and who must be distinguished by a holy and devoted life and spirit.

13. "*The office of a deacon.*" *Is this correct?*

It is, *lit.*, for those having served well, etc. It is of faithful service and not of office that Paul is speaking here.

15. *Was the Church the pillar and ground of the truth?*

No. It was Timothy, who, being made an exponent of the truth in Ephesus, is exhorted and instructed how to behave himself in the church, being a pillar and stay of the truth. Paul uses a like term of James, Cephas, and John, who seemed to be pillars (in Jerusalem). Timothy had received the truth, and is urged by Paul to uphold it.

16. "*Without controversy.*" *What does this mean?*

A literal rendering of Paul's words would have been far better than this mere paraphrase of them. He simply says, *And confessedly great is the secret of godliness*, and then adduces those wondrous facts which form the great scheme of redemption.

Is " God was manifest in the flesh" a correct reading ?

Scholars say there is not sufficient evidence to support it, and they now read, " He who was manifested in flesh was justified in spirit, was seen by messengers, was proclaimed among the nations, was believed on in the world, was received up in glory," and these facts apply to the Lord Jesus, and to no other being.

CHAPTER IV.

1. *What does Paul mean by " seducing spirits" who should lead away from the faith ?*

Teachers, who by false teaching should cause the people to wander from the right way.

" In the latter times." What period does Paul refer to ?

It is, *lit.*, *latter seasons*, and may refer to opportunities granted in these last days, when the secular power of the apostacy has been overthrown. It is indeed a gracious season, but false teachers are leading away from the truth.

What is meant by " doctrines of devils " ?

It is, *lit.*, *teachings of demons, i.e.*, the thoughts, ideas, etc., of departed heroes, teachers, and other distinguished men would be embodied in religious systems, and thus taught and received by the people. In this way the teaching of Christ and His apostles would be set aside. The Greeks evidently apply the word demon to persons who had lived in the world, and whose teaching, power, etc., they reproduced and honoured in their gods.

3. *Paul says that marriage and meats would be forbidden by these teachers. Does history point to any who have done so ?*

The Church of Rome does forbid her priests to marry, and commands her members to abstain on certain days from certain kinds of food, " which God has created to be received with thanksgiving," and she thus answers to Paul's " seducing spirits" to the very letter.

4. *" Every creature of God is good, and nothing to be refused." May we conclude that there need not be any discrimination ?*

Paul cannot mean that. There are things which would be injurious and destructive, and these must be avoided. He evidently refers to things which are good, from which seducers would debar, and not to evil things which no man should use.

10. *How is God the Saviour of all men, and also specially of them that believe ?*

If we use the word saviour or preserver in its providential bearing, we shall see that he is speaking not of the salvation of the soul, but of the body. As their Creator, God upholds or preserves all His creatures, but believers have His promise, both of present and future life ; and therefore trusting in Him, says Paul, we both labour and suffer reproach.

13. *Till I come, give attendance to reading." Was this to be in the church ?*

The reading was to be connected with exhortation and teaching, and would therefore be in the church. It would doubtless be the writings of Moses and the prophets that would be read, and, when read in the light of the faith which had been delivered to the saints, they would furnish most valuable instruction. In this way these ancient writings should still be read, and, when opened in the light of New Testament truths, could not fail to instruct and profit.

14. *How could the gift possessed by Timothy come to him through prophecy ?*

The gift would be bestowed by the

hands of the apostle, but the prophets of the church made known its sphere of exercise, and the elders, by the laying on of hands, set him apart to it. Paul's exhortation was, doubtless, needed to urge him to be earnest in what was evidently to be the work of his life.

CHAPTER V.

1. *" Rebuke not an elder."* Does Paul refer to one having oversight in the church ?

I think not, but to elderly men, whose age claimed respect, even from Timothy. And though left to restrain evil in the church, and set right whatever might be wrong, he is exhorted to approach the brethren with that Christian courtesy becoming the family of God. The elder men were to be entreated as fathers, the elder women as mothers, the younger men and women as brothers and sisters, in all purity. The church was also a family, and Paul directs that all its members should look upon each other in the spirit of their one heavenly Father. These directions are worthy of being regarded by all the members of the Church of Christ.

3, 4. *" Honour widows that are widows indeed."* What does this involve ?

Helping them according to their necessity. This duty rested upon the church, unless such had children, or grandchildren, then this act of piety devolved upon them; and they are exhorted to show it to their own parents, as being good and acceptable before God.

8. *" If any provide not for his own."* Does he mean through indolence or indifference ?

No, but through unwillingness to do what was clearly a duty. To refuse to help those who had a claim upon them was to Paul a denial of Christianity.

2 c

9, 10. *Widows from threescore years old were to be enrolled on the list. Was this for support or for service ?*

Possibly both. Such widows as are here named by Paul would not only call for the practical sympathy of the church, but would be fitted for needed service. No sister who had been faithful in the opportunities afforded her in early life could fail to be useful in declining years. There is a sphere of work for the young, and there is one for the aged. May all watch and pray to use it well.

11–13. *Is it wrong for young widows to marry again, because Paul seems to condemn some for so doing ?*

He cannot mean that it is wrong for a widow to marry again, because in his first epistle to the Corinthians (vii. 39) he writes, "She is at liberty to be married to whom she will, only in the Lord." But when they wax wanton against Christ, and cast off their first faith, they would form improper associations, and become tattlers and busybodies, speaking evil rather than good. All such were to be refused for service in the Church ?

17. *What does Paul mean by " double honour" to be shown to elders who rule and work well ?*

His illustrations of the ox, which under the law God commanded to be unmuzzled while treading out corn, and the hire of the toiling labourer, of which he is said to be worthy, would lead us to conclude that he is teaching that those who labour in spiritual work are worthy of being sustained by the Church. It is no doubt an obligation resting upon all who belong to Christ to work for Him as they have ability and opportunity, while the Church is responsible to help all who do so if their need so require.

19. *Why are elders exempt from accusation, except before two or three witnesses?*

It is due to their years and long standing in the faith that they be not lightly accused; but when two or three bear witness against them, the evidence must be accepted, and they must be dealt with according to the law of Christ.

20. *" Them that sin rebuke before all." Does this apply to elders, or to any others in the Church?*

From the context I should judge that he refers to elders, while there is nothing in the passage to prevent its application to any who sin.

Some churches publicly rebuke those of their number, who after some public offence seek restoration to the church, and base their action upon this verse. Do they do right in this?

I think they misunderstand in this matter, and administer the rebuke at the wrong time. It is when they sin that they are to be rebuked, and not when they repent. They should then be encouraged in their return to the right way, and should not be rebuked. Besides, the word *elenche*, rendered rebuke, should be rendered convict—*i.e.*, when the charge is made.

21, 22. *Why does Paul charge Timothy so solemnly " before God, and the Lord Jesus, and the elect angels"?*

Because of the importance of the work he had to do. It is as if he said, God, and Christ, and the elect angels—*i.e.*, the chosen messengers the apostles of Christ—are all looking at you, to see whether or not you will be faithful to the trust reposed in you. You will have to judge between brethren that differ; be not partial. You will have to appoint overseers of the church; but lay hands suddenly on no man.

23. *Why did Paul urge Timothy to drink no longer water, but use a little wine?*

Because there was a necessity for it in his often infirmities. Had Timothy been in health, it would not have been commanded.

Was it intoxicating wine?

It may have been fermented, it may not, we cannot tell. It was proper for a sickly man to use, and was prescribed by Paul as proper in his case. It is sad for any one to use the apostle's direction as a plea for his carnal indulgence, and this command is seldom quoted for any other purpose.

CHAPTER VI.

1–3. *Why did these Christian servants require to be exhorted to faithfulness?*

These bondservants or slaves were under peculiar temptation to be unfaithful. Their position supplied no motive to be just, but rather the contrary, and Paul reminds them of their relation to God, and exhorts them to honour Him by being faithful. These things Timothy was to urge upon them.

Believing masters appear to have held believing slaves. How could this be reconciled with the law of love?

That will depend upon the nature of the bond between master and slave, and we cannot learn this now, and must therefore decide that if this form of service had been wrong, Paul would have forbidden it. Slavery, for a limited period, was common among the Jews, and it may have been so at Ephesus. Besides, a person under bond may have had a voice in fixing it, and should be faithful until it expire. Christ is honoured by the faithfulness of a servant, and the gentleness of a master, and both are responsible to the Judge of all.

5. *How could these men suppose that "gain is godliness"?*

Scholars now arrange the sentence *supposing that godliness is gain.* It is gain they are seeking, and their highest thought about godliness is, that it is a means to this end. Such are truly men of corrupt minds.

6–8. *Why does he teach that god-iness with contentment is great gain?*

What he really teaches is, that godliness with sufficiency is great gain, and having this they should be satisfied. For as nothing was brought into the world by us, so nothing can be taken out of it.

9. *"They that will be rich." Is it wrong to possess riches?*

Not if possessed lawfully; but to covet them is to surround the path-way to another world with great peril. To seek to be rich is soul-ruin according to Paul.

12. *Paul says of Timothy that he had professed a good profession before many witnesses. What had he done?*

He had literally *confessed the good confession,* or openly declared that "Jesus is the Christ, the Son of the living God."

13. *Why did Jesus make the good confession?*

He did not make it, but witnessed it before (*lit.,* upon, *i.e.,* under the administration of) Pontius Pilate. It was before the High Priest, who said, "Art thou the Son of the Blessed?" that Jesus replied, "Thou has said" (Matt. xxvi. 63); and thus witnessed to this cardinal truth of Christianity. It was God the Father who said of Him, as He rose from His immersion in the Jordan, out of which as from a womb He entered upon His new life of service to God, "This is My beloved Son, in whom I am well pleased." This acknow-ledging of Him in His humanity, was attested by Himself before the Jew-ish Sanhedrin, though in doing so He was condemned to die. And

now, as the ascended Lord of all, He claims the honest confession of this truth by all that would be His dis-ciples. This "good confession" Timothy had *confessed before many witnesses,* and he is here charged to be faithful till this despised Jesus should be manifested in glory.

15. *"Who is the blessed and only potentate." Is this Jesus, or God the Father?*

Our translators, by adding the words "who is," have made Paul to say that Jesus is the "blessed and only potentate," and hinder us from feeling the force of his statements concerning Him. Paul makes two statements concerning Jesus, which when viewed together form a striking contrast—(1.) That His true char-acter had been denied before Pilate, and He had thus been put to shame. (2.) That God, the blessed and only potentate, the King of kings, and Lord of lords, would, in His own times—*lit.,* seasons—manifest Him in His true character. For this glorious manifestation Timothy, and all other faithful disciples, must pa-tiently wait.

16. *"Who only hath immortality." Does this apply to God the Father?*

This is almost certain, and when read along with other Bible state-ments, is deeply instructive. God is essentially and truly immortal, be-cause He cannot die. Adam received life from God, and had he continued obedient, through the tree of life, his existence must have continued; still he was not immortal, because capable of death. Then in Christ the risen One, we have not only life, but im-mortality brought to light through the Gospel. And this blessed life and immortality, this deathlessness, is now promised to all who are in Christ; and through Him this high privilege will be realised, and is now the hope of the believer.

"Whom no man hath seen, nor can

see." *In Exodus xxiv.* 10 *it is written,* "*And they saw the God of Israel.*" *How can these statements be reconciled?*

Paul is speaking of the Father, and of Him this is absolutely true, as declared also by Jesus : " No man hath seen God at any time ; the only begotten Son, who is in the bosom of the Father, He hath declared Him " (John i. 18). Here we get a simple revelation of this important truth. The Father has always been invisible to man, but was revealed during the past dispensations to Adam, Moses, Isaiah, and others, by Jehovah, the one God of Israel (one, be it noted, in contrast with the many gods of the nations, and not with the Father) ; and, again, by Him in flesh, for " the Word was made flesh, and dwelt among us, full of grace and truth." There are aspects of these great matters that we cannot fully comprehend, but we may receive them because they are revealed.

17–19. " *Charge them that are rich in this world, that they be not high minded,*" etc. *Do these spiritual dangers always attend riches?*

Always. Riches bring the snares which the apostle warns against to all who possess them ; and it is only by following the Spirit's directions that these snares can be overcome. Riches exalt the possessor, and may beget high-mindedness ; they are a visible supply for present need, and may induce independence of God—a trust in what is so often proved to be uncertain, instead of the living and unchanging God. Paul suggests —as a preventive of all these evils —humility, confidence in God, heavenly wealth by an abundance of good works, a willingness to be a channel of God's communications to others, and thus " that they may lay hold on eternal life."

20. " *Avoiding profane and vain babblings.*" *What were these ?*

The empty, profitless harangues of Judaising teachers, which being out of date, were useless, and being against Christ, were profane.

"*And oppositions of science falsely so-called.*" *What is this ?*

The reasonings of philosophers, which were, *lit., a falsely-named science or knowledge,* simply because they were in opposition to revelation, or the true knowledge, which Paul and others had received. These ensnaring things Timothy was to avoid, and to guard the trust of truth which had been committed to his care.

THE SECOND EPISTLE OF PAUL THE APOSTLE TO

TIMOTHY.

CHAPTER I.

From what place did Paul write this second letter to Timothy ?

The subscription at the close of the epistle says, that it was "written from Rome, when Paul was brought before Nero the second time." But as this subscription has only a traditional basis, and as there are internal evidences that he was not in Rome when he wrote it, we object to the tradition, and avail ourselves of these internal proofs to the contrary. In his letter to the Philippians (i. 19), he is confident that he should be delivered, and should see them again. In his letter to Philemon, sent from Rome by Onesimus, he writes, " But withal prepare me also a lodging : for I trust that through your prayers I shall be given to you." In this letter he informs Timothy that he "was delivered out of the mouth of the lion" (Nero Cæsar), a fact which he wished all the Gentiles to hear, and that he should be delivered from every evil work. In his letter to Titus he is able to arrange for his winter residence at Nicopolis, and directs him to meet him there, and also requests Timothy to come to him before winter, and bring his cloak and books and parchments. Presuming, therefore, that Paul reached the home of his friend Philemon, and then wrote his letter to Titus, and his second letter to Timothy, and thus, as a warrior whose warfare is nearly closed, he casts his mantle over these true sons in the faith, and commits the work to them and other kindred spirits. His work of preaching and toil and travel is nearly over, for the dissolving of the tent is keenly felt, and only one thing remains for him to do—viz., to marshal the forces that remain, and cheer them on in their noble work. To this end important directions are given in these epistles, and others would be laid before them in his winter quarters at Nicopolis, where possibly his worn out body would quietly sink to rest. Be this as it may, this is the last place to which, by arrangement, we can trace this noble champion of the cross. True, tradition says that he was again arrested, and tried by Nero, and ordered to be beheaded. Outside of Rome, it is said, the public executioner severed his head from his body with a sword, and weeping friends buried it in the Catacombs, the great Roman cemetery. But then the same voice that speaks thus says that Peter also suffered death in Rome, by order of Nero, and the guides in the Mamer-

tine prison still point out the pillar to which they say he was fastened, and where he sealed the truth with his blood. But can we believe this report of Peter dying there ? Again and again men have asked for proofs, and have even offered large premiums for them, but the evidence has never been produced. And if we were to make the same claim in relation to Paul's martyrdom there, reliable evidence could not be furnished. We know that Paul was prepared to suffer anything for Christ, but he who possibly suffered more in life than all the apostles together, may have been spared a cruel death. We will, however, now examine the epistle itself, from which further confirmation of the things suggested may be obtained.

1. *"Paul an apostle . . . according to the promise of life which is in Christ Jesus." What promise was this, and when was it given ?*

It will be well to compare his statement here with the opening statement of his letter to Titus, written as we presume about the same time. He is evidently referring to the same promise in both, but presents it in different aspects. In Timothy it is simply *the promise of life which is in Christ Jesus ;* and in verse 3, where he refers to *his forefathers,* we presume that Abraham, Isaac, and Jacob were intended, for to them this promise of life for the nations through the Christ was given ; and according to it he was an apostle of Jesus Christ. Then to Titus he says that he was "an apostle of Jesus Christ according to the faith of God's elect." Now these patriarchs were God's elect, who having received this promise of life for the nations of the earth, believed it, and looked for its fulfilment under the Messiah. Thus we see that in the one epistle he speaks of the promise made to the fathers, and in the other of their faith in the promise, according to which he had been constituted an apostle, being sent by Christ to make known salvation even to those called the "ends of the earth."

3. "*I thank God, whom I serve from my forefathers with a pure conscience.*" *What does this mean?*

It is in the light of his great mission that we shall best understand his meaning. He had just stated that he was an apostle according to the promise of life which is in Christ Jesus; and in this verse he simply states that he was *serving God* from his *forefathers;* that is, he was carrying out His will according to the promise made to them, *with a pure conscience,* or in all sincerity. Thomson, and also Dr Conquest render it, "whom I serve *as did* my forefathers," but this is not in harmony with his thought which is more clearly expressed to Titus (i. 1), "An apostle *according* to the faith of God's elect;" and now here, *an apostle serving according to* (the promise made unto) *my forefathers.* Then we have to mark his joy over Timothy who was fitted and willing to carry forward the same great work.

4. "*Being mindful of thy tears.*" *Why refer to his weeping? or why did Timothy weep?*

Paul has not stated, and the only just inference must be from the subject in hand. The letter indicates that there were many faithless ones, but especially among those of the circumcision, nearly all of whom turned from the apostle. Now the grief of the apostle on this account was very great, and in this grief Timothy had a large share. He had been circumcised that he might be more acceptable to the Jews, but had failed to win them to Christ as well as Paul. He however remembered his grief, which his tears

manifested, and his zeal for Christ had encouraged Paul to look upon him as a genuine child in faith, and one fitted to carry on the great work with which he had been entrusted, but was now about to lay down.

5. *Paul remembers the faith of Timothy's mother and grandmother. Why refer to it?*

These distinguished women were Jewesses, and as their unfeigned faith—held no doubt in the midst of much opposition — had triumphed over all hindrance, the apostle counts upon their son exhibiting the same bold and noble daring for Christ. The faith of these mothers furnished a fine example to their son, and Paul was persuaded that it was being reproduced in him.

8. "*Be not thou, therefore, ashamed of the testimony of our Lord, nor of me his prisoner.*" *Why call himself the Lord's prisoner, if he had been set free?*

It may be well to mark this peculiar phrase "His prisoner;" as it may help us to understand the nature of the confinement. He was not Cæsar's prisoner, nor a prisoner "for you Gentiles," but "His prisoner." He was laid aside by weakness and infirmity, and the time of his departure was at hand. No plans of labour for himself are marked out in this epistle, no going to "regions beyond" is spoken of here. He is simply cheering on his co-workers in the field, and inviting some of them to come and receive his parting instruction, and then he is ready to pass away. He had long endured shame for the truth of Christ, and his name must remain inseparably connected with it; and he now asks Timothy not to be ashamed of him, nor of the testimony of his Lord. A solemn crisis was at hand, the old standard-bearers of the cross were passing away, and Timothy is urged to gird himself for conflict and suffering, which he and others would have to endure.

9–11. *Why does he introduce this epitome of God's gracious scheme of mercy?*

He had been speaking in the preceding verse of his afflictions in connection with the Gospel, and was urging Timothy to jointly suffer with him; but no sooner does the Gospel of the grace of God come before his mind, than he is led to recapitulate the scheme of redemption, as it had been made known in his own ministry, and to embrace those aspects of it which deserve special notice. We can scarcely fail to note the repetition of this epitome in his epistles, and its importance is thereby established. We find it in Romans i. 1–5; xvi. 25, 26; Ephesians i. 3–12; Titus i. 1–3. Sometimes he alludes to it in the utmost brevity, as, "according to my Gospel," "according to the promise of life," "according to the faith of God's elect," etc. Now to understand Paul in any one of these statements, is to possess the key to his teaching in all the others, and enables one to study the truth in the varied aspects in which it is presented by him. In this epitome of God's gracious scheme of salvation as here given to Timothy, we notice nearly all the peculiar facts and principles of his preaching and teaching. "God, who saved us" (us who believe), "and called us with an holy calling, not according to our works" (works of law), "but according to His own purpose and grace, which was given us in Christ Jesus before the world began;"—*lit., before the times of the ages*, being given to Abraham, for those who should believe in Christ before the ages of the law,—"but is now made manifest by the appearing of our Saviour Jesus Christ." The Gospel then was first made known among the Jews, its privileges being fully realised by those who believed in Jesus; and was then carried forward among the Gentiles by the mission of Paul for their acceptance and life. It was the fulfilment of Ezekiel's vision of the holy waters (chap. xlvii.), which after issuing from under the threshold of the house, flowed onward to the desert and the sea, deepening and healing at every measure of its progress. Now we would not like to indulge in mere fanciful interpretations of God's Word, but we do think, that for every symbolic or figurative representation of these things by the prophets, there are corresponding facts and privileges named in the Gospel records, and it is there we must look for explanations of what they have fore-revealed. Indeed the facts which are given us in the Acts of Apostles, correspond to these holy waters, which issued from under the threshold of the house, and are a figure of the water of life which issued from Him whom envious Pharisees and haughty scribes had rudely trampled under foot. The first measure of a thousand cubits, and the waters were to the ancles, and here we have the Jews who believed in Jesus at Pentecost, drinking of this flowing water of life. Another thousand, and the waters were to the knees, and the Samaritans are reached by the preaching of Philip. A thousand cubits further, and we have Peter in the house of Cornelius, for the waters are to the loins. A still further measure and the water of life reached Antioch, and became a river too deep to be passed over, for here various nationalities of men were gathered into one assembly in the name of Jesus. From Antioch Paul and Barnabas were sent out to preach the Gospel, and had no limits to their mission, so that the river became an ocean, a sea without a shore. That the vision of the prophet was figurative of the first preaching of the Gospel, and which ultimately reached the nations, ought not, I think, to be questioned. In this God-like scheme of mercy Paul rejoiced, and laboured with all his heart and strength to help forward the work. True, he suffered sorely in the work, but every stripe was to him a scar of honour, and every wound a brandmark of the Lord Jesus. He was "in prisons more frequent" (than other apostles), "in death oft," and yet we hear him say, "Nevertheless I am not ashamed, for I know whom I have believed."

12–14. *"He is able to keep that which I have committed unto Him against that day." What had Paul committed to Christ ?*

It is, strictly, *powerful He is my deposit to guard unto that day.* Paul is here referring to the deposit or trust which had been committed to him by Jesus. He had been entrusted with a message to the nations, and with a secret for the saints, and to this trust he had been faithful ; and now that he is transferring this solemn trust to Timothy, who had proved himself to be a true son in the Gospel, and with all confidence that Jesus was able to guard the trust reposed in him, he exhorts, " Hold fast the form of sound words, which thou hast heard of me." And again, " That good thing "—*lit.,* good deposit—"which was committed unto thee, keep by the Holy Spirit which dwelleth in us."

15. *" This thou knowest, that all they which are in Asia be turned away from me." Why does Paul refer to these apostates from the faith ?*

Simply to remind Timothy of the true state of things, as his own work would doubtless be affected by it. It is evident that—on his return from Rome—he had become acquainted with the apostacy of these

brethren, but the sad fact had been revealed to Paul only on his own return into Asia. We must, however, note that Paul refers only to Jewish brethren. There were many from among the Gentiles who stood by him in his work, but the circumcised in Asia had turned away from the truth—Phygellus and Hermogenes being specially named.

16–18. *Why does Paul refer first to the house of Onesiphorus, and then to himself ?*

It is rather suspicious that he does so, and the reason is easily discovered, especially as he is spoken of in connection with these apostate brethren. Both in Rome, when on a visit there, and in Ephesus, where he probably lived, he had showed great sympathy with the apostle, and his kindness had been deeply felt. But now he can only offer a prayer for him, " The Lord grant unto him that he may find mercy of the Lord in that day," *i.e.,* that day of wrath which would soon overwhelm the nation. Such a prayer could not have been offered for a faithful man. Onesiphorus had turned away with other Jews, and is here remembered only with grief ; his household had remained faithful, since they were to be saluted with Prisca and Aquila (iv. 19). And even here blessings are invoked on his house and not on himself.

CHAPTER II.

1, 2. *" Thou therefore, my son, be strong in the grace that is in Christ Jesus." What does this imply ?*

It is, *lit.,* be empowering thyself in the favour, etc., and the exhortation must be listened to in the light of preceding facts. By *the favour which is in Christ Jesus,* Paul refers to the wondrous display of it among the nations, to whom he had been sent with a message of salvation, and of their reception into the body, and on account of which there had been such a sad separation from him. Phygellus, Hermogenes, Onesiphorus, with others, had yielded to the strong current of Jewish prejudice, and held that the Gentiles must pass through the gates of Judaism to reach the position which Paul claimed for them, on the ground of their simple faith in Jesus. Against their dogged persistence in this fatal error he had often fought single handed, and gathered into the fold of Christ Greek, Barbarian, and Scythian, with other Gentiles in every Roman province. When Paul ceased hostilities against the saints, and began to preach Jesus as the Anointed in the synagogue of Damascus and elsewhere, Jewish believers glorified God in him; but when the true character of his mission was unfolded, by Jesus sending him far hence unto the Gentiles, one by one they fell away from him, until at last, as far as Jewish sympathy was concerned, we find him standing in Asia alone. But in what spirit do we find him when his own share in the struggle is nearly at an end? Does he waver in the fight, and counsel Timothy to compromise the matter, and meet these Judaisers half way, and thus prevent trouble? Not a word of it. The old champion of the cross can fight no longer, but he can counsel at least one. "Thou therefore, my son, be strong in the grace that is in Christ Jesus. And the things that thou hast heard of me among many witnesses, the same commit thou to faithful men, who shall be able to teach others also."

3–7. Why does Paul, in his exhortation to Timothy, refer to the soldier, the combatant in the games, and the toiling husbandman?

To remind him that self-denial and labour must precede conquest and reward, and to this end the illustrations are strikingly suggestive. The soldier must be free from everything that would interfere with his warfare. The one striving in the games must strive lawfully, or he would not be crowned; and the husbandman must toil ere he reap the harvest. These are all self-evident illustrations, which Timothy must apply to himself, and fulfil in himself in order to be a good soldier of Jesus Christ. From entanglements of life he must keep himself free; with the truth he must strive, or his contest would not be acknowledged, while fruit in the Gospel could only follow persevering labour.

8. Why does he refer to Christ, who was raised from the dead?

It is a still further illustration of the truth he was teaching, viz., that trial precedes reward. Christ died before He could be raised up out of death; and became of David's seed, that He might be the Son of God with power, according to the testimony of the Spirit of holiness, by the resurrection from the dead. To which he adds, "Wherein I suffer trouble, as an evil doer, even unto bonds."

10. Who were these elect ones for whom he was enduring all things?

Gentile believers, because it was on their account that so much suffering was endured. His mission to them brought upon him, not only the wrath of his own nation, but also the hostility of many of the brotherhood of Jewish believers. Believing however that, if faithful, Gentile believers would be glorified, he preached and taught, and suffered on their behalf, until his labours were crowned with great success.

11–13. "It is a faithful saying." To what does Paul apply this faithful word?

To the glorification of these Gentile believers who, through the grace of God, were as eligible for the privileges provided in Christ as were those Jews who first trusted in Him.

In order that we may more clearly discern the purport of the apostles' teaching here, I will give the very literal rendering of this section by J. B. Rotherham.

"Faithful is the saying! for—
If we jointly-died,—we shall also jointly-live;
If we are enduring,—we shall also jointly-reign;
If we shall deny,—He too will deny us;
If we are faithless,—He abides faithful;
For—deny Himself—He cannot!"

Jointly-died; jointly-live. Jointly with whom?

The apostle is repeating the same truth as is stated in Eph. ii. 5, where he teaches that God, by means of Christ, jointly made alive, jointly raised, and jointly seated in the heavenlies in Him, believing Gentiles with Jews, and made of the two one body—one new man. Here the apostle is claiming for those on whose behalf he suffered a full participation in all the results of the grace and power of Christ, even unto glorification with Him.

"If we deny Him;" "If we believe not." Does he refer to any person specially?

Yes; he had spoken already of some who denied Him, and here he points out their fearful doom. The unfaithfulness of men will not make Christ unfaithful; and all who are faithful will share His great and glorious reward.

16–18. Hymenæus and Philetus held and taught that the resurrection was past. What does this mean? and why does Paul hold it to be such a serious error?

The error of these men was nothing less than the old Sadducean heresy of *no resurrection*, with the addition of what was held by some, according to Tertullian, that the resurrection was nothing more than the rising of the soul from the death of ignorance to the light of knowledge. Now this error was a denial of the resurrection of Christ, and also of the resurrection of others, and was most destructive in its tendency. The reception of this error would be like the abnormal growth of a cancer in the human body that would eat out the natural flesh, and at last destroy it. Paul counsels that even the discussion of such matters was to be avoided, and the ministry of the truth so adjusted that the workman would not have to be ashamed.

19. What is this "foundation of God that standeth sure"? and what is the seal affixed to it?

Christ Jesus is the firm foundation which God has laid, and His resurrection, to which so many bore witness, is the seal affixed to it. A living Jesus is as the blossoming rod of Aaron among the dead rods of the tribes of Israel; and no one need mistake the choice of God.

"The Lord knoweth them that are His." How is this statement connected with the foundation and the seal?

It is generally read as if Paul was speaking of believers, whereas he is speaking of Christ, whom God knew as His Son, raised from the dead, and manifested to chosen witnesses.

"Let every one that nameth the name of Christ depart from iniquity." Does this apply to believers?

Yes; it is a most solemn admonition to all who bear the name of the living Christ. As He has been raised up from death, so must they be separate from all iniquity.

20. Does the "great house," with its "vessels of gold and silver," etc., represent the Church of God?

There ought not to be any dishonourable vessels connected with God's house, and if cleansed by His truth, they are all fitted for His use.

But if any are the subjects of persistent error and ungodliness, they will certainly be dishonoured. The illustration is intended both to instruct and warn.

24–26. *In directing Timothy how to deal with opposers he also adds, " If God peradventure will give them repentance." Is God's help uncertain ?*

Not to those who sincerely seek it. But here is a class who set themselves in opposition to God, and Paul directs that such should be brought under discipline and instruction, that, if God should favour them with an opportunity, they might be brought to a full knowledge of the truth, and recover themselves out of Satan's snare, though they had been taken captive by him for his will or pleasure.

CHAPTER III.

1–5. *Would you call this teaching about the last days a prophecy ?*

It is a revelation of the future condition of things, which Paul could not have known except by the Holy Spirit.

Would these sad traits of character be manifested by religious persons ?

It is of such persons that he is writing, because he says of them, " Having a form of godliness, but denying the power thereof."

What is it that will make the times so perilous ?

The abounding impiety of those who profess to be the disciples of Christ. Young converts are fashioned more by the example of older professors than by the precepts of the Word, and seldom rise above the pattern set before them. Hence, when elder brethren and sisters are worldly, and selfish, and formal, the young will be educated by their example.

Do you think we are now in the last days ?

It is certain that there is not one sin named here by Paul that is not filled up by professors of religion of one type or other. No doubt there are many noble exceptions, but there are too many who practise the vices named. The worst stage of it may not even yet be reached, and as impiety prevails the peril will be the greater.

Will persecution and violence be a part of the peril ?

Paul does not even name persecution. It is rather the peril of prevailing selfishness that will come out in pride, and covetousness, and love of pleasure, all mixed up with a form of piety.

What is the remedy for this evil ?

Paul has given it in one brief sentence : " From such [persons and things] turn away." In such a spirit and purpose we may rise above them, and in self-denial and love serve the Lord Jesus. The struggle in every case will be between self and Christ.

6. *Why do these aggressors against piety and devotedness to Christ select women as their victims, and, as I presume, agents in their work ?*

Women more easily yield to teaching than men, and when interested are most powerful for good or evil. It was woman that the serpent first ensnared and used for his evil purpose, and his emissaries always, as far as they can, adopt the same plan. Women have power, and when employed on the side of evil the results are often fearful. It was the daughters of men who drew off the sons of God from their first estate, and all perished together in the deluge that came upon the ungodly. It was the daughters of Midian who succeeded in seducing the sons of Israel into idolatry, which brought thousands of them to shame. If I could gain the ear of sisters in the Lord, I would say,

Your influence for good or evil is great, beware lest Satan succeed in using you for his evil designs. And though Eve, through being deceived, was the first in transgression, yet through you the Great Deliverer entered into the world to save men; and if your hearts and lives are only yielded to Him, many through your efforts will be delivered out of the evil, and Jesus will be glorified in and by you.

7. *" Ever learning, and never able to come to a knowledge of the truth." How is this?*

Because they have accepted teachers of error, and confusion and uncertainty is the result. If the Spirit, through Christ and His apostles had been their teacher, they would have learned all the truth, and by obedience would have been perfected in all His will.

8. *" Jannes and Jambres withstood Moses." Who were these men, and why does Paul refer to them?*

They were magicians in Egypt, and while we learn of their opposition to Moses, he has not given us their names. Scholars say that they are given in the Targum of Jonathan, a book of paraphrase on the Scriptures, and from that source Paul may have learnt their names. These magicians withstood Moses when testifying for God, and in this spirit of opposition they could not learn the truth concerning Jehovah. So, says Paul, do these opposers act, and with corrupted minds they resist the teachers of the truth, and as concerning the faith are disapproved.

9. *" But they shall proceed no further." What would cut short their career?*

The judgment of God which soon after fell upon the nation of Israel, and with it came the end of all Judaising efforts. Their system was so broken up, that from that time they ceased to make proselytes; and

though they persistently hold their faith, they have ceased to ask the nations to share it with them.

11. *Why does Paul remind Timothy of his own deliverances from trial?*

Because he knew that trial awaited his faithful successor, and wished to encourage him by this cheering fact in his own eventful life.

14, 15. *Why does Paul refer Timothy to the Old Testament when urging him to abide in the teaching he had received?*

Because those scriptures contained the promise of blessing to the nations through Abraham's seed, and to give effect to these had been the work of Paul's life. These scriptures were well known to Timothy, even from his childhood, and through the faith they could make wise to salvation all who received the truth contained in them.

Does Paul refer to Scripture to prove its inspiration?

No. He affirms it to have been given by inspiration — *lit.*, God-breathed—and refers to it in order to show the end for which it was given, and to urge the application of it to all manifest departures from righteousness. He had spoken prophetically of these departures from the faith, and here shows that the scriptures, which from a child Timothy had known, and those truths in which he had been instructed by the apostle, were the only means by which these evils were to be dealt with.

Are the terms in which this fourfold purpose is rendered sufficiently clear?

It would be better to render "doctrine" by *teaching;* "reproof" by *conviction;* and "instruction in righteousness" by *discipline* which is in righteousness, that ready may be the man of God, fully fitted unto every good work.

CHAPTER IV.

1. "*I charge thee therefore before God, and the Lord Jesus Christ.*" *Why give this solemn charge ?*

In order to arouse Timothy to the importance of the great work committed into his hands. Paul's appeal to God is on the ground of His love in giving His Son to save the world, and to the Lord Jesus, because He is appointed to be its judge.

"*Who shall judge the quick and the dead at His appearing and His kingdom.*" *Will the kingdom begin only with the appearing of Jesus ?*

The present rendering does not convey Paul's meaning. It will be better to read, *Who is coming to judge living and dead, according to His appearing and His kingdom.* It is what He has done and revealed concerning His love and claims that will be the standard of judgment in that day, and not anything that has yet to be revealed. Jesus has died for sin that men might be reconciled to God, and He has been exalted to reign over those who by Him will return in loving allegiance to God, and also to judge all who refuse God's gracious arrangement. By this standard both Timothy and those to whom he ministered would be judged, and therefore Paul appeals to it as the only ground of judgment.

2. "*Be instant in season, out of season.*" *What does this mean ?*

Be urgent in the season afforded you for doing good, and when you have not one, make one—a hint worth remembering by all labourers for Christ. There are, however, two reasons assigned by Paul why Timothy is thus urged to be in earnest. (1.) That a time would come when *sound teaching* would not be received ; and (2.) that Paul himself was about to be removed.

3. "*They shall heap to themselves teachers, having itching ears.*" *What condition of things is this ?*

A very sad state indeed, but by this rendering his meaning is not perceived. A more correct rendering would be, *tickling the ears,* and refers to the kind of teachers the people who would not endure sound teaching would gather to themselves. These teachers would minister reasonings and genealogies that would amuse and beguile them, and so they would be turned away from the truth. The Word that would separate from evil and turn to righteousness was not taught by them, and in this way the perilous times began.

6. *What does Paul mean when he says,* "*For I am now ready to be offered, and the time of my departure is at hand*" ?

It is, *lit., I am ready to be poured out, and the season of my release has come near.* Paul evidently felt the loosing down of his tabernacle, and knew that his end was at hand. His strife with the foes of Christ and truth was over, and he was looking for death to break the tie that held him here. Noble warrior, thou hast indeed fought a good fight, and received many a scar in thy spiritual contest. Earnest runner in the heavenly race, with wearied limbs thy goal has been reached. Zealous watchman of thy Master's trust, thou wouldest allow none to tamper with His rights. As a servant of thy Lord, we owe much to thee for thy faithful discharge of duty in handing down to us in written testimony the truth received from Him. Fain would we give thee our poor tribute of praise, but thou sought it not; the smile of thy Saviour alone was sought by thee.

7. *When he says* "*I have kept the faith,*" *does he refer to his own confidence ?*

It is strictly, *I have guarded the faith.* With a holy jealousy he had watched over the trust of truth given to him by his Master. He had kept the deposit inviolate, and was laying it down only with his life. It was not his own faith, but "the faith" which he had guarded from all admixture.

9. "*Do thy diligence to come shortly unto me.*" *Why does Paul hasten him?*

His end was not far off, and he has much to say, therefore *come quickly*, or make haste, for I shall soon be gone.

10. "*Demas hath forsaken me.*" *Why refer to this faithless one?*

Demas had ministered to his need both in Rome and Asia. Indeed Paul seems to have been his special charge; but the snare of the "present world" overcame him, and for it he abandoned his charge. Twice the apostle had sent from Rome his greeting to the saints, but here he has to write, "Demas hath forsaken me, having loved the present world."

11. "*Take Mark, and bring him with thee.*" *Was this the Mark that once left him to go to Jerusalem?*

I judge so. But though he left Paul, for some reason not named, he did not leave Christ, and knowing the value of his service, Paul desires again to see him, and to direct him in his work.

13. *Paul had left his cloak, books, and parchments at Troas with Carpus. When did he leave them there?*

On his return journey from Rome, from which place, having been set at liberty, as stated in verse 17, he returned to Asia to fulfil the engagements he had made when expecting deliverance. Philemon, who lived at Colosse, had been asked to prepare him a lodging (Philemon 21); and in his letter to Titus, possibly written soon after Paul arrived in Asia, Nicopolis was named as the place where he would winter, and where he, Timothy, and other named

associates, are asked to meet him. Only a few incidents of his journey from Rome are given, but the references show the route over which he travelled. He had passed through Corinth, for Erastus remained there (ver. 20); and Miletus, for there he left Trophimus sick; and Troas, where his cloak, etc., were left, and which he now desires Timothy to bring with him, when he should come. At verse 21, Timothy is urged, "Do thy diligence to come before winter," and whether the kindred spirits he had summoned to Nicopolis arrived before he departed this life or not we cannot tell. The record is closed, and his last words are the sweet benediction that finished all his letters, "Grace be with you, Amen."

16. "*At my first answer no man stood with me.*" *To what does he refer?*

To his trial before Nero Cæsar, to which he but briefly alludes. In the soul-cheering vision which had been given to him during the storm on the Adriatic Sea, the angel of God said to him, "Fear not, Paul; thou must be brought before Cæsar." The interview, however, was delayed much longer than might have been expected, but the two years in his own hired house was a most interesting period, and was filled up with work which will bear fruit until the Lord returns. Those "prison epistles," as they have been not unfitly termed, are, to those who will hear an apostle of Jesus, as precious as when first received by the churches to which they were written. Then there was a change from the hired house which he was so long permitted to occupy, to some more secret place, which Onesiphorus, on his visit to Rome, discovered only with diligent search. Tradition still points to the Mamertine prison where he was confined prior to his trial, but beyond this legend of the mediæval church we know nothing. When Paul appealed from Festus to the higher court of Cæsar, he doubtless expected justice and protection from that powerful monarch, who up to that period had shown no hostility to Christians. But while Paul was at Rome, a great change had taken place in Nero, and so cruel had he become, that even Paul's friends were afraid to stand by him, and all forsook him. " Not-withstanding," said he, " the Lord stood with me, and strengthened me; . . . and I was delivered out of the mouth of the lion." Being thus set at liberty, he would speedily prepare for his departure, and after a while regained the scene of early labours and former associates, but only to find that his work on earth must cease. The trust reposed in Christ during the service of his life, was not changed in the prospect of death. The summons found him prepared to meet it, and he could say, " I am ready to be offered"—*lit.*, to be poured out—" and the time of my departure is at hand." Faithful warrior of the cross, may thy unselfish spirit yet animate many a fainting, feeble soldier of Jesus, and arouse to yet higher and truer service those who are trembling in the fight.

THE EPISTLE OF PAUL TO

TITUS.

CHAPTER I.

1–3. " *Paul* . . . . *an apostle of Jesus Christ, according to the faith of God's elect.*" *What does he mean by this ?*

God's elect, to whom Paul here refers, were the patriarchs, Abra-ham, Isaac, and Jacob ; and to whom the promise of blessing for the nations through the Messiah had been made. Why such a promise should have been made to them, and why its fulfilment should have been so long delayed was (1.) on account of God's delay in sending the Mes-siah, the one only source of blessing to men ; and (2.) that during this in-terval, a very numerous seed was given to Abraham, and upon them very many favours were bestowed. In fact, during this long period, the family of Abraham seemed to possess all the attention and favour of God, while the nations—the world outside —were lying in the wicked one, very much like an unpitied captive in the grasp of a victor. The fulness of the time, however, did arrive, and He who was to bless the nations did ap-pear, and ultimately—as recorded in the Acts of Apostles—the proclama-tion of grace and life was made known to them. The loving welcome which many of them gave to Him, and how they were led to believe and be bap-tised into Him, the records of this valuable historical document will supply in detail, and should be care-fully studied to become fully ac-quainted with it. Now this blessing of Abraham coming on the Gentiles through faith, was the fulfilment of the promise made to him, and be-lieved or expected by him ; and it is to this that Paul refers when he writes " an apostle of Jesus Christ, according to the faith of God's elect."

" *And the acknowledging of the truth which is after godliness.*" *Is this also connected with his apostle-ship ?*

Yes, but we should read instead, *a full knowledge of the truth—i.e.,* a full revelation of the truth—by which those who receive it are made godly. Paul was fitted by this full revelation of the truth, to lead the Gentiles into pardon of sins, and also purity of heart and life.

How could this promise of eternal life to the nations, which is said to have been promised before the world began, be held by Paul to have been first given to the patriarchs?

It is our Authorised Version that has made him speak thus, and which is so far misleading. His words strictly rendered would read, *before the times of the ages—i.e.,* before the dispensation of the law—the true God, to these patriarchs, promised eternal life for the nations through His Son; and in due season His Word was manifested in a proclamation committed unto Paul.

4. *Why does he call Titus his " own son after the common faith "?*

It is, *lit.,* a genuine or true child according to the common faith—*i.e.,* one who believed and preached the same glad-tidings that Paul preached. Just as a true son is sure to forward the business or interests of his father, so Titus was sustaining and carrying forward the work which had been entrusted to Paul. He was his true son in the Gospel, and his apostolic benediction, " grace [omit mercy] and peace," could be given to him.

5. *" For this cause left I thee in Crete; that thou shouldest set in order,"* etc. *Why did Paul not do this himself?*

We must not suppose that he would leave the church in disorder, or without proper instruction, but time alone would reveal how far they had conformed to his instruction, or how faithfully they might continue " in the apostles' doctrine "; and for this purpose Titus was left among them, that any manifest deficiency might be corrected. Paul names specially the appointing of overseers, and these could not be appointed until their fitness became manifest, and for this time was required.

6–9. *Does this list of qualifications for oversight differ from that given to Timothy?*

The difference is not great, but it will be helpful to study them together, and to note any explanation or variation of detail which is given. For instance, in Timothy we get "bishop"—*lit.,* overseer—only, while in Titus we get both " elder " and " bishop." Then in Timothy the bishop must be " apt to teach "; whilst in Titus, it is required that he be " holding fast the faithful word as he hath been taught." Now this is an important addition, and should have special attention. The elder must not only be " apt to teach," but it must be the " faithful word " in which his skill is shown. A mere eloquent talker is not enough, but he must be sound in the faith, that the church may be built up.

Should the Church receive as overseers those who lack some *of these required qualifications?*

Paul says that overseers *must* be thus fitted, and it would be a daring violation of the Spirit's directions to accept of them otherwise. It would be far better for the church to continue steadfastly in the apostle's doctrine, and the fellowship, the breaking of bread, and prayers, as detailed in the New Testament, than to appoint as overseers those not fitted for the work. If the directions of the Spirit are followed, the results will justify the selection made; but if elders are chosen otherwise, the church must suffer loss.

10–14. *Were these circumcised persons who were to be restrained by Titus, Cretians or Jews?*

They were most likely circumcised

Cretians; who having obtained some knowledge of Jewish tradition, were seeking to stand foremost as teachers of the Church. Paul directs that their mouths be stopped—*lit.*, muzzled; because not only was their teaching injurious to the saints, but their lives also were immoral, and to them the grave charge of one of their own poets—Epimenidus, a poet of the sixth century, B. C.—was applicable. "The Cretians are always liars, evil beasts, slow bellies." They must therefore be rebuked, and prevented from turning men from the faith.

How did these "deceivers" obtain so much influence in the Church?

They confessed that they knew God, and so deceived the simple; but in works they were denying Him, and must therefore be prevented from subverting the people.

CHAPTER II.

1. *What did Paul mean by the "sound doctrine," that Titus was exhorted to speak?*

The doctrine or teaching according to godliness, was that which produced purity of heart and reformation of life. The claims of Christ when honestly accepted will result in separation from evil, and these claims must be put forth in order to acceptance.

Is a preacher or teacher responsible for results?

Yes; according to the measure his teaching is received, so will be the result. If a man teach infidelity, and his teaching be received, he will make infidels. Or, if he teach Romanism, or spiritualism, or Methodism, or Presbyterianism, or any other ism, the receivers of the doctrine will be moulded by it. Or if a man teach Christianity according to the New Testament, he will make Christians. Every teacher or preacher therefore is responsible for results,

2 D

as the teaching moulds the disciple who receives it.

11. *Has salvation appeared to all men?*

Our translators have made Paul to say so, but it should be—The grace of God, that bringeth salvation to all men hath appeared.

Does Paul refer to this universal provision for any special purpose?

His reference is in relation to its effects on all who receive it. He had been exhorting men and women, the aged and the young, to so live that Christ might be honoured; and that denying ungodliness and worldly lusts, they should live "soberly, righteously, and godly, in the present world."

13. *What is the relation between purification of heart and life, and the glorious appearing of the great God, etc.*

No person can intelligently look for that glorious appearing—*lit.*, appearing of the glory of the great God and our Saviour Jesus—who has not been purified by His truth; since that glory is not for the unholy, but for the saints in Christ.

14. *Is redemption from iniquity the great end for which Christ gave Himself?*

This is what Paul affirms in this statement; and while pardon of sin is a necessity in man's guilty condition, and stands first on the list of Gospel promises, yet the great end of the administration of grace, is a restoration of the lawless to loving obedience to God. If this is not secured, the end of His death is frustrated as far as the sinner is concerned.

"A peculiar people." What does this mean?

It is strictly a people purchased or acquired for Himself. Jesus gave His life for us, and thus made us His own, and is now seeking to make His disciples like Himself, obedient in all things.

CHAPTER III.

1. *Why does Paul urge submission to principalities, and powers, and magistrates?*

Because these governments and authorities are of God, and in this submission God is obeyed. This certainly is a high motive for all the saints.

But if rulers should command what is contrary to God's will, what must the saints do then?

They must resist, since an opposing authority cannot be obeyed. When Christ sent out His disciples to bear witness to His resurrection, the rulers at Jerusalem forbade them to do so, and the reply of Peter is most decisive : " We ought to obey God rather than men."

3. *Why does Paul refer to the past sinful life of himself and other believers?*

In order to remind Titus of the result of their own submission to Christ. They had been the subjects of almost every form of vice and disobedience, and yet they had been turned by the Gospel from evil to good, and from sin to holiness. He wishes to remind him that what the love of God had done in himself and other saints it could do for these debased and vice-ruled Cretians. But as this must be effected by the truth, he is exhorted to urge and teach and direct them to the great end for which Jesus gave His life, that the redeeming power of the Gospel might be seen in all.

4. *Why does he refer to the kindness and love of God our Saviour, which had been so manifest in their salvation?*

He wishes to note the striking manifestation of His love, who, in the face of all their past vileness and iniquity, had showed mercy to them. It is as if he had said, our iniquities did not hinder the outflow of His great mercy, and this should be remembered in all our labours for others.

5. *" The washing of regeneration."* *What does this mean?*

It is well to note that two things are named here, viz., regeneration and the washing—*lit.*, bath of regeneration—and these must neither be confounded nor separated. The regeneration is by the Word of truth —*i.e.*, the Gospel. " Of His own will or desire begat He us with the Word of truth " (James i. 18) ; while the bath is the immersion in water which Christ has appointed to follow. The language must not be thought strange for Paul to use, since Ananias had used similar language to him. " Arise, and be baptised, and wash away thy sins, calling on the name of the Lord."

What is this " renewing of the Holy Spirit "?

It is the effect of his teaching and truth, as manifested in a new life. In the bath of regeneration, or, in other words, their burial with Christ in baptism, they voluntarily separated themselves from the sins of the old life ; and in accepting the teaching and guidance of the Spirit, it was a renewing of the Holy Spirit —a new creation.

10. *What constituted any one a heretic?*

A heretic, according to Paul, is one who forms a sect or party by departing from apostolic teaching ; which is always the result of such a departure. After the failure of admonition, such persons were to be condemned and rejected.

12. *" Be diligent to come to me to Nicopolis." From what place did Paul write this direction to Titus?*

Both this letter and his second letter to Timothy were written in Asia, after his arrival from Rome ; but in what part of it we cannot say. If he did reach the home of Philemon, as suggested in his letter to him, then it might be at his house that these letters were written, and Nicopolis is named as the meeting-place of old associates in the work. Paul arranged to winter in Nicopolis, and Timothy was urged to get there with books, cloak, and parchments before winter. Whether the meeting took place or not we have no means of knowing. We see his anxious desire to meet again those from whom he had been so long separated, and a number of these are specially named, and then the curtain falls and hides him from our view. The truth had been proclaimed and written down; the authority of Christ had been established; and in this we rejoice—yea, and will rejoice.

THE EPISTLE OF PAUL TO

PHILEMON.

If Onesimus had not run away from his master Philemon, I suppose we should not have had this beautiful letter from Paul?
Onesimus might have run away, as many other slaves have done, without Paul writing about it. It was not his running away, but his noble surrender to the rightful claim of Philemon after his conversion, that became the occasion of this letter.

Was it not strange that Onesimus should visit Paul in his hired house?
It is not strange that he should do so, although in so doing he might expect a rebuke. Possibly there was not another face in Rome that he knew except the apostle. He might gaze with interest for a while upon the crowds as they rushed to and from the busy amphitheatre; or he might stand by the gate of the Forum, and watch the train of busy merchants hurrying by, but none of them turned a familiar glance upon Onesimus. In no position would a lone heart feel its loneliness more than in the crowded thoroughfare of a great city. Not a face smiled upon him, not a hand stretched out to welcome him among all the passers by. Such, we presume, would be the condition of Onesimus in Rome. But he knew Paul, and most likely had washed his feet, and cleaned his sandals, and brushed the dust from his cloak, and heard his kind words, and proved his sympathy in his enslaved position. He would doubtless have heard from his master about Paul's imprisonment, and now he must seek that familiar face, although he might reprove him.

While conversion to Christ must always be through the truth of the Gospel, may not circumstances have something to do with it?
They are often helpful, and when rightly improved may lead to a crisis. Here we have Onesimus, through a previous acquaintance with Paul, led to visit him. It is an opportunity both for sympathy and faithfulness, and Paul uses it for making known the Gospel, and the man is turned to Christ. The case is deeply suggestive, and we may all profit by it. Quite unexpectedly people may be brought under our influence. It may be a child, a servant, a friend, or a needy one; and it is an opportunity we should use wisely. To be unfaithful to our trust may be to

them an eternal loss. I have known a serious young woman call at the house of a teacher in the church, in the hope that he would speak to her about her need of Christ, but she waited only to hear jesting and trifling talk. Need I say that she was greatly disappointed, and left that house with every desire for being a Christian quenched in her spirit; and which never returned until many years after. If Christians do not feel able to do much good, let them not do harm by frivolity and mirth.

Would Paul urge Onesimus to return to his master?

It is more likely to have been a proposal on his own part, as a fruit of honest conversion to Christ. Every true convert is sure to repair as far as possible past wrongs, and to meet all lawful claims. The professed conversion of any one who ignores just claims should be questioned.

1. *Where did Philemon live?*

We presume at Colosse, as Archippus, who is named here, is named in Paul's letter to the Colossians (iv. 17).

2. *Who was Apphia?*

Most likely she was the wife of Philemon, and the reading in several MSS. is, " and to our sister Apphia."

5–7. *What were the distinguishing features of the life of Philemon?*

Faith, love, and benevolent sympathy with the saints. Paul knew of these, and could refer to them with deep satisfaction.

8. *Why does he say that he might be " much bold in Christ to enjoin that which is convenient "?*

He means that as an apostle, as one to whom Philemon owed his conversion, and having even suffered on his behalf, he might have put forth a claim, but he will not use these things for himself but rather plead in love the request he has to make for another.

10. *What has he to request?*

That Philemon would receive as a beloved brother in the Lord his runaway slave; once unprofitable, but now profitable to both himself and Paul.

21. *Did he expect that Philemon would comply with his request?*

He expected that his love would even exceed the request, and that Onesimus would be received as a brother in the Lord.

22. *" Withal prepare me a lodging." Did he get free?*

Yes. In his last letter to Timothy he reports his deliverance, and he would then leave for Asia. Erastus and Trophimus became his travelling companions, but according to 2 Tim. iv. 20, were left at Corinth, etc.

THE EPISTLE OF PAUL THE APOSTLE TO THE

HEBREWS.

CHAPTER I.

" God, who at sundry times and in divers manners spake," etc. Is not this a very abrupt introduction to this epistle?

Yes, when contrasted with the other epistles, nearly all of which begin with the name of the author, and for this departure from the usual method there must be some important reason. We think the reason is to be found in the argument itself, and shows divine wisdom in affixing the name of God to it, rather than that of any man. The writer is led to affirm to these Hebrews, that a new law-giver, a new administration, a new sacrificial death, a new covenant, a new priesthood, etc., had been introduced by God, and accepted by them, but the truth of which some of them were beginning to doubt. Now, it was to prevent them falling away from Christ that this epistle was written; and the wisdom and skill of the writer in proving that every part of the old economy had been set aside by the introduction of a new and better institution, is manifestly inspired. That the Mosaic economy was of God was evidently accepted by both parties; but the writer goes on to adduce facts and types and prophecies to prove, not only that there must of necessity be another institution following the first, but that it had been truly established. Hence it is not the name of the writer that begins the letter, or could properly be appended to it, but the name of the Founder of both institutions; and between Him who had spoken once more, not by prophets but by a Son, and those who rejected this new oracle, the issue must now rest. Hence the writer begins with " God," *i.e.*, the same God, " who at sundry times and in divers manners spake in time past unto our fathers by the prophets, hath in these last days spoken unto us by His Son."

" *At sundry times and in divers manners.*" *What does this mean ?*

It is, *lit.*, *in many parts, and in many ways, i.e.*, fragmentary and diverse. God did not give His will through one person, nor in one method, as Jewish history so fully attests.

2. " *Hath in these last days spoken.*" *Does the writer refer to the Gospel dispensation ?*

It is, *lit.*, *in the last of these days, i.e.*, of the old dispensation; for when Jesus, the new oracle of God, began to speak to men—to us, the Jews—the old economy had not closed. Paul, therefore,—who is assumed to be the author of this epistle, whoever may have been the writer,—notes distinctly, that God, who spoke to the fathers by prophets, spoke to their children by a Son. It is literally *in* the prophets, and *in* (the person of) a Son, whom He appointed, etc. The communication therefore was divine, and had a special claim upon their attention.

" *By whom also He made the worlds.*" *Does he refer to the material universe ?*

It is, *lit., the ages ;* and may be read, *on whose account He made or formed the ages.* That is, the ages of the Jewish dispensation were all arranged to set forth Christ, the appointed heir of God. Indeed, the whole institution was filled with types and shadows of the coming Christ; and but for Him who was to come and fulfil them all, the Jewish economy could have had no existence.

3. *Why does he refer to the many excellences of this new claimant ?*

In order to show that not only did He equal former messengers of God, but that He far surpassed them all. In Him the glory of God, and the character of God, and the power of God were all manifested ; and that He might be fitted for the great work of redemption, He made a purging—*lit.*, a purification—for sins, and was then seated at the right hand of the Majesty on high.

4. " *Being made so much better than the angels.*" *Does he refer to celestial beings ?*

It is, *lit., having become so much superior to the messengers, i.e.*, the messengers of the former dispensation, as Moses, Aaron, and the prophets. It is with their official standing and work that He is contrasted all through the epistle, and not celestial beings who never had any official connection with it. It is very important to note this, or the force of the writer's statements will be lost. It was not the word of heavenly beings on which their destiny rested, but that of Moses and the prophets; and it is so far misleading to ordinary readers, to have angels (as we now apply the word) as a rendering of *angelois*, instead of messengers, the proper rendering of the word.

" As He hath by inheritance obtained a more excellent name than they." What name was this ?

The name of " Son," which was never given to messengers of that former economy. They were called servants, as " Moses my servant" (Josh. i. 2). He a Son, as " This is my Son the beloved" (Matt. iii. 17).

May not the title " Lord," be the more excellent name inherited ?

Lord, the name which is above every name, is not inherited, but given to Him as a recompense for His humiliation in the death of the cross. Lord is added as the crowning title of the Son.

5–13. In this section there are a number of quotations from the prophets, which are put by the writer in the form of a challenge. Why is this challenge given ?

It is given to show that sonship, worship, creation, immutability, and lordship, were never applied to the official messengers of that old dispensation ; but that all had been applied to Him in whom God had spoken to them, even His Son Jesus. It is a grand summary of prophetic utterances, which, being formed into a wreath and placed on the head of Him that was once crowned with thorns, was to claim for Him, by consent of these prophetic messengers, the homage and dominion which had become His right ; and which they never did claim for themselves.

14. " Are they not all ministering spirits." Were not these heavenly beings ?

No ; they were Jewish prophets, who prophesied of the grace that should come to believers in the Gospel age. It was revealed to them, that they did not minister or reveal things about themselves but to others, and their service is here claimed for the heirs of salvation. Spirits are here used for prophets who spoke by the Holy Spirit (see 1 Peter i. 10–12).

CHAPTER II.

1–3. Does this part of the argument of the writer terminate with Chapter I. ?

No, it is only suspended, to allow of a word of needed exhortation ; a feature very noticeable in all the letters of Paul. He had just shown the dignity and exaltation of the Son in whom God was speaking to them, and at once he perceives the higher responsibility thus laid upon them, and seeks to impress it upon their attention. So he exhorts, " Therefore we ought to give the more earnest heed to the things which we have heard, lest at any time we should let them slip. For if the word spoken by messengers" (Moses, Joshua, etc.,) "was stedfast, and every transgression and disobedience " (to their word) "received a just recompence of reward; how shall we escape, if we neglect so great salvation?"

" Lest we should let them slip." Is " them " a proper addition ?

It conveys a different thought from Paul, who says, *we should give heed lest we should let slip or glide away*, and not " let *them* slip." The things they had heard were to have their most earnest attention, that by the truth they might be preserved from gliding away from Christ.

Was Christ the Lord the first to proclaim salvation?

So it is here affirmed, and we presume that the writer refers to the ministry of the Lord while on the earth, and labouring among the Jewish people. There is not a single aspect of the great salvation that He did not proclaim and illustrate while ministering among them. The kingdom was proclaimed, and pardon of sins bestowed. Demons were dispossessed, and death vanquished by raising up the dead to life again; and even glorification in His own person was manifested to chosen witnesses. These facts were confirmed to the writer and others by those who heard Him.

4. *Why does he refer to the signs, wonders, and gifts that attested the mission of Christ?*

The mission of Moses opened with signs and wonders, which led the children of Israel to accept him as their leader; and the witness borne by God to His Son was every way as marked, and why should they not accept this new leader, on the strength of these new attestations? The God who attested the one also attested the other, and His right to be accepted was beyond all question.

5. *"For unto the angels hath he not put in subjection the world to come, whereof we speak." What does this mean?*

Having previously stated the position which these *angelois* or messengers—as Moses, Joshua, and the prophets—held in that former dispensation, he is now prepared to affirm and prove that the new dispensation, or what he here terms, "the world to come," had not been put under subjection to these former rulers, but that one of higher rank, even God's Son, had been placed over it; and as God was speaking by Him, He alone must be heard. In the preceding chapter (verse 6) this is even more strikingly shown by a quotation from the Septuagint version of Deut. xxxii. 43, "When He bringeth in the first begotten into the world," by His resurrection, "He saith, And let all the angels or messengers of God worship Him." Or, as it was seen in the transfiguration, when Moses and Elias, the representatives of that old institution, laid down their authority at the feet of Jesus; and after the three apostles had seen this visible surrender of position to Him who was glorified in the presence of all, there came a voice out of the cloud, even the voice of God, saying, "This is my beloved Son: hear Him."

What is the meaning of "world" in this verse?

Oikoumene, which occurs here and in chap. i. 6, and is rendered "world" in both places, cannot, we think, be fully rendered by any single word in our language; and, therefore, whatever word is used to render it, it must fail to convey the idea intended. If we could make ourselves familiar with the idea which *oikoumene* conveyed to the Greeks and Romans in their day, we might get over the difficulty created by the want of a proper word, and thus be able to perfectly understand it. According to Robinson (Greek and English Lexicon), the Greeks, and afterwards the Romans, used *oikoumene* to denote the country inhabited by them, and over which they ruled, in opposition to the lands or country occupied by barbarian nations. It conveyed therefore to them and to all familiar with it a very definite idea. When the command went out from Cæsar Augustus, that all the world—the *oikoumene*—should be taxed or enrolled, every Roman official would understand how far the enrolment would extend, and that no one outside Roman territory could be entered on their lists. When Jesus said (Matt.

xxiv. 14), " And this Gospel of the kingdom shall be preached in all the world—the *oikoumene*—for a witness," every disciple understood that He referred to the Jews who were then scattered over the Roman empire, and that in the good providence of God, and before the judgment came upon the nation, they would all hear what God had so graciously done for them, whether it would lead to their condemnation or salvation. Now, as it pleased God, who selected *ecclesia*, the term used to denote a lawful assembly in every Greek city, to designate the gathering of His people for worship ; and *baptizo*, the ordinary term which denoted the action of dipping or covering over, to express the discipling ordinance of the new institution ; so it pleased Him to consecrate *oikoumene* to denote the acquired possession of His Son ; a possession which should be subjected not to angels or rulers of the former economy, but only to Him who purchased the Church with His own blood. We may have to train our minds to properly feel the force of the term employed to denote this special portion of the dominion of Jesus, but it is doubtless the best that could be employed. It is not *kosmos*, the beautiful universe over which God reigns as its Creator ; nor *gee*, the earth on which man is physically located ; nor *aion*, the age, whether good or evil; but *oikoumene*, the commonwealth which is ruled by the laws and statutes of its gracious Head, and includes only those who are obedient to His will.

If the writer refers to the Christian economy, why does he speak of it as " to come " ?

It is well to notice that he is viewing nearly all the great questions discussed in this epistle, first of all from the Jews position under the law, and then proves and applies the fulfilment. From the Jewish side of the old institution, the *oikoumene*, the priestly king, the new covenant, etc., were all to come ; but from the Christian side, they were all accomplished facts.

6–9. Why does he quote from the 8th Psalm about the Son of man being made lower than the messengers ?

It is simply to show in the history of Jesus—the Son of man of the Psalm — the fulfilment of its prophetic announcements, in that He was made lower than other messengers, and then raised higher than they.

How was He made lower, and then raised higher than other messengers ?

By becoming a victim for sin, and suffering death for others, which neither Moses nor any of the prophets ever did; and then was crowned with glory and honour at God's right hand, to which none of them were ever raised.

" Thou hast put all things under His feet, ... but now we see not yet all things put under Him." *How was this ?*

It is a simple statement of two facts, both of which were true. All authority had been given into His hands, but His enemies, the Jews, had not been made His footstool. But as the coronation had taken place, so in due time would be the humbling subjection of His enemies. " For He must reign till He has put all enemies under His feet."

10. Was the tasting of death, and bringing many sons to glory, inseparable ?

Most certainly, for whoever claimed the latter must also take the former. The messengers of the law period had not tasted death for others, and could not therefore lead to glory.

11–14. Why does he refer to the sanctified and the sanctifier being of one (Father), and to the prophecies about Jesus singing in the midst of the assembly?

These prophecies having been delivered, they must of necessity be fulfilled, and as Jesus had instructed His disciples to call God Father, "Our Father who art in heaven," and as He joined them in praise at the memorial feast, so it is claimed that these prophecies were fulfilled in Him.

How did the devil get the "power of death"? And how did Jesus destroy him by death?

God gave it to him when He said of the woman's seed, "thou shalt bruise His heel." The opportunity for this deadly work was deferred four thousand years; but as soon as Jesus, the woman's seed, and also the seed of Abraham, was born in Bethlehem, then, through Herod, a daring attack was made upon the child to destroy Him. The occasion failed, but not the purpose, and at last He was given into his hand. Judas, who betrayed Him, and the chief priests and rulers who crucified Him, were willing agents in the hand of the evil one. They might not understand what He meant by saying, "This is your hour, and the power of darkness," but in the light of facts we can discern His meaning. Yes, the devil had indeed the power of death, but by the resurrection of Jesus this power was destroyed, or annulled, for He became the Saviour of all who believe in Him.

16. *"For verily he took not on him the nature of angels." What does this mean?*

It is, *lit., For not indeed of messengers he takes hold, but of the seed of Abraham he takes hold;* and if we understand this to apply to Jesus, the seed of Abraham, of whom it had been written, "Thou shall make His soul an offering for sin," we shall then see his meaning. God did not lay hold of any one of the messengers of the former economy as a victim for sin, but He "laid on Him" (the seed of Abraham) "the iniquity of us all." In the application of this testimony to the Lord Jesus we see an overwhelming reason why they should no longer cling to the leaders of that old institution, but to Him who, though made lower than all by the suffering of death, yet being crowned with glory, is the only deliverer from guilt and death which God has in grace provided.

17. *How did this "merciful and faithful High Priest" make reconciliation for the sins of the people?*

It should be *propitiation* for the sins of the people, this being the ground of reconciliation; and in being tried by suffering, He is able to succour those who are tempted or tried.

CHAPTER III.

1. *Why does he address them as "holy brethren"?*

The writer was a Hebrew, so that there was a fleshly brotherhood; but it is only through that higher spiritual brotherhood that he can speak of their "heavenly calling."

"Heavenly calling." What was that?

The high calling of God to glory. The phrase is used in contrast with the earthly calling of their fathers, which was to the land of Canaan.

Why does he call Jesus "the Apostle and High Priest of our profession"?

An apostle is one sent by another, and as Christ Jesus has been sent by God to be the head of His house, and also their High Priest, He is truly the Apostle and High Priest of our profession,—*lit.,* confession. And having confessed Him to be the Son of God, His claim to their obedience and confidence in Him to the end is earnestly pressed upon their attention.

2–6. *Why does he refer to Moses ?*

Moses had been the God-appointed servant of His house from the time that he brought the people of Israel out of Egypt; but having sent His Son to form a new house or institution, and to be its head and Lord, it was counted as a rival interest which the greater part of the nation refused to accept. This obstinate and continued rejection on their part was beginning to act injuriously even upon those who had accepted Jesus as the Messiah, and many were wavering in mind who had once nobly suffered for Christ. It was to hinder this growing apostacy among the saints that this epistle was written, and the merits of the two institutions laid side by side. In the first part the references are more general, but here he distinctly names the leader of the old economy, and Moses and Christ are now contrasted in their official standing.

In what are they contrasted here ?

In the position which each sustained to the house of God. Both were faithful, but one was only a servant, the other a son. Moses was a servant in God's house, but Christ the son in the house built by Himself; therefore He had more glory than Moses.

7–11. *Why does he refer to the provocation and judgment of Israel in the wilderness ?*

He had just stated that, as confessors of Christ, they had become His house, and are exhorted to hold fast their confidence and rejoicing of the hope firm unto the end ; and when about to exhort them to beware of the evil heart of unbelief, which is ready to start aside from God, he is led first of all to repeat the warning of the Spirit as found in the 95th Psalm.

Their fathers lost the land of Canaan. Does he refer to it for the purpose of warning them against a similar loss ?

He evidently intended them to feel that it was as possible for them to lose the prize of glory through unbelief as it was for their fathers to lose the land of Canaan. He therefore exhorts, "Take heed, brethren, lest there be in any of you an evil heart of unbelief in departing from the living God."

14. *For we are made partakers of Christ if we hold the beginning of our confidence stedfast unto the end." Does he mean that those who fail never were partakers ?*

It is well to keep before us that the object of Christ was to lead into glory, as the purpose of God was to bring to Canaan. The failure of their fathers did not ignore their previous deliverance from Egypt, nor would their own failure their previous illumination. It was through the after rising up of unbelief that Canaan was lost, but into which Joshua led their children. Christ reached the glory, and it was only they who continued faithful that would be partakers with Him in glory.

15–19. *Why does he repeat and dwell upon this sad story of the fall in the wilderness ?*

In order to show that God did not act arbitrarily in rejecting their fathers, but was upholding the authority of Moses, and thus to assure them that He would also uphold the authority of His Son.

CHAPTER IV.

1. *Why does he exhort, " Let us therefore fear" ?*

Their fathers had lost the land of Canaan—God's typical rest—through their disobedience, and he now earnestly warns them against losing that higher rest promised through the Son.

2. *What was the Gospel preached to them?*

The glad tidings of the land which through want of faith they were not allowed to enter.

And what the " Gospel preached to us"?

The salvation of Jesus, with eternal glory, which the faithful alone can enjoy.

The doctrine that " once in grace always in grace" appears to be ignored in the apostle's warning; is the doctrine not Scriptural?

It is a dogma of a human creed, and is never taught in the Scriptures. To hold it seems a most solemn trifling with all the exhortations, warnings, and examples with which the Word of God abounds. Only think of the Holy Spirit, by an apostle, bringing forward the fact of their fathers being destroyed through unbelief after being saved out of Egypt, to warn these Hebrews against a like spiritual result, when, according to this doctrine, the like could not happen; the thing is preposterous. It is a blind assumption, which has led many to trust to a supposed eternal decree instead of the Lord Jesus.

3. *" We which have believed do enter into rest." What rest is this?*

It is the rest which a weary sinburdened heart finds in Jesus. It is the rest of salvation, which He alone can give.

What is meant by " My rest"?

God's rest in creation. His own work unblighted by transgression. There was not a stain on the work of His hands. It was "good," yea, "very good," and He could rest, *i.e.*, find satisfaction in it. But then sin entered through His creature man, and His rest was broken up, and He must either abandon it wholly to judgment, or create a new basis on which He can meet and dwell with His creatures. To provide this rest God began to work again, and all through the ages, in types, and shadows, in promises, and illustrations, the work of His gracious hand was seen. "My Father worketh hitherto" (John v. 17), said Jesus, "and I work," but the Pharisees only stumbled at what He did. Instead of seeing a proof that the heavenly husbandman had not abandoned His vineyard, they counted it a sin that He should heal a man on the sabbath day.

6–9. *" They to whom it was first preached entered not in because of unbelief." Could they have entered?*

Yes, by faith in God's promise they might have entered that Canaan rest to which God called them, and which was a type of the Christian inheritance. But instead of believing the gracious purpose of God, they turned back in heart to Egypt, and so lost both the shadow and the substance.

" It remaineth that some must enter therein." Why must some enter?

Because the promise being given, it remained for their seed to inherit, and under the command of Joshua they were led into Canaan, and a triumphant possession of the land was obtained. Still, that which was typified by it was not obtained, and the promise therefore remained for others to possess. "For if Jesus,"—*lit.*, Joshua—"had given them rest, then would He not afterward have spoken of another day," as is done in Ps. xcv. "To-day if ye will hear His voice," etc. Paul's conclusion therefore is, that as the rest had not been realised, the promise remained for enjoyment. "There remaineth therefore a rest to the people of God."

Is heaven the rest that remains for enjoyment?

It is the rest of faith, or rest in Christ that he is speaking of, which though perfected in glory, begins on earth. " For we which have believed do enter into rest." *Sabbatismos,* the Greek word of this 9th verse, which is rendered rest, does not occur elsewhere in the New Testament. It has evidently been selected to express a very important thought, viz., that the rest,—*lit.,* sabbath-keeping—intended for the believer, is in some respects similar to the rest of God, *i.e.,* a holy rest—a ceasing from selfishness—which is really man's "own work," in relation to which there is no rest, *i.e.,* no satisfaction. God's work in creation was purely unselfish, there was no blot in it, and He could rest from His work ; and when Christ, God's rest, is accepted, a new principle of action is formed, and the service is in righteousness and true holiness. It was to this rest and to this work that Jesus invited when He said, " Come unto Me, all ye that labour and are heavy laden, and I will give you rest. Take My yoke upon you and learn of Me, . . . and ye shall find rest unto your souls."

11–13. *"For the Word of God is quick, and powerful, . . . and dividing asunder of soul and spirit," etc. What does this mean ?*

It is evidently connected with the "example of unbelief," with God swearing that "they shall not enter into My rest." That living and powerful word took hold of the whole nation, and only two escaped from that life and spirit-dividing sentence, that was sharper than a two-edged sword, from which some might escape. It is a solemn and instructive warning not to trifle with the threatenings of God, to whom all things are naked and opened.

14. *Why should the passing of Jesus into heaven be a spur to faithfulness ?*

Because when on earth there was undoubted sympathy with men in trial, although in trial Himself ; but now that He is in heaven and has become our High Priest, what may we not expect from Him ?

Is there anything strange in Jesus passing into the heavens ?

Yes, it is most wonderful, because it is not only as the Son of God that He goes there, but as the man who was under judgment and death. To know that Jesus is there, is to know that humanity is raised from death and seated in glory. And now He is pledged to do the same for all who trust Him. Well might Paul exhort, " Let us hold fast our confession."

When he speaks of Jesus being tempted like them in all things apart from sin, does he refer to nature or to circumstances ?

To circumstances. There was not a trial incident to human position with which He was not tested. So that He was like them in all things except sin. They had sin, He knew no sin, and in this He stood alone.

16. *What is meant by the " throne of grace " ?*

The throne of grace is, to the believer under Christ, what the mercy-seat was to the priesthood under Aaron. It was the place of access to those who sought the favour of God. When sprinkled by the High Priest with blood, it became the seat of both authority and mercy, and from it the worshipper was both directed and blessed. So Jesus our great High Priest is seated upon a " throne of grace," *i.e.,* His administration is with authority and mercy combined, and to Him let us boldly come, *i.e.,* confident of access through Him.

Why does he say " mercy and grace " ?

Because it is as sinners we have to come to Him to obtain mercy, and it is as worshippers that we need

His gracious mediation. Both are provided and enjoyed in Him.

CHAPTER V.

1–3. *Why does he now refer to the officiating High Priest ?*

Because under that administration there were two official persons, Moses, the lawgiver, of whose authority he had spoken in the preceding chapters ; and Aaron, the officiating High Priest, whose divine call and ministry he now sets forth. He is very careful to state that both were appointed of God for men. Moses was appointed over the house as a ruling servant, and Aaron as a ministering priest ; and both were types of Him who was to come.

" That he may offer both gifts and sacrifices for sins." Were these two kinds of offerings.

Yes ; there were sacrifices for sins, and also gifts, *i.e.,* thank-offerings of the accepted worshippers, and both had to be presented by the priest upon the altar. The nation might provide a bullock for atonement, but the priest alone could carry the blood into the holy place. An individual might bring his lamb or turtle-dove and kill it before the Lord, but the priest alone could sprinkle its blood upon the altar, or wave his offering for acceptance. The priest was to the worshipping Israelite an absolute necessity, so is Jesus to all who would worship acceptably in spirit and in truth.

4. *Some persons hold that as Aaron was called to the priesthood by God, and could not otherwise have officiated, so no person ought to preach the Gospel unless divinely called. Is this true ?*

No ; unless the call of the Church be a divine call. Every disciple of Christ is under obligation to make known His Gospel ; but any one who pretends to have a call from God, apart from the Church and his own necessary obligation, is certainly deceiving himself, and may deceive others. It is simply stated here that Aaron was called of God to the priesthood, and could not have taken it otherwise ; and then it is added, " So also Christ glorified not Himself to be made an High Priest;" but was called of God to this high position. This reference, therefore, to the divine call of Aaron, by which he was received of the people, was in order to show that Christ, who was called of God, should also be received.

5, 6. *How was Christ called to His priesthood ?*

By a prophetic announcement, which doubtless belongs to the Messiah. The writer claims for Him that He who said, " Thou art my Son, this day have I begotten Thee," said also, " Thou a priest for ever, after the order of Melchisedec."

" Thou a priest for ever." Is His priesthood eternal ?

It is, *lit., Thou a priest for the age,* and is a most important declaration. His appointment was not for a generation, as the priests of old, but for the whole dispensation. His priesthood therefore abides for the age, because He, ever liveth to make intercession for us.

7. *" Who in the days of His flesh." Does this apply to Melchisedec or to Christ ?*

To Christ, I have no doubt. To His " prayers and supplications with strong crying and tears," the apostles bear ample testimony.

When was Christ saved from death ?

It is, *lit., out of death,* and should be understood of His resurrection. Jesus was not saved from dying, and never wished to be.

8. *" Though He were a Son, yet learned He obedience by the things*

He suffered." Might He as a Son have claimed exemption ?

It is rather intended to teach that He proved His sonship by His obedience to the Father, and thus showed how sonship is to be proved in others.

9. *" Being made perfect." How could an already perfect Jesus be made perfect ?*

He was perfected as a Saviour by His obedience in death, and then became the author—*lit.*, a cause—of eternal salvation to all obeying Him.

11. *Why was it so difficult for them to understand his teaching about Melchisedec ?*

Because they were dull—*lit.*, they had *become sluggish in the hearing about* Christ, and so were hindered by their want of interest.

12. *What were these "first principles of the oracles of God" ?*

The teaching of the Old Testament concerning the coming of the Messiah, whether in type or prophecy.

What was the " milk " with which —from their babe condition—they required to be fed ?

The milk is still the teaching spoken of ; but as the figure is changed from a scholar to a babe, we get the appropriate term *milk* instead of instruction.

What is meant by "strong meat" ?

The facts and truths, privileges and promises, of the new covenant ; or, in other words, the truth concerning Christ, as having come in the flesh, as having been put to death, raised, and glorified ; and through whom repentance, remission, and sonship were bestowed on all who accepted Jesus as the God-provided Saviour of men. This meat was so strong that many of the Jews —through their unbelief—could not eat of it, and so perished by their disobedient rejection of Jesus.

CHAPTER VI.

1, 2. *Are not the first two verses of this chapter very difficult to understand ?*

They are like many other portions of Scripture, difficult until we get the key, and then they are plain enough. Of one thing we should be certain, viz., that they are sure to be in harmony with all other revealed truth. It will aid us very much to remember that Paul was writing about two dispensations, and to a people who were leaving the one, and yet through their sluggishness they were making very slow progress towards the other. Indeed, at times they appear to be almost standing still, as if afraid of the new ground upon which they had advanced ; and as the great bulk of the nation had refused to accept of Christ as their Lord and Saviour, it must have been a cause of stumbling to the few who had believed. If we, therefore, decide that these " principles of the doctrine of Christ," or more *lit.*, *the beginning of the Word of Christ,* which they were to leave, were those things of the past dispensation—the types and teaching concerning the Coming One—and the "perfection" to which they were to advance were the facts and privileges of the new covenant, we shall find it easy enough to understand, and this is what seems to be its proper application. We may not clearly perceive the force of everything in this Jewish ritual, but the main thought of the writer is plain enough.

4–6. *" For it is impossible for those who were once enlightened," etc. Is this of general or special application ?*

Paul is speaking of believing Jews, and not at all of Gentiles. There is a wide difference between a Jew enlightened by the preaching of the apostles and also receiving spiritual gifts—the powers or signs of the Christian age—and then on some pretence trampling underfoot this specially prepared evidence on behalf of Christ, and a Gentile who, through carelessness and temptation, falls into sin. The latter may regret his folly, and confess, and forsake it, and turn again to the provided Advocate; but the Jew, who renounced Christ for Moses, had no Saviour to go to. By going back to sacrifices and temple-worship he reversed God's plan entirely, and thus crucified the Son of God afresh, putting Him to an open shame.

How could Jesus be crucified afresh ?

He was typically crucified in every victim offered on the sacrificial altar, and this is why He is called "the Lamb slain from the foundation of the world" (Rev. xiii. 8); and to renew these sacrifices when He had fulfilled them was to crucify Him afresh, and was also a denial of the propitiation offered to God; and thus He was put to an open shame.

7–12. Why does he refer to the cursing of the fruitless ground ?

It is intended as a warning, though he is "persuaded," or would rather think "better things" of them; for they had endured much suffering for the truth, and their work and labour of love was not forgotten. Still he has his fears, and in order to prove them he submits a crucial test.

What is the test submitted ?

Endurance to the end, without which the hope could not be realised. They must be "imitators of those who through faith and patience inherit the promises."

Why does he refer to Abraham obtaining the promise through endurance ?

In order to show them by this striking instance that if they would realise the blessed hope, they must endure to the end. Abraham received the promise long before he obtained the oath which secured to him the Messiah as his Son. The promise, according to the reasoning here, was conditional until Isaac was offered upon the altar. To have refused to offer his son in death would have been a refusal of the only condition on which God could bless and save guilty men— viz., through the death and resurrection of His Son. To turn away, therefore, from this God-provided source of blessing would render their salvation an impossibility.

But Isaac did not die ; might not Abraham have expected that it would be so ?

He had not the slightest ground of hope for his release ; and as Isaac was his heir, he had already counted upon his resurrection, in order to his inheriting the promises. Abraham really offered up his son. He had bound him on the altar, and taken his knife, and in a few seconds the great artery would have been severed, and life would have ceased. It was at that moment that the angel arrested his hand, and declared that by his faith God was honoured. Isaac did not die ; but a ram caught in a thicket did, and from the altar he received him back in a figure. The promise was then given absolutely, and was not to hang upon another contingency. God "sware by Himself, saying, surely blessing I will bless thee, and multiplying I will multiply thee. And so," *i.e.,* in this way, "after he had patiently endured, he obtained the promise." And the lesson Paul wishes to teach these Hebrews is, that only by enduring faith in a crucified and risen Jesus could eternal life be secured to them.

18–20. What are these "two immutable things" in which believers have such strong consolation ?

The throne and priesthood of the Christ, through whom salvation and blessing is secured to all who believe in Him. Abraham had seen these things typified in Melchisedec, and had confessed him as a representative of the Messiah, by giving tithes of all he possessed. The bread and wine received in return were symbols of kingly and priestly blessing, and prepared Abraham for those daring acts of faith by which he became afterward so distinguished. And as God, who cannot lie, promised with an oath that His Son the Messiah should have a Melchisedec priesthood, the apostle claims it to have been fulfilled, and to have become the basis of their hope.

" *Which entereth into that within the veil.*" *What does this mean?*

He means that as Christ had entered into the glory, so had He become their hope, and His promise of the same glory was the anchor of their soul. Their hope, therefore, was within the veil.

CHAPTER VII.

May this discourse about Melchisedec be called milk, or strong meat?

In chapter v. he had shown that they were babes, *i.e.*, unskilled ones, because needing milk, *i.e.*, instruction in first principles about Christ, when they ought to have been teachers ; we may therefore conclude that it is milk, and not strong meat, which is given in this discourse. No doubt it is a privilege to learn how much instruction is contained in such an Old Testament narrative, but it is only such as we might have heard from Paul when reasoning with the Jews in their synagogues. It is sad that he should have to present such reasoning to these Hebrews as is given in this chapter, when they should have been prepared for higher truth. No doubt we have lost some valuable teaching even about Melchisedec which Paul could have given, had they only been prepared for it. He tells them that he had many things to say about him which were hard to be understood, because they were dull of hearing, and therefore not prepared to receive it. So in their dulness he has to show them that Christ fills up the order of Melchisedec, instead of showing the exalted privileges which believers have in their exalted kingly Priest.

Is it possible for persons now to be like these Hebrews, and fit only for milk?

One fears that there are many who, through their sluggishness, know only an historical Christ. They are acquainted with the facts of His birth, baptism, miracles, trial, death, resurrection, and ascension to glory, and that is about as far as they can go. Upon these matters they preach, and teach, and write, and sing ; but of the new life in Christ, of being risen with Christ, of being in the new creation, and being accepted in the beloved, they seem to know very little. There are, no doubt, on that earth side of the sepulchre many things done for us which are truly wonderful ; but, on the heaven side of it, there are things to be enjoyed in union with an exalted Saviour that are more wonderful still, and of these things many professed teachers know nothing.

1, 2. *In what did the Melchisedec priesthood differ from that of Aaron?*

Aaron was only a priest. Melchisedec was both king and priest. By name he was king of righteousness, by rule he was king of Salem, and priest of the Most High God. Again, in the Levitical priesthood, of which Aaron was the first, the right of succession belonged to the son, but the right of succession to the Melchisedec priesthood was given to Him whom God seated in royal power at His right hand; and for Him it waited all through the ages. Again, the sphere of the Aaronic priesthood was first in the tabernacle, and then in the temple, and for the fleshly seed of Abraham only could he minister. And when the temple was destroyed, and not a stone left upon a stone, his sphere of service was broken up—was indeed mercifully, though abruptly, terminated, because the true and rightful successor to Melchisedec had been installed into office; not on earth, but at God's right hand; not for one nation only, but to minister for all who receive Him, as their Lord and Saviour.

3. *" Without father, without mother," etc. How could this be ?*

The writer is not speaking of his natural descent, but of his priestly standing. It is the priesthood that is in question, not fleshly descent. Aaron was made a priest because he was the son of Levi, and at death his garments were put upon Eleazer, his son and successor in the priestly office. But it was not so with Melchisedec, whose priesthood takes precedence of Aaron's. From no priestly father did he receive office, but from God, whose priest he became; and to no son did he resign his commission, but left it for Him to whom it was promised; and in due time the unbroken order was resumed and perfected in Christ.

4. *" Now consider how great this man was." Why does he refer to Abraham's acknowledgment of the greatness of Melchisedec ?*

Possibly to break up that vain trust which they had placed in Abraham, and which was manifestly dividing their interest. If their father Abraham owned the superior official standing of Melchisedec—and it was only in position that he was greater

2 E

—surely his children should be prepared to accept Christ, of whom Melchisedec was but a type. Abraham was returning from the slaughter of the kings when Melchisedec met him, but the priest of God was acknowledged and blessing received.

5–7. *Why should the giving of tithes indicate inferiority in the giver ?*

It is an acknowledgment of an inferior position, and the reception of blessing is an indication that he who blesses is superior. So that Abraham, and Levi in Abraham, owned that Melchisedec was higher in standing than themselves.

8. *" Of whom it is witnessed that he liveth." If this is spoken of Melchisedec, how did he live through the ages until Christ ?*

On the principle that the king never dies, because there is one to succeed him. In Melchisedec God founded an order which was to be perpetuated in and by Christ his successor, so that as a priest the Melchisedec priesthood lives in Jesus, or as Paul states, " it is witnessed that he liveth."

11–13. *The imperfection of the Levitical priesthood is here implied. In what was it imperfect ?*

In being (1.) a priesthood without governmental power, and therefore it was set aside for that higher and royal priesthood; (2.) in pertaining only to the flesh, and could not perfect the conscience of the guilty. A better priesthood therefore was needed, and was introduced by God in His Son.

19–23. *" For the law made nothing perfect." Why did God ordain such an imperfect system ?*

The law was not imperfect, it was holy, and just, and good. Paul does not say that it was imperfect, but that it made nothing perfect. It was a system of types, shadows, and figures of good things to come, and as such was perfect. But when the substance had come, and the Jews wished to dwell among the shadows, then the folly of such a course had to be shown, and this is done by an exposition of the nature and design of the whole institution. When Paul speaks of the weakness and un-profitableness of the law, it is no re-flection upon God who does all in wisdom, but upon those who per-verted His arrangements. The law, the priesthood, the covenant, were all that God wished them to be, but when used by the Jews to fulfil some intention of their own, then failure was inevitable. Had they looked through the law to the Gospel, and through the imperfect dying priest to Him who continued ever, there would have been no necessity for such an exposition as Paul has here given. It was their folly that called forth such a rebuke.

CHAPTER VIII.

1. *" Now of the things which we have spoken this is the sum." Is the writer bringing his argument to a close ?*

After stating the facts concerning Melchisedec, he is now prepared to affirm, " We have such a High Priest,"—*i.e.*, we have one who is like Melchisedec — both king and priest. Or as stated by Zechariah (vi. 13), " He shall be a priest upon his throne : and the counsel of peace shall be between them both,"—*i.e.*, the throne and the priesthood were to combine in this new administra-tion.

2. *What does he mean by the " sanctuary, and the true tabernacle," of which Jesus was a minister ?*

Facts will best explain his mean-ing. The holy place of the taber-nacle where the priests worshipped, was a type of the Church over which

Jesus our High Priest now presides, while the most Holy—*lit.*, the Holies of Holies — into which the High Priest entered once a year with blood, was a type of heaven, in which Jesus now dwells. He is a minister of the Holies—*i.e.*, heaven—and of the true tabernacle,—the church on earth.

What does a " minister" here mean ?

It is, *lit.*, a public serving one— *i.e.*, one serving those who are re-lated to his position. Christ Jesus, though in heaven, is now serving the saints on earth, both as their kingly Priest and Mediator.

4. *Why could he not be a priest on earth ?*

Because there were priests divinely appointed for that carnal service. But one being required for the higher spiritual ministry, He was appointed to that which was more excellent, and to heaven where He ministers for the spiritual priesthood.

5. *" According to the pattern showed to thee in the mount." Why does he quote this statement ?*

He had just stated that the insti-tution was a " shadow of heavenly things," and here he recalls their attention to the word *pattern* as sup-porting this statement, and applies it to the whole institution.

6. *Of this " better covenant" Jesus is said to be " the Mediator." What does He do as mediator ?*

A mediator is one who interposes between parties sustaining a certain relation to each other, and who pre-vents the breaking up of that rela-tion, when failure might justly have caused it. Now this is what Jesus has done on behalf of the priestly family, over whom He so graciously presides. But in order to feel the force of this reference to Him as mediator, we must refer to the event upon which it is based, which, though not stated here, was well known to these Hebrews, and is thus recalled to their remembrance. When their fathers accepted the blood-sealed covenant at Sinai, and were formed into a nation, and while Moses was in the mount receiving all necessary instruction for the tabernacle, etc., they made a molten calf, and worshipped it as their deliverer from Egypt. By this act of disobedience their position was forfeited, and their sin called for either their removal or the allowance of a mediator. At first God threatened to remove them, and make of Moses a great nation; but this he refused, and became instead their mediator, and was allowed to go before them, though assured by God, " In the day when I visit, I will visit their sin upon them," *i.e.*, their personal or national sin shall bring judgment upon them, although as a nation they shall not be removed until the end be accomplished (see Exod. xxxii.). Now, in this transaction we have an illustration of the mediatorial work of Christ. As believers in Him we have been delivered from bondage, brought into the new covenant, and made the children of God by the faith in Jesus; but unless God can mercifully deal with the failure of His children, and by some proper arrangement can forgive and secure the true spirit of obedience, His purpose must have been frustrated. This end, however, He has provided for in making Jesus a mediator, as well as a Priest and Lord. Through Him, therefore, failure under the New Covenant is forgiven, when the required conditions are met. So John in his First Epistle teaches, " My little children, these things write I unto you, that ye sin not. And if any man sin, we have an advocate with the Father, Jesus Christ the righteous." From this we learn that He is mediator in relation to the failure of the saints, and but for this gracious help we could not

gain the glory. We are exhorted to sin not, but should we sin we shall be forgiven upon confessing and forsaking it through Jesus our mediator, or advocate, or intercessor, all of which terms are employed to set forth this aspect of His ever-blessed work.

7–10. What is a covenant?

A covenant is a fixed institution or arrangement of God, and designed by Him for the protection and benefit of all who become the subjects of it. Not only are the claims of God set forth in it, but also the privileges secured to all who accept it, as well as the penalties which must follow either unfaithfulness or rejection of it. Paul here refers, not only to the covenant which God made with their fathers, when He took them by the hand, but also to that which He promised to make, and which by the Gospel should be written on the hearts of all who received it. By the introduction of this new covenant the former is made old, and must therefore vanish away.

" *With the house of Israel and with the house of Judah.*" *When did God make it with both?*

When it was proclaimed by the apostles at Pentecost, and was then accepted by many from Parthia, Elam, Mesopotamia, etc., and who were doubtless out of all the tribes of Israel, as well as those of Judah. Indeed James, when addressing his letter to them afterwards, speaks to them as the " twelve tribes," *i.e.*, persons out of all these tribes, and owns them as his brethren in " the faith of our Lord Jesus Christ." This covenant was formulated while Jesus was on earth, and after being sealed with His blood, was in due time proclaimed in His name, and entered by those who believed in Him.

What was the essential difference between these two covenants?

While both covenants were made by God, both sealed with blood, both entered by birth, both secured privileges to the obedient, both threatened judgment on transgressors, and both were for the age in which they were given; yet in the nature of these things there was a wide difference. God prepared them for the old covenant in taking them by the hand, i.e., delivering them from Egypt by power, but for the new by the Gospel, and thus writing it on their hearts. The former was sealed by the blood of bulls and goats, the latter by the blood of His Son. The birth into the Old Covenant was a birth of the flesh, the birth into the New was of water and the Spirit. The privileges under the former were the good things of the life that now is; the privileges of the latter not only the life that now is, but also that which is to come. That covenant waxed old, and was ready to vanish away; this will issue in immortality.

11. *"For all shall know me, from the least to the greatest." Is this prophetic of the future condition of the world?*

No; it is the condition of those who are under the New Covenant, and began as soon as Christ was received through the Gospel. All such knew Him by the Gospel of His grace. The Jewish child entered into the Old Covenant by its birth of Jewish parents, and had to be instructed afterward; while the believer learns concerning God by the truth through which he enters.

CHAPTER IX.

1. *Did the tabernacle and its service belong to the first covenant?*

The covenant seems to have included the entire Jewish ritual; the pattern of it being given to Moses before the covenant was broken by the people, and was all designed to set forth Christ and His people in Him. There are also many aspects of worship and privilege provided for Christians, which are shadowed forth in those " ordinances of divine service."

Is there not much precious truth to be learned from Paul's teaching about the tabernacle, and ought we not to be thankful for the instruction he has given?

There is no doubt as to its preciousness, or our indebtedness for the lessons received; but it is very sad to think that after he had been preaching the Gospel for at least twenty years, and proving by signs and wonders and gifts of the Holy Spirit, that sinners could be saved by Christ without the deeds of the law, that he should have had to write a letter to these Hebrews to prove that the institution around which their hearts were clinging so tenaciously, was after all but a shadow or pattern of the good things to come. The fact that he is compelled to do so is, to say the least, very suspicious.

But as there are lessons of instruction that have come out of their dulness of apprehension, is not the gain a great advantage to us?

No doubt we gain instruction from their lingering about the " mount that might be touched," though with death; but how much more should we have gained had they been prepared for the things " of which we cannot now speak particularly,"—things they might have heard had they not been dull of hearing? The lessons of instruction were in the things referred to, but these scholars were not ready for them, and so the instruction could not be given.

2. *" For there was a tabernacle made; the first wherein was the candlestick," etc. What does this first mean?*

The first part of the tabernacle, the holy place, and beyond which there was the Holies of Holies, or the most Holy; each of them being a type of spiritual and heavenly things, and each having its furniture corresponding thereto.

Of what is this first part of the tabernacle, with its furniture and worshippers a type?

Of the Church, the spiritual priesthood, worshipping and serving in Christ. They have the lamp of His word, and in its light they worship; and also a table on which are the memorials of His life and death, who is their spiritual food; and they have also an altar, even the name of Jesus, on which they can offer all their sacrifices with acceptance.

3. *Of what is the second part, the Holies of Holies, a type?*

Of heaven, where Jesus, the true ark of the covenant, now is.

4. *What is shadowed forth by the "golden censer"?*

The censer was filled with coals from the golden altar, and incense sprinkled upon it, and was then carried by the High Priest into the Holies of Holies, and is a most impressive illustration of Jesus entering into heaven with the sweet savour of His own life and death on earth; and also of the prayers of saints when offered in His name.

What do the "golden pot that had manna, and Aaron's rod that budded, and the tables of the covenant" represent?

As all these things stood related to the pilgrim life of the children of Israel, so Christ is shadowed forth by them in His relation to the pilgrim life of the believer. As the manna which fell every day—and of which an omer was put into the ark—was their food, so Christ, the daily food of the Church by the truth, is in heaven. As the quickened rod of Aaron, which budded, blos-

somed, and brought forth almonds, silenced the murmurings of the congregation with respect to the man of God's choice; so the resurrection of Jesus out from among dead ones, has for ever settled the question of God's glorified and chosen High Priest. The tables of the covenant laid up in the ark, under the mercy seat, the place of rule and favour, teach that in Christ, the true ark of the covenant, both authority and mercy are combined.

5. *What do the cherubims on the mercy-seat represent?*

They are symbols of redeemed humanity made one with Christ in glory, and as they owe their glorification to Him, so they look down upon Him with adoring gratitude.

7. *"But into the second went the High Priest alone once every year, not without blood." Why refer to the High Priest entering the Holies?*

It is well to note here that while the apostle states these facts concerning the priest, it was not so much to illustrate the work of Christ, as to show the deficiency of the Aaronic priesthood. The High Priest entered once a year, but could not remain there. Then the blood which he carried in had been shed for himself as well as others, thus marking the imperfection, both of himself and his work.

8. *Since the High Priest entered with blood "into the holiest of all," why does he say that the way was not yet manifest?*

It was manifest for him, but for no one else. How any other person could enter into the anti-typical heaven, was never learned from that tabernacle service. The priestly family were brought into the holiest, but beyond it they could not advance. Here was another mark of its imperfection.

9. *If the gifts and sacrifices offered in connection with the tabernacle did*

not perfect the worshipper, why did God appoint them to be offered?

They did "sanctify to the purifying of the flesh," and this was all God intended them to do. These animal sacrifices could never purge the conscience, and were never designed for this purpose. It was therefore a sad mistake to continue their use, when the conscience-cleansing blood of Christ had been shed. It was because of this divine provision which was made for man's need, that the institution had become unprofitable, and this the apostle was trying to teach them.

14. *"Christ, who through the eternal Spirit, offered Himself without spot to God." What does this mean?*

That all the revelations given by the Spirit during that age, whether in testimony, prophecy, type, or illustration, had all been met and fulfilled by Christ. Or, in other words, the Holy Spirit had written beforehand the life, sufferings, and death of Jesus, and He in due time fulfilled them all, and thus offered Himself without spot—*i.e.*, without failure—to God.

15. *"For this cause He is the Mediator of the New Testament." What cause?*

That by preserving the believer in his priestly standing, when through failure it might be forfeited, He might purge the conscience from dead works, and maintain in him a life of loving obedience.

"That by means of death." Whose death?

The death of Christ. It would be better to read, *death having taken place for redemption of transgressions under the first covenant*, etc., *i.e.*, Christ having died, those who sinned under the first covenant might through believing in Him be forgiven, and receive the promise of the ever-abiding inheritance.

"Under the first testament." Why is it rendered "testament" instead of covenant?

There is no just reason why it should be so rendered. *Diatheke*, which in this chapter is rendered six times by testament, is in many other places rendered covenant, and should have been so rendered here. Paul's reference to men who make a *Diatheke* or covenant, or what we now call a will, is not sufficient to change the rendering, since in principle a man's covenant is the same as God's. It is his arrangement of the things over which he has power, and, when his death has taken place, it must become an administration to all who are interested, and be accepted or rejected by them.

16–20. *"For where a testament is, there must also of necessity be the death of the testator." Why must there be the death of the testator?*

It pleased God to make a covenant or arrangement for blessing consequent upon the death of His Son, so that the Old Covenant which prefigured it, must be sealed with blood, which, to be in harmony with its material character, was that of bulls and goats, and the covenant of a man, which is referred to as illustrating it, could only be administered after his death. There must therefore be the death of the covenanter, before there could be an administration of his effects. This is true of men, and also of God, whose New Covenant had been sealed with the blood of Christ.

21, 22. *Is sprinkling with blood, and purging with blood, the same thing?*

No. Sprinkling was the act of Moses when consecrating the covenant, purging or purifying was the effect.

26. *What is meant by "the end of the world"?*

It is, *lit., upon the consummation*

of the ages, and possibly refers to the prophecy of Daniel (ix. 26), where it is stated, that after sixty-nine hebdomads or weeks of years, the Messiah would be cut off, but not for Himself. At this specified time Jesus did appear to put away sin by the sacrifice of Himself.

Did He put away sin unconditionally?

No. In addition to His own life being given for sin, that it might be put away, the Gospel reveals the requirement of faith, or acceptance of Him by all from whom the charge of sin is removed. The statement here can only be intelligently read in the light of the Gospel proclamation, or the commission of the Lord Jesus.

27. *Why does he bring forward the fact of God appointing men "once to die," to prove the sufficiency of the one offering of Christ?*

It is important to notice that whilst in some things the priest was a type of Christ, in others he was a striking contrast. He had just stated that the High Priest had to offer a victim every year when he entered into the holy place, but that Jesus, by one offering of Himself, secured an abiding place in heaven, and His sacrifice once for all procured salvation for all who believe in Him. Then to sustain the equity of Christ being but once offered, he affirms that men die but once as the effect of Adam's sin. The judgment that follows will be upon their own sin, in rejecting the Christ.

CHAPTER X.

1. *"For the law having a shadow of good things to come." Do these good things belong to the Christian age, or to the yet future state?*

The word *mellonta,* rendered here by "things to come," occurs ten times in this epistle, and in nearly all these places points to the Christian economy. It is from the region of shadows and patterns that Paul looks towards the good things brought in by Christ. The shadows of things in that Jewish age, whether of Christ or the saints, were all fulfilled in the Christian administration, while those things which are yet future to believers are to be learned from Christ and His apostles.

Did not the continual offering of sacrifices show the faith of the worshippers?

Yes; but it also showed the inefficacy of the things offered. Had the sacrifices been equal to their need, they would not have required repetition.

4. *Paul here says, "For it is not possible that the blood of bulls and goats should take away sins;" while Moses (Levit. iv. 32–35) says, The man who brought his sin-offering for atonement should have his sin forgiven. How can these diverse statements be reconciled?*

The statements are not diverse, as both are true. The blood of animals could not take away sin, but God, who directed these offerings to be made for offences against the law, could forgive those who obeyed His command. The appointed offerings, while specially connected with the institution, and offered in relation to offences committed under it, were also a medium through which they could look to the coming Messiah, and all who did so obtained acceptance through Him.

5–10. *Why does he refer to the 40th Psalm?*

To show that the sacrifices and offerings under the law failed to satisfy God, and that their removal was anticipated when He who had the prepared body should be here to say, "Lo, I come" (in the volume of the book it is written of me) " to do Thy will, O God." Then Paul adds, " He taketh away the first " (the offerings under the law) " that He might establish the second " (the sacrifice of Jesus once offered) for acceptable worship. The first could not perfect the worshipper, while the second will or arrangement sanctifies those who through it draw nigh to God.

11, 12. *The earthly priest stood to minister, while the heavenly priest sat down. Why does he take note of posture ?*

Posture evidently indicated the character of the work of both. There was no seat provided for the priest in the tabernacle, which plainly intimated that he could not abide there, while Jesus, after offering one sacrifice for sins, sat down at God's right hand.

13. *" From hence expecting till His enemies be made His footstool " (Ps. cx. 1). Why quote this psalm to these Hebrews ?*

To show that the Christ-rejecters of that nation, to whom special reference is made here, would have to be put in this humiliating position. Time did prove their persistent rejection of Christ, and in that final overthrow of Jerusalem they were put under His feet. They saw, indeed, in that overthrow, what they had so often scoffingly asked for, " the sign of the Son of man in heaven."

15–18. *Why does Paul quote the testimony of the Spirit in relation to the New Covenant ?*

To show from one item of it how superior is the result of the offering of Christ to that of the offerings under the law. They only brought sin to remembrance ; while under the Gospel sin, when forgiven, was not to be remembered by God any more: thus proving that sin so removed did not require another offering.

How can God cease to remember sin ?

He can treat the forgiven one as if he had never sinned, and this is what is meant by not remembering sin.

19. *" Having, therefore, brethren, boldness to enter." What does this imply ?*

The privilege of access to God, through the once - offered life of Jesus.

20. *" By a new and living way." What does this mean ?*

The old way of access was through dead victims, but the way opened to believers is through a living Christ. The rending of the veil— that is to say, His flesh—has opened a new way to God ; for He, being raised from death, now invites us to draw nigh through Himself.

22. *What is this " assurance of faith " in which they were to draw nigh ?*

It is the assurance of believed testimony respecting their acceptance.

How can the heart be sprinkled from an evil conscience ?

It can be *cleansed* from an evil conscience, and this is what Paul means. He is speaking of spiritual privileges in language connected with the outer court of the tabernacle, with which every Jew was familiar. Sprinkling with blood seven times for cleansing the unclean, and bathing with water at the laver, were every-day occurrences in that old economy ; and in the language of these shadows he is now speaking of spiritual things. A heart sprinkled from an evil conscience, and the body washed with pure water, are only symbols of faith and immersion into Christ. It is the facts which prove the meaning of the types.

23. *Why does he exhort, " Let us hold fast the profession of our faith" ?*

It is, *lit., the confession of the hope.* The hope was glory and immortality through Christ, and to possess these a believing confession of Him was demanded. This confession had been made both by the writer and the persons addressed, and now he urges, Let us hold fast, or firm, this confession. Two things are implied in this exhortation : (1.) That the hope promised by God was true, since He was faithful ; and (2.) that there was a tendency to apostatise from Christ, even among those who had once confessed Him as the Son of God. Now it is to prevent the apostacy that the instruction and warnings of the epistle are given.

23. *" Not forsaking the assembling of yourselves together." What was the purport of this meeting ?*

It was the "breaking of bread" doubtless ; for this ordinance being appointed by Christ to be attended to by His disciples upon the first day of the week, they could not be true to Him without meeting for this purpose. But in doing this they stood committed to the great facts of the Gospel, and this was becoming a very serious test. The great body of the Jewish nation denied these facts, and persecuted their brethren who believed them to be true. Hence this pressure was felt, and some were holding back from this feast of the Lord. Paul here exhorts them not to so neglect, but to stir up each other in view of the approaching day.

What day was this ?

The day of judgment upon the nation, which was then not far off. It was indeed approaching, and their faith in Christ, or doubt concerning Him, would materially affect their destiny.

26. *Why should the case of those who " sin wilfully " be so hopeless ?*

It could not be otherwise. There is but one sacrifice accepted for sin, and but one Saviour appointed by God, and to turn from Him entails nothing but judgment and fiery indignation, which shall devour all who thus offend. To the Christ-rejecting Jew there is no hope. God can only show mercy through Jesus, and when He is despised, which is implied in sinning wilfully, nothing but judgment remains.

Does this fearful testimony apply to Gentiles as well as Jews ?

There is a wide difference between a Jew who denies God's beloved Son and a Gentile who falls into sin. The latter, possibly, will not have denied the Christ, but only proved unfaithful, and may avail himself of provided forgiveness.

28. *Why does he refer to the hopeless condition of the convicted despiser of Moses' law ?*

Simply to show how certain must be the doom of those who despise One greater than Moses.

32–34. *These Hebrews acted a noble part in the beginning of their Christian course. Why did Paul fear their apostasy ?*

Their withdrawal from the assembly excited his fear, and to him it was the beginning of their sad end. Their sacrifices for Christ at first were all that could be desired, but these were followed by temptations, to which they were beginning to yield. Their fathers made a noble exit from Egypt, but afterwards fell in the wilderness, and he warns them against a like result in sinning against Christ.

35. *Is " cast not away therefore your confidence," etc., an effort to prevent this ?*

Yes ; and his exhortations and instructions are wisely blended. The recompense is sure and great, but patience is needed. The Coming One is faithful, but the just live—*i.e.,* continue—by faith. To draw back

—*lit.*, shrink back—is to fall into perdition, and to save the soul there must be abiding confidence. Such are his instructive appeals at the close of this part of his argument.

CHAPTER XI.

1. *" Now faith is the substance of things hoped for."* How can faith be the substance of the things referred to ?

It is rather strange that Dean Alford, and other recent translators, should have given us exposition rather than a translation of this first verse. They evidently assumed —though without any just reason— that Paul was giving a definition of faith, and accordingly have written, *Now faith is the confidence of things hoped for ;* which is no more than saying, Now faith is believing—a statement Paul was not likely to make. Besides, this statement completely hides his thought, not only in this verse, but through the entire chapter. He is evidently using the word "faith," by metonymy, for testimony, and this should be clearly seen in order to feel the force of his statements. The apostle is looking for glory, life, and immortality, and he here shows why he does so. Now faith—*i.e.*, the believed testimony of God—is the substance (or that which stands under, or is the basis) of the things hoped for, the evidence—*lit.*, the conviction—of things not seen. Paul's affirmations are both simple and instructive, and it would be a loss to have them hidden from our view. What he really says is, We hope for these things, and the testimony of God is the ground upon which our hope is resting ; and although we have not seen them, we are assured of them by His Word.

2. *" For by it the elders obtained a good report."* Who are these elders?

and by what did they obtain this report ?

These elders are Abel, Enoch, Noah, etc., who, by believing God's testimony, and by their faithful action, obtained His attestation.

3. *" Through faith we understand that the worlds were framed,"* etc. Does he refer to the universe ?

No ; it is, *lit.*, By faith (in God's testimony) *we apprehend that the ages were adjusted by a declaration of God.* So that it is not of the framing of worlds that Paul is writing, but of the ages in which Jesus and the dispensation of grace were shadowed forth. We get the same truth in chap. i. 2 : " By whom also He made the worlds "—*lit.*, the ages. The Christian economy was after a plan of the ages, and not of things then appearing—*i.e.*, of that institution —and as this plan was given into their keeping during the ages, they should have been prepared for its working out in the appointed time.

The persons who are named in this chapter are all said to have distinguished themselves by faith. Is testimony always implied when faith is named ?

Without testimony they could not have believed. We must, therefore, in reading mentally supply this fact, that in every instance God's testimony preceded their faith. God testified, and they believed, and acted according to His testimony. Thus we might read : By faith—in God's testimony — Abel offered a more excellent sacrifice than Cain ; and Enoch walked with God ; and Noah built the ark, etc. To all these persons something was declared or promised, and called forth action in conformity with the promise made by God.

Do these three cases typify any aspects of truth which are embodied in Christianity ?

Since what was written aforetime was for our instruction, we may expect to find it even thus early in the world's history. Hence, in Abel we have an illustration of present acceptance through faith; in Enoch of glorification; and in Noah of deliverance out of judgment. These truths are continually set before us in the teachings of the new covenant, and we are not surprised to find illustrations of them, even in the Book of Genesis, which has been not unfitly termed "the seed-bed of the dispensations." That is to say, there is hardly a truth made known in the Gospel that has not been illustrated in this first book of the ways of God with men.

8. *Abraham is the next on Paul's list, which includes many others distinguished by their faith. Why give such an epitome to these Hebrews?*

The reason is a very important one, and should be clearly understood in order to feel the force of these examples. He had shown them distinctly that it was only through faith and patience that they would inherit the promises, and here he brings forward these cases to sustain his statements. Each of these persons named had received God's testimony, which contained His promise, and which only could be reached by enduring faith. Now by their faith God was honoured, and though not permitted to see Christ, the object of their faith and hope—that privilege being reserved for a future generation—yet they became examples to all who would seek through Him the promised glory.

9, 10. *Why did Abraham sojourn in the land of promise instead of possessing it?*

It was promised to him before he left Mesopotamia, but as he went with his father to Haran, instead of obeying God, he lost the promise, as stated by Stephen (Acts vii. 2–5), and when he did arrive in Canaan, he had to learn that it would then be given to his seed. Ultimately, however, he became a sojourner in that land, and waited the fulfilment of the promise as declared to him.

Why did he not return when he found it was lost for personal possession?

In verse 15 Paul says that "they" (both Abraham, Isaac, and Jacob) might have returned to the country from whence they came out, but learning that the land was typical of a better inheritance, they voluntarily became types of that pilgrim life, which those should afterward lead, who through faith in Jesus should become heirs of the heavenly country. The object of Paul in thus bringing before these Hebrews the sojourning of Abraham in the typical land of promise, was to help them to hold fast the position to which they had been called by Christ, and of which Abraham in faith so nobly became a type or illustration.

11. *Did Sarah receive strength to conceive seed through her faith?*

Yes, she received strength from God, whose promise she believed, when there was no human probability of having a child; and thus from Abraham, who had become as dead, there sprung this innumerable multitude of the nation of the Jews.

13. *"These all died in faith, not having received the promises." What were these unfulfilled promises?*

The things by which the Christian economy has been so signally distinguished, viz., the coming of Christ, and the nations being blessed in Him. Neither of these promises were fulfilled during their lifetime, nor were they expected: they saw them afar off, and embraced—*lit.*, greeted—them as the promises of a faithful God; and confessed that they were strangers and pilgrims on the earth. Such indeed was the confession of

Abraham before the sons of Heth (Gen. xxiii. 3, 4), when asking them to entreat with Ephron the Hittite to sell to him the cave of Machpelah.

Ephron offered to give him the field and the cave therein; why did he refuse this generous gift?

In the spirit of true submission to God. God would not give him even so much as a foot-breadth, and therefore being denied by Him, he would not become an inheritor through man. The weighing of the silver, and obtaining the pledges of purchase, were sacred things to Abraham, because thereby he endorsed the decision of God.

17. *" By faith Abraham, when he was tried, offered up Isaac." In what did the trial consist?*

In being called to offer up Isaac, he had either to question the promise made to him, or believe that God would raise him from the dead. In offering him up he counted God faithful, and able to raise him from from death; and though Isaac did not die, yet in receiving him from the altar, he received him in a figure —*lit.*, in a parable—*i.e.*, he was so instructed by what he saw, that the day of Christ was unveiled to him, and in joy he looked forward to his appearing.

20. *Isaac, Jacob, Joseph, Moses, Rahab, etc., are said to have distinguished themselves " by faith." Had all these persons received a testimony from God?*

Yes, either directly or indirectly the testimony of God concerning Christ was made known to them. And as His coming into the world to establish a reign of blessing was to be through them to the peoples or nations in it, those who understood and appreciated this high mission, were led to do those remarkable things which are here recorded.

In what way did Isaac show his faith in God's testimony?

To him and to his seed God confirmed the promise made to Abraham, and believing this promise he prophetically blessed his two sons— Jacob, as heir of the Messianic promises, and Esau as heir of worldly possessions.

21. *Jacob blessed both the sons of Joseph when dying. How did this show his faith?*

By this act of blessing the sons of Joseph as he was a dying, Jacob gave them a place as head of tribes in the nation that was being formed. Joseph, who had become as dead to his father, was set aside, but his two sons were incorporated in his stead, so that Jacob really got increase, through him that was separated from his brethren, in the " ten thousands of Ephraim, and the thousands of Manasseh " (Deut. xxxiii. 16, 17). This incident is not without instruction to those who care to follow it. " For whatsoever things were written aforetime were written for our learning." Jesus was indeed separated by His brethren, but who can number the increase that has followed to God's family by that cruel separation?

" By faith Jacob . . . worshipped, leaning upon the top of his staff." Why refer to his staff?

The staff seems to have been taken with him during all his wanderings, and to have been to him a symbol of his need and dependence on One greater than himself. At his first halting-place for the night, when leaving his father's home, and while sleeping with a stone for a pillow, he had a dream, and saw the ladder which reached from earth to heaven, and the angels ascending and descending upon it, and above it stood the Lord, the God of Abraham. It was a wondrous sight granted to the lonely traveller, but more wondrous still the message he received. The promise which had been given to Abraham by oath, and confirmed unto Isaac, was also given unto him, that through his Seed all the families of the earth should be blessed. Jacob must have left that hallowed spot with feelings of wondering inquiry how such a thing could be, since between the staff, the only thing he possessed, and the promise he had just received, which embraced the whole human family, there was a striking contrast. Twenty years after, when returning from Padan-aram with wives and children, flocks and herds, and when invoking protection from God against Esau his brother, the staff is again brought into view. God had done much for him during his struggles in a strange land, and he feels that he owes his success to Him, and not to himself. "I am not worthy of the least of all the mercies, and of all the truth, which Thou hast showed unto Thy servant; for with my *staff* I passed over this Jordan; and now I am become two bands" (Gen. xxxii. 10). The staff was remembered, and the fulfilment of the promise had already begun. Then in Egypt, when the time came that he must die, the promise of God had developed much further, and the heads of tribes were being formed, with Ephraim and Manasseh joined to them. No wonder that Jacob worshipped, *i.e.*, adored the God of Israel, but he bowed himself upon the top of his staff. Jacob kept his staff to remind both himself and his seed what he was, and what God Himself had done.

22. *Had Joseph received any testimony concerning their departure from Egypt?*

He knew that God had promised to their fathers that their seed should inherit Canaan, and such was his confidence that He would fulfil His promise, that he commanded his bones to be kept in Egypt until they were called out of it. Yes, by faith in God's word, he assured them that He would bring them out of it.

23. *Had the parents of Moses any testimony from God respecting Moses as a deliverer?*

Most certainly, or how could they have acted in faith. They saw that he was a proper child, and hid him for God. So it was with Moses himself, and all that are named in this chapter. It was by faith in God's promise concerning the coming Messiah that they were strong and did exploits. Even Gideon and Barak, Samson and David, by delivering the people, became types of the higher deliverances to be effected by the woman's conquering Seed.

35. *Is the "better resurrection," which some sought, a contrast with that of the unsaved at the last day?*

Not at all. If we read *but* instead of "and," the intended contrast will then be seen. (Some) women received their dead raised to life again, *but* others were tortured, not accepting deliverance, that they might obtain a better resurrection. A resurrection to eternal life would indeed be *better* than mere temporal deliverance. And while we have not been made acquainted with the facts, it is evident that suffering saints of that period had not only knowledge of the resurrection to glory, but preferred to wait for it as their highest privilege rather than dishonour God.

40. "*God having provided some better thing for us.*" What was this better thing?

The fulfilment of the promise which they believed, and in the faith of which they died. Their faith is perfected or completed in our possession of Christ, and in the salvation promised to the nations through Him.

———

CHAPTER XII.

1. *" Wherefore seeing we also are compassed about with so great a cloud of witnesses." Were these witnesses visible or invisible ?*

Not invisible, as many presume, and for which thought there is no foundation in either the verse or its context, but visible spectators of those running in the Christian race. All the persons named in the previous chapter had to evince their faith in the presence of others—Abel before his brother, Enoch before those living around him, and Noah before the world. In fact, the persons named had to show their faith before a scoffing world, and " others had trials of cruel mockings and scourgings, yea, moreover, of bonds and imprisonments." "Wherefore seeing *we also* are compassed about," *i.e.*, people are looking at us as men looked at them.

Who were this cloud of witnesses ?

Their own Jewish brethren, who no doubt were jealously watching them, as the eager spectators of a race-course, and hoping to see a defeat of their Christian purpose, by means of Judaising teachers employed against them.

What is the difference between the " weight" and the " sin which easily beset them," both of which were to be laid aside ?

A weight is anything that would hinder the speed of the runner, while sin is a positive stepping aside from the right way. Their persistent clinging to the Old Covenant was a weight in their Christian race ; for whilst holding to the law they could not be perfected through Christ. Then the sin which so easily beset them was unbelief—a tendency to doubt the supplanting of the law of Moses by the Gospel of Christ.

Do Gentile believers need these exhortations ?

We are not surrounded by the same circumstances, but there are others equally dangerous, so that we need both watchfulness and self-denial.

" Let us run with patience the race." Does this mean mere quietude of spirit ?

It is very important to maintain even a " meek and quiet spirit, which is in the sight of God of great price " (1 Peter iii. 4). But *endurance* or *perseverance* would better express the writer's thought than patience. The race is, *lit.*, an *agony* or contest, and therefore perseverance in the truth, or endurance under trial, was necessarily called for in order to a successful issue.

2. *" Looking unto Jesus." Why look to Him ?*

As an example of both endurance and triumph, He " endured the cross, despising the shame, and is set down at the right hand of God."

Why does he call Jesus the " author and finisher of faith " ?

It is, *lit.*, *the chief leader and finisher of the faith,* and is stated to show how superior Jesus is to Moses, who, though he led them out of Egypt, could not bring them into Canaan. Joshua had to be appointed to complete his work. But Jesus, the Captain of salvation, not only leads out from bondage of sin but also into salvation, and will lead into glory, all who follow Him.

4. *" Ye have not yet resisted unto blood, striving against sin." Was this sin in general ?*

It is, *lit.*, *the sin, i.e.*, of apostasy. They had endured a great fight of afflictions, and had suffered the loss of goods after their conversion to Christ ; but the contest was waxing hotter, and life was in danger, and from this trial they were shrinking. Paul would rather they had met the trial boldly, and as their Master had gone to the cross for them, they should have been willing to have yielded their lives also.

5–8. Chastisement appears to be inseparable from Christian life. What is this chastisement to which every child of God must yield ?

If we use the word discipline instead of chastisement, and understand this to be carried on by means of instruction, we shall not only see its simplicity, but admire the divine provision for our spiritual training. God as a Father instructs all His children, and when we yield to His instruction we prove ourselves to be so. Hence subjection to His commands is absolutely necessary to prove our sonship while insubordination to His word, will prove us bastards and not sons.

9. What is meant by " Father of spirits " ?

We can scarcely mistake its meaning, since it is used in contrast with " fathers of our flesh," *i.e.*, our fleshly fathers, through whom we obtained our present fleshly standing as children ; and whose control we acknowledged with reverent submission. And, says Paul, "shall we not much rather be in subjection to the Father of spirits, and live?" Not intending by this that He is the creator of spirits, however true that may be, but that He has become our spiritual Father by the truth, through which we have been begotten and born into His family.

12. " Hands that hang down, and the feeble knees." Is it not sad that such a state of things should be found among the disciples of Jesus ?

Yes, very sad indeed, but it was so then, and has often been so since ; and wherever found, it involves a grave responsibility to meet it in the spirit of the good Samaritan. It is a kind of nurse work, for which there is need in every Christian assembly. The church is at times like an infirmary, where the sick, and lame,

and drooping meet us at every turn. Then is the time to heed this exhortation, " Wherefore lift up the hands which hang down, and the feeble knees ; and make straight paths for your feet, lest that which is lame be turned out of the way ; but let it rather be healed." Here is plenty of work for all who will labour for the Master. To smile and cheer, to soothe and sympathise for Christ's sake, is a needful and blessed work ; and is but a feeble compensation for all He has done for us.

16. Why does he refer to this action of Esau ?

To Esau belonged by birth the right to be in the line from Abraham to Christ, but his estimate of the privilege was so low, that he sold it for a mess of pottage ; and Paul here warns against any having been so foolish as to part with their spiritual birthright for fleshly things.

Had these Jews a spiritual birthright ?

Yes ; they were the firstborn into the kingdom of the God of heaven, and to part with their position, and return to the law of Moses, was to sell their birthright. The Gospel was " to the Jew first, and also to the Greek," but in returning to Judaism, the first became last, and the last first.

Was Esau a fornicator, and profane ?

Yes, he married wives in opposition to God's law, and so became a fornicator. He was also profane, in bartering heavenly for earthly things.

18–21. Why does Paul contrast the two dispensations ?

In order to show the folly of going back from the last to the first, as some of them were doing. Their fathers who saw the introduction of the law, trembled at the sight, and intreated that the blackness, and tempest, and awful words might cease. Even Moses said, " I exceedingly fear and quake." How foolish to think of returning to such a covenant, when a better had been brought in.

22–24. " *But ye are come to Mount Sion.*" *Do the things here contrasted with the Old Covenant belong to the New, or are they yet future ?*

They must be matters of present enjoyment, or how could he say, "ye are come," if they were still future? It is true, that many of these descriptive terms belong primarily to the Jewish economy, but then every careful reader will have noticed that there is scarcely a privilege in the Christian economy that is not described by some term taken from the Mosaic. The type generally furnishes a name for the antitype, while the difference is that of shadow and substance. Hence mount and city, messengers and assembly, the firstborn and the enrolment, the Mediator and the covenant, the blood and the sprinkling, became familiar symbols of higher truths and more blessed facts. Ye are come to Jesus, said Paul : do not go back to Moses.

What is intended by " *Mount Sion,*" " *the city,*" *and* " *the heavenly Jerusalem* " *?*

The Church based upon Jesus. This is expressly stated in the next verse, Ye are come . . . . to the church of first-born ones.

Does not " *general assembly* " *point to the final gathering of the saints in glory ?*

No, because they had not come to that. They had come to the church, into which believers had gathered out of every synagogue, every Jewish sect, and every tribe, and formed one general assembly, just as it is said in Acts ii. 44, " And all that believed were together." It was a general assembly of those who believed in Christ, and into which all were welcomed who did so.

" *And to the spirits of just men*

made perfect." *What does this mean ?*

" Spirits of just men " is here put for prophets. Had he but written, You are now permitted to see their prophecies fulfilled, we should have had no difficulty in understanding it, and this is what, by metonymy, he really means.

" *And to the blood of sprinkling.*" *What does this mean ?*

They had come to Jesus, the Mediator of the New Covenant, and to the truth of His death for sins, which alone cleansed the conscience. How foolish to go back to animal sacrifices ! The " blood of sprinkling " is, by metonymy, the blood of cleansing.

Why does he refer to the blood of Abel ?

The blood of Abel, which Cain shed, called for vengeance (Gen. iv. 10) ; but the blood of Jesus, which they had shed, called for cleansing and blessing on all who receive Him:

25–29. " *Yet once more I shake not the earth only, but also heaven.*" *What is intended by this shaking ?*

If we carefully note the comment of the apostle, " And this word, yet once more, signifieth the removing of those things that are shaken, as of things that are made, that those things which cannot be shaken may remain ; " we shall see that he refers not to the physical universe, but to the Jewish economy with its people and institutions, so often termed by the prophets in symbol, earth and heaven. See Isa. i. 2, " Hear, O heavens, and give ear, O earth : for the Lord hath spoken," and in many other places. So that when Paul read in Haggai about earth and heaven being shaken in order to removal, he knew that the Jewish institution was intended. Indeed, so certain was he that the house had become desolate, and would fall in ruins upon all who remained in it, that he could never be induced to re-enter it. The kingdom which had been established in grace could not be shaken, and its full acceptance was earnestly urged upon them. The old covenant had been shaken by the death of Jesus, and would be removed; the new had been established, and would stand till He returned in glory.

CHAPTER XIII.

In this closing chapter the apostle has given twelve exhortations, each differing from the other. Why has he given so many distinct appeals after so much teaching?

For this special reason, that he saw in them a tendency to fail in each of the things to which he exhorts,—in brotherly love, in hospitality, especially to Gentile believers, in sympathy with those imprisoned for preaching to them, and in the ordinance of marriage, etc. In all these things, as well as other duties named in the chapter, there was a decline of interest, and selfishness and worldliness was prevailing; it was needful therefore to warn against such declension. No doubt circumstances had much changed, and things unlooked for had formed new temptations. Many of them had colonised in heathen cities, and were yielding to the influences by which they were surrounded; and required to be warned that the law of Christ had not changed. There is a tendency in altered circumstances to make excuses for neglect of duties, instead of making all bend to the claims of Christ. To demand that our love to Him shall be greater than to all beside may appear a very high claim, but He who makes it once gave His life for us.

1. *" Let brotherly love continue."* *Why has he to exhort believers to do so?*

Respect of persons was prevailing, and so brotherly love declined.

2. *" Be not forgetful to entertain strangers." Does he refer to believers?*

Yes; and most likely to Gentile believers, against whom Jewish prejudice was very strong, so that it was much needed.

3. *" Remember them that are in bonds." Would the writer refer to himself?*

This was most probably written near the close of Paul's imprisonment, and others were suffering in like manner. To sympathise with such was identification with the body of Christ.

4. *Why does he exhort about marriage?*

Because it was being violated through the example of the heathens, hence he warns them that God will judge adulterers and whoremongers.

5. *" Let your conversation be without covetousness." Does he forbid talking about worldly things?*

It is not the talking that he warns against, but the life. Let your manner of life be without the love of money, and be satisfied with present things; for God has promised never to leave you. Such a promise should remove all anxiety, and leave us free to worship and serve Him in all faithfulness.

7. *" Remember them which have the rule over you." To what rulers does he refer?*

To the apostles of Jesus who were appointed to this high position, for they were to sit on thrones, judging the twelve tribes of Israel. The Jews who were converted to Christ at Pentecost fully endorsed this appointment, for "they continued stedfastly in the apostles' doctrine;" but when Paul wrote—and it is most likely that they were the same Jews —they were beginning to question the apostles' teaching.

2 F

9. *"Grace" and "meats." What do these terms signify?*

They are intended to represent the two institutions, and are inclusive of what belongs to each. Meats could not profit the spirit, since they pertained only to the flesh; the grace of God which brought salvation by Jesus alone could do that.

10. *"We have an altar." To what does he refer?*

Malachi calls the table of showbread both table and altar (i. 7), and it is most likely that altar is here used for table, not as that on which something is offered sacrificially, but as commemorative of something done. From the table of the Lord the believer does eat, and thereby acknowledges that Christ has both died and risen again. Now, it would be confusion for a Jew to perform tabernacle service, which was all typical of a coming institution, and then eat at the table which was expressive of the fact that all had been fulfilled. Paul here speaks very positively that they had no right to do so.

11. *Why does he refer to the great annual atonement of the Jews?*

The burning of the bodies of beasts outside the camp—by the virtue of whose blood the high priest gained access into the Holies of Holies—prefigured in a striking manner the death of Jesus outside the city, and His entrance into glory, by virtue of His death. That yearly sacrifice was for the nation, and Jesus having suffered for the people, why should they repeat what had been abrogated?

13. *What is going "without the camp"?*

The decided course to which he urges them is based upon what took place at Sinai. When the tribes made and worshipped a golden calf, Moses took the tabernacle of witness and pitched it outside the camp, and then cried, "Who is on the Lord's side? let him come unto me" (Exod. xxxii. 26). Now Paul here plainly intimates that the old institution had become a camp instead of the dwelling-place of God, and urges that they should identify themselves with Jesus, the rejected one.

15. *"By Him therefore let us offer." Was it by Christ?*

Yes; and it must appear strange that he should have to draw them away from priestly mediation by means of sacrifices, to that of offering praise by Jesus for salvation received; or as it is, *lit., the fruit of lips confessing to His name.* Yet so it was, but from such confusion Paul sought to deliver them.

18. *He asks their prayers for restoration. What does this imply?*

Imprisonment, but with assurance of release, and he desired prayer that it might be hastened. It is with pleasure that he informs them of the release of Timothy, and that he was anxiously looking for his own.

23. *If this letter was written by Paul, why does he here call Timothy a "brother" when in his epistle to him he calls him a "son"?*

In the family of God Timothy was a brother, in the Gospel he was a son, and so both terms are beautiful and appropriate.

24. *"They of Italy salute you." From what place in Italy did these saints send their greeting to these Hebrew Christians?*

From Rome, we judge; and the greetings of these Italian saints, which were sent to them through the writer of this letter, furnish a further proof that Paul is its author. We know that Timothy was with him in Rome, as his name is joined to several of what are termed his "prison epistles," and that for a while he was his fellow-prisoner, but was set at liberty—a release which encouraged Paul to expect the same, and purposed seeing them along with him. That he did see some of these Hebrews on his return into Asia is very likely, but only to find that they had become unfaithful, as afterwards referred to in his second letter to him. "This thou knowest, that all they which are in Asia be turned away from me" (2 Tim. i. 15), referring doubtless to faithless Jews. He had indeed been faithful to them, both personally and by letter, but only to prove their unfaithful requital of his labours and sufferings to preserve them from the much-feared apostacy.

25. *"Grace be with you all." What is indicated by this benediction?*

There are at least two things plainly indicated by it. (1.) That the epistle was written by an apostle of Christ, since no one else but an apostle could authoritatively pronounce it. (2.) That it was written by Paul, being the token of his salutation in all his epistles . . . (2 Thes. iii. 17).

THE GENERAL EPISTLE OF

JAMES.

CHAPTER I.

Why did James write this epistle?
To warn his brethren in the flesh, those who had confessed the Lord Jesus, that unless they repented of their manifest departures from truth and righteousness, the judgment of God would speedily overtake them. It is very sad that he should have had to write such a letter, but their behaviour had become so bad that it had to be condemned, and this almost final effort is made to save them from impending wrath.

It may be well to note here that we have three epistles, which were written directly to believing Hebrews, and in which we are able to trace very accurately the course pursued by them from their conversion at Pentecost to the near approach of the judgment which desolated the nation. The first of these was written by Peter shortly after their dispersion, a dispersion which was caused by the great persecution which had been raised against them chiefly through Saul of Tarsus. This first epistle of Peter was written to comfort them in their trial, and contains a full exposition of their acceptance, calling, and privileges, with directions how to walk so as to please God. These dispersed saints, through the apostles' teaching, had shown a truly noble spirit; and being assured that they had a portion in heaven, they had taken joyfully even the spoiling of their goods. After locating themselves among the nations and countries around, several things seem to have operated unfavourably upon them, and ultimately induced many of them to return to Judaism, and to the impiety of which James here complains. They had been carefully instructed by the apostles that judgment would fall upon their nation, but when in the forbearance of God this judgment was delayed, and the temple, priesthood, etc., remained as before, their faith in the testimony was considerably weakened. Even rulers over the spiritual house began to say, "My Lord delayeth His coming," and then tyranny and dissipation speedily followed this delusive thought. The claims of the old institution were again revived among them, and their interest was evidently divided between the two covenants. This appears to have become fully manifest when the second special letter—the Epistle to the Hebrews—was written to them. In this epistle we have a most elaborate argument in defence of Christ Jesus, the God-appointed leader, priest, and mediator of the new covenant. Now it is very suspicious indeed, to say the least, that the writer should have to set up a defence of that which had been previously accepted, to have to try to prevent them from going back to that which they had left, and yet this was truly the case. Every phase and aspect of the argument, and these are numerous; every exhortation and warning given, and these are multiplied to an almost painful extent, very clearly indicates a lurking mistrust of their confidence in Christ. What the issue would be remained to be proved, and this third letter—the epistle of James—seems to make manifest what they had become. Judaism had in a large measure been accepted, and the fruit of it—tyranny, oppression, self-exaltation, injustice, and worldliness—everywhere prevailed. And, instead of weeping and howling for the miseries that were at hand, for the coming of the Lord in judgment against them was near, they lived in pleasure and were wanton, and nourished their hearts as in a day of slaughter. This epistle by James was the last warning cry of danger that was being raised by a spiritual watchman, and we fear with but little success. It was a last effort to preserve from apostasy those who still remained faithful, but whose faithfulness was much weakened by the unbelief and worldliness of their Jewish brethren. To these three epistles of instruction, warning, and defence of the truth, we might add

the first epistle of John, which was also written to believing Jews, and, along with this by James, was a last effort to preserve from the power of antichrist any who had ears to hear the truth. John's defence of the truth must have preceded the judgment on the nation but a very short period, because he adds, "Little children, it is the last time," *lit.*, the last hour (1 John ii. 18), and possibly no further warnings were added to these.

1. *Why does James address his letter to the twelve tribes ?*

It is "to the twelve tribes which are scattered abroad,"—*lit., which are in the dispersion ;* and from this descriptive sentence we see at once who are intended. It is not to the scattered remnants of the Assyrian and Babylonian captivities that he writes, but to those of the twelve tribes, who, after suffering for Christ, had been driven from Jerusalem, or had otherwise shared in the consequences of that dispersion named by Luke (Acts viii. 1). Peter in his epistle to them addresses them as the *elect sojourners of a dispersion,* and thus owns them as God's elect ones, and not merely the fleshly seed of Abraham.

"James, a servant of God." What is suggested by this lowly title ?

A very plain fact, viz., that he was working for God, and for the Lord Jesus. It is a very different title indeed from the pompous prefixes which men now attach to their names, and which serve only to exalt the flesh, but out of which there is nothing for the Master. Here is a man employed by God, and who assumes to be called nothing higher than what he really is, "a servant of God, and of the Lord Jesus." When we contrast this simple matter of fact title with the titles which men now assume, from "his holiness the Pope," through all the grades of clerical distinctions, it is certainly very striking. We are not questioning their right to wear these humanly-imposed titles, we only say that the distinctions are curious enough.

2. *" My brethren, count it all joy when ye fall into divers temptations." Is not this strange advice?*

Yes, very strange indeed, unless we look to the end, as James directs them to do. It would look strange to see a man casting bushels of seed into the ground, unless we think of the harvest that is expected to follow. It would be strange to spend years in acquiring a knowledge of some business, unless we take into account the acquisition of wealth which the knowledge thus possessed may secure. So in regard to trial and suffering endured here; if that trial is forming our character and fitting us for glory, we should indeed joy in it.

3. *What is this " patience" which is to follow the " trying of faith"?*

It is, *lit.*, endurance,—*i.e.*, abiding the test, and remaining firm in the truth, when hard pressed to swerve from it.

4. *" But let patience have her perfect work." How could this be?*

It is simply, let your endurance be perfected—*i.e.*, by your obedience in all things that God may require from you. You will then be entire, deficient in nothing.

5. *" If any of you lack wisdom, let him ask of God." Does this privilege apply to everything we might desire?*

To everything necessary to form a Christ-like character. Whenever wisdom is needed to enable us to please God, and do what is right before Him, we may be sure of obtaining it. For such a purpose he will give liberally, and not upbraid those who seek His help.

6. *" But let him ask in faith," in order to obtain. Does he mean simple faith?*

If by this very common phrase is meant faith without the required obedience, I should say no, because in the second chapter he affirms that faith without works is dead.

8. *What is a double-minded man?*

It is, *lit.*, *a two-souled man,—i.e.*, one who is ruled by circumstances, and therefore unstable in his actions. He is like water driven with the wind, and tossed hither and thither.

9–11. *Is " the brother of low degree" a poor brother?*

I should judge so, because James is contrasting the state of the poor with the rich.

How is the brother of low degree exalted?

By becoming, through the Gospel, a child of God and an heir of glory. There is no position higher than this.

How were the rich made low?

Possibly he alludes to some who had been deprived of their earthly possessions through accepting Jesus, and he urges all such to rejoice, because, though riches that perish had been taken from them, an unfading crown of life was set before them.

12. *What is this " crown of life" which those who endure shall receive?*

It is the deathlessness which shall encircle those who become victors in the strife, for they shall be ever with the Lord. The crown of life is a fit symbol of immortality.

13. *James will not have God charged with tempting men, and yet we read " God did tempt Abraham." How are these statements to be reconciled?*

The apparent contradiction is easily removed. The word tempt means to test or try, whether spoken of God or man, or Satan; but with this difference, Satan and man tempt to evil, God never. He may and does try or test our sincerity, love, and obedience, and it is for this purpose that God did tempt or try Abraham. He tested his spirit of obedience by asking him to offer up his son, his only son Isaac, and found him willing to obey. And this is what is implied in James's statement, "Neither tempteth he any man" (to do evil).

14. *Does James teach here that lust or desire is the chief factor in temptations to evil?*

Yes. There are first the circumstances inciting to evil, by appealing to the senses or the flesh, then, if there is desire, conception takes place, and in the action or birth sin is brought forth, and death or condemnation follows.

Is man responsible for the circumstances of evil that so continuously surround him?

No; only for yielding to the evil or temptation which may arise. There is no sin in being tempted, but only in doing the wrong to which we may be tempted.

17. *" The Father of lights." Why is God so designated?*

It was in order to set aside a prevailing thought, viz., that God tempted men to do evil. This charge is denied by showing that He is the source of all good, the creator of the orbs of day and night, and whose love and benevolence is always the same.

18. *" Of His own will begat He us with the word of truth." Was this begetting unconditional, or why does he refer to it in this way?*

It is in order to show the graciousness of God, and not that He acts arbitrarily, or seeks to make them His children without the necessary means. It is rather to stir them up to respond to the grace that had brought to them, first of all, the salvation which is by Jesus. It was indeed of His own will that the apostles should begin at Jerusalem to tell of pardon and life in Christ; but it was that their love, and purity, and obedience, should for ever commend His grace to others. Peter expresses the same thought when he says "That ye should show forth the praises,"—*lit.*, the excellences—" of Him who called you out of darkness into His marvellous light" (1 Peter ii. 9). It was by the fruit of a holy life that they were to extol God.

19. *" Let every man be swift to hear." To hear who, or what?*

To hear God, who seeks to instruct His children in truth and righteousness.

" Slow to speak." Why is this necessary?

There is more mischief caused by the lips than all other members of the body. The tongue can kindle a fire which the hands cannot put out. There is divine wisdom in the direction, for thereby evil is prevented. It is the same as to command carefulness of speech, or to speak as in God's sight.

21. *What is superfluity of naughtiness?*

It is, *lit.*, the overflowing of badness or vice, which he assumes must be laid aside, and the engrafted word must be received in order to their final salvation.

" The engrafted word." What is that?

We had better read the *implanted word,*—*i.e.*, the word received and ruling in their minds,—so that instead of being ruled by pride, or worldliness, or malice, they might be ruled by the purifying truth of God.

22–24. *" But be ye doers of the Word, and not hearers only." Is this a rebuke?*

It would seem as if they had heard more than they practised, and required to be stirred up to obedience. It is easy to read and hear; but if the simile of the man looking into the mirror, and going away straightway *forgets* his appearance, be applied to us, our reading and hearing is in vain.

But since looking into the mirror cannot change the face, how does forgetfulness apply to one who hears and does not act ?

The man is supposed to look into the mirror to see if his face is clean, and then to wash it when it is not clean ; but to see that the face is dirty and forget to wash it is a true picture of one who hears the correcting word and fails to apply it to his own heart and life. Do not act in that foolish way, says James.

25. *What is this "perfect law of liberty" ?*

It is the law of the New Covenant, which reveals a new life, and sets free from the old one all who yield to its claims. The Gospel not only shows us what we are, but what we should be. The Gospel of Christ brings freedom from the law of sin and death to all who obey it. Such are truly blessed in their deed.

26. *Does bridling the tongue differ from " slow to speak " ?*

There is a difference which possibly only some persons will understand. To be slow to speak will be only nature to some, but to curb the tongue will be obedience to God, and by some will be done only by a daily victory over self. Still, it is not the much speaking that is condemned, but display of self. We can never speak too much of Jesus, our danger is in speaking too much of ourselves. It is in this vain display that we are to bridle or restrain our tongues, that we may thus restrain our pride and vanity.

27. *" To visit the fatherless and widows in their affliction." What does " to visit " imply ?*

It is, *lit., to oversee*, which means practical care of those who are needy. To maintain purity of heart and practical sympathy with the needy is pure religion, and undefiled before God. James hints that

there had been more talk than work, and suggests a reversal of such a vain and profitless course.

CHAPTER II.

1. *In condemning partiality in the assembly, does James ignore the civil relation which one man bears to another ?*

By no means. In the state the servant is subject to his master, and magistrates rule over their subjects ; but in the Church of Christ these distinctions vanish, and the poor are as high as the rich. He who made them one body made them equal, and with Him is no partiality.

In condemning " respect of persons," why does he refer to the Lord of glory ? and why does he forbid them to associate such conduct with " the faith " ?

Because His example formed such a contrast to theirs. He had stooped from glory to men of low estate, while they despised the poor ; and such a haughty behaviour to their brethren could not be tolerated, being altogether unlike the spirit and action of the Lord Jesus.

2. *The " gold ring " and the " goodly apparel " were indications of wealth. Should it not be respected ?*

God does not look at rings and costly garments, but at the heart. It may be but vanity to wear them, and, to say the least, it is weakness to esteem the wearer more worthy of respect on that account. God is no respecter of persons on account of their riches, and the Church should possess His spirit. The assembly is in a sad state when the influence of wealth rules in it instead of Christ.

5. *" Hath not God chosen the poor ?" Was this intended as a rebuke to the rich ?*

Yes ; and indicates the sad condition of the assembly. Poor believers were despised on account of their poverty, whilst the rich, with the mere semblance of piety, were honoured. It was indeed well to remind them that though poor in this world's goods they were rich in faith, because heirs of the kingdom, and should not be despised. It is well, however, to understand that poverty gives no claim to the kingdom of God, nor do riches debar their possessor from the privilege. Both riches and poverty are often the result of circumstances altogether outside the will of man. God never despises the poor on account of his poverty, nor esteems the rich on account of his riches, but the spirit manifested by each is alone regarded by Him. God chooses in Christ all who accept Him, and rejects those who reject Him, whether poor or rich.

6. *" But ye have despised the poor." Were these poor saints?*

He is writing to his brethren, who had professedly accepted Christ, and these were their poor brethren, from whom protection had been withheld in their persecutions. Hence they were drawn to judgment by oppressors, and the worthy name named upon them was despised.

7. *What name was this?*

It is, *lit., the good name which was called upon them.* Now, according to 1 Peter iv. 14–16, the believing Jews had accepted the divinely-imposed name of Christian, and for this they were reproached. This name distinguished them as belonging to Christ, and aroused the blasphemy of those who were in opposition.

8, 9. *" If ye fulfil the royal law," etc. Why does James seek to convict believers in Jesus by appealing to the law of Moses?*

It is well to understand that this part of the law, though given by God through Moses, was re-enacted through the Lord Jesus, and hence, along with many other precepts of the law, its authority was renewed. It is not inappropriately termed by James the "royal or kingly law." If you show respect of persons, he says, you are convicted by this law as transgressors.

10–13. *How is a person who keeps the whole law, except in one point, guilty of all?*

His meaning must be understood by his own teaching, which is, that though the law contains various precepts, yet it is from one law-giver, and he who violates any part of it becomes a transgressor of law, and is guilty before God. He wishes by this reference to show them that in showing respect of persons they had violated a law of God, and were therefore guilty before Him.

" So speak ye, and so do." Is this an exhortation?

Yes. It is an appeal to them to be governed in their spirit and life by that higher law of liberty or love. And to urge and influence them to do so, he adds, " For he shall have judgment,"—*i.e.,* condemnation without mercy,—" that hath showed no mercy, and mercy rejoiceth against judgment." The Alexandrian MS. is, " But let mercy rejoice against judgment,"—*i.e.,* by you showing mercy instead of judgment.

14. *James here begins a deeply-interesting argument to prove the absolute necessity of works in order to justification; while Paul, in his epistle to the Romans, as strongly contends that a man is justified by faith in Christ Jesus, without the deeds of the law. How do you reconcile their statements?*

Those who think these are statements to be reconciled, do so because they have concluded that both are writing of the same class of persons; whereas Paul is writing of *sinners* being justified by their faith in Jesus without obedience to the law of Moses; while James is writing of *believers*, who, he affirms, cannot be justified,—*i.e.*, approved,—while living in disobedience to the claims of Christ, or, as he terms it, "works" not of the law, but of the faith. There is therefore no variance between them, nor could there be any difficulty if their words only applied to those for whom they were intended. If James had been writing of penitent sinners he would have affirmed with Paul that God could justify them through faith in Jesus without the deeds of the law; indeed, he could not have been a servant of Jesus had he affirmed otherwise; and Paul when writing to saints could say, "if ye live after the flesh ye shall die." Thus we learn that between Paul and James there was no difference in their teaching. Both were guided by the one Spirit, and spoke and wrote the same things. Paul wrote that God would justify them that believe in Jesus; and James wrote that justification so freely bestowed would not avail for final acceptance unless they continued in obedience to Christ. The Master, indeed, had spoken the same thing when He said "to those Jews which believed on Him," "If ye continue in my word, then are ye my disciples indeed" (John viii. 31).

17. "*Even so faith, if it hath not works, is dead, being alone.*" *Would it be right to call it a dead faith?*

We think not. The terms are no more in harmony than it would to say a *dead life*. What James does say is, that if works are not seen, faith has expired.

19. "*Thou believest that there is one God.*" *What is the purport of contrasting their faith with that of devils or demons?*

The demons believed in coming judgment and trembled, as was owned by them before Jesus, "Art thou come hither to torment us before the time?" (Matt. viii. 29). But these Jews, though they believed in "one God," or that God is one,—*i.e.*, in God's unity,—yet they sinned without fearing the consequence. They are, indeed, reproved for trifling with future consequences, while demons trembled on account of them.

21-23. *Both James and Paul quote the statement, "Abraham believed in the Lord, and He counted it unto him for righteousness" (Gen. xv. 6), but make a very different application of it. How can their diverse application of these words be reconciled?*

I observe that Paul says, that when Abraham believed in the Lord it was counted unto him for righteousness, and this was before the birth of Isaac; while James says that this Scripture was fulfilled when he had offered up his son; and this will possibly perplex some. There is, however, no contradiction in their application of this Scripture, since both expositors were guided by the one Spirit, and together they teach us two very distinct aspects of truth —the one referring to the beginning of Christian life through faith in Jesus; the other, to the perfecting of that life, and obtaining the final promise of God by continued obedience to the Lord Jesus. Abraham believed the promise made known to him concerning the coming Jehovah, and God counted it to him for righteousness,—*i.e.*, Jehovah,—He that is to be, became to him the source of a new life; and Paul quotes this fact to show that God, through Christ Jesus, can bless and pardon the sinner who receives Him, even though he may have nothing else to commend him; and uses this fact, both in his epistle to the Romans (iv. 3) and Galatians (iii. 6), against the prevailing Jewish thought that obedience to the law was necessary for obtaining salvation. Abraham also offered up his son Isaac at God's command, and obtained the absolute promise of blessing which could only be obtained through obedience to that requirement; and James uses this fact to show these professedly-believing Jews, that unless there was a life-conformity to "the faith of our Lord Jesus," they could not be counted "heirs of the kingdom which God promised to them that love Him." It is, indeed, striking that Paul, when writing to Hebrew Christians (vi. 11–15), should use this fact of the offering of Isaac, and concludes, "And so, after he had patiently endured" (the trial), "he obtained the promise."

"*And he was called the Friend of God.*" *Why was this endearing title given to Abraham ?*

I presume it was because he became a sharer with God in the painful experience of giving up His well-beloved Son. Abraham not only obeyed God, but in so doing he became a friend and associated sufferer in spirit with Him in this painful surrender.

24. "*Ye see then how that by works a man is justified, and not by faith only.*" *Does not this sound very unevangelical ?*

Yes; if you place it alongside of the proposition which is supported by almost every pulpit, and endorsed by almost every treatise on the way of salvation, viz., that men are justified *by faith alone.* But as James writes by the Spirit, we must accept his statement as true, whatever may be affirmed against it. It is but right, however, to state that this variance, which has arisen between such persons and the Scriptures, seem to have arisen from two causes, —(1.) a misapplication of Paul's statement, "that a man is justified by faith without the deeds of the law," as if by the deeds of *the law,* Paul

meant the requirements of the Gospel, which is a sad perversion of his words ; and (2.) a wrongly-attached meaning of *diakosune,* here rendered justified, and thought to mean the same as pardoned. A more correct rendering would be *made righteous,* and when so rendered we can read James intelligently, "Ye see then" (from this act of Abraham) "how that by work" (things commanded) "a man is made righteous, and not by faith only."

25. "*Likewise was not Rahab the harlot justified by works ?*" *Paul says,* "*By faith the harlot Rahab perished not*" (*Heb. xi.* 31). *Why does James here differ from Paul ?*

The difference is only in words, not in teaching ; and since both are writing to believing Hebrews—possibly to the same persons—and both under the one Spirit, we could not conceive of any other difference. It is, however, instructive that we are enabled to study this case as presented by both. Paul says that it was by faith—*i.e.,* in God's testimony concerning Israel—which she proved by her acts or works, for she received the spies in peace. James says she was made righteous by works when she received the messengers and had sent them out another way. Her faith is implied and proved here, but not stated. She showed her faith by her works. From these cases James wished them to see that if there was not obedience to God, they were like a body without a spirit, and their professed faith was dead.

CHAPTER III.

1. "*My brethren, be not many masters.*" *Why would they be condemned for this ?*

It is, *lit., be not many teachers ;* and James must be understood, not as forbidding them to teach those truths which had first been taught by Christ, and then by the apostles through the Spirit, but as warning them against Jewish tradition and endless genealogies, by which they had become so much entangled. Indeed, they were striving to become teachers of the law rather than the Gospel, and for this they would receive greater condemnation.

2. *"In many things we all offend."* *Does James include himself?*

His words imply that both he and they would offend or stumble if they taught these things. The man who would refrain from uttering or teaching the imaginings either of himself or others would be perfect, and able to bridle or govern all his actions.

3-6. *Why does he refer to the horse, the ship, and the small fire?*

They well knew that an unbridled horse would dash its rider, and an ungoverned ship would bring ruin to those involved, and a small fire would set a forest in flames; even so, an unbridled tongue would cause great mischief. To curb and control it, therefore, was of great moment. For as the horse by the bit could be turned wherever the rider wished, and as the ship though large could be turned about with the helm, and the fire could be quenched while yet a spark; so could the tongue be controlled, and its possible evils be hindered.

"And the tongue is a fire, a world of iniquity." *What does this mean?*

The simile of the fire in the forest is still before him, so he compares it to the tongue among the members, which, through its evil, defiles the whole body and sets on fire the course, *lit.*, the wheel of nature,—*i.e.*, setting in motion its evil passions,—and it is set on fire of hell.

"Fire of hell." *What is that?*

It is, *lit.*, *fire of Gehenna*, which was the fire of judgment, which was ever burning and consuming that which was cast into it. Such, James intimates, will be the doom of those whose unbridled tongues produce so much mischief; the consuming wrath of God will surely overtake them.

7-9. *"For every kind of beasts and of birds, etc., . . . hath been tamed of mankind; but the tongue can no man tame."* *Does he mean our own tongue or the tongue of another.*

The tongue of another, most certainly. The most savage beast may be tamed and do your bidding, but the tongues of men never.

Can we tame our own?

Yes; when we become obedient to Christ we shall use it for good instead of evil, for blessing instead of cursing, for telling of Jesus and His love, instead of slander and reproach. Our speech may minister grace to the hearers instead of inflaming the passions; and when we do these things our tongue is tamed, because the heart is right with God.

10. *"Out of the same mouth proceedeth blessing and cursing."* *Does he mean that the same person did this?*

Yes; and he has to condemn such an iniquitous blending of curse and blessing. Even nature condemned such a mixture as well as God, and it ought to be abandoned by all who profess to fear Him.

CHAPTER IV.

1-4. *"From whence come wars and strife among you?"* *Is it to personal or national strife that he refers?*

To personal, I presume. It was the strong against the weak, the rich against the poor, and the ambitious against the lowly. We do not wonder that he should warn them against associating such a course with the faith of the Lord of glory.

*What was their object in this un-
righteous course?*

A gratification of fleshly desire.
A lusting of power for selfish purposes.

*Is it not strange that he should
have called them brethren?*

Well, they had been brought into
the family through their faith in
Jesus, and he begins his letter by
acknowledging their once-established
claim. But here he has to mark
their degeneracy, and, through their
unfaithfulness to the Bridegroom,
he has to call them (adulterers omit)
adulteresses.

*Is there any warning for us in
their sad degeneracy?*

Yes; we get in these unfaithful
Jews an illustration of what is possible to ourselves. They began in
the Spirit and were ending in the
flesh, they began in humility and
were ending in pride, they accepted
Jesus and were proving themselves
unfaithful; and against such a change
we have need to watch and pray.

5, 6. *"Do ye think that the Scripture saith in vain, the spirit that
dwelleth in us lusteth to envy." What
does he mean?*

These sayings in the Scriptures
are of very great moment, because
in them we have character and
principles, both bad and good, fully
revealed, and these may afterwards
be embodied in the life and spirit.
Now, in quoting one of these sketches,
James asks, Are you going to fill it
up? because if you do you will
suffer; "For God resisteth the proud,
but giveth grace to the humble," and
Scripture does not speak in vain.

7. *" Submit yourselves therefore to
God." What is submission to Him?*

Obedience to all His will, letting
God rule, and not the flesh and the
devil.

*"Resist the devil." How could
they resist him?*

The devil is resisted when his
temptations to evil are not obeyed.
It is not by force that Satan succeeds,
but by tempting men and women to
disobedience, and these temptations
may all be resisted.

11. *"Speak not evil one of another,
brethren." Is it wrong to speak of the
sins and failings of others?*

Yes; when it is only for personal
ends that we do so, because we put
ourselves in the place of the judge.
It is only when the claims of the
Church require it that we are free
to deal with those who may have
sinned.

13–17. *"If the Lord will, we shall
live, and do this, or that." What
should we learn from this exhortation?*

Several very important lessons:—
(1.) That life is uncertain, and that
we cannot be sure of the morrow, or
even of a moment. (2.) That this
should be felt and acknowledged in
every action of life. "If the Lord
will" should be our constant motto.
(3.) We may judge that these persons had become reckless of these
truths, and boasted as if life was in
their own hands. James warns them
against this self-dependence, and
urges them rather to depend on
God.

17. *"To him that knoweth to do
good, and doeth it not, to him it is
sin." Would you call it the sin of
omission?*

Yes; or of neglect of known or
revealed duty. God holds it as disobedience, and will punish those
who do so.

CHAPTER V.

1–6. *What does James mean by
the "last days," in which judgment
was to overtake these unrighteous rich
men?*

As the persons addressed were to
suffer personally in this threatened
judgment, we have no difficulty in

concluding that he refers to the *last days* of the dispensation, in which, not only was their temple destroyed and their city burnt with fire, but also in every province in the Roman empire the Jews suffered in a measure from the same judgment. Their goods were taken from them, their property was confiscated, and no eye pitied them. James knew this would come upon them, for even Moses had declared in his Song of Judgment (Deut. xxxii.) that such calamities would overtake the disobedient. The prophets had prophesied of the " days of vengeance," and Jesus Himself had given to the apostles a most minute detail of this " great tribulation," which He said should have no parallel. Well might He say, " Weep and howl for your miseries that shall come upon you."

7. *" Be patient therefore, brethren, unto the coming of the Lord." Is it another class that is here exhorted?*

Yes. There were the faithless and the faithful, tyrants and their victims ; and it is the latter that James exhorts to patience until the Lord should come.

8. *"The coming of the Lord draweth nigh." Does he refer to what we now call His second coming?*

That could not be, since that has not yet taken place, and this was something to be realised in that generation. The word rendered " coming " here is, *lit., presence,* and when we learn from James that these afflicted ones were to be delivered, and that that deliverance was near, even at the door, we feel assured that in some way the presence of Jesus was associated with that judgment. His power manifestly shone out in the deliverance of all His disciples. They saw His hand in their freedom, and the overthrow of those who persecuted them.

In urging them to be patient unto the coming of the Lord, he refers to the husbandmen waiting for the early and the latter rain. Why does he do so?

Until these rains fell in their season there was neither sowing of seed nor pasture for their flocks ; therefore, for these periodical rains the husbandman waited, and must wait until God supplied the necessary boon. So James teaches these suffering saints, that until the Lord interposed they would have to endure their afflictions. That He would not disappoint their trust was to him an absolute truth, and His presence—*i.e.*, the shining of His delivering power—was drawing nigh.

11. *Job is a second instance of patient suffering. Why does James bring forward his case?*

Not merely to show how patiently some can endure, but what is also a very precious truth, to show how God feels towards those who suffer. They might think that God was unkind in allowing so much trial to fall upon them, but in the case of Job they saw the end or character of the Lord, that He was pitiful and of tender mercy. It is a blessed truth, full of consolation to all sufferers, that God feels for them, and will in the end set them free.

12. *" Swear not at all." Is it wrong to swear in courts of law?*

Both Christ and James forbid swearing or taking of oaths: it must therefore be wrong to do so. Men are compelled by law to take oaths when called upon as witnesses, but as Christ forbids His disciples to do so, it is their duty to refuse. Christians should speak the truth everywhere without being bribed by oath, ever remembering that untruthfulness of spirit separates from the kingdom of God. It is very suspicious that James should have to refer to this matter, as it indicates a condition of things very much unlike Christian discipleship.

13. *"Is any among you afflicted?
let him pray."　To what kind of
affliction does James refer?*

To evil endured in the cause of
Christ and truth, and the direction
how to act should be carefully followed. To seek human redress for
any wrong or injury done to us is
man's method; to pray is the Spirit's
direction, and they alone are safe
who follow it.

*"Is any merry? let him sing
psalms."　Why give this direction?*

It is properly a supplementary
contrast to the former condition, and
is a direction that all Christians
should heed. The word "merry"
scarcely conveys the writer's meaning. James refers to two states—
a state of trial, and directs that they
should pray; and freedom from trial,
when happy feelings are produced,
and then there should be praise.
The singing of psalms or songs of
praise is suggested, and as these are
so largely, filled with praise and
thanksgiving, they are fitted for that
devotion of spirit which Christians
should labour to cultivate.

14–16. *"Is any sick among you?
let him call for the elders of the
Church," etc.　Was it for ordinary
sickness that James directs that
prayer and anointing with oil should
be used?*

It was for sickness, inflicted as a
penalty against some. violation of
apostolic authority, and not ordinary
sickness or common infirmities of
the body, that James here directs
these things to be done. That there
were gifts of healing bestowed
through the apostles in their day is
evident, but such were bestowed for
the special purpose of confirming the
truth of the Gospel they preached,
and were to cease with them; but
it is equally plain that there was
no standing law given to the Church
for the cure of ordinary bodily infirmities or sickness. Had such a

law been given by the Spirit, then
Paul, acting under His guidance,
would surely have acknowledged
it. Timothy had a weak stomach,
and his "often infirmities." Why is
he directed to use a little wine for
it, if there was, in the Church, a
standing law for the healing of such
complaints? And why did Paul
leave Trophimus at Miletum sick,
if such a provision had been made
for his recovery? These facts appear
to forbid such a thought. That
penalties, or infliction of death and
suffering, did follow defiance of apostolic authority, is duly recorded;
and it is to the removal of these,
upon repentance and confession,
that James here refers; and anointing and prayer, for the removal
of these evils, was a standing law
in the Church. Ananias and Sapphira were struck with death, and
for this punishment no remedy was
provided. The fornicator in the
Church at Corinth was delivered
unto Satan for the destruction of
the flesh, but through his confession
and repentance he was restored,
possibly in the way that James
directs. John also speaks of the
"sin unto death," for which prayer
should not be offered; and of the
"sin which is not unto death," for
which it might be offered. These
things should be understood, and
not perverted. That God has provided remedies for our ordinary
sickness, just as He has provided
food for the sustaining of health,
we fully believe, and the proper use
of both involves responsibility.
That God does permit His children
to seek His help in their need is
clearly revealed, and to those who
do so there are often marvellous
interpositions; but let us not be reproached if we do not anoint with
oil for every ache and pain, as if
we were neglecting a rule which was
intended only for special cases.

17–20. *Is the case of Elias brought forward to show the power of prayer?*

Not exactly for that purpose, but it is cited to bear upon the case already alluded to. The nation of Israel became idolatrous, and Elijah prayed that rain might be withheld, a witness against their sin. Here punishment followed transgression; then James gives the parallel case of recovery, by saying that Elijah prayed again, and the heavens gave rain, and blessing rested upon those who had been chastened. James had exhorted them to confess their faults one to another and to pray one for another, that, in the way directed, they might be healed. He also directed that they should strive for this end, assuring them that by leading to repentance a soul would be saved from death and a multitude of sins would be hidden.

THE FIRST EPISTLE GENERAL OF PETER.

CHAPTER I.

1. *To whom was this epistle by Peter written?*

A more literal rendering of the first verse will supply a correct answer. *Peter, an apostle of Jesus Christ, to elect sojourners of a dispersion—of Pontus, Galatia, etc.* In Acts viii. 1 we read, "And at that time there was a great persecution against the Church which was at Jerusalem; and they were all scattered abroad," etc. It is to these dispersed saints that this epistle by Peter was written, and was divinely adapted to their peculiar trial, and shows how perfectly God provided for their spiritual instruction.

By whom were these persons converted? and when did their conversion take place?

There is sufficient evidence to prove that they were converted by Peter, and that their conversion took place at Pentecost, when the Gospel of Jesus was first proclaimed. We learn from Acts ii. that those who heard and received Peter's testimony were from Pontus, Cappadocia, etc., and in this epistle Peter notes the same thing. We should, however, read here, not *throughout* Pontus, but *of* Pontus, etc. They had gone up to Jerusalem from Pontus, Cappadocia, and other countries, and had located at Jerusalem, but shortly after their conversion were dispersed throughout Judea and Samaria. We think it is evident that these tried saints, to whom Peter wrote this letter, were the same that so gladly received his word at Pentecost; and we also see the divine adaptation of both the sermon and the epistle. They were the same persons, but not in the same state. The *sermon* at Pentecost was preached to them as *sinners*, and was intended to prove to them that Jesus of Nazareth, who had been crucified, was the anointed and ascended Son of God; and to lead them to accept of Him as their exalted Lord. This *letter* was written to them as *believers* in Jesus; and as they had been driven away from their teachers, and thus deprived of instruction, it was intended to supply the place of the oral teaching they might have received had they been permitted to remain. In this letter, Peter, guided by the Spirit, and acting under the authority of Jesus, assures them of their standing in Christ, and of their imperishable inheritance, and of the obligations resting upon them to live in loving conformity to the example and will of their Lord and Master during their allotted sojourn on the earth. The sermon and the letter together are the keys—*i.e.*, the authority—committed to him in relation to the kingdom of Christ and of God. And now, having opened it, it stands open to all who will enter on the terms proposed.

2. *" Elect according to the fore-knowledge of God." Must "elect" be omitted here ?*

Peter only uses the word in the first verse, but it is implied in connection with "according to fore-knowledge." It is instructive as revealing the principle on which such a privilege was realised.

What is meant by "fore-know-ledge," according to which they were chosen ?

Fore-knowledge is used, by metonymy, for fore-revelation. God revealed or made known beforehand by the prophets, not only the sufferings and death of Jesus, but the salvation and acceptance of those who should receive Him. Now it is according to these testimonies, as stated in verse 11, that these believing ones were elected of God.

" Through santification of spirit." What does this mean ?

It is, *lit.*, *in sanctification of spirit* —*i.e.*, in a separation from their former state, and spirit, and practice. Just as their fathers, when chosen in Egypt, through the promise made to Abraham, were separated from it, so they, being chosen in Christ, were separated from their former life and state.

Is " Unto obedience and sprinkling of the blood of Jesus Christ"

connected with this " sanctification of spirit " ?

Yes. This shows to what they had been separated—*i.e.*, unto obedience and sprinkling of the blood. God had elected them to live, not as in their former state, but to serve the Lord Jesus.

How could they be sprinkled with blood ?

Peter writes as a Jew to Jews, naming the action for the result. Under the law the priest sprinkled the blood for cleansing, and had Peter written, unto cleansing of the blood of Jesus Christ, it would have been plain to us Gentiles, as this is what he means. In 1 John i. 7 we get the same thought as here, but in other words.

3. *"Blessed be the God," etc. Why does Peter in this eulogy of praise join himself with these elect ones ?*

Because he had shared with them in the "abundant mercy" bestowed, and therefore owns the favour in this ascription of praise. It may be well, however, to state that the word *eulogetos*, here rendered "blessed," implies not merely what *is* said of Him, but what *ought* to be said. The word would be well rendered by *worthy of all praise* is the God and Father of our Lord Jesus Christ.

Why does he say "Who according to His abundant mercy "?

This abundant mercy has a special bearing upon them as Jews. They had the law and the prophets, but had been unfaithful to their opportunities, and were therefore guilty before God. Their sins were indeed as scarlet; but when Jesus arranged for the proclamation of the Gospel, His apostles were directed to begin at Jerusalem, and this "abundant mercy" issued in a new life.

" Begotten again unto a lively hope." What does this imply ?

It is, *lit.*, *a living hope*, because a

living Jesus by His resurrection had become their hope. As the Jewish nation, to whom the Messiah was promised, received through its fulfilment the hope of which Paul speaks : "Unto which promise our twelve tribes . . . . hope to come" (Acts xxvi. 7); but having mistaken the object of His coming, their carnal hope expired with His death. Now the hope which Peter and these persecuted saints possessed had been obtained by regeneration, or a begetting again by the incorruptible seed. It was therefore both a new life, a new birth, and a new hope, through the resurrection of Jesus.

4. *" To an inheritance incorruptible and undefiled." With what is this inheritance contrasted ?*

With their inheritance in the land of Canaan, which had been defiled by iniquity, and was passing away. In fact they had been driven out of their earthly portion, and they are now encouraged with the assurance of a better and higher portion.

" Reserved in heaven for you." Is there anything special in this statement ?

It is a very noticeable contrast to the location of their former estate. That was on earth, this in heaven ; that was lost to them, this was reserved, and therefore their hope. Besides, it is well to note that this is in harmony with all the promises made under the Gospel. The reward of the saints is in heaven, not on the earth.

5. *" Salvation ready to be revealed in the last time." When was this ?*

It is, *lit., a last season*, and refers to the deliverance which they would prove in that gracious season by the mighty power of Jesus. It was ready to be revealed when the season should arrive, and for this they would have to wait.

6. *How could joy and heaviness*

2 G

exist in the same mind at the same time ?

These very opposite experiences have often been felt. Paul felt both when he wrote, "sorrowful, yet always rejoicing." These saints were put to grief in their many trials, but they could rejoice in Christ the hope of glory. No doubt these experiences were often of an alternating character, and struggled together in fierce conflict. Trials would press heavily upon their spirits, and then the promises with sustaining power would bear upward ; thus their strength was renewed, and their faith victorious.

7. *Why does Peter contrast the trial of their faith with the testing of gold by fire ? and why was it needed ?*

This reference to the testing of gold is in order to show the reason for the severe trial through which they were called to pass. A piece of ore, said to be gold, is put into the hands of a refiner, but before it can be counted as wealth it must be tested, and the test by fire is deemed sufficient. So with these saints ; they had confessed Christ, had endured a measure of trial already, and this was being continued in order to prove them thoroughly. If there was gold in the furnace, it would come out purified from its dross ; and if there was true appreciation and faith in Christ, it would be found unto praise and honour and glory at the appearing of Jesus Christ.

8. *" Full of glory." What does this imply ?*

It is, *lit., glorified*, and specially refers to Christ. These saints had not seen Christ, but they had heard of His love through the Gospel, and this had begotten love in them. Then having believed His promises they rejoiced with an unspeakable joy, (He having been) glorified.

9–11. *The salvation attained by these elect ones had been the subject of prophecy. Would you call this fore-knowledge?*

Yes, or fore-revealing, which is the same thing. This electing and saving was not an afterthought with God. It was, as Paul states, *according to a plan of the ages* (Eph. iii. 11); and as Peter states here "according to the fore-knowledge of God," verse 2; and "testified beforehand," verse 11. These prophets therefore prophesied of the grace that should be shown to them, and thus being made known beforehand, it is very properly called fore-knowledge.

"*Not to themselves, but to us they did minister." Are these the same as Paul's "ministering spirits" in Heb. i. 14?*

Yes; both Peter and Paul refer to the ministry of the prophets, who, they assure us, revealed beforehand the privileges of the saints under the Christian economy; and as the proclamation of these glad-tidings had been attested by the Holy Spirit, the evidence of this truth was most conclusive.

"*Which things the angels desire to look into." Are these celestial beings?*

No; they are the messengers who first "preached the Gospel with the Holy Spirit sent down from heaven," into which things they were desiring to look more closely.

13. "*Wherefore gird up the loins of your mind." How were they to do this?*

By the truth which they had received, and by which they would be fitted for their heavenly journey. Truth would be to the Christian, what a girdle would be to an eastern traveller, and the force of this illustration they would perfectly understand.

"*The grace that is to be brought unto you at the revelation of Jesus Christ." What future favour was this?*

It will be better to read, *Hope perfectly for the favour which is being brought unto you in a revelation of Jesus Christ.* It was the favour already provided in Jesus that he wished them to enjoy.

17. "*And if ye call on the Father." Is Peter doubtful respecting this?*

It is better to read, *And if (as) Father ye call on Him who without respect of persons judges according to the work of each, (then) in reverence pass the time of your sojourn.* It is a very important exhortation which is based upon their new relationship.

18. *Why does he refer to a redemption by silver and gold?*

Under the law every man had to pay a ransom for his own life. It was known as redemption money, and gave the ransomed a title to be registered in the congregation, but had no moral influence over the heart. But the blood of Christ had redeemed them from a vain life, and is referred to as a caution against their returning to that state from which they had been delivered.

"*Who verily was fore-ordained before the foundation of the world." Was this before creation?*

"Fore-ordained" is not a proper word to use here, as the sentence literally reads, *Having indeed been fore-known before a laying down of a world;* by which Peter refers to the founding of the Jewish economy, as before that dispensation the Coming One was certainly known, and must therefore have been revealed to those who expected His appearance, and whose faith was seen in their obedient life. He was certainly fore-known to Abel, when by faith he offered his more excellent sacrifice; and to Noah, when he offered clean beasts; and to Abraham who built his altar in whatever place he pitched his tent. This fore-revealing and fore-knowledge of the Christ not only preceded the manifestation of Him, but also the dispensation under which the Jews lived.

23. *"Being born again." In what does this differ from "begotten again" of verse 3 ?*

It is the same Greek word in both places, so that there should be no difference in the rendering. The word regenerated would be a proper word in both verses. In the first this is said to be " by [the truth of] the resurrection," and here is said to be by the " Word of God," who, he declares, " liveth and abideth for ever."

Has man any part in this regeneration ?

He is responsible for receiving this preached Gospel, or incorruptible seed, without which it will never take place. To expect regeneration before faith, and so without it, is to ignore the whole Gospel arrangement.

24. *" All flesh is as grass." Does this refer to the general frailty of humanity, or to dispensational standing ?*

Peter evidently refers to the dispensational standing of the nation, and quotes these words from Isa. xl. 6, as a warning respecting it. A solemn crisis had arrived, the dispensation had virtually closed, and all connected with it were as grass, ready to be cut down. The contrast is between the fading things of the old economy, and the abiding privileges of the Gospel institution.

CHAPTER II.

1. *" Wherefore laying aside all malice." Why has Peter to exhort them to do so ?*

It would be better to read, Having put away therefore all malice, and all guile, etc. Indeed, so thorough had been their reformation, that their

souls are said to have been purified by the truth. Hence the exhortation begins with them as " new-born babes."

2. *Why does Peter urge them to desire the sincere milk of the word, when Paul condemns the Hebrews for continuing to require it ?*

The reason for the difference appears to be this. Paul blames the Hebrews for remaining so long among the types and shadows of the Old Covenant—the milk of the word— when they ought to have advanced into the full use of the facts and revelations of the New ; while Peter urges a rational use of these instructions in their then infant state ; as by such use they might grow thereby, —*lit.*, grow into salvation,—*i.e.*, into full deliverance from the elements of their former state. He then adds, " If so be,"—*i.e.*, if you so use this instruction,—you will indeed show that you have tasted that the Lord is gracious.

Why does he call them " new-born babes " ?

They had been but newly begotten by the Gospel, and the phrase is very appropriate. The epistle was written shortly after their dispersion, and is therefore the earliest of all the apostolic epistles.

4. *" A living stone." Why did Peter apply such a simile to the Lord ?*

The prophets had termed the Messiah a stone, and Jesus being raised from death, He had become a living stone, a foundation on which they were built, and were therefore secure.

When was Christ the stone, disallowed or rejected of men ?

When He was denied by the nation and put to death.

And when " chosen of God " ?

When raised from the dead, He was laid by God as the living foundation of a new temple, and was then

" chosen of God and precious,"—*lit.*, had in honour,—because exalted to God's right hand.

5. " *Lively stones.*" *What does this imply?*

It is, *lit.*, *living stones.* Being quickened by Christ the living foundation stone, they received a new life in Him, and in union with Him formed a new house, and He being a priest, they formed under Him a new priesthood. This was to them authoritative instruction, and was required by them in their new and gracious position.

6–8. *Two prophecies are here quoted by Peter; what does he intend to show by them?*

That there will be two results from what God had done in laying Christ as a foundation. (1.) That those who believe in Him will be saved and honoured ; " Unto you, therefore, which believe, He is precious,"—*lit., is this honour.* (2.) That those who disbelieve the word, through the spirit of disobedience, will stumble over this stone into judgment.

" *Being disobedient; whereunto also they were appointed.*" *Was it to disobedience?*

No. God appoints no one to disobey His testimony, but He has appointed that those who do so shall suffer. And this the prophet declares (Isa. viii. 15), " And many among them shall stumble, and fall, and be broken." The stumbling is through their unbelief, but the doom of all who do so is, " shall be broken." This is implied but not stated by Peter, and it is to this they were appointed.

9. " *But ye are a chosen generation,*" etc. *On what ground did Peter apportion these privileges to those scattered ones?*

Those persons were Jews, but it was not as such that this honour was accorded to them, but as the elect of God, through faith in Jesus. Under the Old Covenant election, priesthood, etc., belonged to them as the fleshly seed of Abraham ; but when the New Covenant was introduced, there was a transfer of these privileges to believers. This declaration by Peter is of immense importance to all who believe in Jesus.

10. " *Which in time past were not a people.*" *If these were Jews how could it apply to them?*

These persons addressed were from the provinces, and possibly most, if not all, were of the ten tribes, whose nationality had been lost by their dispersion. Now by faith in Jesus, they had obtained mercy, and so became the people of God.

11–18. " *Dearly beloved, I beseech you as strangers and pilgrims, abstain from fleshly lusts.*" *What does this exhortation indicate?*

The immoral character of their past life, from which they had been redeemed, and that their present life must be in harmony with their high calling. Besides, being scattered in cities where vice predominated, and where persecution might further be expected, they are exhorted to holy behaviour, to be orderly and submissive to governors, to be patient under trial, to live as the servants of God, that in all things they might be acceptable to Him.

19–23. *Is it not strange that Peter should warn them against self-defence in cases of injustice, and suffering wrongfully?*

Yes, very strange when viewed according to our thoughts. So it was when Christ was reviled, and reviled not again ; and when He suffered, and threatened not ; and Peter wishes Him to be their example.

25. " *Ye were as sheep going astray.*" *Does this term* sheep *apply to other than Jews?*

It was never applied to Gentiles,

because in their natural state they were not the flock of God. The Jews were His flock, and were under the care of His shepherds, the priests and prophets ; but, as was so marked in the case of the ten tribes, they had gone astray as lost sheep. They had indeed become the prodigal, and were restored to their Father only through the Gospel, and were then placed under the Shepherd and Bishop of their souls.

CHAPTER III.

1. *" Likewise, ye wives, be in subjection to your own husbands." Is not this a strange exhortation ?*

He is exhorting believing women, whose unbelieving husbands might show undue tyranny over them. Hence Peter exhorts them to lead such an obedient, chaste, and reverential life, that even their husbands might be won over by it to serve Christ. Such a result they were to seek by living a subjected and holy life.

Why should Peter be so particular about women plaiting the hair, and wearing of gold, and adorning the body ?

Because these things have an influence against the truth, and it is not strange that the Holy Spirit should wish the disciples of Jesus to understand this, and so fashion themselves that He should be honoured. And since it is a matter of pleasing or displeasing Christ, and of helping or hindering His cause that was involved in their conduct, it is not strange that he should exhort even about the clothing of the body.

Is it wrong for women now to wear gold and plait the hair ?

It is wrong to do what the Spirit forbids, and when His mind is revealed it becomes a test to all hearts. No doubt it is far easier to adorn the body so as to please self, than to adorn

the mind with a meek and quiet spirit, but it is the latter only that God approves.

6. *" Whose daughters ye are." Does he mean of Abraham, or Sarah, since both are named ?*

Of Sarah, whose example is commended for their imitation. Her reverence of her husband is specially commended, and in having her spirit they became her children.

7. *Why is the husband permitted to rule the wife ? And why must it be in knowledge and sympathy ?*

The husband is permitted to rule, because he is a representative of Christ ; and in His loving spirit this rule must be exercised; and the wife is required to submit, because she represents the Church. Both are positions of responsibility, and both husband and wife are to fill their place so that Christ may be honoured.

8. *" Finally, be ye all of one mind." How was this possible ?*

By all having the mind of Christ ; and with His Spirit dwelling in them they would then be compassionate one of another, and would love as brethren.

9. *" Not rendering evil for evil," etc. Was Peter charging them with doing this ?*

No, he is only instructing them in Christian behaviour. It would be out of place in an epistle, which might very properly be called the great charter of their standing, privileges, and obligations, to deal with failure under it. A charter could properly contain only those specifications of privilege, etc., which those to whom it is given could rightly claim, while behaviour in relation to it must be dealt with afterward. These favoured Jews, who had been blest with all spiritual blessings in Christ, had to be tested by their behaviour, and then praise or blame, encouragement or warning, had to be awarded. And this we find to have been done in the epistle to the Hebrews, and the epistle by James, as well as the first epistle of John. These four epistles have an inseparable relation to these first Jewish converts ; and, if overlooked, will certainly hinder a right application of their contents. The order of these four epistles is doubtless a moral one, and the state of those to whom each is addressed must always be kept before us, in order to feel the force of the appeals, ,tc., that are made.

15. " *But sanctify the Lord God in your hearts.*" *What does this mean ?*

The Revised Version reads, " But sanctify in your hearts Christ as Lord ; " and this reading is now accepted as correct. At Pentecost Jesus had been received by them as both Lord and Christ, and here Peter asks them to sanctify Him in their hearts, and to be ready to give a reason for their hope of glory through Him to any asking for it.

19. " *By which also he went and preached unto the spirits in prison.*" *Is not this a very strange circumstance ?*

Its strangeness or otherwise will depend upon our understanding of Peter's reference to this matter. If we suppose him to say that while the body of Jesus lay in the sepulchre, He by the Spirit went to that part of Hades, where the spirits of those who were disobedient in the days of Noah were confined, and preached to them, then we might very properly call it a strange circumstance, because we have nothing like it in any other part of the Bible. But if we understand him to mean that during that period of long-suffering while the ark was preparing, Noah by the Spirit, through whom all testimony is given, did preach to them of righteousness and a coming

judgment, then there is nothing strange about it. God has always warned transgressors of judgment, and sought to dissuade them from continuing to rebel.

But why does Peter refer to it at all, even supposing him to refer to the time of Noah ?

This question is seldom asked, although a very important one, as a correct answer will help to remove any difficulty which may have arisen in connection with it. But we must first notice how Peter introduces this interesting fact. These saints, to whom he was writing, had suffered for the truth's sake, and that from their own brethren, the Jews, who through their disobedience were under the judgment, as stated by Christ in Matt. xxiv., as the Antidiluvians had been under the judgment of the deluge ; and to both the long-suffering of God was shown by delaying the threatened doom, in order that they might repent and be saved. Now Peter, who well knew of this coming doom—having heard it pronounced by Jesus — exhorts these saints in all their trials endured from these unbelieving ones to manifest such a Christ-like spirit, rendering good for evil, blessing for cursing, that those who would not be won to obedience by the testimony might be won by their behaviour. And in order to encourage them to witness for Christ, he brings forward the example of Christ (1.) in His own personal suffering for sins, to bring them to God ; and (2.) by the Spirit in Noah preaching to the men of a former age, while God's long-suffering waited, a case so strikingly parallel to their own. The Antidiluvians did not profit by the favour shown to them, but were drowned by the flood—out of which only eight were saved—and are stated by Peter as being in his day "spirits in prison." These striking illustrations are therefore given to show that as Noah preached to those under judgment, and as Christ bore witness to the men of that generation, so they were to witness for Christ, even to their judgment-doomed brethren the Jews, that so they might be without excuse.

There is nothing strange in this aspect of it. Would you press this view as the correct one?

Most certainly, since the Spirit of God never reveals what is merely to gratify curiosity, but always for some practical purpose. Hence this reference to Noah, warning the impenitent to shun the coming judgment by turning to the Lord, was an example to these saints to live and labour in the truth, that during the patience of God their brethren might turn and live in the salvation of Jesus.

21. *" The like figure whereunto baptism doth now save us." Why call it a figure?*

It is, *lit., an antitype, even baptism, which also now saves us.* That is, our baptism, in which we are saved by the resurrection of Christ, who is now in heaven, corresponds to the water through which Noah was saved from the world on which judgment rested, and carried in the ark into the world where the rainbow assured him the deluge would never return. Noah was under the judgment as well as others, for it rested on the world; but being moved by the revelation of God, he prepared an ark, and in it was carried safely through. So these Jews had been under judgment; but a Saviour being provided, they believed in Him, and in their immersion into His death they passed through judgment on to resurrection ground, and so reached the promise of life. " There is therefore now no condemnation to them that are in Christ Jesus." Baptism

into Christ is with Peter a transitional ordinance, and is likened to Noah passing from judgment to deliverance.

Why does he say that baptism is " not the putting away the filth of the flesh "?

Peter is writing to Jews, who knew that immersions under the law were always ceremonially for the cleansing of the flesh, whilst under the Gospel baptism is never done for this purpose. Baptism is not a mere bodily act, but is for the mind, or, as we read here, " the answer of a good conscience toward God."

"The answer of a good conscience." How could it be that?

We should read, Asking or demanding a good conscience, and not " answer." The law was satisfied when the flesh was purged, but Christ claims a good conscience from all who are immersed—*i.e.,* an honest, hearty acceptance of Him as their Lord and Saviour. It is a sincere, conscientious purpose that baptism, or Christ in baptism, demands from all who will be His disciples.

CHAPTER IV.

1–5. Why does Peter refer to the sufferings of Christ?

It was not merely to show that Christ suffered, but that having suffered on account of sin, He was for ever released. This was the position he urges them to occupy, or to be armed with the same mind. Their past life, while living among Gentiles, had been stained with vices peculiar to them, but, having been set free by the Gospel, he now urges them to be like Christ, and have done with sin for ever. And though the people among whom they were now cast would think their refusal to walk with them strange, yet, as all were responsible to the judge of both quick and dead, they should keep themselves from these surrounding evils.

6. *"The Gospel preached also to them that are dead." To whom does he refer?*

To those to whom Noah preached, and who are here spoken of as "them that are dead." The object of the preaching was their restoration to God, and failing this, judgment. So, he teaches, it would be with men now living in the flesh, judgment would follow their disobedience.

7. *"The end of all things is at hand." What things does he refer to?*

To the end of the Jewish dispensation, which he knew must soon take place, and for which sobriety, watchfulness, and prayer would be their best preparation.

12. *What was this fiery trial that would try them?*

I know of nothing historically except the judgment which fell upon the nation. As the Romans were the executers of that judgment, the Jews living in Roman provinces would be more or less involved in the calamity. As Jews they would suffer nationally from the Romans, and as Christians they would suffer from their own brethren. It was indeed a fiery trial through which they were called to pass, and would test their faith exceedingly.

17. *"For the time is come that judgment must begin at the house of God." Was this the Church?*

No; it was the Jewish temple, and was called by Jesus on one occasion, His "Father's house." But as it had become a "den of thieves" —*i.e.*, an assembly of dishonest hypocritical worshippers—the whole institution had to be removed by judgment; and when Peter wrote the time was hastening on, and the overwhelming demonstrations of wrath

were soon to be poured out on all connected with it. That Peter refers to the end of the Jewish institution could scarcely be questioned, since the disobedient under the Gospel are warned of a more fearful doom than would rest upon the unfaithful connected with that former house of God.

18. *"And if the righteous scarcely be saved." Saved from what?*

Saved from that overwhelming judgment, I presume. The Saviour promised that they should be saved out of it, but only by faithfully attending to his directions. Israel had become a leprous house all through, and according to the law must be pulled down. In doing this there was danger to all, but the faithful were to be delivered.

CHAPTER V.

1. *"The elders who are among you I exhort." To what were they exhorted?*

To faithfully feed and take oversight of the flock.

"Who am also an elder." When and by whom was Peter made an elder?

By the Lord Jesus when he appeared to them by the Sea of Galilee, and commanded him to feed His lambs, and shepherd His sheep. Peter was made both an apostle and an overseer by the Lord Jesus; and having fulfilled the former in his proclamations, he is here fulfilling the latter in teaching and directing the saints.

2–4. *"Taking the oversight thereof." Is self-appointment to the work intended here?*

No; Peter is exhorting those who were already elders in the church to do the work of Christ faithfully, not even by constraint or for a sordid motive. To assume that he is exhorting persons to take office who may be impressed that they ought to do so, as some have understood, is to fall into a serious mistake. It is not old men but recognised elders that are addressed.

5–8. *" Likewise, ye younger, submit yourselves unto the elder."* *Why exhort them to submission ?*

Both the elder and the younger of the assembly were responsible to God, and therefore both are exhorted. The elders were to so teach and live, that their example should be worthy of imitation, and to such examples the younger were to submit themselves. And since a common foe sought the ruin of all, they were to be humble, sober, vigilant, and so escape his evil purpose.

" Your adversary the devil, as a roaring lion, walketh about seeking whom he may devour." *Was this a visible or an invisible foe ?*

Possibly an invisible one, but working through some visible agency —a power to be resisted in the faith, for which steadfastness was required ere a final victory would be obtained.

13. *" The church that is at Babylon."* *Where was this ?*

It is, *lit., She (who is) at Babylon, . . . salutes you.* We judge that Babylon is used by Peter as a symbolic name, and that Jerusalem is intended. Babylon of old persecuted and enslaved God's people and Jerusalem had done the same thing, as they had so painfully experienced in being scattered abroad. Those who remained, for some did remain, are referred to by *she* or the Church, as the Sinaitic MS. reads, for he adds, "elected together with you." The "election of God," of both foreign and home-born Jews, took place together upon their joint-acceptance of Christ, for Luke records that "all that believed were together, and had all things common." After the death of Stephen, those from Pontus, etc., were expelled, while the others remained, and when Peter wrote this consolatory and instructive epistle, their greeting of love is sent to their persecuted brethren.

THE SECOND EPISTLE GENERAL OF
PETER.

CHAPTER I.

Why did Peter write this second epistle ?

As his first epistle was written to believing Jews, and was an important sequel to his first proclamations to them, as affirming their standing and security by continued obedience to Christ ; so this second epistle, written to believing Gentiles, was necessary to assure them that in being faithful to Christ an entrance into the everlasting kingdom of Jesus would be administered unto them. Together, these sermons and epistles are the keys of the kingdom of heaven given to him by Christ, and being opened by these authoritative announcements, it stands open for all who wish to enter upon the terms proposed. This new administration being opened by the authority of Jesus, none can shut it, or authoritatively change its mode of entrance ; and the old being closed, none can open it again. He openeth, and no man shutteth ; and shutteth, and no man openeth.

1. *On what ground does Peter*

acknowledge the election of these believing Gentiles ?

When Peter led the house of Cornelius to believe in Jesus, they were sealed with the Holy Spirit, and this removed all doubt from his mind ; so that in writing to them as believing Gentiles he can say, "to them that have obtained like precious faith with us through the righteousness of God and our Saviour Jesus Christ." Thus showing that they were permitted to share what had now become the common privilege of all believers.

"Through the righteousness of God." Why was it righteous in God to accept of them ?

Because Jesus had died for their sins, and as Peter said in that noted conference on Gentile acceptance, "God . . . put no difference between us and them, purifying their hearts by faith" (Acts xv. 9).

2. *Is not the benediction the same in both epistles ?*

It is "Grace to you, and peace be multiplied" in both, only in the first it is "according to the fore-knowledge of God the Father," *i.e.*, the revelations made known by the prophets ; whilst in the second, it is "through the knowledge,"—*lit.*, in the full knowledge,—"of God, and of Jesus our Lord,"—*i.e.*, as made known by the apostles of Jesus. Because it is through them that the privileges of believing Gentiles were fully made known.

3. *"According as His divine power hath given us all things," etc. Who does he mean by "us"?*

Us Jews, who first believed on Him. To us all things that pertain to life and godliness have been given, through the knowledge of Him who called us to glory and virtue.

4. *"Whereby are given unto us exceeding great and precious promises; that by these ye might be partakers." Who are the ye referred to ?*

These believing Gentiles, who through their faith in Jesus, were made to have fellowship with them, and are here assured of a full share of all provided privileges.

5-7. *"And beside this, giving all diligence, add to your faith virtue," etc. Why does Peter insist upon the perfecting of these graces ?*

These graces were necessary to form Christian character, and prepare them for final acceptance. They had been received through grace, and must now be obedient in all that is required. Nor must it be thought a matter of human judgment for Péter to insist upon these graces being added to each other: he is using the key of the everlasting kingdom, or speaking in the name of Jesus, and those who wish to enter must observe the terms or conditions on which entrance will be granted.

Seven graces or traits of character were to be added to their faith ; is there anything essential in the order in which they stand ?

It is quite possible that even the order is important. For instance, "Add to your faith virtue,"—*lit.*, courage or fortitude,—and then note how essential this is for all that is to follow. Then again, how essential is knowledge to help us in being temperate or self-controlled. Yes, even the order is important, as the adding of one will help us to add the next on the list with greater ease than if we overlooked it. It is rather singular that the Greek word translated "add" should be derived from the name of a chorus-leader among the Greeks, or the person who was responsible for bringing together all that was necessary to complete the festival music. So Peter teaches the responsibility of the Christian to bring together into one life all the requisites of a pure Christian character, so that it might form one grand harmonious chorus in the ears of God—the sweet music of a life redeemed to Him.

8. *Is "neither barren nor unfruitful" a further result of this adding together ?*

It is, *lit.*, neither idle nor unfruitful in the knowledge, etc., *i.e*, there will be much Christian activity and also fruit to God in such a life as here commended.

9. *"But he that lacketh these things is blind." In what respect is he blind ?*

He is blind to the claims of Christ. Or if he knew them he has forgotten the purifying of his old sins,—*i.e.*, the putting from him the sins or disobedience of his past life. It was presumed that in his immersion every convert to Christ did so, and rose from the grave of water to walk in newness of life. Now, Peter teaches here that those who do not add to their faith the things required, are idle and unfruitful, and that ruin will be the result.

10–13. *If their calling and election were of God, how did it require to be made sure ?*

Because the final salvation and glory, which is the end of the calling and choice of God, could only follow the continued obedience of those elected. Peter well knew that his own brethren in the flesh had been chosen and called to Canaan, but were not allowed to enter through their unbelief; and he now assures these Gentiles that an undoubted entrance into the everlasting kingdom would only be given to the obedient. Of this truth he would not fail to remind them as long as permitted to remain in the tabernacle, and even to stir them up by putting them in remembrance.

14. *"I must shortly put off this my tabernacle, even as our Lord Jesus Christ hath showed me." To what does he refer ?*

To the personal statement of Jesus, that he would die a violent death (John xxi. 18, 19), and which he knew was not far off.

16–18. *Why does he refer to transfiguration ?*

Because he had been assuring them of glory through a glorified Christ, and at once he refers to the fact that he had seen Him glorified, and heard the voice of God affirming Jesus to be His Son, in whom He was well pleased. It was to Him a demonstration of the whole truth of their proclamation and teaching.

19. *"We have also a more sure word of prophecy." How could prophecy be more sure than the sight of glory ?*

Peter is not contrasting prophecy with the vision on the mount, but is affirming that through the vision the word of prophecy was more firm or sure to them. To prophecy itself they would do well to take heed, because it was as a lamp shining in a dark place, or through the night, and being from God would be fulfilled.

"Till the day dawn, and the day star arise in your hearts." Does this imply that the day of Gospel fact had not arrived ?

No. This would be contrary to all apostolic testimony. Indeed, his words "in your hearts" should lead us to see that the light was truth, and entered the mind only as admitted by the understanding and faith; and this is why he urges the heeding of prophecy given in old time, and to mark its fulfilment in the evidences of an ascended and glorified Christ. The day had dawned, but many through ignorance saw not the light.

"No prophecy of the Scripture is of any private interpretation." What does this mean ?

I understand him to mean that the prophecies were not concerning those who wrote them, but were about

Christ and the saints of the present dispensation. The prophets spoke by the Holy Spirit of things to come, and so he urges them to take heed, for the prophecies concerned themselves.

CHAPTER II.

1. *" But there were false prophets also among the people, even as there shall be false teachers among you." What security did God provide against these perverters of the truth?*

When God sent His prophets He gave evidence of the truth of their mission; and when Jesus sent preachers they also had their divine attestations. In relation to prophets that might arise, it was proposed as a test by Isaiah, " To the law and to the testimony, if they speak not according to this, it is because there is no light or divine revelation in them" (viii. 20). The law of Moses, and the testimony of prophets, was the standard by which the words of all could be tried, and this was the security of the people. When Jesus sent forth His apostles He affirmed, " He that heareth you, heareth Me," and as their preaching and teaching under the special guardianship of the Holy Spirit was for the age, it must be the standard of appeal all through the dispensation. Teachers did arise then, and every century has added to their number, who taught doctrines contrary to the apostles, or who set aside what they taught in the name of Jesus. No doubt a terrible doom awaits all such false teachers, but with the apostles' writings in hand, or within reach, every one who is led aside is personally responsible for his own deception. A person who trades in counterfeit notes, who has an opportunity of testing them at the bank, is liable to be arrested as well as those who issued them.

What does he mean by " damnable heresies"?

It is, *lit., sects destructive—i.e.,* sects that destroy and mutilate the truth, even denying the Lord that bought them—*i.e.,* denying His authority or right to rule over them.

3. *Whose judgment now of a long time lingereth not. Who might those persons be?*

At first he speaks of them as if yet future, but further on he speaks of them as actually in their midst, even joining with them in their love-feasts. And though he has sketched a most vivid portrait of their uncleanness and insubordination; of their covetousness and vanity, he has not told us who they were. It is from Paul that we learn that they were Jews, and that their Judaising efforts, as they spread themselves over the churches of the Gentiles, caused him no little trouble. They were doubtless mere hired mercenaries, whose god was their belly, and who minded earthly things. Their judgment, however, was fast approaching, for the doom of the nation was not far off, and with it these deceivers fell to rise no more.

4-9. *We learn here that judgment fell upon " the angels that sinned," the " old world," and " Sodom and Gomorrah." Why does Peter refer to these cases?*

Simply to show that since God so signally punished these ancient offenders, those who denied the authority of Jesus the ascended Lord need not hope to escape.

Who were these angels that sinned?

It is better to read *the messengers,* and these in Gen. vi. 2 are called the " sons of God," being of the line of Seth, and who, after calling themselves by the name of Jehovah, and being counted as witnesses for the truth for which Abel suffered death, were seduced by the daughters of men; and thus, through the lusts of the flesh, their high position as the sons of God was abandoned. That special judgment from God followed their sin, although Genesis furnishes no record of it, must, I think, from this statement be inferred. God spared them not, but cast them down to hell — *lit.*, to Tartarus — to chains or dens of gloom He gave them over, reserving them for judgment, and if not before the deluge, they were certainly judged then.

In speaking of the judgment of the world by water, and of Sodom by fire, why does Peter refer to the deliverance of Noah and Lot ?

Because in the coming judgment, to which Peter alludes, the faithful were to be delivered from it ; and for their encouragement he shows that, while God could reserve for judgment the ungodly, He could deliver the godly out of the trial. The deliverance of both Noah and Lot were proofs of what God could do for those who honoured Him.

10–15. If those whose vices are detailed in these six verses were Jews, how was it that they became so unclean in their desires, and so immoral in their lives ?

It is indeed strange that those who had the oracles of God should have become so vile. It is, however, a striking fact, that while the Jew would never give up his religion, he managed to tack on to it all the abominations derived from association with Gentiles, in every age in which he has mixed with them ; whether they have been Moabites, Canaanites, Babylonians, Romans, or Asiatics. Here we get them thoroughly steeped in the vices of the age, and a party of them, those who were corrupted hirelings, actually seeking to corrupt by their mixed Judaism those who from among the Gentiles had turned to Christ.

What are the proofs that they were Jews, and that they were hired to Judaise the Gentile converts ?

That they were hired is very clear, for like Balaam they loved the wages of unrighteousness ; and that they were Jews is also evident, for they had gone astray from the right path, which was applicable then only to Jews who had once professed conversion to Christ.

20. *" They are again entangled and overcome." Does he refer to the false teachers, or to those deceived by them ?*

To those who were deceived by their empty boasting words. By the truth the Gentiles were purified, but when their teaching was received, they went back like the dog to his vomit, and the washed sow to wallowing in mire. And this is why Peter so earnestly seeks to guard these converts, and to prevent the evil influence of these false teachers.

CHAPTER III.

1. *" This second epistle, beloved, I now write unto you ; in both which I stir up,"* etc. *Does not this imply that both letters were written to them ?*

No. It only implies that he had written a previous letter, which if read might also profit them. This second epistle, beloved, I now write to you, in which (letters) I stir up your pure or sincere mind, by reminding you of what prophets and apostles have spoken. The object of Peter was the same in both letters, viz., to help those who had accepted Jesus as their Lord and Saviour, but the first was most likely written to believing Jews, and at an early period of their Christian standing. When he did write to these Gentile saints, he had almost reached the end of his life, and was waiting for his decease —*lit.*, his exodus—but ere he goes out of his tabernacle, these words of teaching and warning are written for their preservation from evil.

Since the first letter was written to believing Jews, how could believing Gentiles appropriate what had been written to others?

Peter informs them at the beginning of this 'letter that having obtained like precious faith with believing Jews, they were entitled to receive "grace and peace," which includes all that God has provided, and that saints could enjoy, so that the privileges of the one became the privileges of the other, in and through the Lord Jesus. The Jews were the first to receive "according to His abundant mercy," but the Gentiles being afterward saved by grace, became partakers with them. Thus the privileges detailed in the first letter could be appropriated to themselves through their being also in Christ.

3. *"There shall come in the last days scoffers." What days are these?*

The last days of this dispensation —the days in which the unfulfilled promise of God should call out their denial of the promise being ever fulfilled.

Have these scoffers yet appeared?

Every century since Jesus left the earth has furnished its deriding scoffers; but it is a question whether this form of unbelief, based upon the delay of the Saviour's coming, has ever been manifested to such an extent as to fulfil this prophecy of Peter. Certainly the promised presence of Jesus has been delayed beyond the time which many who ardently expected Him have calculated. The time, according to those who have made the appearing of Jesus a special study, has often been affirmed, and that with an assurance and vehemence that has induced thousands to accept their dicta, and, in the light of their statements, to

believe that they saw the time of the end so clearly as to make the event a fixed expectation. The results in many of these cases have been both ludicrous and painful. We know of men and women who, having been led to fix upon a certain day or night as the time beyond which they thought the Saviour's coming could not extend, have parted with home, business, goods, indeed everything but their hope, which on the appointed day left them ashamed, since Jesus did not come according to their expectations, but the body and its claims continued as before. Others were more shrewd and business-like in their actions, for while they affirmed as confidently the time of the Lord's advent, managed to lease their dwellings for a much longer period, or kept on their business, although they made no secret of their assurance that then they would have to depart and greet the descending Christ at the time they stated. "I fully expect the Lord will be here in September," writes a friend, but that was in 1879, and He has not yet met such expectation. Now the delay of the Lord has actually gone beyond every date fixed by man for His return, at least as far as known to me, the Rev. M. Baxter excepted. For after persuading thousands by his plausible reasoning that Louis Napoleon was "the destined monarch of the world," and would be destroyed by the personal appearing of Jesus about 1873, he has now pushed that event to about 1890, beyond which, as I heard him publicly state, it cannot far extend, as the lines of prophecy and dates come to a close about that time; and for this fresh date, which is only another delusion of all who believe it, there is not a single valuable reason given. Now, I suppose that through teachers of this school millions have expected Christ to appear during the last thirty years, whose hopes have all been disappointed. Now this disappointment may continue until the very state of things predicted by Peter shall really take place, and instead of expecting Him they may in their vexed disappointment raise the question, Where is the promise of His coming? and this very form of unbelief become the ruling feature of that period.

How is it that so many earnest men have made such mistakes as it is now plain to all they have made?

They have mistaken events that were to take place under the government of Christ for His actual return. But as the time of His return has not been revealed, it is impossible for any to say when it will take place, and it is only presumption in all who have done so.

5-7. Are the arguments which Peter advances against this form of scepticism satisfactory?

I think so. He first shows their ignorance or careless oversight of a well known fact, viz., that the world had once been destroyed by water, so that things had not continued as they were from creation. Then, second, he affirms prophetically that the world that now is, is reserved unto fire against the day of judgment and perdition of ungodly men, so that however long the promise may be delayed, it is certain to be fulfilled.

8. " One day is with the Lord as a thousand years." Does this mean that time is nothing to God?

He is not speaking of God's nature, but of His faithfulness. Length of time does affect man's action, but God's never. Man through delay often forgets both promise and obligation, but God never forgets. If He threatens judgment, a thousand years' delay will not alter His word. This is

what Peter means by a "thousand years as one day."

10. " But the day of the Lord will come." What is this " day of the Lord"?

It is the day in which He will manifest His displeasure against man's rejection of Himself during the dispensation. The present, according to Paul, is *man's day*—i.e., the time of his opportunities, however he may use them or abuse them. Peter has given us a threefold aspect of this day, calling it the " day of the Lord," and the "day of God," and the "day of judgment and perdition of ungodly men." Paul has given us the three aspects in one sentence : " He [God] hath appointed a day, in the which He will judge the world in righteousness by that man whom He hath ordained " (Acts xvii. 31).

10-12. What is meant by the day coming as a thief?

A thief enters when men are most secure, and takes away their treasures before they are aware of it. Many profess to be looking for Him now, but His chariot does not appear, and His long delay may beget in many the thought that all things will continue as they were. This vain thought will no doubt embolden men to be careless, and when least expected, " in a moment, in the twinkling of an eye," the crisis will have come; or, as Dr Young writes :—

" Sudden as the spark
From smitten steel ; from nitrous grain the blaze,
Man, starting from his couch, shall sleep no more !
The day is broke which never more shall close!
Above, beneath, around, amazement all !
Terror and glory joined in their extremes !
Our God in grandeur, and our world on fire ! "

Peter affirms that the heavens shall pass away, that the elements shall melt with fervent heat, the earth also, and the works therein shall be burned up. In view of these solemn events, the exhortation to a holy life and godliness is most appropriate. May the delay of the Lord never embolden us to trifle, nor lead us to question the truth of all He has spoken.

"*Nevertheless we, according to His promise, look for new heavens, and a new earth, wherein dwelleth righteousness." Will this precede or follow the dissolved elements?*

I am inclined to believe that these new heavens and new earth will precede the burning and destruction of the world. I say believe, because there is prophetic teaching as to what God intends by these terms, and this must guide our decision. The Scriptures do not teach that a renovated earth is to be the dwelling-place of the glorified; nor, indeed, should we expect it, since heaven, where Jesus now is, is the home of promise. " I go to prepare a place for you," said Jesus to His disciples, " that where I am, there also ye may be." We will, however, look to the prophecy from which Peter quotes. " Behold I create new heavens, and a new earth, and the former shall not be remembered nor come into mind" (Isa. lxv. 17). Now if God had said nothing further on this statement, we should have been left to infer, as best we could, what was really intended. But God has not left His meaning so closed up that we cannot see into it. He has seen fit to explain these symbols, and thus instructed we can learn their meaning. Hence He adds, " But be ye glad and rejoice for ever in that which I create : for, behold, I create Jerusalem a rejoicing, and her people a joy " (ver. 18). Here we are instructed, that it is not a material universe that God purposed to create, but a new order of things—a new constitution, or what Paul terms a " heavenly Jerusalem." Now, it is according to His promise that we look for this fulfilment, which of course must precede the

destruction of the world on which it will be displayed.

But when God says heavens and earth, is it not wrong to say that He means something else?

But He has told us Himself that He means something else than the material things, and He surely knows what He does mean. Besides, this is by no means a solitary instance. Malachi wrote that Elijah would come before the Messiah, but the disciples had to learn that John, and not the veritable Elijah, was intended. It may be well to note a matter here which we should all thoroughly understand, viz., that the nature of things is always according to the constitution or covenant to which they belong, and that even though the same name is used under the New Covenant as was employed under the Old, yet the fact of its higher character demands a different and higher order of things. If we look only at names, we shall be deceived, as were the disciples while looking for a repetition of the Old economy instead of the higher blessings of the New.

15. *How is the long-suffering of God to be accounted as salvation?*

The delay of judgment afforded opportunity for men to embrace God's offered mercy, and manifested His unwillingness that men should perish.

16. *Was it Paul that was hard to be understood, or the things about which he wrote?*

The things themselves were difficult, because unmanifested, and the unstable wrested or misapplied them to their own destruction. The possibility of doing this should make all of us careful how we use the Word of God.

18. "*But grow in grace and in the knowledge of our Lord," etc. What does this mean?*

Grace is favour and specially relates to the privileges which had been conferred upon them as believing Gentiles. It is the same thought which we get in the first chapter, but is here expressed in a figure. There he addresses them as having " obtained like precious faith with us " (Jews), and then exhorts " add to your faith virtue," etc. ; here he compares them to trees planted in a good soil, and exhorts to growth,— *i.e.*, that fruits of righteousness may be, by Jesus Christ, to the praise and glory of God. To grow in the knowledge of Jesus was to receive the revelations of Him which apostles and prophets had given, and which were essential to the upholding of their spiritual life. To grow in grace is to possess ourselves of all the privileges which Jesus has provided for us ; and to grow in knowledge is to advance into all the revelation which has been made concerning Him.

THE FIRST EPISTLE GENERAL OF

JOHN.

CHAPTER I.

Why did John write this Epistle, and to whom was it written ?

The Epistle was written to prove to the professed disciples of Jesus—and these are most likely to have been his Jewish brethren—the pure and holy character of His claims and service ; and also to show what fellowship with God, with Christ, and with the apostles really involved. It is evident — from the fact that holiness of heart and life is so urgently insisted upon, and its necessity illustrated in such a variety of aspects — that Christianity was either not understood by them, or that the claims of Christ were being trifled with. In his argument, John not only affirms the direct purpose of the mission of Christ—*i.e.*, to put away sin—but also shows the relationship which is being established between God or Satan by the good or evil actions of life. " Little children, let no man deceive you : he that doeth righteousness is righteous, even as He is righteous. He that committeth sin is of the devil." And while these professing Jews—

2 H

who were treating Christ much as their fathers had treated Moses, viz., using the traditions of the elders instead of His sayings—are fully answered, and are shown that their plan will never succeed with God, the truth delivered should be a warning to all other professors of religion, and to every age. This epistle is the final appeal of one of the apostolic witnesses in defence of the truth, and with it the Jewish dispensation closed. "*Little children, it is the last hour.*"

1. " *That which was from the beginning.*" *If John is writing about the personal Christ here, why does he use words in the neuter gender ?*

He is most certainly writing about Christ, but he is also writing of "life" manifested through the Christ, and therefore he very appropriately writes, " That which was from the beginning."

Is John trying to prove the incarnation of Jesus ?

No ; but His life by resurrection from death. About the former there was no question, but to the latter there were grave objections ; hence the scrutiny to which He was subjected even by His apostles. We have seen Him with our eyes, said John, we have gazed upon Him, and our hands have handled of the Word of life. "For the life was manifested, and we have seen it, and bear witness, and show unto you that eternal life, which was with the Father, and was manifest to us," in the Christ.

3, 4. What was there peculiar to this life which had been reached by Jesus ?

Entire separation from that which caused His death. What John really intends by this fellowship with Him is more fully expressed by Paul, "In that He died, He died unto sin once : but in that He liveth, He liveth unto God. Likewise reckon ye also yourselves to be dead indeed unto sin, but alive unto God through Jesus Christ our Lord" (Rom. vi. 10, 11). The fellowship, of which John is speaking here, is fellowship in redemption from all iniquity, and this important purpose these believers had entirely overlooked, and this is what he is trying to teach them.

5. " God is light," etc. What does this mean ?

That God is holy, and in His action there is no impurity. This was the revelation they had received of His character, and He had so declared it to them.

6. Why does he refer to this message concerning God ?

In order to show that if they walked in darkness or sin while professing fellowship with Him, their lives were a practical condemnation of their profession. If we say we walk with Him when we walk in sin, " we lie, and do not the truth."

7. What is walking in the light ?

Walking in the truth, *i.e.,* walking in obedience to God, and in

conformity to His will, as manifested in Jesus.

" Fellowship one with another." Is this with fellow-believers ?

According to Tischendorf, the Alexandrian MS. reads *fellowship with Him,* and this reading is most in harmony with the context.

" And the blood of Jesus Christ His Son cleanseth us from all sin." Does this refer to pardon or purity ?

To purity of both heart and life ; but the true force of this statement can only be understood by reading it in relation to the former part of the verse. If we walk in the light or truth, as He (God) is in the light, or according to the revelation of Himself, we have fellowship with Him, and the blood of Jesus Christ His Son cleanseth us from all sin. This latter sentence must not be read as if it taught that all sin *can be pardoned* through His blood, however true that may be ; nor that it *can cleanse* from the love of sin, as John is not teaching that either; but rather, as there is no darkness in God, so, in the blood or death of Jesus, there is no toleration or allowance of any sin. It cleanseth from *all.* It is not the power of the death of Christ that John is discussing here, but the extent of its moral claims. The fact that Christ died for sin is a proof that He could not allow transgression.

8. " If we say that we have no sin," etc. Does John apply this to believers ?

Not to those who were walking in the light, and yielding their members as instruments of righteousness unto God, but to those who rested in ceremonial cleansing, and deemed it sufficient, while really living in the practice of evil. If we do this, says John, we deceive ourselves, and the truth is not in us. The reference is to those Jews who accepted of Christ very much as their fathers accepted of Joshua when Moses was dead, viz., as completing a work which the other had begun, and not as an atoning Saviour, whose death proved their guilt and ruin. To be satisfied with law-service in relation to sin was to ignore the necessity of the death of Jesus, and to make God a liar when affirming its necessity.

9. "*If we confess our sins,*" etc. *Does this apply to alien sinners or to believers?*

John is writing to believers, and here announces the great law of forgiveness which applies to those who, having placed themselves under the administration of Christ, have failed in their obligations. Now failure or offence under any wise administration, even a parental one, must be dealt with. The offender must be liable to be called to account, and must be amenable to authority, and by some arrangement, calculated to prevent wrong-doing and uphold authority, he may be forgiven. Now it is not for us to arrange what we think should be, but to learn what is really the arrangement of God in relation to these matters ; and these being revealed to us, we are able to understand them. In the Gospel proclamation we learn that upon sincere faith, confession of Christ, and immersion into Him, the penitent sinner is freely pardoned, and is thus born into the family of God. Now this fixed gracious law of mercy shown to the returning sinner, can no more be repeated to those who have become unfaithful, in order to their required forgiveness, than could marriage be repeated by one who had become unfaithful to the marriage vow. Some other law must meet the case which will be in just harmony with it. Now, in this 9th verse, John states the law which relates to believers who have sinned against God, " If we confess our sins

He is faithful and just to forgive us our sins." Now this law of forgiveness is for those who are under the administration of Christ, and not for the penitent unsaved. It is exceedingly simple and wisely adapted to all concerned. The sin committed must be confessed to God, the forsaking of it being implied though not stated, and God is "faithful" to forgive, because He has promised to do so, and "just," because it is done through Jesus the gracious Mediator. It is one of the most solemn blunders of the age to reverse these arrangements of God, and direct the alien sinner to seek forgiveness by prayer and confession of sin, when the divine law requires faith in Jesus, confession of Him as the Son of God with the mouth, and immersion into Him, in order to attain the forgiveness promised. When this law is violated, the result is confusion in the minds of all who do so, and more or less uncertainty as to what God may do, must be felt. No penitent sinner who changes the constitutional law of the Lord Jesus, and seeks forgiveness by prayer and confession of sin, instead of yielding to His authority, can know that his sins are forgiven, since He is speaking only through His Word, and this is violated by all who adopt some other method. Such misdirected persons may be sincere, and may reason plausibly as to results, but they must wait to know whether or not He will accept the change which they have made.

CHAPTER II.

1. " *My little children.*" *Why does John say "little"?*

It is so rendered five times in this epistle, but as *teknia*, by metonymy, expresses affection, it is better to read in each instance *my dear child-*

ren, as expressing the yearning affection which he felt towards them.

" *These things write I unto you that ye sin not.*" *Did John expect they could live without committing sin ?*

Of course he did, or why write these things for the purpose of preventing it ? He teaches afterward that sin is transgression of law, or lawlessness, the practice of which allies with the devil, and he wrote these things that they might not sin.

" *If any man sin, we have an advocate with the Father.*" *Does he not here admit the possibility of sin?*

Yes, and then shows the gracious provision which God has made against possible failure. So that while he writes these things, " that ye may not sin," he can also write, " If any man sin,"—*lit.,* should sin, —" we have an advocate with the Father."

" *An advocate with the Father.*" *What is an advocate?*

One who pleads or intercedes for another. It is another aspect of the office of mediator or intercessor. It has special reference to the failures of believers, and but for this advocacy their position would be forfeited through transgression. A strictly just God could not allow transgression and uphold His throne. But, as God allowed Moses to become the mediator of the children of Israel after their sin at Sinai, so Christ is made a mediator of the believing family, in order to meet their possible failure, and through confessing and forsaking sin, they are restored and forgiven. Let us beware of transgression, but when we have sinned let us confess it and be forgiven. Jesus ever lives to make intercession for us.

2. " *And He is the propitiation for our sins.*" *What is meant by this?*

That Jesus offered Himself to God for our sins, and as a result of this sacrifice, God can now deal propitiously with sinners.

" *Our sins.*" *To whom does John refer ?*

To Jews, for whose transgressions, according to the prophets, Jesus was wounded or suffered. But John adds, " not for ours only, but also for the sins of the whole world."

May it not be believers who are contrasted with the " whole world" ?

No, because the propitiation is not for any as believers but as sinners. The Jews to whom John is writing this, did question about this offering being for the sins of the nations, but he affirms that it was not for " ours only, but also for the whole world."

3–6. " *And hereby we do know that we know Him.*" *By what?*

By keeping His commandments, which is only another aspect of " fellowship with Him," and of " walking in the light," and also of " perfecting the love of God." Here John affirms that the doing of these things was a test of their profession. It was only a deception to say " I know Him," and walk contrary to His will. And the reason why he refers to Christ being a propitiation for sins, seems to be for the purpose of giving force to his exhortations, viz., that if He gave Himself for sins, to be a covering from the consequence of transgression ; they should be induced to put them away by obedience to God, or, to walk as He, Christ, walked.

7–11. *What does John mean by an " old commandment," and a " new commandment" ?*

John was insisting upon obedience to God, and says that it was not a new command that he should do so, but that from the beginning this had been required. The old commandment therefore was obedience to God. But when he speaks of a new commandment, he refers specially to that which Jesus had given. "This is My commandment, that ye love one another, as I have loved you" (John xv. 12). He had seen in their action toward each other that which indicated a spirit of hatred, and he now proposes a practical test by which their state might be proved. "He that loveth his brother abideth in the light . . . But he that hateth his brother is in darkness."

"Again, a new commandment I write unto you, which thing is true in Him and in you." What does this mean?

The new command was love to each other, and this was "true" in Jesus, because His love to others was manifested, "and [only] in you," when the same spirit is manifest.

What does he mean by "the darkness is past, and the true light now shineth"?

It is, *lit.*, the darkness is passing, etc., *i.e.*, there had been such a manifestation of what ought to be, in the life and spirit of Jesus, that there was no longer any excuse. His example made plain all that was required of His disciples.

12. *"I write unto you, dear children, because your sins are forgiven." Why refer to their forgiveness?*

To remind them how God in His mercy had acted towards them. There is a claim for gracious action towards their brethren, and it was needful to refer to God's gracious dealing with themselves.

Why does he add "For His name's sake"?

It is, *lit.*, *through His name.* Their forgiveness had been declared by the apostles, but it was by the authority of Jesus, or in His name they did so. Christ is the God-appointed medium through whom forgiveness is proclaimed and enjoyed.

13. *"Fathers," "young men," and "little children." Does John use*

these terms in a literal or in a spiritual sense?

It is in relation to their faith and knowledge of Christ that John uses these terms, and not of the years of either their natural or spiritual life. Both Peter and Paul use the term "babes" to denote the condition of those who had but a limited knowledge of the truth, in contrast with those who were "of full age,"—*i.e.*, perfected in the knowledge of Christ. The explanatory statements appended by John,—"ye have known Him that is from the beginning," and "ye have known the Father,"—will enable us to understand the spiritual state of each class referred to. The knowledge of Christ by the one class, and the knowledge of the Father only by the other, will show how widely they were separated from each other.

"I write unto you, little children, because ye have known the Father." Is this a lower grade of knowledge than knowing Jesus, or "Him that is from the beginning"?

Most certainly. The little children addressed here are not a very hopeful class; but, since they had known the Father, through the Old Covenant under which they had been educated, John wishes to impart instruction in this epistle, which would be helpful even to them. We must, however, note here—in order to remove a difficulty that might be felt by some—that "little children" of verse 12 are not the same as "little children" of verse 13. The former, the *teknia, lit.*, dear children, whose sins were forgiven, included both fathers and young men; while the latter, the *paidia*, were those who were under the restraints of Judaism, and to whom John could speak naturally as a father to children in the flesh, but not as children in the faith.

14. *"I have written unto you,*

fathers," *but in verse* 13 *he says,* "*I write unto you.*" *Why this change of tense ?*

In the latter statement he is referring to the epistle, in which he is urging their full conformity to the will of God, and in the former to the Gospel he had written, with which these fathers were familiar.

15–17. "*Love not the world,*" *etc. Why should they not love the world, when it belongs to God ?*

It is not the material universe to which John refers, because that is of God, but to those things which are in it, which are not of Him. These he explains to be the "lust of the flesh, and the lust of the eyes, and the pride of life ;" these are "not of the Father, but of the world," and it is these things which are not to be loved. "If any man love the world" —*i.e.,* indulges these fleshly desires —"the love of the Father is not in Him."

18. "*Little children, it is the last time.*" *What does this mean ?*

It is, *lit., a last hour,*—*i.e.,* a last of the dispensational day. The closing of the day during that generation had been positively declared by Jesus, and though events and not dates were given to mark its close, yet as some of these had become manifest, John could write, *it is the last hour.* Antichrist was to appear before the close of the day, and John says, "Even now are there many antichrists," *whereby we know that it is the last hour.*

Who is antichrist? Has he appeared, or is he yet to come ?

John is the only writer in the New Testament who uses the term antichrist, and only in his epistles. According to him antichrist is not any particular false teacher, but was applied to any who denied that Jesus was the anointed of God. These saints had heard that antichrist should come, and, said John, "even now

are there many antichrists." "They went out from us, but they were not of us." The history of these persons, although not then called antichrist, is continually before us in the Acts, and the epistles. James and the elders called Paul's attention to their standing and influence. "Thou seest, brother, how many thousands of Jews there are which believe ; and they are all zealous of the law" (Acts xxi. 20). Paul also refers to them as "false brethren unawares brought in" (Gal. ii. 4), and whose object, viz., to bring Gentiles under the law of Moses, was completely frustrated. After doing what mischief they could, but not so much as they purposed, these separated themselves, sensual, having not the Spirit (Jude 19). The antichrist of John, therefore, was not some one to arise in the future, but was then manifest among them. Besides, the Gentiles have never been charged with the sin of antichrist, nor are likely to be. It was therefore strictly confined to that Jewish period.

But did not Paul prophesy of the "man of sin," who was to appear at some future time ?

Yes ; but he does not call him antichrist, neither does John call antichrist the man of sin. They are therefore not the same, and must not be confounded.

20. "*But ye have an unction from the Holy One.*" *What does this mean?*

It is *lit., an anointing,*—*i.e.,* the gift of revelation—which, being received from the Spirit on behalf of the Christ, they were to use against this lie of antichrist. They had in themselves by this gift an evidence of the truth which antichrist denied.

23. "*Whoso denieth the Son, the same hath not the Father.*" *Why does John say this ?*

These persons were evidently Jews, who thought as Paul once did, that in denying Jesus they were honouring the Father. John here affirms that the Father and the Son were so closely united in the great scheme of redemption, that to deny the Son separated from the Father, who had testified of His Son.

Why is the latter half of this verse printed in italics?

Some MSS. and versions do not contain the portion so marked, and we judge that our translators have been ruled by this fact to mark it as doubtful. There are, however, so many MSS. which contain it, that scholars have decided that it is a genuine reading.

27. "*Ye need not that any man teach you.*" *Does this imply independence of all teaching?*

We must note what follows, "but as the same anointing teacheth you." These saints had received gifts of the Spirit by the hands of the apostles, and could therefore test all teaching. They must not therefore listen to seducers, but test them whether they were of God. They required instruction, but if not in harmony with that given by the Spirit, it must be rejected.

CHAPTER III.

1. *Why does John introduce the matter of sonship?*

For a very practical purpose, viz., that the character of the Father must be reproduced in the child. This is stated in a very plain way at the close of chapter ii. "Every one that doeth righteousness is born [or begotten] of Him."

How is being sons a fruit of love?

It is—*lit., children*—a privilege which follows faith in Jesus. By believing in Jesus, who died and rose again, we are begotten of God, and in our new birth we become His children, and being His children we are to dwell in His home, and this is why we are to be like

Him. Purity is necessary for fellowship with God.

"*The world knoweth us not, because it knew Him not.*" *What does this mean?*

The world knew Him not as the Son of God, and because of His witness to this truth they condemned Him to die. And it is as His children that the world knoweth us not.

"*Beloved, now are we the sons of God.*" *Why does he say* now *are we* sons?

It is a very precious revelation that believers are as truly the children of God on earth as they will be in heaven. The relationship begins on earth, and is perfected in glory, where saints are made like Jesus.

3. *Why does the possession of this hope demand purification?*

The two, according to John, are inseparable, and to expect to enter heaven while walking in darkness, or under the power of evil, is only self-deception. Hence John adds, "Every man that hath this hope in him purifieth himself, even as He [Christ] is pure."

4–6. *Why does John refer to the transgression of law by sin?*

It is, *lit., sin is lawlessness*, and is a new phase of his argument in defence of holiness in heart and life. He states that Christ was manifested to take away sin, and those who sin are lawless to His great purpose, being in opposition or rebellion against Him.

7–8. *Is our spiritual relationship to God and Satan manifested by our obedience and disobedience?*

So John affirms, and warns against being deceived otherwise. "He that doeth righteousness is righteous, even as He is righteous," *i.e.*, right action determines our character as well as God's. "He that committeth sin is of the devil"—*i.e.*, is joined with him in disobedience, and is a child of the devil.

"*That He might destroy the works of the devil.*" *Is this to put an end to all evil?*

John teaches that Jesus came to put an end to disobedience by means of the truth, and not by force of omnipotence. It is the same truth as affirmed by the angel, "Thou shalt call His name Jesus, for He shall save His people from their sins" (Matt. i. 21), and should not be pressed as teaching the extermination of all evil.

9. "*Whosoever is born of God doth not commit sin.*" *Is this absolutely true?*

It is true according to the reason assigned by John, "for His seed"— *i.e.*, His truth—"remaineth in him," and in no other way. He had expressed the same truth in verse 6, "Whosoever abideth in Him sinneth not." To presume, as some do, that believers may do wrong, and yet not sin, is to pervert John's teaching, viz., that " all unrighteousness is sin." What he really does teach is, that as long as God's truth rules the hearts and lives of His children, they cannot sin. Obedience to Christ is man's only preservative from transgression.

11–15. *Why does he refer to the murder of Abel?*

He had stated that God required them to love one another, and this case is brought forward to show what may follow where love is not. Had Cain loved his brother he would not have done this deed of blood. The murder commenced in his heart, and the act speedily followed; so John adds, "Whosoever hateth his brother is a murderer."

Why cannot a murderer have life?

John does not say he cannot have life, but that while he hates his brother eternal life cannot abide in him. The hatred and the life cannot dwell together.

16. *Why refer to the love of God?*

"God" is improperly added to this verse; it is Christ Jesus who laid down His life, and John uses the fact to show what love really does. He who loves his brother will not only feel for him in his need, but will help in that need ; and where this is wanting, the love of God may be fairly questioned.

18–22. "*If our heart condemn us.*" *Why appeal to the heart?*

By the heart consciousness based upon knowledge is implied. If we love in word only, we are conscious of wrong, and open to God's condemnation; but if in deed and truth, we have inward conscious approval, and have confidence in our approach to Him.

CHAPTER IV.

1–3. "*Beloved, believe not every spirit.*" *What does John mean by "spirit" here?*

A prophet, either true or false. There were true prophets—*i.e.*, men speaking by the Spirit of God, and making revelations from Him to the Church ; and John here designates them by the source from whence their revelations were derived. But there were also false prophets, or spirits, who had gone forth, and therefore all were to be tested.

How could these spirits or professed prophets be tested?

There was imparted to some in the Church, by the apostles, the gift of "discerning of spirits" or prophets—*i.e.*, knowing whether or not they were from God ; but the trying or testing which John here proposes is their doctrine. Jesus Christ had come in the flesh, and by their confession of this fact these prophets were to be tested. These false prophets held, as the Jews hold to this day, that Jesus of Nazareth was not the Christ of God, but that He was still to come. The one who holds this doctrine, says John, is not of God, but is antichrist, because the truth of which we bear witness is denied. It is evident from this epistle of John—and his statements are fully sustained by all New Testament writers—that one great proposition, viz., that Jesus of Nazareth was raised from death, and exalted to the right hand of God, was affirmed and proved by His chosen witnesses ; and that this truth was opposed by the nation, and ultimately by many who first believed in Him. This opposition was continued until their overthrow, and ceased externally for ever. The Jews never persecuted the Gentiles after the destruction of Jerusalem.

6. *" He that knoweth God heareth us." Does John affirm this as a further test of these pretenders ?*

Yes. The apostles were the accredited ambassadors of Christ, and to hear them was to hear Jesus, and to refuse their message proved that all such were not of God. No liberty of dissent from their divinely accredited message could be tolerated.

" The spirit of truth and the spirit of error." What was this ?

The " spirit of truth " was the testimony which the apostles had delivered, and the " spirit of error " was the testimony which denied their teaching ; and by these provided tests they were called to discern truth from error.

7-11. *Why is it that John uses the word love so frequently in his epistles, while Peter, James, and Paul insist as earnestly upon obedience ?*

John uses the word in his epistles some forty times, and there must be some important reason why it is so frequently employed. The great precept of the law was, Thou shalt love the Lord thy God with all thy heart; and we presume that those to whom

John wrote held that they fulfilled this precept. This has led him to show so fully what love is, and his teaching is valuable to all who desire not to be deceived. Love, with John, includes obedience to all requirements, and where obedience is not manifest love is wanting. Even God is referred to as an illustration that love is not mere sympathy of feeling or good wishes, but practical ministry to real need. " Herein is love, not that we loved God, but that He loved us, and sent His Son to be the propitiation for our sins."

12. *What has " No man hath seen God at any time " to do with this question of love ?*

John wishes to show that God is revealed by His acts, and if they acted like Him, then He dwelt in them, and His love was perfected in them.

Is this test concerning the way in which God dwells in men continued to us ?

It cannot be changed, because the testimony of the Spirit is for the age, and must therefore be applied to all. It is by our acceptance of it that we prove our relationship to God.

14. *" The Father sent the Son, the Saviour of the world." How is He the Saviour of the world, since so many are not saved by Him ?*

This declaration must be read in the light of other statements, by which its meaning may be understood. Christ Jesus is the only God-appointed Saviour of men, and only those are declared to be saved who have accepted of Christ as made known in the Gospel. This testimony respecting the purpose of God towards the world is invaluable. Our faith should be as wide as apostolic testimony, and if men are not saved it is because Christ is rejected.

15. *Why is confession of Jesus as the Son of God so important a matter?*

From the opened heavens God declared that Jesus was His Son, and to confess Him, for the purpose for which He was sent into the world, is to unite with God. God dwells in all such, and they in God. His sending His Son into the world, and then owning Him when in the world, was a twofold development of His love, and shows what love really means.

17. *"Herein is our love made perfect." Perfected in what?*

In being like God by our love one to another. Love is completed, or perfected, in godlike action.

How will perfected love give boldness in the day of judgment?

Perfected love is obedience to God, and when we become like Him, we cannot fear the test to which all will be subjected.

19. *Why does John say, "We love Him," etc.?*

Scholars now reject the word "Him" from the text, and read, "We love, because He first loved us"—*i.e.*, we are loving our brethren because of His love first shown to us. Love to the brethren is prompted by His love to us, and is a proof of our love to Him.

CHAPTER V.

1–3. *" Whosoever believeth that Jesus is the Christ is born of God." Is this a proper rendering?*

Nearly all recent translators render it *begotten of God*, this being in strict harmony with the context. It is the Father who begets by the truth concerning Jesus, which, being received into the heart, shows itself in the spirit and life of those who receive it. Thus God becomes their father, and they are His children.

If John refers to begetting by the truth, why does he make no reference to birth?

It would be out of place to speak of birth to persons who professed to have been born again. John is helping them to test their professed relation to God by their action towards each other, and the test is an important one. It is assumed by him that a child will love its father, and he holds that love to the father is proved by love to a brother; and as God the Father has commanded His children to love each other, then their love to Himself is proved by their obedience to this command, "that he who loveth God love his brother also."

4, 5. *What does John mean by " overcoming the world"?*

The spirit of the world is disobedience to God, and hatred of men, and this is overcome by believing in Jesus. The children of God love God, and love each other, and thus are not of the world.

6. *" This is He that came by water and blood." "And it is the Spirit that beareth witness." When did He bear witness to Christ?*

At His baptism, when the Spirit rested upon Him; and at His death, being quickened by the Spirit. Jesus was indeed the Son of God, and to this the Spirit bore witness on these occasions.

7. *" There are three that bear record in heaven," etc. To whom do they witness?*

Nearly all Biblical scholars now hold that the sentence is spurious; and though found in some of the early Latin MSS., it is not found in any Greek MS., nor any Greek father, nor in any version written before the 16th century. We should therefore read, " There are three that bear record,—the Spirit, the water, and the blood:" and omit all that comes in between " record " and " the Spirit."

8. *" These three agree in one." In what do they agree ?*

In one unanswerable proof that Jesus is the Son of God. This is the one great subject of attestation, and therefore of belief. But when John speaks of Spirit, and water, and blood bearing witness that Jesus is the Christ, it is most likely that, by metonymy, he refers to those who form the three great sources of testimony to Jesus the anointed, viz., the prophets, John the Baptist, and the apostles. All these unitedly testified to this great truth. " For the testimony of Jesus is the spirit of prophecy " (Rev. xix. 10), *i.e.*, the prophets all point to Him, as the One that was to come. Then John bore witness to the representatives who came to him from Jerusalem, that he was sent to make straight the way of the Lord. And to these the apostles added their joint-testimony that Jesus was glorified at the right hand of God. To question this triad of witnesses, who are all of God, is to make God a liar, because refusing the witnesses He has brought forward.

10. *" He that believeth on the Son of God hath the witness in himself." What does this mean ?*

Alford says that most of the oldest MSS. read *in Him*, and if this reading is accepted, we can then read, *He that believes on the Son of God, hath or receives the witness of God in or concerning Him*, i.e., *Jesus : he that believes not God makes Him false ; because he believes not the record that God gave of His Son.*

11. *What is this " eternal life," which God gives to those who believe in Jesus ?*

Spiritual life is the favour of God, as stated in Ps. xxx. 5, and is enjoyed only through Christ. It is called eternal or everlasting, because it continues, not only through the present age, but is enjoyed in the future.

It forms a striking contrast to the ceremonial national life of the Jewish age, which closed with the dispensation. This life in Jesus is life for evermore.

If the life received by the believer is eternal, would this not preclude the possibility of losing it, or of being lost ?

Believers cannot be lost, or cast away, as long as they have eternal life abiding in them, which is the same as having Christ abiding in them. But as Christ is received by faith, so He may be afterward rejected in unbelief. The life is eternal because Christ is eternal, but abiding in Him is essential to its continued enjoyment. Hence Paul writes to the Romans, " Thou standest by faith : be not high-minded, but fear."

13. *Did their knowledge of life depend upon the apostles' testimony concerning it ?*

Yes ; this was the only God-appointed channel of instruction concerning their standing and life. They were sent by Jesus to proclaim the terms of life in His name, hence their affirmations were essential to assurance. This is why he says, " These things have I written unto you that believe on the name of the Son of God ; that ye may know that ye have eternal life."

Is their proclamation and teaching necessary for our assurance of the same privileges ?

There is no other way ; just as there is no other name given among men by which we can be saved. We may think we shall be saved in this way, or that way, but we are only guessing when we do so, and our guesses must end in failure. Jesus has spoken to us by those on whom the Spirit rested, and if we are guided by their directions, we shall not only be sure of forgiveness, but have the promise of eternal life secured to us by a faithful and merciful High Priest.

14. *"If we ask anything according to His will, He heareth us." Is John speaking of prayer in general, or of some special aspect of it?*

To be heard by God, when our petitions are according to His will, is certain to us, whatever they may be, though here I have no doubt that John is referring to a special case, because he names the "sin which is not unto death," for which they might pray, and obtain "life for them that sin not unto death."

16. *"There is a sin unto death." Is this physical or spiritual death?*

It is physical death, which the apostles in some cases had power to inflict, as seen in the case of Ananias and Sapphira; and also bodily suffering, as in the case of Elymas, who was struck with blindness for a season, and also the incestuous man at Corinth, who upon his repentance was set free from this infliction of bodily trouble. There was a sin unto death, for recovery from which they were not to pray; the judgment inflicted must have its course. It is a solemn truth that there are physical consequences brought on by sin which God will not remove, although He may, upon repentance and confession, forgive.

18. *"We know that whosoever is born of God sinneth not." Why does John repeat this statement from chap. iii. 9?*

Because it is appropriate to his teaching about sinning against God. It is to show that if sin is committed the truth has been abandoned. If the truth by which they have been begotten of God is held, then they will not sin.

"He that is begotten of God keepeth himself." How does he keep himself?

Some MSS. read *him* instead of himself, while the Vatican and Alexandrine MSS. read *it keepeth him*—i.e., the truth keepeth him—which is most likely to be the true reading, as showing how saints are kept from sinning against God.

19. *"The world lieth in wickedness." Is this a correct rendering?*

It should be *in the evil one;* a sad contrast to the saints who abide in Christ.

THE SECOND EPISTLE OF

JOHN.

In what does this epistle differ from the first epistle of John?

His first epistle was written to believers in their varied stages of holy attainments, while this was written to a Christian lady and her children, in whose piety John expresses great confidence, and who is exhorted to withstand the assaults which would be made upon the truth which she and her children had received.

1. *Why did John term himself* "the elder" when he might have called himself an apostle?

If it had been a question of authority he might have done so, but he is writing to one who had received apostolic testimony with unquestioning confidence, and in this term "elder" both sympathy and experience are fitly combined, and most appropriately presented to a faithful disciple of Jesus.

Is it not rather strange that such a brief letter, and one written to a lady, should have a place in the New Testament canon?

Whatever was written by inspired men was counted as the common property of the saints, and as such has a place in holy writings.

"Whom I love in the truth." Does John here explain the nature of this love?

John was practically fulfilling his own teaching, that he who loveth God loveth his brother also. It was not natural amiability or fleshly position that called out this love, but the truth, and on account of the truth which she had received. It was the love of a brother to a sister in Christ—a love which pervaded the whole holy brotherhood, "And not I only, but also all they that have known the truth." It was because Christ was received and honoured by this lady and her family, that John could say, "Whom I love in the truth."

3. *"Grace be with you, mercy, and peace." Why does John use the apostolic benediction to this lady and her children?*

A now accepted reading of this verse is, *There shall be with us grace, mercy, and peace,* etc. It is not the announcement of the benediction by John that had been done in all the churches of the saints, but the assurance that it should not fail to any who honoured Christ.

"In truth and love." John here names but two graces of Christian life, while Paul names "faith, hope, and love, these three." Why this difference?

The truth of John includes the faith and hope of Paul, as both are produced by the truth as testimony concerning Jesus; and it is instructive to note the varied way in which the same truth is presented in the Scriptures. It is not that one apostle contradicts or sets aside the testimony of another: they all spoke the same thing; but to meet the condition of the people it was often variously expressed. A full knowledge of the truth in one place will go far to help our understanding of it in others.

7. *" For many deceivers are entered into the world, who confess not that Jesus Christ is come in the flesh." Did they deny His incarnation?*

I understand John to say that these persons did not confess Jesus Christ, who had come in the flesh. They were Jewish missionaries who travelled far and wide to uphold the authority of Moses, and thus ignored the authority of Christ. They were opposed to Christ, and of each John says, "This is a deceiver and an antichrist."

8. *" Look to yourselves, that we lose not those things which we have wrought." What does John mean?*

" We " is used three times in this verse, and in each instance we should read *ye* instead. If they yielded to these deceivers they would lose the reward which Christ Jesus would bestow on the faithful, and their former labour and sacrifice would avail them nothing.

What was this "doctrine of Christ" against the rejection of which John so earnestly warns this lady?

It was the teaching concerning Him which had been set forth by the apostles, and by continuing in it the first disciples so distinguished themselves. "They continued stedfastly in the apostles' doctrine." The apostles taught that Jesus was raised from the dead, and exalted to power as the Lord of all; and to receive Him as the exalted of the Father, was to receive both the Father and the Son.

10. *Why were they forbidden to entertain and bid God speed to those who did not hold this doctrine?*

Because he who refused this teaching was antichrist, and to wish him success was to be a partaker of his evil deeds. With those who uphold the authority of Christ we should cordially unite, but with those who set it aside we should refuse all participation. In the religious denominations of the present day their principal differences are maintained by the authority of man being pitted against the authority of Christ, the very thing against which John is warning this lady and her children, and against this evil all should watch and strive. It should be the aim of every disciple of Jesus to uphold His authority against all human usurpation.

THE THIRD EPISTLE OF

JOHN.

1. *Who was Gaius to whom John wrote this brief letter?*

Either a citizen of Corinth who had been immersed by Paul, and with whom he occasionally sojourned, or else another Gaius who is counted by John as one of his children in the faith. If there were two persons of this name, then both were distinguished for hospitality, piety, and faithfulness. John calls him the "well-beloved Gaius."

2. *Is it not curious that the health of his soul should furnish a standard for the wish of John respecting his bodily health and prosperity?*

It was a rare case, and a most blessed illustration of pure devotedness to the cause of truth. Would that these were more numerous.

May we conclude that his bodily health and circumstances were not so good as they should have been?

It is difficult to say whether or not Gaius was out of bodily health. John had heard from brethren of his holy and obedient walk in the truth, and he now wishes that both body and circumstances may be equally prosperous.

3. *"Thou walkest in the truth." What does this imply?*

A life in conformity to the will of Jesus. He had exercised himself unto godliness, and his sympathetic help was shown both to brethren and to strangers.

5–8. *What strangers were these to whom John refers?*

Most likely they were Jews who were faithfully labouring for Christ, and at the same time refusing help from Gentile believers, to whom they might justly have looked for help. There were not many of this Paul-like spirit, but there were some, and Gaius is commended for helping and encouraging such in their work of faith and labour of love. Indeed, we might conclude from this statement, "We therefore ought to receive such," that Gaius was a Jew.

9. *"I wrote unto the Church: but Diotrephes . . . receiveth us not." Why refuse an apostle?*

Through his ambition for pre-eminence. John could speak with authority, and had to guide the church into the truth, but Diotrephes dared to oppose even an apostle. It was the outcome of that selfish desire for eminence that sought to set aside one whom the Lord had sent.

"I wrote unto the church." Does he refer to his first epistle?

Possibly he does. There was enough in that epistle to offend an ambitious self-seeking man. When

John says, "He that loveth not his brother is not of God," it went right home to Diotrephes, who most likely in his "prating against us" would say that it would be better for John to mind his own business, and to let other people alone. Even brethren were influenced against the associates of the apostle, and were not allowed to receive them, but were cast out of the church whenever they did receive them.

"*Wherefore, if I come, I will remember his deeds." What do these words imply?*

The apostles were sustained in their authority by the power of the Spirit, and some who resisted it were visited with judgment. Had John visited that church, there would have been a contest between apostolic authority and the usurpation of Diotrephes that would have made it a serious matter for him.

12. *Who was Demetrius that is named in this letter?*

All we know of him is contained in this verse, in which we have a threefold testimony that he will not be ashamed of in the day of judgment, viz., a "good report of all," *i.e.*,—the church, "and of the truth itself," and also of the apostles. It is a noble record which John bore to Demetrius; may we all strive to obtain a like witness to our faithfulness.

THE GENERAL EPISTLE OF

JUDE.

"*The General Epistle of Jude." Was this inscription prefixed by Jude himself?*

Scholars tell us that ancient MSS. do not contain it; it must therefore have been added by some one. The epistle is not a "general epistle," addressed to any and everybody, but to believing Gentiles well known to the writer, and who were in danger of being led away from the truth by the beguiling words of false teachers.

1. *Was Jude an apostle?*

He does not style himself an apostle, but simply a "servant of Jesus Christ, and brother of James." And, although there were two apostles so named, yet he is more likely to be the Jude referred to in Matthew xiii. 55, and who became an earnest evangelist of the glad tidings of Jesus.

"*To them that are sanctified by God the Father." What does this mean?*

A now accepted reading is *beloved* not "sanctified" which has a very important bearing upon their Gentile standing, and the grace of God shown towards them. Dean Alford renders this part of the verse, *To the called, beloved in God the Father, and preserved for Christ Jesus.* They had been called by the Gospel, in which the love of God to the world had been proved by the gift of His Son.

3. *What does Jude mean by the "common salvation," about which he was purposing to write?*

I presume that he refers to the privileges which believers in Jesus, whether Jews or Gentiles, enjoyed alike, or in common with each other. The Jews, being placed under the law, occupied a much higher position than Gentiles, but under the Gospel, their standing and privileges were equal. Being raised up together, and made sit together in heavenly places, it is very appropriately called by Jude, "the common salvation."

Why did he change his purpose? and what is meant by "the faith once delivered to the saints"?

He had come to know that ungodly men were turning the grace of God into lasciviousness, and that by their teaching and example they would ensnare the saints, and lead them to set aside the authority of Jesus. Hence warning had become necessary, and at once he writes to hinder the evil policy of these deceivers. "The faith once,"—*lit.*, once for all, —"delivered to the saints," was the entire testimony delivered by the apostles, delivered by them in the name of Jesus, and to which nothing could be added, and from which nothing could be lawfully taken away. "The faith" is not mere belief, but denotes what has been done and commanded, and therefore what has to be believed and obeyed, and for the upholding of such they were earnestly to contend.

These men, of whom Jude complains, "were before of old ordained to this condemnation." How can this be reconciled with their freedom?

If we render this sentence, *Whose condemnation was written long ago,* we shall more easily apprehend his meaning. These ungodly men, who crept in privily, were doing the things against which God had declared judgment long before, or by the prophets; and, whilst warning these saints against yielding to their seductions, he thus intimates that wrath would certainly overtake them; or, as Peter (ii. 3) says, "Whose judgment, now of a long time [recorded] lingereth not, and their damnation slumbereth not."

"Denying the only Lord God," etc. *What does this mean?*

They denied the authority of Him who was "the only Lord"—*lit.*, Master (God omit)—"and our Lord Jesus Christ."

5-7. Why does Jude refer to the Israelites, to the angels, and to Sodom?

In order to show that no previously enjoyed privilege could shield from judgment when the obligations were violated. The children of Israel were saved out of the land of Egypt, but those who believed not were afterward destroyed. The angels or high ones—*i.e.*, the sons of God of the first age—which kept not their first estate, were placed in bonds, under darkness, unto the judgment of the great day; while Sodom and adjoining cities, on account of their filthy lives, were set forth as an example, suffering the vengeance of eternal fire. By these examples, Jude teaches that crime and evil will bring judgment on all who practise them.

9. Why does he refer to the contention between Michael and the devil about the body of Moses? and how did Jude get to know about it?

We know nothing of the dispute beyond what Jude has recorded, nor how he obtained the information. That God buried Moses in the land of Moab, in a secret sepulchre, is revealed—a work which Michael may have been commissioned to do—and that possibly over this secret interment the contention took place. Jude refers to it in order to show that these presumptuous men would dare what even Michael would not permit himself to do; or, as expressed by one in cutting irony, "Fools rush in where angels fear to tread." These dreamers despised dominion, and spoke against dignities, and yet disciples must not rail against them, but rather imitate Michael, who said, "The Lord rebuke thee."

10. *Why does he compare them to brute beasts?*

There are two aspects of their character, as named by Jude, which show how needful it was for these saints to beware of their influence. (1.) They were presumptuous in speaking against things which they did not understand ; and (2.) those things which could be known naturally to be wrong, in these they corrupted themselves ; so that they were worse than the unreasoning animals or " brute beasts."

Why does he refer to Cain, Balaam, and Core?

Each of these persons had manifested a distinct form of evil, which was being reproduced in these insubordinate spirits—viz., love of self, love of money, and love of honour. The " way of Cain " was separation from the control of God, and then to make himself happy without God. He had art, science, and music, but no God to restrain him, and this was his self-chosen way. Balaam sought reward—*i.e.*, wealth—and though God restrained him, yet by craft he obtained his desire. To affirm that the spirit of Balaam was in these men is to reveal to us that they were the paid agents of some Jewish society, whose object was to corrupt Gentile believers. Then Korah sought honour, and daringly aspired to be equal with God's anointed priest, and perished in his ambition. To associate with such persons was dangerous, and Jude warns against fellowship with any who practised such things.

Can these evils be still practised?

Yes, in spirit, though not in the same form. Evil things are very much like garments, the fashion of which may change, while the material of which they are made is from the same loom. We may substitute hatred—*i.e.*, want of loving action—

for murder, and worldliness for the altar of Baal, and think it a great improvement, but He that searcheth the heart knoweth that the spirit is the same. We have need to examine ourselves, lest, while condemning these ancient sinners, we may be repeating their sin in another form. God looks at us much like a physician at his patient, and thinks far more seriously of the impure condition of the blood, than of the symptoms which arise from it. He knows that the symptoms are only the result of circumstances, while the source is within. The same thought, under another figure, was expressed by Jesus, when He said, " Make the tree good, and his fruit [will be] good."

12. *" These are spots in your feasts of charity, when they feast with you." What does this mean?*

An established reading is, *These are hidden rocks, when in your love-feasts they feast with you*, and is only one of a number of figures which Jude employs to describe their utterly vile, worthless, and dangerous character. To admit them to their love-feasts, when so lawless to Christ, was like sailing a vessel over hidden rocks, and a wreck would be almost certain. To look to them for spiritual help was like expecting a shower from clouds without water ; for they were carried about by whatever wind might blow. To expect spiritual refreshment from these deceivers was like expecting fruit from a withered tree. These trees had twice died, and were sure to be uprooted.

What does he mean by " twice dead "?

These persons were Jews, who, as trees, had been planted in God's vineyard, but died, though heavenly culture was bestowed upon it. In accepting Jesus, as they seem to have done, they were planted in His

2 I

spiritual garden that they might grow and bear fruit to His glory ; but, living after the flesh instead of after the spirit, they died. Thus they twice died, and, as dead trees, were sure fuel for the burning.

The figures and facts which Jude employs are much the same as those given by Peter in the 2nd chapter of his Second Epistle. How is this to be accounted for?

It may be well to notice that Peter writes prophetically of what would come to pass; Jude, when the fulfilment was looking them in the face, and this will account for the repetition of both the facts and figures which Jude reproduces in his epistle. It is the one Spirit sending the same message by two messengers, and has its appropriate place and force from both. The same thing by other inspired writers may be noticed again and again. It was not to produce something fresh that led the Spirit to select so many to communicate the needful truth, but to meet cases as specially required, and the same truths and precepts and facts are in their measure used by them all : all of them are enlisted in one common cause, and preaching and teaching for one Master, with one result. No language could more fully describe the character and spirit of these "filthy dreamers" than that which Peter has given in his prophecy, and Jude most impressively confirms it by pointing to its corroboration in these men. The cases also in which judgment followed transgression were familiar to the transgressors, and this reproduction of them should have had its proper effect upon their minds.

14. *" And Enoch, the seventh from Adam, prophesied of these." How could Jude apply this early prophecy by Enoch to the men of his day?*

God is true to His word, whether given by Enoch or by Peter, and when men fill up the crimes recorded, He will fill out the judgment also. These hypocritical deceivers had filled up the list of evil things, which had been spoken of before, and Jude could then affirm, upon you the judgment will fall.

17, 18. *What period does Jude refer to by " the last time "?*

The last period of the Jewish dispensation, because they are urged to remember the words of the apostles, and had therefore specially to do with it. The love of many of the Jews had waxed cold, and iniquity was abounding, and judgment was near, and these saints are warned against the evil examples that might ensnare them.

20, 21. *Were the special directions given by Jude sufficient to preserve the saints from apostacy?*

These four specific directions were given by the Spirit through Jude, and were not only sufficient to preserve from the evils which surrounded them, but are adapted for preservation in every period of the dispensation. The evils to which Jude refers existed then, and in one form or other will continue till the Lord shall return; but here is a God-provided remedy : (1.) " Building up youselves on your most holy faith,"—*i.e.*, building up your Christian character by the apostle's teaching. This would certainly preserve from false teaching. (2.) " Praying in the Holy Spirit,"—*i.e.*, by His guidance. This would preserve from vain words, and carnal desires. (3.) " Keep yourselves in the love of God,"—*i.e.*, an unwavering confidence that they were beloved of God—a truth which gives present power and blessing. (4.) " Looking for the mercy of our Lord Jesus Christ unto eternal life." This was the hope set before them, and was to be the girdle of their loins.

22, 23. *" And of some have compassion making a difference, and others* save with fear." Why does he suggest discrimination in the suggested work of restoration ?

Because there was a difference of spirit, even among those who had gone astray. Some were confirmed apostates, who would never be reclaimed, but others had been deceived by being careless, and might be restored. Upon some they were to look with compassion, and others they were to save with fear—i.e., to themselves. There is, however, another reading of these verses, and though, according to scholars, the ancient MSS. are divided, yet the evidence has led several translators to accept of it as most probable. Dean Alford renders : " Some indeed convict, when they contend with you ; but others save, pulling them out of the fire ; and of others have compassion with fear, hating even the garment spotted by the flesh." This reading suggests a twofold course to all faithful disciples :—(1.) To convict deceivers by the proofs they were able to produce ; and (2.) to save, if possible, the deceived.

" Hating even the garment spotted by the flesh." What does this mean ?

Under the law, a garment worn by a leprous person if put on a clean person would defile ; such contact, therefore, had to be carefully guarded against. The garment was typical of a person's habits of life, and Jude here warns them against clothing themselves with the practices of those who were walking in uncleanness. The garment spotted by the flesh— i.e., defiled by its lusts — must be avoided.

24. Why does Jude close with this doxology ?

It is a very appropriate relief to the dark picture which he has drawn. The surroundings of a believer could scarcely be more perilous, and yet their mighty Helper was equal to all their need. " He is able to keep you from falling, and to present you faultless before the throne of His glory with exceeding joy."

THE REVELATION

OF

ST JOHN THE DIVINE.

CHAPTER I.

Is " The Revelation of St John the Divine," a proper title for this book ?

" St John the Divine " has been added to the " The Revelation " by a later hand, and should be omitted. That John was a saint there can be no doubt, but when appended as here done, it is a mark of canonisation by the Church of Rome. The true and proper title of the book is given in the first verse, " A Revelation of Jesus Christ," and is properly designated by " The Revelation."

Why is it called a revelation, when it is so difficult to understand ?

The difficulty arises from its revelations being made in symbols, and hieroglyphs, the meaning of which must first be understood before the book can be intelligibly read ; but when the meaning of these symbols are learnt, the difficulty is very greatly diminished.

Is it possible to learn the meaning of these symbols ?

The Revealer Himself has given the meaning of several of them, and these explanations form a key to much of the book. John was told, "the seven candlesticks which thou sawest are the seven churches," and "the seven stars are the angels of the seven churches." John also saw a beast with ten horns, and was told that these were ten kings; and also a woman sitting upon many waters, and these are said to be peoples, multitudes, etc. Then many of the symbols used in this book are taken from the prophets, and from them the meaning of many signs may be ascertained, and thus learning the given alphabet of signs, we shall be better fitted to read this "Revelation of Jesus Christ."

1. *" Which God gave unto Him." Does not this giving of revelation by God, show that the standing of Christ was inferior to the Father?*

It is in perfect keeping with what is largely taught in the New Testament, viz., the servant character of Jesus. "He was in the form of God, and thought it no robbery to be equal with God, but made Himself of no reputation, and took upon Him the form of a servant." Hence this giving and receiving is in harmony with His humiliation as a servant, for "the servant knoweth not what his lord doeth."

"And He sent and signified it," etc. Does this word "signified" mean simply to declare to John?

Declaring or revealing is doubtless implied in the word, but it is the manner of doing it that is chiefly intended. If we pronounced the word sign-ified, the meaning would be more clearly perceived. The angel made known the revelation by signs, and in these mystic characters we have to search out the things that were to be done.

3. *" Blessed is he that readeth, and they that hear the words of this pro-*phecy." *Do those who cannot understand this prophecy, lose the promised blessing?*

The Saviour claims for His prophecy personal attention and obedience, but while many may not understand it, yet from their faithfulness to Him as learnt from the epistles, the claims of Christ are really met. Submission to Jesus the Lamb and leader of the flock of God, is that which is demanded here, and those who follow Him enjoy this promise.

" For the time is at hand." What time was this?

It is, *lit., the season,—i.e.,* of fulfilment of the things first referred to, —viz., judgment upon the faithless churches, and also upon the Jewish nation, whose season of judgment was at hand.

4. *" John to the seven churches which are in Asia." Why are these churches selected in preference to other churches named in the epistles?*

These seven churches seem to present every possible type of condition; and are thus dealt with, not for their sakes alone, but to show, through all time, what Christ approves and what He disapproves. Every church on earth may find itself dealt with in one or other of these letters, and should be encouraged or warned as their case may be. In relation, however, to the district named, it may be well to note that it is not Asia proper that is intended here, nor even Asia Minor, but proconsular Asia; comprising Phrygia, Mysia, Caria, and Lydia, within which boundaries these churches were situated.

This salutation of " grace and peace" is, " from Him who is, and who was, and who is to come, . . . and from Jesus Christ." Does this refer to one, or different beings?

It is to one person to whom all these things apply, even to Him who appeared to John in Patmos, "who is," the One filling all in all; and "who was," in the beginning God; "and who is to come," *i.e.*, He will return from the heavens into which He entered. Or, as stated by Himself, "I will come again."

The " seven spirits which are before His throne," are also joined with John in his salutation. What are these seven spirits ?

In chaps. iv. and v. they are said to be "lamps of fire before His throne," which is only another aspect of the seven-branched lamp,—*i.e.*, the Church,—which is united with Jesus and John in their salutation to these seven assemblies. The benediction is directly from Jesus, but in it He is joined by the apostle and the churches in the spirit of their loving sovereign head.

5. *"The faithful witness." Why is Jesus so called ?*

Because when challenged by the High Priest as to whether He was the Son of the Blessed or not, He affirmed that He was, although He knew that in doing this He would bring upon Himself the sentence of death. The truth of God was at stake, therefore He hesitated not, and is here appropriately called "the faithful witness."

How is Jesus the "first-begotten from the dead," when others rose before Him ?

He was the first-begotten from the dead into immortality, and though others were raised by Him to manifest His power, they had to return to corruption. In Him alone was life and immortality brought to light.

" The prince of the kings of the earth." Why is He so called ?

It is, *lit., the chief of the kings of the earth.* They rule, each in his own kingdom, but He was exalted far above all principality, and power, and might, and dominion; and is therefore chief or above them all,

being "King of kings, and Lord of lords."

" Unto Him that loved us." Does John refer to His love in dying for them ?

A more approved reading is, *Unto Him that loves us.* It was a present love that cheered the saints of those days, and should cheer us still. It had been shown on the cross, but it also came from the throne, and as a reality was most precious.

" And washed us from our sins in His own blood." Does John refer to His pardoning grace, as shown towards them when sinners ?

No; but to the power of the truth of His sacrifice upon them as believers. It is the same thought which we get in his first epistle, i. 7, "His blood cleanseth us from all sin." The "cleanseth" in the one is the same as "washed us" in the other. His death has effected what Jewish sacrifices could never effect, viz., purging the conscience from dead works.

6. *" And hath made us kings and priests unto God." How are believers made kings ?*

A more correct reading would be, *And made us a kingdom ; priests unto God,* etc. That is, believers, who are priests to God under the New Covenant, are by Him constituted into a kingdom for Christ, or, as we read in the Syriac version, "and hath made us a priestly kingdom ;" so that, along with the rule of Jesus in creation, He has rule over the saints through the Gospel, which is the rod of His power. Believers are thus made a "royal priesthood," or a priesthood under Christ the king.

" Behold He cometh with clouds, and every eye shall see Him." Does John refer to the clouds of the sky ?

We are reading about events that were "at hand"—*i.e.*, soon to take place—but as these are given to us in symbols, we must take heed lest we put the sign for the thing sign-ified. The sign is a cloud or clouds; the things referred to are armies of men, through which the "wrath of the Lamb" against His foes was to be manifested. The prophets were wont to use this symbol when referring to the armies wherewith God chastised His enemies. Hence we read, "The burden of Egypt. Behold, the Lord rideth upon a swift cloud, and shall come into Egypt" (Isa. xix. 1). In Ezek. xxxviii. 15 we have a prophecy which relates to this very period to which John refers, and in which this symbol is used to denote the force which God would employ for judgment. "And thou [Gog, the Roman forces] shalt come from thy place out of the north parts, thou, and many people with thee, all of them riding upon horses, a great company, and a mighty army: And thou shalt come up against My people of Israel, as a cloud to cover the land; *it shall be in the latter days*, and I will bring thee against My land." "Behold He cometh with clouds," said John—*i.e.*, with judgment; and as He names those who pierced Him as wailing because of Him, so we judge that John refers to the Roman army, as the clouds upon which Jesus came to the judgment of the Jewish nation.

"*Every eye shall see Him.*" *If this applies only to the Jews, how could John affirm its universality?*

There were not only those who cried "to the mountains and rocks, Fall on us;" but also the nations who inflicted the judgment—all saw the power of Him they had once put to death.

Had not the destruction of Jerusalem taken place when John wrote the Revelation?

No; and although in our reference Bibles the chronology is printed A.D. 96, yet scholars maintain that this arises from some copyists mistaking the name of the emperor who is said to have reigned at the time John wrote. According to R. Young, in his brief "Commentary on the Book of Revelation," "it was written in Patmos (about A.D. 68), whither John had been banished by Domitius Nero, as stated in the title of the Syriac version of the book; and with this concurs the express statement of Iræneus (A.D. 175), who says it happened in the reign *Domitianou*—*i.e.*, Domitius (Nero). Sulpicius Severus, Orosius, etc., stupidly mistaking Domitia*nou* for Domitian-*ikos*, supposed Iræneus to refer to *Domitian* (A.D. 95), and most succeeding writers have fallen into the same blunder. The internal testimony is wholly in favour of the earlier date." That John saw these visions in the reign of Nero, and that they were written by him during his banishment by that emperor, is confirmed by Theophylact, Andreas, Arethas, and others. We judge, therefore, that this Book was written about A.D. 68, and this agrees with other facts of history. About the year A.D. 62, Paul appealed to (Nero) Cæsar for protection against the injustice of his countrymen, and for a season he obtained from him, and those who ruled under him, all the protection he desired; but when called to stand before him, about three years after, he narrowly escaped with his life. During the early part of his reign, and whilst under the influence of Seneca, his tutor, Nero was all that might have been expected from him; but, even whilst Paul was in Rome, a great change became manifest, and from being gentle and considerate, he had become bloodthirsty, and from being a protector of the liberties of the Christians, he had become a furious persecutor. After the conflagration in Rome, which had been wrongly charged upon Christians, a most fearful onslaught was made upon them by his direction, and in that persecution John was banished to Patmos. There are also several statements in this Book which can only be understood on the ground that the judgment upon Jerusalem was then future, as "The time is at hand," "Behold I come quickly," "Behold He cometh with clouds, and every eye shall see Him, and they also which pierced Him, and all kindreds of the earth shall wail because of Him." In Matt. xxiv. Jesus used this very symbol of "clouds" in relation to that judgment, and I presume that every Jew throughout the Roman empire felt the effect of that visitation.

8. "*I am Alpha and Omega, the beginning and the ending.*" *What did Jesus mean by this?*

I presume that "Alpha and Omega," the first and last letters of the Greek alphabet, are symbols of the testimony revealed by Jesus. As all words are formed by letters, they become suggestive of this application. The first proclamation was made by Christ through the apostles; and this "Revelation," which is also given by Him, through John, is the last. He opened the testimony, and closed it, and no promise of further revelation has been given.

10. "*I was in the Spirit on the Lord's day.*" *What is intended by this statement?*

It is understood by many, to teach that John was — as expressed by Barnes in his commentary on this verse—in a spirit of elevated devotion; a state of high and uncommon religious enjoyment; and that this took place on the first day of the week. Others again understood that by being "in the Spirit," prophetic inspiration is intended, and that the "Lord's day" is not the first day of the week, but the day in which His power will be manifested in those special triumphs which are afterwards revealed by John. Now, to all who revere the first day of the week,—and it is frequently so termed in the New Testament,—it would be pleasant to know that it was called the "Lord's day" by inspiration here, although not so called in any other place; but as "Lord's day" is more likely to point forward to judgment upon His enemies, and His triumph over them, than to the first day of the week,—as that could in no way that we now perceive affect the nature of the revelation given to John,—we must forego that pleasure, and rather receive those revelations which are afterwards given of Him as the victorious Lamb of God. The prophets had written much concerning "the day of the Lord." Zephaniah (i. 7–18) had spoken of it as a day of wrath, a day of trouble and distress, and when the whole land should be devoured by the fire of His jealousy. John was permitted to see in vision the fulfilment of these prophecies of the day of the Lord, and very properly names this period "the Lord's day," and afterwards, "the great day of His wrath" (Rev. vi. 17).

11–16. *Who was it that commanded John to write?*

The speaker was behind him, and on turning round he saw seven golden candlesticks, and one standing in their midst like unto the Son of man, with seven stars in His right hand: And out of His mouth went a sharp two-edged sword.

What do these candlesticks, stars, and sword indicate?

They were seen by John as symbols of things to be revealed, and are afterwards explained to him (ver. 20). The candlesticks are said to be the seven churches to which he had been directed to write, whilst the sword of the Spirit—and we presume that Jesus used this sword—was the Word of God.

The sword in the mouth of Jesus was a two-edged sword. What does this mean?

The sword is a symbol of magisterial authority, and legislative administration, and, being two-edged, indicates its action both on unfaithful churches and the opposing forces of the world.

17. "*I fell at His feet as dead.*" *Why was John so afraid of Jesus?*

We cannot be surprised at the effect of this august appearance of the Master upon His servant, before whom he fell as dead. He had seen Him in all His lowliness on earth, and here he saw Him in all the majesty of heaven, and was overpowered at the sight. Jesus, however, could raise up His servant, and cheer and fit him to reveal those things which he was about to see and hear.

"*I am the first and the last.*" *Does this mean the same as "Alpha and Omega" of verse 11.*

No. The latter refers to the divine testimony, the former to His divine existence. It was soul-cheering to John, and to those who still read his testimony, to hear Jesus exclaim, Fear not, for behold I am alive for evermore—*lit.*, into the ages of the ages—and have the keys of hell and of death.

What does He mean by having the "keys of hell and death"?

Having authority over death and hades, the unseen world. The order of the words are, death and hell, literally hades.

CHAPTER II.

1–7. "*Unto the angel of the church of Ephesus write.*" *Who is this angel, and why write to the angel?*

There was in every Jewish synagogue a person who had the charge of its books or scrolls, bringing them out when required, and receiving them again for safe keeping, and was known as the angel of the synagogue. It would be from this person that Jesus received the book of the prophet Isaiah, when He stood up to read in the synagogue of Nazareth, and gave it again to him when He had read the section for that day. Now, there was a person of this class in every church; one who had the charge of its MSS. and apostolic letters, and who is here called "the angel of the church." The letter was therefore very properly sent to him, and through him to the assembly. He was not its pastor, elder, or even a deacon in the ordinary acceptation of that title of service, but was the custodian of all its communications, and under the symbol of a star, was held in the right hand of Jesus. When God led Israel out of Egypt, He directed their way by means of a cloud—a symbol of His presence and authority—and which was afterwards called the "angel or messenger of God" (Exod. xiv. 19). Now this symbol of Jehovah's authority, as we here see, is transferred to him who had the charge of divine revelations, which testimonies are made the standard of appeal by Christ, and by these their life and spirit were to be tested. It is also important to notice that as the conduct of these churches is reproved, and as no standard of appeal is formally given in the letters, it is only right to presume that the judgment of Christ is based upon the inspired records which they had already received; and which were in the keeping of the angel of the church. To write to him, therefore, was not only to bring the charges made against them through him, but to appeal to the testimonies already in possession.

Why have we the condition of just seven churches brought before us?

Because they appear to embrace every variety of spiritual condition possible, while recognised by Jesus as His churches; and as we get His estimate of them all, according to their state, we are able to make a proper application of His promises or threatenings.

It is assumed by some that the condition of these seven churches is prophetic of the Church as it will be found at different periods of the dispensation. Is this true?

There is nothing in the letters to favour such a conclusion. The true condition of these churches is unveiled by Jesus, and they are approved or condemned by Him. Thus we have valuable instruction furnished to other churches all through the dispensation. To suppose that the condition of the church in Ephesus gives us the first stage of the Church of Christ, and the condition of the church in Smyrna the second stage, and the state of the Laodiceans the seventh and last stage, is without any foundation whatever. There were churches that were faithful then, while others were unfaithful and worldly, and such I have no doubt there will be when Jesus returns. The assemblies then presented every possible phase of Christian life, and they present the same to-day; both of that at Ephesus and that of Laodicea, the first and last of the seven churches.

What is the most marked failure of the church in Ephesus?

The decline of their first love, and for this lack of affection nothing could atone. No amount of labour, or endurance of evil, or resistance of false claims to apostolic power, could be allowed as a substitute for love. He who loved them unto death must have their love in return.

Does this stringent claim of Christ upon the church in Ephesus present any lesson to us?

We should learn from it that religion without love is not esteemed by Christ.

6. *What were these doings of the Nicolaitanes?*

Subjecting the people to human authority, and thus supplanting the authority of Jesus. Nicolaitanes is derived from Nicolaus—*i.e.*, a conqueror of the people—and being given to these usurpers at once indicates the nature of their deeds. This incipient apostasy, which at last developed the "man of sin," was even then beginning to appear in some of the churches. The church in Ephesus is commended for their opposition to it; but, alas! they failed in their love.

7. *The fruit of the tree of life was promised to "him that overcometh." What privilege was this?*

Creation had its paradise with its tree of life, which Adam lost through transgression; but through Christ the paradise of God has again been opened to the faithful, in which also stands the tree of life. It is no doubt outside the present scene—*i.e.*, man's fleshly standing, or where sin has placed him—but it is nevertheless a reality which all the faithful enjoy. A tree in the Revelation is a symbol of a man, and here points to the man Christ Jesus—the Tree of Life, who not only gives life to those who receive Him, but sustains that life for ever.

LETTER TO THE CHURCH IN SMYRNA.

8. *Jesus here declares Himself to be "the first and the last, who was dead and is alive." To what does He refer?*

To His former existence as Jehovah of the Old Covenant, and to His present position as the anointed of the New. Jesus is here simply repeating the declaration of Isaiah (xliv. 6), "I am the first and I am the last," and though He died He rose again, and is now able to meet every promise and fulfil every threatening.

There is not a single charge against this church in Smyrna. To what do you attribute this exception?

To their persistent faithfulness in the midst of surrounding evils. Their position was as trying as any of the churches, but they held fast the truth, and honoured Christ.

9. *What were their chief trials?*

There was a synagogue of blaspheming Jews in Smyrna, whose arrogant claims to the sole recognition of God caused them much annoyance. These Jews claimed to be the assembly of God, but were practically the "synagogue of Satan." Besides, the municipal authority was about to interfere with their liberty, and they were soon called to choose between a prison and the service of Christ.

10. *" Be thou faithful unto death." Did Jesus mean as long as they lived?*

He points to a far more trying issue than faithfulness all through life, as what He asks is the yielding up of that life itself. His words mean, be faithful even unto dying for me. It was a very high claim, but He who made it promised to give them a " crown of life,"—*i.e.*, a never ending life.

" Ye shall have tribulation ten days." What did this mean?

Ten is a symbolic number for an indefinite period, and is so used in the Scriptures. Jacob said of Laban that he had changed his wages ten times, and his family would understand by it that the terms of his service had often been changed, and that there was no certainty in serving him. These Smyrneans were in tribulation when John wrote, and nothing definite about its termination is stated. It is even hinted that it might result in the taking of their lives, and they are exhorted to be faithful.

LETTER TO THE CHURCH IN PERGAMOS.

12–17. *The opening sentence in all these letters is taken either from the sayings or appearance of Jesus when seen by John. What may we learn from this peculiar application?*

The whole appearance and words of Jesus seem to have been arranged in harmony with the solemn relation which He sustained to these churches, and the application is made according to the condition in which they are severally found. The sharp sword with two edges is the symbol to the church in Pergamos—a most solemn sign of judgment.

Satan had his " seat " in Pergamos. What was that?

It is, *lit.*, the " throne of Satan," throne being a symbol of authority. Satan ruled in that city through its civil authorities, and the nature of his rule is indicated by their action against the name and faith of Jesus. This name they sought to supplant by some other name, and the laws of Jesus by the laws of man. These things were resisted by the church, and in one instance unto death, and Jesus did not forget their hard struggle with an outside enemy.

What were the things He had against them?

They are said to be the doctrine of Balaam, and of the Nicolaitanes, which being tolerated by the church brought upon itself the judgment of the sword of His mouth—*i.e.*, His condemnation.

What was this doctrine of Balaam, which was held by some in the church at Pergamos?

The teaching of Balaam is but briefly stated here, but the nature of it may be easily understood. Balaam was a prophet of the Gentiles, and when sent for by Balak the king of Moab to curse Israel, some very striking prophecies concerning them and other nations were delivered by him, and with which the king was greatly offended. Still as a prophet of God Balaam was afraid to do otherwise, and faithfully delivered the words of God concerning Israel. But when his work as a prophet was finished— for the wages of unrighteousness— Balak was counselled as a friend. Balaam advised the king to be sociable, to encourage intercourse in worship and lust, and the result was according to his crafty design, viz., trespass against the Lord, and a fearful judgment upon the people of Israel. The people whom Balaam could not curse, he could by seducing lead into disobedience, and more than twenty thousand perished on account of their sin. So in the church at Pergamos, there were those that held for worldly conformity, and thus bridged over the gulf that separated the Church from the world. Christ insisted upon separation from all evil, while these persons suggested intercourse, which at last led to trespass against the Lord. The Church ought to know that her separation from all evil is demanded by her Lord, and on no pretext should His will be violated.

What was the doctrine of the Nicolaitanes?

Pre-eminence in the church, which while some eagerly sought, others assisted them to attain. The evil began with Nimrod, the mighty hunter before the Lord (Gen. x. 9); a subjecter not of beasts but of men, out of whom, in opposition to Jehovah, he formed his kingdom which was called Babel. It was also manifest in Israel when they said to Samuel "make us a king to judge us like all the nations" (1 Sam. viii. 5). It was this same evil of human supremacy that was showing itself in the church at Pergamos, and Jesus offered but one alternative—

repentance or removal by judgment.

What was this hidden manna that Christ promised to " him that overcometh"?

The manna of the wilderness was a type of the soul-sustaining truth by which His people are sustained on earth; but the manna hidden or put in the ark of the covenant, was a type of glorification, and that is what Jesus promised to the conqueror.

What is the white stone and the new name?

The new name belongs to the period of the feast of hidden manna, and will be known only when the feast time arrives. The white stone, the symbol of purity, is the divine qualification for the new name, and the hidden manna.

LETTER TO THE CHURCH IN THYATIRA.

18–29. " *The Son of God, who hath His eyes like unto a flame of fire, and His feet are like unto fine brass." What do these symbols indicate?*

Omniscience and judgment. " His eyes as a flame of fire " searched the reins and hearts of the church; while " His feet as fine brass" showed Him dealing with them in judgment.

How is it that among so many good things in this church, as faith, and love, and patience, there should be such a mixture of evil?

The evil complained of by Jesus was caused by the unsubjected hearts of some persons in power in the church. For a time the church presented some noble traits of character, and faith and patience abounded; then some one introduced the Jezebel heresy, and the evil was tolerated, and ultimately prevailed.

What was this Jezebel heresy?

The sins named are the same as those of Balaam, viz., worldly conformity, with this difference, Balaam was without, a counsellor against

Israel, while Jezebel was within, a patroness of evil and insubordination to Christ. Jezebel was a queen in the nation of Israel, and prompted Ahab to sin; and so in the church in Thyatira, we see this evil principle accepted, and then it ruled over the people, to the dishonour of Christ, and to their own shame.

There were some in the church who had " not known the depths of Satan." What does this mean?

There were in that church some faithful souls, who like Elijah bore witness against the evil, and like Naboth would not sell the inheritance of the Lord; and these are exhorted to hold fast unto the end.

" He that overcometh, . . . to him will I give power over the nations." When will this be fulfilled?

When the Lamb triumphs over the dragon, then His associates will triumph with Him.

CHAPTER III.

LETTER TO THE CHURCH IN SARDIS.

1–6. The introduction to this church is from Him who hath the seven spirits of God, and the seven stars. Do these represent what He is, or what He claims?

I think that both are represented. A spirit is a symbol of a prophetic messenger, while the seven spirits set forth a perfect testimony. A star is the shining forth of that truth through those who receive it. Jesus gave a perfect testimony, and holds it as a star in his right hand—a witness for Himself.

They professed to have spiritual life. Why are they accounted as dead?

Because they had ceased to act for Christ. Still, although spiritually dead, their responsibility was not dead, hence they are urged to strengthen the things that remain,

or judgment would overtake them. This matter of relationship and responsibility to Christ is full of instruction to all who have accepted Him as their Lord. We may refuse to allow His word to live in us, but we cannot set aside His power to judge us.

" I will come on thee as a thief." What coming was this?

A visitation in judgment, from which they could not escape.

What lesson may we learn from these faithful few in Sardis?

We may learn that it is possible to be pure and faithful in the midst of surrounding apostasy.

What is this " book of life"?

A record of the faithful, or those who are alive in Christ.

How may persons know whether or not their name is in the book?

By knowing whether or not they are on the side of Jesus. All who obey Him are recorded as such.

LETTER TO THE CHURCH IN PHILADELPHIA.

7–13. Is there anything peculiar in the preface to this letter?

Yes; we have the Lord, not only telling the church what He has, but what He is. In each letter we find Him meeting their state with His own fitness for blessing or judgment. It is their condition that calls forth from Himself whatever is in keeping with it. The message to this faithful assembly is not about the sword with two edges, but of purity and power to bless. Their character was in harmony with His will, and His authority was vouchsafed for their protection and privilege.

What is this " key of David"?

The key is a symbol of authority. David was placed over the house of Israel, and all its forces were put under him; so Christ was set over the House of God, and all the forces of heaven were under His control.

This He declares for the encouragement of these persecuted saints.

What was this synagogue of Satan?

It was professedly a synagogue of Jews, for there were such in most of the cities of Asia. But while claiming to be the people of God, their impure lives were a disgrace to themselves and a snare to converted Gentiles. Jesus refused to own them, and declared their true character and doom.

" Behold, I will come and make them to worship before thy feet." What is this ?

It is prophetic of the change which was soon to take place among the Jews. For nearly forty years they had persecuted and reproached the disciples of Jesus, but their judgment was at hand. Their revolt against the Romans in Judea turned the tide of favour against them in every Roman province, so that they had then to bow at the feet of those they had so cruelly treated.

Does " Behold I come quickly " refer to this period ?

I do not know any other to which it can apply. It was near at hand, and the preservation of the faithful was then signally manifest.

LETTER TO THE CHURCH IN LAODICEA.

14–22. *" These things saith the Amen, the faithful and true witness." What is the bearing of this testimony upon the church ?*

It forms a striking contrast to their own spirit and life—He witnessing unto death, while they were so careless about the truth.

Why is Jesus called the "Amen" ?

The meaning of Amen is affirmation—*i.e.*, " so shall it be." It is a most solemn word to write to a faithless church. Jesus was the executer of the judgment of God, and unless they took timely warning He would most surely fulfil it.

Why is He called "the faithful and true witness" ?

Because He bore witness to His sonship before the High Priest, although He knew it would cost Him His life ; and before Pilate to His kingship, although it formed a plea for His condemnation—a striking contrast to their unfaithfulness.

This letter was sent to the church in Laodicea. How may we profit by it ?

By learning what is pleasing or displeasing to Christ, and acting so as to secure His approval. We learn here that He abhors lukewarmness, and if we shun this sin we shall have profited by the lesson.

The church made a false estimate of itself. How may we profit by their folly ?

By judging ourselves by a divine standard, and thus avoiding their mistake.

The Saviour advised them to obtain from Him gold for riches, white raiment for clothing, and eye salve for their defective sight. What is the meaning of those symbols ?

The truth of Christ is the basis of them all. Gold is a symbol of His glorification beyond death, a striking contrast to earthly riches, which are all to perish. The white raiment is that holy life which they were to copy from His example. His pure life was to be embodied in their own, and thus would be clothed in white. The eye salve was also the truth, by which everything would appear in its true light.

What does Christ standing at the door indicate ?

Both His rejection and His grace. By their adoption of self rule they had put Jesus outside, but He stood there for a while intreating for admission, and promised a feast if they would only admit Him to be a guest.

" My throne." Is this distinct from the Father's throne ?

There is but one throne, and that is the Father's, but it was won by Jesus when He conquered Satan and death, and was then transferred to Him. "All authority is given unto me," and in His triumph all victors are called to share.

CHAPTER IV.

1. *"After this I looked, and behold a door was opened in heaven."* What does this mean ?

"Heaven," in the "Revelation," is a symbol of the sphere of the Church, or of that system of which the Lamb, in this book, is the distinctly recognised head ; while "door" is a symbol of opportunity or privilege, which was granted to John, of looking upon the scene of its struggles and triumphs. It is, however, important to notice that here we get a marked division of the book. John had written of the "things which he had seen," viz., the Son of God in the midst of the golden lamps, with seven stars in His right hand, with eyes as a flame of fire, and with a two-edged sword going out of His mouth. He had seen Jesus on the cross, in shame and death, and he is now permitted to see Him in majesty and glory, and to be a witness to attest the same to others. He had also been instructed in the "things that are," viz., the house of God under judgment, and letters were to be written and sent to the churches specially named. And then he is invited to look upon the "things which must be hereafter" —*lit.*, after these.

2. *What is meant by the "throne set in heaven"* ?

A throne is a symbol of authority, and as one sat upon it, we learn that authority was maintained in the sphere upon which John was permitted to gaze.

Who was the occupant of this throne ?

God, who is not only the rightful ruler of the universe, but also of the Church, which is specially named the "Church of God." But in chapters iv. and v., which are introductory to the "Revelation" proper, we not only see God seated upon this throne, invested with all authority, and acknowledged by the elders and the living creatures which were about His throne ; but we also see a transfer of this power and glory to Him who now appears, and is afterward to be distinguished in this book as "the Lamb," who is also to be the leader of the saints who assemble under His banner, and who suffer and triumph with Him.

3. *Of what is this rainbow a symbol ?*

Of a covenant of unfailing privilege, which He who sat upon the throne was pledged to maintain on behalf of all who accepted His authority. A bow was set in the cloud after the deluge, and was God's token that the judgment would never return. So this rainbow round about the throne — the resurrection of Christ—was to these elders a pledge that the dispensational judgment would never rest upon those who had accepted Him.

4. *What do the twenty-four elders represent ?*

The saved of the Jewish nation in both dispensations. Twelve is the symbol of the unity of the nation, but is doubled here, as the saved in both institutions are represented.

6. *There are "four beasts" taking a part in this scene. What do they represent ?*

"Beasts" is an unhappy translation of *zoa*, which should be rendered *living ones*, because we have beast, as a symbol of an empire, employed in different parts of the Revelation, and it is therefore confusing and misleading to so render it. These *living ones* are symbols of the redeemed from among the nations of the earth, and in chap. vii. we see them as the " great multitude out of every nation," etc.

Why have we but " four " to symbolise redeemed humanity ?

Four is all inclusive, as the four winds, the four quarters of the earth ; so four is used to denote all who own the worthiness of Jesus.

7. *Each of the four living ones distinctly represent the figure of an animal, as a lion, a calf, a man, and an eagle. Why are these animal likenesses employed ?*

They are doubtless symbols of qualities, or dispositions, or principles common to the saints, as conquest in the lion, service in the calf, intelligence in the man, and aspiration in the eagle, which, either singly or combined, are developed in those who love and honour Jesus, no matter in what quarter of the earth they are found. In Jesus, when on earth, these features were all combined, and those who sincerely accept Him as their leader become in a measure like unto Him.

8. *Each of these living creatures had six wings. Of what are these a symbol ?*

Wings are for ascent, and as it is by truth that spiritual ascent is effected and humility and obedience secured, we judge them to be symbols of truth by which these important results are secured, and which is derived from divine history, law, and prophecy, as given in connection with both dispensations. Isaiah, who " saw the Lord sitting upon a throne " (the throne of grace), says, " Above it stood the seraphims : each one had six wings ; with twain he covered his face "—*i.e.*, humbled by the truth—" and with twain he covered his feet "—*i.e.*, walking in the truth—" and with twain he did fly "—*i.e.*, soaring upward by the truth.

What does the united action of the elders and the living ones or cherubims represent ?

The united ascription of praise to God by all the faithful, whether Jews or Gentiles. It is an united testimony that He who sat on the throne was worthy of glory and honour.

CHAPTER V.

1. *In the right hand of Him that sat on the throne John saw a sealed book. What does this book represent ?*

It is a symbol of testimony or revelation, and contained the fortune or destiny of the cause of the Lamb on earth, with an account of His foes and their judgment. The book, which was sealed with seven seals—*i.e.*, perfectly sealed—was in the hand of God, and the messenger cried with a loud voice, " Who is worthy to open the book, and loose the seals thereof ? And no man in heaven "—*i.e.*, among the Jewish rulers—" nor in earth "—*i.e.*, among the Jewish people—" neither under the earth "—*i.e.*, among the nations —" was able to open the book." No one was found able to unfold the history of that new enterprise which had commenced under the auspices of the Lamb that was slain.

Could the writing outside the sealed book be read ?

Time had unfolded a part of its history, and with this John and others were familiar. This was not sealed, but written on the outside, but beyond this all was secret. John wept because no man was found to open the book, but he was afterward cheered by the assurance that the Lion of the tribe of Judah had prevailed to open the book, and to loose the seven seals.

6, 7. *Why is Jesus called both a Lion and a Lamb ?*

Both are symbols of His character. As the meek oppressed one He is the Lamb, and as the conquering one He is the Lion. As a Lamb He patiently endured for a while the tyranny of His foes, but afterward rose in His strength against them.

As a Lamb He had seven horns and seven eyes. What are these ?

The seven horns are a symbol of His perfect kingship, or rule : " All authority is given to me ; " and the seven eyes or spirits are His complete laws of truth, which are " sent forth into all the earth."

7–9. *" And He [the Lamb] came and took the book . . . and the four beasts, or living ones, and four and twenty elders fell down," etc. Was this seen by John in vision only, or was it a real occurrence ?*

It was only a representation of things, and these were seen by John in the Spirit, or in vision. God gave the book, and Jesus the Lamb received it, and this " Revelation " is the book opened. From this vision of John we learn that, upon this assumption of power by Jesus, those who had worshipped God did in like manner render homage to the Lamb who was slain. " Thou art worthy . . . for Thou wast slain, and hast redeemed us to God by Thy blood." This was the new song, which, after Pentecost, was sung to Jesus, and will continue to be sung by all who believe in Him.

10. *" We shall reign on the earth." What does this mean ?*

It is the triumph of the saints over the direful opposition which was put forth against their Lord, the Lamb of the " Revelation ; " and which was continued against His followers until it was terminated by a complete overthrow of their power. As long as their opportunity and power continued, the saints were kept in most ignoble bondage, but when it ceased, they triumphed, and may very properly be said to " reign on the earth."

Have the saints reached this period of triumph, or reign, or is it yet future ?

The Jews were the first to trample upon the liberties of the saints, but their power was broken by the Lamb soon after John saw the vision ; but the persecuting spirit of Pagan Rome, and the more despotic power of Papal Rome which succeeded it, rested upon them for centuries. These governments, however, both the secular and the spiritual have now ceased to exist, so that spiritual freedom and triumph are now fully enjoyed by the followers of the Lamb. The saints are no longer under bondage to secular powers, but reign with their Leader on the earth,—*i.e.*, through Jesus they now triumph over that which enslaved and degraded them ; and from verse 11–14, we have the united praises of all these, in their varied relations, to Him who alone is worthy.

CHAPTER VI.

1. *When the Lamb opened one of the seals, what may He be said to have done ?*

Simply revealed in symbol a part of the history of this dispensation.

At what period of time was this seal opened ?

At Pentecost, with the first proclamation of the Gospel of Jesus. And although the seven seals were all opened under the Christian administration, yet they specially apply to the Jews, and in that period of their history from A.D. 33½ to about A.D. 70, when their national power ceased.

2. *What does the horse symbolise ?*

As animals are very frequently employed as symbols by the Spirit through the prophets, it will be well to carefully note the use which is made of them. For instance, we have the lion, the bear, the leopard, the goat, the dragon, the wolf, the lamb, etc., all employed as symbols of the prevailing spirit of nations, or of those who rule or represent them ; and we may therefore expect conformity to this rule in any selection that may be made. It is in the light of these facts that we are able to decide that when an animal is selected in various instances in the prophets to symbolise the animus or spirit of a nation, or a company of people, we are at liberty to follow out this God-given rule in the "Revelation." We judge, therefore, that the horse, which was seen in four of these seals when opened, is a symbol of war and aggression of one party against another. This is implied in the further detail, that He who sat upon the horse had a bow given to Him, and He went forth conquering and to conquer. But when we speak of war, it is not human slaughter and bloodshed that is to be thought of here ; the colour of the horse, and the name of Him that sat upon it, afterward given to us as the "Word of God" (xix. 20), forbids the thought. The prophets are the first to supply the symbols, "Gird thy sword upon thy thigh, O most mighty, with thy glory and thy majesty. And in thy majesty ride prosperously because of truth and meekness and righteousness; and thy right hand shall teach thee terrible things. Thine arrows are sharp in the heart of the king's enemies; whereby the people fall under thee" (Ps. xlv. 3). It is a war scene that the prophet foresees, and in Acts ii. we get the first view of this battle-field. It was by the apostles, of whom this " white

2 K

horse " is a symbol, that the Lord Jesus began His aggressive war against sin and unrighteousness, "and He went forth conquering," and though fearful opposition followed and hindered His progress, we have the sequel in the words, " and to conquer."

But John knew these things already; how can this be called a Revelation ?

We must not forget the direction given to John, "Write the things which thou hast seen," as well as " the things which shall be hereafter."

3, 4. *When the second seal was opened, John saw another horse that was red, and to him that sat thereon a great sword was given. To what things are these symbols applied ?*

The horse is still the symbol of a person, nation, or people forming for war, but the red colour denotes rage and revengeful opposition to the first. It is not the same person, nor the same party as the first, but one that goes forth in opposition. Two things he is seen to possess, (1.) an opportunity for mischief: "there was given to him that sat thereon to take peace from the earth, and that they should kill one another ; " and (2.) authority : "and there was given to him a great sword," a symbol of magisterial power, which he is ready to use. As the first horse represents the spiritual aggressions of Pentecost and onward, so the second horse represents the deadly opposition that was awakened in the nation, in both its rulers and people. They had the opportunity and the authority, and they were not slow to use them. The book of the "Acts of Apostles" is the key to this symbolic picture.

5, 6. *At the opening of the third seal a black horse is seen, and he that sat on him had a pair of balances in his hand. Of what are these things symbols ?*

It is still war, a threatened aggression, for the horse is present, and the symbol betokens invasion. The colour is a symbol of night, for blackness begins to show itself everywhere in that Jewish dispensational sky, and as the horse advances the midnight will cover all. We must, however, notice that the rider differs from the former two. The first rider was the "Word of God." The second, Jewish magisterial authority opposed to the Lamb; and the third, Roman imperialism, whose forces became to these first opposers the executers of the wrath of the Lamb.

What do the balances indicate?

The balances are the symbol of justice, which is being meted out to the enemies of the Lamb. They are being weighed by an impartial hand, and found wanting.

Does "a measure of wheat for a penny" indicate scarcity?

No, it is rather a providential supply, which the people of the Lamb were to experience through that great tribulation. For their penny they would get their measure, and even the oil and the wine, symbols of gracious provision and privileges, were not to be unrighteously trampled upon by the executers of the divine will.

7, 8. Of what is this fourth and last horse a symbol?

It is the final onslaught of the war horse, who is led over this section of the earth, to kill with sword, and with hunger, and with death, and with the beasts of the earth.

Is it the physical death of the body that is intended here?

Possibly not; although we are sure that many would die in that terrible revolution, yet that may not be the death intended here. It was the theocracy, or God-ruled nation, that died, and was also buried, for hell, —*lit.*, hades,—followed death, and thus put their national form out of sight. They were, in fact, scattered among the nations, and thus were swallowed up, not as individuals, for as such they still exist in the world, but their national life is no more.

9–12. Why have we no horse under this fifth seal?

The second, third, and fourth horses have done their sad work, and when the remainder of the seals are opened, it is not the furious tramping of the war horses that John sees, but rather a glance over the battle field, when the dread strife had partially ceased. On the opening of this fifth seal, John saw the effect of the march of the red horse and his rider, and heard the cry of those who were slain for the Word of God, while seeking to serve Him under a new and better covenant.

John saw under the altar the souls of them that were slain for the Word of God. Who are these?

The altar is the symbol of priestly prerogative, and those who are said to be under it are those who, during such tyrannical sway, were deprived of lawful rights and privileges which, as citizens of the commonwealth, justly belonged to them. John saw the souls, *i.e*, the persons who were thus slain for the Word of God. And as "they cried with a loud voice, saying, How long, O Lord, holy and true, dost Thou not judge and avenge our blood on them that dwell on the earth?" they are told to rest for a little season, until others were killed as they had been.

12–17. What does the opening of the sixth seal denote?

The result of the going forth of the fourth horse, the symbol of the Roman forces, whose visitation was as a cloud eclipsing the orbs of heaven, and as an earthquake displacing and throwing the whole economy into hopeless confusion.

Indeed, we get, in symbol in these six verses what we get in testimony in Matt. xxiv. John heard the testimony from the lips of Jesus, and saw the symbols as they were sketched on the page of the book, which had just been unsealed and opened before him.

Do all these seals refer to the Jewish nation?

Directly or indirectly all are connected with their action or sufferings. These six seals reveal their history, from Pentecost to the destruction of their city. Every seal opened is a stage in their eventful career, and depicts their terrible overthrow. It is full of solemn instruction, respecting the faithfulness of God, both to reward and punish.

Some people think the end of the world is here described; may it not be so?

If the language was literal, it would indicate a convulsion of nature, but as these are signs in connection with a system, it can only indicate a convulsion or breaking up of that system. When the Lamb closed that dispensation in His wrath, the people sought to hide from it in dens and rocks of the mountains, but where can men hide from the personal presence of Jesus? When the herald announces His approach by the last trump, one moment will change the whole scene. The twinkling of an eye, and the transition from time to eternity, will have taken place. This solemn crisis, though certain to all who then shall be found on the earth, is not the event which John is here permitted to reveal.

CHAPTER VII.

1. *Four angels, standing on the four corners of the earth, are seen by John restraining the violence of the four winds of the earth. What do these things mean?*

John had just gazed upon the symbolic scene in which the overthrow of the Jewish nation had been vividly sketched, and in connection with this event we have the deliverance of those who obeyed the directions of Jesus. Now, in the opening of this chapter, John sees in symbol the gracious providence of God towards those who escaped into the various parts of the world. The winds, symbol of the fury of the nations in sympathy with Rome, are actually restrained from all who thus escape, in each of the four quarters of the earth. Jesus had said, "In your patience possess ye your souls,"—*i.e.*, your lives,—and this was proved by all who believed Him.

2–8. *What was this sealing of the servants of God?*

It was the visible mark of divine protection, which was granted to all who believed the testimony of Jesus, and who had become His disciples. Twelve thousand out of each of the twelve tribes were thus sealed and protected, in relation to that sad crisis. It was but a small number compared with the nation that suffered; and of their experience we have no historical record. Yet we are bound to accept this revelation, and rejoice that, in the general refusal of the nation to believe in Christ, there should have been so many Jews, chiefly from the provinces, who accepted Jesus as Lord and Christ. It is very likely that twelve thousand out of each of the twelve tribes are only symbolic of a large number who honoured Jesus by their trust, and were in return honoured by His protecting care. That thousand and thousands are used as symbols of a large number, a glance at a concordance under this head will suffice to show. It is evident from the revelation here (1.) That there was a great number out of the twelve tribes of Israel who had been led by the ministry of the apostles to believe in Jesus, because, in chap. xiv. 4, they are said to be "the first fruits unto God and to the Lamb"; and (2.) That these were sealed, *i.e.*, delivered from the judgment which overwhelmed the unbelieving nation. True, in the records of the labours of the apostles, we have no account of such a large number of converts as are named in this chapter; but they were known to God, and in these symbolic figures He has given this very pleasing revelation. We must indeed confess that, after reading of the fierce opposition which the apostles received, we are somewhat startled at this result, and see that their labours were not in vain.

9. "*After this I beheld, and lo, a great multitude.*" *Who are these?*

The saved from among the Gentiles, and this vision is prophetic concerning them. After the destruction of Jerusalem there were but few converts from among the Jews, whilst Gentile converts became a multitude; and being purified by the truth, the full provision of the Gospel was enjoyed.

CHAPTER VIII.

"*And when he had opened the seventh seal, there was silence in heaven about the space of half-an-hour.*" *What does this mean?*

Heaven is a symbol of the Jewish institution,—an administration of a very exalted character, and which was upheld by God during a lengthened period. When the sixth seal was opened John saw the whole institution a complete wreck. The sun was eclipsed, the moon became as blood, the stars fell, and the heaven was rolled up as a scroll, and departed. Or, as Haggai writes (ii. 6), "Yet once, it is a little while,

and I will shake the heavens, and the earth, and the sea, and the dry land," etc. And this "yet once more" Paul explains to mean "the removing of things that are shaken," *i.e.*, the old institution, "that the things which cannot be shaken," *i.e.*, the kingdom we are receiving, "may remain" (Heb. xii. 27). Now, on the opening of this seventh seal, the collapse of everything belonging to that Jewish institution must be understood as having taken place. The titles, privileges, sacrifice, worship, priesthood, and power, which had once been the boast of the Jews, had passed away for ever. From the arrest of Peter and John in Solomon's Poreh (Acts iii.) to the entrance of the Roman army into Judea under Titus, at the "time of the end," as spoken to Daniel, the Jews never ceased to persecute and annoy the disciples of Christ. With that overthrow their power and persecution ceased, and this "silence in heaven" is most expressive. The limit of the silence to "about the space of half-an-hour" is also to be noted. The respite granted to the disciples of Jesus by the removal of these opponents was soon followed by Pagan persecution; but the nature and extent of this renewed trial, and their deliverance from it also, is brought forward in the after revelations of the Lamb.

Does the opening of the seventh seal terminate the "Revelation" concerning the Jewish people?

The opening of the seventh seal terminates a series of events which reached from the beginning of the Gospel era to the effect of God's judgment poured upon them by the Romans. But in chap. viii. 2, we get a new series of events happening to the same people, thus furnishing in these sketches of their history a further detail of their opportunities, their misuse of them, and the sad troubles which followed the sounding of the seven trumpets. These new revelations of this people under privilege and judgment, and of God's determination to fully execute all He had purposed, reach down to the close of chap. xi.

What is the evidence that chapters viii. to xi. inclusive are to be applied to the Jews?

There are several reasons which lead to this conclusion. The symbols used in this section are strictly Jewish. The trumpets, censer, incense, altar, temple, court, candlestick, etc., all point to that people and their institution. They were first used as types, and here as symbols of their doom, and John could not fail to see the application. We may also note that these Jewish symbols are never used after chap. xi. It is a new scene which then opens,—a contest between the followers of the Lamb and the governments of the world, and the symbols employed are in harmony with this new struggle. The reign of the Lamb was at first opposed by the house of Israel, whose priestly influence—the last fragment of its power—was put forth to prevent His rightful sway. Then imperialism—the head of pagan despotism—made a furious onslaught, and those who were identified with the Lamb had to endure the brunt of its rage. Then the opposition was renewed by an apostate church, which unrighteously obtained worldly governmental power; and the contest between these parties, and the triumph of the Lamb over them all, is fully revealed. The symbols which are used, descriptive of these operations, are quite distinct and appropriate to each, and if some of them are applied to all, it is because they are of general application.

2. *Of what are these seven angels a symbol?*

Of God's perfect testimony, which had its seven-fold application to Israel, during that eventful period in which it was applied.

Of what are the trumpets a symbol?

It may be well to refer to their appointed use under the law. The trumpet was largely employed to express the will of God, and direct the varied movements of His people during their journeys in the wilderness. Not only was the new moon announced, and the congregation gathered; the sacrifice proclaimed, and the jubilee ushered in by sounding of trumpets, but its clarion note aroused the host, and sent them forth to battle. In the land it was chiefly used for military operations, and was a signal for preparation for hostilities. To John all this would be familiar, and as trumpet after trumpet sounded, he was prepared to note the calamities that were coming on his people. As a nation they had often heard its certain sound, and prepared themselves for the battles of the Lord, but now John hears it summoning other hosts to do their direful work on them, because they had become the enemies of God and the Lamb. The trumpet is therefore a symbol of God's proclamation of His will, and here we see its fulfilment along the stages of their sad history.

3–5. *What does this angel standing by the altar represent?*

A two-fold result of the testimony of God. It is by the side of the golden altar that he stands with golden censer, and with the much incense given him the prayers of saints ascend to God; while from that same altar the burning coals are cast into the earth, and exciting commotions are felt by all concerned. It is a striking symbol of the two-fold mission of the Lamb, viz., as an intercession for the royal priesthood, and an avenger of the disobedient. He was then, as he still is, a friend or an emeny, according as He was accepted or rejected.

6–12. In describing the effect of the sounding of these four trumpets, the whole creation is laid under tribute to supply the requisite symbols— as sun, moon, stars, waters, earth, grass, hail, fire, blood, etc. What do all these mean?

We must read them as signs of things or people, whether we can discover their meaning or not. To read them as a literal description of events that were to happen would lead to disappointment and confusion. In connecting these events with that period of Jewish history which followed the ascension of Jesus, and remembering that many of the Jews were scattered over the Roman empire, and suffered very much from the revolts and struggles of their nation, we shall, I think, find many of those things which followed the sounding of these trumpets set forth in these symbols. They were indeed but the beginning of sorrows—the evening shadows of the dark night of judgment that was so soon to close over them.

Is this indicated in the yet greater woes that were to follow?

It is evidently manifest that the nearer the dispensation came to a close, the more terrible were the judgments that fell upon the people, until the days of vengeance closed the scene.

CHAPTER IX.

1–3. Were these remaining trumpets connected with that dispensation?

The whole seven were undoubtedly connected with one people, although we get alternate views of both the executers and their victims. Nor must we think it strange that so large a space of the "Revelation" should be occupied with the sufferings and destiny of that people, when we remember that they killed the Lord Jesus and their own prophets, and persecuted the apostles; and were opposed to all whom God sent to bless them.

What is this star that fell?

Some one who possessed authority for seduction and evil. Their own history supplies the answer.

What is this "bottomless pit"?

It is strictly the *abyss*, or place out from which evil arose, and which blinded the minds of those who believed not. And as smoke bedims the atmosphere and renders vision difficult, so did the blinding smoke of error arise out of that Jewish abyss, when the chief priests persuaded the people that Jesus was stolen out of the sepulchre; and in the shade of this dense gloom, clouds of locusts swarmed the earth to consume and destroy; and only those who believed the truth concerning Jesus, as attested by the apostles, were enabled to resist the error, and so were not hurt by it.

4–10. What are we to understand by these locusts, whose destructive work was limited to those men who had not the seal of God on their foreheads?

If we are to abide by the statement already made,—and we see no reason to change it,—viz., that this section of the Revelation, from chap. vi. to xi., has special reference to the Jews and their varied experiences, from the first proclamation of the ascended Jesus, to their final overthrow, then we must conclude that we get here a reference to some trouble through which they were called to pass before that final crisis. The destructive operations of these locusts, which are given in symbol by John, were a part of those wars, famines, pestilences, and quakings, "the beginning of sorrows" foretold by Jesus, and which preceded the end.

What were the grass and herb and trees which the locusts were not to touch ?

Trees were a symbol of the righteous, who are often likened to them by the prophets, as in Isaiah lxi. 3, " But ye shall be called trees of righteousness," etc., while the grass and green things growing out of the earth, are symbols of their liberties, which for a long time were not meddled with or hurt by the Romans, the stinging scorpions of the Revelation. Even Paul, when annoyed by the Jews at Jerusalem, could appeal unto Cæsar, and in his name found protection from their rage.

11. " *And they had a king over them, the angel of the bottomless pit. What does this mean ?*

This king was the leader of this tormenting host, and to him was given power over the abyss, and was God's scourging rod against the nation of Israel. In the Greek tongue his name was, *lit.*, the destroyer, and history supplies the name of this agent.

14. *Four angels were bound in the great river Euphrates, and were afterward loosed for the work of destruction. What is meant by this river and these angels ?*

" The waters which thou sawest, where the whore sitteth, are peoples, and multitudes, and nations " (xvii. 15) ; and this will help us to understand the meaning of river, one of the divisions of waters. The army of the king of Assyria is spoken of as of the waters of a river, strong and many, and which for a time were bounded or restrained by its banks ; but when loosed they overflowed the land of Israel (Isa. viii. 7, 8). So these angels or messengers of God's wrath were the military forces of Rome, which for a while were bound or restrained, but when set free overflowed the land for judgment. Josephus distinctly states that when Titus was forming his army for subduing Jerusalem, many soldiers were released from their duties in other parts of the empire, in order to assist the expedition ; and that many auxiliaries were united to help against the Jews ; John says, " for an hour, and a day, and a month, and a year," or as long as required.

CHAPTER X.

1. *Is this tenth chapter a continuation of Jewish history ?*

It is rather a revelation of God's gracious purposes, and which still remained for the world. That dispensation closed with judgment, but grace remained for humanity through Jesus Christ. The mighty angel which came down from heaven was clothed with a cloud, a symbol of a desolating army, but a rainbow encircled his head, and God's gracious covenant was remembered by Him. This tenth chapter forms a sequel to the preceding section somewhat similar to chap. vii. In chap. vi. we see the storm of wrath bursting over the Jewish nation, and many seeking to hide from it ; then in chap. vii. we get a view of the sealed out of the twelve tribes, and of the great multitude. So in chap. x. we get some blessed revelations connected with this dispensation, to which the " rainbow," and the " mystery," and the " little book," so unmistakably point.

2. *What is the meaning of this " little book "?*

Book is a symbol of revelation. When the book is sealed, the matters within are secret, and when open they are known. This little book, which John afterward ate, contained those testimonies which he had before received from Jesus, but which he is now informed he has still more widely to make known.

3. *What did these seven thunders utter ?*

We cannot know, because John was forbidden to write them, so that neither in symbol nor testimony have they been recorded.

5, 6. *" The angel . . . sware . . . that there should be time no longer." To what does this apply?*

Scholars now render this last clause, *There shall be delay no longer.* The reference, therefore, is not to the end of time, but to some event which had been delayed or kept back from its fulfilment.

7. *What is this "mystery of God," that was to be finished during the sounding of the seventh angel?*

The word "mystery" in the New Testament—and it is there applied to various things—is simply a secret, or something hidden from the un-initiated, but when revealed is no longer a secret. For instance, we have the "mystery of the kingdom of God," and yet it was given unto the disciples, by the ministry of Jesus, "to know the mysteries of the kingdom of heaven." We have also the "mystery of Christ," *i.e.*, His hidden purpose concerning the Gentiles being "fellow-heirs, and of the same body," and this was clearly revealed to Paul, and through him to all believers. In addition to these, we have the "mystery of godliness," *i.e.*, God's gracious sys-tem revealed in the facts of the Gos-pel ; and "the mystery of iniquity," the hidden lawlessness, but after-wards manifest ; and here the "mys-tery of God," which "should be finished,"—*i.e.*, God's secret, respect-ing the time of judgment upon the nation of Israel—should be veiled no longer. When Jesus announced to His disciples the doom of the temple, they modestly asked, "When shall these things be?" and His reply will help us to understand what is meant by the *secret of God.* After stating the facts of its overthrow, Jesus said, " But of that day and hour knoweth no man, no, not the angels of heaven, but My Father only " (Matt. xxiv. 36.) The time, therefore, of that Jewish judgment was kept secret un-til the seal which concealed it was opened by the Lamb ; and in the time of the sounding of the seventh angel, this secret was to be finished.

What was the purport of the sounding of this seventh angel?

It was the announcing of what may be called a new era. The testi-mony of God among the Jews was finished, the secret was consummated, and John must after this deliver his testimony to peóples, and nations, and kings.

9. *Why had John to eat the little book?*

To symbolise his reception of a message that must be delivered in a new field. "Thou must prophecy again, not now among thine own people, but among the nations and potentates of the earth."

Why was the book first sweet, and then bitter?

It was sweet to him to receive it as a testimony from Jesus, but bitter in his experience when he had to suffer for that testimony.

CHAPTER XI.

1. *What temple was this which John had to measure?*

It is said to be the temple of God, but as God had a temple at Jerusa-lem, and also a house built up of living stones, the former a type of the latter ; it may be well to enquire to which of these John's measuring rod was to be applied. And, lest there should be any mistake as to which is intended, the "altar," the symbol of God's claim, and "them that worship therein," are specially named, so that the old temple at Jerusalem is referred to.

To what period does this measuring apply?

To the period just preceding the removal of both temple and worshippers, which was not far distant when John had his vision. The temple and its altar were still standing, and the worshippers were still gathering to that once hallowed shrine ; but God was about to destroy it, and scatter those who gathered to it. It would be a question with John and many others, Was it right in God to do so ? John's measuring rod was to furnish the answer. The truths he had preached and taught had only to be applied to the old temple worshippers, to make their sad deficiency apparent. Animal sacrifices and formal services could never satisfy God, who claimed to be worshipped in spirit and in truth. He never intended that even fleshly services should be offered by unclean hearts ; and after long protest against such abominations, He now determined to sweep it all away ?

2. *The Gentiles were to tread under foot the holy city forty and two months. What does this mean ?*

According to historians, this was the length of the Roman siege, or, as stated by R. Young, in his commentary on the New Testament, " the exact time the Romans besieged Jerusalem," or kept it under guard.

3. *Did the two witnesses prophesy in sackcloth during the same period ?*

The same length of time is stated, only it is given in days instead of months. The 1260 days being 42 months, and the treading under foot of the holy city, and their witnessing in sackcloth were going on together.

Who were these two witnesses ?

The faithful from among the Jews and the Gentiles, the two classes who during that lengthened siege had to witness in sackcloth—a symbol of mourning. Again and again these two witnesses come before us in the Revelation. We see them in their representatives, the elders, and the living creatures, and we see them in the sealed from among the Jews and the great multitude. They witnessed for God, and were preserved by God all through that eventful time.

4. *Why were they called " olive trees" and " candlesticks " ?*

Because they were both receivers and dispensers of light and truth. The olive tree was a symbol of the Spirit of Truth, the candlestick or lamp the shining out of that truth in believers. These things are first given to us in type in connection with the tabernacle, and then by Zechariah (chap. iv.), who in vision saw the two olive trees and the seven-branched lamp, which through golden pipes received the oil from the olive trees. The source of revelation, the Holy Spirit; the medium, prophets and apostles ; and the receivers, the Church, are here distinctly before us in symbol. John indeed learned that these two trees and two candlesticks were the two witnesses—*i.e.*, two sections of believers—who united in one testimony to the faithfulness of God.

If the faithful of that age were the " anointed ones" in symbol, how could they inflict such fearful judgments on their persecutors ?

It must not be overlooked that these faithful ones had the promise of divine protection, while the judgments that followed were only prophetic denunciations fulfilled. We must not think of vindictiveness in the witnesses, but of God's defence of those who held fast His testimonies. Then we must not understand this turning waters into blood, and closing the windows of heaven, etc., as literal, but as signs of judgment peculiar to the age. Rain is a symbol of blessing, and most righteously was blessing withheld from Christ-rejecting and saint-persecuting Jews.

7. *What is this beast that ascended*

out of the pit and made war against the witnesses?

It is strictly "the wild beast," and this symbol at once suggests that it is a foe outside the Jewish nation, and, as we afterwards learn, rises out of the sea—*i.e.*, the nations— thus showing that a passing reference is here made to the Roman power, the symbolic wild beast which succeeded the Jews as persecutors of the saints. The witnesses finished their testimony to the former, the rejection of which closes with judgment, and then the wild beast begins a deadly onslaught upon them, and deprives them of life—*i.e.*, their civil rights —which are ruthlessly taken from them. It is, however, only a passing allusion.

8. "*In the street of the great city, which spiritually is called Sodom and Egypt, where also our Lord was crucified." Was He not crucified at Jerusalem?*

The great city—which spiritually is called Sodom, on account of its corruption; and Egypt, because it was an oppressive world-power—was imperialism, with Rome for its centre, whether wielded by the dragon or the woman that sat upon the beast. Jerusalem, "where also our Lord was crucified," was only a street or broad way of this city, a thoroughfare in its widely acquired dominion. Here the lifeless forms of the witnesses were also exposed for a brief period, as other troubles which came upon their enemies, and the gracious interference of God prevented a longer manifestation of injustice at that time.

15. *At the sounding of the seventh angel our Lord's possession of the kingdoms of this world is announced. What does this mean?*

If is strictly "the kingdom of the world" has become, or passed over to our Lord and His Anointed, and He shall reign for ever and ever.

This marks a crisis in that once God-ruled kingdom of Israel, but which apostatised and assumed world-power, which under the sounding of the seventh trumpet was at an end. The putting down of this kingdom was a proof that Jesus was exalted.

How can He "reign for ever and ever" if His kingdom is to be given up?

It is, *lit.*, "into the ages of the ages," which is simply through the Christian administration. The ages in which Jesus reigns are those that follow the Jewish ages, and when all enemies are subdued, then He will give up the kingdom to God the Father.

18, 19. "*The nations were angry, and thy wrath is come." When did this take place?*

At the close of the Jewish dispensation. The nation had long given up its life, and at last the time came when the dead were to be judged. This verse is a recapitulation of the closing scene—the angry nations, the wrath of the Lamb, the opened ark of God rebounding with judgment upon the rebellious, close this very solemn crisis; and after this scene in the revelations of the Lamb we are led over another and very different field.

CHAPTER XII.

If chapter xi. closes a section of history in which we see a marked triumph of the Lamb over His enemies, what is the character of the revelations of chapter xii.?

A very marked section of the book begins here, in which we trace that further opposition which the followers of Christ had to endure, and of their full triumph through their victorious leader. True, the first view that John gets here is the jealousy and opposition of the dragon against the man-child—one foe against another—while both became foes to the Lamb ; and when combined, as they afterwards were in the woman-dragon empire, the opposition became fearful.

1. *What heaven was this in which John saw a great wonder ?*

It is the symbolic heaven of the Church, the exalted sphere in which she moves. As the earth has its physical heaven, beneath which it moves, so the Church is in a corresponding exalted sphere, or what Paul terms the heavenlies.

What did the woman represent ?

The Church, of which in the "Revelation" she is a symbol, or as she is called here "a wonder,"—lit., a sign,—"a woman clothed with the sun, and the moon under her feet, and upon her head a crown of twelve stars;" these planetary names being transferred from the unfaithful house of Israel to the Church of God, which also became the receiver of divine light—i.e., the truth—through the twelvefold medium, the apostles, and a reflector of the light which she had received.

2. *If the woman represents the Church, what is indicated by her being with child ?*

She was not only with child,—i.e., a child in conception,—but pained to be delivered. What made her a marvel was that she had conceived,—i.e., in her mind,—and was pained to give birth to a man-child or ruler, when the Lamb was her rightful Lord and ruler.

3. *What is this "great red dragon, having seven heads and ten horns" ?*

The dragon is a symbol of a government, which had been formed by the union of several kingdoms, and which was then known as the Roman empire, over which the Cæsars ruled, the representatives of this dragon power. Daniel, in his night-vision, saw this beast rise up out of the sea, a symbol of the

nations, and describes it as a beast "dreadful and terrible, and strong exceedingly," and it had ten horns, symbols of the kingdoms of which it was composed.

Why did the dragon seek to devour the child ?

This man-child was evidently a ruler, and his rule began to encroach upon the rule of the dragon ; hence the attempt made by the dragon to destroy him.

Who was this man-child that the woman brought forth ?

The Lord Jesus placed in the Church, of which this woman was a symbol, pastors, overseers, and deacons, to teach, oversee, and serve her for her Lord and head ; but in her unfaithfulness the woman conceived and brought forth one who sought to rule not only over all those named, but also "all nations with a rod of iron." And the one who was a Metropolitan Bishop thus became head of all other bishops or overseers ; this is the man-child she brought forth, and is now known as papa or Pope, who ruled nations with the acquired iron rod of imperial Rome.

5. *" And her child was caught up to God and his throne." How was this exaltation effected ?*

We must not read as if God had caught him up and set him on His throne, because this is not stated. By what means this elevation was reached must be learned from other sources. That there were agents and circumstances helping to this result is implied in the phrase "caught up," but these are not given here. The man-child appears passive, but this is only one side of the matter, and we must look elsewhere for the other. In 2. Thess. ii. 4, Paul gives us the other side, and completes the picture. There we see the personal ambition of the "man of sin" exalting himself until he is seated as a god in the temple of God, and thus we learn how his exaltation was effected. Had he been content to have been joined with others in loving oversight of the flock of God, it would never have been well, and we should never have heard or read of the birth of a man-child, a symbol of human headship. But, alas! the spirit of the mother of Zebedee's children was in the Church, and her offspring was ready for pre-eminence; while times and seasons favoured his daring ambition and bore him up-ward, until, at last, we see him alongside of God, and a daring usurper of His throne.

6. *What is meant by the woman fleeing into the wilderness?*

The children of Israel, who were a type of the Church of Christ, supply the symbols which are here em-ployed. When Moses, the appointed servant of God, was rejected by them, they were doomed to wander forty years in the wilderness, and through the favour of God were supplied with manna during that long period. So when the woman, the Church in symbol, became un-faithful to Christ by giving birth to a human ruler, the wilderness neces-sarily became her place of sojourn, while the truth—the God-provided manna—was prepared for her suste-nance during the period which John names. Still it remained to be proved whether she would eat and live, or neglect it and die. We are sorry to add that the latter became her sad lot. The leaven that was put into the meal leavened the whole lump, and not a single congregation remained as planted by the apostles of Christ.

What length of time is indicated by the 1260 *days — the time the woman was said to be in the wilder-ness?*

Many writers affirm that the 1260 days are so many years, and extend over the period of the Papal assump-tion of civil power—viz., from 606 to its termination. This we think a mistake. It is evident that the woman was in the wilderness during the supremacy of the dragon, and that the 1260 days denote some period of that rule. Indeed, the whole of the chapter is connected with the Pagan rulers of Rome, whose determination to put down Christianity,—or, in the words of John, make "war with the remnant of her seed,"—has stained the page of history with fearful crimes.

7–9. *" There was war in heaven." What heaven was this, and when did it take place?*

It was the struggle between the forces of that dragon-empire and the ecclesiastical system, which was then rising into prominence. That once dominant Pagan power could no longer prevail, and its place was finally lost, being cast out into the earth. This heaven in which war raged was not the home of God or of celestial beings, but that exalted sphere connected with governments, whether secular or spiritual, for the symbol is applied to both.

10. *To what does this triumphant song of the saints refer?*

To their triumph over their Pagan opposer—a triumph gained by the blood of the Lamb who died for them, by the word of their testi-mony which they used in their warfare, by their death for the truth, and by the power of Him who is seated on the throne; for by the union of all these their de-liverance was effected.

CHAPTER XIII.

1, 2. *Is not this vision of the beast rising up out of the sea, somewhat similar to Daniel's vision of the beasts?*

Daniel saw four beasts rise out of

the sea, which he understood to be symbols of empires, whereas John saw only the last of these, the three former having passed away, and even this beast was a changed form of empire.

The beast rose out of the sea. Of what is the sea a symbol?

The sea is a collection of waters, and is a symbol of nations united for one object. Daniel says that the four winds were striving upon the great sea, and this stormy scene applies to all the beasts. It is a fit symbol of the condition of the nations when these kingdoms came into existence.

This beast that John saw had seven heads and ten horns. What do these represent?

The ten horns are kingdoms, of which the empire is composed, and which for the time being coalesce, and form one symbolic beast; while the seven heads are the seven internal powers which are controlled by the beast. In fact, the whole administrative power so fully centres in the beast that it is fitly represented in symbol by having appended to its head ten horns—*i.e.*, the kingdoms which composed this huge monster beast — and seven heads, the entire internal rule of these kingdoms. See notes on chap. xvii.

This beast which John saw could not be the dragon, because the dragon gave him power and his seat. What was this beast?

The dragon was strictly imperialism in its Pagan form, but Paganism declined, even while the empire stood in its strength. Constantine renounced Paganism, and formally declared for Christianity, even while possessing the rule of the Cæsars. The renunciation of Paganism as a state religion was the wounding to death one of its heads, but this deadly wound was healed by formal Christianity being made to take its place. The world wondered after the beast, for though one source of power was slain, and thus its life was imperilled by this loss, it was soon renewed by a fresh source of power obtained by a new religion.

5–9. Blasphemy against God and the saints, with persecutions that continued forty and two months, are here said to follow the readoption of the old Pagan religion by the nation. What was the cause of this change?

We have only to refer to the well-known career of the emperor Julian, the Apostate—so named because of his apostacy from Christianity. Julian who at first privately and then publicly avowed infidelity, encouraged all of a kindred spirit, and persecuted many of the Christian faith. This trouble continued only for a limited time, as this power over kindreds, and tongues, and nations, was permitted only forty and two months.

11. What was this two-horned beast that came up out of the earth?

It was an empire, for the beast is still a symbol of imperial rule. But the beast now shown to John united in its head two distinct forms of authority. It had two horns like a lamb, but spake as a dragon. Now we have never had but one such ruler or class of rulers in the world, and therefore have no difficulty in deciding that it was the man-child, who not only assumed to sit on the throne of God, or ruled over the church, but also ruled all nations with a rod of iron. In form a lamb, because professedly belonging to Christ, but in power a dragon, because ruling nations. To say that the Bishop of the Church of Rome did seek and ultimately attain this position is only to repeat what history has written on her open page; and while assuming the title of Pope, or Father in the Church, has had his name on the published list of the kingdom-rulers of this world. His rule, it is true, though gradually diminishing during the last 400 years, was continued until 1870, when, upon the withdrawal of French troops from Rome, Italy wrenched the last fragment of unlawful rule out of his hand. In one form or other this power has been wielded for ages—first in the dragon, then in the beast that came out of the sea, and then in the two-horned beast that came up out of the earth.

What does " coming up out of the earth" mean?

The sea is a symbol of the nations, —*i.e.*, the world,—while the earth is a symbol of the Church in its apostate condition ; the ten-horned beast came up out of the former, while the two-horned beast came up out of the latter.

12–14. *Why did the latter make use of signs to sustain his authority?*

His secular authority was secured by the sword, but conviction of his sacred rule was sought by signs, which his position gave him power to perform, although deceptive in their nature. He sought to be feared not only as a ruler on earth, but as having power over heaven.

15. *What was this image of the beast?*

A reproduction or likeness of the power of the former beast, which had a wound by a sword, but lived in its successor.

16. *What was the mark of the beast?*

His sovereign authority, which, like the head of Cæsar stamped on the penny, all who circulate must acknowledge it. Hand and head in work or thought must yield to this despotism, or suffer. To accept this arrogant rule secured to the subject certain privileges, while to refuse, exposed to a denial of every civil and sacred right.

18. *Why does John give the name of this despotic person in numerals?*

It is in keeping with the book to use symbols, and as the man was then living, it would have been dangerous to have done otherwise ; as the safety of the disciples would have been imperilled by it.

Who was this man?

It is stated by Irenæus that Nero Cæsar was judged to be the person, and this early conviction I am most inclined to accept. Scholars also tell us that Irenæus reports that there were two readings of this number, 666, and 616. Now it is said that, in full Hebrew form, Neron Cæsas does count 666, the number now read, while the shorter Greek form, Nero Cæsar, counts 616. This is remarkable, and we question whether any other name will give these two readings.

CHAPTER XIV.

1, 2. *Who is this Lamb that stood on Mount Sion?*

It is a symbol of a person, who, in several deeply important aspects, has been before us already. John saw Him as the Lamb that had been slain, and lived again to receive homage ; then as leading to living fountains of water those who had followed Him in the strife ; and here we see Him as victorious leader of a faithful host.

Are these hundred forty and four thousand, a symbol of faithful saints, or is it a literal reckoning?

It is the symbolic unity of the saints that is here set forth, and this symbolic mark in their forehead, is their open faithful confession of His sovereign authority.

Is the triumph of the Lamb and His faithful associates the purport of this section?

Most certainly, and it forms a striking contrast to the previous triumph of their foes. John had seen the triumph of the dragon over the seed of the woman, then of the beast that came out of the sea, that made war with the saints and overcame them, and also of the beast that came out of the earth, deceiving and enslaving, or else destroying, those who would not submit to his claims. For a long time the enemy was victorious, but John saw a turn in the fearful tide of opposition. There had been faithful ones all through the struggle,—faithful ones from among the Jews, and faithful ones from among the Gentiles,—and as time moved on their number increased. John saw the scales slowly turn, and the lowly were being raised up. There was a rift in the dark cloud which had spread its gloom so long over the saints. Shouts of triumph were rising here and there, mingled with moans of defeat by their enemies; and at last the Lamb is seen on Mount Sion as a victor.

3. *What was this new song they sung?*

The song of victory, which none but the associates of the Lamb could sing.

The defeat of the dragon was after a long period; how could the firstfruits unto God and the Lamb share in it?

It is in their successors that they triumph, the cause is one, and the party is one on both sides. It is the dragon and the Lamb whose destinies we have to watch, and all who join with them have the glory or the shame as the issue may be.

6, 7. *What Gospel had this flying angel to proclaim among the nations of the earth?*

The word Gospel means glad tidings, and it may appear strange when we say, that these were tidings of judgments upon the enemies of the Lamb. They were of course glad tidings only to the followers of the Lamb, as by these judgments they were set free from former oppression.

Why is it called "the everlasting Gospel"?

It is, *lit.*, "an age-lasting glad message," and in this form conveyed the cheering assurance that the privilege would continue all through the age. The triumph of the enemy was over, and the freedom from tyranny was age-lasting.

What is the proof that this glad message to the saints everywhere was of judgment and not the Gospel of Christ?

The angel gives the message, and this removes all doubt, "Saying with a loud voice, fear God and give glory to Him, for the hour of His judgment is come."

8. *Why does another angel announce the fall of Babylon?*

The proclamation of the two angels are inseparable. One heralds forth the hour of judgment, the other announces that it has fallen upon the great city Babylon.

Is the fall of Babylon contemporary with the rise of truth and liberty?

Most certainly. The two forces have their alternate effects as markedly as day and night. When day advances, night recedes. When the cause of the Lamb triumphed, the cause of the dragon under every phase suffered defeat. Of course it is important to discern what triumph and defeat means in relation to these two forces. Under the rule of the dragon the Word of God is closed, liberty is denied, and men use these at their peril; while under the rule of the Lamb we have an open Bible, and can read and obey it without fear of consequences. This is what we mean by triumph and defeat, by having life instead of death. Happy is the heart that can understand and appreciate this blessed change.

Has Babylon yet fallen?

She has fallen, there can be no doubt. Like her from whom she derived her mystic name, that which made her known and feared has been taken from her. The dread imperialism of ancient Babylon, by which power she made nations bow to her idolatrous claims, and even enslaved the people of God until that power was wrested from her hand, has been faithfully imitated by the mother of harlots. She who made nations drink of the cup of her fornication, and held under tyranny the people of God, can do so no longer. Her sceptre has been torn from her grasp, never again to be restored. Yes, she has fallen, fallen, who once made the earth tremble.

9. *Has this third angel anything to do with the fall of Babylon?*

His proclamation is a solemn warning to all who own her authority, and receive her mark—*i.e.*, acknowledge her authority—that they will share her doom, and drink of her unmixed cup of divine indignation.

10. *Is the fire and brimstone with which they were to be tormented literal fire?*

By the law of the book we must conclude it to be wrath in symbol. The torment is real, but not physical; the minds of all connected will feel it, but it is in relation to their state.

11. *"The smoke of their torment ascendeth up for ever and ever." Is not this eternal suffering?*

It is, *lit.*, "into ages of ages," a suffering continued through the ages. It is of time, not of eternity, that John is revealing. Babylon, the saint-enslaving city, like the Gospel-rejecting Jew, has been cast into a furnace of fire, and gnashing of teeth, and torment that will not cease, are indications of the sad experience of both. This declaration, that the smoke of their torment will ascend

from age to age, is a plain enough intimation that what they have lost they will never regain.

13. *Does this reference to those who " die in the Lord" apply to believers now?*

Yes; but the words "from henceforth" denote a great change of circumstances. Under the rule of the dragon, the pains and penalties inflicted on the saints were often fearful, but under the rule of the Lamb these penalties ceased. When Babylon of old lost her power, she could no longer threaten with a furnace of fire those who would not bow down to her golden image; neither can her antitype, or rather her successor, now that her rule is taken away. Under her despotism the saints who died in the Lord rested from suffering, now they "rest from their labours; and their works do follow them."

14. *" And I looked, and behold a white cloud." Of what is this white cloud a symbol?*

A cloud is a type or symbol of that by which God's authority is represented and executed, whether in relation to His testimonies, of which the cloud which led the children of Israel was a type, or of armies or hosts, which were the executioners of His will, and are frequently referred to under this symbol. The Assyrians were God's "swift cloud," upon which He rode into Egypt (Isa. xix. 1); and the Romans—in their united hosts—were the clouds upon which Jesus came to judge Israel (Matt. xxiv. 30 ; Rev. i. 7); but here John saw a white cloud—upon which sat the Son of man—a symbol of His own faithful host, by whom, through the truth, His victories were to be established.

15. *" The harvest of the earth is ripe." What does this mean?*

The earth, in the Revelation, is the symbol of the apostate church, as the sea is a symbol of the nations which surround her. "The harvest," said Jesus, when predicting the end of the Jewish economy, "is the end of the world" or age; and the harvest here is the end of the dragon dynasty, which being ripe for judgment, the sickle was prepared to cut it down.

18–20. *What is this "vine of the earth"?*

The vine had been a symbol of God's people Israel, and is here transferred to His Church. When the vineyard yielded nothing but wild grapes, He took away the hedge thereof, and the wild beasts trampled upon it. So with the Church, which the Lord purchased for Himself, when it became carnal there was no fruit for the Master of the vineyard. His forbearance with her unfaithfulness was truly marvellous, but at last the crisis came, and her clusters of the vine were thrown into the winepress of the wrath of God, and a deep stream of blood flowed out of the city.

Was this human blood that flowed out from the city?

It was the blood of the grapes that were trodden in the winepress that was seen to flow out, and not human blood. What this symbolic blood may signify, may be best learnt from a description of the results of the same judgment, as given in chap. xviii., especially from ver. 10–14. Here we see that gold, silver, and every possible form of wealth and pleasure had been acquired, and this was the fruit brought forth for herself, and was all taken from her. This was the blood, which on being trodden in the winepress, flowed out from the city.

CHAPTER XV.

1. *Do the seven plagues of these seven angels follow the preceding events?*

2 L

They evidently belong to the same tragic scene, but here we get another view of the troubles of the fallen, and the triumphs of the delivered. These triumphs are seen and heard in the beginning of this chapter, while the nature and extent of the troubles of their enemies are detailed on to the end of chap. xvi.

2. *What was this "song of Moses the servant of God, and the song of the Lamb," which was sung by those who stood "upon the sea of glass"?*

It was the song of victory and of judgment combined. Moses stood upon the shores of the Red Sea with his delivered host, and they sung their song of freedom; and here the host of the Lamb celebrate a similar triumph.

3. *Why is their deliverer called the "king of saints"?*

Scholars now read *king of nations*, which is most appropriate to Him who has triumphed over their most persistent opposition. That He is above them is manifest, because He has thoroughly checked their tyranny.

5–8. *Is the opening of the temple of the tabernacle of testimony, at all connected with the rule of the dragon?*

While the dragon ruled in the plenitude of his power, the temple was closed, and testimony was silenced everywhere. But when the crisis of judgment began, a door was opened for testimony, and with this crisis, the plagues which these appointed messengers of God inflicted upon the foes of the Lamb commenced.

When did this take place?

I am inclined to think that the pouring out of these vials of wrath extend from the first waning of the power of the beast to its final overthrow, and include all the varied forms of judgment, with which God was pleased to visit that gigantic apostasy.

————

CHAPTER XVI.

1. *These seven angels are said to pour out their vials upon the earth, the sea, the rivers, the sun, and the air. What do these symbols indicate?*

They all refer to results endured by the nations, according to their varied relation to the empire of the dragon. Every nation which had given its power to the beast suffered through that relation, and ultimately sought a separation, which fact history fully attests. So that though the pouring out of these vials caused immense trouble in many places, yet all resulted in the accomplishment of that final judgment, the binding of the dragon.

12. *What was this "river Euphrates"?*

A symbol of a nation no doubt, but what nation we venture not to affirm. The prophet Isaiah (viii. 7) applied it to the Assyrian power, but when John wrote that power had perished from the earth. The river Euphrates flowed through ancient Babylon, and was for a long time a source of its strength, but ultimately of its overthow. According to this symbol some great nation was a source of supply to mystic Babylon, but, under the vial of the sixth angel, this source was dried up, or drained off, so that the way of the kings of the east might be prepared for the work they had to do. The dragon power had to be crippled and destroyed by the very kings which had upheld it, and the pouring out of these vials upon themselves aroused them for this strange reverse.

13–16. *Of what are these frogs a symbol?*

Of uncleanness, which was manifest in all the systems, out of the mouths of which they are said to come. It was manifest in the dragon, the symbol of the Cæsar administration; of the beast, the symbol of the secular rule which followed in the Roman empire; and of the prophet, the symbol of spiritual rule—all of these being united in what is now known as the Papacy. It is a sad fact that tyranny, deception, and impiety characterised them all, and all have been judged and overthrown. This overthrow is the result of the battle of the great day of God Almighty, called in the Hebrew tongue Armageddon, or the battle of the mountains —*i.e.*, the governments of the earth. Such a contest has already occurred, and the result history has written on her open page. Where is now the rule of any of these three once dominant powers? They have all been put down, and are things of the past. The sound of their voice made the earth tremble, and now the last of them only mutters from the dust—"Verily there is a God that judgeth the earth." The Lamb has triumphed, and they who are on His side rejoice.

17, 18. *The seventh angel poured out his vial into the air. Of what is air a symbol?*

Air is in symbol the atmosphere of thoughts, reasonings, and imaginations, and after the great battle of Armageddon, in which the nations overcame the representative of the dragon rule, a great revolution followed in this sphere.

19. *What is this "great city" with its divisions?*

It is that great religious political institution that once ruled over the kings of the earth. Its divisions are already manifest. It has been separated from the nations and its secular from its spiritual power.

What are these "cities of the nations" which are said to fall?

Their religious establishments, the churches of states which are in symbol "the cities of the nations," are falling, and must fall, for their doom is written. The doom of the mother is the doom of all her children, for the people who have been compelled to live in them will ultimately destroy them all.

CHAPTER XVII.

1. *" The great whore." To whom does this apply ?*

To that ecclesiastical system called the "Church of Rome," whose acquired power, actions, and doom, John is permitted prophetically to record. She is in symbol a woman, because it is a church—professedly the Church of Christ—which she represents, and she is called a whore, because she has prostituted herself to the will and dictation of others, instead of remaining the faithful affianced bride of her Lord. She was also seen by John to sit upon—by means of the beast that carried her — "many waters." John is afterwards told by the angel, who was his instructor, that the waters were "peoples, and multitudes, and nations, and tongues." Now, that the Church of Rome has occupied this position of secular rule, I presume no one will deny.

2. *How have the kings of the earth committed fornication with her ?*

They have sinned by her license and example. Not only has she waxed wanton through the flesh, but has sold the right to these kings of the earth to use spiritual power for national purposes.

4. *The woman was arrayed in purple, and decked with gold and precious stones and pearls, while in her hand she held a golden cup full of abominations. What do all these things symbolise ?*

The wealth and corruption of the system, of which this woman and these things are a symbol. When John saw her it was a revelation, but history has filled up the picture which all may now read in living characters. If the Roman Catholic Church, so called, which through its head the Pope has ruled over kings and nations, which has amassed enormous wealth, and tolerated every form of corruption, and by wars and persecutions has put millions to death, answer not to this picture which John saw, then glass can never make face answer to face. Well might he wonder when he saw in these symbols what the Church of Christ by her apostasy would become.

5. *Why is this forehead inscription written in capital letters ?*

To give it special prominence, although there is no authority to distinguish it in type. It is a most singular inscription, and being embroidered on her forehead indicates her open daring practice of all these things.

Why is she called " a mystery " ?

It is, *lit.*, a secret—*i.e.*, something known only to the initiated. John saw the woman in power, wealth, and splendour. He saw her also drunken with the blood of saints, and he wondered with great astonishment. The secret, however, is opened to him, and the source from whence her power, and wealth, and cruelty are derived is stated in symbols, the meaning of which John doubtless understood, and this is why he wondered.

Why is she called " Babylon the great " ?

Because of the imperial power she had obtained and used. Her ancient prototype ruled over nations, magistrates, teachers, soldiers, priests, etc., and the Church of Rome—of which this woman is a symbol—sat upon this beast, and wielded all his power. In the zenith of her power none could withstand her claims, and kings held their thrones only at her will.

How is she the " mother of harlots " ?

She herself became the whore of the dragon, and though betrothed to Christ, her first husband, she committed adultery by union with a world ruler ; or, in other words, she, as the Church of Christ, to whom she had vowed obedience, united herself with the State, and imperiously grasped its power. Other religious sects have followed her example, and have elected their rulers or lords, who appoint laws and ordinances which Christ never ordained, and have thus drunk of her cup. To be under the rule of such, whether kings, queens, synods, conferences, or parliaments, is harlotry, and must be conscientiously repudiated. Christ alone must rule His own bride. What He appoints His people must do, though others forbid ; and what man appoints must be resisted, though loss and trial be the result.

7. *" I will tell thee the mystery of the woman," etc. Of what use are these explanations, when further explanation is required to understand them ?*

Although clothed in symbols they were of great use to John, who, no doubt, knew their meaning and application. Besides, some of these things are plain enough even to us. We learn that the horns are kings, that the waters are peoples, etc., and that the woman is a city—*i.e.*, a system—which ruled over kings, and this explanation can be applied to many other parts of the Revelation, where these things are spoken of.

8. *" The beast that was, and is not, and yet is." What is this ?*

" The beast that was " came up out of the sea, and ruled for a season ; then the woman, the Church, obtained the rule and became the beast of the earth (see chap. xiii.).

Of the former beast it then was strictly true, " and is not;" while the authority, being continued with the latter, it was also true, " and yet is."

9. *What were these seven mountains ?*

A mountain is a symbol of internal government, a mountain being an exalted part of the earth on which it stands ; and a horn is a symbol of a kingdom or external government. The seven heads or mountains on which the woman was sitting, was that sevenfold or complete internal administrative process which belongs to all kingdoms, viz., its legislative, its military, its magisterial, its ecclesiastical, its commercial, its educational, and its domestic rule. All these were controlled by the beast, and from the senate house to the inner circle of domestic life, its all-pervading influence was felt.

10. *Do these seven kings, the sixth of which was reigning at that time, belong to the woman-dragon reign ?*

No ; they are connected with the first stage of the empire. The seven kings were to arise before the threatened judgment fell upon the Jewish nation. This reference also serves to mark the period of the beast's supremacy when John wrote the Revelation. It is the internal evidence which decides the chronology of the book. " There are seven kings " (before the execution of the first judgment), " five are fallen " (these were Julius, Augustus, Tiberius, Caligulus, and Claudius Cæsar), " and one is " (Nero Cæsar, under whose auspices Paul went to Rome about the year A.D. 62. And as Nero died about A.D. 67, it was towards the close of his finally cruel reign that John received in Patmos this Revelation), " the other [Galba] is not yet come ; and when he cometh, he must continue a short space." Five months only did Galba reign, and was succeeded by Vespasian, the general of the Roman troops, who, by the hand of Titus his son, overthrew Jerusalem, A.D. 71.

12. *The ten horns or kings upon the head of the beast on which the woman sat, had received no kingdom when John had his vision. When did they receive their kingdoms and give their power and strength unto the beast?*

This could only be after the well-known Gothic invasion under Theodoric, and as these Gothic kingdoms ultimately received Roman laws, as published by Justinian, they became Roman kingdoms. Justinian, in his famous Decretal Epistle to the Pope, recognised him as the supreme head of all holy churches, both in the Eastern and Western kingdoms, which decree was accepted by the Pope, and both decree and acceptance of it was enrolled by Justinian in the volume of the civil law, which was really accepted by these ten kingdoms. In this legislative act by the representative of the Cæsars, the Revelation by John was fulfilled. " The dragon gave him his power, and his seat, and great authority." And, as stated here, " These have one mind, and shall give their power and strength unto the beast."

These ten horns or kings support the cause of the woman and then hate her. Does history mark this change?

This change is distinctly noted in history. First, these kings which received their kingdoms in the same hour as the beast, did give their strength and power unto her. Then a change commenced, and her right to rule was at last questioned and rejected. Some German states led the way, other nations followed, and at last they symbolically made her naked—*i.e.*, stripped her of her dominion—and did eat her flesh—*i.e.*, her riches—and did burn her with fire, until not a vestage of her former secular rule remained. In 1870 the Italians entered Rome, and

wrested the last portion of her greatly contracted rule from her hand, and from that date her secular rule terminated, and the Revelation by John has been fulfilled. Futurists may deny these conclusions, and affirm that these ten kingdoms have yet to arise, and first support and then destroy antichrist, who, they say has also yet to come. It is surely a mistake to look for that which has been already. The ten kingdoms have had their existence along with the whore, and have done all that John revealed concerning her. Instead of looking for the fulfilment of fulfilled prophecy, we should rather give glory to God who has given already this triumph unto the Lamb.

At what period were there exactly ten kingdoms supporting this woman, or upholding the secular power of the Church of Rome?

The number ten when used as a symbol is indefinite, and does not require the exact number to fulfil it (see remarks on chap. ii. 10). It is misleading to search for a period when there was just ten kingdoms forming this empire. It was simply formed of a number of kingdoms, and this is all that is intended.

CHAPTER XVIII.

1–10. *To what periods of time do the proclamations of this angel refer?*

John refers to two periods in relation to the woman which sat upon many waters, and was called " Babylon the great," which it would be well to note, viz., her apostasy, and her judgment. A voice from heaven revealed her judgment, but the angel had first disclosed the reason for the harsh treatment she was to receive. The declaration " Babylon the great is fallen, is fallen, and is become the habitation," etc., should be rendered, *She fell, Babylon the great, and became the habitation of demons*, etc., and this at once reveals what she had done in the past. It was her sins that led God to prepare the full cup of wrath, and the nations she seduced were the agents which God used to make her drink it. It was her past impiety that led God to deal with her in such severity, and break the rod of her strength for ever.

11. *Who were these merchants who were made rich by her ?*

Those who traded in the special wares of her system, and in the hour of her judgment her traffic with the world was broken. Her mart was once the market-place of the earth, and her merchants were enriched by her special commodities. Here we see them mourning because no man buyeth their merchandise any more.

12, 13. *Is this long list of merchandise, from gold and silver, to slaves and souls of men, to be understood literally ?*

We must read it as connected with the huge system of barter that was carried on by the woman that sat upon the beast. It is a fact of history, that not a privilege for the body or the soul, for time or eternity, could be enjoyed except as purchased from her through her appointed spiritual merchants. Enjoyment otherwise was both forbidden and hindered. That unjust monopoly is now broken up, and her permission is no longer sought. The judgment therefore, here spoken of, has come upon her, and her loud wail ascends in vain.

21. *Of what is this millstone cast into the sea a symbol ?*

Of her final and irrevocable doom.

Does this mean that Romanism, as a religious system, will come to an end ?

No ; that system remains, and may continue, along with other heresies, to the end. This book deals with its secular power, and this, it reveals, would be violently wrested

out of its hand, never to be grasped again. There are errors and sects, evils and abominations, that God removes only by the reception of His truth ; and there are forms of despotic tyranny that He removes out of the way by the strength of His arm, or, in other words, by force. This twofold operation must be carefully noted.

CHAPTER XIX.

1–6. *What is the purport of this chapter ?*

It is a revelation of the triumph of the saints, consequent upon the destruction of the power of the great whore.

This " Alleluia ; salvation, and glory," was heard by John in the heavens ; was this the home of God ?

It was out of the symbolic heaven, that the shout of triumph came—the ringing cheer of praise from the heavenlies, in which, though not acknowledged by her foes, Jesus had seated His bride.

7–9. *" For the marriage of the Lamb is come." Had it never taken place before.*

It is not the marriage that was to take place, but rather the marriage festival, or, as afterwards called, " the marriage supper," or feast of the Lamb, which had been so long delayed, and was about to take place, because of the judgment of the " great whore." Jesus, like His prototype Adam, had once been cast into a death-sleep, and also had His side opened, out of which, or by believing in Him as the crucified and risen Saviour, the disciples at Pentecost were received as His bride. But, owing to the jealousy of the typical bride, which, though bidden to the wedding, would not come, the festival—the public rejoicing— did not take place. And this strife and jealousy continuing all through that age, the feast could not be celebrated, and at last, the bond-woman, and her scoffing son, were cast out of the house, and had there been no foolish hindrance, it might have been celebrated then. At this juncture, the man-child was born, and the woman, instead of being honoured with a public feast, was driven into the wilderness, and had to wait during the long years of the apostacy, the promised rightful festival. The "great whore," who had become mistress of the house, would not believe that believers, simply Christians, were the bride of the Lamb, and even the hint of such a blessed truth was put down with violence. In the preceding chapter, the woman sitting upon many waters is judged, her city is with violence thrown down, and in this chapter the bride is heard to say, "Let us be glad and rejoice, and give honour to Him : for the marriage of the Lamb is come, and his wife,—'arrayed in fine linen,'—hath made herself ready."

10. *Why did John fall in adoration at the feet of the messenger ?*

He was filled with adoring gratitude at the revelations he had received, and was ready to honour the messenger who had brought them ; but he was at once prevented from so doing. The direction given by this fellow-servant is of the greatest moment,—let God be honoured, not His messengers.

11. *John saw heaven opened, and a white horse, and a royal rider ; What does this mean ?*

It is a soul-cheering scene that is here presented—a revelation of the conquests of the Lamb. In chap. vi. John saw the white horse go forth conquering—*i.e.*, winning hearts to Jesus,—and some marked results followed. Then he saw other horses enter the field, red, black, and pale ; and frightful results became manifest.

He might wonder whether or not the white horse was really driven from the field. But here he again appears ; a royal rider is seated upon him, and diadems encircle His head. He is a conqueror, with vesture dipped in blood, and is seen returning from the battle-field. A triumphant host follow Him, upon white horses, clothed in fine linen, the righteousness of saints ; and behind them are the vanquished, upon which the fowls that fly in the midst of heaven are summoned to feed. This grand apocalyptic picture, glowing with the symbols already opened, must be viewed only in the light in which they are reflected. John saw the struggle between the dragon and the Lamb, and here he beheld the triumph. That power is put down, the nations feed upon the spoil, and the saints have freedom from the long continued despotic tyranny that the ten-horned beast inflicted upon them. Let us give glory to Him who sits on the throne, and reigns for ever and ever.

CHAPTER XX.

1. *Of what is this key and chain a symbol ?*

Of authority over the abyss, and power to restrain the evil coming out of it.

2. *Is this binding of the dragon a reality ?*

It is a reality, but presented in a figure or symbol, the meaning of which we must learn.

What is the dragon that was bound ?

A government or empire, as seen in chap. xii.—there, at liberty to persecute and injure ; here, bound and set aside.

Is it Satan that was bound ?

Not the being that is usually denominated Satan, but the dragon, —*i.e.*, a kingdom here characterised as the "ancient serpent,"—*i.e.*, the cunning one, "who is a devil,"—*i.e.*, a thruster through or accuser, "and Satan,"—*i.e.*, a shutter-up or adversary; all these being characteristics of that ten-horned kingdom.

3. *What is this bottomless pit?*

It is strictly *the abyss*, and is a sign of a state of subjection, not a literal pit, but a once-dominant power humbled and restrained or bound.

When was the dragon bound?

When his secular dominion was taken away, which it most certainly was when the Italians entered Rome in 1870, and claimed it for Italy. That act completed the consuming which had been going on for centuries. It was the last link of that great chain which had been gradually enclosing the body of the monster, and with it the binding was complete.

Are these thousand years literal years?

I cannot say that they denote a thousand ordinary years, since in this book some numbers are certainly used as symbols of indefiniteness, and others of completeness. That a period of considerable duration is intended, I have no doubt; a period of liberty and privilege which the dragon would never have granted, and which he cannot now even control. It is a privilege enjoyed through the power of the Lamb.

Is this millennium of liberty and privilege a complete removal of all evil?

It would be deceptive either to affirm or expect such a result. Some evils are removed by force, others only by the reception of evil-removing truth. There are evils which God has determined to restrain, because they are destructive of the liberty of others, but there are evils for the removal of which we become personally responsible.

4. *What do these thrones symbolise?*

Rule and victory. The beast had his throne, and ruled over the saints; here John saw the saints seated on thrones, which implied their rule over him. It is a marvellous change effected by the power of God.

What is meant by "the souls of them that were beheaded"?

The persons who were deprived of their liberties under the dragon rule. To deprive a man of his right to worship and serve God according to His direction, is in symbol to behead him. This was the sad lot of many, but when the dragon was bound this scene was reversed, "and they lived and reigned with Christ." And this triumph over their foes was not to be of an ephemeral character, but to continue for "a thousand years."

Do all who have suffered enjoy this prolonged triumph on the earth?

Not personally, since many who enjoy and share the triumph will not have suffered personally. Neither will those who are put down be the same persons that began the "war with the saints." The struggle had been going on for nearly two millenniums, but from the day that the white horse went forth (chap. vi.) to the binding of the dragon, there were but two leaders, the Lamb and the dragon, and but two parties, who were arranged under, and carrying out the spirit and purpose of their respective leaders. It has been like the besieging of a fortress that has dealt many heavy blows on the besiegers, and troop after troop have been cut down, and battalion after battalion have been drafted in to the conflict, ere the enemy was conquered; some arriving only to hear the shout of victory, and share the rejoicing when the strife had ceased. The Lamb triumphed, and all who were on His side shared the triumph as they had shared the strife.

5. *Who are these "rest of the dead," who live not again until the thousand years are finished?*

It is the dragon party, whose national power was so completely extinguished, as very appropriately to be described as dead, a symbolic death from which they will not recover for a thousand years.

What is this first resurrection?

Not a resurrection of bodies from literal corruption, but a resurrection of the saints from a state in which a symbolic death and burial is implied. The condition of the saints during the rule of the dragon-empire was similar to that of Israel when in Babylon. Their national life was entombed by that subjection, and when brought out of it they are said to have been brought out of their graves (Ezek. xxxvii. 12). "The resurrection" is a settled definition of that rising again of the literal dead from death, and belongs exclusively to that event; but in this Book of Revelation we are told distinctly that symbols are used to describe events, and for this all should be prepared. This resurrection of the saints, therefore, is their rising from a former state of symbolic and not literal death.

A first resurrection implies a second; what is the second resurrection?

The rising again of the dragon-party, who are to be loosed from the abyss into which they were cast and entombed so long.

6. *Why is it the holy alone that are to share that first resurrection?*

Because it was they alone who were buried, and it can apply to no others.

What is this "second death"?

The first death was that subjection endured by the saints, the second death is the subjection and punish-

2 M

ment of the dragon, as now endured by that party. This death will have no power over the saints during this thousand years. As "priests of God and of Christ, they shall reign with Him a thousand years," *i.e.*, they shall enjoy their privileges unmolested by this tyrant, and shall thus reign with Christ during this promised period.

Why limit it to a thousand years?

That it should be limited at all, indicates that it is to be enjoyed on earth, and belongs only to this fleshly state, as there is no limit to the joys of the glorified. But that it should continue through these generations of the saints, is a most blessed revelation.

When the thousand years are expired, Satan shall be loosed again. What does this mean?

That the chain or restraint now laid on the dragon will be removed. We must not think it strange that in her season or opportunity, the woman should seek to regain her lost power. She would possess it to-day if she could, but not a single horn or king will help her, and she cannot do it alone. Ritualism is the growing influence, through which she will get the help of Gog and Magog,—*i.e.*, the multitude, through which she will seek to regain her lost seat,—and for this result the sects are really though unconsciously preparing themselves. Ritualism is a religion of the flesh, and will, in the turn of the tide, seek state power to carry out all its desires. The stained window and the towering steeple, the surpliced priest and the pealing organ, and such like things, which almost every congregation seeks to obtain, may appear but small matters; but they are the seeds of a harvest that would astonish the sowers, could they only return to witness it. Now Rome is the mother of all these ecclesiastical adornments, and as she gave them birth, the parentage will be acknowledged. She who once won her power by strategy will yet attempt to regain it by the same method.

Will she regain it?

It will be attempted, and by deception a strong force will be gathered, and an onslaught on the saints will be made, but at this juncture judgment from God will arrest their purpose, and His enemies will be called to their final account. Into the matter of this future crisis we are not disposed to enter. There are solemn issues still pending, but the Judge of all the earth will do right. "Blessed are all they that go in the way of His commandments."

CHAPTER XXI.

1. *Is this "new heaven and new earth" a new constructed or created physical universe?*

If the heaven, earth, sea, sun, moon, and stars, which have been so frequently before us in this book, were literally parts of this universe, we should not hesitate for a moment to so use them; but as they have been used all through as symbols of churches, states, nations, etc., we could hardly expect that a change would be made without due notice being given. The book opens with a distinct intimation that its revelations would be made in signs, it seems therefore only right to so read it to the end; and as some of these signs have become fixed in their application, we should not venture to change them. We therefore conclude that it is not a new sky above, nor a new earth beneath, but a new spiritual polity which will take the place of that which the Lamb had thrown down,—new only in contrast with the heaven and earth of the dragon. The heaven and earth belonging to the old apostate system being removed, there is room made for a new heaven and new earth, in harmony with the administration of the Lamb. "The first heaven and the first earth had passed away; and there was no more sea," that is, these former related systems, while they remained in their position, hindered the manifestation of the Church of Christ, and were therefore removed out of the way.

2. *Is this coming down of the holy city a symbolic view of the Church?*

It is a scenic view of her open manifestation on the earth; in symbol it is a city, but it is in fact a bridal festival. The Church is as a bride adorned for her husband, and her long delayed recognition is here said to take place.

If this holy city is a symbol of the Church on earth, how can it be that tears and pain and death are said to be removed away from her?

These tears and sorrow and death are in relation to the oppressions of a former tyrannical system, and not what belongs to our present physical state through the fall of Adam and other transgressions. These will remain till death is swallowed up in victory. When God improves our condition, physically, it will be by giving us an immortal body. There is a period when this will take place, but every purpose of God has its type preceding and illustrating what He will do. Every calamity named here has been inflicted — by the woman that sat upon the beast— upon His affianced bride, but now her power is arrested, these tears are dried, and her suffering from this source ends.

9–27. *One of the seven angels invited John to view the bride, the Lamb's wife. How can we discern her in this chapter?*

Only by observing the symbol

under which she is set forth. As the apostate harlot had been described as a great city, which ruled over the kings of the earth, so the bride, the Lamb's wife, is symbolised as a city. "I will show thee the bride," said the angel, and, says John, he "showed me that great city, the holy Jerusalem."

Some say this is a description of a literal city; may it not after all be so?

If it is a city it is rather strange that nothing is said about its inhabitants. John is distinctly told that it is the bride of the Lamb, but literal stones and pearls are not His bride, however precious they may be. The twelve foundations are its symbolic unity, for the signatures of the apostles are inscribed upon them. Her twelve gates are always open, for their testimony, by which men enter, has never been withdrawn. Her light is the Lamb, and, by His undimmed testimony, He always shines upon her.

CHAPTER XXII.

1. *Is this chapter connected with the previous one?*

It would have been better not to have divided them, as it is a continued description of the city. Here we have an account of its hallowed furnishings, all appropriate to His great purpose. The river of water of life and the tree of life, with its twelve fruits, with leaves of healing for the nations around, are all there. There also is the throne of God and the Lamb, and the light of truth which never grows dim.

What is this water of life?

It is the truth of the Gospel of Christ, which gives life to all who drink of it—*i.e.*, all who receive Him.

Why is it said to proceed out of the throne of God and the Lamb?

Because all spiritual life proceeds from the gracious government of God, through the Lamb. There is no life but through Jesus.

2. *There is but one tree. How does it bear twelve fruits?*

There is but one Saviour, but there are twelve apostles to represent Him from whom every healing blessing flows.

The leaves of this tree are said to be for the healing of the nations. What is the use of the fruit?

The fruit and its leaves are fit symbols of the twofold provision which is in Christ, viz., salvation for the sinner, and righteousness, and sanctification, and redemption for the saint.

Might not this be a description of a heavenly scene?

It is a heavenly scene, but not in heaven as you may mean. It is where sickness dwells and spiritual healing is needed, and God has richly provided for man's deepest need.

6, 7. *If the binding of the dragon has only been completed in our day, how could the angel speak of "things which must shortly be done"?*

Some of the things which John saw were shortly to transpire, but not all that he saw. Some things were near at hand when the Revelation was given, as the overthrow of the first antichristian opposition, and associated events. Then others were more remote, as the overthrow of Pagan hostility, and the binding of the dragon, and here we must discern in relation to promised execution.

7. *Must we understand "Behold I come quickly" in the same way?*

We cannot apply it to the final judgment of sinners and glorification of believers, since that has not even yet taken place; we must, therefore, conclude that Jesus referred to those earlier judgments, with which He visited those who opposed His claims in the world. Those who first received the testimony must have so understood it.

"Blessed is he that keepeth the sayings of the prophecy of this book." What sayings are these?

Those special appeals to the churches, I presume, and which had been written and received by them. There were many sayings of Jesus in these epistles, and many blessings promised to those who should keep them.

10–12. *" He that is unjust let him be unjust still." What does this indicate?*

The close of opportunities to all directly concerned. Privileges had been enjoyed by many who had abused them, and they were about to be withdrawn. The coming crisis was intended to seal the position of each, whether obedient or disobedient.

14. *"Blessed are they that do His commandments, that they may have right to the tree of life," etc. Is not this like life promised to works?*

The life here promised is the continuance of blessing which the faithful should enjoy. The accepted reading now is " Blessed are they who are washing their robes." It is such who shall have access to the tree of life, and dwell in the city of God. These things were to be testified in the churches, that all might know that grace demanded obedience, and that the obedient alone could be blessed.